FORD

FULL-SIZE VANS
1989-96 REPAIR MANUAL

CHILTON'S

Covers all U.S. and Canadian models of
Ford E150, E250, E350, Club Wagon, Cutaway and
Motor Home Chassis; gasoline and diesel engines

by Thomas A. Mellon, A.S.E., S.A.E.

CHILTON Automotive Books

PUBLISHED BY **HAYNES NORTH AMERICA**, Inc.

AUTOMOTIVE
PARTS &
ACCESSORIES
ASSOCIATION MEMBER

Manufactured in USA
© 1998 Haynes North America, Inc.
ISBN 0-8019-8848-9
Library of Congress Catalog Card No. 97-78114
5678901234 9876543210

Haynes Publishing Group
Sparkford Nr Yeovil
Somerset BA22 7JJ England

Haynes North America, Inc
861 Lawrence Drive
Newbury Park
California 91320 USA

ABCDE
FGHI

7H2

Contents

Contents

DRIVE TRAIN **7**

STEERING AND SUSPENSION **8**

BRAKES **9**

BODY AND TRIM **10**

GLOSSARY

MASTER INDEX

SAFETY NOTICE

Proper service and repair procedures are vital to the safe, reliable operation of all motor vehicles, as well as the personal safety of those performing repairs. This manual outlines procedures for servicing and repairing vehicles using safe, effective methods. The procedures contain many NOTES, CAUTIONS and WARNINGS which should be followed, along with standard procedures to eliminate the possibility of personal injury or improper service which could damage the vehicle or compromise its safety.

It is important to note that repair procedures and techniques, tools and parts for servicing motor vehicles, as well as the skill and experience of the individual performing the work vary widely. It is not possible to anticipate all of the conceivable ways or conditions under which vehicles may be serviced, or to provide cautions as to all possible hazards that may result. Standard and accepted safety precautions and equipment should be used when handling toxic or flammable fluids, and safety goggles or other protection should be used during cutting, grinding, chiseling, prying, or any other process that can cause material removal or projectiles.

Some procedures require the use of tools specially designed for a specific purpose. Before substituting another tool or procedure, you must be completely satisfied that neither your personal safety, nor the performance of the vehicle will be endangered.

Although information in this manual is based on industry sources and is complete as possible at the time of publication, the possibility exists that some car manufacturers made later changes which could not be included here. While striving for total accuracy, the authors or publishers cannot assume responsibility for any errors, changes or omissions that may occur in the compilation of this data.

PART NUMBERS

Part numbers listed in this reference are not recommendations by Haynes North America, Inc. for any product brand name. They are references that can be used with interchange manuals and aftermarket supplier catalogs to locate each brand supplier's discrete part number.

SPECIAL TOOLS

Special tools are recommended by the vehicle manufacturer to perform their specific job. Use has been kept to a minimum, but where absolutely necessary, they are referred to in the text by the part number of the tool manufacturer. These tools can be purchased, under the appropriate part number, from your local dealer or regional distributor, or an equivalent tool can be purchased locally from a tool supplier or parts outlet. Before substituting any tool for the one recommended, read the SAFETY NOTICE at the top of this page.

ACKNOWLEDGMENTS

This publication contains material that is reproduced and distributed under a license from Ford Motor Company. No further reproduction of distribution of the Ford Motor Company material is allowed without the express written permission from Ford Motor Company.

1

GENERAL INFORMATION AND MAINTENANCE

HOW TO USE THIS BOOK

Chilton's Total Car Care manual for 1989–96 Ford Full-Size Vans is intended to help you learn more about the inner workings of your vehicle while saving you money on its upkeep and operation.

The beginning of the book will likely be referred to the most, since that is where you will find information for maintenance and tune-up. The other sections deal with the more complex systems of your vehicle. Operating systems from engine through brakes are covered to the extent that the average do-it-yourselfer becomes mechanically involved. This book will not explain such things as rebuilding a differential for the simple reason that the expertise required and the investment in special tools make this task uneconomical. It will, however, give you detailed instructions to help you change your own brake pads and shoes, replace spark plugs, and perform many more jobs that can save you money, give you personal satisfaction and help you avoid expensive problems.

A secondary purpose of this book is a reference for owners who want to understand their vehicle and/or their mechanics better. In this case, no tools at all are required.

Where to Begin

Before removing any bolts, read through the entire procedure. This will give you the overall view of what tools and supplies will be required. There is nothing more frustrating than having to walk to the bus stop on Monday morning because you were short one bolt on Sunday afternoon. So read ahead and plan ahead. Each operation should be approached logically and all procedures thoroughly understood before attempting any work.

All sections contain adjustments, maintenance, removal and installation procedures, and in some cases, repair or overhaul procedures. When repair is not considered practical, we tell you how to remove the part and then how to install the new or rebuilt replacement. In this way, you at least save the labor costs. Backyard repair of some components is just not practical.

Avoiding Trouble

Many procedures in this book require you to "label and disconnect . . ." a group of lines, hoses or wires. Don't be lulled into thinking you can remember where everything goes—you won't. If you hook up vacuum or fuel lines incorrectly, the vehicle will run poorly, if at all. If you hook up electrical wiring incorrectly, you may instantly learn a very expensive lesson.

You don't need to know the official or engineering name for each hose or line. A piece of masking tape on the hose and a piece on its fitting will allow you to assign your own label such as the letter A or a short name. As long as you remember your own code, the lines can be reconnected by matching similar letters or names. Do remember that tape will dissolve in gasoline or other fluids; if a component is to be washed or cleaned, use another method of identification. A permanent felt-tipped marker can be very handy for marking metal parts. Remove any tape or paper labels after assembly.

Maintenance or Repair?

It's necessary to mention the difference between maintenance and repair. Maintenance includes routine inspections, adjustments, and replacement of parts which show signs of normal wear. Maintenance compensates for wear or deterioration. Repair implies that something has broken or is not working. A need for repair is often caused by lack of maintenance. Example: draining and refilling the automatic transmission fluid is maintenance recommended by the manufacturer at specific mileage intervals. Failure to do this can ruin the transmission, requiring very expensive repairs. While no maintenance program can prevent items from breaking or wearing out, a general rule can be stated: MAINTENANCE IS CHEAPER THAN REPAIR.

Two basic mechanic's rules should be mentioned here. First, whenever the left side of the vehicle or engine is referred to, it is meant to specify the driver's side. Conversely, the right side of the vehicle means the passenger's side. Second, most screws and bolts are removed by turning counterclockwise, and tightened by turning clockwise.

Safety is always the most important rule. Constantly be aware of the dangers involved in working on an automobile and take the proper precautions. See the information in this section regarding SERVICING YOUR VEHICLE SAFELY and the SAFETY NOTICE on the acknowledgment page.

Avoiding the Most Common Mistakes

Pay attention to the instructions provided. There are 3 common mistakes in mechanical work:

1. Incorrect order of assembly, disassembly or adjustment. When taking something apart or putting it together, performing steps in the wrong order usually just costs you extra time; however, it CAN break something. Read the entire procedure before beginning disassembly. Perform everything in the order in which the instructions say you should, even if you can't immediately see a reason for it. When you're taking apart something that is very intricate, you might want to draw a picture of how it looks when assembled at one point in order to make sure you get everything back in its proper position. We will supply exploded views whenever possible. When making adjustments, perform them in the proper order; often, one adjustment affects another, and you cannot expect even satisfactory results unless each adjustment is made only when it cannot be changed by any other.

2. Overtorquing (or undertorquing). While it is more common for overtorquing to cause damage, undertorquing may allow a fastener to vibrate loose causing serious damage. Especially when dealing with aluminum parts, pay attention to torque specifications and utilize a torque wrench in assembly. If a torque figure is not available, remember that if you are using the right tool to perform the job, you will probably not have to strain yourself to get a fastener tight enough. The pitch of most threads is so slight that the tension you put on the wrench will be multiplied many times in actual force on what you are tightening. A good example of how critical torque is can be seen in the case of spark plug installation, especially where you are putting the plug into an aluminum cylinder head. Too little torque can fail to crush the gasket, causing leakage of combustion gases and consequent overheating of the plug and engine parts. Too much torque can damage the threads or distort the plug, changing the spark gap.

There are many commercial products available for ensuring that fasteners won't come loose, even if they are not torqued just right (a very common brand is Loctite®). If you're worried about getting something together tight enough to hold, but loose enough to avoid mechanical damage during assembly, one of these products might offer substantial insurance. Before choosing a threadlocking compound, read the label on the package and make sure the product is compatible with the materials, fluids, etc. involved.

3. Crossthreading. This occurs when a part such as a bolt is screwed into a nut or casting at the wrong angle and forced. Crossthreading is more likely to occur if access is difficult. It helps to clean and lubricate fasteners, then to start threading with the part to be installed positioned straight in. Then, start the bolt, spark plug, etc. with your fingers. If you encounter resistance, unscrew the part and start over again at a different angle until it can be inserted and turned several times without much effort. Keep in mind that many parts, especially spark plugs, have tapered threads, so that gentle turning will automatically bring the part you're threading to the proper angle, but only if you don't force it or resist a change in angle. Don't put a wrench on the part until it's been tightened a couple of turns by hand. If you suddenly encounter resistance, and the part has not seated fully, don't force it. Pull it back out to make sure it's clean and threading properly.

Always take your time and be patient; once you have some experience, working on your vehicle may well become an enjoyable hobby.

TOOLS AND EQUIPMENT

◗ **See Figures 1 thru 15**

Naturally, without the proper tools and equipment it is impossible to properly service your vehicle. It would also be virtually impossible to catalog every tool that you would need to perform all of the operations in this book. Of course, It would be unwise for the amateur to rush out and buy an expensive set of tools on the theory that he/she may need one or more of them at some time.

The best approach is to proceed slowly, gathering a good quality set of those tools that are used most frequently. Don't be misled by the low cost of bargain tools. It is far better to spend a little more for better quality. Forged wrenches, 6 or 12-point sockets and fine tooth ratchets are by far preferable to their less expensive counterparts. As any good mechanic can tell you, there are few worse experiences than trying to work on a vehicle with bad tools. Your monetary savings will be far outweighed by frustration and mangled knuckles.

Begin accumulating those tools that are used most frequently: those associated with routine maintenance and tune-up. In addition to the normal assortment of screwdrivers and pliers, you should have the following tools:

• Wrenches/sockets and combination open end/box end wrenches in sizes from ⅛–¾ in. or 3mm–19mm (depending on whether your vehicle uses standard or metric fasteners) and a ¹³⁄₁₆ in. or ⅝ in. spark plug socket (depending on plug type).

➡**If possible, buy various length socket drive extensions. Universal joint and wobble extensions can be extremely useful, but be careful when using them, as they can change the amount of torque applied to the socket.**

• Jackstands for support.
• Oil filter wrench.
• Spout or funnel for pouring fluids.
• Grease gun for chassis lubrication (unless your vehicle is not equipped with any grease fittings—for details, please refer to information on Fluids and Lubricants found later in this section).
• Hydrometer for checking the battery (unless equipped with a sealed, maintenance-free battery).
• A container for draining oil and other fluids.
• Rags for wiping up the inevitable mess.

In addition to the above items there are several others that are not absolutely necessary, but handy to have around. These include Oil Dry® (or an equivalent oil absorbent gravel—such as cat litter) and the usual supply of lubricants, antifreeze and fluids, although these can be purchased as needed. This is a basic list for routine maintenance, but only your personal needs and desire can accurately determine your list of tools.

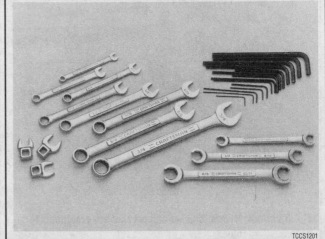

Fig. 2 In addition to ratchets, a good set of wrenches and hex keys will be necessary

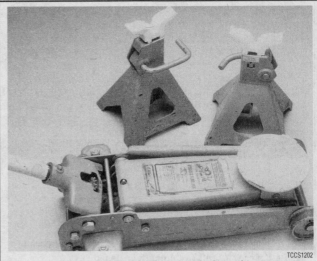

Fig. 3 A hydraulic floor jack and a set of jackstands are essential for lifting and supporting the vehicle

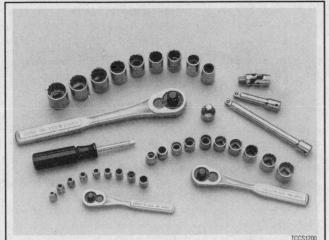

Fig. 1 All but the most basic procedures will require an assortment of ratchets and sockets

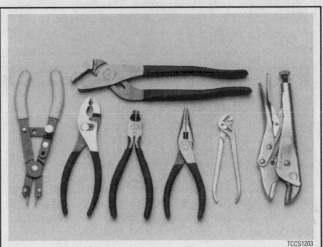

Fig. 4 An assortment of pliers, grippers and cutters will be handy for old rusted parts and stripped bolt heads

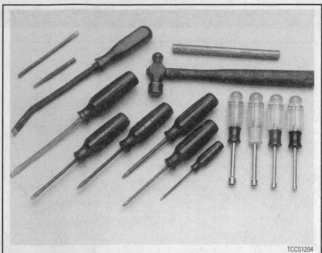

Fig. 5 Various drivers, chisels and prybars are great tools to have in your toolbox

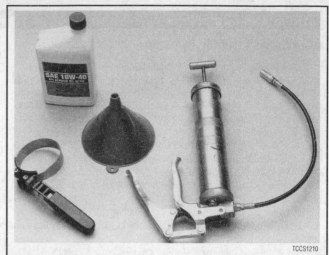

Fig. 8 A few inexpensive lubrication tools will make maintenance easier

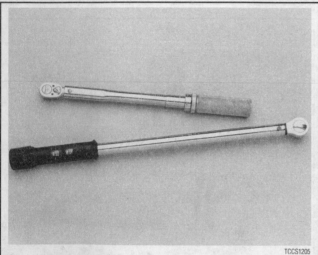

Fig. 6 Many repairs will require the use of a torque wrench to assure the components are properly fastened

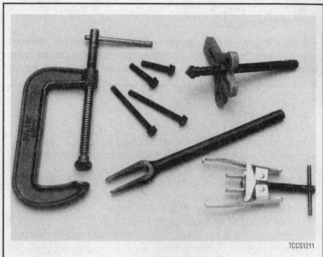

Fig. 9 Various pullers, clamps and separator tools are needed for many larger, more complicated repairs

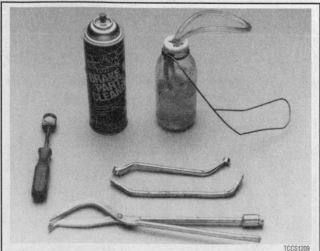

Fig. 7 Although not always necessary, using specialized brake tools will save time

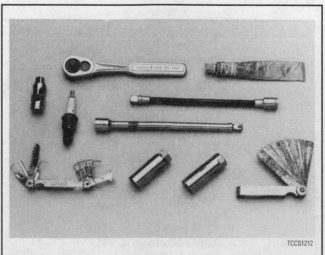

Fig. 10 A variety of tools and gauges should be used for spark plug gapping and installation

After performing a few projects on the vehicle, you'll be amazed at the other tools and non-tools on your workbench. Some useful household items are: a large turkey baster or siphon, empty coffee cans and ice trays (to store parts), ball of twine, electrical tape for wiring, small rolls of colored tape for tagging lines or hoses, markers and pens, a note pad, golf tees (for plugging vacuum lines), metal coat hangers or a roll of mechanic's wire (to hold things out of the way), dental pick or similar long, pointed probe, a strong magnet, and a small mirror (to see into recesses and under manifolds).

A more advanced set of tools, suitable for tune-up work, can be drawn up easily. While the tools are slightly more sophisticated, they need not be

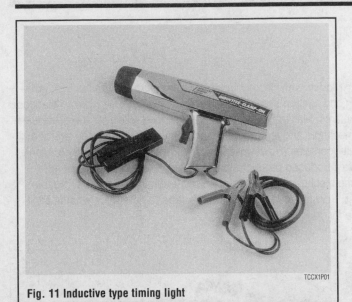

TCCX1P01

Fig. 11 Inductive type timing light

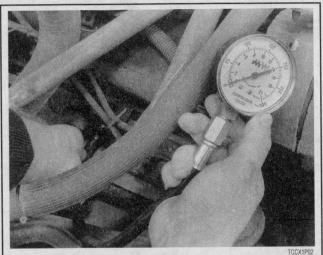

TCCX1P02

Fig. 12 A screw-in type compression gauge is recommended for compression testing

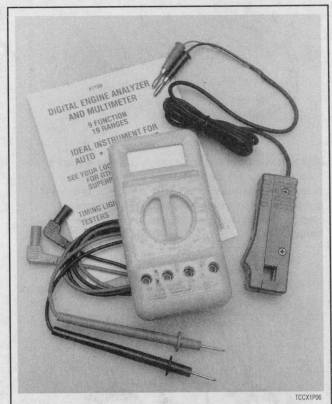

TCCX1P06

Fig. 14 Most modern automotive multimeters incorporate many helpful features

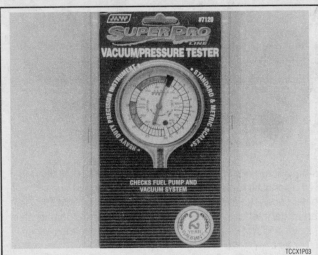

TCCX1P03

Fig. 13 A vacuum/pressure tester is necessary for many testing procedures

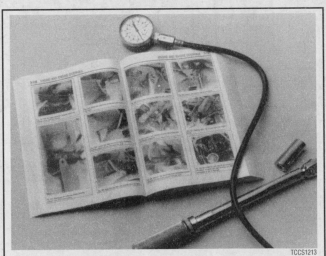

TCCS1213

Fig. 15 Proper information is vital, so always have a Chilton Total Car Care manual handy

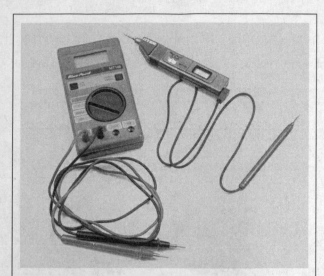

Digital multimeters come in a variety of styles and are a "must-have" for any serious home mechanic. Digital multimeters measure voltage (volts), resistance (ohms) and sometimes current (amperes). These versatile tools are used for checking all types of electrical or electronic components

Modern vehicles equipped with computer-controlled fuel, emission and ignition systems require modern electronic tools to diagnose problems. Many of these tools are designed solely for the professional mechanic and are too costly and difficult to use for the average do-it-yourselfer. However, various automotive aftermarket companies have introduced products that address the needs of the average home mechanic, providing sophisticated information at affordable cost. Consult your local auto parts store to determine what is available for your vehicle.

Trouble code tools allow the home mechanic to extract the "fault code" number from an on-board computer that has sensed a problem (usually indicated by a Check Engine light). Armed with this code, the home mechanic can focus attention on a suspect system or component

Sensor testers perform specific checks on many of the sensors and actuators used on today's computer-controlled vehicles. These testers can check sensors both on or off the vehicle, as well as test the accompanying electrical circuits

Hand-held scanners represent the most sophisticated of all do-it-yourself diagnostic tools. These tools do more than just access computer codes like the code readers above; they provide the user with an actual interface into the vehicle's computer. Comprehensive data on specific makes and models will come with the tool, either built-in or as a separate cartridge

outrageously expensive. There are several inexpensive tach/dwell meters on the market that are every bit as good for the average mechanic as a professional model. Just be sure that it goes to a least 1200–1500 rpm on the tach scale and that it works on 4, 6 and 8-cylinder engines. (If you have one or more vehicles with a diesel engine, a special tachometer is required since diesels don't use spark plug ignition systems). The key to these purchases is to make them with an eye towards adaptability and wide range. A basic list of tune-up tools could include:

- Tach/dwell meter.
- Spark plug wrench and gapping tool.
- Feeler gauges for valve or point adjustment. (Even if your vehicle does not use points or require valve adjustments, a feeler gauge is helpful for many repair/overhaul procedures).

A tachometer/dwell meter will ensure accurate tune-up work on vehicles without electronic ignition. The choice of a timing light should be made carefully. A light which works on the DC current supplied by the vehicle's battery is the best choice; it should have a xenon tube for brightness. On any vehicle with an electronic ignition system, a timing light with an inductive pickup that clamps around the No. 1 spark plug cable is preferred.

In addition to these basic tools, there are several other tools and gauges you may find useful. These include:

- Compression gauge. The screw-in type is slower to use, but eliminates the possibility of a faulty reading due to escaping pressure.
- Manifold vacuum gauge.

- 12V test light.
- A combination volt/ohmmeter
- Induction Ammeter. This is used for determining whether or not there is current in a wire. These are handy for use if a wire is broken somewhere in a wiring harness.

As a final note, you will probably find a torque wrench necessary for all but the most basic work. The beam type models are perfectly adequate, although the newer click types (breakaway) are easier to use. The click type torque wrenches tend to be more expensive. Also keep in mind that all types of torque wrenches should be periodically checked and/or recalibrated. You will have to decide for yourself which better fits your purpose.

Special Tools

Normally, the use of special factory tools is avoided for repair procedures, since these are not readily available for the do-it-yourself mechanic. When it is possible to perform the job with more commonly available tools, it will be pointed out, but occasionally, a special tool was designed to perform a specific function and should be used. Before substituting another tool, you should be convinced that neither your safety nor the performance of the vehicle will be compromised.

Special tools can usually be purchased from an automotive parts store or from your dealer. In some cases special tools may be available directly from the tool manufacturer.

SERVICING YOUR VEHICLE SAFELY

▶ **See Figures 16, 17, 18 and 19**

It is virtually impossible to anticipate all of the hazards involved with automotive maintenance and service, but care and common sense will prevent most accidents.

The rules of safety for mechanics range from "don't smoke around gasoline," to "use the proper tool(s) for the job." The trick to avoiding injuries is to develop safe work habits and to take every possible precaution.

Do's

- Do keep a fire extinguisher and first aid kit handy.
- Do wear safety glasses or goggles when cutting, drilling, grinding or prying, even if you have 20–20 vision. If you wear glasses for the sake of vision, wear safety goggles over your regular glasses.

- Do shield your eyes whenever you work around the battery. Batteries contain sulfuric acid. In case of contact with the eyes or skin, flush the area with water or a mixture of water and baking soda, then seek immediate medical attention.
- Do use safety stands (jackstands) for any undervehicle service. Jacks are for raising vehicles; jackstands are for making sure the vehicle stays raised until you want it to come down. Whenever the vehicle is raised, block the wheels remaining on the ground and set the parking brake.
- Do use adequate ventilation when working with any chemicals or hazardous materials. Like carbon monoxide, the asbestos dust resulting from some brake lining wear can be hazardous in sufficient quantities.
- Do disconnect the negative battery cable when working on the electrical system. The secondary ignition system contains EXTREMELY HIGH VOLTAGE. In some cases it can even exceed 50,000 volts.

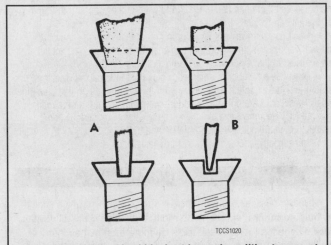

TCCS1020

Fig. 16 Screwdrivers should be kept in good condition to prevent injury or damage which could result if the blade slips from the screw

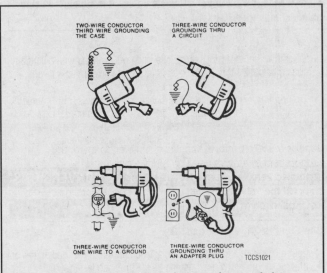

TWO-WIRE CONDUCTOR THIRD WIRE GROUNDING THE CASE

THREE-WIRE CONDUCTOR GROUNDING THRU A CIRCUIT

THREE-WIRE CONDUCTOR ONE WIRE TO A GROUND

THREE-WIRE CONDUCTOR GROUNDING THRU AN ADAPTER PLUG

TCCS1021

Fig. 17 Power tools should always be properly grounded

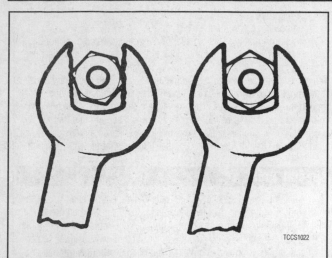

Fig. 18 Using the correct size wrench will help prevent the possibility of rounding off a nut

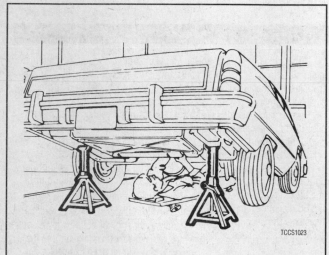

Fig. 19 NEVER work under a vehicle unless it is supported using safety stands (jackstands)

• Do follow manufacturer's directions whenever working with potentially hazardous materials. Most chemicals and fluids are poisonous if taken internally.
• Do properly maintain your tools. Loose hammerheads, mushroomed punches and chisels, frayed or poorly grounded electrical cords, excessively worn screwdrivers, spread wrenches (open end), cracked sockets, slipping ratchets, or faulty droplight sockets can cause accidents.

FASTENERS, MEASUREMENTS AND CONVERSIONS

Bolts, Nuts and Other Threaded Retainers

▶ See Figures 20, 21, 22 and 23

Although there are a great variety of fasteners found in the modern car or truck, the most commonly used retainer is the threaded fastener (nuts, bolts, screws, studs, etc). Most threaded retainers may be reused, provided that they are not damaged in use or during the repair. Some retainers (such as stretch bolts or torque prevailing nuts) are designed to deform when tightened or in use and should not be reinstalled.

• Likewise, keep your tools clean; a greasy wrench can slip off a bolt head, ruining the bolt and often harming your knuckles in the process.
• Do use the proper size and type of tool for the job at hand. Do select a wrench or socket that fits the nut or bolt. The wrench or socket should sit straight, not cocked.
• Do, when possible, pull on a wrench handle rather than push on it, and adjust your stance to prevent a fall.
• Do be sure that adjustable wrenches are tightly closed on the nut or bolt and pulled so that the force is on the side of the fixed jaw.
• Do strike squarely with a hammer; avoid glancing blows.
• Do set the parking brake and block the drive wheels if the work requires a running engine.

Don'ts

• Don't run the engine in a garage or anywhere else without proper ventilation—EVER! Carbon monoxide is poisonous; it takes a long time to leave the human body and you can build up a deadly supply of it in your system by simply breathing in a little every day. You may not realize you are slowly poisoning yourself. Always use power vents, windows, fans and/or open the garage door.
• Don't work around moving parts while wearing loose clothing. Short sleeves are much safer than long, loose sleeves. Hard-toed shoes with neoprene soles protect your toes and give a better grip on slippery surfaces. Jewelry such as watches, fancy belt buckles, beads or body adornment of any kind is not safe working around a vehicle. Long hair should be tied back under a hat or cap.
• Don't use pockets for toolboxes. A fall or bump can drive a screwdriver deep into your body. Even a rag hanging from your back pocket can wrap around a spinning shaft or fan.
• Don't smoke when working around gasoline, cleaning solvent or other flammable material.
• Don't smoke when working around the battery. When the battery is being charged, it gives off explosive hydrogen gas.
• Don't use gasoline to wash your hands; there are excellent soaps available. Gasoline contains dangerous additives which can enter the body through a cut or through your pores. Gasoline also removes all the natural oils from the skin so that bone dry hands will suck up oil and grease.
• Don't service the air conditioning system unless you are equipped with the necessary tools and training. When liquid or compressed gas refrigerant is released to atmospheric pressure it will absorb heat from whatever it contacts. This will chill or freeze anything it touches. Although refrigerant is normally non-toxic, R-12 becomes a deadly poisonous gas in the presence of an open flame. One good whiff of the vapors from burning refrigerant can be fatal.
• Don't use screwdrivers for anything other than driving screws! A screwdriver used as an prying tool can snap when you least expect it, causing injuries. At the very least, you'll ruin a good screwdriver.
• Don't use a bumper or emergency jack (that little ratchet, scissors, or pantograph jack supplied with the vehicle) for anything other than changing a flat! These jacks are only intended for emergency use out on the road; they are NOT designed as a maintenance tool. If you are serious about maintaining your vehicle yourself, invest in a hydraulic floor jack of at least a 1½ ton capacity, and at least two sturdy jackstands.

Whenever possible, we will note any special retainers which should be replaced during a procedure. But you should always inspect the condition of a retainer when it is removed and replace any that show signs of damage. Check all threads for rust or corrosion which can increase the torque necessary to achieve the desired clamp load for which that fastener was originally selected. Additionally, be sure that the driver surface of the fastener has not been compromised by rounding or other damage. In some cases a driver surface may become only partially rounded, allowing the driver to catch in only one direction. In many of these occurrences, a fastener may be installed and tightened, but the

Fig. 20 Here are a few of the most common screw/bolt driver styles

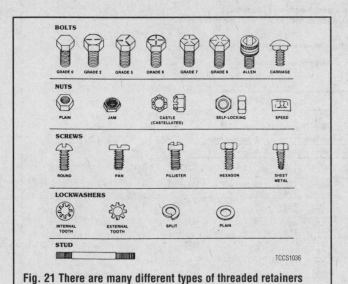

Fig. 21 There are many different types of threaded retainers found on vehicles

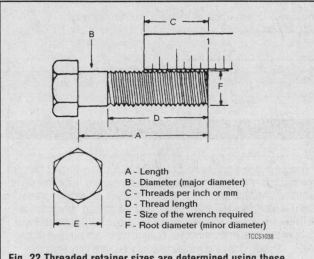

A - Length
B - Diameter (major diameter)
C - Threads per inch or mm
D - Thread length
E - Size of the wrench required
F - Root diameter (minor diameter)

TCCS1038

Fig. 22 Threaded retainer sizes are determined using these measurements

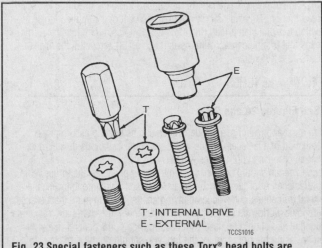

T - INTERNAL DRIVE
E - EXTERNAL

TCCS1016

Fig. 23 Special fasteners such as these Torx® head bolts are used by manufacturers to discourage people from working on vehicles without the proper tools

driver would not be able to grip and loosen the fastener again. (This could lead to frustration down the line should that component ever need to be disassembled again).

If you must replace a fastener, whether due to design or damage, you must ALWAYS be sure to use the proper replacement. In all cases, a retainer of the same design, material and strength should be used. Markings on the heads of most bolts will help determine the proper strength of the fastener. The same material, thread and pitch must be selected to assure proper installation and safe operation of the vehicle afterwards.

Thread gauges are available to help measure a bolt or stud's thread. Most automotive and hardware stores keep gauges available to help you select the proper size. In a pinch, you can use another nut or bolt for a thread gauge. If the bolt you are replacing is not too badly damaged, you can select a match by finding another bolt which will thread in its place. If you find a nut which threads properly onto the damaged bolt, then use that nut to help select the replacement bolt. If however, the bolt you are replacing is so badly damaged (broken or drilled out) that its threads cannot be used as a gauge, you might start by looking for another bolt (from the same assembly or a similar location on your vehicle) which will thread into the damaged bolt's mounting. If so, the other bolt can be used to select a nut; the nut can then be used to select the replacement bolt.

In all cases, be absolutely sure you have selected the proper replacement. Don't be shy, you can always ask the store clerk for help.

✳✳ WARNING

Be aware that when you find a bolt with damaged threads, you may also find the nut or drilled hole it was threaded into has also been damaged. If this is the case, you may have to drill and tap the hole, replace the nut or otherwise repair the threads. NEVER try to force a replacement bolt to fit into the damaged threads.

Torque

Torque is defined as the measurement of resistance to turning or rotating. It tends to twist a body about an axis of rotation. A common example of this would be tightening a threaded retainer such as a nut, bolt or screw. Measuring torque is one of the most common ways to help assure that a threaded retainer has been properly fastened.

When tightening a threaded fastener, torque is applied in three distinct areas, the head, the bearing surface and the clamp load. About 50 percent of the measured torque is used in overcoming bearing friction. This is the friction between the bearing surface of the bolt head, screw head or nut face and the base material or washer (the surface on which the fastener is rotating). Approximately 40 percent of the applied torque is used in overcoming thread friction. This leaves only about 10 percent of the applied torque to develop a useful clamp load (the force which holds a joint together). This means that friction can account for as much as 90 percent of the applied torque on a fastener.

TORQUE WRENCHES

♦ **See Figures 24 and 25**

In most applications, a torque wrench can be used to assure proper installation of a fastener. Torque wrenches come in various designs and most automotive supply stores will carry a variety to suit your needs. A torque wrench should be used any time we supply a specific torque value for a fastener. A torque wrench can also be used if you are following the general guidelines in the accompanying charts. Keep in mind that because there is no worldwide standardization of fasteners, the charts are a general guideline and should be used with caution. Again, the general rule of "if you are using the right tool for the job, you should not have to strain to tighten a fastener" applies here.

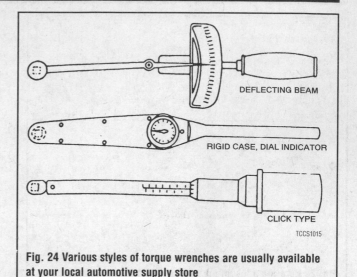

DEFLECTING BEAM

RIGID CASE, DIAL INDICATOR

CLICK TYPE

TCCS1015

Fig. 24 Various styles of torque wrenches are usually available at your local automotive supply store

Standard Torque Specifications and Fastener Markings

In the absence of specific torques, the following chart can be used as a guide to the maximum safe torque of a particular size/grade of fastener.
- There is no torque difference for fine or coarse threads.
- Torque values are based on clean, dry threads. Reduce the value by 10% if threads are oiled prior to assembly.
- The torque required for aluminum components or fasteners is considerably less.

U.S. Bolts

SAE Grade Number	1 or 2			5			6 or 7		
Number of lines always 2 less than the grade number.									
Bolt Size (Inches)—(Thread)	Maximum Torque			Maximum Torque			Maximum Torque		
	Ft./Lbs.	Kgm	Nm	Ft./Lbs.	Kgm	Nm	Ft./Lbs.	Kgm	Nm
¼ — 20	5	0.7	6.8	8	1.1	10.8	10	1.4	13.5
— 28	6	0.8	8.1	10	1.4	13.6			
⁵⁄₁₆ — 18	11	1.5	14.9	17	2.3	23.0	19	2.6	25.8
— 24	13	1.8	17.6	19	2.6	25.7			
⅜ — 16	18	2.5	24.4	31	4.3	42.0	34	4.7	46.0
— 24	20	2.75	27.1	35	4.8	47.5			
⁷⁄₁₆ — 14	28	3.8	37.0	49	6.8	66.4	55	7.6	74.5
— 20	30	4.2	40.7	55	7.6	74.5			
½ — 13	39	5.4	52.8	75	10.4	101.7	85	11.75	115.2
— 20	41	5.7	55.6	85	11.7	115.2			
⁹⁄₁₆ — 12	51	7.0	69.2	110	15.2	149.1	120	16.6	162.7
— 18	55	7.6	74.5	120	16.6	162.7			
⅝ — 11	83	11.5	112.5	150	20.7	203.3	167	23.0	226.5
— 18	95	13.1	128.8	170	23.5	230.5			
¾ — 10	105	14.5	142.3	270	37.3	366.0	280	38.7	379.6
— 16	115	15.9	155.9	295	40.8	400.0			
⅞ — 9	160	22.1	216.9	395	54.6	535.5	440	60.9	596.5
— 14	175	24.2	237.2	435	60.1	589.7			
1 — 8	236	32.5	318.6	590	81.6	799.9	660	91.3	894.8
— 14	250	34.6	338.9	660	91.3	849.8			

Metric Bolts

Relative Strength Marking	4.6, 4.8			8.8		
Bolt Markings						
Bolt Size Thread Size x Pitch (mm)	Maximum Torque			Maximum Torque		
	Ft./Lbs.	Kgm	Nm	Ft./Lbs.	Kgm	Nm
6 x 1.0	2–3	.2–.4	3–4	3–6	4–.8	5–8
8 x 1.25	6–8	.8–1	8–12	9–14	1.2–1.9	13–19
10 x 1.25	12–17	1.5–2.3	16–23	20–29	2.7–4.0	27–39
12 x 1.25	21–32	2.9–4.4	29–43	35–53	4.8–7.3	47–72
14 x 1.5	35–52	4.8–7.1	48–70	57–85	7.8–11.7	77–110
16 x 1.5	51–77	7.0–10.6	67–100	90–120	12.4–16.5	130–160
18 x 1.5	74–110	10.2–15.1	100–150	130–170	17.9–23.4	180–230
20 x 1.5	110–140	15.1–19.3	150–190	190–240	26.2–46.9	160–320
22 x 1.5	150–190	22.0–26.2	200–260	250–320	34.5–44.1	340–430
24 x 1.5	190–240	26.2–46.9	260–320	310–410	42.7–56.5	420–550

TCCS1098

Fig. 25 Standard and metric bolt torque specifications based on bolt strengths—WARNING: use only as a guide

Beam Type

▶ See Figure 26

The beam type torque wrench is one of the most popular types. It consists of a pointer attached to the head that runs the length of the flexible beam (shaft) to a scale located near the handle. As the wrench is pulled, the beam bends and the pointer indicates the torque using the scale.

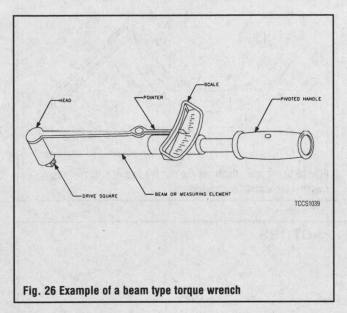

Fig. 26 Example of a beam type torque wrench

Click (Breakaway) Type

▶ See Figure 27

Another popular design of torque wrench is the click type. To use the click type wrench you pre-adjust it to a torque setting. Once the torque is reached, the wrench has a reflex signaling feature that causes a momentary breakaway of the torque wrench body, sending an impulse to the operator's hand.

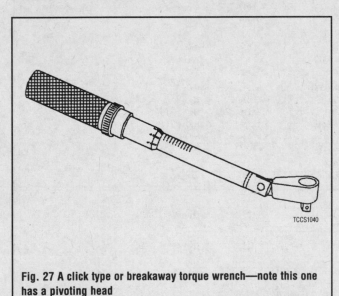

Fig. 27 A click type or breakaway torque wrench—note this one has a pivoting head

Pivot Head Type

▶ See Figures 27 and 28

Some torque wrenches (usually of the click type) may be equipped with a pivot head which can allow it to be used in areas of limited access. BUT, it must be used properly. To hold a pivot head wrench, grasp the handle

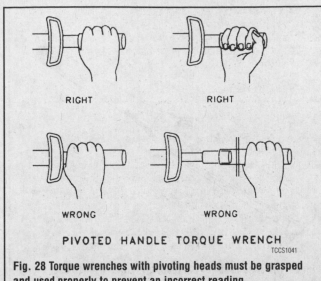

Fig. 28 Torque wrenches with pivoting heads must be grasped and used properly to prevent an incorrect reading

lightly, and as you pull on the handle, it should be floated on the pivot point. If the handle comes in contact with the yoke extension during the process of pulling, there is a very good chance the torque readings will be inaccurate because this could alter the wrench loading point. The design of the handle is usually such as to make it inconvenient to deliberately misuse the wrench.

➡️It should be mentioned that the use of any U-joint, wobble or extension will have an effect on the torque readings, no matter what type of wrench you are using. For the most accurate readings, install the socket directly on the wrench driver. If necessary, straight extensions (which hold a socket directly under the wrench driver) will have the least effect on the torque reading. Avoid any extension that alters the length of the wrench from the handle to the head/driving point (such as a crow's foot). U-joint or Wobble extensions can greatly affect the readings; avoid their use at all times.

Rigid Case (Direct Reading)

▶ See Figure 29

A rigid case or direct reading torque wrench is equipped with a dial indicator to show torque values. One advantage of these wrenches is that they can be held at any position on the wrench without affecting accuracy. These wrenches are often preferred because they tend to be compact, easy to read and have a great degree of accuracy.

TORQUE ANGLE METERS

▶ See Figure 30

Because the frictional characteristics of each fastener or threaded hole will vary, clamp loads which are based strictly on torque will vary as well. In most applications, this variance is not significant enough to cause worry. But, in certain applications, a manufacturer's engineers may determine that more precise clamp loads are necessary (such is the case with many aluminum cylinder heads). In these cases, a torque angle method of installation would be specified. When installing fasteners which are torque angle tightened, a predetermined seating torque and standard torque wrench are usually used first to remove any compliance from the joint. The fastener is then tightened the specified additional portion of a turn measured in degrees. A torque angle gauge (mechanical protractor) is used for these applications.

Standard and Metric Measurements

▶ See Figure 31

Throughout this manual, specifications are given to help you determine the condition of various components on your vehicle, or to assist you in

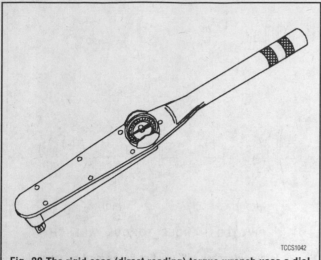

Fig. 29 The rigid case (direct reading) torque wrench uses a dial indicator to show torque

TCCS1042

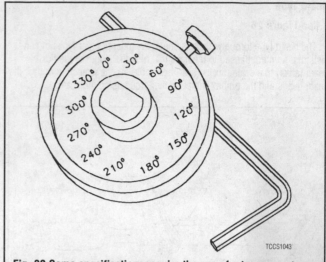

Fig. 30 Some specifications require the use of a torque angle meter (mechanical protractor)

TCCS1043

CONVERSION FACTORS

LENGTH–DISTANCE

Inches (in.)	x 25.4	= Millimeters (mm)	x .0394	= Inches
Feet (ft.)	x .305	= Meters (m)	x 3.281	= Feet
Miles	x 1.609	= Kilometers (km)	x .0621	= Miles

VOLUME

Cubic Inches (in3)	x 16.387	= Cubic Centimeters	x .061	= in3
IMP Pints (IMP pt.)	x .568	= Liters (L)	x 1.76	= IMP pt.
IMP Quarts (IMP qt.)	x 1.137	= Liters (L)	x .88	= IMP qt.
IMP Gallons (IMP gal.)	x 4.546	= Liters (L)	x .22	= IMP gal.
IMP Quarts (IMP qt.)	x 1.201	= US Quarts (US qt.)	x .833	= IMP qt.
IMP Gallons (IMP gal.)	x 1.201	= US Gallons (US gal.)	x .833	= IMP gal.
Fl. Ounces	x 29.573	= Milliliters	x .034	= Ounces
US Pints (US pt.)	x .473	= Liters (L)	x 2.113	= Pints
US Quarts (US qt.)	x .946	= Liters (L)	x 1.057	= Quarts
US Gallons (US gal.)	x 3.785	= Liters (L)	x .264	= Gallons

MASS–WEIGHT

Ounces (oz.)	x 28.35	= Grams (g)	x .035	= Ounces
Pounds (lb.)	x .454	= Kilograms (kg)	x 2.205	= Pounds

PRESSURE

Pounds Per Sq. In. (psi)	x 6.895	= Kilopascals (kPa)	x .145	= psi
Inches of Mercury (Hg)	x .4912	= psi	x 2.036	= Hg
Inches of Mercury (Hg)	x 3.377	= Kilopascals (kPa)	x .2961	= Hg
Inches of Water (H_2O)	x .07355	= Inches of Mercury	x 13.783	= H_2O
Inches of Water (H_2O)	x .03613	= psi	x 27.684	= H_2O
Inches of Water (H_2O)	x .248	= Kilopascals (kPa)	x 4.026	= H_2O

TORQUE

Pounds–Force Inches (in–lb)	x .113	= Newton Meters (N·m)	x 8.85	= in–lb
Pounds–Force Feet (ft–lb)	x 1.356	= Newton Meters (N·m)	x .738	= ft–lb

VELOCITY

Miles Per Hour (MPH)	x 1.609	= Kilometers Per Hour (KPH)	x .621	= MPH

POWER

Horsepower (Hp)	x .745	= Kilowatts	x 1.34	= Horsepower

FUEL CONSUMPTION*

Miles Per Gallon IMP (MPG)	x .354	= Kilometers Per Liter (Km/L)	
Kilometers Per Liter (Km/L)	x 2.352	= IMP MPG	
Miles Per Gallon US (MPG)	x .425	= Kilometers Per Liter (Km/L)	
Kilometers Per Liter (Km/L)	x 2.352	= US MPG	

*It is common to covert from miles per gallon (mpg) to liters/100 kilometers (1/100 km), where mpg (IMP) x 1/100 km = 282 and mpg (US) x 1/100 km = 235.

TEMPERATURE

Degree Fahrenheit (°F)	= (°C x 1.8) + 32
Degree Celsius (°C)	= (°F – 32) x .56

TCCS1044

Fig. 31 Standard and metric conversion factors chart

their installation. Some of the most common measurements include length (in. or cm/mm), torque (ft. lbs., inch lbs. or Nm) and pressure (psi, in. Hg, kPa or mm Hg). In most cases, we strive to provide the proper measurement as determined by the manufacturer's engineers.

Though, in some cases, that value may not be conveniently measured with what is available in your toolbox. Luckily, many of the measuring devices which are available today will have two scales so the Standard or Metric measurements may easily be taken. If any of the various measuring tools which are available to you do not contain the same scale as listed in the specifications, use the accompanying conversion factors to determine the proper value.

The conversion factor chart is used by taking the given specification and multiplying it by the necessary conversion factor. For instance, looking at the first line, if you have a measurement in inches such as "free-play should be 2 in." but your ruler reads only in millimeters, multiply 2 in. by the conversion factor of 25.4 to get the metric equivalent of 50.8mm. Likewise, if the specification was given only in a Metric measurement, for example in Newton Meters (Nm), then look at the center column first. If the measurement is 100 Nm, multiply it by the conversion factor of 0.738 to get 73.8 ft. lbs.

SERIAL NUMBER IDENTIFICATION

Vehicle

▶ See Figures 32 and 33

The Vehicle Identification Number (VIN) is located on the left side of the dash panel behind the windshield.

A seventeen digit combination of numbers and letters forms the VIN. Refer to the illustration for VIN details.

Vehicle Safety Compliance Certification Label

▶ See Figures 34 and 35

The English certification label is attached to the driver's door or lock pillar. The French certification label is attached to the passenger's or driver's

SAMPLE VIN

1 F T E E 11 H 5 T L A00001

POSITIONS 1, 2 AND 3 — MANUFACTURER, MAKE AND TYPE (WORLD MANUFACTURER IDENTIFIER)

POSITION 4 — BRAKE SYSTEM/GVWR CLASS FOR FORD-COMPLETED TRUCKS AND MPV'S. FOR BUSES AND INCOMPLETE VEHICLES, BRAKE SYSTEM (ONLY).

POSITIONS 5, 6, AND 7 — MODEL OR LINE, SERIES, CHASSIS, CAB OR BODY TYPE

POSITION 8 — ENGINE TYPE

POSITION 9 — CHECK DIGIT

POSITION 10 — MODEL YEAR (FORD-COMPLETED VEHICLES)

POSITION 11 — ASSEMBLY PLANT

POSITIONS 12 THROUGH 17 — SEQUENCE NUMBER BEGINS AT A00001. CONSTANT A UNTIL SEQUENCE NUMBER OF 99,999 IS REACHED, THEN CHANGES TO CONSTANT B AND SO ON.

88481G01

Fig. 33 This sample VIN will help to decode what each symbol represents on the label

door or lock pillar. The label contains the name of the manufacturer, production month and year of the vehicle, certification statement and VIN. The label also contains gross vehicle weight and tire data.

Engine

▶ See Figures 36, 37, 38 and 39

The engine identification tag identifies the cubic inch displacement of the engine, the model year, the year and month in which the engine was built, where it was built and the change level number. The change level is usually the number one (1), unless there are parts on the engine that will not be completely interchangeable and will require minor modification.

The engine identification tag is usually located on the valve cover on all engines except the 7.3L diesels. The diesel engine ID number is stamped on the front of the block in front of the left cylinder head.

Fig. 32 The Vehicle Identification Number (VIN) is visible through the driver's side of the windshield

88481P01

VEHICLE IDENTIFICATION CHART

Engine Code						Model Year	
Code	Liters	Cu. In. (cc)	Cyl.	Fuel Sys.	Eng. Mfg.	Code	Year
C	7.3	444 (7270)	8	DI	Navistar	K	1989
F	7.3	444 (7270)	8	DI	Navistar	L	1990
G	7.5	460 (7536)	8	MFI/SFI	Ford	M	1991
H	5.8	351 (5766)	8	MFI/SFI	Ford	N	1992
M	7.3	444 (7270)	8	DSL	Navistar	P	1993
N	5.0	302 (4942)	8	MFI/SFI	Ford	R	1994
R	5.8	351 (5766)	8	MFI	Ford	S	1995
Y	4.9	300 (4917)	6	MFI/SFI	Ford	T	1996

MFI - Multi-port Fuel Injection
DSL - Diesel
DI - Direct Injection (turbo diesel)
SFI - Sequential Fuel Injection

88481C01

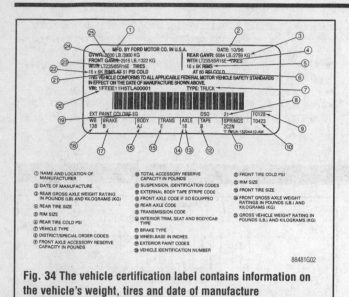

① NAME AND LOCATION OF MANUFACTURER
② DATE OF MANUFACTURE
③ REAR GROSS AXLE WEIGHT RATING IN POUNDS (LB) AND KILOGRAMS (KG)
④ REAR TIRE SIZE
⑤ RIM SIZE
⑥ REAR TIRE COLD PSI
⑦ VEHICLE TYPE
⑧ DISTRICT/SPECIAL ORDER CODES
⑨ FRONT AXLE ACCESSORY RESERVE CAPACITY IN POUNDS

⑩ TOTAL ACCESSORY RESERVE CAPACITY IN POUNDS
⑪ SUSPENSION, IDENTIFICATION CODES
⑫ EXTERNAL BODY TAPE STRIPE CODE
⑬ FRONT AXLE CODE IF SO EQUIPPED
⑭ REAR AXLE CODE
⑮ TRANSMISSION CODE
⑯ INTERIOR TRIM, SEAT AND BODY/CAB TYPE
⑰ BRAKE TYPE
⑱ WHEELBASE IN INCHES
⑲ EXTERIOR PAINT CODES
⑳ VEHICLE IDENTIFICATION NUMBER

㉑ FRONT TIRE COLD PSI
㉒ RIM SIZE
㉓ FRONT TIRE SIZE
㉔ FRONT GROSS AXLE WEIGHT RATINGS IN POUNDS (LB.) AND KILOGRAMS (KG)
㉕ GROSS VEHICLE WEIGHT RATING IN POUNDS (LB.) AND KILOGRAMS (KG)

88481G02

Fig. 34 The vehicle certification label contains information on the vehicle's weight, tires and date of manufacture

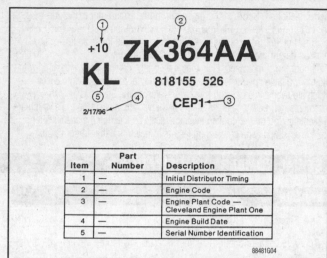

Item	Part Number	Description
1	—	Initial Distributor Timing
2	—	Engine Code
3	—	Engine Plant Code — Cleveland Engine Plant One
4	—	Engine Build Date
5	—	Serial Number Identification

88481G04

Fig. 37 Engine code information label—5.0L and 5.8L gasoline engines

88481P02

Fig. 35 The vehicle safety compliance label can be found on the inside edge of the door or lock pillar

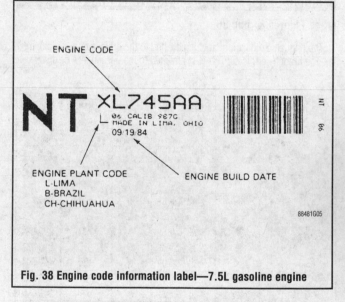

88481G05

Fig. 38 Engine code information label—7.5L gasoline engine

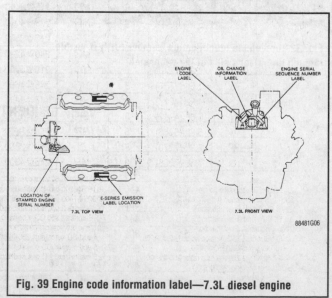

88481G03

Fig. 36 Engine code information label—4.9L gasoline engine

88481G06

Fig. 39 Engine code information label—7.3L diesel engine

GENERAL ENGINE SPECIFICATIONS

Year	Engine ID/VIN	Engine Displacement Liters (cc)	No. of Cyl.	Fuel System Type	Net Horsepower @ rpm	Net Torque @ rpm (ft. lbs.)	Bore x Stroke (in.)	Compression Ratio	Oil Pressure (lbs. @ rpm)
1989	Y	4.9L (4917)	6	EFI	①	②	4.00x3.98	8.8:1	40-60@2000
	N	5.0L (4942)	8	EFI	185@3800	270@2400	4.00x3.00	9.0:1	40-60@2000
	H	5.8L (5766)	8	EFI	210@3800	315@2800 ③	4.00x3.50	8.8:1	40-65@2000
	M	7.3L (7270)	8	DSL	180@3300 ④	345@1400 ⑤	4.11x4.18	21.5:1	40-70@3300
	G	7.5L (7536)	8	EFI	230@3600	390@2000	4.36x3.85	8.5:1	40-65@2000
1990	Y	4.9L (4917)	6	EFI	①	②	4.00x3.98	8.8:1	40-60@2000
	N	5.0L (4942)	8	EFI	185@3800	270@2400	4.00x3.00	9.0:1	40-60@2000
	H	5.8L (5766)	8	EFI	210@3800	315@2800 ③	4.00x3.50	8.8:1	40-65@2000
	M	7.3L (7270)	8	DSL	180@3300 ④	345@1400 ⑤	4.11x4.18	21.5:1	40-70@3300
	G	7.5L (7536)	8	EFI	230@3600	390@2000	4.36x3.85	8.5:1	40-65@2000
1991	Y	4.9L (4917)	6	EFI	①	②	4.00x3.98	8.8:1	40-60@2000
	N	5.0L (4942)	8	EFI	185@3800	270@2400	4.00x3.00	9.0:1	40-60@2000
	H	5.8L (5766)	8	EFI	210@3800	315@2800 ③	4.00x3.50	8.8:1	40-65@2000
	M	7.3L (7270)	8	DSL	180@3300 ④	345@1400 ⑤	4.11x4.18	21.5:1	40-70@3300
	G	7.5L (7536)	8	EFI	230@3600	390@2000	4.36x3.85	8.5:1	40-65@2000
1992	Y	4.9L (4917)	6	EFI	①	②	4.00x3.98	8.8:1	40-60@2000
	N	5.0L (4942)	8	EFI	185@3800	270@2400	4.00x3.00	9.0:1	40-60@2000
	H	5.8L (5766)	8	EFI	210@3800	315@2800 ③	4.00x3.50	8.8:1	40-65@2000
	M	7.3L (7270)	8	DSL	180@3300 ④	345@1400 ⑤	4.11x4.18	21.5:1	40-70@3300
	G	7.5L (7536)	8	EFI	230@3600	390@2000	4.36x3.85	8.5:1	40-65@2000
1993	Y	4.9L (4917)	6	EFI	⑥	⑦	4.00x3.98	8.8:1	40-60@2000
	N	5.0L (4942)	8	EFI	185@3800	270@2400	4.00x3.00	9.0:1	40-60@2000
	H	5.8L (5766)	8	EFI	200@3800	310@2800	4.00x3.50	8.8:1	40-65@2000
	R	5.8L (5766)	8	EFI	240@4200	340@3200	4.00x3.50	8.8:1	40-65@2000
	C	7.3L (7270)	8	IDI	190@3000	395@1400	4.11x4.18	21.5:1	40-70@3300
	M	7.3L (7270)	8	IDI	185@3000 ⑧	360@1400 ⑨	4.11x4.18	21.5:1	40-70@3300
	G	7.5L (7536)	8	EFI	230@3600	390@2200	4.36x3.85	8.5:1	40-88@2000
1994	Y	4.9L (4917)	6	EFI	⑥	⑦	4.00x3.98	8.8:1	40-60@2000
	N	5.0L (4942)	8	EFI	185@3800	270@2400	4.00x3.00	9.0:1	40-60@2000
	H	5.8L (5766)	8	EFI	200@3800	310@2800	4.00x3.50	8.8:1	40-65@2000
	R	5.8L (5766)	8	EFI	240@4200	340@3200	4.00x3.50	8.8:1	40-65@2000
	F	7.3L (7270)	8	DI	210@3000	425@2000	4.11x4.18	17.5:1	40-70@3300
	K	7.3L (7270)	8	IDI	190@3000	395@1400	4.11x4.18	21.5:1	40-70@3300
	M	7.3L (7270)	8	IDI	185@3000 ⑧	360@1400 ⑨	4.11x4.18	21.5:1	40-70@3300
	G	7.5L (7536)	8	MFI	245@4000	400@2200	4.36x3.85	8.5:1	40-88@2000
1995	Y	4.9L (4917)	6	MFI	145@3400 ⑩	265@2000 ⑩	4.00x3.98	8.8:1	40-60@2000
	N	5.0L (4942)	8	MFI	205@4000	275@3000	4.00x3.00	9.0:1	40-60@2000
	H	5.8L (5766)	8	MFI	210@3600	325@2800	4.00x3.50	8.8:1	40-65@2000
	R	5.8L (5766)	8	MFI	240@4200	340@3200	4.00x3.50	8.8:1	40-65@2000
	F	7.3L (7270)	8	DI	210@3000	425@2000	4.11x4.18	17.5:1	40-70@3300
	G	7.5L (7536)	8	MFI	245@4000	400@2200	4.36x3.85	8.5:1	40-88@2000
1996	Y	4.9L (4917)	6	SFI	145@3400 ⑩	265@2000 ⑩	4.00x3.98	8.8:1	40-60@2000
	N	5.0L (4942)	8	SFI	199@4200	270@2400	4.00x3.00	9.0:1	40-60@2000
	H	5.8L (5766)	8	SFI	210@3600	325@2800	4.00x3.50	8.8:1	40-65@2000
	F	7.3L (7270)	8	DI	210@3000	425@2000	4.11x4.18	17.5:1	40-70@3300
	G	7.5L (7536)	8	MFI	245@4000	400@2200	4.36x3.85	8.5:1	40-88@2000

DSL - Diesel
DI - Direct Injection (turbo diesel)
IDI - Indirect Injection (turbo diesel)
EFI - Electronic Fuel Injection
MFI - Multi-port Fuel Injection
SFI - Sequential Fuel Injection
① E-150 with 2.73/3.08 axle ratio: 145@3400
  All other models: 150@3400
② E-150 with 2.73/3.08 axle ratio: 265@2000
  All other models: 260@2000

③ 310@2800 on vans over 8500 lbs. GVWR
④ 160@3300 on high altitude applications
⑤ 305@1400 on high altitude applications
⑥ E-series 3 spd automatic: 150@3400
  E-series 4 spd OD automatic: 145@3400
⑦ 3 spd automatic: 260@2000
  4 spd OD automatic: 265@2000
  5 spd manual OD or 4 spd automatic OD: 265@2000
  5 spd manual HD or 4 spd automatic OD: 260@2000

⑧ High altitude: 165@3000
⑨ High altitude: 325@1600
⑩ Ratings are for the E150-250 van and regular wagon with 4 spd OD automatic (E40D). Use 150hp@3400 rpm and 260 ft. lbs. @2000rpm for all other applications

The engine identification code is located in the VIN at the eighth digit. The VIN can be found in the safety certification decal and the VIN plate at the upper left side of the dash panel. Refer to the "Engine Application" chart for engine VIN codes.

Transmission

♦ **See Figures 40, 41, 42, 43 and 44**

The transmission identification letter is located on a metal tag or plate attached to the case or it is stamped directly on the transmission case. Also, the transmission code is located on the Safety Certification Decal.

Drive Axle

♦ **See Figures 45 and 46**

The drive axle code is stamped on a flat surface on the axle tube, next to the differential housing, or on a tag secured by one of the differential housing cover bolts. A separate limited-slip tag is attached to the differential housing cover bolt. The letters L-S signify a limited-slip differential.

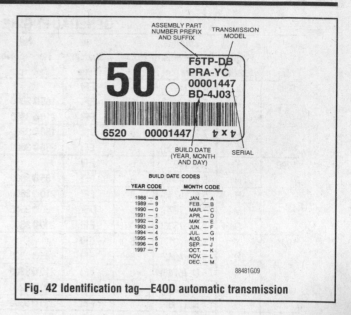

Fig. 42 Identification tag—E40D automatic transmission

Fig. 40 Service identification tag—Mazda M50D manual transmission

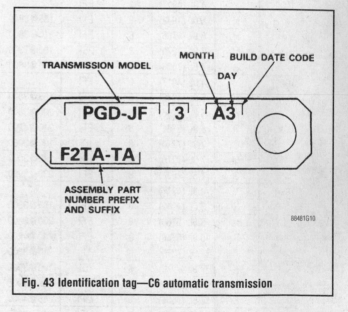

Fig. 43 Identification tag—C6 automatic transmission

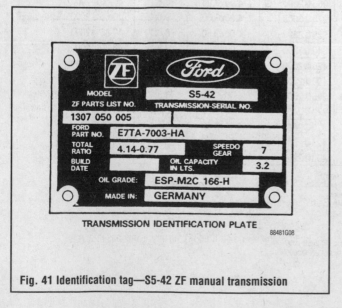

Fig. 41 Identification tag—S5-42 ZF manual transmission

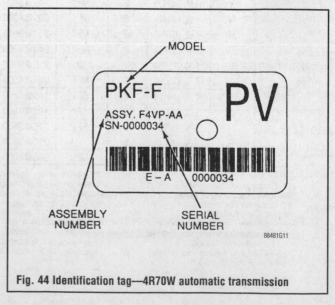

Fig. 44 Identification tag—4R70W automatic transmission

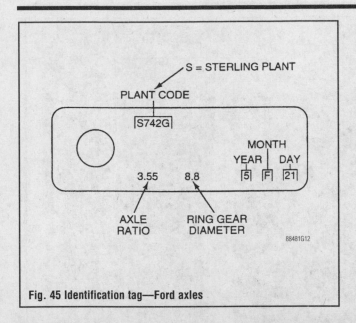

Fig. 45 Identification tag—Ford axles

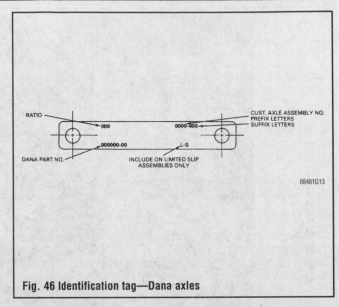

Fig. 46 Identification tag—Dana axles

ROUTINE MAINTENANCE AND TUNE-UP

Proper maintenance and tune-up is the key to long and trouble-free vehicle life, and the work can yield its own rewards. Studies have shown that a properly tuned and maintained vehicle can achieve better gas mileage than an out-of-tune vehicle. As a conscientious owner and driver, set aside a Saturday morning, say once a month, to check or replace items which could cause major problems later. Keep your own personal log to jot down which services you performed, how much the parts cost you, the date, and the exact odometer reading at the time. Keep all receipts for such items as engine oil and filters, so that they may be referred to in case of related problems or to determine operating expenses. As a do-it-yourselfer, these receipts are the only proof you have that the required maintenance was performed. In the event of a warranty problem, these receipts will be invaluable.

The literature provided with your vehicle when it was originally delivered includes the factory recommended maintenance schedule. If you no longer have this literature, replacement copies are usually available from the dealer. A maintenance schedule is provided later in this section, in case you do not have the factory literature.

Air Cleaner

The air cleaner is a paper element type.

The paper cartridge should be replaced according to the Preventive Maintenance Schedule in the owner's manual, or at the end of this section.

→**Check the air filter more often if the vehicle is operated under severe dusty conditions and replace or clean it as necessary.**

REPLACEMENT

1989–94 Models

GASOLINE ENGINES

▶ **See Figures 47, 48 and 49**

1. Loosen the two clamps that secure the hose assembly to the air cleaner.
2. Remove the two screws that attach the air cleaner to the bracket.
3. Disconnect the hose and inlet tube from the air cleaner.

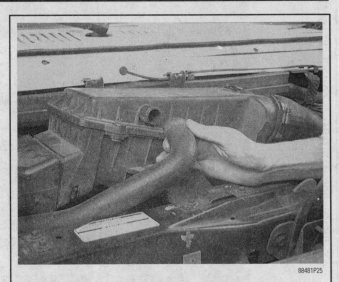

Fig. 47 Disengage the hose from the air cleaner housing

4. Remove the screws attaching the air cleaner cover.
5. Remove the air filter and tubes.

To install:

6. Install the air filter and tubes.
7. Install the screws attaching the air cleaner cover. Don't overtighten the hose clamps! A torque of 12–15 inch lbs. (1.36–1.69 Nm) is sufficient.
8. Connect the hose and inlet tube to the air cleaner.
9. Install the two screws that attach the air cleaner to the bracket.
10. Tighten the two clamps that secure the hose assembly to the air cleaner.

DIESEL ENGINES

▶ **See Figure 50**

1. Open the engine compartment hood.
2. Remove the wing bolt holding the air cleaner assembly.

UNDERHOOD MAINTENANCE COMPONENT LOCATIONS

1. Battery
2. Battery cable
3. Radiator cap
4. Air filter housing
5. Engine oil filler cap
6. Brake master cylinder
7. Engine oil dipstick
8. Washer fluid reservoir
9. Transmission dipstick (located under snorkel)

8481P06

Fig. 48 Loosen the housing retainers . . .

Fig. 49 . . . then lift the housing cover and withdraw the filter element

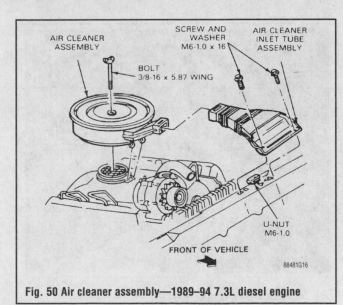

Fig. 50 Air cleaner assembly—1989–94 7.3L diesel engine

3. Remove the air cleaner housing, then remove the filter element.
4. Remove and discard the old filter element, and inspect the condition of the air cleaner mounting gasket. Replace the gasket if necessary.
5. Place the new filter element in the air cleaner body and install the cover.
6. Install the air cleaner assembly and tighten the wing bolt.

1995–96 Models

ALL ENGINES

♦ See Figures 51 and 52

1. Tag, disconnect and set aside any tubes, hoses or ducts that interfere with removal of the air cleaner cover.

❊❊ CAUTION

Whenever the element, air cleaner housing and/or outlet tube are removed, use a clean rag to prevent contamination of the air intake system.

2. Loosen the air cleaner cover retainers (clamps or screws) and remove the cover.
3. Remove the filter element.
To install:
4. Install the filter element and cover.
5. Fasten the air cleaner retainers.
6. Engage any hoses, tubes or ducts disconnected during removal.

Fuel Filter

REMOVAL & INSTALLATION

Gasoline Engines
♦ See Figures 53 thru 59

1989–93 MODELS
♦ See Figure 60

The filter on these engines is located on the left frame rail. The filter should be changed either every 15,000 miles (24,000 km) or 15 months, whichever comes first. The filter should also be changed whenever a fuel delivery module is replaced.

➡To prevent siphoning of fuel from the tank when the filter is removed, raise and support the front end of the van above the level of the tank.

1. Relieve fuel system pressure, as described in Section 5. When working in hot weather, work quickly to complete filter replacement before the fuel pressure rebuilds!
2. Disconnect the negative battery cable.
3. Loosen the screw clamp so that the filter slides rearward easily.
4. Detach the quick-connect couplings and remove the filter.
5. Remove the filter from the bracket by rotating the fuel line, being careful not to kink the line, then slide the filter rearward and out of the bracket.
To install:

➡Note the direction-of-flow arrow on the new filter.

6. Place the filter into the bracket, making sure the flow arrow is pointing towards the tab of the bracket, then slide the filter forward until it rests against the tab of the bracket.
7. Tighten the screw on the clamp to 1.3–2.1 ft. lbs. (1.8–2.8 Nm).
8. Install the quick-connect fittings onto the filter ends.
9. Turn the ignition switch from **OFF** to **RUN** several times—without starting the engine—and check for leaks.
10. Lower the van.

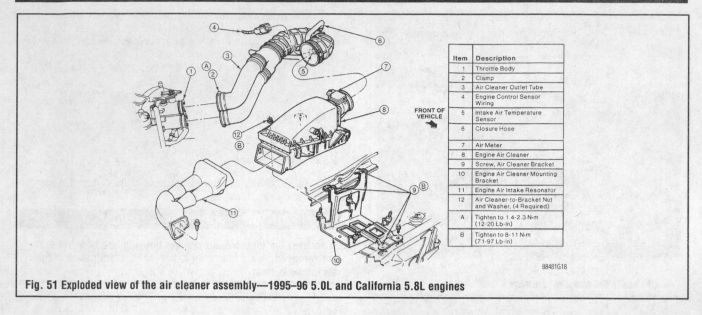

Item	Description
1	Throttle Body
2	Clamp
3	Air Cleaner Outlet Tube
4	Engine Control Sensor Wiring
5	Intake Air Temperature Sensor
6	Closure Hose
7	Air Meter
8	Engine Air Cleaner
9	Screw, Air Cleaner Bracket
10	Engine Air Cleaner Mounting Bracket
11	Engine Air Intake Resonator
12	Air Cleaner-to-Bracket Nut and Washer, (4 Required)
A	Tighten to 1.4-2.3 N·m (12-20 Lb-In)
B	Tighten to 8-11 N·m (71-97 Lb-In)

FRONT OF VEHICLE

88481G18

Fig. 51 Exploded view of the air cleaner assembly—1995–96 5.0L and California 5.8L engines

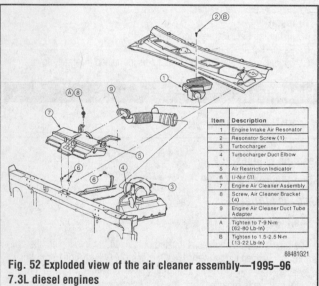

Item	Description
1	Engine Intake Air Resonator
2	Resonator Screw (1)
3	Turbocharger
4	Turbocharger Duct Elbow
5	Air Restriction Indicator
6	U-Nut (3)
7	Engine Air Cleaner Assembly
8	Screw, Air Cleaner Bracket (4)
9	Engine Air Cleaner Duct Tube Adapter
A	Tighten to 7-9 N·m (62-80 Lb-In)
B	Tighten to 1.5-2.5 N·m (13-22 Lb-In)

88481G21

Fig. 52 Exploded view of the air cleaner assembly—1995–96 7.3L diesel engines

88481P13

Fig. 54 . . . then disconnect the clamp from the negative battery terminal

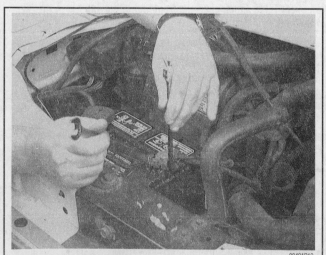

88481P12

Fig. 53 Use a back-up wrench and loosen the battery clamp retainer . . .

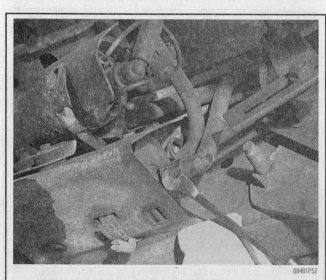

88481P52

Fig. 55 Use a prytool to disengage the fuel filter clips

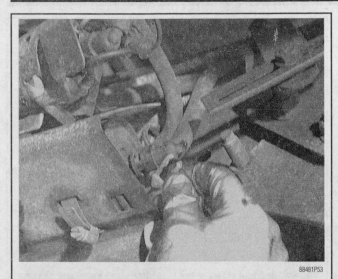

Fig. 56 After the clip has been disengaged, pull it from the hose

Fig. 57 Loosen the fuel filter retaining clamp

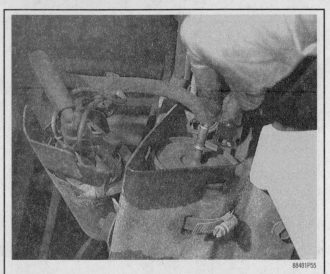

Fig. 58 Disconnect the fuel lines from the ends of the filter . . .

Fig. 59 . . . and remove the filter from the bracket

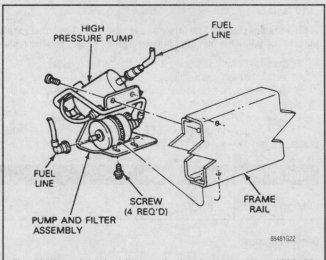

Fig. 60 View of the fuel filter and related components—1989–93 models

1994–96 MODELS

▶ See Figure 61

1. Relieve fuel system pressure. See Section 5.

➡When the battery is disconnected and reconnected, some abnormal drive symptoms may appear temporarily. Do not be unduly concerned. The vehicle must be driven for at least 10 miles to allow the engine management computer to relearn its adaptive strategy.

2. Disconnect the negative battery cable.
3. Raise and safely support the vehicle.
4. Remove the filter-to-fuel line retainer clips.
5. Disconnect the quick-connect couplings from both ends of the filter.
6. Push the arms of the filter bracket apart and pull out the filter.

✵✵ WARNING

Be careful to avoid kinking the fuel lines!

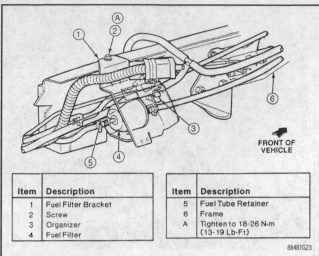

Item	Description
1	Fuel Filter Bracket
2	Screw
3	Organizer
4	Fuel Filter

Item	Description
5	Fuel Tube Retainer
6	Frame
A	Tighten to 18-26 N·m (13-19 Lb-Ft)

Fig. 61 The fuel filter and related components are located on the left frame rail

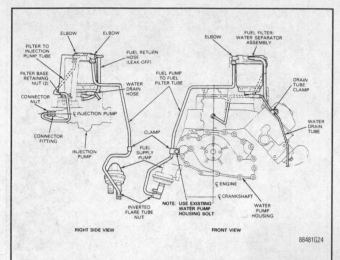

Fig. 62 Sectional views of the fuel filter/water separator assembly

To install:

➡Note the direction-of-flow arrow on the new filter. The arrow should point to the tab of the fuel filter bracket against which the filter rests.

7. Install the filter by snapping it into place on the bracket.
8. Install the push-connect fittings to the filter ends.
9. Snap on the the filter-to-fuel line clips, making sure the long legs of the clips go onto the fuel lines.
10. Lower the vehicle and connect the negative battery cable.
11. Turn the ignition switch from **OFF** to **RUN** several times—without starting the engine—and check for leaks.

Fuel Filter/Water Separator

REMOVAL & INSTALLATION

Diesel Engines

1989–94 MODELS

♦ See Figure 62

The 7.3L diesel engines use a one-piece spin-on fuel filter. Do not add fuel to the new fuel filter. Allow the engine to draw fuel through the filter.

1. Disconnect the negative battery cables.
2. Place a suitable container under the filter and drain the fuel from filter by opening the water separator drain valve.
3. Remove the drain tube, then unscrew the water separator from the bottom of the filter.
4. Remove the spin-on filter by unscrewing it counterclockwise with your hands or a strap wrench.

To install:
5. Clean the filter mounting surface.
6. Coat the gasket or the replacement filter with clean diesel fuel. This helps ensure a good seal.
7. Tighten the filter by hand until the gasket touches the filter mounting surface.
8. Tighten the filter an additional 180–300°.
9. Apply clean diesel fuel to the water separator seal and install it to the bottom of the fuel filter.
10. Connect the drain tube and make sure all drain valves are closed.
11. Connect the negative battery cables and check for leaks.

➡After changing the fuel filter, the engine will purge the trapped air as it runs. The engine may run roughly and smoke excessively until the air is cleared from the system.

1995–96 MODELS

♦ See Figure 63

1. Disconnect the negative battery cable.
2. Remove the turbocharger assembly.
3. Remove the baffle and the air inlet crossover manifold.
4. Place a suitable container under the drain hose and open the filter drain.
5. Remove the two capscrews securing the fuel filter base to the crankcase.
6. Disconnect the water drain hose from the filter.
7. Disconnect the fuel outlet hose, located between the fuel and filter housing, and the fuel return hose from the fuel pressure regulator valve.
8. Disconnect the two fuel supply hoses that connect the regulator block to the cylinder head fuel rails.
9. Loosen the clamp at the fuel pump end of the hose which connects the fuel filter to the inlet of high pressure stage at the fuel pump.
10. Disengage the wiring harness from the right side of the filter housing.
11. Disengage the electrical connections from the Water In Fuel (WIF) sensor and the fuel heater.

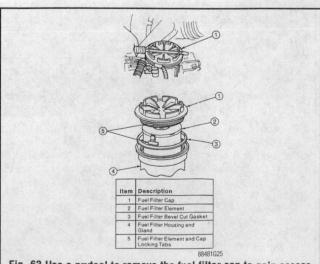

Item	Description
1	Fuel Filter Cap
2	Fuel Filter Element
3	Fuel Filter Bevel Cut Gasket
4	Fuel Filter Housing and Gland
5	Fuel Filter Element and Cap Locking Tabs

Fig. 63 Use a prytool to remove the fuel filter cap to gain access to the filter element

12. Remove the fuel filter.

13. Use a prybar to remove the fuel filter cap and the filter element will come out with the cap.

14. Depress the element locking tabs and remove the element from the cap.

To install:

15. Clean the mating surfaces and install the filter element onto the cap, making sure the tabs engage.

16. Install the filter gap and press down firmly, but gently, to engage it.

17. Engage the wiring connections to the fuel heater and WIF sensor.

18. Engage the wiring harness to the filter housing.

19. Tighten the clamp at the fuel pump end of the hose which connects the fuel filter to the inlet of high pressure stage at the fuel pump.

20. Engage the two fuel supply hoses that connect the regulator block to the cylinder head fuel rails.

21. Connect the fuel outlet hose, located between the fuel and filter housing, and the fuel return hose from the fuel pressure regulator valve.

22. Connect the water drain hose to the filter.

23. Install the two capscrews securing the fuel filter base to the crankcase.

24. Install the air inlet crossover manifold and baffle.

25. Install the turbocharger assembly.

26. Connect the negative battery cable.

Fuel/Water Separator

DRAINING

The 7.3L diesel engines are equipped with a fuel/water separator in the fuel supply line. A "Water in Fuel" indicator light is provided on the instrument panel to alert the driver. The light should glow when the ignition switch is in the **START** position to indicate proper light and water sensor function. If the light glows continuously while the engine is running, the water must be drained from the separator as soon as possible to prevent damage to the fuel injection system.

1. Shut off the engine. Failure to shut the engine **OFF** before draining the separator will cause air to enter the system.

2. Place a suitable container under the drain tube.

3. Unscrew the drain valve to open it and allow the valve to remain open for 15 seconds or until clear, water-free fuel is flowing.

4. Close the drain securely until liquid is no longer flowing.

5. Start the engine and check the "Water in Fuel" indicator light; it should not be lit. If it is lit and continues to remain on, there is a problem somewhere else in the fuel system.

PCV Valve

GASOLINE ENGINES

▶ See Figures 64 thru 69

➡**Some models require the removal of the upper intake manifold in order to remove the PCV valve.**

Check the PCV valve to see if it is free and not gummed up, stuck or blocked. To check the valve, remove it from the engine and work the valve by sticking a screwdriver in the crankcase side of the valve. It should move. It is possible to clean the PCV valve by soaking it in a solvent and blowing it out with compressed air. This can restore the valve to some level of operating order. This should be used only as an emergency measure. Otherwise, the valve should be replaced.

1. Disconnect the oil separator hose from the PCV valve.

2. Remove the PCV valve from the grommet in the crankcase.

3. Inspect the grommet for deterioration.

To install:

4. If necessary, replace the crankcase grommet.

5. Install the PCV valve.

6. Install the hose.

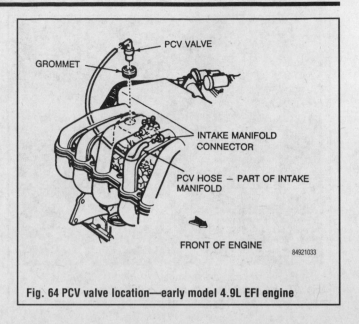

Fig. 64 PCV valve location—early model 4.9L EFI engine

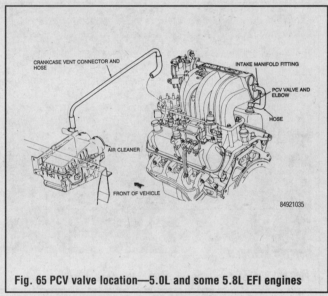

Fig. 65 PCV valve location—5.0L and some 5.8L EFI engines

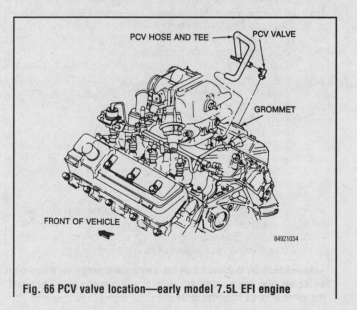

Fig. 66 PCV valve location—early model 7.5L EFI engine

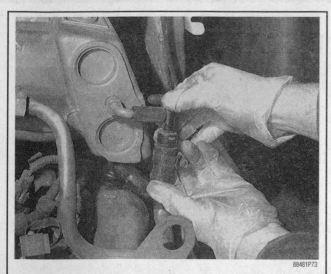

Fig. 67 Disconnect the hose from the PCV valve . . .

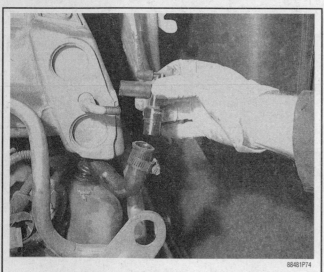

Fig. 68 . . . and pull the valve from the hose or grommet

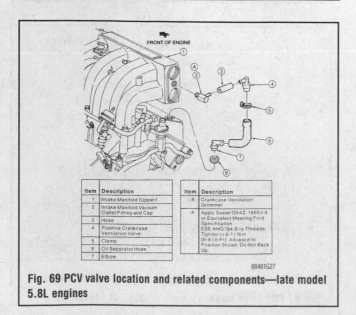

Fig. 69 PCV valve location and related components—late model 5.8L engines

Item	Description	Item	Description
1	Intake Manifold (Upper)	8	Crankcase Ventilation Grommet
2	Intake Manifold Vacuum Outlet Fitting and Cap	A	Apply Sealer D8AZ-19554-A or Equivalent Meeting Ford Specification ESE-M4G 194-B to Threads Tighten to 8-11 N·m (6-8 Lb-Ft). Advance to Position Shown. Do Not Back Up
3	Hose		
4	Positive Crankcase Ventilation Valve		
5	Clamp		
6	Oil Separator Hose		
7	Elbow		

Battery

PRECAUTIONS

Always use caution when working on or near the battery. Never allow a tool to bridge the gap between the negative and positive battery terminals. Also, be careful not to allow a tool to provide a ground between the positive cable/terminal and any metal component on the vehicle. Either of these conditions will cause a short circuit, leading to sparks and possible personal injury.

Do not smoke, have an open flame or create sparks near a battery; the gases contained in the battery are very explosive and, if ignited, could cause severe injury or death.

All batteries, regardless of type, should be carefully secured by a battery hold-down device. If this is not done, the battery terminals or casing may crack from stress applied to the battery during vehicle operation. A battery which is not secured may allow acid to leak out, making it discharge faster; such leaking corrosive acid can also eat away at components under the hood.

Always visually inspect the battery case for cracks, leakage and corrosion. A white corrosive substance on the battery case or on nearby components would indicate a leaking or cracked battery. If the battery is cracked, it should be replaced immediately.

GENERAL MAINTENANCE

♦ See Figure 70

A battery that is not sealed must be checked periodically for electrolyte level. You cannot add water to a sealed maintenance-free battery (although not all maintenance-free batteries are sealed); however, a sealed battery must also be checked for proper electrolyte level, as indicated by the color of the built-in hydrometer "eye."

Always keep the battery cables and terminals free of corrosion. Check these components about once a year. Refer to the removal, installation and cleaning procedures outlined in this section.

Keep the top of the battery clean, as a film of dirt can help completely discharge a battery that is not used for long periods. A solution of baking soda and water may be used for cleaning, but be careful to flush this off with clear water. DO NOT let any of the solution into the filler holes. Baking soda neutralizes battery acid and will de-activate a battery cell.

Batteries in vehicles which are not operated on a regular basis can fall victim to parasitic loads (small current drains which are constantly drawing current from the battery). Normal parasitic loads may drain a battery on a vehicle that is in storage and not used for 6–8 weeks. Vehicles that have

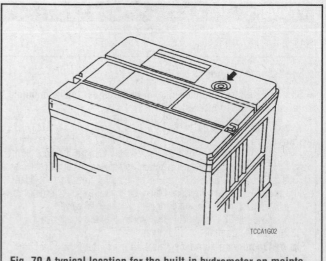

Fig. 70 A typical location for the built-in hydrometer on maintenance-free batteries

additional accessories such as a cellular phone, an alarm system or other devices that increase parasitic load may discharge a battery sooner. If the vehicle is to be stored for 6–8 weeks in a secure area and the alarm system, if present, is not necessary, the negative battery cable should be disconnected at the onset of storage to protect the battery charge.

Remember that constantly discharging and recharging will shorten battery life. Take care not to allow a battery to be needlessly discharged.

BATTERY FLUID

Check the battery electrolyte level at least once a month, or more often in hot weather or during periods of extended vehicle operation. On non-sealed batteries, the level can be checked either through the case on translucent batteries or by removing the cell caps on opaque-cased types. The electrolyte level in each cell should be kept filled to the split ring inside each cell, or the line marked on the outside of the case.

If the level is low, add only distilled water through the opening until the level is correct. Each cell is separate from the others, so each must be checked and filled individually. Distilled water should be used, because the chemicals and minerals found in most drinking water are harmful to the battery and could significantly shorten its life.

If water is added in freezing weather, the vehicle should be driven several miles to allow the water to mix with the electrolyte. Otherwise, the battery could freeze.

Although some maintenance-free batteries have removable cell caps for access to the electrolyte, the electrolyte condition and level on all sealed maintenance-free batteries must be checked using the built-in hydrometer "eye." The exact type of eye varies between battery manufacturers, but most apply a sticker to the battery itself explaining the possible readings. When in doubt, refer to the battery manufacturer's instructions to interpret battery condition using the built-in hydrometer.

➡**Although the readings from built-in hydrometers found in sealed batteries may vary, a green eye usually indicates a properly charged battery with sufficient fluid level. A dark eye is normally an indicator of a battery with sufficient fluid, but one which may be low in charge. And a light or yellow eye is usually an indication that electrolyte supply has dropped below the necessary level for battery (and hydrometer) operation. In this last case, sealed batteries with an insufficient electrolyte level must usually be discarded.**

Checking the Specific Gravity

▶ **See Figures 71, 72, 73 and 74**

A hydrometer is required to check the specific gravity on all batteries that are not maintenance-free. On batteries that are maintenance-free, the spe-

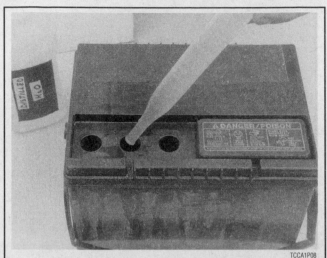

Fig. 72 If the fluid level is low, add only distilled water through the opening until the level is correct

cific gravity is checked by observing the built-in hydrometer "eye" on the top of the battery case. Check with your battery's manufacturer for proper interpretation of its built-in hydrometer readings.

✳✳ CAUTION

Battery electrolyte contains sulfuric acid. If you should splash any on your skin or in your eyes, flush the affected area with plenty of clear water. If it lands in your eyes, get medical help immediately.

The fluid (sulfuric acid solution) contained in the battery cells will tell you many things about the condition of the battery. Because the cell plates must be kept submerged below the fluid level in order to operate, maintaining the

Fig. 71 On non-maintenance-free batteries, the fluid level can be checked through the case on translucent models; the cell caps must be removed on other models

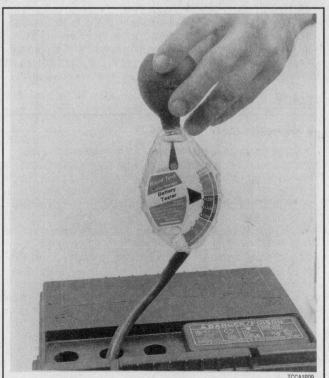

Fig. 73 Check the specific gravity of the battery's electrolyte with a hydrometer

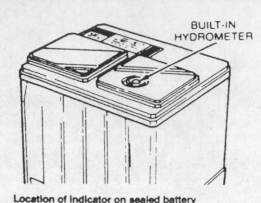

BUILT-IN HYDROMETER

Location of indicator on sealed battery

BATTERY TOP

DARKENED INDICATOR

WITH GREEN DOT

BATTERY TOP

DARKENED INDICATOR

NO GREEN DOT

MAY BE JUMP STARTED

BATTERY TOP

LIGHT YELLOW OR BRIGHT INDICATOR, NO GREEN DOT DO NOT JUMP START

Check the appearance of the charge indicator on top of the battery before attempting a jump start; if it's not green or dark, do not jump start the car

TCCS1253

Fig. 74 A typical sealed (maintenance-free) battery with a built-in hydrometer—NOTE that the hydrometer eye may vary between battery manufacturers; always refer to the battery's label

fluid level is extremely important. And, because the specific gravity of the acid is an indication of electrical charge, testing the fluid can be an aid in determining if the battery must be replaced. A battery in a vehicle with a properly operating charging system should require little maintenance, but careful, periodic inspection should reveal problems before they leave you stranded.

As stated earlier, the specific gravity of a battery's electrolyte level can be used as an indication of battery charge. At least once a year, check the specific gravity of the battery. It should be between 1.20 and 1.26 on the gravity scale. Most auto supply stores carry a variety of inexpensive battery testing hydrometers. These can be used on any non-sealed battery to test the specific gravity in each cell.

The battery testing hydrometer has a squeeze bulb at one end and a nozzle at the other. Battery electrolyte is sucked into the hydrometer until the float is lifted from its seat. The specific gravity is then read by noting the position of the float. If gravity is low in one or more cells, the battery should be slowly charged and checked again to see if the gravity has come up. Generally, if after charging, the specific gravity between any two cells varies more than 50 points (0.50), the battery should be replaced, as it can no longer produce sufficient voltage to guarantee proper operation.

CABLES

▶ **See Figures 75, 76, 77, 78 and 79**

Once a year (or as necessary), the battery terminals and the cable clamps should be cleaned. Loosen the clamps and remove the cables, negative cable first. On batteries with posts on top, the use of a puller specially made for this purpose is recommended. These are inexpensive and available in most auto parts stores. Side terminal battery cables are secured with a small bolt.

Clean the cable clamps and the battery terminal with a wire brush, until all corrosion, grease, etc., is removed and the metal is shiny. It is especially important to clean the inside of the clamp thoroughly (an old knife is useful here), since a small deposit of foreign material or oxidation there will prevent a sound electrical connection and inhibit either starting or charging. Special tools are available for cleaning these parts, one type for conventional top post batteries and another type for side terminal batteries. It is also a good idea to apply some dielectric grease to the terminal, as this will aid in the prevention of corrosion.

After the clamps and terminals are clean, reinstall the cables, negative cable last; DO NOT hammer the clamps onto battery posts. Tighten the clamps securely, but do not distort them. Give the clamps and terminals a thin external coating of grease after installation, to retard corrosion.

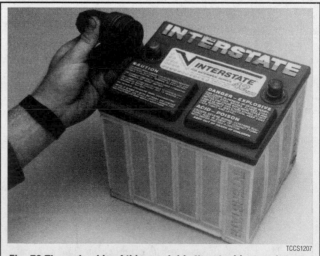

TCCS1206

Fig. 75 Maintenance is performed with household items and with special tools like this post cleaner

TCCS1207

Fig. 76 The underside of this special battery tool has a wire brush to clean post terminals

Fig. 77 Place the tool over the battery posts and twist to clean until the metal is shiny

TCCS1208

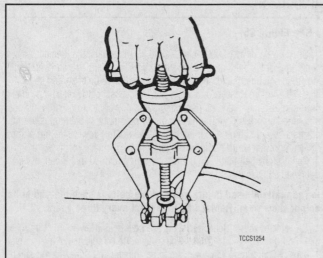

TCCS1254

Fig. 78 A special tool is available to pull the clamp from the post

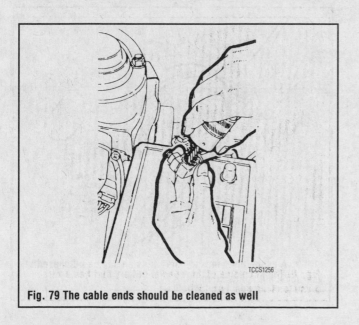

TCCS1256

Fig. 79 The cable ends should be cleaned as well

Check the cables at the same time that the terminals are cleaned. If the cable insulation is cracked or broken, or if the ends are frayed, the cable should be replaced with a new cable of the same length and gauge.

CHARGING

✷✷ CAUTION

The chemical reaction which takes place in all batteries generates explosive hydrogen gas. A spark can cause the battery to explode and splash acid. To avoid serious personal injury, be sure there is proper ventilation and take appropriate fire safety precautions when connecting, disconnecting, or charging a battery and when using jumper cables.

A battery should be charged at a slow rate to keep the plates inside from getting too hot. However, if some maintenance-free batteries are allowed to discharge until they are almost "dead," they may have to be charged at a high rate to bring them back to "life." Always follow the charger manufacturer's instructions on charging the battery.

REPLACEMENT

When it becomes necessary to replace the battery, select one with an amperage rating equal to or greater than the battery originally installed. Deterioration and just plain aging of the battery cables, starter motor, and associated wires makes the battery's job harder in successive years. The slow increase in electrical resistance over time makes it prudent to install a new battery with a greater capacity than the old.

Belts

INSPECTION

▶ **See Figures 80, 81, 82, 83 and 84**

Inspect the belts for signs of glazing or cracking. A glazed belt will be perfectly smooth from slippage, while a good belt will have a slight texture of fabric visible. Cracks will usually start at the inner edge of the belt and run outward. All worn or damaged drive belts should be replaced immediately. It is best to replace all drive belts at one time, as a preventive maintenance measure, during this service operation.

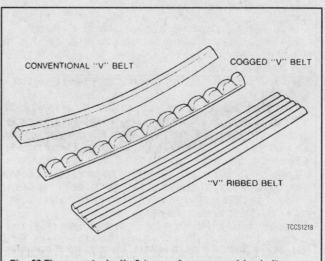

CONVENTIONAL "V" BELT

COGGED "V" BELT

"V" RIBBED BELT

TCCS1218

Fig. 80 There are typically 3 types of accessory drive belts found on vehicles today

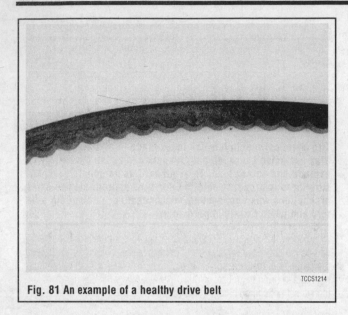
Fig. 81 An example of a healthy drive belt

TCCS1214

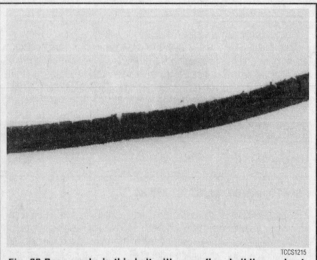
Fig. 82 Deep cracks in this belt will cause flex, building up heat that will eventually lead to belt failure

TCCS1215

Fig. 83 The cover of this belt is worn, exposing the critical rein-forcing cords to excessive wear

TCCS1216

Fig. 84 Installing too wide a belt can result in serious belt wear and/or breakage

TCCS1217

ADJUSTMENT

▶ **See Figure 85**

Once a year or at 12,000 mile (19,308 km) intervals, the tension (and condition) of the alternator, power steering (if so equipped), air conditioning (if so equipped), and Thermactor air pump drive belts should be checked and, if necessary, adjusted. Loose accessory drive belts can lead to poor engine cooling and diminish alternator, power steering pump, air conditioning compressor or Thermactor air pump output. A belt that is too tight places a severe strain on the water pump, alternator, power steering pump, A/C compressor or air pump bearings.

Replace any belt that is so glazed, worn or stretched that it cannot be tightened sufficiently.

➡ **The material used in late model drive belts is such that the belts do not show wear. Replace belts at least every three years.**

On vehicles with matched belts, replace both belts. New ½ in. (13mm), ⅜ in. (10mm) and ¹⁵⁄₃₂ in. (12mm) wide belts are to be adjusted to a tension of 140 lbs.; ¼ in. (6mm) wide belts are to be adjusted to 80 lbs., as measured on a belt tension gauge. Any belt that has been operating for a minimum of 10 minutes is considered a used belt. In the first 10 minutes, the belt should

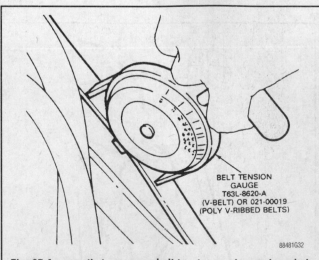

BELT TENSION
GAUGE
T63L-8620-A
(V-BELT) OR 021-00019
(POLY V-RIBBED BELTS)

88481G32

Fig. 85 A gauge that measures belt tension can be purchased at your local auto parts store

stretch to its maximum extent. After 10 minutes, stop the engine and recheck the belt tension. Belt tension for a used belt should be maintained at 110 lbs. (all except ¼ in. wide belts) or 60 lbs. (¼ in. wide belts). If a belt tension gauge is not available, the following procedures may be used.

Except Serpentine Belt

✳✳ CAUTION

On models equipped with an electric cooling fan, disengage the negative battery cable or fan motor wiring harness connector before replacing or adjusting drive belts. The fan may come on, under certain circumstances, even though the ignition is off.

ALTERNATOR BELT

▶ **See Figures 86 and 87**

1. Position the ruler perpendicular to the drive belt at its longest straight run. Test the tightness of the belt by pressing it firmly with your thumb. The deflection should not exceed ¼ in. (6mm).
2. If the deflection exceeds ¼ in. (6mm), loosen the alternator mounting and adjusting arm bolts.

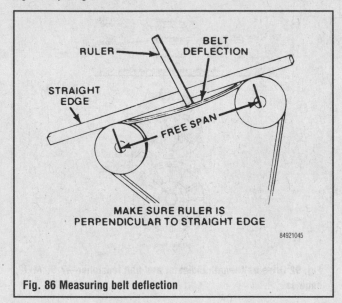

Fig. 86 Measuring belt deflection

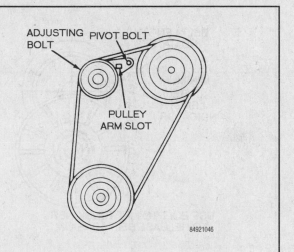

Fig. 87 Some pulleys have a rectangular slot to aid in moving the accessory to be tightened

3. Place a 1 in. open-end or adjustable wrench on the adjusting ridge cast on the body, and pull on the wrench until the proper tension is achieved.
4. Holding the alternator in place to maintain tension, tighten the adjusting arm bolt. Recheck the belt tension. When the belt is properly tensioned, tighten the alternator mounting bolt.

POWER STEERING BELT—4.9L ENGINE

1. Hold a ruler perpendicular to the drive belt at its longest run, and test the tightness of the belt by pressing it firmly with your thumb. The deflection should not exceed ¼ in. (6mm).
2. To adjust the belt tension, loosen the adjusting and mounting bolts on the front face of the steering pump cover plate (hub side).
3. Using a prybar on the pump hub, move the power steering pump toward or away from the engine until the proper tension is reached. Do not pry against the reservoir, as it is relatively soft and easily deformed.
4. Holding the pump in place, tighten the adjusting arm bolt and then recheck the belt tension. When the belt is properly tensioned, tighten the mounting bolts.

POWER STEERING BELT—V8 MODELS

1. Position a ruler perpendicular to the drive belt at its longest run. Test the tightness of the belt by pressing it firmly with your thumb. The deflection should be about ¼ in. (6mm).
2. To adjust the belt tension, loosen the three bolts in the three elongated adjusting slots at the power steering pump attaching bracket.
3. Turn the steering pump drive belt adjusting nut as required until the proper deflection is obtained. Turning the adjusting nut clockwise will increase tension and decrease deflection; counterclockwise will decrease tension and increase deflection.
4. Without disturbing the pump, tighten the three attaching bolts.

AIR CONDITIONING COMPRESSOR BELT

▶ **See Figure 88**

1. Position a ruler perpendicular to the drive belt at its longest run. Test the tightness of the belt by pressing it firmly with your thumb. The deflection should not exceed ¼ in. (6mm).
2. If the engine is equipped with an idler pulley, loosen the idler pulley adjusting bolt, insert a prybar between the pulley and the engine (or in the idler pulley adjusting slot), and adjust the tension accordingly. If the engine is not equipped with an idler pulley, the alternator must be moved to accomplish this adjustment, as outlined under Alternator (Fan Drive) Belt.
3. When the proper tension is reached, tighten the idler pulley adjusting bolt (if so equipped) or the alternator adjusting and mounting bolts.

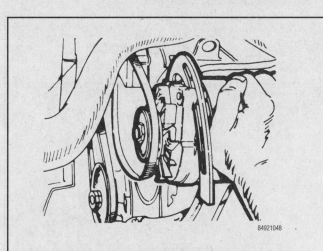

Fig. 88 If there is no idler pulley, adjust A/C compressor belt tension by moving the alternator toward or away from the engine

THERMACTOR® AIR PUMP BELT

1. Position a ruler perpendicular to the drive belt at its longest run. Test the tightness of the belt by pressing it firmly with your thumb. The deflection should be about ¼ in. (6mm).

2. To adjust the belt tension, loosen the adjusting arm bolt slightly. If necessary, also loosen the mounting belt slightly.

3. Using a prybar, pry against the pump's rear cover to move the pump toward or away from the engine, as necessary.

✳✳ WARNING

Do not pry against the pump housing itself, as damage to the housing may result.

4. Holding the pump in place, tighten the adjusting arm bolt and recheck the tension. When the belt is properly tensioned, tighten the mounting bolt.

Serpentine Belt

◗ **See Figures 89, 90, 91, 92 and 93**

Most models feature a single, wide, ribbed V-belt that drives the water pump, alternator, and (on some models) the air conditioner compressor.

Fig. 89 On some models, belt tension can be observed using the belt length indicator mark

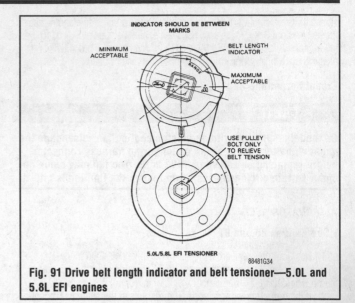

Fig. 91 Drive belt length indicator and belt tensioner—5.0L and 5.8L EFI engines

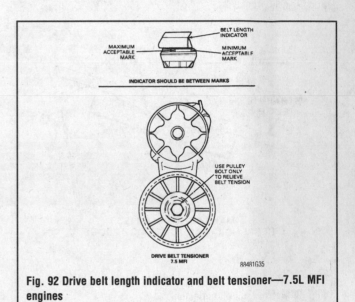

Fig. 92 Drive belt length indicator and belt tensioner—7.5L MFI engines

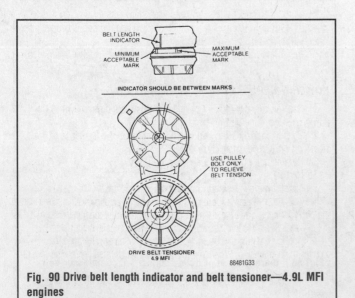

Fig. 90 Drive belt length indicator and belt tensioner—4.9L MFI engines

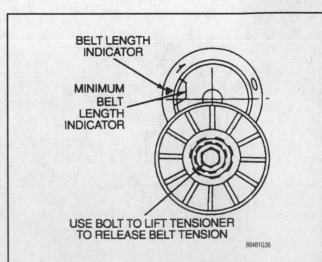

Fig. 93 Drive belt length indicator and belt tensioner—7.3L diesel engines

The spring powered tensioner eliminates the need for periodic adjustments.

On some models, proper tension of the belt can be verified by confirming that the belt length indicator is between the minimum and maximum acceptable marks.

REMOVAL & INSTALLATION

Except Serpentine Belt

◆ See Figure 94

ALTERNATOR BELT

◆ See Figures 95, 96 and 97

1. Remove any component or belt that obstructs the removal of the alternator belt, if applicable.
2. Loosen the alternator mounting and adjusting arm bolts to allow sufficient slack in the belt.
3. Remove the alternator belt.

To install:
4. Install the alternator belt on the pulleys.

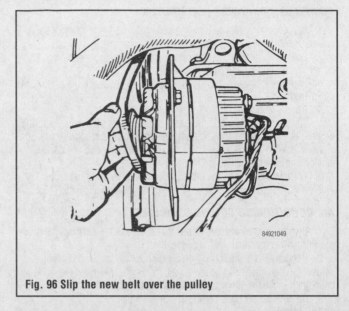

Fig. 96 Slip the new belt over the pulley

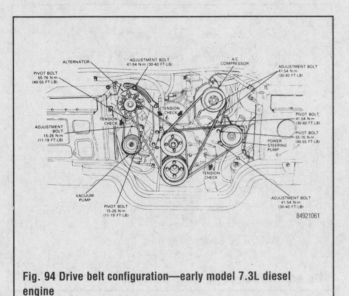

Fig. 94 Drive belt configuration—early model 7.3L diesel engine

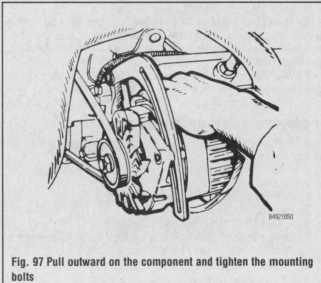

Fig. 97 Pull outward on the component and tighten the mounting bolts

Fig. 95 To change belts, first loosen the component's mounting and adjusting bolts slightly

5. Holding the alternator in place to maintain tension, tighten the adjusting arm bolt. Recheck the belt tension. When the belt is properly tensioned, tighten the alternator mounting bolt.
6. Install any component or belt that was removed to allow this procedure.

POWER STEERING BELT—4.9L ENGINE

1. Remove any component or belt that obstructs the removal of the power steering drive belt, if applicable.
2. Loosen the adjusting and mounting bolts on the front face of the steering pump cover plate (hub side).
3. Remove the power steering drive belt.

To install:
4. Install the power steering drive belt.
5. Using a pry bar or broom handle on the pump hub, move the power steering pump toward or away from the engine until the proper tension is reached. Do not pry against the reservoir as it is relatively soft and easily deformed.
6. Holding the pump in place, tighten the adjusting arm bolt and then recheck the belt tension. When the belt is properly tensioned tighten the mounting bolts.
7. Install any component or belt that was removed to allow this procedure.

POWER STEERING BELT—V8 MODELS

1. Remove any component or belt that obstructs the removal of the power steering drive belt, if applicable.

2. Loosen the three bolts in the three elongated adjusting slots at the power steering pump attaching bracket.

3. Remove the power steering drive belt.

To install:

4. Install the power steering drive belt.

5. Turn the steering pump drive belt adjusting nut as required until the proper deflection is obtained. Turning the adjusting nut clockwise will increase tension and decrease deflection; counterclockwise will decrease tension and increase deflection.

6. Without disturbing the pump, tighten the three attaching bolts.

7. Install any component or belt that was removed to allow this procedure.

AIR CONDITIONING COMPRESSOR BELT

1. Remove any component or belt that obstructs the removal of the air conditioning compressor belt, if applicable.

2. If the engine is equipped with an idler pulley, loosen the idler pulley adjusting bolt. Otherwise, loosen the alternator adjusting and mounting bolts, then move the alternator to relieve belt tension.

3. Remove the air conditioning compressor belt.

To install:

4. Install the air conditioning compressor belt.

5. Insert a prybar between the pulley and the engine (or in the idler pulley adjusting slot), and adjust the tension accordingly. If the engine is not equipped with an idler pulley, the alternator must be moved to accomplish this adjustment, as outlined under Alternator (Fan Drive) Belt.

6. When the proper tension is reached, tighten the idler pulley adjusting bolt (if so equipped) or the alternator adjusting and mounting bolts.

7. Install any component or belt that was removed to allow this procedure.

THERMACTOR® AIR PUMP DRIVE BELT

1. Remove any component or belt that obstructs the removal of the air pump belt, if applicable.

2. Loosen the adjusting arm bolt slightly. If necessary, also loosen the mounting belt slightly.

3. Remove the Thermactor® air pump drive belt.

To install:

4. Install the Thermactor® air pump drive belt.

5. Using a prybar or broom handle, pry against the pump rear cover to move the pump toward or away from the engine, as necessary.

✲✲ WARNING

Do not pry against the pump housing itself, as damage to the housing may result.

6. Holding the pump in place, tighten the adjusting arm bolt and recheck the tension. When the belt is properly tensioned, tighten the mounting bolt.

7. Install any component or belt that was removed to allow this procedure.

Serpentine Belt

◗ **See Figures 98 thru 105**

The serpentine belt drives the water pump, alternator, and (on some models) the air conditioner compressor.

✲✲ WARNING

Check to make sure that the V-ribbed belt is located properly in all drive pulleys before applying tensioner pressure.

1. Install a closed end wrench on the tensioner pulley bolt, then lift the tensioner arm away from the belt.

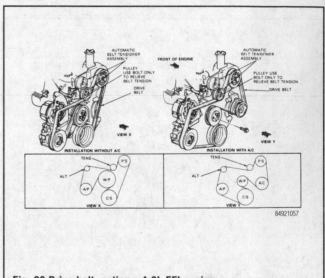

Fig. 98 Drive belt routing—4.9L EFI engine

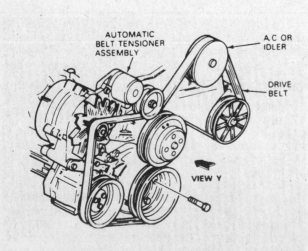

Fig. 99 Drive belt routing—early model 5.0L and 5.8L engines

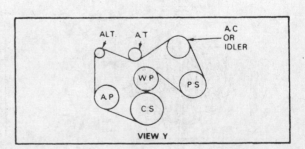

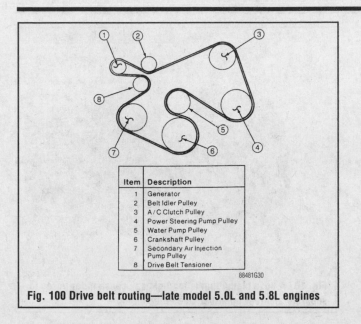

Item	Description
1	Generator
2	Belt Idler Pulley
3	A/C Clutch Pulley
4	Power Steering Pump Pulley
5	Water Pump Pulley
6	Crankshaft Pulley
7	Secondary Air Injection Pump Pulley
8	Drive Belt Tensioner

88481G30

Fig. 100 Drive belt routing—late model 5.0L and 5.8L engines

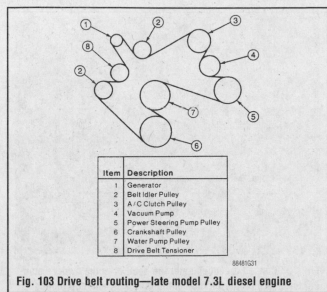

Item	Description
1	Generator
2	Belt Idler Pulley
3	A/C Clutch Pulley
4	Vacuum Pump
5	Power Steering Pump Pulley
6	Crankshaft Pulley
7	Water Pump Pulley
8	Drive Belt Tensioner

88481G31

Fig. 103 Drive belt routing—late model 7.3L diesel engine

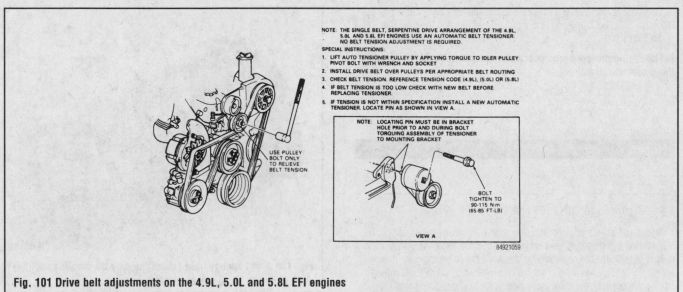

NOTE: THE SINGLE BELT, SERPENTINE DRIVE ARRANGEMENT OF THE 4.9L, 5.0L AND 5.8L EFI ENGINES USE AN AUTOMATIC BELT TENSIONER. NO BELT TENSION ADJUSTMENT IS REQUIRED.

SPECIAL INSTRUCTIONS:

1. LIFT AUTO TENSIONER PULLEY BY APPLYING TORQUE TO IDLER PULLEY PIVOT BOLT WITH WRENCH AND SOCKET.

2. INSTALL DRIVE BELT OVER PULLEYS PER APPROPRIATE BELT ROUTING

3. CHECK BELT TENSION. REFERENCE TENSION CODE (4.9L), (5.0L) OR (5.8L)

4. IF BELT TENSION IS TOO LOW CHECK WITH NEW BELT BEFORE REPLACING TENSIONER.

5. IF TENSION IS NOT WITHIN SPECIFICATION INSTALL A NEW AUTOMATIC TENSIONER. LOCATE PIN AS SHOWN IN VIEW A.

USE PULLEY BOLT ONLY TO RELIEVE BELT TENSION

NOTE: LOCATING PIN MUST BE IN BRACKET HOLE PRIOR TO AND DURING BOLT TORQUING ASSEMBLY OF TENSIONER TO MOUNTING BRACKET

BOLT TIGHTEN TO 90-115 N·m (65-85 FT-LB)

VIEW A

84921059

Fig. 101 Drive belt adjustments on the 4.9L, 5.0L and 5.8L EFI engines

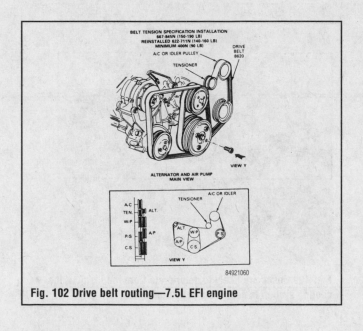

BELT TENSION SPECIFICATION INSTALLATION
667-845N (150-190 LB)
REINSTALLED 622-711N (140-160 LB)
MINIMUM 400N (90 LB)

DRIVE BELT 8620

A/C OR IDLER PULLEY

TENSIONER

VIEW Y

ALTERNATOR AND AIR PUMP MAIN VIEW

VIEW Y

84921060

Fig. 102 Drive belt routing—7.5L EFI engine

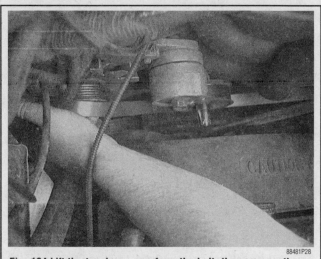

88481P28

Fig. 104 Lift the tensioner arm from the belt, then remove the belt from the pulleys

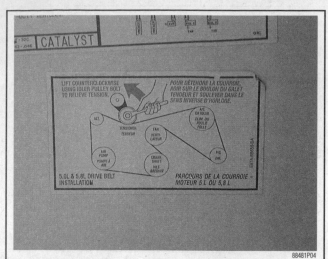

Fig. 105 Consult the label under the hood or in the owner's manual to ensure proper rotation of the tensioner and belt routing

2. Remove the old belt and release the tensioner slowly. Do not let the tensioner snap back into position, as this could damage the tensioner.

To install:

➡ **The spring powered tensioner automatically adjusts the belt to the proper tension.**

3. Install a closed end wrench on the tensioner pulley bolt and rotate the tensioner.
4. Install the belt and release the tensioner.

Hoses

INSPECTION

◆ **See Figures 106, 107, 108 and 109**

Upper and lower radiator hoses, along with the heater hoses, should be checked for deterioration, leaks and loose hose clamps at least every 15,000 miles (24,000 km). It is also wise to check the hoses periodically in early spring and at the beginning of the fall or winter when you are performing other maintenance. A quick visual inspection could discover a weakened hose which might have left you stranded if it had remained unrepaired.

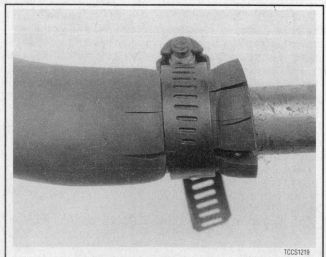

Fig. 106 The cracks developing along this hose are a result of age-related hardening

Fig. 107 A hose clamp that is too tight can cause older hoses to separate and tear on either side of the clamp

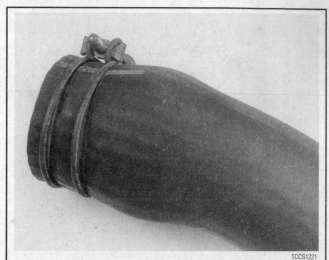

Fig. 108 A soft spongy hose (identifiable by the swollen section) will eventually burst and should be replaced

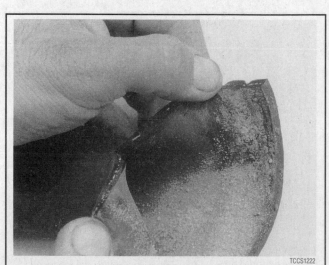

Fig. 109 Hoses are likely to deteriorate from the inside if the cooling system is not periodically flushed

Whenever you are checking the hoses, make sure the engine and cooling system are cold. Visually inspect for cracking, rotting or collapsed hoses, and replace as necessary. Run your hand along the length of the hose. If a weak or swollen spot is noted when squeezing the hose wall, the hose should be replaced.

REMOVAL & INSTALLATION

♦ See Figures 110, 111 and 112

1. Remove the radiator pressure cap.

❋❋ CAUTION

Never remove the pressure cap while the engine is running, or personal injury from scalding hot coolant or steam may result. If possible, wait until the engine has cooled to remove the pressure cap. If this is not possible, wrap a thick cloth around the pressure cap and turn it slowly to the stop. Step back while the pressure is released from the cooling system. When you are sure all the pressure has been released, use the cloth to turn and remove the cap.

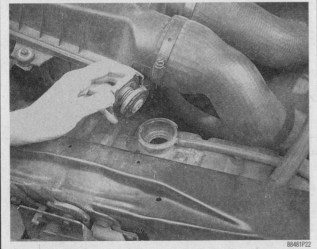

Fig. 110 Remove the radiator cap after the engine has sufficiently cooled

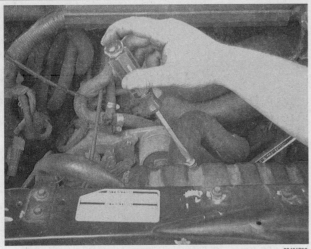

Fig. 111 Loosen the hose clamp at each end of the hose

Fig. 112 Twist and pull each end of the hose to disconnect it from the fittings, and remove the hose from the van

2. Position a clean container under the radiator and/or engine drain-cock or plug, then open the drain and allow the cooling system to drain to an appropriate level. For some upper hoses, only a little coolant must be drained. To remove hoses positioned lower on the engine, such as a lower radiator hose, the entire cooling system must be emptied.

❋❋ CAUTION

When draining coolant, keep in mind that cats and dogs are attracted by ethylene glycol antifreeze, and are quite likely to drink any that is left in an uncovered container or in puddles on the ground. This will prove fatal in sufficient quantity. Always drain coolant into a sealable container. Coolant may be reused unless it is contaminated or several years old.

3. Loosen the hose clamps at each end of the hose requiring replacement. Clamps are usually either of the spring tension type (which require pliers to squeeze the tabs and loosen) or of the screw tension type (which require screw or hex drivers to loosen). Pull the clamps back on the hose away from the connection.

4. Twist, pull and slide the hose off the fitting, taking care not to damage the neck of the component from which the hose is being removed.

➡️ If the hose is stuck at the connection, do not try to insert a screwdriver or other sharp tool under the hose end in an effort to free it, as the connection and/or hose may become damaged. Heater connections especially may be easily damaged by such a procedure. If the hose is to be replaced, use a single-edged razor blade to make a slice along the portion of the hose which is stuck on the connection, perpendicular to the end of the hose. Do not cut deep, so as to prevent damaging the connection. The hose can then be peeled from the connection and discarded.

5. Clean both hose mounting connections. Inspect the condition of the hose clamps and replace them, if necessary.

To install:

6. Dip the ends of the new hose into clean engine coolant to ease installation.

7. Slide the clamps over the replacement hose, then slide the hose ends over the connections into position.

8. Position and secure the clamps at least ¼ in. (6mm) from the ends of the hose. Make sure they are located beyond the raised bead of the connector.

9. Close the radiator or engine drains and properly refill the cooling system with the clean drained engine coolant or a suitable mixture of ethylene glycol coolant and water.

10. If available, install a pressure tester and check for leaks. If a pressure tester is not available, run the engine until normal operating temperature is reached (allowing the system to naturally pressurize), then check for leaks.

✳✳ CAUTION

If you are checking for leaks with the system at normal operating temperature, BE EXTREMELY CAREFUL not to touch any moving or hot engine parts. Once temperature has been reached, shut the engine OFF, and check for leaks around the hose fittings and connections which were removed earlier.

Spark Plugs

♦ See Figure 113

A typical spark plug consists of a metal shell surrounding a ceramic insulator. A metal electrode extends downward through the center of the insulator and protrudes a small distance. Located at the end of the plug and attached to the side of the outer metal shell is the side electrode. The side electrode bends in at a 90° angle so that its tip is just past and parallel to the tip of the center electrode. The distance between these two electrodes (measured in thousandths of an inch or hundredths of a millimeter) is called the spark plug gap.

The spark plug does not produce a spark but instead provides a gap across which the current can arc. The coil produces anywhere from 20,000 to 50,000 volts (depending on the type and application) which travels through the wires to the spark plugs. The current passes along the center electrode and jumps the gap to the side electrode, and in doing so, ignites the air/fuel mixture in the combustion chamber.

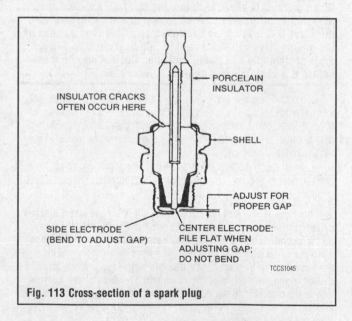

Fig. 113 Cross-section of a spark plug

SPARK PLUG HEAT RANGE

♦ See Figure 114

Spark plug heat range is the ability of the plug to dissipate heat. The longer the insulator (or the farther it extends into the engine), the hotter the plug will operate; the shorter the insulator (the closer the electrode is to the block's cooling passages) the cooler it will operate. A plug that absorbs little heat and remains too cool will quickly accumulate deposits of oil and carbon since it is not hot enough to burn them off. This leads to plug fouling and consequently to misfiring. A plug that absorbs too much heat will have no deposits but, due to the excessive heat, the electrodes will burn away quickly and might possibly lead to preignition or other ignition problems. Preigni-

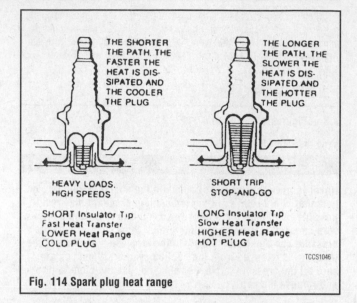

Fig. 114 Spark plug heat range

tion takes place when plug tips get so hot that they glow sufficiently to ignite the air/fuel mixture before the actual spark occurs. This early ignition will usually cause a pinging during low speeds and heavy loads.

The general rule of thumb for choosing the correct heat range when picking a spark plug is: if most of your driving is long distance, high speed travel, use a colder plug; if most of your driving is stop and go, use a hotter plug. Original equipment plugs are generally a good compromise between the 2 styles and most people never have the need to change their plugs from the factory-recommended heat range.

REMOVAL & INSTALLATION

♦ See Figures 115, 116 and 117

A set of spark plugs usually requires replacement after about 20,000–30,000 miles (32,000–48,000 km), depending on your style of driving. In normal operation, plug gap increases about 0.001 in. (0.025mm) for every 2,500 miles (4,000 km). As the gap increases, the plug's voltage requirement also increases. It requires a greater voltage to jump the wider gap and about two to three times as much voltage to fire the plug at high speeds than at idle. The improved air/fuel ratio control of modern fuel injection, combined with the higher voltage output of modern ignition systems, will often allow an engine to run significantly longer on a set of standard spark

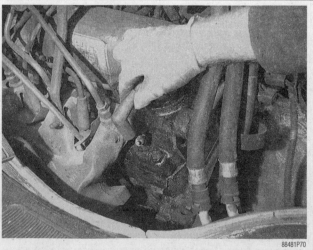

Fig. 115 Grasp the boot of the spark plug wire and gently pull it from the spark plug

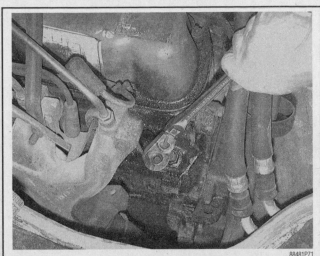

Fig. 116 Use a spark plug socket and a ratchet to loosen the spark plugs

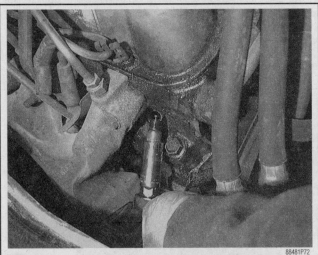

Fig. 117 Withdraw the socket to remove the spark plug from the engine

plugs, but keep in mind that efficiency will drop as the gap widens (along with fuel economy and power).

When you're removing spark plugs, work on one at a time. Don't start by removing the plug wires all at once, because, unless you number them, they may become mixed up. Take a minute before you begin and number the wires with tape.

1. Disconnect the negative battery cable, and if the vehicle has been run recently, allow the engine to thoroughly cool.

2. Raise the front of the vehicle and support it with jackstands.

3. Remove the engine cover to access to the spark plugs.

4. Carefully twist the spark plug wire boot to loosen it, then pull upward and remove the boot from the plug. Be sure to pull on the boot and not on the wire, otherwise the connector located inside the boot may become separated.

5. Using compressed air, blow any water or debris from the spark plug well to assure that no harmful contaminants are allowed to enter the combustion chamber when the spark plug is removed. If compressed air is not available, use a rag or a brush to clean the area.

➡Remove the spark plugs when the engine is cold, if possible, to prevent damage to the threads. If removal of the plugs is difficult, apply a few drops of penetrating oil or silicone spray to the area around the base of the plug, and allow it a few minutes to work.

6. Using a spark plug socket that is equipped with a rubber insert to properly hold the plug, turn the spark plug counterclockwise to loosen and remove the spark plug from the bore.

✻✻ **WARNING**

Be sure not to use a flexible extension on the socket. Use of a flexible extension may allow a shear force to be applied to the plug. A shear force could break the plug off in the cylinder head, leading to costly and frustrating repairs.

To install:

7. Inspect the spark plug boot for tears or damage. If a damaged boot is found, the spark plug wire must be replaced.

8. Using a wire feeler gauge, check and adjust the spark plug gap. When using a gauge, the proper size should pass between the electrodes with a slight drag. The next larger size should not be able to pass while the next smaller size should pass freely.

9. Carefully thread the plug into the bore by hand. If resistance is felt before the plug is almost completely threaded, back the plug out and begin threading again. In small, hard to reach areas, an old spark plug wire and boot could be used as a threading tool. The boot will hold the plug while you twist the end of the wire and the wire is supple enough to twist before it would allow the plug to crossthread.

✻✻ **WARNING**

Do not use the spark plug socket to thread the plugs. Always carefully thread the plug by hand or using an old plug wire to prevent the possibility of crossthreading and damaging the cylinder head bore.

10. Carefully tighten the spark plug. If the plug you are installing is equipped with a crush washer, seat the plug, then tighten about ¼ turn to crush the washer. If you are installing a tapered seat plug, tighten the plug to specifications provided by the vehicle or plug manufacturer.

11. Apply a small amount of silicone dielectric compound to the end of the spark plug lead or inside the spark plug boot to prevent sticking, then install the boot to the spark plug and push until it clicks into place. The click may be felt or heard, then gently pull back on the boot to assure proper contact.

12. Install the engine cover.

INSPECTION & GAPPING

◗ **See Figures 118 thru 127**

Check the plugs for deposits and wear. If they are not going to be replaced, clean the plugs thoroughly. Remember that any kind of deposit will decrease the efficiency of the plug. Plugs can be cleaned on a spark plug cleaning machine, which can sometimes be found in service stations, or you can do an acceptable job of cleaning with a stiff brush. If the plugs are cleaned, the electrodes must be filed flat. Use an ignition points file, not an emery board or the like, which will leave deposits. The electrodes must be filed perfectly flat with sharp edges; rounded edges reduce the spark plug voltage by as much as 50%.

Check spark plug gap before installation. The ground electrode (the L-shaped one connected to the body of the plug) must be parallel to the center electrode and the specified size wire gauge (please refer to the Tune-Up Specifications chart for details) must pass between the electrodes with a slight drag.

➡**NEVER adjust the gap on a used platinum type spark plug.**

Always check the gap on new plugs, as they are not always set correctly at the factory. Do not use a flat feeler gauge when measuring the gap on a used plug, because the reading may be inaccurate. A round wire type gapping tool is the best way to check the gap. The correct gauge should pass through the electrode gap with a slight drag. If you're in doubt, try one size smaller and one larger. The smaller gauge should go through easily, while

Fig. 118 A normally worn spark plug should have light tan or gray deposits on the firing tip

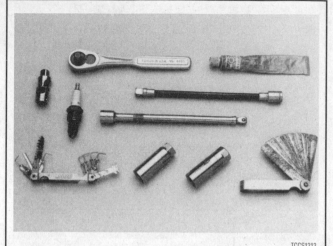

Fig. 120 A variety of tools and gauges are needed for spark plug service

the larger one shouldn't go through at all. Wire gapping tools usually have a bending tool attached. Use that to adjust the side electrode until the proper distance is obtained. Absolutely never attempt to bend the center electrode. Also, be careful not to bend the side electrode too far or too often, as it may weaken and break off within the engine, requiring removal of the cylinder head to retrieve it.

Fig. 119 A carbon fouled plug, identified by soft, sooty, black deposits, may indicate an improperly tuned vehicle. Check the air cleaner, ignition components and engine control system

Fig. 121 A physically damaged spark plug may be evidence of severe detonation in that cylinder. Watch that cylinder carefully between services, as continued detonation will not only damage the plug, but could also damage the engine

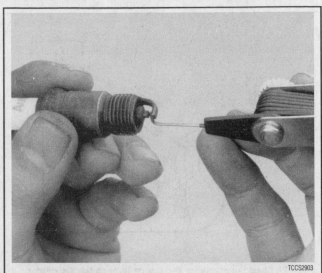

Fig. 122 Checking the spark plug gap with a feeler gauge

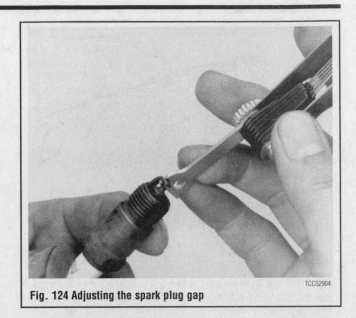

Fig. 124 Adjusting the spark plug gap

Fig. 123 An oil fouled spark plug indicates an engine with worn piston rings and/or bad valve seals, allowing excessive oil to enter the combustion chamber

Fig. 125 This spark plug has been left in the engine too long, as evidenced by the extreme gap. Plugs with such an extreme gap can cause misfiring and stumbling accompanied by a noticeable lack of power

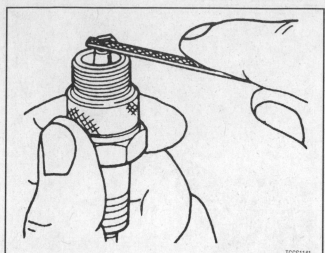

Fig. 126 If the standard plug is in good condition, the electrode may be filed flat—WARNING: do not file platinum plugs

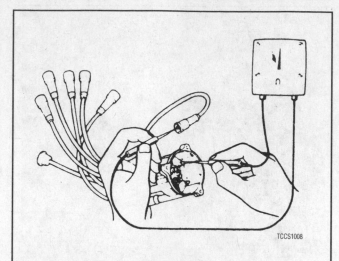

Fig. 128 Checking plug wire resistance through the distributor cap with an ohmmeter

Fig. 127 A bridged or almost bridged spark plug, identified by a build-up between the electrodes, and caused by excessive carbon or oil build-up on the plug

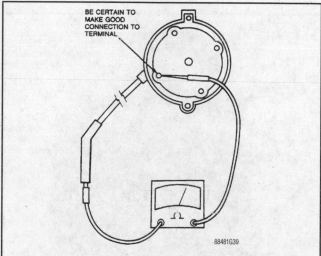

Fig. 129 Checking individual plug wire resistance with an ohmmeter

Every 50,000 miles (80,000 km) or 60 months, the resistance of the wires should be checked with an ohmmeter. Wires with excessive resistance will cause misfiring, and may make the engine difficult to start in damp weather.

To check resistance, an ohmmeter should be used on each wire to test resistance between the end connectors. Remove and install/replace the wires in order, one-by-one.

Resistance of these wires must not exceed 7,000 ohms per foot. To properly measure this, remove the wires from the spark plugs, and remove the distributor cap. Do not remove the wires from the cap. Measure the resistance through the terminal in the distributor cap. Do not pierce any ignition wire for any reason. Measure only from the two ends.

➡Whenever the high tension wires are removed from the plugs, coil, or distributor, silicone grease must be applied to the boot before reconnection. Coat the entire interior surface with Ford silicone grease D7AZ-19A331-A, or its equivalent.

Spark Plug Wires

TESTING

♦ **See Figures 128 and 129**

At every tune-up/inspection, visually check the spark plug cables for burns, cuts, or breaks in the insulation. Check the boots and the nipples on the distributor cap and/or coil. Replace any damaged wiring.

REMOVAL & INSTALLATION

♦ **See Figures 130 and 131**

1. If the wires are to be re-used, label all the wires prior to removal.
2. If the wires are being replaced, remove and replace them one-by-one.

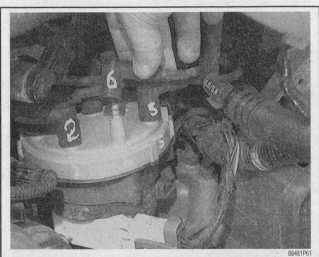

Fig. 130 Matchmark the wires to their respective distributor cap towers before removal

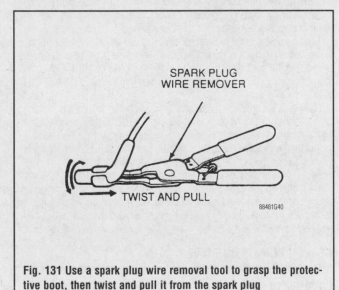

Fig. 131 Use a spark plug wire removal tool to grasp the protective boot, then twist and pull it from the spark plug

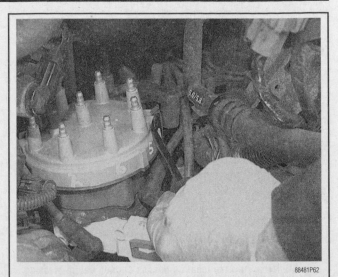

Fig. 132 Disengage the distributor cap retainers . . .

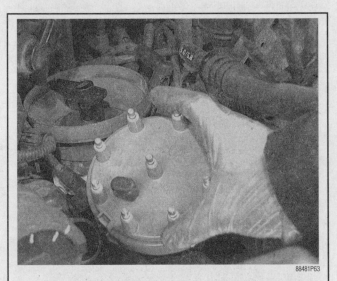

Fig. 133 . . . then remove the cap from the distributor

3. In all cases, use a spark plug removal tool to grasp the protective boot at the connector. Do not pull on the wires. Grasp and twist the boot to remove the wire.

➡ Whenever the high tension wires are removed from the plugs, coil, or distributor, silicone grease must be applied to the boot before reconnection. Coat the entire interior surface with Ford silicone grease D7AZ-19A331-A, or its equivalent.

Distributor Cap and Rotor

REMOVAL & INSTALLATION

▶ See Figures 132, 133, 134 and 135

1. If necessary, tag and disengage the spark plug wires and bracket(s).
2. Loosen the distributor cap hold-down retainers (spring clips or screws).
3. Remove the cap and sit it aside.
4. Grasp the rotor and pull it up and off the shaft.
To install:
5. Install the rotor by aligning the locating boss and pressing it firmly, but gently, onto the shaft until it is firmly seated.

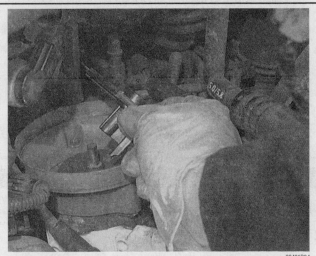

Fig. 134 Pull the rotor straight up and off the shaft

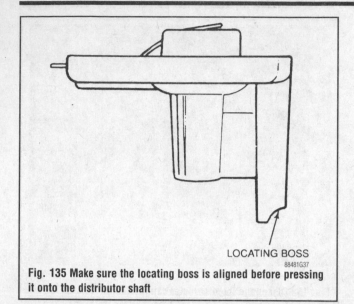

Fig. 135 Make sure the locating boss is aligned before pressing it onto the distributor shaft

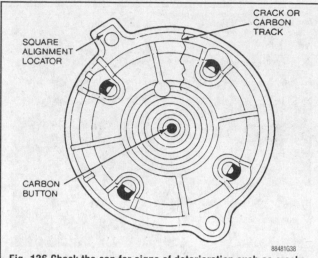

Fig. 136 Check the cap for signs of deterioration such as cracks, a broken carbon button or carbon tracks

6. If applicable, align the distributor cap's square locator with the notch on the base and fasten the retainers.

7. Install the spark plug wires and, if removed, the bracket(s).

INSPECTION

◆ **See Figure 136**

1. Remove the distributor cap and rotor.
2. Wash the inside and outside of the cap and wash the rotor with soap and water, then dry them thoroughly with compressed air or a lint-free cloth.
3. Look closely at the distributor cap, inspecting it for signs of deterioration such as cracks, a broken carbon button or carbon tracks.
4. Inspect the terminals for dirt or corrosion.
5. Inspect the rotor for carbon build-up, cracks or damage to the blade or spring.
6. If damage is found, replace the distributor cap and/or rotor.

Ignition Timing

GENERAL INFORMATION

Ignition timing is the measurement, in degrees of crankshaft rotation, of the point at which the spark plugs fire in each of the cylinders. It is measured in degrees before or after Top Dead Center (TDC) of the compression stroke.

Ideally, the air/fuel mixture in the cylinder will be ignited by the spark plug just as the piston passes TDC of the compression stroke. If this happens, the piston will be beginning the power stroke just as the compressed and ignited air/fuel mixture starts to expand. The expansion of the air/fuel mixture then forces the piston down on the power stroke and turns the crankshaft.

Because it takes a fraction of a second for the spark plug to ignite the mixture in the cylinder, the spark plug must fire a little before the piston reaches TDC. Otherwise, the mixture will not be completely ignited as the piston passes TDC and the full power of the explosion will not be used by the engine.

The timing measurement is given in degrees of crankshaft rotation before the piston reaches TDC (BTDC, or Before Top Dead Center). If the setting for the ignition timing is 5°BTDC, each spark plug must fire 5° before each piston reaches TDC. This only holds true, however, when the engine is at idle speed.

As the engine speed increases, the piston go faster. The spark plugs have to ignite the fuel even sooner if it is to be completely ignited when the piston reaches TDC.

If the ignition is set too far advanced (BTDC), the ignition and expansion of the fuel in the cylinder will occur too soon and tend to force the piston down while it is still traveling up. This causes engine ping. If the ignition spark is set too far retarded after TDC (ATDC), the piston will have already

passed TDC and started on its way down when the fuel is ignited. This will cause the piston to be forced down for only a portion of its travel. This will result in poor engine performance and lack of power.

Timing marks consist of O marks or scales can be found on the rim of the crankshaft pulley and the timing cover. The mark(s) on the pulley correspond(s) to the position of the piston in the number 1 cylinder. A stroboscopic (dynamic) timing light which is hooked into the circuit of the No. 1 cylinder spark plug.

Every time the spark plug fires, the timing light flashes. By aiming the timing light at the timing marks while the engine is running, the exact position of the piston within the cylinder can be easily read since the stroboscopic flash makes the pulley appear to be standing still. Proper timing is indicated when the mark and scale are in proper alignment.

Because these vehicles utilize high voltage, electronic ignition systems, only a timing light with an inductive pickup should be used. The pickup simply clamps to the No. 1 spark plug wire, eliminating the adapter. It is not susceptible to cross-firing or false triggering, which may occur with a conventional light, due to the greater voltages produced by electronic ignition.

INSPECTION AND ADJUSTMENT

TFI-IV and DI Systems

◆ **See Figure 137**

The ignition timing adjustment is not required unless the distributor has been moved from its factory setting or has been removed from the engine.

1. Place the transmission in **Park** or **Neutral** position.
2. Place the heater and A/C controls in the **OFF** position.
3. Connect an inductive timing light following the tool manufacturer's instructions.
4. Disengage the single wire in-line SPOUT connector or remove the shorting bar from the double wire SPOUT connector.
5. Start the vehicle and allow it to reach normal operating temperature.

➡**A remote starter should not be used. Use the ignition key only to start the vehicle. Disconnecting the start wire at the starter relay will cause the TFI module to revert to the start mode timing and the timing will be improperly adjusted.**

6. With the engine running at the specified rpm, check the initial timing. If adjustments must be made, loosen the distributor hold-down bolt and rotate the distributor while watching the timing marks.
7. Once the proper adjustment has been reached, make sure the distributor is not disturbed until the hold-down bolt is secured..
8. After the bolt has been secured, engage the single wire in-line SPOUT connector or the shorting bar on the double wire SPOUT connector.

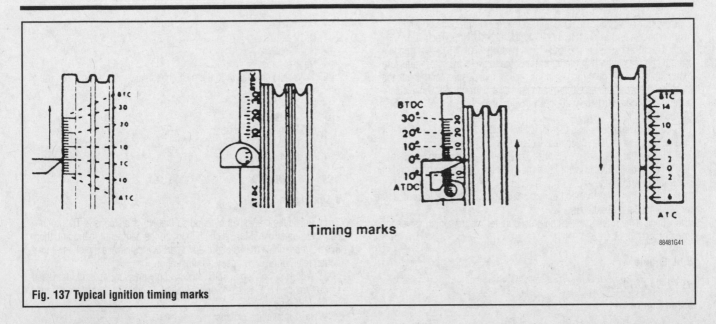

Timing marks

88481G41

Fig. 137 Typical ignition timing marks

9. Recheck the timing advance while varying the engine speed to verify that the distributor is advancing beyond its initial setting.

10. Disconnect the timing light and road test the vehicle to check for proper operation.

Valve Lash

No periodic valve lash adjustments are necessary or possible on these engines. The gasoline engines utilize hydraulic valve trains to automatically maintain proper valve lash. If the engine is determined to have a valve tap, the following inspection procedures can help determine if the hydraulic lifter is to blame.

INSPECTION

▶ See Figures 138 and 139

4.9L Engine

▶ See Figure 140

1. Rotate the crankshaft by hand so that No. 1 piston is at TDC of the compression stroke. Make a chalk mark on the damper at that point, then make 2 more chalk marks about 120° apart, dividing the damper into 3 equal parts.

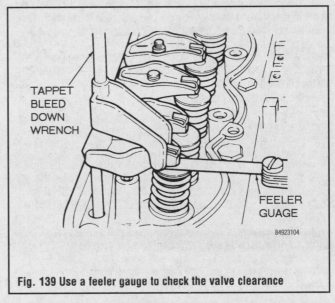

84923104

Fig. 139 Use a feeler gauge to check the valve clearance

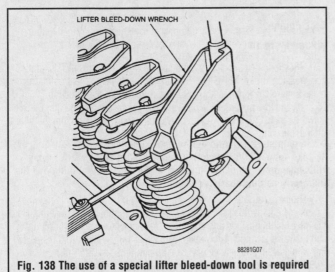

88281G07

Fig. 138 The use of a special lifter bleed-down tool is required to check valve adjustment

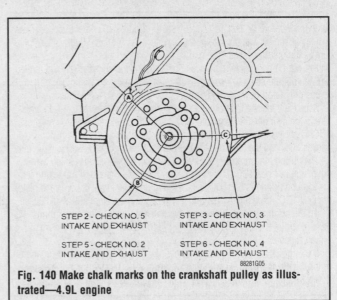

STEP 2 - CHECK NO. 5 INTAKE AND EXHAUST

STEP 3 - CHECK NO. 3 INTAKE AND EXHAUST

STEP 5 - CHECK NO. 2 INTAKE AND EXHAUST

STEP 6 - CHECK NO. 4 INTAKE AND EXHAUST

88281G05

Fig. 140 Make chalk marks on the crankshaft pulley as illustrated—4.9L engine

2. With No. 1 piston at TDC, tighten the rocker arm bolts on No. 1 cylinder intake and exhaust to 17–23 ft. lbs. (23–31 Nm). Then, slowly apply pressure, using Lifter Bleed-Down Wrench T70P-6513-A, or equivalent, to completely bottom the lifter. Take care to avoid excessive pressure that might bend the pushrod. Hold the lifter in this position and check the clearance between the rocker arm and the valve stem tip. Allowable clearance is 2.5–5.0mm (0.10–0.20 in.) with a desired clearance of 3.0–4.5mm (0.125–0.175 in.).

3. If the clearance is less than specified, install a shorter pushrod. If the clearance is greater than specified, install a longer pushrod.

4. Rotate the crankshaft clockwise (as viewed from the front) until the next chalk mark is aligned with the timing pointer. Repeat the procedure for No. 5 intake and exhaust.

5. Rotate the crankshaft to the next chalk mark and repeat the procedure for No. 3 intake and exhaust.

6. Repeat the rotation/checking procedure for the remaining valves in firing order, that is: 6–2–4.

5.0L Engine

1989–94 MODELS

▶ See Figure 141

1. Rotate the crankshaft by hand so that No. 1 piston is at TDC of the compression stroke. Make a chalk mark on the damper at that point, then make 2 more chalk marks about 90° apart in a clockwise direction. If in doubt, refer to the accompanying illustration.

2. With No. 1 piston at TDC, slowly apply pressure, using Lifter Bleed-Down Wrench T70P-6513-A, or equivalent, to completely bottom the lifter, on the following valves:
- No. 1 intake and exhaust
- No. 7 intake
- No. 5 exhaust
- No. 8 intake
- No. 4 exhaust

Take care to avoid excessive pressure that might bend the pushrod. Hold the lifter in this position and check the clearance between the rocker arm and the valve stem tip. Allowable clearance is 1.8–4.3mm (0.071–0.171 in.) with a desired clearance of 2.3—3.8mm (0.091—0.151 in.).

3. If the clearance is less than specified, install a shorter pushrod. If the clearance is greater than specified, install a longer pushrod.

4. Rotate the crankshaft clockwise—as viewed from the front—180°, until the next chalk mark is aligned with the timing pointer. Repeat the procedure for:

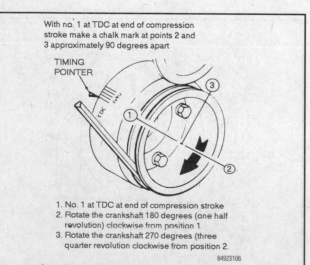

With no. 1 at TDC at end of compression stroke make a chalk mark at points 2 and 3 approximately 90 degrees apart

TIMING POINTER

1. No. 1 at TDC at end of compression stroke
2. Rotate the crankshaft 180 degrees (one half revolution) clockwise from position 1
3. Rotate the crankshaft 270 degrees (three quarter revolution clockwise from position 2.

84923106

Fig. 141 Mark the crankshaft positions as illustrated for checking the positive stop-type valve adjustment—5.0L and 5.8L engines

- No. 5 intake
- No. 2 exhaust
- No. 4 intake
- No. 6 exhaust

5. Rotate the crankshaft to the next chalk mark—90°—and repeat the procedure for:
- No. 2 intake
- No. 7 exhaust
- No. 3 intake and exhaust
- No. 6 intake
- No. 8 exhaust

1995–96 MODELS

▶ See Figure 141

1. Rotate the crankshaft by hand so that No. 1 piston is at TDC of the compression stroke. Make a chalk mark on the damper at that point, then make 2 more chalk marks about 90° apart in a clockwise direction. If in doubt, refer to the accompanying illustration.

2. With No. 1 piston at TDC, slowly apply pressure, using Lifter Bleed-Down Wrench T70P-6513-A, or equivalent, to completely bottom the lifter, on the following valves:
- No. 1 intake and exhaust
- No. 4 intake
- No. 3 exhaust
- No. 8 intake
- No. 7 exhaust

Take care to avoid excessive pressure that might bend the pushrod. Hold the lifter in this position and check the clearance between the rocker arm and the valve stem tip. Allowable clearance is 1.8—4.3mm (0.071—0.171 in.) with a desired clearance of 2.3—3.8mm (0.091—0.151 in.).

3. If the clearance is less than specified, install a shorter pushrod. If the clearance is greater than specified, install a longer pushrod.

4. Rotate the crankshaft clockwise—as viewed from the front—180°, until the next chalk mark is aligned with the timing pointer. Repeat the procedure for:
- No. 3 intake
- No. 2 exhaust
- No. 7 intake
- No. 6 exhaust

5. Rotate the crankshaft to the next chalk mark—90°—and repeat the procedure for:
- No. 2 intake
- No. 4 exhaust
- No. 5 intake and exhaust
- No. 6 intake
- No. 8 exhaust

5.8L Engine

▶ See Figure 141

1. Rotate the crankshaft by hand so that No. 1 piston is at TDC of the compression stroke. Make a chalk mark on the damper at that point, then make 2 more chalk marks about 90° apart in a clockwise direction.

2. With No.1 piston at TDC, slowly apply pressure, using Lifter Bleed-Down Wrench T70P-6513-A, or equivalent, to completely bottom the lifter, on the following valves:
- No. 1 intake and exhaust
- No. 4 intake
- No. 3 exhaust
- No. 8 intake
- No. 7 exhaust

Take care to avoid excessive pressure that might bend the pushrod. Hold the lifter in this position and check the clearance between the rocker arm and the valve stem tip. Allowable clearance is 1.8—4.3mm (0.071—0.171 in.) with a desired clearance of 2.3—3.8mm (0.091—0.151 in.).

3. If the clearance is less than specified, install a shorter pushrod. If the clearance is greater than specified, install a longer pushrod.

GENERAL INFORMATION AND MAINTENANCE

4. Rotate the crankshaft clockwise—as viewed from the front—180°, until the next chalk mark is aligned with the timing pointer. Repeat the procedure for:
- No. 3 intake
- No. 2 exhaust
- No. 7 intake
- No. 6 exhaust

5. Rotate the crankshaft to the next chalk mark—90°—and repeat the procedure for:
- No. 2 intake
- No. 4 exhaust
- No. 5 intake and exhaust
- No. 6 intake
- No. 8 exhaust

7.5L Engine

▶ See Figure 142

1. Rotate the crankshaft by hand so that No. 1 piston is at TDC of the compression stroke. Make a chalk mark on the damper at that point.

2. With No. 1 at TDC, slowly apply pressure, using Lifter Bleed-Down Wrench T70P-6513-A, or equivalent, to completely bottom the lifter, on the following valves:
- No. 1 intake and exhaust
- No. 3 intake
- No. 4 exhaust
- No. 7 intake
- No. 5 exhaust
- No. 8 intake and exhaust

Take care to avoid excessive pressure that might bend the pushrod. Hold the lifter in this position and check the clearance between the rocker arm and the valve stem tip. Allowable clearance is 1.9–4.4mm (0.075–0.175 in.) with a desired clearance of 2.5–3.8mm (0.100–0.150 in.).

3. If the clearance is less than specified, install a shorter pushrod. If the clearance is greater than specified, install a longer pushrod.

4. Rotate the crankshaft clockwise—viewed from the front—360°, until the chalk mark is once again aligned with the timing pointer. Repeat the procedure for:
- No. 2 intake and exhaust
- No. 4 intake
- No. 3 exhaust
- No. 5 intake
- No. 7 exhaust
- No. 6 intake and exhaust

Idle Speed and Mixture Adjustments

GASOLINE ENGINES

The engines covered in this manual contain sophisticated fuel injection systems, in which an engine control computer utilizes information from various sensors to control idle speed and air/fuel mixtures. Periodic adjustments are neither necessary, nor possible, on these systems. If a problem is suspected, please refer to Sections 4 and 5 of this manual for more information on electronic engine controls and fuel injection.

DIESEL ENGINES

Curb Idle

1989–94 MODELS

▶ See Figure 143

1. Bring the engine up to normal operating temperature.
2. Place the manual transmission in Neutral or automatic transmission Park. Firmly set the parking brake.

➡**Idle speed is measured with the manual transmission in Neutral or the automatic transmission in Drive, with the wheels blocked and the parking brake ON.**

3. Check the curb idle speed, using a magnetic pickup tachometer suitable for diesel engines. The part number of the Ford tachometer is Rotunda 055-00108 or its equivalent. Adjust the idle speed to 600–700 rpm.

➡**Always check the underhood emissions control information sticker for the latest idle and adjustment specifications.**

4. Place the transmission in Neutral (M/T) or Park (A/T) and momentarily speed up the engine. Allow the rpm to drop to idle and recheck the idle speed. Readjust if necessary.

1995–96 MODELS

No curb idle speed adjustment is possible, nor should any be attempted.

Fast Idle

1989–94 MODELS

1. Start the engine and bring it up to normal operating temperature.
2. Place the transmission in Neutral (manual transmission) or Park (automatic transmission).

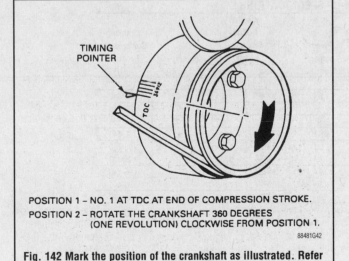

POSITION 1 – NO. 1 AT TDC AT END OF COMPRESSION STROKE.
POSITION 2 – ROTATE THE CRANKSHAFT 360 DEGREES (ONE REVOLUTION) CLOCKWISE FROM POSITION 1.

Fig. 142 Mark the position of the crankshaft as illustrated. Refer to the text for details—7.5L engines

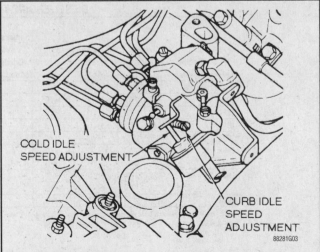

Fig. 143 Diesel injection pump showing idle speed adjustment. Pump is mounted on top (front) of the intake manifold

GASOLINE ENGINE TUNE-UP SPECIFICATIONS

Year	Engine ID/VIN	Engine Displacement Liters (cc)	Spark Plugs Gap (in.)	Ignition Timing (deg.) MT	Ignition Timing (deg.) AT	Fuel Pump (psi)	Idle Speed (rpm) MT	Idle Speed (rpm) AT	Valve Clearance In.	Valve Clearance Ex.
1989	Y	4.9L (4917)	0.044	10B	10B	50-60	①	①	HYD	HYD
	N	5.0L (4942)	0.044	10B	10B	35-45	①	①	HYD	HYD
	H	5.8L (5766)	0.044	10B	10B	35-45	①	①	HYD	HYD
	G	7.5L (7536)	0.044	10B	10B	35-45	①	①	HYD	HYD
1990	Y	4.9L (4917)	0.044	10B	10B	50-60	①	①	HYD	HYD
	N	5.0L (4942)	0.044	10B	10B	35-45	①	①	HYD	HYD
	H	5.8L (5766)	0.044	10B	10B	35-45	①	①	HYD	HYD
	G	7.5L (7536)	0.044	10B	10B	35-45	①	①	HYD	HYD
1991	Y	4.9L (4917)	0.044	10B	10B	50-60	①	①	HYD	HYD
	N	5.0L (4942)	0.044	10B	10B	35-45	①	①	HYD	HYD
	H	5.8L (5766)	0.044	10B	10B	35-45	①	①	HYD	HYD
	G	7.5L (7536)	0.044	10B	10B	35-45	①	①	HYD	HYD
1992	Y	4.9L (4917)	0.044	10B	10B	50-60	①	①	HYD	HYD
	N	5.0L (4942)	0.044	10B	10B	35-45	①	①	HYD	HYD
	H	5.8L (5766)	0.044	10B	10B	35-45	①	①	HYD	HYD
	G	7.5L (7536)	0.044	10B	10B	35-45	①	①	HYD	HYD
1993	Y	4.9L (4917)	0.044	10B	10B	50-60	700	575	HYD	HYD
	N	5.0L (4942)	0.044	10B	10B	35-45	775	675	HYD	HYD
	H	5.8L (5766)	0.044	10B	10B	35-45	775	675	HYD	HYD
	R	5.8L (5766)	0.044	10B	10B	35-45	775	675	HYD	HYD
	G	7.5L (7536)	0.044	10B	10B	35-45	775	675	HYD	HYD
1994	Y	4.9L (4917)	0.044	10B	10B	50-60	700	575	HYD	HYD
	N	5.0L (4942)	0.044	10B	10B	35-45	775	675	HYD	HYD
	H	5.8L (5766)	0.044	10B	10B	35-45	775	675	HYD	HYD
	R	5.8L (5766)	0.044	10B	10B	35-45	775	675	HYD	HYD
	G	7.5L (7536)	0.044	10B	10B	35-45	775	675	HYD	HYD
1995	Y	4.9L (4917)	0.044	10B	10B	50-60	700	575	HYD	HYD
	N	5.0L (4942)	0.044	10B	10B	35-45	775	675	HYD	HYD
	H	5.8L (5766)	0.044	10B	10B	35-45	775	675	HYD	HYD
	R	5.8L (5766)	0.044	10B	10B	35-45	775	675	HYD	HYD
	G	7.5L (7536)	0.044	10B	10B	35-45	775	675	HYD	HYD
1996	Y	4.9L (4917)	0.044	10B	10B	50-60	700	575	HYD	HYD
	N	5.0L (4942)	0.044	10B	10B	35-45	775	675	HYD	HYD
	H	5.8L (5766)	0.044	10B	10B	35-45	775	675	HYD	HYD
	G	7.5L (7536)	0.044	10B	10B	35-45	775	675	HYD	HYD

NOTE: The Vehicle Emission Control Information label often reflects specification changes made during production.
The label figures must be used if they differ from those in this chart.
B - Before top dead center
HYD - Hydraulic
① Refer to the underhood emission label

88481C03

DIESEL ENGINE TUNE-UP SPECIFICATIONS

Year	Engine ID/VIN	Engine Displacement cu. in. (cc)	Valve Clearance Intake (in.)	Valve Clearance Exhaust (in.)	Intake Valve Opens (deg.)	Injection Pump Setting (deg.) ①	Injection Nozzle Pressure (psi) New	Injection Nozzle Pressure (psi) Used	Idle Speed (rpm)	Cranking Compression Pressure (psi) ③
1989	M	7.3L (7270)	HYD	HYD	—	8.5B	1875	1425	②	195-440
1990	M	7.3L (7270)	HYD	HYD	—	8.5B	1875	1425	②	195-440
1991	M	7.3L (7270)	HYD	HYD	—	8.5B	1875	1425	②	195-440
1992	M	7.3L (7270)	HYD	HYD	—	8.5B	1875	1425	②	195-440
1993	M	7.3L (7270)	HYD	HYD	—	8.5B	1875	1425	②	195-440
1994	M	7.3L (7270)	HYD	HYD	—	8.5B	1875	1425	②	195-440
	F	7.3L (7270)	HYD	HYD	—	④	1875	1425	②	195-440
1995	F	7.3L (7270)	HYD	HYD	—	④	1875	1425	②	195-440
	M	7.3L (7270)	HYD	HYD	—	8.5B	1875	1425	②	195-440
1996	F	7.3L (7270)	HYD	HYD	—	④	1875	1425	②	195-440

NOTE: The Vehicle Emission Control Information label often reflects specification changes made during production.
The label figures must be used if they differ from those in this chart
HYD - Hydraulic
B-Before top dead center
NA-Not available
① At 2000 rpm
② Refer to the underhood emission label
③ Compression pressure in the lowest cylinder must be at least 75% of the highest cylinder
④ PCM controlled

88481C04

3. Disconnect the wire from the fast idle solenoid.
4. Apply battery voltage to activate the solenoid plunger.
5. Speed up the engine momentarily to set the plunger.
6. The fast idle should be 850–900 rpm. Adjust the fast idle by turning the solenoid plunger in or out.
7. Speed up the engine momentarily and recheck the fast idle. Readjust if necessary.
8. Remove the battery voltage from the solenoid and reconnect the solenoid wire.

1995–96 MODELS

No fast idle speed adjustment is possible, nor should any be attempted.

Air Conditioning System

SYSTEM SERVICE & REPAIR

➡It is recommended that the A/C system be serviced by an EPA Section 609 certified automotive technician utilizing a refrigerant recovery/recycling machine.

The do-it-yourselfer should not service his/her own vehicle's A/C system for many reasons, including legal concerns, personal injury, environmental damage and cost. The following are some of the reasons why you may decide not to service your own vehicle's A/C system.

According to the U.S. Clean Air Act, it is a federal crime to service or repair (involving the refrigerant) a Motor Vehicle Air Conditioning (MVAC) system for money without being EPA certified. It is also illegal to vent R-12 and R-134a refrigerants into the atmosphere. Selling or distributing A/C system refrigerant (in a container which contains less than 20 pounds of refrigerant) to any person who is not EPA 609 certified is also not allowed by law.

State and/or local laws may be more strict than the federal regulations, so be sure to check with your state and/or local authorities for further information. For further federal information on the legality of servicing your A/C system, call the EPA Stratospheric Ozone Hotline.

➡Federal law dictates that a fine of up to $25,000 may be levelled on people convicted of venting refrigerant into the atmosphere. Additionally, the EPA may pay up to $10,000 for information or services leading to a criminal conviction of the violation of these laws.

When servicing an A/C system you run the risk of handling or coming in contact with refrigerant, which may result in skin or eye irritation or frostbite. Although low in toxicity (due to chemical stability), inhalation of concentrated refrigerant fumes is dangerous and can result in death; cases of fatal cardiac arrhythmia have been reported in people accidentally subjected to high levels of refrigerant. Some early symptoms include loss of concentration and drowsiness.

➡Generally, the limit for exposure is lower for R-134a than it is for R-12. Exceptional care must be practiced when handling R-134a.

Also, refrigerants can decompose at high temperatures (near gas heaters or open flame), which may result in hydrofluoric acid, hydrochloric acid and phosgene (a fatal nerve gas).

R-12 refrigerant can damage the environment because it is a Chlorofluorocarbon (CFC), which has been proven to add to ozone layer depletion, leading to increasing levels of UV radiation. UV radiation has been linked with an increase in skin cancer, suppression of the human immune system, an increase in cataracts, damage to crops, damage to aquatic organisms, an increase in ground-level ozone, and increased global warming.

R-134a refrigerant is a greenhouse gas which, if allowed to vent into the atmosphere, will contribute to global warming (the Greenhouse Effect).

It is usually more economically feasible to have a certified MVAC automotive technician perform A/C system service on your vehicle. Some possible reasons for this are as follows:

• While it is illegal to service an A/C system without the proper equipment, the home mechanic would have to purchase an expensive refrigerant recovery/recycling machine to service his/her own vehicle.

• Since only a certified person may purchase refrigerant—according to the Clean Air Act, there are specific restrictions on selling or distributing A/C system refrigerant—it is legally impossible (unless certified) for the home mechanic to service his/her own vehicle. Procuring refrigerant in an illegal fashion exposes one to the risk of paying a $25,000 fine to the EPA.

R-12 Refrigerant Conversion

If your vehicle still uses R-12 refrigerant, one way to save A/C system costs down the road is to investigate the possibility of having your system converted to R-134a. The older R-12 systems can be easily converted to R-134a refrigerant by a certified automotive technician by installing a few new components and changing the system oil.

The cost of R-12 is steadily rising and will continue to increase, because it is no longer imported or manufactured in the United States. Therefore, it is often possible to have an R-12 system converted to R-134a and recharged for less than it would cost to just charge the system with R-12.

If you are interested in having your system converted, contact local automotive service stations for more details and information.

PREVENTIVE MAINTENANCE

▶ See Figures 144, 145 and 146

Although the A/C system should not be serviced by the do-it-yourselfer, preventive maintenance can be practiced and A/C system inspections can be performed to help maintain the efficiency of the vehicle's A/C system. For preventive maintenance, perform the following:

• The easiest and most important preventive maintenance for your A/C system is to be sure that it is used on a regular basis. Running the system for five minutes each month (no matter what the season) will help ensure that the seals and all internal components remain lubricated.

➡Some newer vehicles automatically operate the A/C system compressor whenever the windshield defroster is activated. When running, the compressor lubricates the A/C system components; therefore, the A/C system would not need to be operated each month.

TCCS1233

Fig. 144 A coolant tester can be used to determine the freezing and boiling levels of the coolant in your vehicle

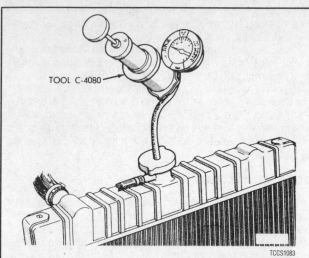

Fig. 145 Cooling systems should be pressure tested for leaks periodically

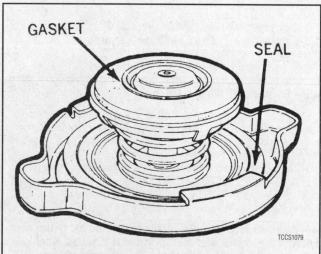

Fig. 146 To ensure efficient cooling system operation, inspect the radiator cap gasket and seal

• In order to prevent heater core freeze-up during A/C operation, it is necessary to maintain proper antifreeze protection. Use a hand-held coolant tester (hydrometer) to periodically check the condition of the antifreeze in your engine's cooling system.

➡**Antifreeze should not be used longer than the manufacturer specifies.**

• For efficient operation of an air conditioned vehicle's cooling system, the radiator cap should have a holding pressure which meets manufacturer's specifications. A cap which fails to hold these pressures should be replaced.

• Any obstruction of or damage to the condenser configuration will restrict air flow which is essential to its efficient operation. It is, therefore, a good rule to keep this unit clean and in proper physical shape.

➡**Bug screens which are mounted in front of the condenser (unless they are original equipment) are regarded as obstructions.**

• The condensation drain tube expels any water which accumulates on the bottom of the evaporator housing into the engine compartment. If this tube is obstructed, the air conditioning performance can be restricted and condensation buildup can spill over onto the vehicle's floor.

SYSTEM INSPECTION

▶ **See Figure 147**

Although the A/C system should not be serviced by the do-it-yourselfer, preventive maintenance can be practiced and A/C system inspections can be performed to help maintain the efficiency of the vehicle's A/C system. For A/C system inspection, perform the following:

The easiest and often most important check for the air conditioning system consists of a visual inspection of the system components. Visually inspect the air conditioning system for refrigerant leaks, damaged compressor clutch, abnormal compressor drive belt tension and/or condition, plugged evaporator drain tube, blocked condenser fins, disconnected or broken wires, blown fuses, corroded connections and poor insulation.

A refrigerant leak will usually appear as an oily residue at the leakage point in the system. The oily residue soon picks up dust or dirt particles from the surrounding air and appears greasy. Through time, this will build up and appear to be a heavy dirt impregnated grease.

For a thorough visual and operational inspection, check the following:

• Check the surface of the radiator and condenser for dirt, leaves or other material which might block air flow.

• Check for kinks in hoses and lines. Check the system for leaks.

• Make sure the drive belt is properly tensioned. When the air conditioning is operating, make sure the drive belt is free of noise or slippage.

• Make sure the blower motor operates at all appropriate positions, then check for distribution of the air from all outlets with the blower on **HIGH** or **MAX**.

➡**Keep in mind that under conditions of high humidity, air discharged from the A/C vents may not feel as cold as expected, even if the system is working properly. This is because vaporized moisture in humid air retains heat more effectively than dry air, thereby making humid air more difficult to cool.**

• Make sure the air passage selection lever is operating correctly. Start the engine and warm it to normal operating temperature, then make sure the temperature selection lever is operating correctly.

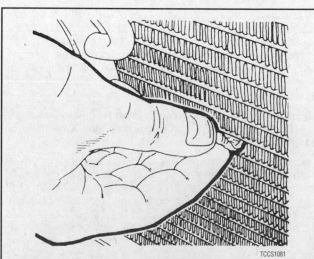

Fig. 147 Periodically remove any debris from the condenser and radiator fins

Windshield Wipers

ELEMENT (REFILL) CARE & REPLACEMENT

▶ **See Figures 148 thru 157**

For maximum effectiveness and longest element life, the windshield and wiper blades should be kept clean. Dirt, tree sap, road tar and so on will cause streaking, smearing and blade deterioration if left on the glass. It is advisable to wash the windshield carefully with a commercial glass cleaner at least once a month. Wipe off the rubber blades with the wet rag afterwards. Do not attempt to move wipers across the windshield by hand; damage to the motor and drive mechanism will result.

To inspect and/or replace the wiper blade elements, place the wiper switch in the **LOW** speed position and the ignition switch in the **ACC** position. When the wiper blades are approximately vertical on the windshield, turn the ignition switch to **OFF**.

Examine the wiper blade elements. If they are found to be cracked, broken or torn, they should be replaced immediately. Replacement intervals will vary with usage, although ozone deterioration usually limits element life to about one year. If the wiper pattern is smeared or streaked, or if the blade

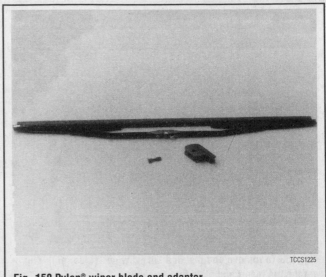

TCCS1225

Fig. 150 Pylon® wiper blade and adapter

TCCS1223

Fig. 148 Bosch® wiper blade and fit kit

TCCS1226

Fig. 151 Trico® wiper blade and fit kit

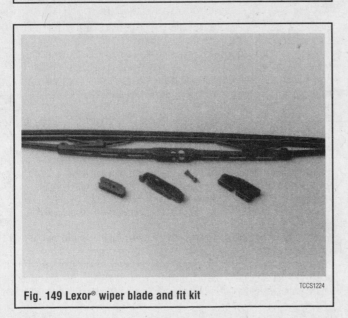

TCCS1224

Fig. 149 Lexor® wiper blade and fit kit

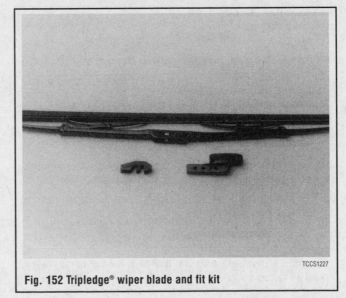

TCCS1227

Fig. 152 Tripledge® wiper blade and fit kit

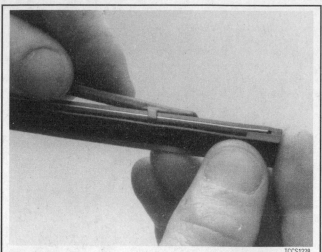

Fig. 153 To remove and install a Lexor® wiper blade refill, slip out the old insert and slide in a new one

TCCS1228

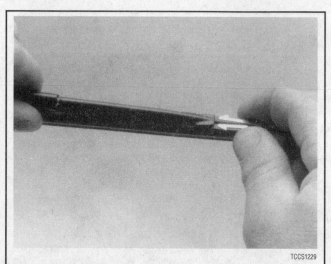

Fig. 154 On Pylon® inserts, the clip at the end has to be removed prior to sliding the insert off

TCCS1229

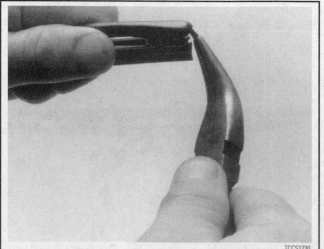

Fig. 155 On Trico® wiper blades, the tab at the end of the blade must be turned up . . .

TCCS1230

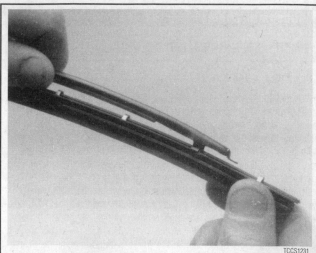

Fig. 156 . . . then the insert can be removed. After installing the replacement insert, bend the tab back

TCCS1231

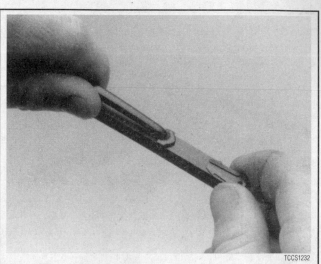

Fig. 157 The Tripledge® wiper blade insert is removed and installed using a securing clip

TCCS1232

chatters across the glass, the elements should be replaced. It is easiest and most sensible to replace the elements in pairs.

If your vehicle is equipped with aftermarket blades, there are several different types of refills and your vehicle might have any kind. Aftermarket blades and arms rarely use the exact same type blade or refill as the original equipment. Here are some typical aftermarket blades; not all may be available for your vehicle:

The Anco® type uses a release button that is pushed down to allow the refill to slide out of the yoke jaws. The new refill slides back into the frame and locks in place.

Some Trico® refills are removed by locating where the metal backing strip or the refill is wider. Insert a small screwdriver blade between the frame and metal backing strip. Press down to release the refill from the retaining tab.

Other types of Trico® refills have two metal tabs which are unlocked by squeezing them together. The rubber filler can then be withdrawn from the frame jaws. A new refill is installed by inserting the refill into the front frame jaws and sliding it rearward to engage the remaining frame jaws. There are usually four jaws; be certain when installing that the refill is engaged in all of them. At the end of its travel, the tabs will lock into place on the front jaws of the wiper blade frame.

Another type of refill is made from polycarbonate. The refill has a simple locking device at one end which flexes downward out of the groove into which the jaws of the holder fit, allowing easy release. By sliding the new refill through all the jaws and pushing through the slight resistance when it reaches the end of its travel, the refill will lock into position.

To replace the Tridon® refill, it is necessary to remove the wiper blade. This refill has a plastic backing strip with a notch about 1 in. (25mm) from the end. Hold the blade (frame) on a hard surface so that the frame is tightly bowed. Grip the tip of the backing strip and pull up while twisting counterclockwise. The backing strip will snap out of the retaining tab. Do this for the remaining tabs until the refill is free of the blade. The length of these refills is molded into the end and they should be replaced with identical types.

Regardless of the type of refill used, be sure to follow the part manufacturer's instructions closely. Make sure that all of the frame jaws are engaged as the refill is pushed into place and locked. If the metal blade holder and frame are allowed to touch the glass during wiper operation, the glass will be scratched.

Tires and Wheels

Common sense and good driving habits will afford maximum tire life. Fast starts, sudden stops and hard cornering are hard on tires and will shorten their useful life span. Make sure that you don't overload the vehicle or run with incorrect pressure in the tires. Both of these practices will increase tread wear.

➡ **For optimum tire life, keep the tires properly inflated, rotate them often and have the wheel alignment checked periodically.**

Inspect your tires frequently. Be especially careful to watch for bubbles in the tread or sidewall, deep cuts or underinflation. Replace any tires with bubbles in the sidewall. If cuts are so deep that they penetrate to the cords, discard the tire. Any cut in the sidewall of a radial tire renders it unsafe. Also look for uneven tread wear patterns that may indicate the front end is out of alignment or that the tires are out of balance.

TIRE ROTATION

▶ See Figures 158 and 159

Tires must be rotated periodically to equalize wear patterns that vary with a tire's position on the vehicle. Tires will also wear in an uneven way as the front steering/suspension system wears to the point where the alignment should be reset.

Rotating the tires will ensure maximum life for the tires as a set, so you will not have to discard a tire early due to wear on only part of the tread. Regular rotation is required to equalize wear.

When rotating "unidirectional tires," make sure that they always roll in the same direction. This means that a tire used on the left side of the vehi-

Fig. 159 Unidirectional tires are identifiable by sidewall arrows and/or the word "rotation"

cle must not be switched to the right side and vice-versa. Such tires should only be rotated front-to-rear or rear-to-front, while always remaining on the same side of the vehicle. These tires are marked on the sidewall as to the direction of rotation; observe the marks when reinstalling the tire(s).

Some styled or "mag" wheels may have different offsets front to rear. In these cases, the rear wheels must not be used up front and vice-versa. Furthermore, if these wheels are equipped with unidirectional tires, they cannot be rotated unless the tire is remounted for the proper direction of rotation.

➡ **The compact or space-saver spare is strictly for emergency use. It must never be included in the tire rotation or placed on the vehicle for everyday use.**

TIRE DESIGN

▶ See Figure 160

For maximum satisfaction, tires should be used in sets of four. Mixing of different types (radial, bias-belted, fiberglass belted) must be avoided. In most cases, the vehicle manufacturer has designated a type of tire on which the vehicle will perform best. Your first choice when replacing tires should be to use the same type of tire that the manufacturer recommends.

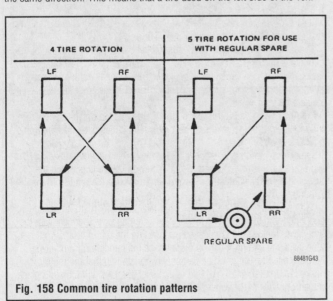

Fig. 158 Common tire rotation patterns

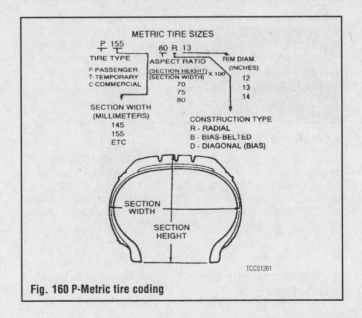

Fig. 160 P-Metric tire coding

When radial tires are used, tire sizes and wheel diameters should be selected to maintain ground clearance and tire load capacity equivalent to the original specified tire. Radial tires should always be used in sets of four.

☀☀ CAUTION

Radial tires should never be used on only the front axle.

When selecting tires, pay attention to the original size as marked on the tire. Most tires are described using an industry size code sometimes referred to as P-Metric. This allows the exact identification of the tire specifications, regardless of the manufacturer. If selecting a different tire size or brand, remember to check the installed tire for any sign of interference with the body or suspension while the vehicle is stopping, turning sharply or heavily loaded.

Snow Tires

Good radial tires can produce a big advantage in slippery weather, but in snow, a street radial tire does not have sufficient tread to provide traction and control. The small grooves of a street tire quickly pack with snow and the tire behaves like a billiard ball on a marble floor. The more open, chunky tread of a snow tire will self-clean as the tire turns, providing much better grip on snowy surfaces.

To satisfy municipalities requiring snow tires during weather emergencies, most snow tires carry either an M + S designation after the tire size stamped on the sidewall, or the designation "all-season." In general, no change in tire size is necessary when buying snow tires.

Most manufacturers strongly recommend the use of 4 snow tires on their vehicles for reasons of stability. If snow tires are fitted only to the drive wheels, the opposite end of the vehicle may become very unstable when braking or turning on slippery surfaces. This instability can lead to unpleasant endings if the driver can't counteract the slide in time.

Note that snow tires, whether 2 or 4, will affect vehicle handling in all non-snow situations. The stiffer, heavier snow tires will noticeably change the turning and braking characteristics of the vehicle. Once the snow tires are installed, you must re-learn the behavior of the vehicle and drive accordingly.

➥**Consider buying extra wheels on which to mount the snow tires. Once done, the "snow wheels" can be installed and removed as needed. This eliminates the potential damage to tires or wheels from seasonal removal and installation. Even if your vehicle has styled wheels, see if inexpensive steel wheels are available. Although the look of the vehicle will change, the expensive wheels will be protected from salt, curb hits and pothole damage.**

TIRE STORAGE

If they are mounted on wheels, store the tires at proper inflation pressure. All tires should be kept in a cool, dry place. If they are stored in the garage or basement, do not let them stand on a concrete floor; set them on strips of wood, a mat or a large stack of newspaper. Keeping them away from direct moisture is of paramount importance. Tires should not be stored upright, but in a flat position.

INFLATION & INSPECTION

▶ **See Figures 161 thru 168**

The importance of proper tire inflation cannot be overemphasized. A tire employs air as part of its structure. It is designed around the supporting strength of the air at a specified pressure. For this reason, improper inflation drastically reduces the tire's ability to perform as intended. A tire will lose some air in day-to-day use; having to add a few pounds of air periodically is not necessarily a sign of a leaking tire.

Two items should be a permanent fixture in every glove compartment: an accurate tire pressure gauge and a tread depth gauge. Check the tire pressure (including the spare) regularly with a pocket type gauge. Too often, the gauge on the end of the air hose at your corner garage is not accurate because it suffers too much abuse. Always check tire pressure when the tires are cold, as pressure increases with temperature. If you must move the vehicle to check the tire inflation, do not drive more than a mile before checking. A cold tire is generally one that has not been driven for more than three hours.

A plate or sticker is normally provided somewhere in the vehicle (door post, hood, tailgate or trunk lid) which shows the proper pressure for the tires. Never counteract excessive pressure build-up by bleeding off air pressure (letting some air out). This will cause the tire to run hotter and wear quicker.

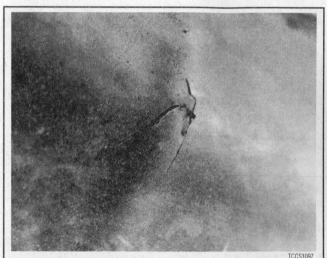

TCCS1097

Fig. 161 Tires should be checked frequently for any sign of puncture or damage

TCCS1095

Fig. 162 Tires with deep cuts, or cuts which show bulging should be replaced immediately

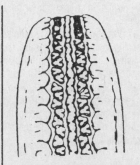

- DRIVE WHEEL HEAVY ACCELERATION
- OVERINFLATION

- HARD CORNERING
- UNDERINFLATION
- LACK OF ROTATION

TCCS1262

Fig. 163 Examples of inflation-related tire wear patterns

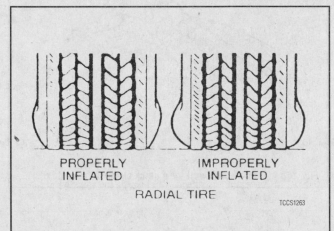

PROPERLY INFLATED   IMPROPERLY INFLATED

RADIAL TIRE

TCCS1263

Fig. 164 Radial tires have a characteristic sidewall bulge; don't try to measure pressure by looking at the tire. Use a quality air pressure gauge

⁂ CAUTION

Never exceed the maximum tire pressure embossed on the tire! This is the pressure to be used when the tire is at maximum loading, but it is rarely the correct pressure for everyday driving. Consult the owner's manual or the tire pressure sticker for the correct tire pressure.

Once you've maintained the correct tire pressures for several weeks, you'll be familiar with the vehicle's braking and handling personality. Slight adjustments in tire pressures can fine-tune these characteristics, but never change the cold pressure specification by more than 2 psi. A slightly softer tire pressure will give a softer ride but also yield lower fuel mileage. A slightly harder tire will give crisper dry road handling but can cause skidding on wet surfaces. Unless you're fully attuned to the vehicle, stick to the recommended inflation pressures.

All tires made since 1968 have built-in tread wear indicator bars that show up as ½ in. (13mm) wide smooth bands across the tire when $\frac{1}{16}$ in. (1.5mm) of tread remains. The appearance of tread wear indicators means that the tires should be replaced. In fact, many states have laws prohibiting the use of tires with less than this amount of tread.

You can check your own tread depth with an inexpensive gauge or by using a Lincoln head penny. Slip the Lincoln penny (with Lincoln's head upside-down) into several tread grooves. If you can see the top of Lincoln's head in 2 adjacent grooves, the tire has less than $\frac{1}{16}$ in. (1.5mm) tread left and should be replaced. You can measure snow tires in the same manner by using the "tails" side of the Lincoln penny. If you can see the top of the Lincoln memorial, it's time to replace the snow tire(s).

CARE OF SPECIAL WHEELS

If you have invested money in magnesium, aluminum alloy or sport wheels, special precautions should be taken to make sure your investment is not wasted and that your special wheels look good for the life of the vehicle.

Special wheels are easily damaged and/or scratched. Occasionally check the rims for cracking, impact damage or air leaks. If any of these are found, replace the wheel. But in order to prevent this type of damage and the costly replacement of a special wheel, observe the following precautions:

• Use extra care not to damage the wheels during removal, installation, balancing, etc. After removal of the wheels from the vehicle, place them on a mat or other protective surface. If they are to be stored for any length of

CONDITION	RAPID WEAR AT SHOULDERS	RAPID WEAR AT CENTER	CRACKED TREADS	WEAR ON ONE SIDE	FEATHERED EDGE	BALD SPOTS	SCALLOPED WEAR
EFFECT							
CAUSE	UNDER-INFLATION OR LACK OF ROTATION	OVER-INFLATION OR LACK OF ROTATION	UNDER-INFLATION OR EXCESSIVE SPEED*	EXCESSIVE CAMBER	INCORRECT TOE	UNBALANCED WHEEL OR TIRE DEFECT *	LACK OF ROTATION OF TIRES OR WORN OR OUT-OF-ALIGNMENT SUSPENSION.
CORRECTION	ADJUST PRESSURE TO SPECIFICATIONS WHEN TIRES ARE COOL ROTATE TIRES			ADJUST CAMBER TO SPECIFICATIONS	ADJUST TOE-IN TO SPECIFICATIONS	DYNAMIC OR STATIC BALANCE WHEELS	ROTATE TIRES AND INSPECT SUSPENSION

*HAVE TIRE INSPECTED FOR FURTHER USE.

TCCS1267

Fig. 165 Common tire wear patterns and causes

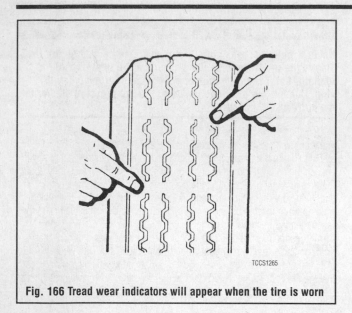

Fig. 166 Tread wear indicators will appear when the tire is worn

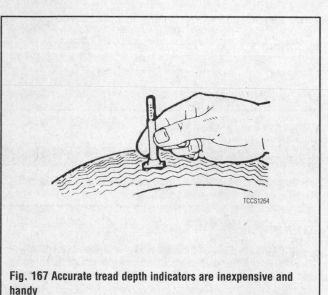

Fig. 167 Accurate tread depth indicators are inexpensive and handy

time, support them on strips of wood. Never store tires and wheels upright; the tread may develop flat spots.

• When driving, watch for hazards; it doesn't take much to crack a wheel.

• When washing, use a mild soap or non-abrasive dish detergent (keeping in mind that detergent tends to remove wax). Avoid cleansers with abrasives or the use of hard brushes. There are many cleaners and polishes for special wheels.

• If possible, remove the wheels during the winter. Salt and sand used for snow removal can severely damage the finish of a wheel.

• Make certain the recommended lug nut torque is never exceeded or the wheel may crack. Never use snow chains on special wheels; severe scratching will occur.

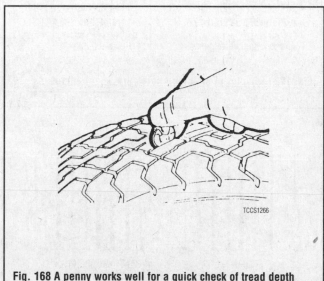

Fig. 168 A penny works well for a quick check of tread depth

FLUIDS AND LUBRICANTS

Fluid Disposal

Used fluids such as engine oil, transmission fluid, antifreeze and brake fluid are hazardous wastes and must be disposed of properly. Before draining any fluids, consult with your local authorities; in many areas waste oil, antifreeze, etc. is being accepted as a part of recycling programs. A number of service stations and auto parts stores are also accepting waste fluids for recycling.

Be sure of the recycling center's policies before draining any fluids, as many will not accept different fluids that have been mixed together.

Fuel and Engine Oil Recommendations

GASOLINE ENGINES

Fuel

All 1987–96 Ford full size vans must use lead-free gasoline with a minimum octane rating of 87(as listed on the pumps), which usually means

regular unleaded. Some areas may have 86 or even lower octane available, which would make 87 midgrade. In such cases, a minimum fuel octane of 87 should STILL be used.

➡**Some fuel additives contain chemicals that can damage the catalytic converter and/or oxygen sensor. Read all of the labels carefully before using any additive in the engine or fuel system.**

The use of a leaded fuel in a vehicle requiring unleaded fuel will plug the catalytic converter and render it inoperative. It will also increase exhaust backpressure to the point where engine output will be severely reduced. Obviously, use of leaded fuel should not be a problem, since most companies have stopped selling it for quite some time.

Fuel should be selected for the brand and octane which performs best with your engine. Judge a gasoline by its ability to prevent pinging, its engine starting capabilities (cold and hot) and general all weather performance. The use of a fuel too low in octane (a measurement of anti-knock quality) will result in spark knock. Since many factors such as altitude, terrain, air temperature and humidity affect operating efficiency, knocking may result even though the recommended fuel is being used. If persistent knocking occurs, it may be necessary to switch to a different brand or grade of fuel. Continuous or heavy knocking may result in engine damage.

➡ **Your engine's fuel requirement can change with time, mainly due to carbon buildup, which will in turn change the compression ratio. If your engine pings or knocks, switch to a higher grade of fuel. Sometimes, just changing brands will cure the problem.**

The other most important quality you should look for in a fuel is that it contains detergents designed to keep fuel injection systems clean. Many of the major fuel companies will display information right at the pumps telling you that their fuels contain these detergents. The use of a high-quality fuel which contains detergents will help assure trouble-free operation of your van's fuel system.

Engine Oil

CONVENTIONAL OIL

▶ **See Figures 169 and 170**

The recommended oil viscosities for sustained temperatures ranging from below 0° (-18°C) to above 32°F (0°C) are listed in the section. They are broken down into multi-viscosities and single viscosities. Multi-viscosity oils are recommended because of their wider range of acceptable temperatures and driving conditions.

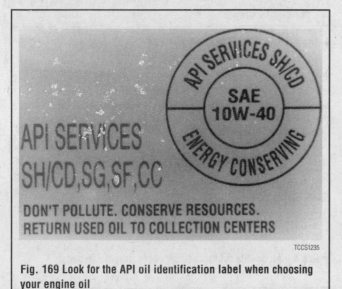

Fig. 169 Look for the API oil identification label when choosing your engine oil

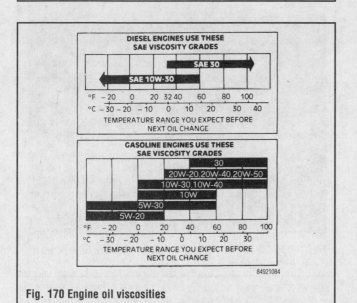

Fig. 170 Engine oil viscosities

When adding oil to the crankcase or changing the oil and filter, it is important that oil of equal quality to the original be used in your van. The use of inferior oils may void the warranty, damage your engine, or both.

The Society of Automotive Engineers (SAE) grade number of the oil indicates the viscosity of the oil—its ability to lubricate at a given temperature. The lower the SAE number, the lighter the oil; the lower the viscosity, the easier it is to crank the engine in cold weather, but the less the oil will lubricate and protect the engine in high temperatures. This number is marked on every oil container.

Oil viscosities should be chosen from those oils recommended for the lowest anticipated temperatures during the oil change interval. Due to the need for an oil that embodies both good lubrication at high temperature and easy cranking in cold weather, multigrade oils have been developed. Basically, a multigrade oil is thinner at low temperatures and thicker at high temperatures. For example, a 10W-40 oil (the W stands for winter) exhibits the characteristics of a 10-weight (SAE 10) oil when the van is first started and the oil is cold. Its lighter weight allows it to travel to the lubricating surfaces quicker and offer less resistance to starter motor cranking than a heavier oil. But after the engine reaches operating temperature, the 10W-40 oil begins acting like straight 40-weight (SAE 40) oil. It behaves as a heavier oil, providing greater lubrication and protection against foaming than lighter oils.

The American Petroleum Institute (API) designations, also found on oil containers, indicate the classification of engine oil used for given operating conditions. Only oils designated Service SH (or the latest superseding designation) should be used in your van. Oils of the SH-type perform many functions inside the engine besides their basic lubrication. Through a balanced system of metallic detergents and polymeric dispersants, the oil prevents high and low temperature deposits and also keeps sludge and dirt particles in suspension. Acids, particularly sulfuric, as well as other by-products of engine combustion are neutralized by the oil. If these acids are allowed to concentrate, they can cause corrosion and rapid wear of the internal engine parts.

✳✳ CAUTION

Non-detergent motor oils or straight mineral oils should never be used in your Ford gasoline engine.

SYNTHETIC OIL

There are many excellent synthetic and fuel-efficient oils currently available that can provide better gas mileage, longer service life, and in some cases better engine protection. These benefits do not come without a few hitches, however; the main one being the price of synthetic oils, which can be three or four times the price per quart of conventional oil.

Synthetic oil is not necessarily for every van and every type of driving, so you should consider your engine's condition and your type of driving. Also, check your van's warranty conditions regarding the use of synthetic oils.

Depending on the type of synthetic oil, brand new engines and older, high mileage engines can be the wrong candidates for synthetic oil. In some cases, the synthetic oil is so slippery that it can prevent the proper break-in of new engines. With the exception of vehicles that are equipped with certain brands of synthetic oil from the factory, most manufacturers recommend that you wait until the engine is properly broken in (3,000 miles) before using synthetic oil. Older engines with wear have a different problem with some synthetics: they "use" (consume during operation) more oil as they age. Slippery synthetic oils get past these worn parts easily. If your engine is "using" conventional oil, it may use synthetics much faster. Also, if your van is leaking oil past old seals you'll have a much greater leak problem with synthetics.

Consider your type of driving, and consult someone knowledgeable on the particular brand of oil you are thinking of using. If most of your accumulated mileage is high speed, highway type driving, the more expensive synthetic oils may be a benefit. Extended highway driving gives the engine a chance to warm up, accumulating less acids in the oil and putting less stress on the engine over the long run. Under these conditions, the oil change interval can be extended (as long as your oil filter can last the extended life of the oil) up to the advertised mileage claims of the synthetics. Trucks with synthetic oils may show increased fuel economy in highway driving, due to less internal friction. However, many automotive experts agree that 50,000 miles (80,000 km) is too long to keep any oil in your engine.

Trucks used under harder circumstances, such as stop-and-go, city type driving, short trips, or extended idling, should be serviced more frequently. For the engines in these trucks, the much greater cost of synthetic or fuel-efficient oils may not be worth the investment. Internal wear increase much quicker on these trucks, causing greater oil consumption and leakage.

DIESEL ENGINES

Fuel

Fuel makers produce two grades of diesel fuel, No. 1 and No. 2, for use in automotive diesel engines. Generally speaking, No. 2 fuel is recommended over No. 1 for driving in temperatures above 20°F (-7°C). In fact, in many areas, No. 2 diesel is the only fuel available. By comparison, No. 2 diesel fuel is less volatile than No. 1 fuel, and gives better fuel economy. No. 2 fuel is also a better injection pump lubricant.

Two important characteristics of diesel fuel are its cetane number and its viscosity.

The cetane number of a diesel fuel refers to the ease with which a diesel fuel ignites. High cetane numbers mean that the fuel will ignite with relative ease or that it ignites well at low temperatures. Naturally, the lower the cetane number, the higher the temperature must be to ignite the fuel. Most commercial fuels have cetane numbers that range from 35 to 65. No. 1 diesel fuel generally has a higher cetane rating than No. 2 fuel.

Viscosity is the ability of a liquid, in this case diesel fuel, to flow. Using straight No. 2 diesel fuel below 20°F (-7°C) can cause problems, because this fuel tends to become cloudy, meaning wax crystals begin forming in the fuel. 20°F (-7°C) is often call the cloud point for No. 2 fuel. In extremely cold weather, No. 2 fuel can stop flowing altogether. In either case, fuel flow is restricted, which can result in no start condition or poor engine performance. Fuel manufacturers often winterize No. 2 diesel fuel by using various fuel additives and blends (no. 1 diesel fuel, kerosene, etc.) to lower its winter time viscosity. Generally speaking, though, No. 1 diesel fuel is more satisfactory in extremely cold weather.

➡️No. 1 and No. 2 diesel fuels will mix and burn with no ill effects, although the engine manufacturer recommends one or the other. Consult the owner's manual for information.

Depending on local climate, most fuel manufacturers make winterized No. 2 fuel available seasonally.

Many automobile manufacturers publish pamphlets giving the locations of diesel fuel stations nationwide. Contact the local dealer for information.

Do not substitute home heating oil for automotive diesel fuel. While in some cases, home heating oil refinement levels equal those of diesel fuel, many times they are far below diesel engine requirements. The result of using dirty home heating oil will be a clogged fuel system, in which case the entire system may have to be dismantled and cleaned.

One more word on diesel fuels. Don't thin diesel fuel with gasoline in cold weather. The lighter gasoline, which is more explosive, will cause rough running at the very least, and may cause extensive damage to the fuel system if enough is used.

Engine Oil

▶ See Figure 170

Diesel engines require different engine oil from those used in gasoline engines. Besides doing the things gasoline engine oil does, diesel oil must also deal with increased engine heat and the diesel blow-by gases, which create sulfuric acid, a high corrosive.

Under the American Petroleum Institute (API) classifications, gasoline engine oil codes begin with an **S**, and diesel engine oil codes begin with a **C**. This first letter designation is followed by a second letter code which explains what type of service (heavy, moderate, light) the oil is meant for. For example, the label of a typical oil bottle will include: API SERVICES SH, CD. This means the oil in the bottle is a superior, heavy duty engine oil when used in a diesel engine.

Many diesel manufacturers recommend an oil with both gasoline and diesel engine API classifications.

➡️Ford specifies the use of an engine oil conforming to API service categories of both SH and CD. DO NOT use oils labeled as only SH or only CD, as they could cause engine damage.

OPERATION IN FOREIGN COUNTRIES

If you plan to drive your van outside the United States or Canada, there is a possibility that fuels will be too low in anti-knock quality and could produce engine damage. It is wise to consult with local authorities upon arrival in a foreign country to determine the best fuels available.

Engine

OIL LEVEL CHECK

▶ See Figures 171, 172, 173 and 174

Check the engine oil level every time you fill the gas tank. The oil level should be above the **ADD** mark and not above the **FULL** mark on the dipstick. Make sure that the dipstick is inserted into the crankcase as far as possible and that the vehicle is resting on level ground. Also, allow a few minutes after turning off the engine for the oil to drain into the pan or an inaccurate reading will result.

1. Open the hood and remove the engine oil dipstick.
2. Wipe the dipstick with a clean, lint-free rag and reinsert it. Be sure to insert it all the way.
3. Pull out the dipstick and note the oil level. It should be between the **SAFE** (MAX) mark and the **ADD** (MIN) mark.
4. If the level is below the lower mark, replace the dipstick and add fresh oil to bring the level within the proper range. Do not overfill.
5. Recheck the oil level and close the hood.

➡️Use a high quality multigrade oil of the proper viscosity.

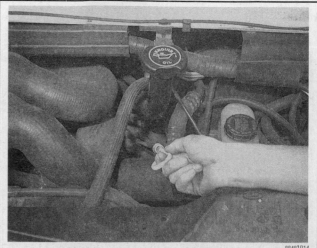

Fig. 171 Withdraw the engine oil dipstick from the tube, wipe it clean, and reinsert it again

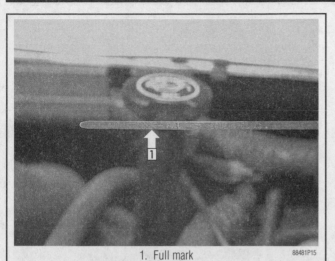

1. Full mark

88481P15

Fig. 172 Remove the dipstick again and check the oil level in reference to the marks on the dipstick

OIL & FILTER CHANGE

♦ See Figures 175 thru 180

➥The engine oil and oil filter should be changed at the recommended intervals on the Maintenance Chart. Though some manufacturers have at times recommended changing the filter only at every other oil change, we recommend that you always change the filter with the oil. The benefit of fresh oil is quickly lost if the old filter is clogged and unable to do its job. Also, leaving the old filter in place leaves a significant amount of dirty oil in the system.

The oil should be changed more frequently if the vehicle is being operated in a very dusty area. Before draining the oil, make sure that the engine is at operating temperature. Hot oil will hold more impurities in suspension and will flow better, allowing the removal of more oil and dirt.

➥It is usually a good idea to place your ignition key in the box or bag with the bottles of fresh engine oil. In this way it will be VERY HARD to forget to refill the engine crankcase before you go to start the engine.

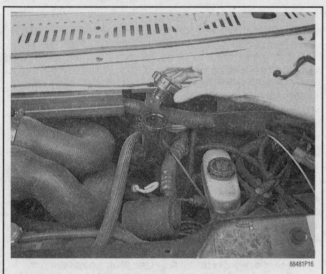

88481P16

Fig. 173 If the level is low, remove the oil filler cap . . .

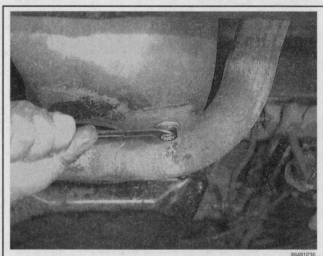

88481P36

Fig. 175 Use a wrench to loosen (but not remove) the oil pan drain plug

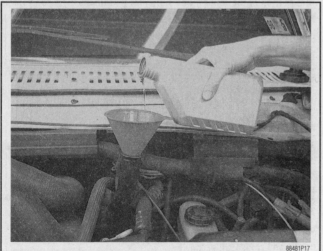

88481P17

Fig. 174 . . . and add the correct grade and amount of engine oil

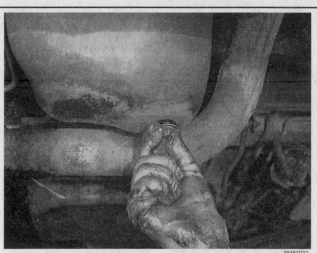

88481P37

Fig. 176 Unthread the plug by hand while keeping an upward pressure until you are ready to remove it

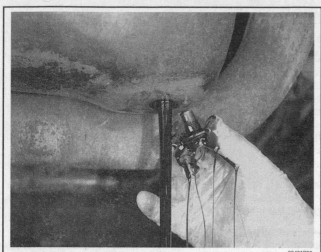

Fig. 177 Remove the plug quickly to avoid getting splashed with oil

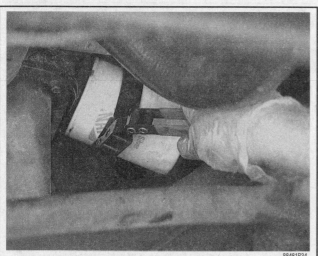

Fig. 178 Use an oil filter wrench, such as the strap type shown here, to loosen the filter from its mounting

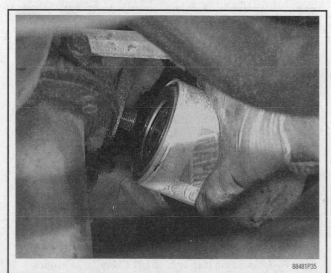

Fig. 179 Reach up to unscrew and remove the filter by hand

Fig. 180 Before installing a new oil filter, lightly coat the rubber gasket with clean oil

1. Raise and support the vehicle safely on jackstands. Make sure the oil drain plug is at the lowest point on the oil pan. If not, you may have to raise the vehicle slightly higher on one jackstand (side) than the other.

2. Before you crawl under the van, take a look at where you will be working and gather all the necessary tools: such as a few wrenches or a strip of sockets, the drain pan, a clean rag, and, if the oil filter is more accessible from underneath the vehicle, you will also want to grab a bottle of oil, the new filter and a filter wrench at this time.

3. Position the drain pan beneath the oil pan drain plug. Keep in mind that the fast flowing oil, which will spill out as you pull the plug from the pan, will flow with enough force that it could miss the pan. Position the drain pan accordingly and be ready to move the pan more directly beneath the plug as the oil flow lessens to a trickle.

➡**Some 5.0L engines are equipped with 2 drain plugs (one in front of the crossmember and one behind it, closer to the transmission). Both should be removed to assure proper pan draining, but if the front end is raised and supported on ramps or jackstands, the oil may not fully drain from the front plug. The best way to assure all oil has been drained is to pull the plugs, then remove the jackstands and carefully lower the vehicle (make sure your drain pans are properly positioned because the relative positioning of the drain holes will change as the vehicle is lowered). Once you are sure the front portion of the oil pan has sufficiently drained, raise the vehicle and support it again with jackstands.**

4. Loosen the drain plug with a wrench (or socket and driver), then carefully unscrew the plug with your fingers. Use a rag to shield your fingers from the heat. Push in on the plug as you unscrew it so you can feel when all of the screw threads are out of the hole (and so you will keep the oil from seeping past the threads until you are ready to remove the plug). You can then remove the plug quickly to avoid having hot oil run down your arm. This will also help assure that have the plug in your hand, not in the bottom of a pan of hot oil.

❄❄ **CAUTION**

Be careful of the oil; when at operating temperature, it is hot enough to cause a severe burn.

5. Allow the oil to drain until nothing but a few drops are coming out of the drain hole. Check the drain plug to make sure the threads and sealing surface are not damaged. Carefully thread the plug into position and tighten it snugly give a slight additional turn. You don't want the plug to fall out (as you would quickly become stranded), but the pan threads are EASILY stripped from overtightening (and this can be time consuming and/or costly to fix).

6. The oil filter is most likely located on the bottom left-hand side of all the engines installed in these vehicles; position the drain pan beneath it. To remove the filter, you may need an oil filter wrench since the filter may have been fitted too tightly and/or the heat from the engine may have made it even tighter. A filter wrench can be obtained at any auto parts store and is well-worth the investment. Loosen the filter with the filter wrench. With a rag wrapped around the filter, unscrew the filter from the boss on the side of the engine. Be careful of hot oil that will run down the side of the filter. Make sure that your drain pan is under the filter before you start to remove it from the engine; should some of the hot oil happen to get on you, there will be a place to dump the filter in a hurry and the filter will usually spill a good bit of dirty oil as it is removed.

7. Wipe the base of the mounting boss with a clean, dry cloth. When you install the new filter, smear a small amount of fresh oil on the gasket with your finger, just enough to coat the entire contact surface. When you tighten the filter, rotate it about a half-turn after it contacts the mounting boss (or follow any instructions which are provided on the filter or parts box).

❊❊ WARNING

Never operate the engine without engine oil; otherwise, SEVERE engine damage will be the result.

8. Remove the jackstands and carefully lower the vehicle, then IMMEDIATELY refill the engine crankcase with the proper amount of oil. DO NOT WAIT TO DO THIS because if you forget and someone tries to start the van severe engine damage will occur.

9. Refill the engine crankcase slowly, checking the level often. You may notice that it usually takes less than the amount of oil listed in the capacity chart to refill the crankcase. But, that is only until the engine is run and the oil filter is filled with oil. To make sure the proper level is obtained, run the engine to normal operating temperature, shut the engine **OFF**, allow the oil to drain back into the oil pan, and recheck the level. Top off the oil at this time to the fill mark.

➡**If the vehicle is not resting on level ground, the oil level reading on the dipstick may be slightly off. Be sure to check the level only when the van is sitting level.**

10. Drain your used oil in a suitable container for recycling and clean-up your tools, as you will be needing them again in a couple of thousand more miles (kilometers?).

Manual Transmission

FLUID RECOMMENDATIONS

The manual transmissions covered by this manual use Mercon® automatic transmission fluid for lubrication. DO NOT use improper fluids such as Dexron® or gear oil. Use of improper fluids could lead to leaks or transmission damage.

LEVEL CHECK

▶ **See Figure 181**

The fluid level should be checked every six months or 6000 miles (9600 km), whichever comes first.

1. Park the van on a level surface, turn the engine **OFF**, FIRMLY apply the parking brake and block the drive wheels.

➡**Ground clearance may make access to the transmission filler plug impossible without raising and supporting the vehicle, BUT, if this is done, the van MUST be supported at four corners and level. If only the front or rear is supported, an improper fluid level will be indicated. If you are going to place the van on four jackstands, this might be the perfect opportunity to rotate the tires as well.**

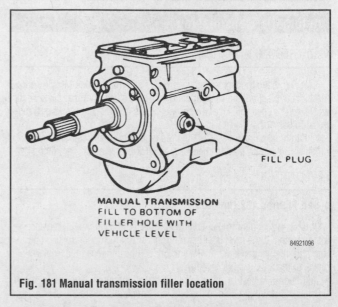

MANUAL TRANSMISSION
FILL TO BOTTOM OF
FILLER HOLE WITH
VEHICLE LEVEL

FILL PLUG

84921096

Fig. 181 Manual transmission filler location

2. Remove the filler plug from the side of the transmission case using a proper size wrench. The fluid level should be even with the bottom of the filler hole.

3. If additional fluid is necessary, add it through the filler hole using a siphon pump or squeeze bottle.

4. When you are finished, carefully install the filler plug, but DO NOT overtighten it and damage the housing.

DRAIN & REFILL

Under normal conditions, the manufacturer feels that manual transmission fluid should not need to be changed. However, if the van is driven in deep water (as high as the transmission casing) it is a good idea to replace the fluid. Little harm can come from a fluid change when you have just purchased a used vehicle, especially since the condition of the transmission fluid is usually not known.

If the fluid is to be drained, it is a good idea to warm the fluid first so it will flow better. This can be accomplished by 15–20 miles of highway driving. Fluid which is warmed to normal operating temperature will flow faster, drain more completely and remove more contaminants from the housing.

1. Drive the vehicle to assure the fluid is at normal operating temperature.

2. Raise and support the vehicle securely on jackstands. Remember that the vehicle must be supported level (usually at four points) so the proper amount of fluid can be added.

3. Place a drain pan under the transmission housing, below the drain plug. Remember that the fluid will likely flow with some force at first (arcing outward from the transmission), and will not just drip straight downward into the pan. Position the drain pan accordingly and move it more directly beneath the drain plug as the flow slows to a trickle.

➡**To ensure that the fill plug is not frozen or rusted in place, remove it from the transmission BEFORE removing the drain plug. It would be unfortunate to drain all of your transmission fluid and then realize that the fill plug is stripped or frozen in place.**

4. Remove the fill plug, then the drain plug and allow the transmission fluid to drain out.

5. Once the transmission has drained sufficiently, install the drain plug until secure.

6. Remove the filler plug, and fill the transmission to the proper level with the required fluid.

7. Reinstall the filler plug once you are finished.

8. Remove the jackstands and carefully lower the vehicle.

Automatic Transmission

FLUID RECOMMENDATIONS

The automatic transmissions covered by this manual use Mercon® automatic transmission fluid for lubrication. DO NOT use improper fluids such as Dexron® or gear oil. Use of improper fluids could lead to leaks or transmission damage.

On automatic transmissions the fluid type is normally stamped on the dipstick. Be sure to double check the dipstick before adding any fluid.

LEVEL CHECK

♦ See Figures 182 thru 189

It is very important to maintain the proper fluid level in an automatic transmission. If the level is either too high or too low, poor shifting operation and internal damage are likely to occur. For this reason, a regular check of the fluid level is essential.

Although it is best to check fluid at normal operating temperature, it can be checked overnight cold, if the ambient temperatures are 50–95°F

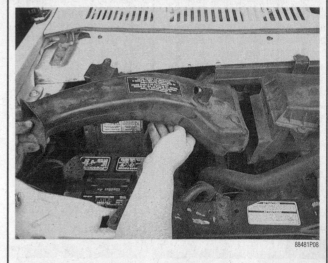

Fig. 184 . . . and remove the snorkel . . .

Fig. 182 The air cleaner snorkel may have to be removed to access the transmission dipstick, as indicated by this label

1. Transmission dipstick

Fig. 185 . . . to gain access to the transmission dipstick, which is located behind the hoses

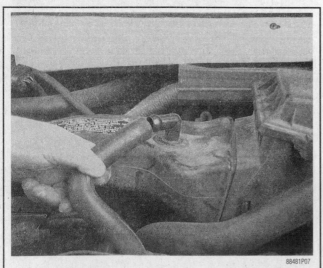

Fig. 183 If necessary, disconnect the hose from the snorkel . . .

Fig. 186 Withdraw the dipstick, wipe it clean and reinsert it again

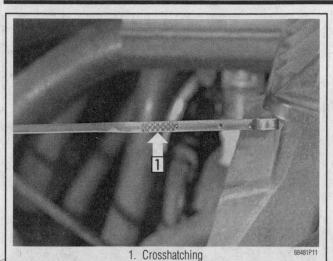

1. Crosshatching

88481P11

Fig. 187 Pull the dipstick out again and check the fluid level in relation to the crosshatching, or ADD and FULL marks

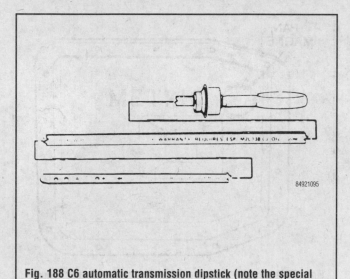

84921095

Fig. 188 C6 automatic transmission dipstick (note the special fluid designation)

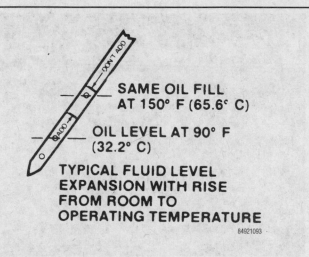

SAME OIL FILL
AT 150° F (65.6° C)

OIL LEVEL AT 90° F
(32.2° C)

TYPICAL FLUID LEVEL EXPANSION WITH RISE FROM ROOM TO OPERATING TEMPERATURE

84921093

Fig. 189 The automatic transmission fluid level will rise as the vehicle reaches operating temperature

(21–35°C). If so, refer to the dots on the transmission dipstick instead of the cross-hatched area and level marking lines.

1. Drive the vehicle for 15–20 minutes, allowing the transmission to reach operating temperature.

➡ **If the van is driven at extended highway speeds, is driven in city traffic in hot weather or is being used to pull a trailer, fluid temperatures will likely exceed normal operating and checking ranges. In these circumstances, give the fluid time to cool (about 30 minutes) before checking the level.**

2. Park the van on a level surface, apply the parking brake and leave the engine idling. Make sure the parking brake is FIRMLY ENGAGED. Shift the transmission and engage each gear, then place the selector in **P** (PARK).

3. Open the hood and locate the transmission dipstick. Wipe away any dirt in the area of the dipstick to prevent it from falling into the filler tube. Withdraw the dipstick, wipe it with a clean, lint-free rag and reinsert it until it fully seats.

4. Withdraw the dipstick and hold it horizontally while noting the fluid level. It should be at the crosshatching or between the upper (FULL) and lower (ADD) marks.

5. If the level is below the lower mark, use a funnel and add fluid in small quantities through the dipstick filler neck. Keep the engine running while adding fluid and check the level after each small amount. DO NOT overfill as this could lead to foaming and transmission damage or seal leaks.

➡ **Since the transmission fluid is added through the dipstick tube, if you check the fluid too soon after adding fluid an incorrect reading may occur. After adding fluid, wait a few minutes to allow it to fully drain into the transmission.**

DRAIN, PAN/FILTER SERVICE & REFILL

Transmission Assembly

◆ **See Figures 190 thru 197**

Under normal service (moderate highway driving excluding excessive hot or cold conditions), the manufacturer feels that automatic transmission fluid should not need periodic changing. However, if a major service is performed to the transmission, if transmission fluid becomes burnt or discolored through severe usage or if the vehicle is subjected to constant stop-and-go driving in hot weather, trailer towing, long periods of highway use at high speeds, fluid should be changed to prevent transmission damage. A preventive maintenance change is therefore recommended for most vehicles at least every 90,000 miles (145,000 km).

➡ **Although not a required service, transmission fluid changing can help assure a trouble-free transmission. Likewise, changing the transmission filter at this time is also added insurance.**

1. Raise the van and support it securely on jackstands.

➡ **The torque converters on some transmissions are equipped with drain plugs. Because it may take some time to drain the fluid from the converter, you may wish to follow that procedure at this time, then come back to the pan and filter removal.**

2. Place a large drain pan under the transmission.

3. On E40D models, loosen the transmission pan drain plug and drain the fluid.

4. On all other models, loosen all of the pan attaching bolts to within a few turns of complete removal, then carefully break the gasket seal allowing most of the fluid to drain over the edge of the pan.

✳✳ CAUTION

DO NOT force the pan while breaking the gasket seal. DO NOT allow the pan flange to become bent or otherwise damaged.

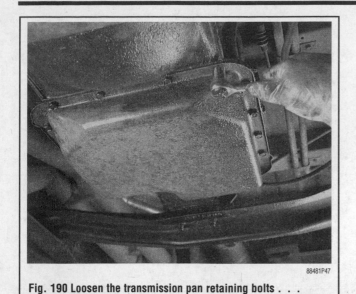

Fig. 190 Loosen the transmission pan retaining bolts . . .

Fig. 193 . . . and the old gasket from the transmission pan

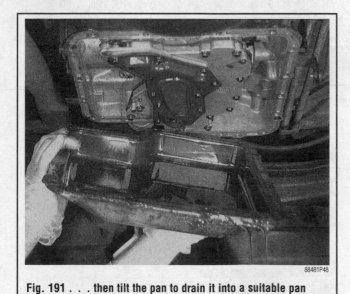

Fig. 191 . . . then tilt the pan to drain it into a suitable pan

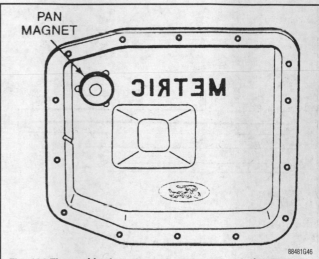

PAN MAGNET

METRIC

Fig. 194 Thoroughly clean the pan and, if equipped, the magnet of dirt and debris—4R70W automatic transmission pan illustrated

Fig. 192 Use a gasket scraper to clean the gasket residue from the transmission pan-to-transmission mating surface . . .

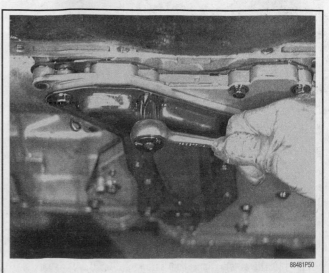

Fig. 195 If necessary, loosen the transmission filter retainers . . .

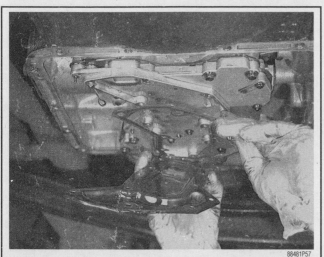

Fig. 196 . . . then remove the transmission filter and gasket from the valve body

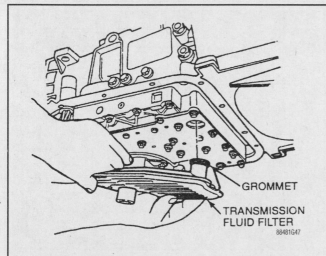

Fig. 197 Install the new fluid filter and grommet—4R70W automatic transmission shown

5. When fluid has drained to the level of the pan flange, remove the pan bolts and carefully lower the pan doing your best to drain the rest of the fluid into the drain pan.

6. Clean the transmission oil pan thoroughly using a safe solvent, then allow it to air dry. DO NOT use a cloth to dry the pan which might leave behind bits of lint. Discard the old pan gasket.

7. If necessary, remove the Automatic Transmission Fluid (ATF) filter retainers, then remove the filter by pulling it down and off of the valve body. Make sure any gaskets or seals are removed with the old filter.

To install:

8. Install the new oil filter screen, making sure all gaskets or seals are in place, then secure using the retaining screws, if applicable.

9. Place a new gasket on the fluid pan, then install the pan to the transmission. Tighten the attaching bolts to 10–12 inch lbs. (14–16 Nm) on E40D models, 8–12 ft. lbs. (11–16 Nm) on C6 models and 107–132 in. lbs. (12–15 Nm) on 4R70W models.

10. On E40D models, tighten the pan drain plug to 15–25 ft. lbs. (20–34 Nm).

11. Add three quarts of fluid to the transmission through the filler tube.

12. Remove the jackstands and carefully lower the vehicle.

13. Start the engine and move the gear selector through all gears in the shift pattern. Allow the engine to reach normal operating temperature.

14. Check the transmission fluid level. Add fluid, as necessary, to obtain the correct level.

Torque Converter

Some torque converters, such as those usually used on the E40D transmission, are equipped with drain plugs. If so, you will probably want to drain the fluid in the converter also at the time of a transmission pan fluid change. Just, make sure that you compensate for the additional fluid drained during the refilling process.

1. Remove the lower engine dust cover or the torque converter drain rubber access plug.

2. Rotate the torque converter until the drain plug comes into view.

3. Remove the drain plug and allow the transmission fluid to drain. This could take some time, so you may wish to perform the other transmission service (fluid pan and filter removal) while waiting.

4. Once the fluid has been drained, install the drain plug.

5. Install the engine dust cover or access plug.

6. Make sure the transmission is properly refilled with fluid before attempting to drive the vehicle.

Rear Axle

FLUID RECOMMENDATIONS

On 1989–93 models, use hypoid gear lubricant SAE 80 or 90.

On 1994–96 models use a premium rear axle lubricant.

On Dana limited slip axles, add 4oz. of friction modifier, Ford specification No. EST–M2C118–A, its equivalent or superseding fluid.

On Ford axles, add 4oz. of friction modifier, Ford specification No. EST–M2C118–A, its equivalent or superseding fluid.

FLUID LEVEL CHECK

▶ **See Figures 198, 199 and 200**

Clean the area around the fill plug, which is located in the housing cover on the Dana axles and the carrier casting on the Ford axles, before removing the plug. The lubricant level should be maintained to the bottom of the fill hole with the axle in its normal running position. If lubricant does not appear at the hole when the plug is removed, additional lubricant should be added. Use hypoid gear lubricant SAE 80 or 90.

➡**If the differential is of the limited slip type, be sure to use special limited slip differential additive.**

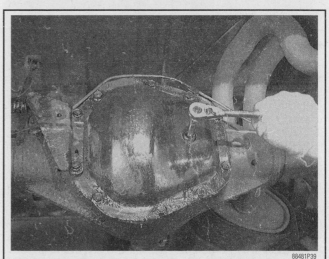

Fig. 198 Loosen and remove the fill plug on the rear axle cover—Dana axle shown

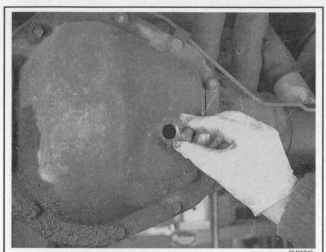

Fig. 199 After the plug has been loosened, unscrew it by hand. If the axle is full, fluid should trickle from the hole

Fig. 201 Loosen all clips and bracket retainers

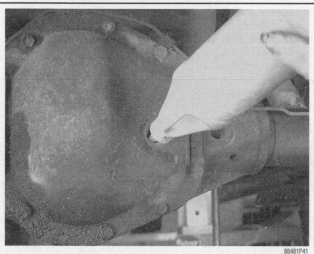

Fig. 200 Add additional lubricant by using a squeeze bottle or pump, until the proper level is reached

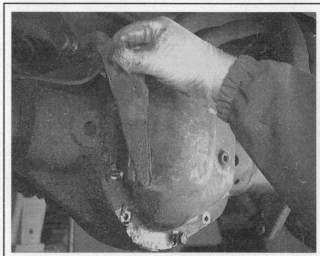

Fig. 202 Move all brackets and clips aside

DRAIN & REFILL

▶ **See Figures 201, 202, 203, 204 and 205**

Drain and refill the rear axle housing every 100,000 miles (160,000 km) or any time the vehicle is driven in high water (up to the axle). Although some fluid can be removed using a suction gun, the best method is to remove the rear cover to ensure that all of any present contaminants are removed. As with any fluid change, the oil should be at normal operating temperature to assure the best flow and removal of fluid/contaminants.

1. Drive the vehicle until the lubricant reaches normal operating temperature.

2. If necessary for access, raise and support the vehicle safely using jackstands, but be sure that the vehicle is level so you can properly refill the axle when you are finished.

3. Use a wire brush to clean the area around the differential. This will help prevent dirt from contaminating the differential housing while the cover is removed.

4. Position a drain pan under the rear axle.

5. Loosen and remove all but 2 of the rear cover upper or side retaining bolts. The remaining 2 bolts should then be loosened to within a few turns of complete removal. Use a small prytool to carefully break the

Fig. 203 Use a prytool to separate the cover from the housing and drain the fluid into a suitable container

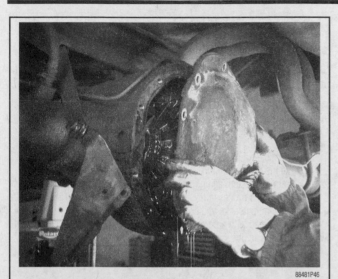

Fig. 204 Remove the cover from the axle housing

Fig. 205 Use a scraper to remove the old gasket and residue from the mating surfaces

gasket seal at the base of the cover and allow the lubricant to drain. Be VERY careful not to force or damage the cover and gasket mating surface.

6. Once most of the fluid has drained, remove the final retaining bolts and separate the cover from the housing.

To fill the differential:

7. Carefully clean the gasket mating surfaces of the cover and axle housing of any remaining gasket or sealer. A putty knife is a good tool to use for this. You may want to cover the differential gears using a rag or piece of plastic to prevent contaminating them with dirt or pieces of the old gasket.

8. Install the rear cover using a new gasket and sealant. Tighten the retaining bolts using a crisscross pattern.

➡**Make sure the vehicle is level before attempting to add fluid to the rear axle, otherwise an incorrect fluid level will result.**

9. Refill the rear axle housing using the proper grade and quantity of lubricant. Install the filler plug, operate the vehicle and check for any leaks.

Cooling System

FLUID RECOMMENDATIONS

▶ **See Figure 206**

Completely draining and refilling the cooling system every two years at least will remove accumulated rust, scale and other deposits. Coolant in late model vans is a 50/50 mixture of ethylene glycol and water for year round use. Use a good quality antifreeze with water pump lubricants, rust inhibitors and other corrosion inhibitors along with acid neutralizers.

Additionally, whenever servicing the cooling system, the pressure cap should be looked at for signs of age or deterioration. Fan belt and other drive belts should be inspected and adjusted to the proper tension. (See checking belt tension).

Hose clamps should be tightened, and soft or cracked hoses replaced. Damp spots, or accumulations of rust or dye near hoses, the water pump or other areas, indicate possible leakage which must be corrected before filling the system with fresh coolant.

✳✳ CAUTION

Never remove the radiator cap under any conditions while the engine is running! Failure to follow these instructions could result in damage to the cooling system and/or per-sonal injury. To avoid having scalding hot coolant or steam blow out of the radiator, use extreme care when removing the radiator cap from a hot radiator. Wait until the engine has cooled, then wrap a thick cloth around the radiator cap and turn it slowly to the first stop. Step back while the pressure is released from the cooling system. When you are sure the pressure has been released, press down on the radiator cap (with the cloth still in position), turn and remove the cap.

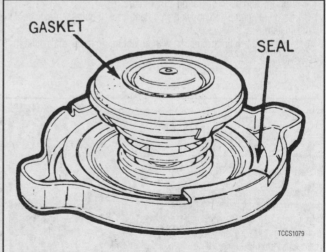

Fig. 206 Be sure the rubber gasket on the radiator cap has a tight seal

LEVEL CHECK

▶ **See Figure 207**

The fluid level can be checked by observing the level indicator marks on the side of the coolant recovery tank, or by removing the radiator cap and looking at the coolant level in the radiator.

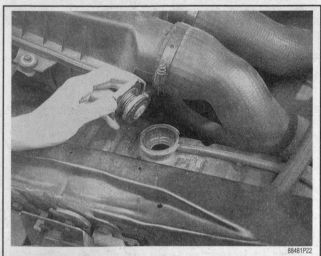

Fig. 207 After the engine has cooled, the radiator cap can be removed to check the coolant level

DRAIN & REFILL

▶ **See Figure 208**

➡**Before opening the radiator petcock, spray it with some penetrating lubricant.**

1. Open the radiator, or disconnect the bottom radiator hose, at the radiator outlet and drain the coolant.

2. Close the petcock or reconnect the lower hose and fill the system with water.

3. Determine the capacity of your coolant system (see the Capacities Specifications chart, later in this section). Add a 50/50 mix of quality antifreeze (ethylene glycol) and water to provide the desired protection.

4. Run the engine to operating temperature.

5. Stop the engine and check the coolant level. If necessary, add coolant to the system

6. Check the level of protection with an antifreeze tester, and adjust if necessary.

7. Install the radiator cap and check for leaks.

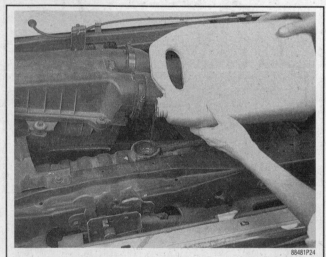

Fig. 208 Add the correct mixture of coolant and water through the radiator filler neck until the system is properly filled

FLUSHING & CLEANING THE SYSTEM

▶ **See Figures 209 and 210**

➡**Before opening the radiator petcock, spray it with some penetrating lubricant.**

1. Open the radiator, or disconnect the bottom radiator hose, at the radiator outlet and drain the coolant.

2. Close the petcock or reconnect the lower hose and fill the system with water.

3. Add a can of quality radiator flush.

4. Idle the engine until the upper radiator hose gets hot.

5. Drain the system again.

6. Repeat this process until the drained water is clear and free of scale.

7. Close all petcocks and connect all the hoses.

8. If equipped with a coolant recovery system, flush the reservoir with water and leave empty.

Fig. 209 Scale deposits, such as those visible here through the filler neck, can be treated and prevented with regular cleaning and flushing

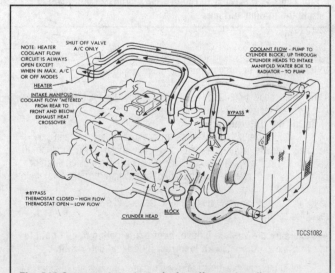

Fig. 210 Cutaway view of a typical cooling system flow

9. Determine the capacity of your coolant system (see capacities specifications). Add a 50/50 mix of quality antifreeze (ethylene glycol) and water to provide the desired protection.

10. Run the engine to operating temperature.

11. Stop the engine and check the coolant level.

12. Check the level of protection with an antifreeze tester, replace the cap and check for leaks.

Brake Master Cylinder

FLUID RECOMMENDATIONS

Use Ford Heavy-Duty Brake Fluid, Ford specification No. ESA–M6C25–, its equivalent, or superseding fluid; do not overfill.

✳✳ WARNING

BRAKE FLUID EATS PAINT. Take great care not to splash or spill brake fluid on painted surfaces. Should you spill a small amount on the van's finish, don't panic, just flush the area with plenty of water.

LEVEL CHECK

▶ **See Figures 211, 212, 213, 214 and 215**

Brake fluid level and condition is a safety related item and it should be checked ANY TIME the hood is opened. Your vehicle should not use brake fluid rapidly (unless there is a leak in the system), but the level should drop slowly in relation to brake pad wear.

The master cylinder reservoir is located under the hood, on the left side firewall. All vehicles covered by this manual should be equipped with a see-through plastic reservoir. This makes checking the level easy and helps reduce the risk of fluid contamination (since you don't have to expose the fluid by opening the cap to check the level). Fluid should be kept near the FULL line or between the MIN and MAX lines, depending on how the reservoir is marked.

1. If it becomes necessary to add fluid to the system, take a moment to clean the area around the cap and reservoir.

2. Use a clean rag to wipe away dust and dirt which could enter the reservoir after the cover is removed.

3. Unscrew the cover and add brake fluid until the proper level is reached.

4. Install and hand-tighten the cover.

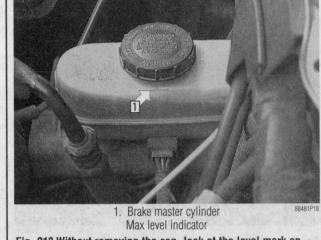

1. Brake master cylinder Max level indicator

Fig. 212 Without removing the cap, look at the level mark on the reservoir to check the brake fluid level

Fig. 213 If fluid must be added, clean the master cylinder cap and the area around it with a rag . . .

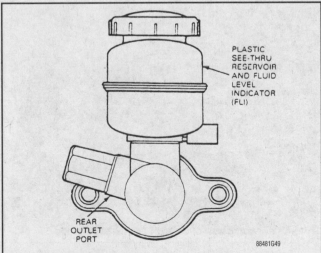

Fig. 211 The master cylinder used on Ford vans is of a see-through design, and has fluid level markings on the side

PLASTIC SEE-THRU RESERVOIR AND FLUID LEVEL INDICATOR (FLI)

REAR OUTLET PORT

Fig. 214 . . . then unscrew the cap and set it aside

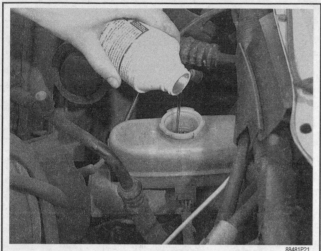

Fig. 215 Add brake fluid until it reaches the MAX level indicator on the side of the reservoir

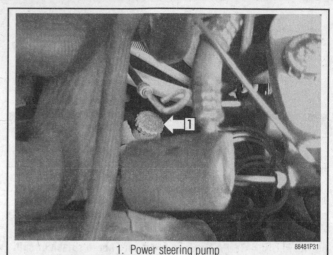

1. Power steering pump

Fig. 216 The power steering pump is located on the driver's side of the engine compartment

→ If the level of the brake fluid is less than half the volume of the reservoir (and the brake pads are not approaching a replacement point), it is advised that you check the brake system for leaks. Leaks in the hydraulic system often occur at the wheel cylinders.

Clutch Master Cylinder

FLUID RECOMMENDATIONS

Keep the reservoir topped up with Ford Heavy-Duty Brake fluid Ford specification No. ESA–M6C25–A, its equivalent or superseding fluid; do not overfill.

LEVEL CHECK

The hydraulic fluid reservoirs on these systems are mounted on the firewall. Fluid level checks are performed like those on the brake hydraulic system. The proper fluid level is indicated by a step on the reservoir.

✳✳ CAUTION

Carefully clean the top and sides of the reservoir before opening, to prevent contamination of the system with dirt, etc. Remove the reservoir diaphragm before adding fluid, and replace after filling.

Power Steering Pump

FLUID RECOMMENDATIONS

Use Ford Premium Power Steering Fluid, or an equivalent power steering fluid that meets Ford specification ESW–M2C33–F.

LEVEL CHECK

▶ See Figures 216, 217, 218 and 219

1. Position the vehicle on level ground. Run the engine until the fluid is at normal operating temperature.
2. Turn the steering wheel all the way to the left and right several times.
3. Position the wheels in the straight ahead position, then shut off the engine.

1. Full hot level mark

Fig. 217 Unscrew the power steering cap/dipstick assembly and read the fluid level. The dipstick has (FULL) HOT . . .

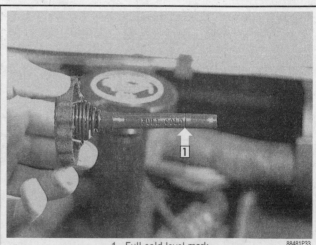

1. Full cold level mark

Fig. 218 . . .and FULL COLD level marks, so the fluid can be checked either before or after the van has been running

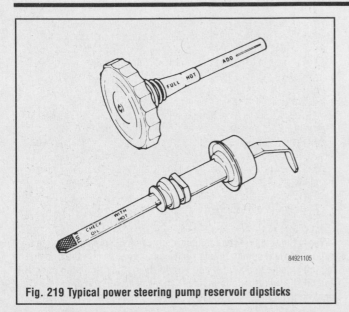

Fig. 219 Typical power steering pump reservoir dipsticks

4. Check the fluid level on the dipstick which is attached to the reservoir cap. The level should be between the ADD and FULL marks on the dipstick.

5. Add fluid if necessary. Do not overfill. Use an approved power steering fluid.

Chassis Greasing

The lubrication chart indicates where the grease fittings are located. The vehicle should be greased according to the intervals in the Preventive Maintenance Schedules at the end of this section.

Front Wheel Bearings

PRECAUTIONS

Before handling the bearings, there are a few things that you should remember to do and not to do. **Remember to DO the following:**

• Remove all outside dirt from the housing before exposing the bearing.
• Treat a used bearing as gently as you would a new one.
• Work with clean tools in clean surroundings.
• Use clean, dry canvas gloves, or at least clean, dry hands.
• Clean solvents and flushing fluids are a must.
• Use clean paper when laying out the bearings to dry.
• Protect disassembled bearings from rust and dirt. Cover them up.
• Use clean rags to wipe bearings.
• Keep the bearings in oil-proof paper when they are to be stored or are not in use.
• Clean the inside of the housing before replacing the bearing. **Do NOT do the following:**
• Don't work in dirty surroundings.
• Don't use dirty, chipped or damaged tools.
• Try not to work on wooden work benches or use wooden mallets.
• Don't handle bearings with dirty or moist hands.
• Do not use gasoline for cleaning; use a safe solvent.
• Do not spin-dry bearings with compressed air. They will be damaged.
• Do not spin dirty bearings.
• Avoid using cotton waste or dirty cloths to wipe bearings.
• Try not to scratch or nick bearing surfaces.
• Do not allow the bearing to come in contact with dirt or rust at any time.

REPACKING

Semi-Floating Front Axle

▶ **See Figure 220**

1. Raise and support the front end on jackstands.
2. Remove the wheel cover. Remove the wheel.
3. Remove the caliper from the disc and wire it to the underbody to prevent damage to the brake hose. See Section 9.
4. Remove the grease cap from the hub. Then, remove the cotter pin, nut lock, adjusting nut and flat washer from the spindle. Remove the outer bearing assembly from the hub.
5. Pull the hub and disc assembly off the wheel spindle.
6. Remove and discard the old grease retainer. Remove the inner bearing cone and roller assembly from the hub.
7. Clean all grease from the inner and outer bearing cups with solvent. Inspect the cups for pits, scratches, or excessive wear. If the cups are damaged, remove them with a drift.
8. Clean the inner and outer cone and roller assemblies with solvent and shake them dry. If the cone and roller assemblies show excessive wear or damage, replace them with the bearing cups as a unit.
9. Clean the spindle and the inside of the hub with solvent to thoroughly remove all old grease.
10. Covering the spindle with a clean cloth, brush all loose dirt and dust from the brake assembly. Remove the cloth carefully so as to not get dirt on the spindle.

To install:

11. If the bearing races were removed, install new ones using a bearing race installer (a suitably sized round driver.
12. It is imperative that all old grease be removed from the bearings and surrounding surfaces before repacking. The new lithium-based grease is not compatible with the sodium base grease used in the past.
13. Pack the bearings with a bearing packer. If done by hand, take great care to force as much grease as possible between the rollers and the cages, scoop the grease in from the top and bottom of the bearing cages.
14. Coat the inner surface of the hub and bearing races with grease.
15. Install the inner bearing in the hub. Lubricate the lip of the seal with grease, then being careful not to distort it, install the oil seal with its lip facing the bearing. Drive the seal in until its outer edge is even with the edge of the hub. A seal installer is best to use for this, but any suitably sized and smooth edge round driver can be used, including a piece of plastic pipe or a socket.
16. Install the rotor.
17. Install the outer bearing cone and roller assembly and the flat washer on the spindle. Install the adjusting nut.

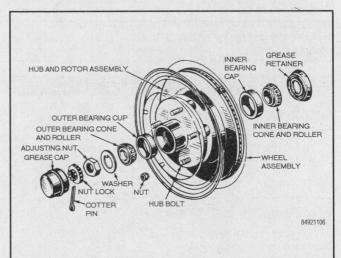

Fig. 220 Exploded view of the front hub, bearing and grease seal

18. Adjust the wheel bearings by torquing the adjusting nut to 17–25 ft. lbs. (23–24 Nm) with the wheel rotating to seat the bearing. Then back off the adjusting nut ½ turn. Retighten the adjusting nut to 10–28 inch lbs. (1.1–3.2 Nm). Install the locknut so that the castellations are aligned with the cotter pin hole. Install the cotter pin. Bend the ends of the cotter pin around the castellations of the locknut to prevent interference with the radio static collector in the grease cap. Install the grease cap.

☀ WARNING

New bolts must be used when servicing floating caliper units. The upper bolt must be tightened first. For caliper service, refer to Section 9.

19. Install the wheels.
20. Install the wheel cover.

Full Floating Rear Axle

♦ **See Figures 221, 222, 223, 224 and 225**

The wheel bearings on full floating rear axles are packed with wheel bearing grease. Axle lubricant can also flow into the wheel hubs and bear-ings, however, wheel bearing grease is the primary lubricant. The wheel bearing grease provides lubrication until the axle lubricant reaches the bearings during normal operation.

1. Set the parking brake and loosen, but do not remove the axle shaft bolts.
2. Raise the rear wheels off the floor and place jackstands under the rear axle housing so that the axle is parallel with the floor.
3. The axle shafts must turn freely, so release the parking brake and, if necessary, back off the rear brake adjustment.
4. Remove the axle shaft bolts and lockwashers. They should not be reused.
5. Place a heavy duty wheel dolly under the wheels and raise them so that all weight is off the wheel bearings.
6. Remove the axle shaft and gasket(s).
7. Remove the brake drum or caliper. See Section 9.
8. Using a special hub nut wrench, remove the hub nut.

➡Verify the thread direction before proceeding. Typically, the hub nut on the right spindle has a right-hand thread, while the one on the left spindle has a left-hand thread. If so, they will be marked RH and LH. If neither side is marked, chances are they both have a right-hand thread. NEVER use an impact wrench on the hub nut!

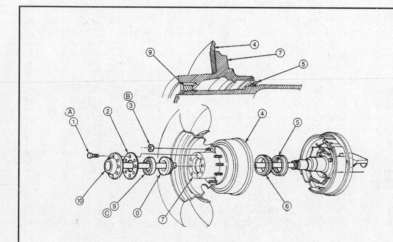

Item	Description
1	Axle Shaft Bolt
2	Rear Wheel Gasket
3	Lug Nut
4	Brake Drum
5	Seal, Hub Inner
6	Rear Wheel Bearing Inner Cone and Roller
7	Rear Hub
8	Rear Wheel Bearing Outer Cone and Roller
9	Hub Nut
10	Axle Shaft

Item	Description
A	Tighten to 122-163 N·m (90-120 Lb-Ft)
B	Tighten to 170-230 N·m (126-170 Lb-Ft)
C	Tighten to 88-102 N·m (65-75 Lb-Ft). To Set Bearings, Back Off Hub Nut 90 Degrees and Retighten to 20-27 N·m (15-20 Lb-Ft).

88481G50

Fig. 221 Exploded view of the wheel bearing assembly—single rear wheel models

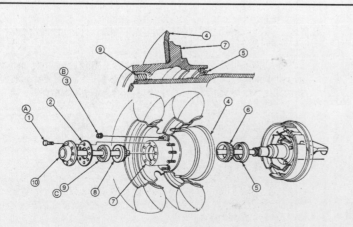

Item	Description
1	Axle Shaft Bolt
2	Rear Wheel Gasket
3	Lug Nut
4	Brake Drum
5	Seal, Hub Inner
6	Rear Wheel Bearing Inner Cone and Roller
7	Rear Hub
8	Rear Wheel Bearing Outer Cone and Roller
9	Hub Nut

Item	Description
10	Axle Shaft
A	Tighten to 122-163 N·m (90-120 Lb-Ft)
B	Tighten to 170-230 N·m (126-170 Lb-Ft)
C	Tighten to 88-102 N·m (65-75 Lb-Ft) While Rotating Hub. After Tightening, Rachet Back 90 degrees, Tighten to 20-27 N·m (15-20 Lb-Ft). The Maximum Torque to Rotate the Hub Is 2-3 N·m (20 Lb-In). Wheel End Play Is 0.00mm (.000 in.).

88481G51

Fig. 222 Exploded view of the wheel bearing assembly—dual rear wheel models (except E-Super Duty)

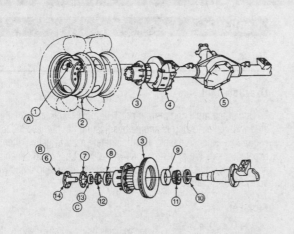

Item	Description	Item	Description
1	Lug Nut	12	Rear Wheel Bearing Outer Cone and Roller
2	Wheel	13	Hub Nut
3	Rear Hub and Rotor Assembly	14	Axle Shaft
4	Disc Brake Caliper	A	Tighten to 170-230 N·m (126-170 Lb-Ft)
5	Dana Full-Floating Axle-Model 80	B	Tighten to 113-153 N·m (83-113 Lb-Ft)
6	Axle Shaft-to-Rear Hub Bolt	C	Tighten to 88-102 N·m (65-75 Lb-Ft) While Rotating Hub. After Tightening, Rachet Back 90 degrees. Tighten to 20-27 N·m (15-20 Lb-Ft). The Maximum Torque to Rotate the Hub is 2-3 N·m (20 Lb-In). Wheel End Play Is 0.00mm (.000 in.).
7	Rear Wheel Gasket		
8	Outer Bearing Cup		
9	Inner Bearing Cup		
10	Inner Hub Seal		
11	Rear Wheel Bearing Inner Cone and Roller		

88481G52

Fig. 223 Exploded view of the wheel bearing assembly—E-Super Duty models

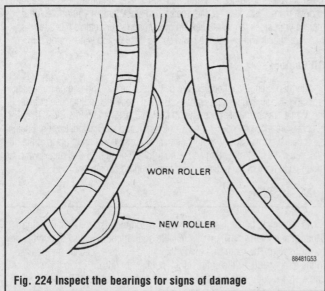

Fig. 224 Inspect the bearings for signs of damage

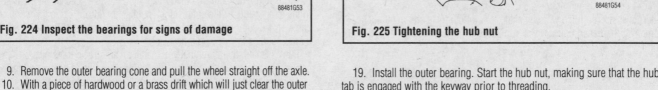

Fig. 225 Tightening the hub nut

9. Remove the outer bearing cone and pull the wheel straight off the axle.
10. With a piece of hardwood or a brass drift which will just clear the outer bearing cup, drive the inner bearing cone and inner seal out of the wheel hub.
11. Wash all the old grease or axle lubricant out of the wheel hub, using a suitable solvent.
12. Wash the bearing cups and rollers and inspect them for pitting, galling, and uneven wear patterns. Inspect the roller for end wear.
13. If the bearing cups are to be replaced, drive them out with a brass drift.
To install:
14. Install the new cups with a block of wood and hammer or press them in.
15. If the bearing cups are properly seated, a 0.0015 in. (0.038mm) feeler gauge will not fit between the cup and the wheel hub. The gauge should not fit beneath the cup. Check several places to make sure the cups are squarely seated.
16. Pack each bearing cone and roller with a bearing packer or in the manner previously outlined for the front wheel bearings. Use a multi-purpose wheel bearing grease.
17. Place the inner bearing cone and roller assembly in the wheel hub. Install a new inner seal in the hub with a seal installation tool.
18. Wrap the threads of the spindle with electrician's tape and carefully slide the hub straight on the spindle. Take care to avoid damaging the seal! Remove the tape.

19. Install the outer bearing. Start the hub nut, making sure that the hub tab is engaged with the keyway prior to threading.
20. Tighten the nut to 65–75 ft. lbs. (88–102 Nm) while rotating the wheel. DO NOT use an impact wrench!

➡The hub will ratchet as torque is applied. This ratcheting can be avoided by using Ford tool No. T88T-4252-AH or its equivalent. Avoiding ratcheting will give more even bearing preloads.

21. Back off (loosen) the adjusting nut 90° (¼ turn). Then, tighten it to 15–20 ft. lbs. (20–27 Nm).
22. Using a dial indicator, check end-play of the hub. No end-play is permitted.
23. Clean the hub bolt holes thoroughly. Replace the hub if any cracks are found around the holes or if the threads in the holes are in any way damaged.
24. Install the axle shaft, new flange gasket, lockwashers and **new** shaft retaining bolts. Coat the bolt threads with thread adhesive. Tighten them snugly, but not completely.
Install the brake drum or caliper.
Install the wheel.
Lower the van to the ground.
Tighten the wheel lug nuts.
Tighten the axle shaft bolts to 70–85 ft. lbs. (94–115 Nm).

TRAILER TOWING

General Recommendations

Your vehicle was primarily designed to carry passengers and cargo. It is important to remember that towing a trailer will place additional loads on your vehicles engine, drivetrain, steering, braking and other systems. However, if you decide to tow a trailer, using the prior equipment is a must.

Local laws may require specific equipment such as trailer brakes or fender mounted mirrors. Check your local laws.

Trailer Weight

The weight of the trailer is the most important factor. A good weight-to-horsepower ratio is about 35:1, 35 lbs. of Gross Combined Weight (GCW) for every horsepower your engine develops. Multiply the engine's rated horsepower by 35 and subtract the weight of the vehicle passengers and luggage. The number remaining is the approximate ideal maximum weight you should tow, although a numerically higher axle ratio can help compensate for heavier weight.

Hitch (Tongue) Weight

▶ See Figure 226

Calculate the hitch weight in order to select a proper hitch. The weight of the hitch is usually 9–11% of the trailer gross weight and should be measured with the trailer loaded. Hitches fall into various categories: those that mount on the frame and rear bumper, the bolt-on type, or the weld-on distribution type used for larger trailers. Axle mounted or clamp-on bumper hitches should never be used.

Check the gross weight rating of your trailer. Tongue weight is usually figured as 10% of gross trailer weight. Therefore, a trailer with a maximum gross weight of 2000 lbs. will have a maximum tongue weight of 200 lbs. Class I trailers fall into this category. Class II trailers are those with a gross weight rating of 2000–3000 lbs., while Class III trailers fall into the 3500–6000 lbs. category. Class IV trailers arc those over 6000 lbs. and are for use with fifth wheel trucks, only.

When you've determined the hitch that you'll need, follow the manufacturer's installation instructions, exactly, especially when it comes to fastener torques. The hitch will subjected to a lot of stress and good hitches come with hardened bolts. Never substitute an inferior bolt for a hardened bolt.

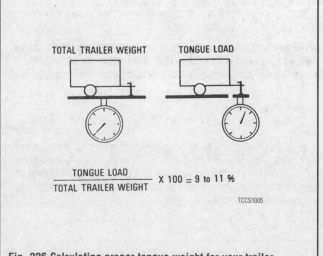

Fig. 226 Calculating proper tongue weight for your trailer

Cooling

ENGINE

Overflow Tank

One of the most common, if not THE most common, problems associated with trailer towing is engine overheating. If you have a cooling system without an expansion tank, you'll definitely need to get an aftermarket expansion tank kit, preferably one with at least a 2 quart capacity. These kits are easily installed on the radiator's overflow hose, and come with a pressure cap designed for expansion tanks.

Flex Fan

Another helpful accessory for vehicles using a belt-driven radiator fan is a flex fan. These fans are large diameter units designed to provide more airflow at low speeds, by using fan blades that have deeply cupped surfaces. The blades then flex, or flatten out, at high speed, when less cooling air is needed. These fans are far lighter in weight than stock fans, requiring less horsepower to drive them. Also, they are far quieter than stock fans. If you do decide to replace your stock fan with a flex fan, note that if your vehicle has a fan clutch, a spaccr will be needed between the flex fan and water pump hub.

Oil Cooler

Aftermarket engine oil coolers are helpful for prolonging engine oil life and reducing overall engine temperatures. Both of these factors increase engine life. While not absolutely necessary in towing Class I and some Class II trailers, they are recommended for heavier Class II and all Class III towing. Engine oil cooler systems usually consist of an adapter, screwed on in place of the oil filter, a remote filter mounting and a multi-tube, finned heat exchanger, which is mounted in front of the radiator or air conditioning condenser.

TRANSMISSION

An automatic transmission is usually recommended for trailer towing. Modern automatics have proven reliable and, of course, easy to operate, in trailer towing. The increased load of a trailer, however, causes an increase in the temperature of the automatic transmission fluid. Heat is the worst enemy of an automatic transmission. As the temperature of the fluid increases, the life of the fluid decreases.

It is essential, therefore, that you install an automatic transmission cooler. The cooler, which consists of a multi-tube, finned heat exchanger, is usually installed in front of the radiator or air conditioning compressor, and hooked in-line with the transmission cooler tank inlet line. Follow the cooler manufacturer's installation instructions.

Select a cooler of at least adequate capacity, based upon the combined gross weights of the vehicle and trailer.

Cooler manufacturers recommend that you use an aftermarket cooler in addition to, and not instead of, the present cooling tank in your radiator. If you do want to use it in place of the radiator cooling tank, get a cooler at least two sizes larger than normally necessary.

➡ **A transmission cooler can, sometimes, cause slow or harsh shifting in the transmission during cold weather, until the fluid has a chance to come up to normal operating temperature. Some coolers can be purchased with or retrofitted with a temperature bypass valve which will allow fluid flow through the cooler only when the fluid has reached above a certain operating temperature.**

Handling A Trailer

Towing a trailer with ease and safety requires a certain amount of experience. It's a good idea to learn the feel of a trailer by practicing turning, stopping and backing in an open area such as an empty parking lot.

JACKING

Your vehicle was supplied with a jack for emergency road repairs. This jack is fine for changing a flat tire or other short term procedures not requiring you to go beneath the vehicle. If it is used in an emergency situation, carefully follow the instructions provided either with the jack or in your owner's manual. Do not attempt to use the jack on any portions of the vehicle other than specified by the vehicle manufacturer. Always block the diagonally opposite wheel when using a jack.

A more convenient way of jacking is the use of a garage or floor jack. You may use the floor jack on any of the frame and suspension points illustrated.

Never place the jack under the radiator, engine or transmission components. Severe and expensive damage will result when the jack is raised. Additionally, never jack under the floorpan or bodywork; the metal will deform.

Whenever you plan to work under the vehicle, you must support it on jackstands or ramps. Never use cinder blocks or stacks of wood to support the vehicle, even if you're only going to be under it for a few minutes. Never crawl under the vehicle when it is supported only by the tire-changing jack or other floor jack.

➡**Always position a block of wood or small rubber pad on top of the jack or jackstand to protect the lifting point's finish when lifting or supporting the vehicle.**

Small hydraulic, screw, or scissors jacks are satisfactory for raising the vehicle. Drive-on trestles or ramps are also a handy and safe way to both raise and support the vehicle. Be careful though, some ramps may be too steep to drive your vehicle onto without scraping the front bottom panels. Never support the vehicle on any suspension member (unless specifically instructed to do so by a repair manual) or by an underbody panel.

Jacking Precautions

The following safety points cannot be overemphasized:
- Always block the opposite wheel or wheels to keep the vehicle from rolling off the jack.
- When raising the front of the vehicle, firmly apply the parking brake.
- When the drive wheels are to remain on the ground, leave the vehicle in gear to help prevent it from rolling.
- Always use jackstands to support the vehicle when you are working underneath. Place the stands beneath the vehicle's jacking brackets. Before climbing underneath, rock the vehicle a bit to make sure it is firmly supported.

SCHEDULED MAINTENANCE INTERVALS
E-150/250 & CLUB WAGON (LIGHT DUTY EMISSIONS UNDER 8500 LBS GVWR) (1989–93)

TO BE SERVICED	TYPE OF SERVICE	VEHICLE MILEAGE INTERVAL (x1000)												
		7.5	15	22.5	30	37.5	45	52.5	60	67.5	75	82.5	90	97.5
Engine oil & filter	R	✓	✓	✓	✓	✓	✓	✓	✓	✓	✓	✓	✓	✓
Automatic transmission fluid & filter	S/I	✓	✓	✓	✓	✓	✓	✓	✓	✓	✓	✓	✓	✓
Automatic transmission shift linkage (Bell crank system)	S/I	✓	✓	✓	✓	✓	✓	✓	✓	✓	✓	✓	✓	✓
Clutch reservoir fluid level	S/I	✓	✓	✓	✓	✓	✓	✓	✓	✓	✓	✓	✓	✓
Engine coolant level, hoses & clamps	S/I	✓	✓	✓	✓	✓	✓	✓	✓	✓	✓	✓	✓	✓
Exhaust system & heat shields	S/I	✓	✓	✓	✓	✓	✓	✓	✓	✓	✓	✓	✓	✓
Steering linkage & driveshaft slip yoke	S/I	✓	✓	✓	✓	✓	✓	✓	✓	✓	✓	✓	✓	✓
Wheel lug nut torque	S/I	✓	✓	✓	✓	✓	✓	✓	✓	✓	✓	✓	✓	✓
Rotate tires	S/I	✓			✓	✓		✓		✓		✓		✓
Fuel filter	R		✓		✓		✓		✓		✓		✓	
Drum brake systems, hoses & lines	S/I		✓		✓		✓		✓		✓		✓	
Air filter	R				✓				✓				✓	
Disc brake system & caliper slide rails & knuckle top & bottom inner pad slots (E-150/250 & Club Wagon)	S/I		✓		✓		✓		✓		✓		✓	
Crankcase emission air filter	R				✓				✓				✓	
Engine Coolant	R				✓				✓				✓	
PCV valve	R					✓			✓				✓	
Spark plugs	R					✓			✓				✓	
Front wheel bearings	S/I					✓			✓				✓	

88481C07

SCHEDULED MAINTENANCE INTERVALS
E-150/250 & CLUB WAGON (LIGHT DUTY EMISSIONS UNDER 8500 LBS GVWR) (1989–93) (Cont.)

TO BE SERVICED	TYPE OF SERVICE	VEHICLE MILEAGE INTERVAL (x1000)												
		7.5	15	22.5	30	37.5	45	52.5	60	67.5	75	82.5	90	97.5
Parking brake system	S/I				✓				✓				✓	
Spindle needle bearing	S/I				✓				✓				✓	
Throttle & kickdown lever ball studs	S/I				✓				✓				✓	
Manual transmission oil	R								✓					
Rear axle oil	R													✓
Drive belts	S/I								✓					
Secondary air injection hoses & clamps	S/I								✓					

R – Replace   S/I – Service or Inspect

FREQUENT OPERATION MAINTENANCE (SEVERE SERVICE)

If a vehicle is operated under any of the following conditions it is considered severe service:
- Extremely dusty areas.
- 50% or more of the vehicle operation is in 32°C (90°F) or higher temperatures, or constant operation in temperatures below 0°C (32°F).
- Prolonged idling (vehicle operation in stop and go traffic).
- Frequent short running periods (engine does not warm to normal operating temperatures).
- Police, taxi, delivery usage or trailer towing usage.
Oil & oil filter change – change every 3000 miles.
Automatic transmission fluid & filter - change every 30,000 miles.
Manual transmission oil - change every 30,000 miles.

Additional items for vehicles operated off-highway:
Front axle spindle pins, steering & clutch linkages, axle & driveshaft U-joints & slip yoke - lubricate every 1000 miles.
Front wheel bearings - check every 1000 miles.
Disc brake system, caliper slide rails - check every 1000 miles.
Drum brake system, hoses & lines - check every 1000 miles.
Exhaust system - check every 1000 miles.
Clutch release lever pivot (7.3L diesel & 7.5L) - lubricate every 1000 miles.

88481C08

SCHEDULED MAINTENANCE INTERVALS
E-250/350 & CLUB WAGON (4.9L,5.8L,7.5L EFI/MFI)
(HEAVY DUTY EMISSIONS OVER 8500 LBS GVWR) (1989−93)

TO BE SERVICED	TYPE OF SERVICE	VEHICLE MILEAGE INTERVAL (x1000)												
		5	10	15	20	25	30	35	40	45	50	55	60	65
Engine oil & filter	R	✓	✓	✓	✓	✓	✓	✓	✓	✓	✓	✓	✓	✓
Automatic transmission fluid & filter	S/I	✓	✓	✓	✓	✓	✓	✓	✓	✓	✓	✓	✓	✓
Automatic transmission shift linkage (Bell crank system)	S/I	✓	✓	✓	✓	✓	✓	✓	✓	✓	✓	✓	✓	✓
Clutch release lever (7.5L)	S/I	✓	✓	✓	✓	✓	✓	✓	✓	✓	✓	✓	✓	✓
Clutch reservoir fluid level	S/I	✓	✓	✓	✓	✓	✓	✓	✓	✓	✓	✓	✓	✓
Engine coolant level, hoses & clamps	S/I	✓	✓	✓	✓	✓	✓	✓	✓	✓	✓	✓	✓	✓
Exhaust system & heat shields	S/I	✓	✓	✓	✓	✓	✓	✓	✓	✓	✓	✓	✓	✓
Front axle spindle pins, steering linkage, driveshaft slip yoke	S/I	✓	✓	✓	✓	✓	✓	✓	✓	✓	✓	✓	✓	✓
Wheel lug nut torque	S/I	✓	✓	✓	✓	✓	✓	✓	✓	✓	✓	✓	✓	✓
Rotate tires	S/I	✓		✓			✓			✓			✓	
Fuel filter	R			✓			✓			✓			✓	
Disc brake system & caliper slide rails & knuckle top & bottom inner pad slots	S/I			✓			✓			✓			✓	
Drive belts	S/I			✓			✓			✓			✓	
Drum brake systems, hoses & lines	S/I			✓			✓			✓			✓	
Air filter	R						✓						✓	

88481C09

SCHEDULED MAINTENANCE INTERVALS
E-250/350 & CLUB WAGON (4.9L,5.8L,7.5L EFI/MFI)
(HEAVY DUTY EMISSIONS OVER 8500 LBS GVWR) (1989−93) (Cont.)

TO BE SERVICED	TYPE OF SERVICE	VEHICLE MILEAGE INTERVAL (x1000)												
		5	10	15	20	25	30	35	40	45	50	55	60	65
Crankcase emission air filter	R						✓						✓	
Engine Coolant	R						✓						✓	
Spark plugs	R						✓						✓	
Engine air induction system (E-350 over 10,000 lbs GVWR)	S/I						✓						✓	
Fan & fan shroud (E-350 over 10,000 lbs (GVWR)	S/I						✓						✓	
Front wheel bearings	S/I						✓						✓	
Parking brake system	S/I						✓						✓	
Throttle & kickdown lever ball studs	S/I						✓						✓	
Ignition wires	R												✓	
Manual transmission & rear axle oil①	R												✓	
PCV valve	R												✓	
Secondary air injection hoses & clamps	S/I												✓	

① Rear axle oil - change every 100,000 miles.
R – Replace   S/I – Service or Inspect

FREQUENT OPERATION MAINTENANCE (SEVERE SERVICE)

If a vehicle is operated under any of the following conditions it is considered severe service:
- Extremely dusty areas.
- 50% or more of the vehicle operation is in 32°C (90°F) or higher temperatures, or constant operation in temperatures below 0°C (32°F).
- Prolonged idling (vehicle operation in stop and go traffic).
- Frequent short running periods (engine does not warm to normal operating temperatures).
- Police, taxi, delivery usage or trailer towing usage.

Oil & oil filter change – change every 3000 miles.
Manual/automatic transmission fluid & filter - change every 30,000 miles.

Additional is for vehicles operated off-highway:
Front wheel bearings, front axle spindle pins, steering & clutch linkages, axle & driveshaft U-joints & slip yoke - lubricate every 1000 miles.
Disc brake system, caliper slide rails, drum brake system, hoses & lines - check every 1000 miles.
Exhaust system - check every 1000 miles.
Clutch release lever pivot (7.5L) - lubricate every 1000 miles.

88481C10

SCHEDULED MAINTENANCE INTERVALS
SUPER DUTY/E-250/350 & CLUB WAGON (7.3L DIESEL) (HEAVY DUTY EMISSIONS OVER 8500 LBS GVWR) (1989–93)

TO BE SERVICED	TYPE OF SERVICE	VEHICLE MILEAGE INTERVAL (x1000)												
		5	10	15	20	25	30	35	40	45	50	55	60	65
Engine oil & filter	R	✓	✓	✓	✓	✓	✓	✓	✓	✓	✓	✓	✓	✓
Automatic transmission fluid & filter	S/I	✓	✓	✓	✓	✓	✓	✓	✓	✓	✓	✓	✓	✓
Automatic transmission shift linkage (Bell crank system)	S/I	✓	✓	✓	✓	✓	✓	✓	✓	✓	✓	✓	✓	✓
Clutch reservoir fluid level	S/I	✓	✓	✓	✓	✓	✓	✓	✓	✓	✓	✓	✓	✓
Drain water from fuel/filter bowl	S/I	✓	✓	✓	✓	✓	✓	✓	✓	✓	✓	✓	✓	✓
Exhaust system & heat shields	S/I	✓	✓	✓	✓	✓	✓	✓	✓	✓	✓	✓	✓	✓
Front axle spindle pins, steering linkage, driveshaft slip yoke	S/I	✓	✓	✓	✓	✓	✓	✓	✓	✓	✓	✓	✓	✓
Wheel lug nut torque	S/I	✓	✓	✓	✓	✓	✓	✓	✓	✓	✓	✓	✓	✓
Engine idle speed	S/I		✓		✓		✓		✓		✓		✓	
Rotate tires	S/I	✓		✓			✓			✓			✓	
Throttle operation & idle return spring	S/I	✓		✓			✓			✓			✓	
Disc brake system & caliper slide rails & knuckle top & bottom inner pad slots	S/I			✓			✓			✓			✓	
Drum brake systems, hoses & lines	S/I			✓			✓			✓			✓	
Engine coolant level, hoses & clamps	S/I	✓	✓	✓	✓	✓	✓	✓	✓	✓	✓	✓	✓	✓
Fan & fan shroud (E-350 over 10,000 lbs GVWR)	S/I			✓			✓			✓			✓	

88481C11

SCHEDULED MAINTENANCE INTERVALS
SUPER DUTY/E-250/350 & CLUB WAGON (7.3L DIESEL) (HEAVY DUTY EMISSIONS OVER 8500 LBS GVWR) (1989–93)(Cont.)

TO BE SERVICED	TYPE OF SERVICE	VEHICLE MILEAGE INTERVAL (x1000)												
		5	10	15	20	25	30	35	40	45	50	55	60	65
Parking brake system	S/I			✓			✓			✓			✓	
Parking brake fluid level (F-Super Duty)	S/I			✓			✓			✓			✓	
Air filter	R						✓						✓	
Crankcase emission air filter	R						✓						✓	
Engine Coolant	R						✓						✓	
Brake master cylinder fluid level	S/I						✓						✓	
Drive belts	S/I						✓						✓	
Engine air induction system (E-350 over 10,000 lbs GVWR)	S/I						✓						✓	
Front wheel bearings	S/I						✓						✓	
Throttle ball stud	S/I						✓						✓	
Fuel filter	R												✓	
Manual transmission fluid	R												✓	
PCV valve	R												✓	
Rear axle oil①	R													

① Rear axle oil - change every 100,000 miles.
R – Replace   S/I – Service or Inspect

FREQUENT OPERATION MAINTENANCE (SEVERE SERVICE)
If a vehicle is operated under any of the following conditions it is considered severe service:
- Extremely dusty areas.
- 50% or more of the vehicle operation is in 32°C (90°F) or higher temperatures, or constant operation in temperatures below 0°C (32°F).
- Prolonged idling (vehicle operation in stop and go traffic).
- Frequent short running periods (engine does not warm to normal operating temperatures).
- Police, taxi, delivery usage or trailer towing usage.
Oil & oil filter change – change every 3000 miles.
Manual/automatic transmission fluid & filter - change every 30,000 miles.

Additional items for vehicles operated off-highway:
Front wheel bearings, front axle spindle pins, steering & clutch linkages, axle & driveshaft U-joints & slip yoke - lubricate every 1000 miles.
Disc brake system, caliper slide rails, drum brake system, hoses & lines - check every 1000 miles.
Exhaust system - check every 1000 miles.
Clutch release lever pivot - lubricate every 1000 miles.

88481C12

SCHEDULED MAINTENANCE INTERVALS
SUPER DUTY/E-150/250/350 & CLUB WAGON (1994-96)

TO BE SERVICED	TYPE OF SERVICE	VEHICLE MILEAGE INTERVAL (x1000)												
		5	10	15	20	25	30	35	40	45	50	55	60	65
Engine oil & filter	R	✓	✓	✓	✓	✓	✓	✓	✓	✓	✓	✓	✓	✓
Automatic transmission shift linkage	S/I	✓		✓		✓		✓		✓		✓		✓
Clutch reservoir fluid level	S/I	✓		✓		✓		✓		✓		✓		✓
Exhaust system & heat shields	S/I	✓		✓		✓		✓		✓		✓		✓
Rotate tires⑥	S/I	✓		✓		✓		✓		✓		✓		✓
Steering linkage suspension, driveshaft U-joint, & slip-yoke (if equipped)	S/I	✓		✓		✓		✓		✓		✓		✓
Clutch release lever (7.3L diesel & 7.5L)	S/I	✓			✓			✓			✓			✓
Fuel filter③	R			✓			✓			✓			✓	
Disc brake system & caliper slide rails	S/I			✓			✓			✓			✓	
Drum brake systems, hoses & lines	S/I			✓			✓			✓			✓	
Parking brake fluid level	S/I			✓			✓			✓			✓	
Engine coolant strength, hoses & clamps	S/I			✓			✓			✓			✓	
Air cleaner filter④	R						✓						✓	
Automatic transmission fluid & filter⑤	R						✓						✓	
Front wheel bearings	S/I						✓						✓	

88481C13

SCHEDULED MAINTENANCE INTERVALS
SUPER DUTY/E-150/250/350 & CLUB WAGON (1994-96)(Cont.)

TO BE SERVICED	TYPE OF SERVICE	VEHICLE MILEAGE INTERVAL (x1000)												
		5	10	15	20	25	30	35	40	45	50	55	60	65
Parking brake system	S/I						✓						✓	
Throttle & TV lever ball studs	S/I						✓						✓	
Crankcase emission air filter	R						✓						✓	
Engine coolant②	R										✓			
Manual transmission & rear axle oil①	R												✓	
PCV valve	R												✓	
Spark plugs	R												✓	
Drive belts	S/I												✓	
Thermactor hoses & clamps	S/I												✓	

① Rear axle oil - change every 100,000 miles.
② Engine coolant - change at 50,000 miles:
     Gasoline - change every 30,000 miles thereafter.
     Diesel - add 8-10 oz. FW-15 every 15,000 miles & 4 pints FW-15 every time coolant is changed.
③ Fuel filter (7.3L diesel) - change filter at 15,000 miles & when ever fuel restriction lamp is illuminated.
④ Air cleaner filter (7.3L diesel) - change filter when restriction gauge is in red zone.
⑤ Automatic transmission fluid & filter - C6 & E40D transmissions do not require regular fluid changes under normal operating conditions.
⑥ Rotate front tires for dual rear wheel vehicles from side to side only.
R – Replace   S/I – Service or Inspect

FREQUENT OPERATION MAINTENANCE (SEVERE SERVICE)
If a vehicle is operated under any of the following conditions it is considered severe service:
- Extremely dusty areas.
- 50% or more of the vehicle operation is in 32°C (90°F) or higher temperatures, or constant operation in temperatures below 0°C (32°F).
- Prolonged idling (vehicle operation in stop and go traffic).
- Frequent short running periods (engine does not warm to normal operating temperatures).
- Police, taxi, delivery usage or trailer towing usage.
Air cleaner filter - check every 3000 miles.
Oil & oil filter change – change every 3000 miles.
Automatic transmission shift linkage - lubricate every 6000 miles.
Clutch reservoir fluid level - check every 6000 miles.
Exhaust system - check every 6000 miles.
Steering linkage suspension, driveshaft U-joint & slip-yoke (if equipped) - lubricate every 6000 miles.
Rotate tires every 9000 miles. (City delivery vehicles & other unique applications that require constant turning, may need more frequent tire rotation.)
Clutch release lever (7.3L diesel & 7.5L) - lubricate every 15,000 miles.
Automatic transmission fluid & filter - change every 21,000 miles.

88481C14

CAPACITIES

Year	Model	Engine ID/VIN	Engine Displacement Liters (cc)	Oil with Filter (qts.)	Transmission (pts.)			Drive Axle Rear (pts.)	Fuel Tank (gal.)	Cooling System (qts.)
					4-Spd	5-Spd	Auto.			
1989	E-150	Y	4.9L (4917)	6.0	7.0	[1]	[2]	[3]	[4]	[5]
	E-150	N	5.0L (4942)	6.0	7.0	[1]	[2]	[3]	[4]	[6]
	E-150	H	5.8L (5766)	6.0	7.0	[1]	[2]	[3]	[4]	[7]
	E-250	Y	4.9L (4917)	6.0	7.0	[1]	[2]	[3]	[4]	[5]
	E-250	N	5.0L (4942)	6.0	7.0	[1]	[2]	[3]	[4]	[6]
	E-250	H	5.8L (5766)	6.0	7.0	[1]	[2]	[3]	[4]	[7]
	E-250	M	7.3L (7270)	10.0	7.0	[1]	[2]	[3]	[4]	31
	E-250	G	7.5L (7536)	6.0	7.0	[1]	[2]	[3]	[4]	28
	E-350	Y	4.9L (4917)	6.0	7.0	[1]	[2]	[3]	[4]	[5]
	E-350	H	5.8L (5766)	6.0	7.0	[1]	[2]	[3]	[4]	[7]
	E-350	M	7.3L (7270)	10.0	7.0	[1]	[2]	[3]	[4]	31
	E-350	G	7.5L (7536)	6.0	7.0	[1]	[2]	[3]	[4]	28
1990	E-150	Y	4.9L (4917)	6.0	7.0	[1]	[2]	[3]	[4]	[5]
	E-150	N	5.0L (4942)	6.0	7.0	[1]	[2]	[3]	[4]	[6]
	E-150	H	5.8L (5766)	6.0	7.0	[1]	[2]	[3]	[4]	[7]
	E-250	Y	4.9L (4917)	6.0	7.0	[1]	[2]	[3]	[4]	[5]
	E-250	N	5.0L (4942)	6.0	7.0	[1]	[2]	[3]	[4]	[6]
	E-250	H	5.8L (5766)	6.0	7.0	[1]	[2]	[3]	[4]	[7]
	E-250	M	7.3L (7270)	10.0	7.0	[1]	[2]	[3]	[4]	31
	E-250	G	7.5L (7536)	6.0	7.0	[1]	[2]	[3]	[4]	28
	E-350	Y	4.9L (4917)	6.0	7.0	[1]	[2]	[3]	[4]	[5]
	E-350	H	5.8L (5766)	6.0	7.0	[1]	[2]	[3]	[4]	[7]
	E-350	M	7.3L (7270)	10.0	7.0	[1]	[2]	[3]	[4]	31
	E-350	G	7.5L (7536)	6.0	7.0	[1]	[2]	[3]	[4]	28
1991	E-150	Y	4.9L (4917)	6.0	7.0	[1]	[2]	[3]	[4]	[5]
	E-150	N	5.0L (4942)	6.0	7.0	[1]	[2]	[3]	[4]	[6]
	E-150	H	5.8L (5766)	6.0	7.0	[1]	[2]	[3]	[4]	[7]
	E-250	Y	4.9L (4917)	6.0	7.0	[1]	[2]	[3]	[4]	[5]
	E-250	N	5.0L (4942)	6.0	7.0	[1]	[2]	[3]	[4]	[6]
	E-250	H	5.8L (5766)	6.0	7.0	[1]	[2]	[3]	[4]	[7]
	E-250	M	7.3L (7270)	10.0	7.0	[1]	[2]	[3]	[4]	31
	E-250	G	7.5L (7536)	6.0	7.0	[1]	[2]	[3]	[4]	28
	E-350	Y	4.9L (4917)	6.0	7.0	[1]	[2]	[3]	[4]	[5]
	E-350	H	5.8L (5766)	6.0	7.0	[1]	[2]	[3]	[4]	[7]
	E-350	M	7.3L (7270)	10.0	7.0	[1]	[2]	[3]	[4]	31
	E-350	G	7.5L (7536)	6.0	7.0	[1]	[2]	[3]	[4]	28
1992	E-150	Y	4.9L (4917)	6.0	7.0	[1]	[2]	[3]	[4]	[5]
	E-150	N	5.0L (4942)	6.0	7.0	[1]	[2]	[3]	[4]	[6]
	E-150	H	5.8L (5766)	6.0	7.0	[1]	[2]	[3]	[4]	[7]
	E-250	Y	4.9L (4917)	6.0	7.0	[1]	[2]	[3]	[4]	[5]
	E-250	N	5.0L (4942)	6.0	7.0	[1]	[2]	[3]	[4]	[6]
	E-250	H	5.8L (5766)	6.0	7.0	[1]	[2]	[3]	[4]	[7]
	E-250	M	7.3L (7270)	10.0	7.0	[1]	[2]	[3]	[4]	31
	E-250	G	7.5L (7536)	6.0	7.0	[1]	[2]	[3]	[4]	28
	E-350	Y	4.9L (4917)	6.0	7.0	[1]	[2]	[3]	[4]	[5]
	E-350	H	5.8L (5766)	6.0	7.0	[1]	[2]	[3]	[4]	[7]
	E-350	M	7.3L (7270)	10.0	7.0	[1]	[2]	[3]	[4]	31
	E-350	G	7.5L (7536)	6.0	7.0	[1]	[2]	[3]	[4]	28
1993	E-150	Y	4.9L (4917)	6.0	7.0 [8]	7.0	24.0	6.0 [9]	[4]	17.5
	E-150	N	5.0L (4942)	6.0	7.0 [8]	7.0	24.0	6.0 [9]	[4]	[10]
	E-150	H	5.8L (5766)	6.0	7.0 [8]	7.0	24.0	6.0 [9]	[4]	[11]
	E-250	Y	4.9L (4917)	6.0	7.0 [8]	7.0	24.0	6.0 [9]	[4]	17.5
	E-250	N	5.0L (4942)	6.0	7.0 [8]	7.0	24.0	6.0 [9]	[4]	[10]
	E-250	H	5.8L (5766)	6.0	7.0 [8]	7.0	24.0	6.0 [9]	[4]	[11]
	E-250	M	7.3L (7270)	10.0	7.0 [8]	7.0	24.0	6.0 [9]	[4]	31.0

88481C05

CAPACITIES

Year	Model	Engine ID/VIN	Engine Displacement Liters (cc)	Oil with Filter (qts.)	Transmission (pts.) 4-Spd	5-Spd	Auto.	Drive Axle Rear (pts.)	Fuel Tank (gal.)	Cooling System (qts.)
1993	E-250	G	7.5L (7536)	6.0	7.0 ⑧	7.0	24.0	6.0 ⑨	④	28.0
	E-350	Y	4.9L (4917)	6.0	7.0 ⑧	7.0	24.0	6.0 ⑨	④	17.5
	E-350	H	5.8L (5766)	6.0	7.0 ⑧	7.0	24.0	6.0 ⑨	④	⑪
	E-350	M	7.3L (7270)	10.0	7.0 ⑧	7.0	24.0	6.0 ⑨	④	31.0
	E-350	C	7.3L (7270)	10.0	7.0 ⑧	7.0	24.0	6.0 ⑨	④	31.0
	E-350	G	7.5L (7536)	6.0	7.0 ⑧	7.0	24.0	6.0 ⑨	④	28.0
1994	E-150	Y	4.9L (4917)	6.0	7.0 ⑧	7.0	24.0	6.0 ⑨	④	14.0
	E-150	N	5.0L (4942)	6.0	7.0 ⑧	7.0	24.0	6.0 ⑨	④	15.0
	E-150	H	5.8L (5766)	6.0	7.0 ⑧	7.0	24.0	6.0 ⑨	④	14.0
	E-250	Y	4.9L (4917)	6.0	7.0 ⑧	7.0	24.0	6.0 ⑨	④	14.0
	E-250	N	5.0L (4942)	6.0	7.0 ⑧	7.0	24.0	6.0 ⑨	④	15.0
	E-250	H	5.8L (5766)	6.0	7.0 ⑧	7.0	24.0	6.0 ⑨	④	15.0
	E-250	M	7.3L (7270)	10.0	7.0 ⑧	7.0	24.0	6.0 ⑨	④	20.0
	E-250	G	7.5L (7536)	6.0	7.0 ⑧	7.0	24.0	6.0 ⑨	④	19.8
	E-350	Y	4.9L (4917)	6.0	7.0 ⑧	7.0	24.0	6.0 ⑨	④	17.5
	E-350	H	5.8L (5766)	6.0	7.0 ⑧	7.0	24.0	6.0 ⑨	④	15.0
	E-350	F	7.3L (7270)	10.0	7.0 ⑧	7.0	24.0	6.0 ⑨	④	20.0
	E-350	M	7.3L (7270)	10.0	7.0 ⑧	7.0	24.0	6.0 ⑨	④	20.0
	E-350	G	7.5L (7536)	6.0	7.0 ⑧	7.0	24.0	6.0 ⑨	④	19.8
1995	E-150	Y	4.9L (4917)	6.0	7.0 ⑧	7.0	24.0	6.0 ⑨	④	14.0
	E-150	N	5.0L (4942)	6.0	7.0 ⑧	7.0	24.0	6.0 ⑨	④	15.0
	E-150	H	5.8L (5766)	6.0	7.0 ⑧	7.0	24.0	6.0 ⑨	④	14.0
	E-250	Y	4.9L (4917)	6.0	7.0 ⑧	7.0	24.0	6.0 ⑨	④	14.0
	E-250	N	5.0L (4942)	6.0	7.0 ⑧	7.0	24.0	6.0 ⑨	④	15.0
	E-250	H	5.8L (5766)	6.0	7.0 ⑧	7.0	24.0	6.0 ⑨	④	15.0
	E-250	M	7.3L (7270)	10.0	7.0 ⑧	7.0	24.0	6.0 ⑨	④	20.0
	E-250	G	7.5L (7536)	6.0	7.0 ⑧	7.0	24.0	6.0 ⑨	④	19.8
	E-350	Y	4.9L (4917)	6.0	7.0 ⑧	7.0	24.0	6.0 ⑨	④	17.5
	E-350	H	5.8L (5766)	6.0	7.0 ⑧	7.0	24.0	6.0 ⑨	④	15.0
	E-350	F	7.3L (7270)	10.0	7.0 ⑧	7.0	24.0	6.0 ⑨	④	20.0
	E-350	M	7.3L (7270)	10.0	7.0 ⑧	7.0	24.0	6.0 ⑨	④	20.0
	E-350	G	7.5L (7536)	6.0	7.0 ⑧	7.0	24.0	6.0 ⑨	④	19.8
1996	E-150	Y	4.9L (4917)	6.0	⑬	7.6	24.0 ⑫	6.0 ⑨	④	14.0
	E-150	N	5.0L (4942)	6.0	⑬	7.6	24.0 ⑫	6.0 ⑨	④	15.0
	E-150	H	5.8L (5766)	6.0	⑬	7.6	24.0 ⑫	6.0 ⑨	④	14.0
	E-250	Y	4.9L (4917)	6.0	⑬	7.6	24.0 ⑫	6.0 ⑨	④	14.0
	E-250	N	5.0L (4942)	6.0	⑬	7.6	24.0 ⑫	6.0 ⑨	④	15.0
	E-250	H	5.8L (5766)	6.0	⑬	7.6	24.0 ⑫	6.0 ⑨	④	15.0
	E-250	G	7.5L (7536)	6.0	⑬	7.6	24.0 ⑫	6.0 ⑨	④	19.8
	E-350	Y	4.9L (4917)	6.0	⑬	7.6	24.0 ⑫	6.0 ⑨	④	17.5
	E-350	H	5.8L (5766)	6.0	⑬	7.6	24.0 ⑫	6.0 ⑨	④	15.0
	E-350	F	7.3L (7270)	14.0	⑬	7.6	24.0 ⑫	6.0 ⑨	④	23.0
	E-350	G	7.5L (7536)	6.0	⑬	7.6	24.0 ⑫	6.0 ⑨	④	19.8

NOTE: Exact automatic transmission fill level determined by use of the dipstick. Motorhome fuel capacity approx. 75 gallons. For limited slip differentials, add the following amounts of friction Modifier Additive: Dana front axle: 2 oz., Dana rear axle: 8 oz., Ford 8.8 in. rear axle: 4 oz. Ford 10.25 in. rear axle 8 oz. 1993-95 Lightning and E-150 w/4.10 axle ratio: 5 oz.

A/C - Air Conditioning
A/T - Automatic Transmission
M/T - Manual Transmission
LWB - Long Wheelbase
SWB - Short Wheelbase

① Mazda M50D transmission: 7.6
S5-42 ZF transmission: 7.0
② C6 transmission: 23.5
AOD transmission: 24.6

③ Dana 60-3:6.3
Dana 60-1V:1989-89:7.0; 1990-92: 6.3
Dana 61: 5.8
Dana 70-2V: 6.6
70HD: 7.4
Dana 80: 8.5
Ford 8.8: 5.5
Ford 10.25: 6.5

④ 124 inch wheel base: 18
138, 158 and 176 inch wheel base—
rear mounted tank:22
front mounted tank:16
⑤ Without A/C: 15
With A/C or supercool:18
⑥ Standard and A/C: 17.5
⑦ Standard cooling: 20

With OD: 4.5 pts.
⑨ Heavy duty: 7.5 pts.
⑩ Manual transmission: 17.5 pts.
Automatic transmission: 18.5 pts.
⑪ Manual transmission: 15 pts.
Automatic transmission: 21 pts.
⑫ With 4R70W: 28 pts.
With E40D: 32.0

68481C06

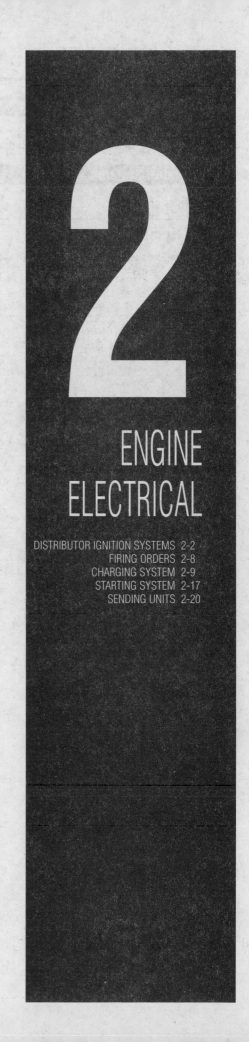

2

ENGINE ELECTRICAL

DISTRIBUTOR IGNITION SYSTEMS

→For information on understanding electricity and troubleshooting electrical circuits, please refer to Section 6 of this manual.

TFI-IV and DI Systems

SYSTEM OPERATION

♦ See Figures 1, 2 and 3

→The TFI ignition system was renamed the DI system in 1995 to conform to OBD II naming standards.

The Thick Film Integrated (TFI-IV) and Distributor Ignition (DI) ignition systems feature a universal distributor using no centrifugal or vacuum advance. The distributor has a die cast base which incorporates a hall effect stator assembly. The Ignition Control Module (ICM) can either be mounted on the distributor or be remotely mounted. No distributor calibration is required and initial timing is not a normal adjustment, since timing advance and related functions are controlled by the Powertrain Control Module (PCM).

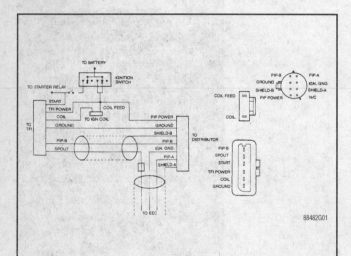

Fig. 1 Wiring schematic of a TFI ignition system with a closed bowl distributor

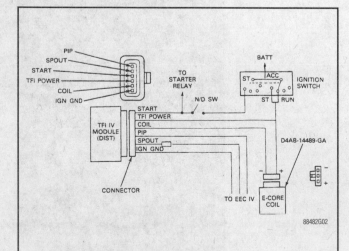

Fig. 2 Wiring schematic of a TFI ignition system with an open bowl distributor

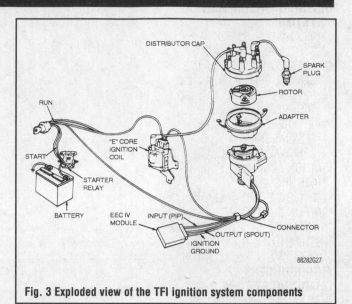

Fig. 3 Exploded view of the TFI ignition system components

Diagnosis and Testing

SERVICE PRECAUTIONS

• Always turn the key OFF and isolate both ends of a circuit whenever testing for shorts or continuity.
• Never measure voltage or resistance directly at the processor connector.
• Always disconnect solenoids and switches from the harness before measuring for continuity, resistance or energizing by way of a 12 volt source.
• When disconnecting connectors, inspect for damaged or pushed-out pins, corrosion, loose wires, etc. Service if required.

PRELIMINARY CHECKS

1. Visually inspect the engine compartment to ensure that all vacuum lines and spark plug wires are properly routed and securely connected.
2. Examine all wiring harness and connectors for insulation damage, burned, overheated, loose or broken conditions. Ensure that the ICM is securely fastened to the front fender apron.
3. Be certain that the battery is fully charged and that all accessories are OFF during the diagnosis.

TEST PROCEDURES

→Perform the test procedures in the order in which they are presented here.

Ignition Coil Secondary Voltage Test

CRANK MODE

♦ See Figure 4

1. Connect a spark tester between the ignition coil wire and a good engine ground.
2. Crank the engine and check for spark at the tester.
3. Turn the ignition switch OFF.
4. If no spark occurs, check the following:
    a. Inspect the ignition coil for damage or carbon tracking.
    b. Check that the distributor shaft is rotating when the engine is being cranked.
    c. If the results in Steps 4a and b are okay, go to the Module Test.

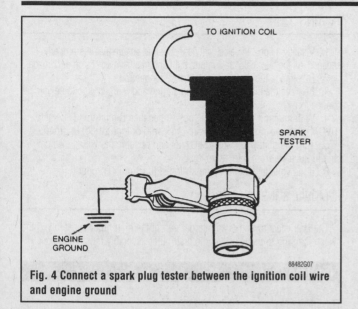

Fig. 4 Connect a spark plug tester between the ignition coil wire and engine ground

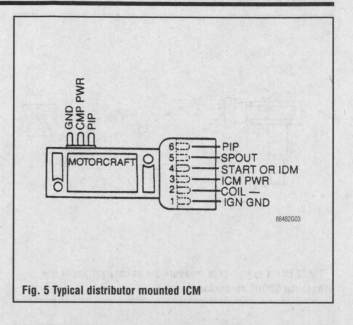

Fig. 5 Typical distributor mounted ICM

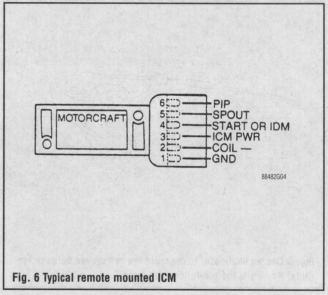

Fig. 6 Typical remote mounted ICM

5. If a spark did occur, check the distributor cap and rotor for damage or carbon tracking. Go to the Ignition Coil Secondary Voltage (Run Mode) Test.

RUN MODE

1. Fully apply the parking brake. Place the gear shift lever in Neutral (manual transmission) or Park (automatic transmission).
2. Disconnect the **S** terminal wire at the starter relay. Attach a remote starter switch.
3. Turn the ignition switch to the **RUN** position.
4. Using the remote starter switch, crank the engine and check for spark.
5. Turn the ignition switch **OFF**.
6. If no spark occurred, the problem lies with the wiring harness. Inspect the wiring harness for short circuits, open circuits and other defects.
7. If a spark did occur, the problem is not in the ignition system.

ICM Test

1989–94 MODELS

1. Remove the ICM.
2. Measure the resistance between the ICM terminals as shown below:
   a. GID—PIP IN: should be greater than 500 ohms.
   b. PIP PWR—PIP IN: should be less than 2,000 ohms.
   c. PIP PWR—TFI PWR: should be less than 200 ohms.
   d. GND—IGN GND: should be less than 2 ohms.
   e. PIP IN—PIP: should be less than 200 ohms.
3. If any of these checks failed, replace the ICM with a new one.

1995–96 MODELS

▶ See Figures 5 and 6

1. Remove the ICM.
2. Measure the resistance between the ICM terminals as shown below:
   a. PIP IN—PIP OUT: should be less than 150 ohms.
   b. CMP PWR—ICM PWR: should be less than 150 ohms.
   c. GND—PIP IN: should be greater than 500 ohms.
   d. GND—IGN GND: should be less than 5 ohms.
   e. CMP PWR—PIP IN: should be between 900 and 1,500 ohms.
3. If any of these checks failed, replace the ICM with a new one.

System Test

1. Disconnect the pin-inline connector near the ICM.
2. Crank the engine
3. Turn the ignition switch **OFF**.
4. If a spark did occur, check the PIP and ignition ground wires for continuity. If okay, the problem is not in the ignition system.
5. If no spark occurs, check the voltage at the positive (+) terminal of the ignition coil with the ignition switch in the **RUN** position.
6. If the reading is not within battery voltage, check for a worn or damaged ignition switch.
7. If the reading is within battery voltage, check for faults in the wiring between the coil and TFI module terminal No. 2 or any additional wiring or components connected to that circuit.

Spark Timing Advance Test

▶ See Figures 7 and 8

Spark timing advance is controlled by the EEC system. This procedure checks the capability of the ignition module to receive the spark timing command from the EEC module. The use of a volt/ohmmeter is required.

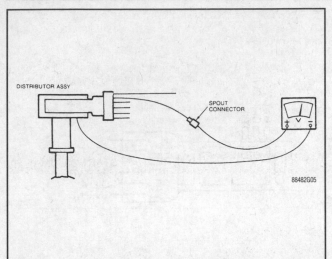

Fig. 7 Use a voltmeter to measure the battery voltage at idle from the SPOUT connector

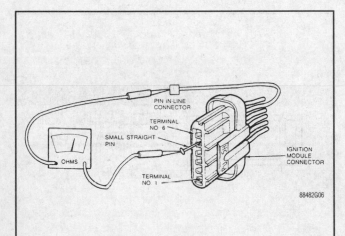

Fig. 8 Use an ohmmeter to measure the resistance between terminal No. 5 and the pin-inline connector

1. Turn the ignition switch **OFF**.
2. Disconnect the pin-inline connector (SPOUT connector) near the TFI module.
3. Start the engine and measure the voltage, at idle, from the SPOUT connector to the distributor base. The reading should be between 30 and 60 percent of the battery voltage.
4. If the result is okay, the problem lies within the EEC-IV system.
5. If the result was not satisfactory, separate the wiring harness connector from the ignition module. Check for damage, corrosion or dirt. Service as necessary.
6. Measure the resistance between terminal No. 5 and the pin-inline connector. This test is done at the ignition module connector only. The reading should be less than 5 ohms.
7. If the reading is okay, replace the TFI module.
8. If the result was not satisfactory, service the wiring between the pin-inline connector and the TFI connector.

Hall Effect Switch

The Hall effect sensor used in the gasoline engine is a three-wire type sensor. This type of sensor requires power and ground to function. When performing this test, backprobe all connectors.

TESTING

1. Visually inspect the electrical connection to ensure that it is properly engaged, all the terminals are straight, tight and free from corrosion or damage.
2. Disengage the distributor electrical connection.
3. Remove the distributor from the engine and then engage the electrical connection.
4. With the ignition **ON**, use a high impedance Digital Volt Ohmmeter (DVOM) and backprobe the PIP wire (gray with orange stripe) to ground.
5. Turn the distributor shaft SLOWLY and observe the voltage which should fluctuate from 0 to 12 volts.
6. If the voltage fluctuates, the switch is functioning properly.

REMOVAL & INSTALLATION

The Hall effect switch is an intergal part of the distributor assembly. If the switch is found to be defective, the distributor assembly must be replaced.

Ignition Coil

TESTING

1. Disconnect the ignition coil connector and check for dirt, corrosion or damage.
2. Substitute a known good coil and check for spark using the spark tester.

✳ CAUTION

Dangerous high voltage may be present when performing this test. Do not hold the coil while performing this test.

3. Crank the engine and check for spark.
4. Turn the ignition switch **OFF**.
5. If a spark did occur, measure the resistance of the ignition coil wire; replace it if the resistance is greater than 7,000 ohms per foot. If the readings are within specification, replace the ignition coil.
6. If no spark occurs, the problem is not with the coil.

REMOVAL & INSTALLATION

◆ See Figures 9, 10, 11 and 12

1. Disconnect the negative battery cable.
2. Tag and disconnect all wiring from the ignition coil.

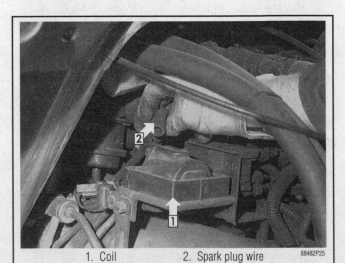

| 1. Coil | 2. Spark plug wire |

Fig. 9 Pull the spark plug wire by the boot to disconnect it from the coil

Fig. 10 Unplug the electrical connection from the coil

Fig. 11 Loosen the coil retaining bolts

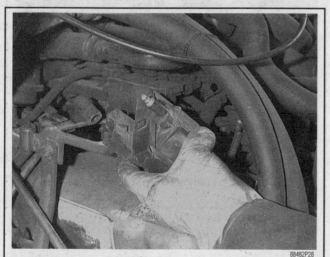

Fig. 12 After all the bolts have been unfastened, lift the coil from the bracket and remove it from the engine compartment

3. Remove the ignition coil-to-bracket bolts, then remove the ignition coil.

4. If necessary, at this time the radio ignition interference capacitor can be removed from the ignition coil.

To install:

5. If necessary, install the radio interference capacitor onto the ignition coil. Tighten the mounting bolt to 25–35 inch lbs. (2.8–4.0 Nm).

6. Position the ignition coil onto the mounting bracket, then install and tighten the mounting bolts to 25–35 inch lbs. (2.8–4.0 Nm).

7. Attach all wiring to the ignition coil, then connect the negative battery cable.

Ignition Control Module (ICM)

REMOVAL & INSTALLATION

1989–94 Models

EXCEPT 7.5L ENGINES

1. Remove the distributor cap from the distributor, and set it aside (spark plug wires intact).

2. Detach the TFI harness connector.

3. Remove the distributor.

4. Remove the two TFI module retaining screws.

5. To disengage the module's terminals from the distributor base connector, pull the right side of the module down the distributor mounting flange and then back up. Carefully pull the module toward the flange and away from the distributor.

✽✽ WARNING

Step 5 must be followed EXACTLY; failure to do so will result in damage to the distributor module connector pins.

To install:

6. Coat the TFI module baseplate with a thin layer of silicone grease (D7AZ-19A331-A, or its equivalent).

7. Place the TFI module on the distributor base mounting flange. Position the module assembly toward the distributor bowl and carefully engage the distributor connector pins.

8. Install and tighten the two TFI module retaining screws to 15–35 inch lbs. (1.7–4.0 Nm).

9. Install the distributor assembly.

10. Install the distributor cap and check the engine timing.

7.5L ENGINES

➥The ignition module is usually located on the left-hand fender apron.

1. Disconnect the negative battery cable.

2. Label and detach all wiring from the TFI module.

3. Remove the TFI module/heatsink-to-fender apron bolts, then remove the TFI module/heatsink.

4. If necessary, at this time the module can be removed from the heat sink.

To install:

5. Apply an approximately 1/32 in. (0.80mm) thick layer of silicone dielectric compound (D7AZ-19A331-A or equivalent) to the baseplate of the ignition module.

6. Install the module onto the heat sink. Tighten the mounting bolts to 15–35 inch lbs. (1.7–4.0 Nm).

7. Attach all wiring to the ICM, then connect the negative battery cable.

1995–96 Models

♦ See Figure 13

➥The ignition module is usually located on the left-hand fender apron.

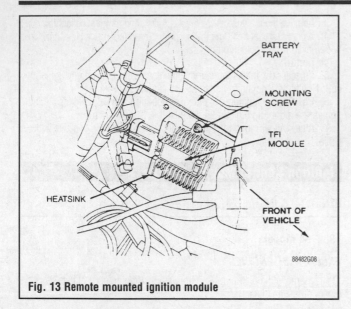

Fig. 13 Remote mounted ignition module

1. Disconnect the negative battery cable.
2. Label and detach all wiring from the ICM.
3. Remove the ICM/heatsink-to-fender apron bolts, then remove the ICM/heatsink.
4. If necessary, at this time the ICM can be removed from the heat sink.

To install:

5. Apply an approximately ⅟₃₂ in. (0.80mm) thick layer of silicone dielectric compound (D7AZ-19A331-A or equivalent) to the baseplate of the ICM.
6. Install the ICM onto the heat sink. Tighten the mounting bolts to 11–16 inch lbs. (1.2–1.8 Nm).
7. Position the ICM onto the front fender apron, then install and tighten the mounting bolts to 80–124 inch lbs. (9–14 Nm).
8. Attach all wiring to the ICM, then connect the negative battery cable.

Distributor

REMOVAL & INSTALLATION

▶ See Figures 14 thru 19

1. Rotate the engine until the No. 1 piston is on Top Dead Center (TDC) of its compression stroke.
2. Disconnect the negative battery cable. Disconnect the vehicle wiring harness connector from the distributor. Before removing the distributor cap, mark the position of the No. 1 wire tower on the cap for reference.
3. Loosen the distributor cap hold-down screws and remove the cap. Matchmark the position of the rotor to the distributor housing. Position the cap and wires out of the way.
4. Remove the rotor.
5. Matchmark the distributor body and engine block to indicate the position of the distributor in the engine.
6. Remove the distributor hold-down bolt and clamp.
7. Remove the distributor assembly from the engine. Be sure not to rotate the engine while the distributor is removed.
8. Cover the distributor opening with a clean shop towel to prevent the entry of dirt or other foreign contaminants.

To install:

➡Before distributor installation, visually inspect the condition of the O-ring which should fit snugly on the shaft. The drive gears should be free of nicks and cracks, and not be excessively worn. Rotate the shaft to make sure it moves freely without binding. Replace any parts if necessary.

9. Remove the shop towel.
10. Make sure that the engine is still with the No. 1 piston up on TDC of its compression stroke.

➡If the engine was disturbed while the distributor was removed, it will be necessary to remove the No. 1 spark plug and rotate the engine clockwise until the No. 1 piston is on its compression stroke. Align the timing pointer with TDC on the crankshaft damper or flywheel, as required.

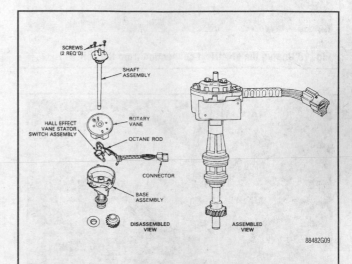

Fig. 14 Exploded view of the closed bowl distributor used on 5.0L, 5.8L and 7.5L engines (4.9L similar)

Fig. 15 Matchmark the position of the rotor in relation to the distributor housing

Fig. 16 Unplug the ignition module electrical connection

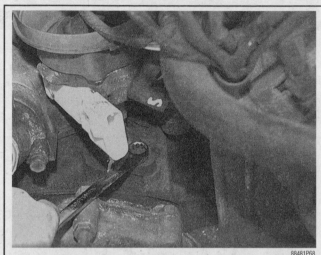

Fig. 18 Loosen the distributor hold-down clamp bolt, then remove the bolt and clamp

Fig. 17 Matchmark the distributor shaft-to-engine block position; this will aid during installation

Fig. 19 Lift the distributor straight up and out of the engine block

11. On all vehicles:
   a. Rotate the distributor shaft so the rotor points toward the mark on the distributor housing made previously.
   b. Rotate the rotor slightly so the leading edge of the vane is centered in the vane switch state assembly.
   c. Rotate the distributor in the block to align the leading edge of the vane with the vane switch stator assembly. Make certain the rotor is pointing to the No. 1 mark on the distributor base.

➡If the vane and vane switch stator cannot be aligned by rotating the distributor in the cylinder block, remove the distributor enough to just disengage the distributor gear from the camshaft gear. Turn the rotor enough to engage the distributor gear on another tooth of the camshaft gear. Repeat Step 9 if necessary.

12. Install the distributor hold-down clamp and bolt(s); tighten them slightly.
13. Attach the vehicle wiring harness connector to the distributor.
14. Install the cap and wires. Install the No. 1 spark plug, if removed.
15. Recheck the initial timing.
16. Tighten the hold-down clamp and recheck the timing. Adjust if necessary.

FIRING ORDERS

▶ See Figures 20, 21, 22 and 23

➡To avoid confusion, remove and tag the spark plug wires one at a time, for replacement.

If a distributor is not keyed for installation with only one orientation, it could have been removed previously and rewired. The resultant wiring would hold the correct firing order, but could change the relative placement of the plug towers in relation to the engine. For this reason, it is imperative that you label all wires before disconnecting any of them. Also, before removal, compare the current wiring with the accompanying illustrations. If the current wiring does not match, make notes in your book to reflect how your engine is wired.

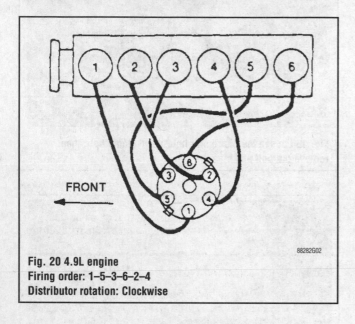

Fig. 20 4.9L engine
Firing order: 1–5–3–6–2–4
Distributor rotation: Clockwise

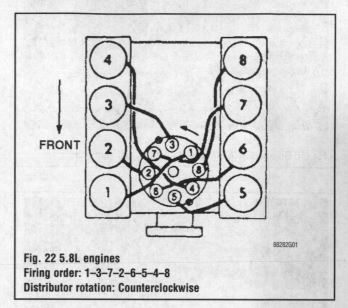

Fig. 22 5.8L engines
Firing order: 1–3–7–2–6–5–4–8
Distributor rotation: Counterclockwise

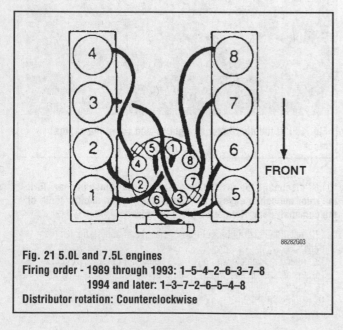

Fig. 21 5.0L and 7.5L engines
Firing order - 1989 through 1993: 1–5–4–2–6–3–7–8
          1994 and later: 1–3–7–2–6–5–4–8
Distributor rotation: Counterclockwise

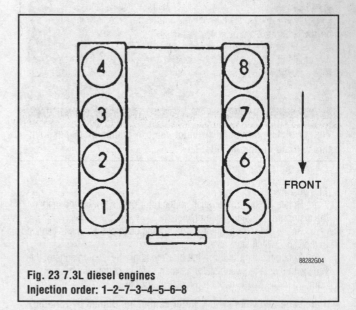

Fig. 23 7.3L diesel engines
Injection order: 1–2–7–3–4–5–6–8

CHARGING SYSTEM

General Information

The alternator charging system is a negative (-) ground system which consists of an alternator, a regulator, a charge indicator, a storage battery and wiring connecting the components, and fuse link wire.

The alternator is belt-driven from the engine. Energy is supplied from the alternator/regulator system to the rotating field through two brushes to two slip-rings. The slip-rings are mounted on the rotor shaft and are connected to the field coil. This energy supplied to the rotating field from the battery is called excitation current and is used to initially energize the field to begin the generation of electricity. Once the alternator starts to generate electricity, the excitation current comes from its own output, rather than from the battery.

The alternator produces power in the form of alternating current. The alternating current is rectified by 6 diodes into direct current. The direct current is used to charge the battery and power the rest of the electrical system.

When the ignition key is turned **ON**, current flows from the battery, through the charging system indicator light on the instrument panel, to the voltage regulator, and to the alternator. Since the alternator is not producing any current, the alternator warning light comes on. When the engine is started, the alternator begins to produce current and turns the alternator light off. As the alternator turns and produces current, the current is divided in two ways: some goes to the battery to charge the battery and power the electrical components of the vehicle, and part is returned to the alternator to enable it to increase its output. In this situation, the alternator is receiving current from the battery and from itself. A voltage regulator is wired into the current supply to the alternator to prevent it from receiving too much current, which would cause it to put out too much current. Conversely, if the voltage regulator does not allow the alternator to receive enough current, the battery will not be fully charged and will eventually go dead.

The battery is connected to the alternator at all times, whether the ignition key is turned on or not. If the battery were shorted to ground, the alternator would also be shorted. This would damage the alternator. To prevent this, a fuse link is installed in the wiring between the battery and the alternator. If the battery is shorted, the fuse link is melted, protecting the alternator.

Alternator Precautions

To prevent damage to the alternator and regulator, the following precautions should be taken when working with the electrical system.
1. Never reverse the battery connections.
2. Booster batteries for starting must be connected properly: positive-to-positive and negative-to-ground.
3. Disconnect the battery cables before using a fast charger; the charger has a tendency to force current through the diodes in the opposite direction for which they were designed. This burns out the diodes.
4. Never use a fast charger as a booster for starting the vehicle.
5. Never disconnect the voltage regulator while the engine is running.
6. Avoid long soldering times when replacing diodes or transistors. Prolonged heat is damaging to AC generators.
7. Do not use test lamps of more than 12 volts (V) for checking diode continuity.
8. Do not short across or ground any of the terminals on the AC generator.
9. The polarity of the battery, generator, and regulator must be matched and considered before making any electrical connections within the system.
10. Never operate the alternator on an open circuit. Make sure that all connections within the circuit are clean and tight.
11. Disconnect the battery terminals when performing any service on the electrical system. This will eliminate the possibility of accidental reversal of polarity.
12. Disconnect the battery ground cable if arc welding is to be done on any part of the vehicle.

Alternator

IDENTIFICATION

There are 4 different types of alternators found on the years and model ranges covered in this manual:
1. Rear terminal, external fan alternator with external regulator
2. Side terminal, external fan alternator with internal regulator
3. Leece-Neville 165 ampere alternator
4. Internal fan alternator with integral rear mount regulator

TESTING

When performing charging system tests, turn off all lights and electrical components. Place the transmission in **P** (AT) or **N** (MT) and apply the parking brake.

To ensure accurate meter indications, the battery terminal posts and battery cable clamps must be clean and tight.

✖✖ WARNING

Do not make jumper wire connections except as instructed. Incorrect jumper wire connections can damage the regulator or fuse links.

Preliminary Inspection (All Types)

1. Make sure the battery cable connections are clean and tight.
2. Check all alternator and regulator wiring connections. Make sure all connections are clean and secure.
3. Check the alternator belt tension. Adjust, if necessary.
4. Check the fuse link between the starter relay and alternator. Replace if burned out.
5. Make sure the fuses/fuse links to the alternator are not burned or damaged. This could cause an open circuit or high resistance, resulting in erratic or intermittent charging problems.
6. If equipped with a heated windshield, make sure the wiring connections to the alternator output control relay are correct and tight.
7. If equipped with a heated windshield, make sure the connector to the heated windshield module is properly seated and there are no broken wires.

External Regulator Alternator

CHARGING SYSTEM INDICATOR LIGHT TEST

1. If the charging system indicator light does not come on with the ignition key in the **RUN** position and the engine not running, check the ignition switch-to-regulator **I** terminal wiring for an open circuit or burned out charging system indicator light. Replace the light, if necessary.
2. If the charging system indicator light does not come on, detach the electrical connector at the regulator and connect a jumper wire between the **I** terminal of the connector and the negative battery cable clamp.
3. The charging system indicator light should go on with the ignition switch in the **RUN** position.
4. If the light does not go on, check the light for continuity and replace, if necessary.
5. If the light is not burned out, there is an open circuit between the ignition switch and the regulator.
6. Check the 500 ohm resistor across the indicator light.

BASE VOLTAGE TEST

♦ See Figure 24

1. Connect the negative and positive leads of a voltmeter to the negative and positive battery cable clamps (respectively).

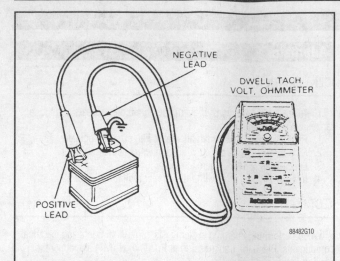

Fig. 24 Connect a voltmeter as illustrated to perform the base voltage test

2. Make sure the ignition switch is in the **OFF** position and all electrical loads (lights, radio, etc.) are OFF.

3. Record the battery voltage shown on the voltmeter; this is the base voltage.

NO-LOAD TEST

1. Connect a suitable tachometer to the engine.

2. Start the engine and bring the engine speed to 1,500 rpm. With no other electrical loads (doors closed, foot off the brake pedal), the reading on the voltmeter should increase, but no more than 2.0 volts above the base voltage.

➡️**The voltage reading should be taken when the voltage stops rising. This may take a few minutes.**

3. If the voltage increases as in Step 2, perform the Load Test.

4. If the voltage continues to rise, perform the Over Voltage Tests.

5. If the voltage does not rise to the proper level, perform the Under Voltage Tests.

LOAD TEST

1. With the engine running, turn the blower speed switch to the high speed position and turn the headlights on to high beam.

2. Raise the engine speed to approximately 2,000 rpm. The voltmeter reading should be a minimum of 0.5 volts above the base voltage. If not, perform the Under Voltage Tests.

➡️**If the voltmeter readings in the No-Load Test and Load Test are as specified, the charging system is operating properly. Go to the following tests if one or more of the voltage readings differs, and also check for battery drain.**

OVER VOLTAGE TESTS

1. If the voltmeter reading was more than 2.5 volts above the base voltage in the No-Load Test, connect a jumper wire between the voltage regulator base and the alternator frame or housing. Repeat the No-Load Test.

2. If the over voltage condition disappears, check the ground connections on the alternator and regulator, and from the engine to the dash panel and to the battery. Clean and securely tighten the connections.

3. If the over voltage condition still exists, disconnect the voltage regulator wiring connector from the voltage regulator. Repeat the No-Load Test.

4. If the over voltage condition disappears (voltmeter reads base voltage), replace the voltage regulator.

5. If the over voltage condition still exists with the voltage regulator wiring connector disconnected, check for a short between circuits **A** and **F** in the wiring harness; service as necessary. Then, reconnect the voltage regulator wiring connector.

UNDER VOLTAGE TESTS

▶️ **See Figure 25**

1. If the voltage reading was not more than 0.5 volts above the base voltage, detach the wiring connector from the voltage regulator and connect an ohmmeter from the **F** terminal of the connector to ground. The ohmmeter should indicate more than 2.4 ohms.

2. If the ohmmeter reading is less than 2.4 ohms, service the grounded field circuit in the wiring harness or alternator and repeat the Load Test.

✳️✳️ WARNING

Do not replace the voltage regulator before a shorted rotor coil or field circuit has been serviced. Damage to the regulator could result.

3. If the ohmmeter reading is more than 3.0 ohms, connect a jumper wire from the **A** to **F** terminals of the wiring connector and repeat the Load Test. If the voltmeter now indicates more than 0.5 volts above the base voltage, the regulator or wiring is damaged or worn. Perform the **S** and **I** Circuit Tests and service the wiring or regulator, as required.

4. If the voltmeter still indicates an under voltage problem, remove the jumper wire from the voltage regulator connector and leave the connector detached from the regulator.

5. Disconnect the **FLD** terminal on the alternator and pull back the protective cover from the **BAT** terminal. Connect a jumper wire between the **FLD** and **BAT** terminals and repeat the Load Test.

6. If the voltmeter indicates a 0.5 volts or greater increase above base voltage, perform the **S** and **I** Circuit Tests and service the wiring or regulator, as indicated.

7. If the voltmeter still indicates under voltage, shut the engine **OFF** and move the positive voltmeter lead to the **BAT** terminal of the alternator. If the voltmeter now indicates the base voltage, service the alternator. If the voltmeter indicates 0 volts, service the alternator-to-starter relay wire.

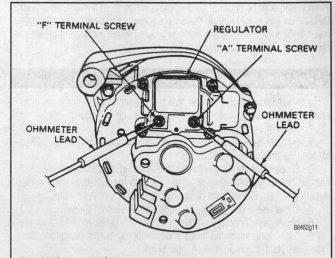

Fig. 25 Connect a jumper wire from the A to F terminals and repeat the Load Test

REGULATOR S AND I CIRCUIT TESTS

▶️ **See Figure 26**

1. Disengage the voltage regulator wiring connector and install a jumper wire between the **A** and **F** terminals.

2. With the engine idling and the negative voltmeter lead connected to the negative battery terminal, connect the positive voltmeter lead to the **S** terminal and then to the **I** terminal of the regulator wiring connector.

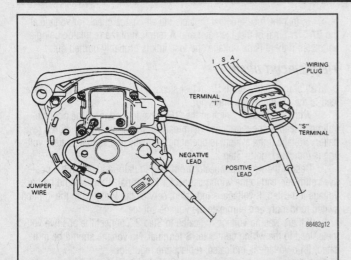

Fig. 26 Connect the positive voltmeter lead to the S terminal and then to the I terminal of the regulator wiring connector

3. The **S** circuit voltage reading should be approximately ½ the **I** circuit reading. If the voltage readings are correct, remove the jumper wire. Replace the voltage regulator and repeat the Load Test.

4. If there is no voltage present, service the faulty wiring circuit. Connect the positive voltmeter lead to the positive battery terminal.

5. Remove the jumper wire from the regulator wiring connector and secure the connector to the regulator. Repeat the Load Test.

FUSE LINK CONTINUITY

1. Make sure the battery is okay (refer to Section 1).

2. Turn on the headlights or any accessory. If the headlights or accessory do not operate, the fuse link is probably burned out.

3. On some vehicles, there are several fuse links. Proceed as in Step 2 to test other fuse links.

4. To test the fuse link that protects the alternator, check for voltage at the **BAT** terminal of the alternator, using a voltmeter. If there is no voltage, the fuse link is probably burned out.

Integral Regulator/External Fan Alternator

CHARGING SYSTEM INDICATOR LIGHT TEST

Two conditions can cause the charging system indicator light to come on when your van is running: no alternator output, caused by a damaged alternator, regulator or wiring; or an over voltage condition, caused by a shorted alternator rotor, regulator or wiring.

In a normally functioning system, the charging system indicator light will be OFF when the ignition switch is in the **OFF** position, ON when the ignition switch is in the **RUN** position and the engine not running, and OFF when the ignition switch is in the **RUN** position and the engine is running.

1. If the charging system indicator light does not come on, detach the wiring connector from the regulator.

2. Connect a jumper wire between the connector I terminal and the negative battery cable clamp.

3. Turn the ignition switch to the **RUN** position, but leave the engine **OFF**. If the charging system indicator light does not come on, check for a bulb socket resistor. If there is a resistor, check the contact of the bulb socket leads to the flexible printed circuit. If they are good, check the indicator light for continuity and replace if burned out. If the light checks out good, perform the Regulator I Circuit Test.

4. If the indicator light comes on, remove the jumper wire and reattach the wiring connector to the regulator. Connect the negative voltmeter lead to the negative battery cable clamp and connect the positive voltmeter lead to the regulator **A** terminal screw. Battery voltage should be indicated. If battery voltage is not indicated, service the **A** circuit wiring.

5. If battery voltage is indicated, clean and tighten the ground connections to the engine, alternator and regulator. Tighten loose regulator mounting screws to 15–26 inch lbs. (1.7–2.8 Nm).

6. Turn the ignition switch to the **RUN** position with the engine **OFF**. If the charging system indicator light still does not come on, replace the regulator.

BASE VOLTAGE TEST

1. Turn the lights ON with the engine **OFF** for 15 seconds to remove any surface charge.

2. Connect the negative and positive leads of a voltmeter to the negative and positive battery cable clamps (respectively).

3. Make sure the ignition switch is in the **OFF** position and all electrical loads (lights, radio, etc.) are OFF.

4. Record the battery voltage shown on the voltmeter; this is the base voltage.

NO-LOAD TEST

1. Connect a suitable tachometer to the engine.

2. Start the engine and bring the engine speed to 1500 rpm. With no other electrical loads (doors closed, foot off the brake pedal), the reading on the voltmeter should increase, but no more than 2.5 volts above the base voltage.

➡**The voltage reading should be taken when the voltage stops rising. This may take a few minutes.**

3. If the voltage increases as in Step 2, perform the Load Test.

4. If the voltage continues to rise, perform the Over Voltage Tests.

5. If the voltage does not rise to the proper level, perform the Under Voltage Tests.

LOAD TEST

1. With the engine running, turn the blower speed switch to the high speed position and turn the headlights on to high beam.

2. Raise the engine speed to approximately 2,000 rpm. The voltmeter reading should be a minimum of 0.5 volts above the base voltage. If not, perform the Under Voltage Tests.

➡**If the voltmeter readings in the No-Load Test and Load Test are as specified, the charging system is operating properly. Go to the following tests if one or more of the voltage readings differs, and also check for battery drain.**

OVER VOLTAGE TESTS

If the voltmeter reading was more than 2.5 volts above base voltage in the No-Load Test, proceed as follows:

1. Turn the ignition switch to the **RUN** position, but do not start the engine.

2. Connect the negative voltmeter lead to the alternator rear housing. Connect the positive voltmeter lead first to the alternator output connection at the starter solenoid and then to the regulator **A** screw head.

3. If there is greater than 0.5 volts difference between the 2 locations, service the **A** wiring circuit to eliminate the high resistance condition indicated by excessive voltage drop.

4. If the over voltage condition still exists, check for loose regulator and alternator grounding screws. Tighten loose regulator grounding screws to 15–26 inch lbs. (1.7–2.8 Nm).

5. If the over voltage condition still exists, connect the negative voltmeter lead to the alternator rear housing. With the ignition switch in the **OFF** position, connect the positive voltmeter lead first to the regulator **A** screw head and then to the regulator **F** screw head. If there are different voltage readings at the 2 screw heads, a malfunctioning grounded brush lead or a grounded rotor coil is indicated; service or replace the entire alternator/regulator unit.

6. If the same voltage is obtained at both screw heads in Step 5 and there is no high resistance in the ground of the **A+** circuit, replace the regulator.

UNDER VOLTAGE TESTS

If the voltmeter reading was not more than 0.5 volts above base voltage, proceed as follows:

1. Detach the electrical connector from the regulator. Connect an ohmmeter between the regulator **A** and **F** terminal screws. The ohmmeter reading should be more than 2.4 ohms. If it is less than 2.4 ohms, the regulator has failed. Also check the alternator for a shorted rotor or field circuit. Perform the Load Test after servicing.

✳✳ WARNING

Do not replace the voltage regulator before a shorted rotor coil or field circuit has been serviced. Damage to the regulator could result.

2. If the ohmmeter reading is greater than 2.4 ohms, fasten the regulator wiring connector and connect the negative voltmeter lead to the alternator rear housing. Connect the positive voltmeter lead to the regulator **A** terminal screw. The voltmeter should indicate battery voltage. If there is no voltage, service the **A** wiring circuit and then perform the Load Test.

3. If the voltmeter indicates battery voltage, connect the negative voltmeter lead to the alternator rear housing. With the ignition switch in the **OFF** position, connect the positive voltmeter lead to the regulator **F** terminal screw. The voltmeter should indicate battery voltage. If there is no voltage, there is an open field circuit in the alternator. Service or replace the alternator, then perform the Load Test after servicing.

4. If the voltmeter indicates battery voltage, connect the negative voltmeter lead to the alternator rear housing. Turn the ignition switch to the **RUN** position, leaving the engine off, and connect the positive voltmeter lead to the regulator **F** terminal screw. The voltmeter should read 1.5 volts or less. If more than 1.5 volts is indicated, perform the **I** circuit tests and service the **I** circuit if needed. If the **I** circuit is normal, replace the regulator, if needed, and perform the Load Test after servicing.

5. If 1.5 volts or less is indicated, unfasten the alternator wiring connector. Connect a set of 12 gauge jumper wires between the alternator **B+** terminal blades and the mating wiring connector terminals. Perform the Load Test, but connect the positive voltmeter lead to one of the **B+** jumper wire terminals. If the voltage increases more than 0.5 volts above base voltage, service the alternator-to-starter relay wiring. Repeat the Load Test, measuring voltage at the battery cable clamps after servicing.

6. If the voltage does not increase more than 0.5 volts above base voltage, connect a jumper wire from the alternator rear housing to the regulator **F** terminal. Repeat the Load Test with the positive voltmeter lead connected to one of the **B+** jumper wire terminals. If the voltage increases more than 0.5 volts, replace the regulator. If the voltage does not increase more than 0.5 volts, service or replace the alternator.

REGULATOR S AND I CIRCUIT TEST

1. Disconnect the wiring connector from the regulator. Connect a jumper wire between the regulator **A** terminal and the wiring connector A lead and connect a jumper wire between the regulator **F** screw and the alternator rear housing.

2. With the engine idling and the negative voltmeter lead connected to the negative battery terminal, connect the positive voltmeter lead first to the **S** terminal and then to the **I** terminal of the regulator wiring connector.

3. The **S** circuit voltage should be approximately ½ that of the **I** circuit. If the voltage readings are correct, remove the jumper wire. Replace the regulator and connect the regulator wiring connector. Perform the Load Test.

4. If there is no voltage present, remove the jumper wire and service the faulty wiring circuit or alternator.

5. Connect the positive voltmeter lead to the positive battery terminal and attach the wiring connector to the regulator. Repeat the Load Test.

FUSE LINK CONTINUITY

1. Make sure the battery is okay (refer to Section 1).

2. Turn on the headlights or any accessory. If the headlights or accessory do not operate, the fuse link is probably burned out.

3. On some vehicles, there are several fuse links. Proceed as in Step 2 to test other fuse links.

4. To test the fuse link that protects the alternator, check for voltage at the **BAT** terminal of the alternator and **A** terminal of the regulator, using a voltmeter. If there is no voltage, the fuse link is probably burned out.

FIELD CIRCUIT DRAIN

In all of the Field Circuit Drain test steps, connect the negative voltmeter lead to the alternator rear housing.

1. With the ignition switch in the **OFF** position, connect the positive voltmeter lead to the regulator **F** terminal screw. The voltmeter should read battery voltage if the system is operating normally. If less than battery voltage is indicated, go to Step 2.

2. Detach the wiring connector from the regulator and attach the positive voltmeter lead to the wiring connector **I** terminal. There should be no voltage indicated. If voltage is indicated, service the **I** lead from the ignition switch to identify and eliminate the voltage source.

3. If there was no voltage indicated in Step 2, connect the positive voltmeter lead to the wiring connector **S** terminal. No voltage should be indicated. If no voltage is indicated, replace the regulator.

4. If there was voltage indicated in Step 3, detach the wiring connector from the alternator rectifier connector. Connect the positive voltmeter lead to the regulator wiring connector **S** terminal. If voltage is indicated, service the **S** lead to the alternator connector to eliminate the voltage source. If no voltage is indicated, the alternator rectifier assembly is faulty.

Integral Regulator/Internal Fan Alternator

BASE VOLTAGE TEST

1. Connect the negative and positive leads of a voltmeter to the negative and positive battery cable clamps (respectively).

2. Make sure the ignition switch is in the **OFF** position and all electrical loads (lights, radio, etc.) are OFF.

3. Record the battery voltage shown on the voltmeter; this is the base voltage.

➥**Turn the headlights ON for 10–15 seconds to remove any surface charge from the battery, then wait until the voltage stabilizes, before performing the base voltage test.**

NO-LOAD TEST

1. Connect a suitable tachometer to the engine.

2. Start the engine and bring the engine speed to 1,500 rpm. With no other electrical loads (doors closed, foot off the brake pedal), the reading on the voltmeter should increase, but no more than 3 volts above the base voltage.

➥**The voltage reading should be taken when the voltage stops rising. This may take a few minutes.**

3. If the voltage increases as in Step 2, perform the Load Test.

4. If the voltage continues to rise, perform the Over Voltage Tests.

5. If the voltage does not rise to the proper level, perform the Under Voltage Tests.

LOAD TEST

1. With the engine running, turn the blower speed switch to the high speed position and turn the headlights on to high beam.

2. Raise the engine speed to approximately 2,000 rpm. The voltmeter reading should be a minimum of 0.5 volts above the base voltage. If not, perform the Under Voltage Tests.

➥**If the voltmeter readings in the No-Load Test and Load Test are as specified, the charging system is operating properly. Go to the following tests if one or more of the voltage readings differs, and also check for battery drain.**

OVER VOLTAGE TESTS

If the voltmeter reading was more than 3 volts above base voltage in the No-Load Test, proceed as follows:

1. Turn the ignition switch to the **RUN** position, but do not start the engine.

2. Connect the negative voltmeter lead to ground. Connect the positive voltmeter lead first to the alternator output connection at the starter solenoid (1992 models) or load distribution point (1993–96 models) and then to the regulator **A** screw head.

3. If there is greater than 0.5 volts difference between the 2 locations, service the **A** wiring circuit to eliminate the high resistance condition indicated by excessive voltage drop.

4. If the over voltage condition still exists, check for loose regulator and alternator grounding screws. Tighten loose regulator grounding screws to 16–24 inch lbs. (1.7–2.8 Nm).

5. If the over voltage condition still exists, connect the negative voltmeter lead to ground. Turn the ignition switch to the **OFF** position and connect the positive voltmeter lead first to the regulator **A** screw head and then to the regulator F screw head. If there are different voltage readings at the 2 screw heads, a malfunctioning regulator, grounded brush lead or grounded rotor coil is indicated; replace the regulator/brush set or the entire alternator.

6. If the same voltage reading (battery voltage) is obtained at both screw heads in Step 5, there is no short to ground through the alternator field/brushes. Replace the regulator.

UNDER VOLTAGE TESTS

If the voltmeter reading was not more than 0.5 volts above base voltage, proceed as follows:

1. Detach the wiring connector from the regulator and connect an ohmmeter between the regulator **A** and **F** terminal screws. The ohmmeter should read more than 2.4 ohms. If the ohmmeter reads less than 2.4 ohms, check the alternator for a shorted rotor-to-field coil or for shorted brushes. Replace the brush holder or the entire alternator assembly. Perform the Load Test after replacement.

☀ WARNING

Do not replace the regulator if a shorted rotor coil or field circuit has been diagnosed, or regulator damage could result. Replace the alternator assembly.

2. If the ohmmeter reading is greater than 2.4 ohms, fasten the regulator wiring connector and connect the negative voltmeter lead to ground. Connect the positive voltmeter lead to the regulator **A** terminal screw; battery voltage should be indicated. If there is no voltage, service the **A** wiring circuit and then perform the Load Test.

3. If battery voltage is indicated in Step 2, connect the negative voltmeter lead to ground. Turn the ignition switch to the **OFF** position, then connect the positive voltmeter lead to the regulator **F** terminal screw. Battery voltage should be indicated on the voltmeter. If there is no voltage, replace the alternator and then perform the Load Test.

4. If battery voltage is indicated in Step 3, connect the negative voltmeter lead to ground. Turn the ignition switch to the **RUN** position, but leave the engine **OFF**. Connect the positive voltmeter lead to the regulator **F** terminal screw; the voltmeter reading should be 2 volts or less. If more than 2 volts is indicated, perform the **I** circuit tests and service the **I** circuit, if needed. If the **I** circuit tests normal, replace the regulator, if needed, then perform the Load Test.

5. If 2 volts or less is indicated in Step 4, perform the Load Test, but connect the positive voltmeter lead to the alternator output stud. If the voltage increases more than 0.5 volts above base voltage, service the alternator-to-starter relay (1992 models) or alternator-to-load distribution point (1993–96 models) wiring. Repeat the Load Test, measuring the voltage at the battery cable clamps after servicing.

6. If the voltage does not increase more than 0.5 volts above base voltage in Step 5, perform the Load Test and measure the voltage drop from the battery to the **A** terminal of the regulator (regulator connected). If the voltage drop exceeds 0.5 volts, service the wiring from the **A** terminal to the starter relay (1992 models) or load distribution point (1993–96 models).

7. If the voltage drop does not exceed 0.5 volts, connect a jumper wire from the alternator rear housing to the regulator **F** terminal. Repeat the Load Test with the positive voltmeter lead connected to the alternator output stud. If the voltage increases more than 0.5 volts, replace the regulator. If voltage does not increase more than 0.5 volts, replace the alternator.

ALTERNATOR S CIRCUIT TEST

1. Detach the wiring connector from the regulator. Connect a jumper wire from the regulator **A** terminal to the wiring connector **A** lead. Connect a jumper wire from the regulator **F** screw to the alternator rear housing.

2. With the engine idling and the negative voltmeter lead connected to ground, connect the positive voltmeter lead first to the **S** terminal and then to the **A** terminal of the regulator wiring connector. The **S** circuit voltage should be approximately ½ the **A** circuit voltage. If the voltage readings are normal, remove the jumper wire, replace the regulator and attach the wiring connector. Repeat the Load Test.

3. If there is no voltage present, remove the jumper wire and service the damaged or worn wiring circuit or alternator.

4. Connect the positive voltmeter lead to the positive battery terminal. Fasten the wiring connector to the regulator and repeat the Load Test.

FUSE LINK CONTINUITY

1. Make sure the battery is okay (refer to Section 1).

2. Turn on the headlights or any accessory. If the headlights or accessory do not operate, the fuse link is probably burned out.

3. On some vehicles, there are several fuse links. Proceed as in Step 2 to test other fuse links.

4. To test the fuse link that protects the alternator, check for voltage at the **BAT** terminal of the alternator and **A** terminal of the regulator, using a voltmeter. If there is no voltage, the fuse link is probably burned out.

FIELD CIRCUIT DRAIN

In all of the Field Circuit Drain test steps, connect the negative voltmeter lead to the alternator rear housing.

1. With the ignition switch in the **OFF** position, connect the positive voltmeter lead to the regulator **F** terminal screw. The voltmeter should read battery voltage if the system is operating normally. If less than battery voltage is indicated, go to Step 2.

2. Detach the wiring connector from the regulator and connect the positive voltmeter lead to the wiring connector **I** terminal. There should be no voltage indicated. If voltage is indicated, service the **I** lead from the ignition switch to identify and eliminate the voltage source.

3. If there was no voltage indicated in Step 2, connect the positive voltmeter lead to the wiring connector **S** terminal. No voltage should be indicated. If no voltage is indicated, replace the regulator.

4. If there was voltage indicated in Step 3, unfasten the 1-pin **S** terminal connector. Again, connect the positive voltmeter lead to the regulator wiring connector **S** terminal. If voltage is indicated, service the **S** lead wiring to eliminate the voltage source. If no short is found, replace the alternator.

REMOVAL & INSTALLATION

▶ **See Figures 27 thru 32**

1. Open the hood and disconnect the battery ground cable.
2. If necessary, remove the shield and fresh air inlet tube.
3. Remove the drive belt.

➡**Some engines are equipped with a ribbed, K-section belt and automatic tensioner. A special tool must be made to remove the tension from the tensioner arm. Loosen the idler pulley pivot and adjuster bolts before using the tool. See the accompanying illustration for tool details.**

4. Label all of the leads to the alternator so that you can install them correctly, then disconnect the leads from the alternator.
5. Remove the adjusting arm bolt.
6. Remove the alternator through-bolt and lower the alternator.
7. Remove the alternator from the vehicle.

To install:

8. Install the alternator and finger-tighten the adjusting arm bolt and through-bolt.
9. Engage the electrical connections.
10. Install the drive belt and, when the proper belt tension is achieved, tighten the through-bolt and adjusting arm bolt.

Fig. 27 Unplug the electrical connection from the alternator

Fig. 30 . . . then loosen the upper mounting bolt

Fig. 28 Loosen the wiring retaining bolt (indicated by the arrow) and disconnect the wiring

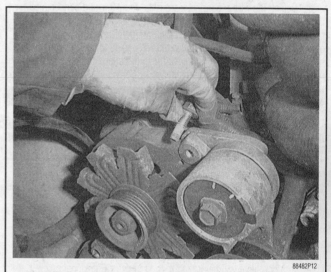
Fig. 31 Remove the bolt from the alternator and bracket . . .

Fig. 29 Loosen the lower retaining bolt . . .

Fig. 32 . . . then remove the alternator from the van

11. Tighten the upper mounting bolts on the 4.9L and 7.5L engines to 16–21 ft. lbs. (21–29 ft. lbs.). Tighten the lower mounting bolt on the 4.9L and 7.5L engines and the mounting bolts on all the other engines to 30–40 ft. lbs. (40–55 Nm).

12. If removed, install the fresh air inlet tube and shield.

Regulator

REMOVAL & INSTALLATION

Leece-Neville Regulator

▶ **See Figures 33 and 34**

The regulator is mounted on the back of the alternator.
1. Disconnect the diode trio lead from the regulator terminal.
2. Remove the 2 nuts retaining the regulator and jumper leads.
3. Carefully pull the regulator from its holder.

➡**The brushes will snap together when the regulator is removed. They can now be checked for length. Brush length minimum is 0.188 in. (4.76mm).**

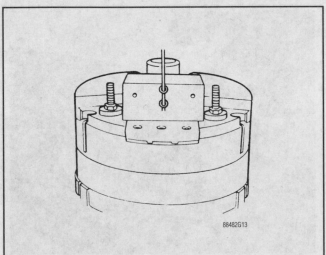

Fig. 33 Hold the brushes in place with a paper clip or similar device

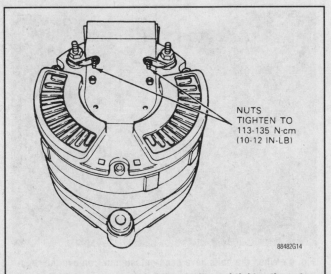

Fig. 34 Withdraw the brush holding device and tighten the nuts

To install:
4. Push the brushes back into their holders and insert a suitable pin through the hole in the housing. This will hold the brushes in place.
5. Carefully push the regulator into place and just start the retaining nuts. Remove the brush holding pin and then tighten the retaining nuts.
6. Connect the diode trio leads.

Integral Rear Mount Regulator

▶ **See Figures 35 and 36**

1. Loosen the four Torx® screws retaining the regulator to the rear of the alternator.
2. Remove the regulator with the brush holder attached.
3. Hold the regulator in one hand and use a prytool to disengage the cap covering the A screw head.
4. Loosen the two Torx® screws engaging the regulator to the brush holder, then separate the regulator from the brush holder.

To install:
5. Engage the brush holder to the regulator and tighten the screws.
6. Install the cap covering the A screw.

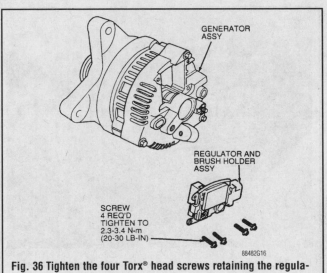

Fig. 35 Use a prytool to disengage the cap covering the A screw head

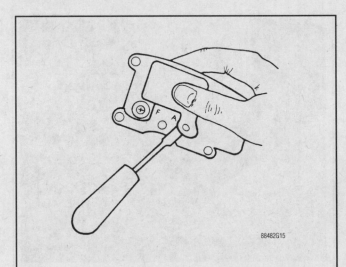

Fig. 36 Tighten the four Torx® head screws retaining the regulator to the proper specification

7. Depress the brushes into the holder and hold the brushes in place by inserting a regular size paper clip, or its equivalent, through the location holes in the brushes.

8. Install the regulator and brush holder assembly, then tighten the screws to 20–30 inch lbs. (2.3–3.4 Nm).

9. Remove the paper clip or its equivalent from the regulator.

Fender Liner Mounted Regulator

◆ **See Figures 37, 38, 39, 40 and 41**

➡**Battery removal may be necessary to access the regulator. If not, disconnect the negative battery cable and skip to Step 2.**

1. Disconnect the negative and then the positive battery cables from the battery. Unfasten and remove the battery.

2. Loosen the regulator mounting retainers.

3. Disengage the regulator electrical connection and remove the regulator.

To install:

4. Engage the electrical connection to the regulator.

5. Install the regulator and tighten the retainers.

6. If applicable, install the battery and fasten it securely.

7. Connect the positive (if applicable) and then the negative battery cable(s).

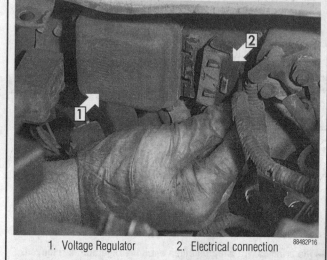

1. Voltage Regulator	2. Electrical connection

88482P16

Fig. 39 Disengage the regulator electrical connections

88482P14

Fig. 37 If required for access, disconnect the battery cables . . .

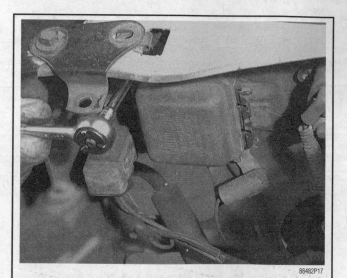

88482P17

Fig. 40 Unfasten the regulator mounting bolts

88482P15

Fig. 38 . . . and remove the battery from the engine compartment

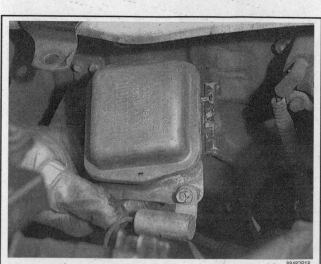

88482P18

Fig. 41 When the bolts have been unfastened, remove the regulator from the engine compartment

STARTING SYSTEM

General Information

The battery and starting motor are linked by very heavy electrical cables designed to minimize resistance to the flow of current. Generally, the major power supply cable that leaves the battery goes directly to the starter, while other electrical system needs are supplied by a smaller cable. During starter operation, power flows from the battery to the starter and is grounded through the vehicle's frame/body or engine and the battery's negative ground strap.

The starter is a specially designed, direct current electric motor capable of producing a great amount of power for its size. One thing that allows the motor to produce a great deal of power is its tremendous rotating speed. It drives the engine through a tiny pinion gear (attached to the starter's armature), which drives the very large flywheel ring gear at a greatly reduced speed. Another factor allowing it to produce so much power is that only intermittent operation is required of it. Thus, little allowance for air circulation is necessary, and the windings can be built into a very small space.

The starter solenoid is a magnetic device which employs the small current supplied by the starting circuit of the ignition switch. This magnetic action moves a plunger which mechanically engages the starter and closes the heavy switch connecting it to the battery. The starting switch circuit usually consists of the starting switch contained within the ignition switch, a neutral safety switch or clutch pedal switch, and the wiring necessary to connect these in series with the starter solenoid or relay.

The pinion, a small gear, is mounted to a one-way drive clutch. This clutch is splined to the starter armature shaft. When the ignition switch is moved to the **START** position, the solenoid plunger slides the pinion toward the flywheel ring gear via a collar and spring. If the teeth on the pinion and flywheel match properly, the pinion will engage the flywheel immediately. If the gear teeth butt one another, the spring will be compressed and will force the gears to mesh as soon as the starter turns far enough to allow them to do so. As the solenoid plunger reaches the end of its travel, it closes the contacts that connect the battery and starter, and the engine is cranked.

As soon as the engine starts, the flywheel ring gear begins turning fast enough to drive the pinion at an extremely high rate of speed. At this point, the one-way clutch begins allowing the pinion to spin faster than the starter shaft so that the starter will not operate at excessive speed. When the ignition switch is released from the starter position, the solenoid is de-energized, and a spring pulls the gear out of mesh, thereby interrupting current flow to the starter.

Some starters employ a separate relay, mounted away from the starter, to switch the motor and solenoid current on and off. The relay replaces the solenoid electrical switch, but does not eliminate the need for a solenoid mounted on the starter to mechanically engage the starter drive gears. The relay is used to reduce the amount of current the starting switch must carry.

TESTING

Place the transmission in **N** or **P**. Disconnect the vacuum line to the Thermactor® bypass valve, if equipped, before performing any cranking tests. After tests, run the engine for 3 minutes before connecting the vacuum line.

Symptoms

STARTER CRANKS SLOWLY

1. Connect a set of jumper cables. If, with the aid of the booster battery, the starter now cranks normally, check the condition of the battery. Recharge or replace the battery, as necessary. Clean the cables and battery posts and make sure all connections are tight.
2. If Step 1 does not correct the problem, clean and tighten the connections at the starter relay and battery ground on the engine. You should not be able to easily rotate the eyelet terminals by hand. Also, make sure the positive cable is not shorted to ground.
3. If the starter still cranks slowly, it must be replaced.

STARTER RELAY OPERATES BUT STARTER DOESN'T CRANK

1. Connect a set of jumper cables. If, with the aid of the booster battery, the starter now cranks normally, check the condition of the battery. Recharge or replace the battery, as necessary. Clean the cables and battery posts and make sure all connections are tight.
2. If Step 1 does not correct the problem, clean and tighten the connections at the starter and relay. Make sure the wire strands are secure in the eyelets.
3. On models with a fender mounted solenoid, if the starter still doesn't crank, it must be replaced.
4. On vehicles with starter mounted solenoid: Connect a jumper cable across terminals **B** and **M** of the starter solenoid. If the starter does not operate, replace the starter. If the starter does operate, replace the solenoid.

※ WARNING

Making the jumper connections could cause a spark. Battery jumper cables or equivalent gauge wires should be used, due to the high current in the starting system.

STARTER DOESN'T CRANK—RELAY CHATTERS OR DOESN'T CLICK

1. Connect a set of jumper cables. If, with the aid of the booster battery, the starter now cranks normally, check the condition of the battery. Recharge or replace the battery, as necessary. Clean the cables and battery posts and make sure all connections are tight.
2. If Step 1 does not correct the problem, remove the push-on connector from the relay (red with blue stripe wire). Make sure the connection is clean and secure and the relay bracket is grounded.
3. If the connections are good, check the relay operation with a jumper wire. Remove the push-on connector from the relay and, using a jumper wire, jump from the now exposed terminal on the starter relay to the main terminal (battery side or battery positive post). If this corrects the problem, check the ignition switch, neutral safety switch and wiring in the starting circuit for open or loose connections.
4. If a jumper wire across the relay does not correct the problem, replace the relay.

STARTER SPINS BUT DOESN'T CRANK ENGINE

1. Remove the starter, as described later in this section.
2. Check the armature shaft for corrosion and clean or replace, as necessary.
3. If there is no corrosion, replace the starter drive.
4. Install the starter.

STARTER SOLENOID DOESN'T OPERATE

1. Using a digital multimeter, check for continuity between the solenoid **M** and **S** terminals and ground (frame).
2. If there is no continuity, make sure the wires and connections are clean and free of dirt.
3. If the condition still exists, replace the solenoid.

REMOVAL & INSTALLATION

Gasoline Engines

▶ See Figures 42, 43, 44, 45 and 46

➡On newer model vehicles, when the battery is disconnected, it may cause some abnormal drive symptoms until the Powertrain Control Module (PCM) relearns its adaptive strategy. The vehicle may need to be driven 10 miles or more for the PCM to relearn its strategy.

1. Disconnect the negative battery cable.
2. Raise the front of the van and install jackstands beneath the frame. Firmly apply the parking brake and place blocks in back of the rear wheels.

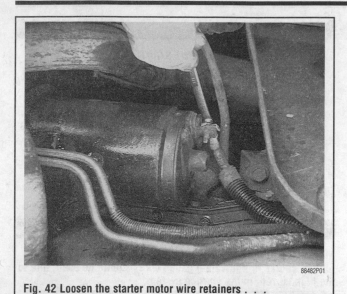

Fig. 42 Loosen the starter motor wire retainers . . .

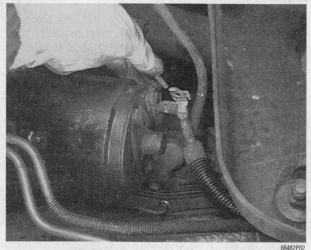

Fig. 43 . . . and disengage the starter motor electrical connection

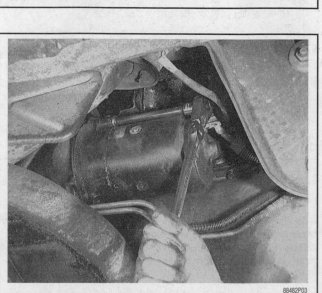

Fig. 44 Loosen the starter motor retaining bolts

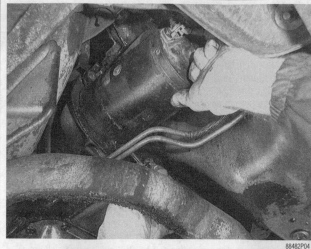

Fig. 45 Before the last bolt is unfastened, support the starter with your hand and remove the last retaining bolt

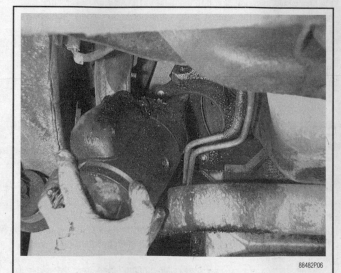

Fig. 46 Remove the starter motor from the vehicle

3. If equipped, remove the heat shield.
4. Tag and disconnect the wiring at the starter.

➡If equipped with a hardshell connector at the S terminal, grasp the plastic shell and pull it off. Do not pull on the wire. Be careful to pull it straight off to prevent damage to the terminal or connector. If any part of the connection is damaged, replace the damaged components.

5. Loosen the starter mounting bolts, then remove the starter.

To install:

6. Install the starter and tighten the mounting bolts to 15–20 ft. lbs. (20–27 Nm).

7. If equipped, engage the connector to the starter solenoid by pushing straight in until it locks in position with a click or detent.

8. Install the starter cable and tighten the nut to 80–120 inch lbs. (9–14 Nm).

9. If applicable, install the heat shield.

10. Remove the jackstands and lower the vehicle.

11. Connect the negative battery cable and check for proper operation.

Diesel Engines

1. Disconnect the battery ground cables.
2. Raise and safely support the vehicle.

3. Disconnect the cables and wires at the starter solenoid.

4. If necessary, turn the front wheels to the right and remove the two bolts attaching the steering idler arm to the frame.

5. Loosen the starter mounting bolts and remove the starter.

To install:

6. Position the starter and install the mounting bolts. Tighten the bolts to 15–20 ft. lbs. (20–27 Nm).

7. Connect the starter wiring.

8. Lower the vehicle.

9. Connect the negative battery cables.

SOLENOID REPLACEMENT

Fender Mounted

◆ See Figures 47 thru 52

1. Disconnect the negative battery cable.

2. With dual batteries, detach the negative cable connecting the two batteries at both ends.

3. Tag the electrical connections and unplug the ignition switch (start) wire.

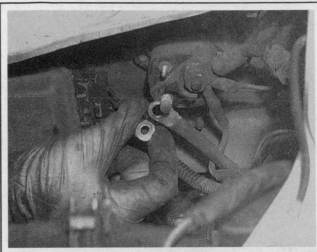

Fig. 49 Remove the nuts and disconnect the wires

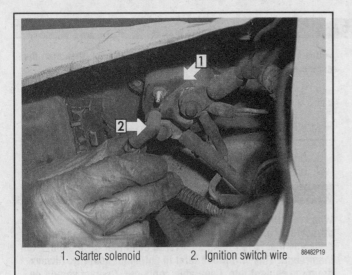

1. Starter solenoid   2. Ignition switch wire

Fig. 47 Unplug the ignition switch wire from the starter solenoid

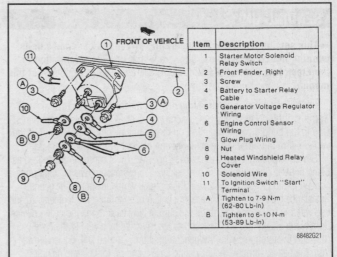

Item	Description
1	Starter Motor Solenoid Relay Switch
2	Front Fender, Right
3	Screw
4	Battery to Starter Relay Cable
5	Generator Voltage Regulator Wiring
6	Engine Control Sensor Wiring
7	Glow Plug Wiring
8	Nut
9	Heated Windshield Relay Cover
10	Solenoid Wire
11	To Ignition Switch "Start" Terminal
A	Tighten to 7-9 N·m (62-80 Lb-In)
B	Tighten to 6-10 N·m (53-89 Lb-In)

FRONT OF VEHICLE

Fig. 50 Exploded view of the fender mounted solenoid's electrical connections—diesel engine shown (gasoline engines similar)

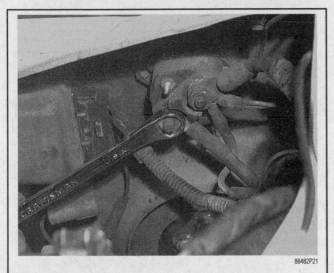

Fig. 48 Loosen the electrical connection retaining nuts

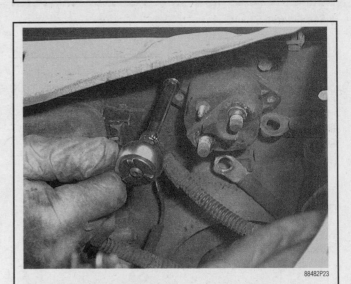

Fig. 51 Loosen the solenoid-to-body retaining bolts

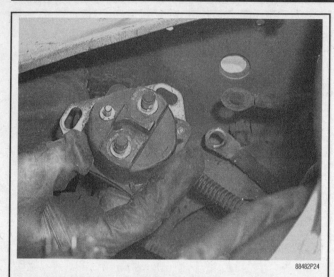

Fig. 52 Remove the solenoid from the van

88482P24

4. Loosen the electrical connection terminal nuts and disengage the wires.
5. Loosen the solenoid retainers and remove the relay.

To install:

6. Install the relay and tighten the retainers to 62–80 inch lbs. (7–9 Nm).
7. Engage the electrical connections on the terminal posts and tighten the nuts to 53–89 inch lbs. (6–10 Nm).
8. Engage the ignition switch (start) wire.
9. Connect the battery cables.

Starter Mounted

1. Disconnect the negative battery cable.
2. Remove the starter.
3. Remove the positive brush connector from the solenoid M terminal.
4. Remove the solenoid retaining screws, then remove the solenoid and, if applicable, adjusting shims.

To install:

5. If removed, install the adjusting shims, then attach the solenoid plunger rod through the drive lever (bottom terminal M should have a metal strip attached to it). Tighten the solenoid retaining screws to 45–89 inch lbs. (5–10 Nm).
6. Attach the positive brush connector to the solenoid M terminal and tighten the retaining nut to 80–124 inch lbs. (9.0–14 Nm).
7. Install the starter and connect the negative battery terminal.

SENDING UNITS

➡ **This section describes the operating principles of sending units, warning lights and gauges. Sensors which provide information to the Electronic Control Module (ECM) are covered in Section 4 of this manual.**

Instrument panels contain a number of indicating devices (gauges and warning lights). These devices are composed of two separate components. One is the sending unit, mounted on the engine or other remote part of the vehicle, and the other is the actual gauge or light in the instrument panel.

Several types of sending units exist; however, most can be characterized as being either a pressure type or a resistance type. Pressure type sending units convert liquid pressure into an electrical signal which is sent to the gauge. Resistance type sending units are most often used to measure temperature and use variable resistance to control the current flow back to the indicating device. Both types of sending units are connected in series by a wire to the battery (through the ignition switch). When the ignition is turned **ON**, current flows from the battery through the indicating device and on to the sending unit.

Coolant Temperature Sender

▶ **See Figures 53 and 54**

OPERATION

When coolant temperature is low, the resistance of the sending unit is high, restricting the flow of current through the gauge and moving the pointer only a short distance. As coolant temperature rises, the resistance of the sending unit decreases, causing a proportional increase in current flow through the sending unit and corresponding movement of the gauge pointer.

The sending unit may only be tested for operation. There is no calibration, adjustment or maintenance required.

TESTING

1. Disconnect the sending unit electrical harness.
2. Remove the radiator cap and place a mechanic's thermometer in the coolant.
3. Using an ohmmeter, check the resistance between the sending unit terminals.
4. Resistance should be high (375 ohms) with engine coolant cold and low (180 ohms) with engine coolant hot.

➡ **It is best to check resistance with the engine cool, then start the engine and watch the resistance change as the engine warms.**

5. If resistance does not drop as engine temperature rises, the sending unit is faulty.

REMOVAL & INSTALLATION

1. Disconnect the negative battery cable.
2. Drain the cooling system into a suitable container.

✳✳ CAUTION

When draining the coolant, keep in mind that cats and dogs are attracted by ethylene glycol antifreeze, and are quite likely to drink any that is left in an uncovered container or in puddles on the ground. This will prove fatal in sufficient quantity. Always drain the coolant into a sealable container. Coolant should be reused unless it is contaminated or several years old.

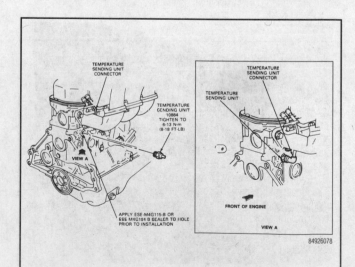

Fig. 53 Coolant temperature sender location—4.9L engine

84926078

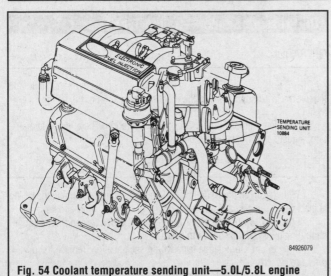

Fig. 54 Coolant temperature sending unit—5.0L/5.8L engine shown, 7.5L engine similar

3. Disengage the electrical connector at the temperature sender/switch.
4. Remove the temperature sender/switch.

To install:

5. Apply pipe sealant or Teflon® tape to the threads of the new sender/switch. Tighten it to 8–18 ft. lbs. (11–24 Nm).
6. Install the temperature sender/switch and connect the electrical connector.
7. Connect the negative battery cable. Fill the cooling system.
8. Run the engine and check for leaks.

Oil Pressure Sender—Indicator Lamp Type

◆ See Figures 55, 56 and 57

OPERATION

A single terminal oil pressure switch is used on vehicles equipped with an oil pressure lamp.

If the pressure is detected to be at an unsafe level, a red indicator lamp will glow on the dashboard. The light should come on when the engine is off but the ignition is in the **RUN** position. Once the engine is started, the light should go out.

The lamp is connected between the oil pressure switch unit (mounted on the engine and the coil terminal of the ignition switch).

TESTING

1. Turn the ignition to the **RUN** position with the engine not running. The indicator lamp should come on.
2. If the indicator lamp does not come on, disconnect the wire from the oil pressure switch terminal and ground the wire.
3. If the indicator light comes on, the pressure switch is inoperative. Replace the switch.
4. If the indicator light fails to come on, either the bulb is burned out, there is no power to the bulb, or the circuit is open somewhere between the bulb and the oil pressure switch.
5. If the lamp stays on with the engine running and the engine has adequate oil pressure, disconnect the wire to the switch. If the lamp goes out, replace the oil pressure switch. If the lamp does not go out, correct the short in the wiring between the switch and lamp.

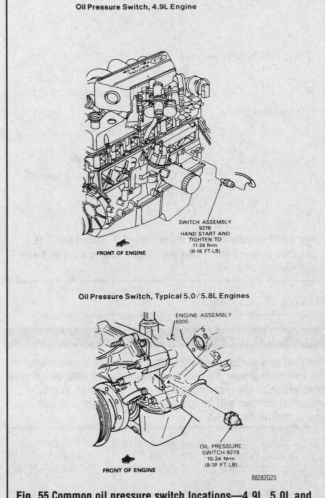

Fig. 55 Common oil pressure switch locations—4.9L, 5.0L and 5.8L engines

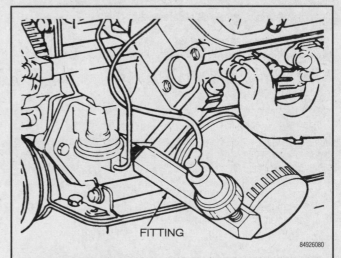

Fig. 56 Some engines have the oil pressure sender mounted on a fitting—5.0L/5.8L engines

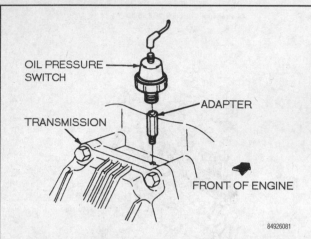

Fig. 57 Oil pressure switch mounting—7.3L diesel and 7.5L gasoline engines. (Note that the adapter is only used on diesel engines)

REMOVAL & INSTALLATION

✳✳ WARNING

The pressure switch used with the oil pressure warning light is not interchangeable with the sending unit used with the oil pressure gauge. If the incorrect part is installed the oil pressure indicating system will be inoperative and the sending unit or gauge will be damaged.

1. Unplug the connector at the unit and unscrew it from its mounting.
2. To install the unit, apply pipe sealant or Teflon® tape to the threads of the new switch and screw it in to its mount. Tighten it to 8–18 ft. lbs. (11–24 Nm).
3. Connect the wiring to the unit.
4. Run the engine and check for leaks and proper operation.

Oil Pressure Sender—Gauge Type

OPERATION

The oil pressure sending unit is a variable resistance type magnetic unit that works in conjunction with the magnetic operation of the gauge system.

The sensing unit may only be tested for operation. There is no calibration, adjustment or maintenance required.

TESTING

1. With the key in the **RUN** position and the engine off, unplug the wiring at the switch. The gauge should read on the LOW graduation or below.
2. Attach the wiring connector to the engine block (ground). The gauge should read just slightly above mid-scale.
3. If the oil pressure gauge tests within specification, replace the oil pressure switch.
4. If the gauge still tests out of calibration, replace the oil pressure gauge.

REMOVAL & INSTALLATION

✳✳ WARNING

The pressure switch used with the oil pressure warning light is not interchangeable with the sending unit used with the oil pressure gauge. If the incorrect part is installed the oil pressure indicating system will be inoperative and the sending unit or gauge will be damaged.

1. Unplug the connector at the unit and unscrew it from its mounting.
2. To install the unit, apply pipe sealant or Teflon® tape to the threads of the new switch and screw it in to its mount. Tighten it to 8–18 ft. lbs. (11–24 Nm).
3. Connect the wiring to the unit.
4. Run the engine and check for leaks and proper operation.

3

ENGINE AND ENGINE OVERHAUL

ENGINE MECHANICAL

Engine

REMOVAL & INSTALLATION

In the process of removing the engine, you will come across a number of steps which call for the removal of a separate component or system, such as "disconnect the exhaust system" or "remove the radiator." In most instances, a detailed removal procedure can be found elsewhere in this manual.

It is virtually impossible to list each individual wire and hose which must be disconnected, simply because so many different model and engine combinations have been manufactured. Careful observation and common sense are the best possible approaches to any repair procedure.

Removal and installation of the engine can be made easier if you follow these basic points:

- If you have to drain any of the fluids, use a suitable container.
- Always tag any wires or hoses and, if possible, the components they came from before disconnecting them.
- Because there are so many bolts and fasteners involved, store and label the retainers from components separately in muffin pans, jars or coffee cans. This will prevent confusion during installation.
- After unbolting the transmission, always make sure it is properly supported.
- If it is necessary to disconnect the air conditioning system, have this service performed by a qualified technician using a recovery/recycling station. If the system does not have to be disconnected, unbolt the compressor and set it aside.
- When unbolting the engine mounts, always make sure the engine is properly supported. When removing the engine, make sure that any lifting devices are properly attached to the engine. It is recommended that if your engine is supplied with lifting hooks, your lifting apparatus be attached to them.
- Lift the engine from its compartment slowly, checking that no hoses, wires or other components are still connected.
- After the engine is clear of the compartment, place it on an engine stand or workbench.
- After the engine has been removed, you can perform a partial or full teardown of the engine using the procedures outlined in this manual.
  1. Drain the cooling system and the crankcase into suitable containers.
  2. Disconnect the negative and positive battery cables.

✳✳ CAUTION

When draining the coolant, keep in mind that cats and dogs are attracted by ethylene glycol antifreeze and are quite likely to drink any that is left in an uncovered container or in puddles on the ground. This will prove fatal in sufficient quantity. Always drain the coolant into a sealable container. Coolant should be reused unless it is contaminated or several years old.

3. On 4.9L engines, remove the front bumper and lower gravel or air deflector.
4. On some engines, it may be necessary to remove the headlight and side market light assemblies.
5. If necessary, remove the grille.
6. Remove the engine cover.
7. Remove the air cleaner housing and ducts.
8. Disconnect the radiator hoses.
9. If equipped with an automatic transmission, disconnect the oil cooler lines from the radiator. Remove the radiator and shroud.
10. Disconnect the heater hoses from the engine.
11. Disconnect the alternator and move it aside.
12. Remove the drive belts.
13. Disconnect power steering pump and support from the engine and set them aside with the lines still attached, if possible. If necessary disconnect the lines.

14. Relieve the fuel system pressure and disconnect the fuel line from the fuel rail. Cover the end of the fuel rail and line to prevent contamination.
15. Tag and disengage the vacuum hoses and electrical connections that will interfere with engine removal.

✳✳ CAUTION

Please refer to Section 1 before discharging the compressor or disconnecting air conditioning lines. Damage to the air conditioning system or personal injury could result. Consult your local laws concerning refrigerant discharge and recycling. In many areas it may be illegal for anyone but a certified technician to service the A/C system. Always use an approved recovery station when discharging the air conditioning.

16. Discharge the air conditioning system and remove the air conditioning condenser.
17. Tag and disconnect the accelerator and transmission kickdown cable (if equipped).
18. Loosen the upper transmission-to-engine bolts and the automatic transmission dipstick tube support bolt from the intake manifold.
19. On 7.5L engines, remove the distributor.
20. On equipped diesel engines, remove the turbocharger.
21. Raise the vehicle and support it safely with jackstands.

✳✳ CAUTION

The EPA warns that prolonged contact with used engine oil may cause a number of skin disorders, including cancer! You should make every effort to minimize your exposure to used engine oil. Protective gloves should be worn when changing the oil. Wash your hands and any other exposed skin areas as soon as possible after exposure to used engine oil. Soap and water, or waterless hand cleaner should be used.

22. Tag and disconnect the starter motor wires and remove the starter.
23. On manual transmission equipped vans:
    a. Remove the flywheel housing lower attaching bolts.
    b. Disconnect the clutch return spring.
24. On automatic transmission equipped vans:
    a. Remove the converter housing access cover assembly.
    b. Remove the flywheel-to-converter attaching nuts.
    c. Secure the converter in the housing.
25. Remove the oil filter.
26. On some diesel engines it may be necessary to remove the fan and clutch assembly. Be careful, the fan clutch may have a right-hand thread nut on some later model engines. Try turning the nut counterclockwise first without using an excessive amount of force.
27. Remove all engine to transmission nuts.
28. Disconnect the exhaust pipe(s) from the exhaust manifold.
29. Loosen the engine mount retainers.
30. Lower the vehicle.
31. Lower the vehicle and position a jack under the transmission and support it.
32. Remove the remaining bell housing-to-engine attaching bolts. Make sure no other component interferes with the engine removal.
33. Attach an engine lifting device and raise the engine slightly and carefully pull it from the transmission. Lift the engine out of the vehicle.
    To install:
34. Installation is the reverse of removal but please note the following steps.
35. On some later model diesel engines where the fan and clutch are removed, the clutch nut may have a right-hand thread. Install the nut by hand turning it clockwise to ensure it threads properly, then tighten the nut.
36. After all the components are installed, have the air conditioning system charged by a qualified technician using a recovery/recycling station.

➡On newer model vehicles when the battery is disconnected it may cause some abnormal drive symptoms until the Powertrain Control Module (PCM) relearns its adaptive strategy. The vehicle may need to be driven 10 miles or more for the PCM to relearn its strategy.

37. Refill the cooling system with the proper type and amount of coolant. If necessary, bleed the cooling system.
38. Refill the engine with the proper amount and grade of engine oil.
39. Check all the other vehicle fluids and replenish as necessary.

Rocker Arm (Valve) Covers

REMOVAL & INSTALLATION

4.9L Engine

1. Disconnect the inlet hose at the crankcase filler cap.
2. Remove the throttle body inlet tubes or air cleaner outlet tube.
3. Disconnect the accelerator cable at the throttle body. Remove the cable retracting spring. Remove the accelerator cable bracket from the upper intake manifold and position the cable and bracket out of the way.
4. Remove the fuel line from the fuel rail. Be careful not to kink the line.
5. Remove the upper intake manifold and throttle body assembly.
6. If applicable, remove the PCV valve from the rocker cover and the crankcase vent filter.
7. Lossen the rocker cover retainers.
8. Remove the rocker arm cover.
9. Remove and discard the gasket.
To install:
10. Check the rocker cover bolts for worn or damaged seals under the bolt heads and replace as necessary.
11. Clean the mating surfaces for the cover and head thoroughly.
12. Place the new gasket on the head with the locating tabs downward. The use of gasket sealer is not necessary.
13. Place the cover on the head making sure the gasket is evenly seated. Tighten the bolts for 1989–91 models to 4–7 ft. lbs. (5–9 Nm). For 1992–96 models, tighten the bolts to 70–124 inch lbs. (8–14 Nm).
14. Install the PCV valve.
15. Install the upper intake manifold and throttle body assembly.
16. Connect the fuel line to the fuel rail.
17. Install the accelerator cable bracket at the upper intake manifold. Install the cable retracting spring. Connect the accelerator cable at the throttle body.
18. Install the throttle body inlet tubes or the air cleaner tube.
19. Connect the inlet hose at the crankcase filler cap.

5.0L and 5.8L Engines

1989–93 MODELS

▶ See Figures 1 thru 10

1. Disconnect the negative battery cable.
2. Remove the air cleaner and inlet duct.
3. If equipped, remove the support brackets from the left-hand cover.
4. Tag and disconnect the crankcase ventilation hoses and tubes.
5. Remove the coil and solenoid brackets.
6. On the right cover, remove the lifting eye and Thermactor® tube.
7. On the left cover, remove the oil filler pipe attaching bolt.
8. Tag and disconnect the spark plug wires.
9. Tag and disengage any vacuum lines, wires or hoses that will interfere with the cover removal.
10. Remove the cover bolts and lift off the cover. It may be necessary to break the cover loose by rapping on it with a rubber mallet. NEVER pry the cover off!

Fig. 1 Remove the left-hand bracket assembly retainers . . .

Fig. 2 . . . then remove the bracket

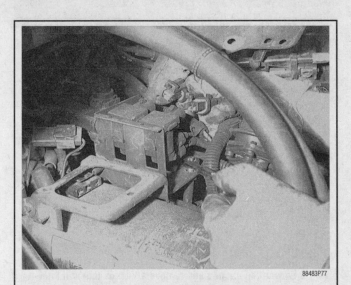
Fig. 3 Loosen the coil and solenoid bracket retainers . . .

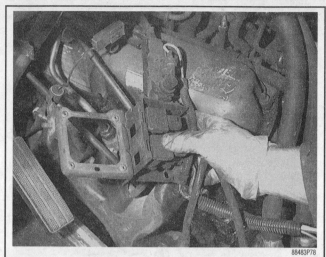

Fig. 4 . . . then slide the coil and solenoid assembly forward . . .

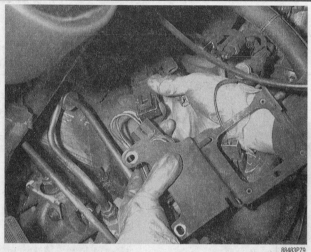

Fig. 5 . . . and disengage the solenoid electrical connections. Remove the bracket assembly

Fig. 6 Loosen the clamps and remove all hoses that will interfere with valve cover removal

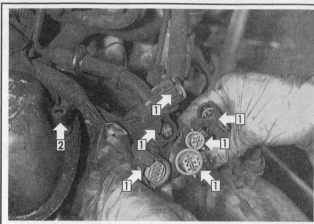

1. Electrical connections
2. Remove the nut retaining the wiring harness to the valve cover

Fig. 7 These wires will hinder valve cover removal, so disconnect them, remove the retaining nut and set them aside

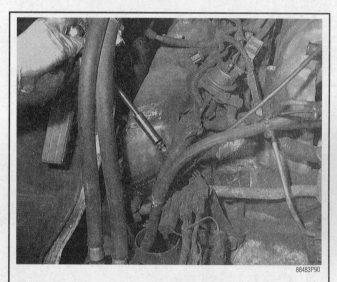

Fig. 8 Loosen the valve cover retaining bolts . . .

Fig. 9 . . . and lift the valve cover up and off the cylinder head to remove it from the engine

Fig. 10 Use a gasket scraper to remove any old material from the valve cover mating surfaces

To install:

11. Thoroughly clean the mating surfaces of both the cover and head.

12. Place the new gasket(s) in the cover(s) with the locating tabs engaging the slots.

13. Place the cover on the head making sure the gasket is evenly seated. Tighten the bolts to 10–13 ft. lbs. (13–17 Nm). After 2 minutes, retighten the bolts to the same specifications.

14. Engage all the vacuum lines, wires and hoses.

15. Connect the spark plug wires.

16. On the right cover, install the lifting eye and Thermactor® tube.

17. On the left cover, install the oil filler pipe attaching bolt.

18. Connect the crankcase ventilation hoses and tubes.

19. Install the coil and solenoids.

20. Install the air cleaner and inlet duct.

21. Connect the negative battery cable.

1994–96 MODELS

▶ See Figure 11

1. Disconnect the negative battery cable.
2. Remove the air cleaner and outlet tube assembly.
3. Remove the oil filler pipe and inside engine cover.

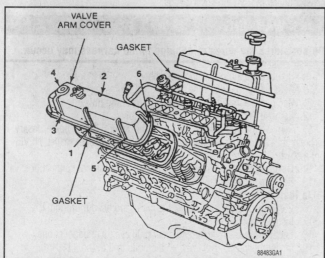

Fig. 11 Rocker arm cover tightening sequence and exploded view of assembly—5.0L and 5.8L engines

4. If equipped with A/C, remove the drive belt, then loosen the compressor retaining bolts and position the unit to one side.

5. Tag and disconnect the spark plug wires.

6. Remove the upper intake manifold.

7. Tag and disengage any vacuum lines, wires or hoses that will interfere with the cover removal.

8. Remove the cover bolts and lift off the cover. It may be necessary to break the cover loose by tapping on it with a rubber mallet. NEVER pry the cover off!

To install:

9. Thoroughly clean the mating surfaces of both the cover and head.

10. Place the new gasket(s) in the cover(s) with the locating tabs engaging the slots.

11. Place the cover on the head making sure the gasket is evenly seated. Tighten the bolts in the indicated sequence to 11–14 ft. lbs. (16–20 Nm). After 2 minutes, retighten the bolts to the same specifications.

12. Install the upper intake manifold.

13. Engage all the vacuum lines, wires and hoses.

14. Connect the spark plug wires.

15. Install the compressor, tighten the retainers, then install the drive belt.

16. Install the engine cover and oil filler pipe.

17. Connect the crankcase ventilation hoses and tubes.

18. Install the air cleaner and outlet tub assembly.

19. Connect the negative battery cable.

7.5L Engine

1989–91 MODELS

1. Disconnect the negative battery cable(s).

2. Remove the air cleaner and intake duct.

3. Remove the Thermactor® exhaust air supply control valve and bracket.

4. Remove the ignition coil bracket and set it aside.

5. Disconnect the MTA hose at the Thermactor® valve.

6. Disconnect the Thermactor® air control valve-to-air pump hose and tube.

7. Mark and remove the spark plug wires.

8. Remove the PCV valve.

9. Tag and disengage any vacuum lines, wires or hoses that interfere with the valve cover removal.

10. Remove the cover bolts and lift off the cover. It may be necessary to break the cover loose by rapping on it with a rubber mallet. NEVER pry the cover off!

To install:

11. Thoroughly clean the mating surfaces of both the cover and head.

12. Place the new cover seal(s) in the cover(s) with the locating tab engaging the slot.

13. Place the cover on the head. Tighten the bolts to 9–11 ft. lbs. (12–15 Nm) from right to left.

14. Install the PCV valve.

15. Engage the vacuum lines, wires and hoses.

16. Install the spark plug wires.

17. Connect the MTA hose at the Thermactor® valve.

18. Connect the Thermactor® air control valve-to-air pump hose and tube.

19. Install the coil mounting bracket.

20. Install the Thermactor® air supply control valve and bracket.

21. Install the air cleaner and inlet duct.

22. Connect the negative battery cable(s).

1992–96 MODELS

1. Disconnect the negative battery cable.

2. Remove the air cleaner and outlet tube.

3. On the right side of the engine, disengage the Thermactor® and bracket. Set them aside.

4. Remove the ignition coil bracket and set it aside.

5. Tag and disconnect the spark plug wires.

6. Remove the PCV valve.

7. Disconnect the oil fill pipe from the left valve cover.

8. Tag and disengage any vacuum lines, wires or hoses that interfere with the valve cover removal.

9. Remove the cover bolts and lift off the cover. It may be necessary to break the cover loose by rapping on it with a rubber mallet. NEVER pry the cover off!

To install:

10. Thoroughly clean the mating surfaces of both the cover and head.

11. Place the new cover seal(s) in the cover(s) with the locating tab engaging the slot.

12. Place the cover on the head. Starting with the rearmost bolt and working forward, tighten the bolts to 9–11 ft. lbs. (12–15 Nm).

13. Install the PCV valve.

14. Engage the vacuum lines, wires and hoses.

15. Install the spark plug wires.

16. Install the coil mounting bracket.

17. Engage the Thermactor® valves, hoses and brackets.

18. Install the air cleaner and outlet tube.

19. Connect the negative battery cable.

➡On newer model vehicles when the battery is disconnected it may cause some abnormal drive symptoms until the Powertrain Control Module (PCM) relearns its adaptive strategy. The vehicle may need to be driven 10 miles or more for the PCM to relearn its strategy.

7.3L Engine

1989–94 MODELS

1. Disconnect both negative battery cables.

2. Remove the fan shroud and the engine cover.

3. On the right-hand valve cover perform the following steps:
   a. Remove the engine oil dipstick tube and valve cover bracket.

4. Remove the transmission filler tube, if applicable.

5. Raise and safely support the front of the vehicle on jackstands.

6. Remove the nuts attaching the right-hand engine mount to the frame.

7. Place a jack under the engine in a suitable location and raise the engine until the fuel filter header touches the vehicle sheet metal. Place a wooden block in the gap and lower the engine so it rests on the block.

8. Lower the vehicle.

9. Remove the cover bolts and lift off the covers. It may be necessary to break the covers loose by rapping on them with a rubber mallet. NEVER pry a cover off!

To install:

10. Clean the mating surfaces of the covers and heads thoroughly, place new gaskets in the covers, position the covers on the heads and tighten the bolts to 6 ft. lbs. (8 Nm).

11. Raise and safely support the front of the vehicle on jackstands.

12. Raise the engine by jacking from a suitable jacking point and remove the wooden block. Install and tighten the engine mount fasteners.

13. Lower the vehicle.

14. Install the transmission filler tube and install the dipstick, if applicable.

15. Install the oil tube and dipstick and valve cover bracket.

16. Install the fan shroud and engine cover.

17. Connect both negative battery cables.

18. Start the van and check for leaks.

1995–96 MODELS—RIGHT COVER

1. Disconnect both negative battery cables.

2. Remove the engine cover and air cleaner assembly.

3. Disengage the alternator electrical connections.

4. Remove the drive belt.

5. Loosen the alternator retaining bolts and remove the alternator from the engine compartment.

6. Loosen the oil level indicator bracket retainer and dipstick.

7. Remove the fuel injector harness clip and disengage the engine harness connectors from the cover gasket.

Do not pierce the wires or damage to the harness may occur.

8. Remove the cover bolts and lift off the covers. It may be necessary to break the covers loose by rapping on them with a rubber mallet. NEVER pry a cover off!

9. Disengage the fuel injector and glow plug electrical connections.

10. Remove the valve cover gasket.

To install:

11. Clean the mating surfaces of the cover and head thoroughly. Install a new gasket.

12. Engage the fuel injector and glow plug electrical connections.

13. Install the valve cover. Tighten the bolts to 8 ft. lbs. (11 Nm).

14. Install the fuel injector harness to the valve cover and engage the harness clip.

15. Install the oil tube and tighten the retainer, then insert the dipstick.

16. Install the alternator.

17. Install the drive belt and engage the alternator electrical connections.

18. Install the air cleaner assembly.

19. Connect both negative battery cables.

20. Start the van and check for leaks.

21. Install the engine cover.

1995–96 MODELS—LEFT COVER

1. Disconnect both negative battery cables.

2. Remove the air cleaner assembly.

Please refer to Section 1 before discharging the compressor or disconnecting air conditioning lines. Damage to the air conditioning system or personal injury could result. Consult your local laws concerning refrigerant discharge and recycling. In many areas it may be illegal for anyone but a certified technician to service the A/C system. Always use an approved recovery station when discharging the air conditioning.

3. Have the A/C system discharged be a qualified technician using an approved recovery/recycling station.

4. Disengage the A/C compressor electrical connections.

5. Disconnect the manifold lines from the compressor.

6. Loosen the compressor bracket retaining bolts and remove the bracket and compressor as a unit.

7. Remove the engine cover.

8. Remove the fuel injector harness clip and disengage the engine harness connectors from the cover gasket.

Do not pierce the wires or damage to the harness may occur.

9. Remove the air intake duct assembly.

10. Remove the oil filler tube.

11. Remove the intake duct bracket and retaining nuts.

12. Remove the crankcase breather assembly.

13. Remove the cover bolts and lift off the covers. It may be necessary to break the covers loose by rapping on them with a rubber mallet. NEVER pry a cover off!

14. Disengage the fuel injector and glow plug electrical connections.

15. Remove the valve cover gasket.

To install:

16. Clean the mating surfaces of the cover and head thoroughly.

17. Install a new gasket.

18. Engage the fuel injector and glow plug electrical connections.

19. Install the valve cover. Tighten the bolts to 8 ft. lbs. (11 Nm).

20. Install the fuel injector harness to the valve cover and engage the harness clip.

21. Install the intake duct tube bracket and retaining nuts. Install the rear nut from the inside of the van and the front nut from outside.

22. Install the engine oil tube, tighten the retainer and insert the dipstick.

23. Install the crankcase breather assembly.

24. Install the intake duct tube assembly.

25. Install the A/C compressor and bracket, tighten the retainers and engage the manifold lines.

26. Engage the compressor electrical connections.

27. Have the system recharged by a qualified technician using an approved recovery/recycling station.

28. Connect both negative battery cables.

29. Start the van and check for leaks.

30. Install the engine cover.

Rocker Arms

REMOVAL & INSTALLATION

4.9L Engine

▶ See Figure 12

1. Remove the rocker arm cover.
2. Loosen the rocker arm bolt, and rocker arm. If removing a pair of rocker arms, also remove the fulcrum guide.

To install:

3. Apply multi-purpose grease such as DOAZ–19584–AA or its equivalent to the top of the valve stems.
4. Apply multi-purpose grease such as DOAZ–19584–AA or its equivalent to the rocker arm seat, fulcrum guide and seat socket in the rocker arm.
5. If removed install the fulcrum guide.
6. Engage the rocker arms and tighten the rocker arm bolts enough to hold the pushrods in place.
7. Adjust the valve clearance as outlined in Section 1.
8. Install the rocker arm cover.

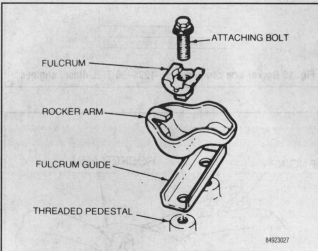

FULCRUM

ROCKER ARM

FULCRUM GUIDE

ATTACHING BOLT

THREADED PEDESTAL

84923027

Fig. 12 Exploded view of rocker arm assembly—4.9L, 5.0L, 5.8L and 7.5L engines

5.0L and 5.8L Engines

▶ See Figures 12 and 13

1. Remove the rocker arm cover.
2. Loosen the rocker arm bolt, and rocker arm. If removing a pair of rocker arms, also remove the fulcrum guide.

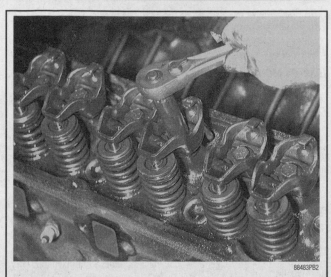

88483PB2

Fig. 13 Loosen the rocker arm bolt—5.8L engine shown

To install:

3. Apply multi-purpose grease such as DOAZ–19584–AA or its equivalent to the top of the valve stems.
4. Apply multi-purpose grease such as DOAZ–19584–AA or its equivalent to the rocker arm seat, fulcrum guide and seat socket in the rocker arm.
5. Install the fulcrum guides, rocker arms, seats and bolts. Tighten the bolts to 18–25 ft. lbs. (24–34 Nm).
6. Install the rocker arm covers.

7.5L Engine

▶ See Figure 12

1. Remove the rocker arm covers.
2. Loosen the rocker arm fulcrum bolts, fulcrum, oil deflector (if equipped), seat and rocker arms. KEEP EVERYTHING IN ORDER FOR INSTALLATION!

To install:

3. Apply multi-purpose grease such as DOAZ–19584–AA or its equivalent to the top of the valve stems.
4. Apply multi-purpose grease such as DOAZ–19584–AA or its equivalent to the rocker arm seat, fulcrum guide and seat socket in the rocker arm.
5. Rotate the crankshaft by hand until No. 1 piston is at TDC of compression. The firing order marks on the damper will be aligned at TDC with the timing pointer.
6. Install the rocker arms, seats, deflectors and bolts on the following valves:
- No. 1 intake and exhaust
- No. 3 intake
- No. 8 exhaust
- No. 7 intake
- No. 5 exhaust
- No. 8 intake
- No. 4 exhaust

Engage the rocker arms with the pushrods and tighten the rocker arm fulcrum bolts to 18–25 ft. lbs. (25–33 Nm).

7. Rotate the crankshaft one full turn (360°) and re-align the TDC mark and pointer. Install the parts and tighten the bolts on the following valves:
- No. 2 intake and exhaust
- No. 4 intake
- No. 3 exhaust
- No. 5 intake
- No. 6 exhaust
- No. 6 intake
- No. 7 exhaust

Engage the rocker arms with the pushrods and tighten the rocker arm fulcrum bolts to 18–25 ft. lbs. (25–33 Nm).

8. Check the valve clearance as outlined in Section 1.
9. Install the rocker arm covers.

Diesel Engines

1989–94 MODELS

▶ **See Figures 14 and 15**

1. Disconnect both negative battery cables.
2. Remove both valve covers.
3. Remove the valve rocker arm post mounting bolts. Remove the rocker arms and posts in order and mark them with tape so they can be installed in their original positions.

To install:

4. Apply multi-purpose grease such as DOAZ–19584–AA or its equivalent to the valve stem tips.
5. Install the rocker arms and posts in their original positions.
6. Turn the engine over by hand until the valve timing mark is at the 11 o'clock position, as viewed from the front of the engine.
7. Install all of the rocker arm post attaching bolts and tighten to 20 ft. lbs. (27 Nm).
8. Install new valve cover gaskets and install the valve cover.

9. Connect both battery cables, start the engine and check for leaks.

1995–96 MODELS

▶ **See Figures 16, 17, 18 and 19**

1. Disconnect both negative battery cables.
2. Remove both valve covers.
3. Loosen the rocker arm bolts, then remove the assembly.
4. Disengage the snap retaining clip, then remove the rocker arm and steel ball from the rocker arm pedestal.

➡ **Be careful when removing the rocker arm snap retaining clip. Do not loose the steel ball.**

To install:

5. Assemble the rocker arm assembly as follows:
  a. Insert the steel ball in the rocker arm cup and lubricate them with engine oil.
  b. Place the rocker arm pedestal on the steel ball.
  c. Install the snap retaining clip over the pedestal groove.
6. If removed, lubricate the ends of the pushrods with engine oil and install then copper end up.

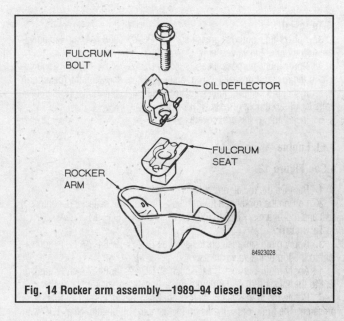

Fig. 14 Rocker arm assembly—1989–94 diesel engines

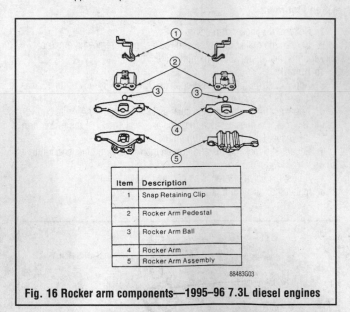

Item	Description
1	Snap Retaining Clip
2	Rocker Arm Pedestal
3	Rocker Arm Ball
4	Rocker Arm
5	Rocker Arm Assembly

Fig. 16 Rocker arm components—1995–96 7.3L diesel engines

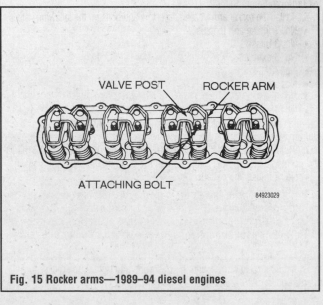

Fig. 15 Rocker arms—1989–94 diesel engines

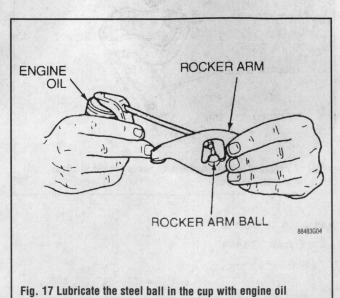

Fig. 17 Lubricate the steel ball in the cup with engine oil

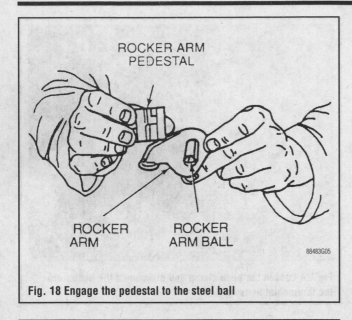

Fig. 18 Engage the pedestal to the steel ball

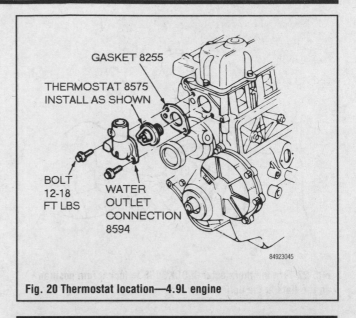

Fig. 20 Thermostat location—4.9L engine

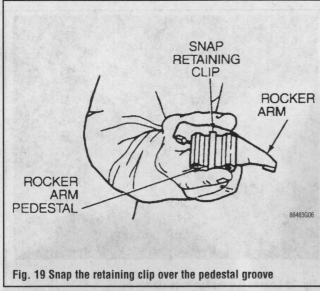

Fig. 19 Snap the retaining clip over the pedestal groove

7. Turn the engine over by hand until the valve timing mark is at the 11 o'clock position, as viewed from the front of the engine.

8. Install the rocker arm assembly and tighten the bolts to 20 ft. lbs. (27 Nm).

9. Install new valve cover gaskets and install the valve cover.

10. Connect both battery cables, start the engine and check for leaks.

Thermostat

REMOVAL & INSTALLATION

➡It is a good practice to check the operation of a new thermostat before it is installed in an engine. Place the thermostat in a pan of boiling water. If it does not open more than ¼ in. (6mm), do not install it in the engine.

4.9L Engine

♦ See Figure 20

1. Drain the cooling system below the level of the coolant outlet housing. Use the petcock valve at the bottom of the radiator to drain the system. It is not necessary to remove any of the hoses.

❋❋ CAUTION

When draining the coolant, keep in mind that cats and dogs are attracted by ethylene glycol antifreeze and are quite likely to drink any that is left in an uncovered container or in puddles on the ground. This will prove fatal in sufficient quantity. Always drain the coolant into a sealable container. Coolant should be reused unless it is contaminated or several years old.

2. Remove the coolant outlet housing retaining bolts and slide the housing with the hose attached to one side.

3. Remove the thermostat and gasket from the cylinder head and clean both mating surfaces.

To install:

4. Coat a new gasket with water resistant sealer and position it on the outlet of the engine.

➡The gasket must be in place before the thermostat is installed.

5. Install the thermostat with the bridge (opposite end of the spring) inside the elbow connection. Turn the thermostat clockwise to engage it in position on the flats cast into the outlet elbow.

6. Position the elbow connection onto the mounting surface of the outlet, so that the thermostat flange is resting on the gasket and install the retaining bolts. Tighten the bolts to 12–15 ft. lbs. (17–20 Nm).

7. Fill the radiator and operate the engine until it reaches operating temperature. Check the coolant level and adjust if necessary.

5.0L, 5.8L and 7.5L Engines

♦ See Figures 22 thru 32

1. Drain the cooling system below the level of the coolant outlet housing. Use the petcock valve at the bottom of the radiator to drain the system. It is not necessary to remove any of the hoses.

❋❋ CAUTION

When draining the coolant, keep in mind that cats and dogs are attracted by ethylene glycol antifreeze and are quite likely to drink any that is left in an uncovered container or in puddles on the ground. This will prove fatal in sufficient quantity. Always drain the coolant into a sealable container. Coolant should be reused unless it is contaminated or several years old.

2. Disconnect the bypass hoses at the water pump and intake manifold.

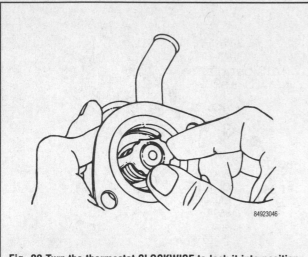

Fig. 22 Turn the thermostat CLOCKWISE to lock it into position on the flats in the outlet elbow

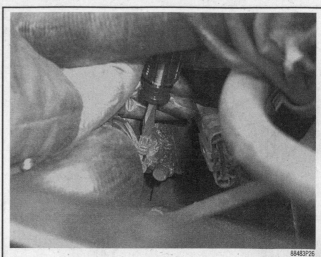

Fig. 24 Loosen the hose clamp and disconnect the hose from the thermostat housing

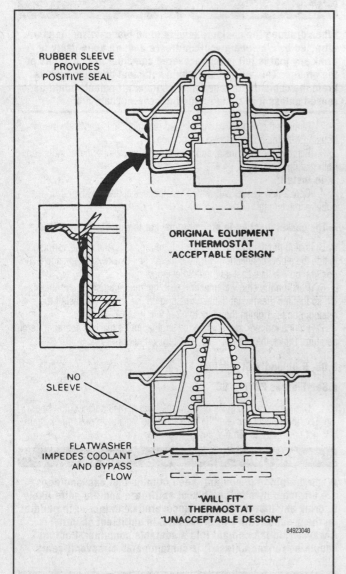

RUBBER SLEEVE PROVIDES POSITIVE SEAL

ORIGINAL EQUIPMENT THERMOSTAT "ACCEPTABLE DESIGN"

NO SLEEVE

FLATWASHER IMPEDES COOLANT AND BYPASS FLOW

"WILL FIT" THERMOSTAT "UNACCEPTABLE DESIGN"

Fig. 23 Be sure that the replacement thermostat is of an acceptable design

Fig. 25 Loosen the bypass hose clamp . . .

Fig. 26 . . . then disconnect the bypass hose from the water pump

Fig. 27 Loosen the thermostat housing retaining bolts

Fig. 30 Use a scraper to clean the gasket mating surfaces

1. Thermostat   2. Thermostat housing

Fig. 28 Remove the housing from the engine block

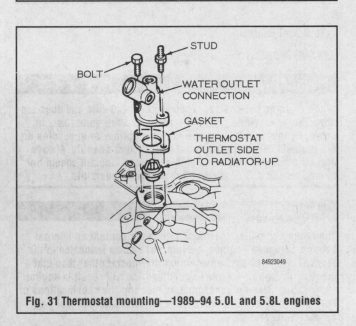

STUD
BOLT
WATER OUTLET CONNECTION
GASKET
THERMOSTAT OUTLET SIDE TO RADIATOR-UP

Fig. 31 Thermostat mounting—1989–94 5.0L and 5.8L engines

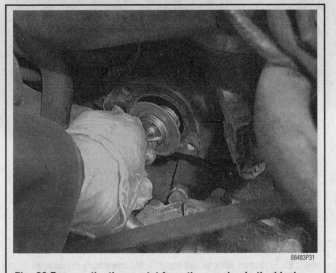

Fig. 29 Remove the thermostat from the opening in the block

3. Remove the bypass tube.
4. Remove the coolant outlet housing retaining bolts, bend the hose and lift the housing with the hose attached to one side.
5. Remove the thermostat and gasket from the intake manifold and clean both mating surfaces.

To install:

6. Install the thermostat on the 5.0L and 5.8L engines as follows:
   a. Coat a new gasket with water resistant sealer and position it on the outlet of the engine.

➡**The gasket must be in place before the thermostat is installed.**

   b. Install the thermostat with the bridge (opposite end of the spring) inside the elbow connection and the thermostat flange positioned in the recess in the manifold. Tighten the bolts to 12–18 ft. lbs. (17–24 Nm).
7. Install the thermostat on the 7.5L engine as follows:
   a. Install the thermostat in the recess, then coat the gasket with a water resistant sealer and position the gasket on top of the thermostat.
   b. Position the elbow connection onto the mounting surface of the outlet.
   c. Tighten the mounting bolts to 23–28 ft. lbs. (32–37 Nm).
8. Install the bypass tube and hoses.
9. Fill the radiator and operate the engine until it reaches operating temperature. Check the coolant level and adjust if necessary.

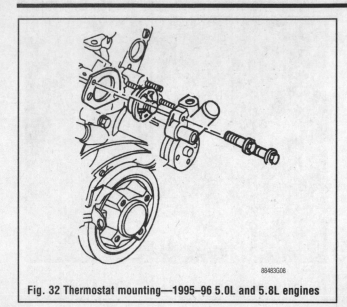

Fig. 32 Thermostat mounting—1995–96 5.0L and 5.8L engines

7.3L Diesel Engines

1987–93 MODELS

> **※※ CAUTION**
>
> When draining the coolant, keep in mind that cats and dogs are attracted by ethylene glycol antifreeze and are quite likely to drink any that is left in an uncovered container or in puddles on the ground. This will prove fatal in sufficient quantity. Always drain the coolant into a sealable container. Coolant should be reused unless it is contaminated or several years old.

> **※※ WARNING**
>
> The factory specified thermostat does not contain an internal bypass. On these engines, an internal bypass is located in the block. The use of any replacement thermostat other than that meeting the manufacturer's specifications will result in engine overheating! Use only thermostats meeting the specifications of Ford part number E5TZ–8575–C or Navistar International part number 1807945–C1.

1. Disconnect both negative battery cables.
2. Drain the coolant to a point below the thermostat housing.
3. Remove the alternator and vacuum pump belt(s).
4. Remove the alternator.
5. Remove the vacuum pump and bracket.
6. Remove all but the lowest vacuum pump/alternator mounting casting bolt.
7. Loosen that lowest bolt and pivot the casting outboard of the engine.
8. Remove the thermostat housing attaching bolts, bend the hose and lift the housing up and to one side.
9. Remove the thermostat and gasket.

To install:

10. Clean the thermostat housing and block surfaces thoroughly.
11. Coat a new gasket with waterproof sealer and position the gasket on the manifold outlet opening.
12. Install the thermostat in the manifold opening with the spring element end downward and the flange positioned in the recess in the manifold.
13. Place the outlet housing into position and install the bolts. Tighten the bolts to 20 ft. lbs. (27 Nm).
14. Reposition the casting.
15. Install the vacuum pump and bracket.

16. Install the alternator.
17. Adjust the drive belt(s).
18. Fill and bleed the cooling system.
19. Connect both battery cables.
20. Run the engine and check for leaks.

1994 MODELS

1. Disconnect both negative battery cables.
2. Drain the coolant to a point below the thermostat housing.
3. Remove the drive belt.
4. Remove the alternator.
5. Disconnect the upper radiator hose.
6. Remove the thermostat housing, its O-ring and the thermostat.

To install:

7. Install the thermostat and the thermostat housing O-ring in the hose connection.
8. Place the outlet housing into position and install the screws. Tighten the retainers to 20 ft. lbs. (27 Nm).
9. Install the upper radiator hose.
10. Install the alternator.
11. Install the drive belt.
12. Fill and bleed the cooling system.
13. Connect both battery cables.
14. Run the engine and check for leaks.

1995–96 MODELS

▶ See Figure 33

1. Disconnect both negative battery cables.
2. Drain the coolant to a point below the thermostat housing.
3. Remove the drive belt.
4. Disconnect the upper radiator hose.
5. Remove the thermostat housing retaining screws and the water hose connection.
6. Remove the thermostat housing, its O-ring and the thermostat.

To install:

7. Install the thermostat and the thermostat housing O-ring in the hose connection.
8. Engage the water hose connection, then place the outlet housing into position and tighten the retainers to 15 ft. lbs. (20 Nm).
9. Install the upper radiator hose.
10. Install the drive belt.
11. Fill and bleed the cooling system.
12. Connect both battery cables.
13. Run the engine and check for leaks.

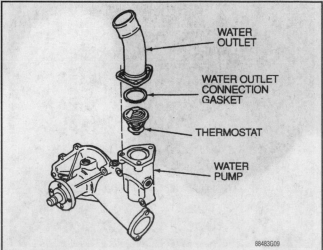

Fig. 33 Exploded view of the thermostat assembly—1995–96 diesel engines

Intake Manifold

REMOVAL & INSTALLATION

1989–93 4.9L Engine

The intake and exhaust manifolds on these engines are sometimes known as "combination manifolds" and are serviced as a unit. Typically, these manifolds are not referred to as a combination manifold, but since the lower intake and exhaust manifolds share the same bolts, and removal of either one requires removal of the other, we will refer to them as such. Refer to the Combination Manifold Removal & Installation procedure later in this section.

1994–96 4.9L Engine

UPPER INTAKE MANIFOLD

▶ See Figure 34

1. Disconnect the negative battery cable.
2. Tag and disengage the electrical connectors from the following components:
   - EGR external pressure valve
   - Throttle Position (TP) sensor
   - Idle Air Control (IAC) valve
   - EGR transducer
3. Tag and disengage the vacuum connections and hoses from the following components:
   - EGR external pressure valve
   - Evaporative emissions (EVAP) system hose from the throttle body and canister purge valve
   - Vacuum lines to the upper intake manifold
4. Tag and disengage the EGR transducer hoses, unfasten the retaining screws, then remove the transducer and bracket.
5. Disconnect the PCV hose from the fitting on the underside of the manifold.

✳✳ CAUTION

When disconnecting the throttle cable ball stud, use a prytool close to the ball stud to pry it off. Never remove the cable by hand, as this may cause damage.

6. Remove the throttle control splash shield.
7. Disconnect the throttle linkage and speed control actuator cable, position the loose cable out of the way.

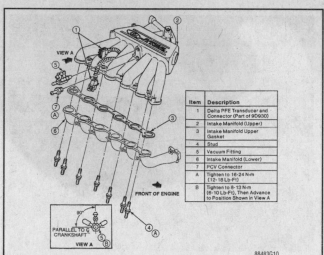

Fig. 34 Exploded view of the upper intake manifold assembly— 1994–96 4.9L engine; 1996 model shown (others similar)

8. Disconnect the air cleaner outlet tube from the throttle body.
9. Disconnect the EGR valve-to-exhaust manifold tube from the EGR external pressure valve and rear exhaust manifold.
10. Remove the EGR valve-to-exhaust manifold tube.
11. Remove the secondary air tube bypass assembly from the lower intake manifold as follows:
    a. Loosen the two retaining nuts.
    b. Loosen the nut attaching the valve bracket to the lower intake manifold.
12. If applicable, disconnect any other component that interferes with the removal.
13. Remove the screw and washer retaining the intake manifold support to the upper intake manifold.
14. Loosen the seven studs retaining the upper manifold.
15. Remove the upper manifold and throttle body as an assembly from the lower manifold.

To install:

16. Clean the mating surfaces as necessary and install a new gasket on the lower manifold half. Position the gasket correctly on the dowels.
17. Install the upper manifold onto the lower manifold, again using the dowels to locate the manifold halves together. Install the seven studs and hand tighten them.
18. Tighten the seven studs to 12–18 ft. lbs. (16–24 Nm).
19. Position the upper intake manifold support onto the boss of the upper intake located under the throttle body. install the screws, tightening them to 22–32 ft. lbs. (30–43 Nm).
20. Install the EGR valve-to-exhaust manifold tube between the external pressure valve and the rear exhaust manifold. The tube should be routed between the No. 5 and No. 6 lower intake runners, located under the throttle body.
21. Tighten both fittings to 25–35 ft. lbs. (34–47 Nm).
22. Connect the PCV hose to the fitting on the valve cover under the upper intake manifold plenum.
23. Install the secondary air bypass tube assembly onto the studs of the lower intake manifold. Tighten the nuts to 8–12 ft. lbs. (11–16 Nm).
24. Connect the accelerator cable, transmission kickdown cable and the speed control actuator, then install the splash shield.
25. Connect the air cleaner outlet tube to the throttle body.
26. Install the EGR transducer, tighten the retainers to 12–18 ft. lbs. (17–24 Nm) and connect the hoses.
27. Engage the vacuum connections and hoses to the following components:
    - EGR external pressure valve
    - Evaporative emissions (EVAP) system hose to the throttle body and canister purge valve
    - Vacuum lines to the upper intake manifold
28. Engage the electrical connectors to the following components:
    - EGR external pressure valve
    - Throttle Position (TP) sensor
    - Idle Air Control (IAC) valve
    - EGR transducer
29. Connect the negative battery cable.

LOWER INTAKE MANIFOLD

The lower intake manifold and exhaust manifolds for the 1994–96 4.9L engine must be removed together. To remove the lower intake manifold, refer to the appropriate Combination Manifold Removal & Installation procedure.

5.0L, 5.8L and 7.5L Engines

➡**Discharge the fuel system pressure before starting any work that involves disconnecting fuel system lines. Refer to Section 5.**

UPPER INTAKE MANIFOLD

▶ See Figures 35 thru 44

1. Disconnect the negative battery cable.
2. Remove the air cleaner assembly from the upper intake manifold.

✳✳ CAUTION

When draining the coolant, keep in mind that cats and dogs are attracted by ethylene glycol antifreeze and are quite likely to drink any that is left in an uncovered container or in puddles on the ground. This will prove fatal in sufficient quantity. Always drain the coolant into a sealable container. Coolant should be reused unless it is contaminated or several years old.

3. Drain the cooling system.

4. Disengage the electrical connectors at the idle air control valve, throttle position sensor and EGR position sensor.

5. Disconnect the throttle linkage at the throttle ball and the transmission linkage from the throttle body.

6. Loosen the bolts that secure the bracket to the intake and position the bracket and cables out of the way.

7. Tag and disengage the upper manifold vacuum fitting connections by removing all the vacuum lines at the vacuum tree (label lines for position identification).

8. Disconnect the vacuum lines to the EGR external pressure valve and fuel pressure regulator.

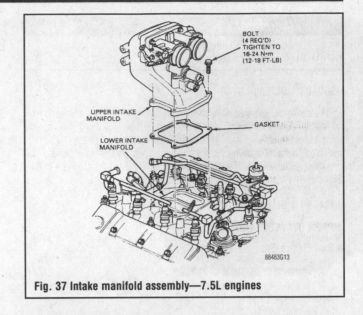

Fig. 37 Intake manifold assembly—7.5L engines

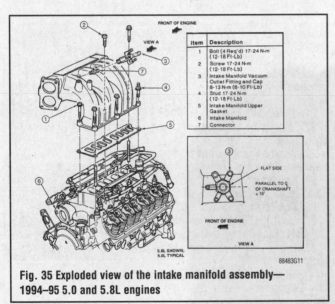

Fig. 35 Exploded view of the intake manifold assembly—1994–95 5.0 and 5.8L engines

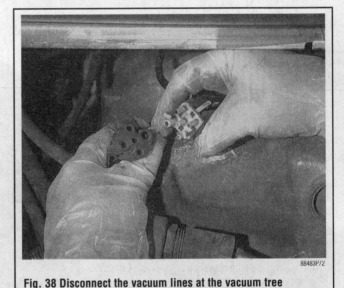

Fig. 38 Disconnect the vacuum lines at the vacuum tree

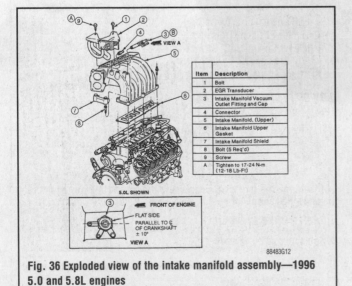

Fig. 36 Exploded view of the intake manifold assembly—1996 5.0 and 5.8L engines

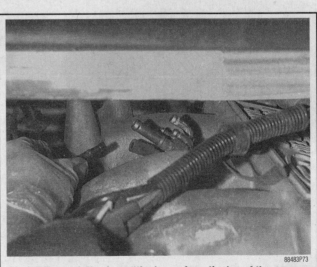

Fig. 39 Tag and disconnect the hoses from the top of the upper intake manifold

9. Disconnect the PCV system by disconnecting the hose from the fitting at the rear of the upper manifold.

10. Disconnect the oil filler pipe.

11. If necessary, remove the EGR transducer by loosening the retainers and disengaging it from the bracket.

12. If equipped, disconnect the two canister purge lines from the fittings at the throttle body.

13. Place a suitable container under the van and disconnect the water heater lines from the throttle body.

14. Disconnect the EGR tube from the EGR external pressure valve by loosening the flange nut.

15. If applicable, disconnect any other component that interferes with the removal.

16. Remove the bolt from the upper intake support bracket to upper manifold.

➡On some 5.0L engines it may be necessary to remove the intake manifold shield before removing the upper intake manifold assembly.

17. Loosen the upper manifold retaining bolts and remove the upper intake manifold and throttle body as an assembly.

18. Clean and inspect all mounting surfaces of the upper and lower intake manifolds.

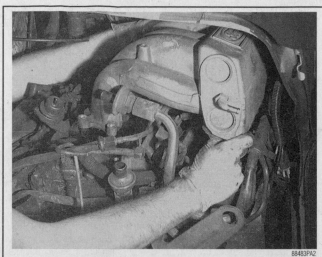

Fig. 42 Lift the upper intake manifold up so that it clears the hoses, pipes and other obstructions . . .

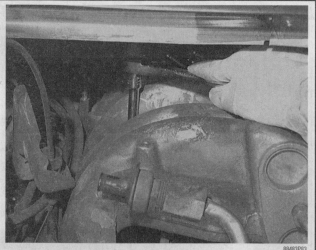

Fig. 40 Unfasten the upper intake manifold center mounting bolts . . .

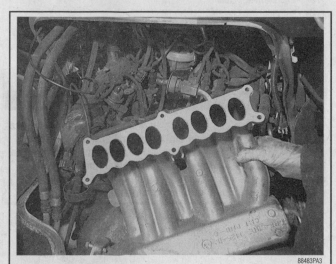

Fig. 43 . . . then remove the manifold from the engine compartment

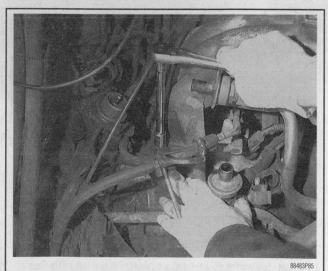

Fig. 41 . . . and the lower mounting bolts

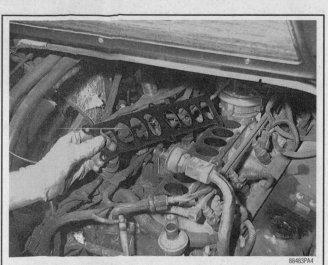

Fig. 44 Remove the upper intake manifold gasket from the lower intake manifold

To install:

19. Position a new mounting gasket on the lower intake manifold.

20. Install the intake manifold shield on the 5.0L models, if applicable.

21. If the EGR transducer was removed, tighten the retainers to 9–12 ft. lbs. (12–16 Nm) on the 5.0L and 12–18 ft. lbs. (17–24 Nm) on 5.8L engines.

22. Install the upper intake manifold and throttle body as an assembly. Install the upper manifold retaining bolts and install the bolt at the upper intake support bracket. Mounting bolts are tightened to 12–18 ft. lbs. (16–24 Nm).

23. Install the lower intake support bracket to the upper manifold attaching bolt.

24. Connect the EGR tube at the EGR valve.

25. Install the two canister purge lines at the fittings at the throttle body.

26. Connect the PCV system hose at the fitting at the rear of the upper manifold.

27. Connect the upper manifold vacuum lines at the vacuum tree. Install the vacuum lines at the EGR valve and fuel pressure regulator.

28. Install the throttle bracket on the intake manifold. Connect the throttle linkage and the transmission linkage at the throttle body.

29. Engage the electrical connectors at the air bypass valve, throttle position sensor and EGR position sensor.

30. Install the air cleaner.

31. Connect the negative battery cable.

LOWER INTAKE MANIFOLD

▶ See Figures 45 thru 53

1. Remove the upper manifold and throttle body.

❊❊ CAUTION

When draining the coolant, keep in mind that cats and dogs are attracted by ethylene glycol antifreeze and are quite likely to drink any that is left in an uncovered container or in puddles on the ground. This will prove fatal in sufficient quantity. Always drain the coolant into a sealable container. Coolant should be reused unless it is contaminated or several years old.

2. Drain the cooling system.

3. Remove the distributor assembly, cap and wires.

4. Disengage the electrical connectors at the engine as applicable, including the Engine Coolant Temperature (ECT) sensor, engine temperature sending unit, Air Charge Temperature (ACT) sensor, Intake Air Temperature (IAT) sensor, Electrical Vacuum Regulator (EVR), thermactor solenoids and Knock Sensor (KS).

Fig. 46 Unfasten the wiring harness retainers

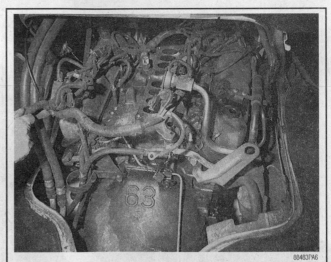

Fig. 47 Move the wiring harness aside to gain access to the manifold bolts

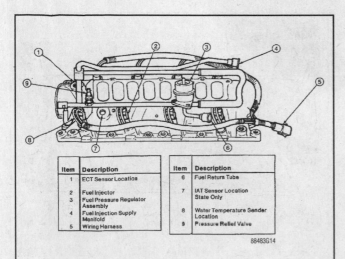

Item	Description
1	ECT Sensor Location
2	Fuel Injector
3	Fuel Pressure Regulator Assembly
4	Fuel Injection Supply Manifold
5	Wiring Harness

Item	Description
6	Fuel Return Tube
7	IAT Sensor Location State Only
8	Water Temperature Sender Location
9	Pressure Relief Valve

Fig. 45 Lower intake manifold assembly—5.0L and 5.8L MFI engines

Fig. 48 Loosen the lower intake manifold retaining bolts and studs

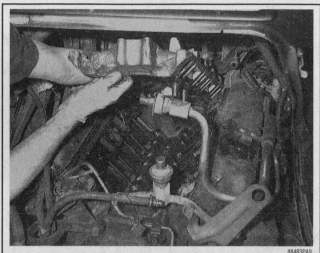

Fig. 49 Remove the lower intake manifold from the engine assembly

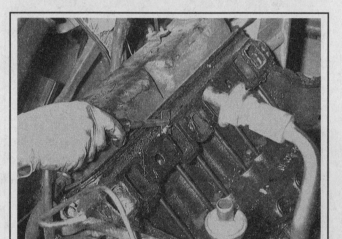

Fig. 50 Use a scraper to remove any gasket material left on the mating surfaces

17. Loosen the intake manifold mounting bolts and studs. Pay attention to the location of the bolts and studs for reinstallation.

18. Remove the lower intake manifold assembly.

To install:

19. Clean and inspect the mounting surfaces of the heads and manifold.

20. Apply a 1/16 in. (1.5mm) bead of RTV sealer to the ends of the manifold seal (the junction point of the seals and gaskets).

➡ **The gaskets must be interlocked with the seal tabs**

21. Install the end seals and intake gaskets on the cylinder heads.

22. Install locator pins at opposite ends of each head and carefully lower the intake manifold into position.

23. On 1989–93 models, install and tighten the mounting bolts and studs to 23–25 ft. lbs. (32–33 Nm) in the sequence illustrated. Wait ten minutes and retighten the retainers to the same specification.

24. On 1994–95 models, install and tighten the mounting bolts and studs in the sequence illustrated and in the following steps:
   a. First pass: 8 ft. lbs. (11 Nm)
   b. Second pass: 16 ft. lbs. (22 Nm)
   c. Final pass: 23–25 ft. lbs. (31–34 Nm)

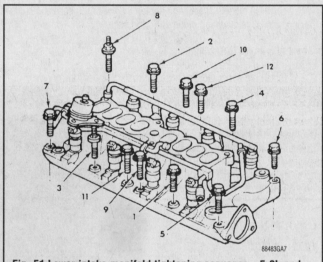

Fig. 51 Lower intake manifold tightening sequence—5.0L and 5.8L EFI engines

5. If equipped, disengage the radio interference capacitor.

6. If equipped, disengage the electrical connector and vacuum harness from the EGR regulator solenoid.

7. If equipped, disengage the electrical connector and vacuum harness from the secondary air injection vacuum regulator solenoid.

8. Disconnect the injector wiring harness from the main harness assembly.

9. If necessary, remove the wiring harness retainers and move the harness aside for clearance.

10. Remove the oxygen sensor ground wire from the intake manifold stud.

➡ **The ground wire must be installed at the same position it was removed from.**

11. Relieve the fuel system pressure.

12. Disconnect the fuel supply and return lines from the fuel rails.

13. Remove the upper radiator hose from the thermostat housing.

14. Remove the water bypass hose.

15. Remove the heater outlet hose at the intake manifold.

16. Loosen the coil bracket retaining nut and set the bracket assembly aside.

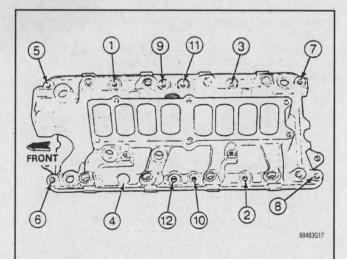

Fig. 52 Lower intake manifold torque sequence—5.0L and 5.8L MFI engines

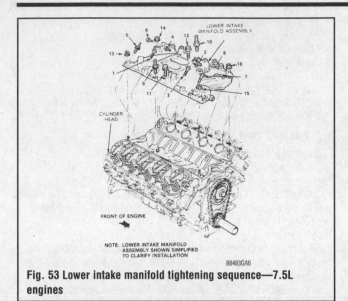

Fig. 53 Lower intake manifold tightening sequence—7.5L engines

25. On 1996 models, install and tighten the mounting bolts and studs in the sequence illustrated and in the following steps:
 a. First pass: 5–10 ft. lbs. (7–14 Nm)
 b. Final pass: 23–25 ft. lbs. (31–34 Nm)
26. Install the coil mounting bracket.
27. Install the upper radiator hose and water bypass tube or hose.
28. Install the heater outlet hose at the intake manifold.
29. Connect the fuel supply and return lines at the fuel rails.
30. Connect the injector wiring harness from the main harness assembly. Install the ground wire from the intake manifold stud.
31. Engage the applicable electrical connectors and vacuum hoses to the engine's sensors, sending units and solenoids.
32. Engage the radio ignition interference capacitor connector.
33. Install the distributor assembly, cap and wires.
34. Fill the cooling system.

7.3L Diesel Engines

1989–94 MODELS

▶ See Figures 54 and 55

1. Disconnect both negative battery cables.
2. Remove the engine cover.
3. Remove the air cleaner and install clean rags into the air intake of the intake manifold. It is important that no dirt or foreign objects get into the diesel intake.
4. Disconnect the fuel inlet and return lines from the fuel filter.
5. Loosen the fuel filter attaching bolts, then remove the filter and bracket assembly.
6. Remove the injection pump as described in Section 5 under Diesel Fuel System.
7. Tag and disengage the glow plug harness and the controller.
8. Label the positions of the wires and remove the engine wiring harness from the engine.

➡The engine harness ground cables must be removed from the back of the left cylinder head.

9. If applicable, disconnect any other component that interferes with the removal.
10. Remove the bolts attaching the intake manifold to the cylinder heads and remove the manifold.
11. Remove the CDR tube grommet from the valley pan.
12. Remove the bolts attaching the valley pan strap to the front of the engine block and remove the strap.
13. Remove the valley pan drain plug and remove the valley pan.

To install:
14. Clean all the mating surfaces.
15. Apply a ⅛ in. (3mm) bead of RTV sealer to each end of the cylinder block as shown in the accompanying illustration.

➡The RTV sealer should be applied immediately prior to the valley pan installation.

16. Install the valley pan drain plug, CDR tube and new grommet into the valley pan.
17. Install a new O-ring and new back-up ring on the CDR valve.
18. Install the valley pan strap on the front of the valley pan.
19. Install the intake manifold and tighten the bolts to 24 ft. lbs. (32 Nm) using the sequence shown in the illustration.
20. Reconnect the engine wiring harness and the engine ground wire located to the rear of the left cylinder head.
21. Install the glow plug controller and wiring.
22. Install the injection pump using the procedure outlined in Section 5 under Diesel Fuel System.
23. Install the fuel filter and bracket, then tighten the retainers to 24–39 ft. lbs. (33–52 Nm).
24. Connect the fuel return and inlet lines.

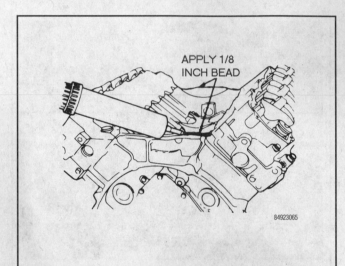

Fig. 54 Apply sealer to the diesel cylinder block-to-intake manifold mating surfaces on each end

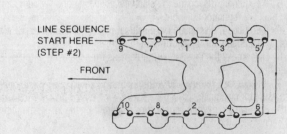

STEP 1. TORQUE BOLTS TO 33 N·m (24 lbf-ft), IN NUMBERED SEQUENCE SHOWN ABOVE
STEP 2. TORQUE BOLTS TO 33 N·m (24 lbf-ft), IN LINE SEQUENCE SHOWN ABOVE.

Fig. 55 Diesel engine intake manifold bolt tightening sequence—1989–94 engines

25. Remove the rag from the intake manifold and replace the air cleaner. Connect both negative battery cables to both batteries.

26. Run the engine and check for oil and fuel leaks.

➡ **If necessary, purge the nozzle high pressure lines of air by loosening the connector one half to one turn and cranking the engine until solid stream of fuel, devoid of any bubbles, flows from the connection.**

✳✳ CAUTION

Keep eyes and hands away from the nozzle spray. Fuel spraying from the nozzle under high pressure can penetrate the skin.

27. Check and adjust the injection pump timing, as described in Section 5 under Diesel Fuel System.

1995–96 MODELS

▶ See Figure 56

1. Loosen the intake manifold hose clamps and the clamp retaining the compressor manifold to the turbocharger.

2. On the left cylinder head it may be necessary to remove the turbocharger.

3. Remove the compressor manifold.

4. Loosen the clamps and remove the intake manifold hoses.

5. Loosen the intake manifold cover retainers and remove the covers.

6. Installation is the reverse of removal. Tighten the intake manifold cover bolts to 18 ft. lbs. (24 Nm).

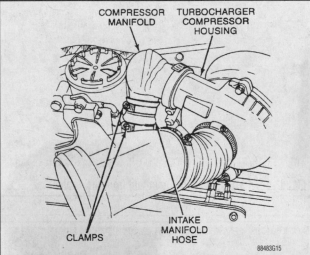

Fig. 56 Loosen the clamps and disconnect the compressor manifold and intake manifold hoses

Exhaust Manifold

REMOVAL & INSTALLATION

4.9L Engine

The intake and exhaust manifolds on these engines are sometimes known as "combination manifolds" and are serviced as a unit. Typically, these manifolds are not referred to as a combination manifold, but since the lower intake and exhaust manifolds share the same bolts, and removal of either one requires removal of the other, we will refer to them as such. Refer to the Combination Manifold Removal & Installation procedure later in this section.

5.0L and 5.8L Engines

1989–94 MODELS

▶ See Figures 57 thru 64

1. Remove the air cleaner and the intake duct assembly, including the crankcase ventilation hose.

2. Loosen the air inlet duct retainers, if equipped.

3. Disconnect the muffler inlet pipes.

4. Loosen the manifold heat shield retainers and remove the shields, if so equipped.

5. If equipped, remove the air injection system lines.

6. On the left-hand manifold, remove the oil tube assembly, speed control bracket and, if equipped, the exhaust heat control valve.

7. Loosen the manifold retainers and remove the heat shield and manifold.

To install:

8. Clean the manifold mating surfaces and cylinder head. Clean the exhaust pipe spherical seat on the manifold and the exhaust pipe sealing area.

9. Inspect the manifold for cracks and damaged gasket surfaces.

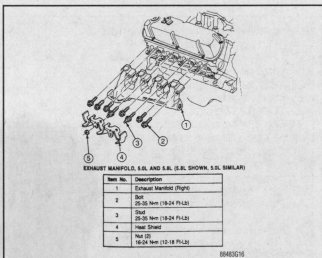

EXHAUST MANIFOLD, 5.0L AND 5.8L (5.8L SHOWN, 5.0L SIMILAR)

Item No.	Description
1	Exhaust Manifold (Right)
2	Bolt 25-35 N·m (18-24 Ft-Lb)
3	Stud 25-35 N·m (18-24 Ft-Lb)
4	Heat Shield
5	Nut (2) 16-24 N·m (12-18 Ft-Lb)

Fig. 57 Exploded view of exhaust manifold and heat shield assembly—1989–94 5.0L and 5.8L engines

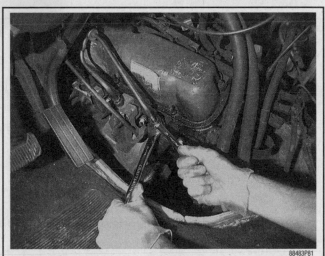

Fig. 58 Loosen the air injection system lines at the manifold using flare nut and back-up wrenches

Fig. 59 Disconnect the lines from the exhaust manifold

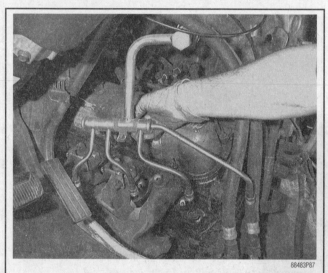

Fig. 60 Remove the lines and set them aside

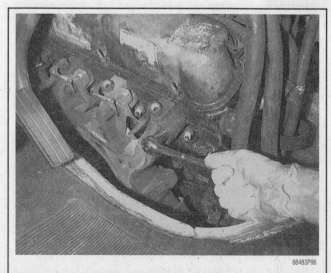

Fig. 61 Unfasten the exhaust manifold retainers

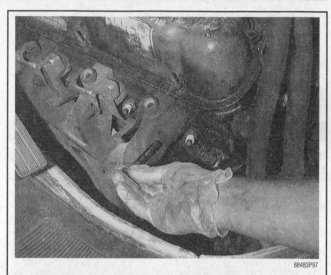

Fig. 62 Remove the heat shield from the manifold

Fig. 63 Separate the exhaust manifold from the engine . . .

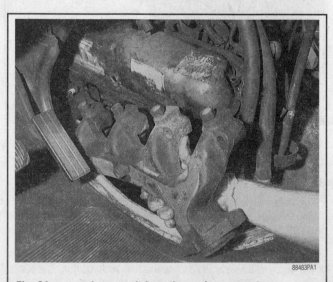

Fig. 64 . . . and remove it from the engine compartment

10. Install a new gasket and the manifold.

11. Install the oil dipstick tube.

12. Install the speed control bracket, if equipped.

13. Working from the center to the ends, tighten the bolts to 18–24 ft. lbs. (25–33 Nm).

14. Install new gaskets, if equipped on the muffler inlet pipe. Position the pipe and exhaust heat control valve (if equipped), into the manifolds. Install the retainers ands tighten them to 25–38 ft. lbs. (34–52 Nm).

15. Install the air cleaner and the duct assembly.

16. Install the crankcase ventilation hose.

1995–96 MODELS

▶ See Figure 65

1. Raise the van and support it with safety stands.

2. Loosen the exhaust manifold-to-pipe nuts, then lower the van.

3. Remove the engine cover.

4. Remove the right-hand exhaust manifold as follows:

   a. Remove the air cleaner assembly and outlet tube.

   b. Loosen the retainers and disengage the upper intake support, transmission dipstick tube, engine oil, dipstick tube and wire brackets.

   c. Loosen the nut securing the EGR tube to the exhaust manifold fitting.

   d. Disengage the EGR valve connector.

   e. Loosen the retainers and remove the EGR external pressure valve and EGR valve as an assembly.

   f. Loosen the spark plug heat shield retainers and remove the shield.

➡ **The exhaust manifold retainers vary in length and type both on the van and on the location. Keep track of what fasteners go where.**

   g. Loosen the studs and bolts, then remove the exhaust manifold and gasket.

5. Remove the left-hand exhaust manifold as follows:

   a. On models with a C6 transmission, remove the secondary air injection manifold tube.

   b. Loosen the lifting eye retainers and remove the eye.

   c. Loosen the spark plug heat shield retainers and remove the heat shield.

   d. Loosen the studs and bolts, then remove the exhaust manifold and gasket.

To install:

6. Clean the manifold mating surfaces and cylinder head. Clean the exhaust pipe spherical seat on the manifold and the exhaust pipe sealing area.

7. Inspect the manifold for cracks and damaged gasket surfaces.

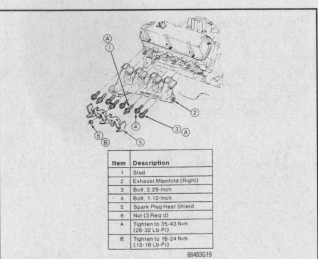

Item	Description
1	Stud
2	Exhaust Manifold (Right)
3	Bolt, 2.25-Inch
4	Bolt, 1.12-Inch
5	Spark Plug Heat Shield
6	Nut (3 Req'd)
A	Tighten to 35-43 N·m (26-32 Lb-Ft)
B	Tighten to 16-24 N·m (12-18 Lb-Ft)

88483G19

Fig. 65 Exhaust manifold and retainers—1995–96 5.0L and 5.8L engines

8. Install the left-hand exhaust manifold as follows:

   a. Install a new gasket and the manifold.

   b. Working from the center to the ends tighten the studs and the bolts to 18–24 ft. lbs. (24–32 Nm) on 1994–95 models and 26–32 ft. lbs. (35–43 Nm) on 1996 models.

   c. Install the spark plug heat shields and tighten the retainers to 12–17 ft. lbs. (16–23 Nm).

   d. Install the front lifting eye and tighten the retainers to 12–17 ft. lbs. (16–23 Nm).

   e. On models with a C6 transmission, install the secondary air injection tube and tighten the retainers to 15–25 ft. lbs. (20–34 Nm) on 1994–95 models and 24–36 ft. lbs. (33–49 Nm) on 1996 models.

9. Install the right-hand exhaust manifold as follows:

   a. Install a new gasket and the manifold.

   b. Working from the center to the ends tighten the studs and the bolts to 18–24 ft. lbs. (24–32 Nm) on 1994–95 models and 26–32 ft. lbs. (35–43 Nm) on 1996 models.

   c. Install the spark plug heat shields and tighten the retainers to 12–17 ft. lbs. (16–23 Nm).

   d. Inspect the EGR valve-to-vent tube for damage or severely rusted and replace if necessary.

   e. Install the EGR valve-to-exhaust manifold tube loosely to the manifold fitting.

   f. Install a new gasket and the valve to the upper intake manifold studs. Tighten the EGR valve retainers to 13–19 ft. lbs. (18–26 Nm), then tighten the tube-to-exhaust manifold fitting nut to 25–35 ft. lbs. (34–47 Nm).

   g. Install the wire, transmission tube, upper intake manifold support brackets and tighten the retainers to 12–18 ft. lbs. (16–24 Nm).

   h. Install the air cleaner assembly and intake tube.

10. Raise the van and support it with safety stands.

11. Install new exhaust pipe-to-manifold gaskets and the pipes. Tighten the retainers to 18–24 ft. lbs. (34–52 Nm) on 1994–95 models and 24–36 ft. lbs. (33–49 Nm) on 1996 models.

12. Lower the van and check for proper operation.

7.5L Engines

▶ See Figure 66

1. If equipped, remove the spark plug heat shield retainers and heat shield.

2. Remove the spark plug wires.

3. If removing the left-hand manifold, disconnect the external EGR tube.

4. Disconnect the manifold at the muffler inlet pipe.

5. Remove the pump-to-exhaust manifold support brace from the back of the power steering pump.

6. If removing the left-hand manifold, remove the oil dipstick tube.

7. Loosen the bolts and washers, then remove the manifold.

8. Inspect the cylinder head joining flanges for evidence of exhaust leaks.

To install:

9. Clean the manifold mating surfaces and cylinder head. Clean the mounting flange of the inlet pipes. Apply a light film of premium long life grease such as XG-1-C or -K or its equivalent to the exhaust manifold.

10. Inspect the manifold for cracks and damaged gasket surfaces.

11. Install a new gasket and the manifold.

12. Starting from the fourth bolt hole from the front of the manifold, tighten the studs and the bolts to 22–30 ft. lbs. (29–40 Nm) on 1989–93 models or 38–48 ft. lbs. (52–65 Nm) on 1994–96 models.

13. Engage the inlet pipe to the manifold and tighten the retainers to 25–38 ft. lbs. (34–52 Nm) on 1989–93 models or 25–36 ft. lbs. (39–49 Nm) on 1994–96 models.

14. If applicable, install the oil dipstick tube and connect the EGR tube.

15. Install the heat shield and spark plug wires.

16. Install the air cleaner and intake duct assemblies.

17. Start the engine and check for leaks.

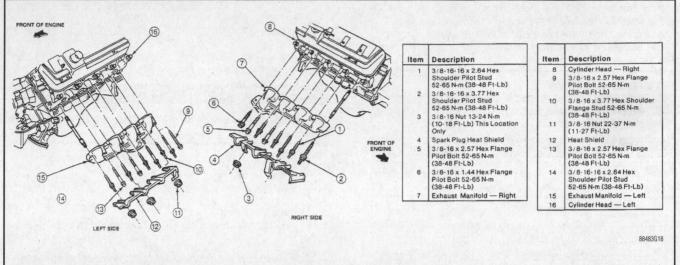

Fig. 66 Exploded view of exhaust manifold and heat shield assembly—7.5L MFI engine

Item	Description	Item	Description
1	3/8-16-16 x 2.64 Hex Shoulder Pilot Stud 52-65 N·m (38-48 Ft-Lb)	8	Cylinder Head — Right
2	3/8-16-16 x 3.77 Hex Shoulder Pilot Stud 52-65 N·m (38-48 Ft-Lb)	9	3/8-16 x 2.57 Hex Flange Pilot Bolt 52-65 N·m (38-48 Ft-Lb)
3	3/8-16 Nut 13-24 N·m (10-18 Ft-Lb) This Location Only	10	3/8-16 x 3.77 Hex Shoulder Flange Stud 52-65 N·m (38-48 Ft-Lb)
4	Spark Plug Heat Shield	11	3/8-16 Nut 22-37 N·m (11-27 Ft-Lb)
5	3/8-16 x 2.57 Hex Flange Pilot Bolt 52-65 N·m (38-48 Ft-Lb)	12	Heat Shield
6	3/8-16 x 1.44 Hex Flange Pilot Bolt 52-65 N·m (38-48 Ft-Lb)	13	3/8-16 x 2.57 Hex Flange Pilot Bolt 52-65 N·m (38-48 Ft-Lb)
7	Exhaust Manifold — Right	14	3/8-16-16 x 2.64 Hex Shoulder Pilot Stud 52-65 N·m (38-48 Ft-Lb)
		15	Exhaust Manifold — Left
		16	Cylinder Head — Left

7.3L Diesel Engine

1989–94 MODELS

◆ **See Figure 67**

1. Disconnect the negative battery cables.
2. If necessary, remove the radiator fan shroud.
3. If necessary, loosen the engine oil dipstick tube and transmission dipstick tube retainers and remove the tubes and dipsticks.
4. Raise the van and support it with safety stands.
5. Loosen the nuts retaining the right-hand engine mount to the frame, then slightly raise the right side of the engine until the fuel filter touches the sheet metal.
6. Install a wood block between the mount and frame, then lower the engine onto the block.
7. Disconnect the pipes from the manifolds.
8. Lower the van, then loosen the bolts and remove the manifold.

To install:

9. Apply anti-seize compound to the manifold retaining bolts.
10. Tighten the bolts to 35 ft. lbs. (47 Nm) in the sequence illustrated.
11. Raise the van and support it with safety stands.

12. Raise the engine so that the block of wood may be removed and lower the engine to the crossmember.
13. On the right-hand engine mount, install and tighten the retainers.
14. Engage the muffler inlet pipe to the manifold and tighten the retainers to 25–36 ft. lbs. (34–39 Nm).
15. Lower the van.
16. If removed, install the engine oil and transmission dipstick tubes, along with the dipsticks, and tighten the retainers.
17. If removed, install the radiator fan shroud.
18. Connect the negative battery cables and install the engine cover.
19. Start the van and check for leaks.

1995–96 MODELS—RIGHT-HAND MANIFOLD

◆ **See Figure 68**

1. Disconnect the negative battery cables.
2. Remove the engine cover.

✳✳ CAUTION

When draining the coolant, keep in mind that cats and dogs are attracted by ethylene glycol antifreeze and are quite likely

---

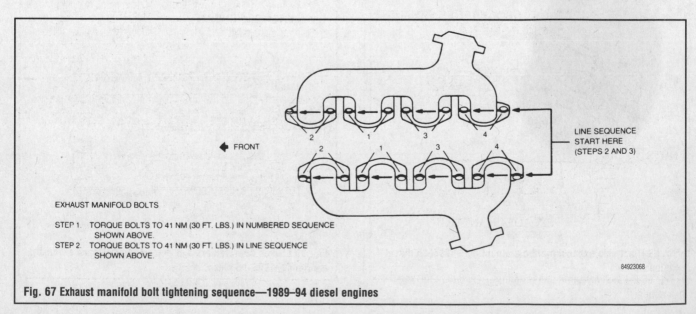

EXHAUST MANIFOLD BOLTS

STEP 1. TORQUE BOLTS TO 41 NM (30 FT. LBS.) IN NUMBERED SEQUENCE SHOWN ABOVE.

STEP 2. TORQUE BOLTS TO 41 NM (30 FT. LBS.) IN LINE SEQUENCE SHOWN ABOVE.

LINE SEQUENCE START HERE (STEPS 2 AND 3)

FRONT

Fig. 67 Exhaust manifold bolt tightening sequence—1989-94 diesel engines

to drink any that is left in an uncovered container or in puddles on the ground. This will prove fatal in sufficient quantity. Always drain the coolant into a sealable container. Coolant should be reused unless it is contaminated or several years old.

3. Drain the cooling system.
4. Remove the air cleaner housing.
5. Disconnect the upper radiator hose and the coolant recovery reservoir hose.

> ✳✳ **CAUTION**

The fan clutch uses a right-hand thread nut. Remove the nut by turning it counterclockwise.

6. Using clutch nut wrench T83T-6312-B and clutch pulley holder T94T-6312-AH or their equivalents, loosen the clutch nut and set the fan and clutch assembly in the fan shroud.
7. Loosen the fan shroud retainers, then remove the shroud and the fan/clutch assembly
8. Remove the drive belt.
9. Disengage the alternator electrical connections, loosen the retainers and remove the alternator.
10. Loosen the engine oil dipstick tube-to-engine retainers and tube.
11. Raise the van and support it with safety stands.
12. Loosen the bolts retaining the right turbocharger exhaust inlet pipe to the exhaust manifold.
13. Lower the van, then disengage the exhaust back pressure line from the manifold.
14. Loosen the exhaust manifold bolts, then remove the manifold.
15. Clean the manifold mating surfaces and check them for warpage using a straightedge. The maximum allowable warpage is 0.005 in. (0.13mm).

To install:
16. Apply anti-seize compound to the manifold bolt threads.
17. If applicable, install the manifold gasket.
18. Install the manifold and the retainers, then tighten the retainers to 45 ft. lbs. (61 Nm).
19. Connect the exhaust backpressure line to manifold.
20. Raise the van and support it with safety stands.
21. Install the right turbocharger exhaust inlet pipe-to-manifold bolts and tighten them to 36 ft. lbs. (49 Nm).

22. Lower the van and install the engine oil dipstick tube and tighten the retainers.
23. Install the alternator and drive belt, then engage the electrical connections.
24. Install the fan shroud and the fan/clutch assembly. Tighten the shroud retainers to 44–71 inch lbs. (5–8 Nm).

> ✳✳ **CAUTION**

The fan clutch uses a right-hand thread nut. Install the nut by turning it clockwise.

25. Using clutch nut wrench T83T-6312-B and clutch pulley holder T94T-6312-AH or their equivalents, tighten the clutch nut.
26. Install the radiator coolant recovery tank hose and the upper radiator hose.
27. Install the air cleaner housing.
28. Refill and bleed the cooling system and connect the negative battery cables.

➡ When the battery is disconnected and reconnected, some abnormal drive systems may occur while the Powertrain Control Module (PCM) relearns the adaptive strategy. The van may need to be driven 10 miles or more for the strategy to be relearned.

29. Install the engine cover.

1995–96 MODELS—LEFT-HAND MANIFOLD

♦ See Figure 69

1. Raise the van and support it with safety stands.
2. Loosen the bolts retaining the turbocharger exhaust inlet pipe to the manifold.
3. Loosen the exhaust manifold retainers and remove the manifold.
4. Clean the manifold mating surfaces and check them for warpage using a straightedge. The maximum allowable warpage is 0.005 in. (0.13mm).

To install:
5. Apply anti-seize compound to the manifold bolt threads.
6. If applicable, install the manifold gasket.
7. Install the manifold and the retainers, then tighten the retainers to 45 ft. lbs. (61 Nm).
8. Install the bolts retaining the turbocharger exhaust inlet pipe to the manifold. Tighten the bolts to 36 ft. lbs. (49 Nm).
9. Lower the van and check for proper operation.

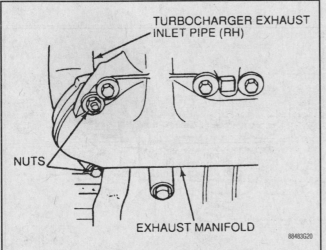

Fig. 68 Right side exhaust manifold mounting—1995–96 diesel engines

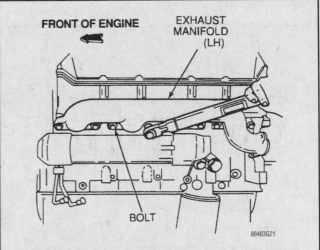

Fig. 69 Loosen the retainers and remove the left-hand exhaust manifold—1995–96 diesel engines

Combination Manifold

REMOVAL & INSTALLATION

4.9L Engine

1989–93 MODELS

▶ See Figure 70

1. Disconnect the negative battery cable.
2. Remove the air inlet hose at the crankcase filter cap.
3. Remove the throttle body inlet hoses.
4. Disconnect the accelerator cable at the throttle body.
5. Remove the cable retracting spring.
6. Remove the cable bracket from the upper intake manifold and position the cable and bracket aside.
7. Disconnect the fuel inlet line at the fuel rail. Don't kink the line!
8. Remove the upper intake and throttle body as an assembly.
9. Tag and disconnect all vacuum lines attached to the parts in question.
10. Disconnect the inlet pipe from the exhaust manifold.
11. Disconnect the power brake vacuum line, if so equipped.
12. Remove the bolts and nuts attaching the manifolds to the cylinder head. Lift the manifold assemblies from the engine. Remove and discard the gaskets.
13. To separate the manifold, remove the nuts joining the intake and exhaust manifolds.

To install:

14. Clean the mating surfaces of the cylinder head and the manifolds.
15. If the intake and exhaust manifolds have been separated, coat the mating surfaces lightly with graphite grease and place the exhaust manifold over the studs on the intake manifold. Install the lockwashers and nuts. Tighten them finger-tight.
16. Install a new intake manifold gasket.
17. Coat the mating surfaces lightly with graphite grease. Place the manifold assemblies in position against the cylinder head. Make sure that the gaskets have not become dislodged.
18. Install the attaching nuts and bolts in the proper sequence on the intake manifold to 22–32 ft. lbs. (30–43 Nm). If the intake and exhaust manifolds were separated, tighten the nuts joining them in the sequence shown to 22–32 ft. lbs. (30–43 Nm).
19. Position a new gasket on the muffler inlet pipe and connect the inlet pipe to the exhaust manifold.

20. Connect the crankcase vent hose to the intake manifold inlet tube and position the hose clamp.
21. Connect the power brake vacuum line, if so equipped.
22. Connect the inlet pipe at the exhaust manifold.
23. Connect all vacuum lines.
24. Install the upper intake and throttle body as an assembly (see Section 5).
25. Connect the fuel inlet line at the fuel rail.
26. Install the accelerator cable bracket at the upper intake manifold.
27. Install the cable retracting spring.
28. Connect the accelerator cable at the throttle body.
29. Install the throttle body inlet hoses.
30. Install the air inlet hose at the crankcase filter cap.

1994–96 MODELS

▶ See Figure 71

1. Disconnect the negative battery cable.
2. Remove the upper intake manifold and throttle body.
3. Remove the two clips and the intake manifold shield.
4. Remove the drive belt.
5. Remove the alternator.
6. Remove the air pump.
7. Remove the alternator bracket.
8. Disconnect the Y-pipe and EGR valve.
9. Disconnect the power brake vacuum line.
10. Remove the manifold, rear exhaust manifold and lower intake manifold to the cylinder head. Lift the manifolds from the engine. Remove and discard the gaskets.

To install:

11. Before installing, clean all mounting surfaces on the cylinder heads and the manifold. Apply an anti-seize compound on the manifold bolt threads.

➡ The EGR valve tube is only on the rear exhaust manifold. If the rear manifold is to be replaced, remove the tube fittings from the discarded manifold as required.

12. On SFI-equipped engines, if either exhaust manifold is to be replaced, remove the heated oxygen sensor from the old manifold and install in the new one.
13. Make sure the dowel pin is in place.
14. Install the rear exhaust manifold with bolts in holes 15 and 16. Tighten the bolts to 22–32 ft. lbs. (30–43 Nm).
15. Install the front exhaust manifold and lifting eye with the stud in hole 13 and bolt in hole 14. Snug the stud and tighten the bolt to 22–32 ft. lbs. (30–43 Nm).

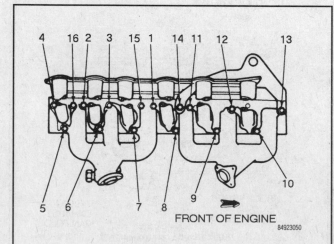

Fig. 70 Intake/exhaust (combination) manifold bolt torque sequence—1989–93 4.9L engines

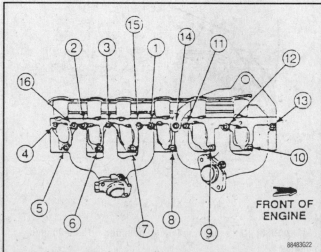

Fig. 71 Intake/exhaust (combination) manifold tightening sequence—1994–96 4.9L engines

16. Install the intake manifold gasket over the dowel pin and line up the port openings in the cylinder head and intake manifold gasket.

17. Install the lower intake manifold onto the dowel pins, then install the remaining bolts.

18. Tighten the bolts to 22–32 ft. lbs. (30–43 Nm) using the proper sequence (see illustration).

19. Connect the power brake vacuum line.

20. Connect the dual converter Y-pipe to the front and rear exhaust manifolds. Tighten the lockwashers and nuts to 25–36 ft. lbs. (34–49 Nm).

21. Install the alternator mounting bracket and three bolts finger-tight. Tighten as follows:

    a. Tighten the bottom rear bolt to 41–54 ft. lbs. (55–74 Nm).
    b. Tighten the center bolts to 41–54 ft. lbs. (55–74 Nm).
    c. Tighten the nut to 41–54 ft. lbs. (55–74 Nm).
    d. Tighten the bottom front bolt to 41–54 ft. lbs. (55–74 Nm).

22. Install the secondary air injection pump and tighten the bolts to 41–54 ft. lbs. (55–74 Nm). Install the air pump pulley and tighten the screws to 12–15 ft. lbs. (16–21 Nm).

23. Connect the alternator wiring.

24. Install the drive belt.

25. Install and clips in place the heat shield.

26. Connect all vacuum lines.

27. Install the upper intake manifold and throttle body.

Turbocharger

REMOVAL & INSTALLATION

1994 Models

▶ See Figure 72

1. Disconnect the negative battery cables.
2. Raise the van and support it with safety stands.
3. Loosen the exhaust crossover pipe-to-left exhaust manifold retainers.
4. Loosen the Y-collector pipe-to-right exhaust manifold retainers.
5. Remove the Y-collector pipe and crossover pipe by twisting the crossover pipe back and forth while also pulling down on it.
6. Lower the van.
7. Remove the air cleaner assembly and the air duct to the turbocharger.
8. Disengage the oil pressure sender connection and remove the turbocharger oil supply line.
9. Loosen the clamp retaining the exhaust down pipe to the wastegate housing.

10. Loosen the bolts retaining the oil drain pedestal to the rear intake manifold.
11. Remove the air chamber hold-down bolt from the intake manifold.
12. Pull the turbocharger assembly up and out of the valley pan grommet.
13. Position the assembly towards the heater box, rotated slightly counterclockwise.
14. Remove the air chamber from the turbocharger.
15. Loosen the oil drain pedestal-to-turbocharger center housing retainers.
16. Remove the oil drain pedestal and set it in the intake manifold valley.
17. Remove the turbocharger assembly.

To install:

18. Install the turbocharger and loosely install the clamp on the wastegate exhaust outlet.
19. Install the oil drain pedestal onto the turbocharger and tighten the retainers to 30 ft. lbs. (40 Nm).
20. Install the air chamber on the compressor.
21. Lift and rotate the turbocharger until the oil drain pedestal is aligned with the valley pan grommet.
22. Push the turbocharger down to seat the oil drain pedestal in the grommet.
23. Loosely install the drain pedestal-to-intake manifold retainers.
24. Raise the van and support it with safety stands.
25. Engage the exhaust crossover pipe to the left exhaust manifold and loosely install the retainers.
26. Install the Y-collector pipe into the turbocharger exhaust inlet housing by tapping the Y-collector flange with long drift punch.
27. Install the Y-collector pipe-to-right exhaust manifold retainers and tighten them to 25–36 ft. lbs. (34–46 Nm).
28. Tighten the exhaust crossover pipe-to-left exhaust manifold retainers and tighten them to 25–36 ft. lbs. (34–46 Nm).
29. Lower the van and tighten the oil drain pedestal bolts to 14 ft. lbs. (19 Nm).
30. Install the turbocharger oil supply line and engage the oil pressure sender wire.
31. Install the air cleaner assembly and intake ducts.
32. Connect the negative battery cables.
33. Start the van and check for oil and exhaust leaks.

1995–96 Models

▶ See Figures 73, 74 and 75

1. Disconnect the negative battery cables and remove the engine cover.
2. Remove the heat shield.
3. Loosen the exhaust Y-pipe-to-turbo inlet adapter bolts from the adapter.

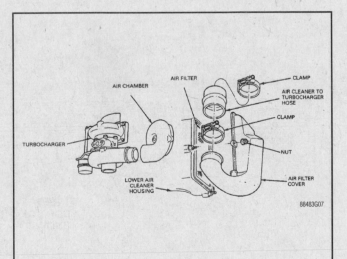

Fig. 72 Exploded view of the turbocharger assembly—1994 diesel engines

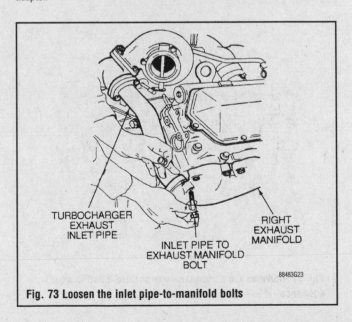

Fig. 73 Loosen the inlet pipe-to-manifold bolts

4. Remove the exhaust outlet clamp from the turbocharger.

5. Loosen the turbocharger exhaust inlet pipe-to-left exhaust manifold retainers.

6. Loosen the intake manifold hose clamps and the clamp retaining the compressor manifold to the turbocharger.

7. Remove the compressor manifold.

➡**The right rear bolt cannot be completely removed.**

8. Loosen the four turbocharger pedestal assembly-to-cylinder block bolts.

9. Remove the turbocharger and disengage the electrical connections.

➡**If the turbocharger is not being removed for service, install fuel/oil/turbo protector cap set T94T-9395-AH or its equivalent.**

10. Remove and discard the oil gallery O-rings.

To install:

11. Install new oil gallery oil rings.

➡**The right rear retaining bolt for the turbocharger pedestal assembly must be installed prior to turbocharger installation.**

12. Engage the electrical connections and install the turbocharger.

13. Install the four turbocharger pedestal assembly-to-engine block bolts and tighten them to 18 ft. lbs. (24 Nm).

14. Loosely install the retainers on the left and right turbocharger exhaust inlet pipes to the exhaust inlet adapter.

15. Install the compressor manifold, intake manifold hoses and clamps making sure the compressor outlet seal is in position.

16. Engage the air inlet hose to the turbocharger compressor and tighten the clamp.

17. Tighten the turbocharger exhaust inlet pipes-to-turbocharger exhaust inlet adapter bolts to 36 ft. lbs. (49 Nm).

18. Tighten the turbocharger exhaust inlet pipes-to-exhaust manifolds bolts to 36 ft. lbs. (49 Nm).

19. Install the exhaust outlet clamp to the turbocharger.

20. Install the heat shield.

21. Install the engine cover and connect the negative battery cables.

22. Start the van and check for proper operation.

Radiator

REMOVAL & INSTALLATION

▶ **See Figures 76 thru 92**

1. Drain the cooling system by opening the radiator cap and then the draincock. The draincock is located at the lower rear corner of the radiator.

✳✳ CAUTION

When draining the coolant, keep in mind that cats and dogs are attracted by ethylene glycol antifreeze and are quite likely to drink any that is left in an uncovered container or in puddles on the ground. This will prove fatal in sufficient quantity. Always drain the coolant into a sealable container. Coolant should be reused unless it is contaminated or several years old.

2. Remove the air cleaner housing, if necessary.

3. Disengage the overflow tube from the recovery tank.

4. Remove the retaining bolts from the shroud, if so equipped, and position the shroud over the fan, clear of the radiator.

5. Disconnect the transmission cooling lines from the bottom of the radiator, if so equipped.

6. Disengage the heated water bypass hose attached to the lower tank, if equipped.

7. Disconnect the upper and lower hoses from the radiator.

8. Remove the radiator retaining bolts or the upper supports and lift the radiator from the vehicle.

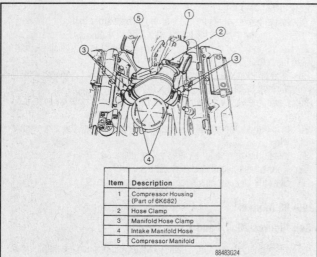

Item	Description
1	Compressor Housing (Part of 6K682)
2	Hose Clamp
3	Manifold Hose Clamp
4	Intake Manifold Hose
5	Compressor Manifold

88483G24

Fig. 74 Loosen the clamps on the illustrated components— 1995–96 diesel engines

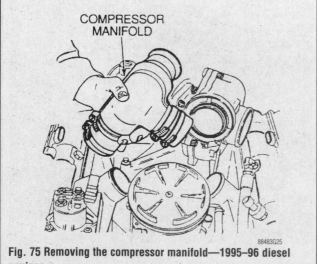

88483G25

Fig. 75 Removing the compressor manifold—1995–96 diesel engines

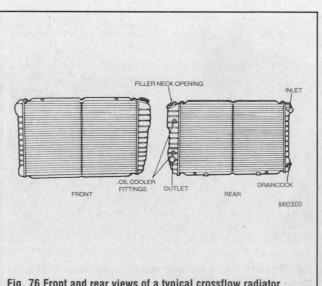

84923033

Fig. 76 Front and rear views of a typical crossflow radiator

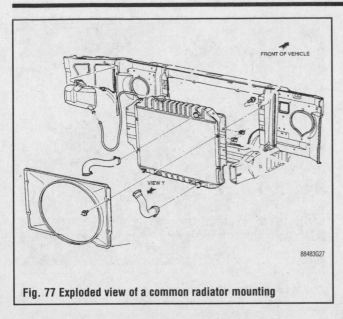

Fig. 77 Exploded view of a common radiator mounting

Fig. 80 Loosen the air cleaner housing hose clamps

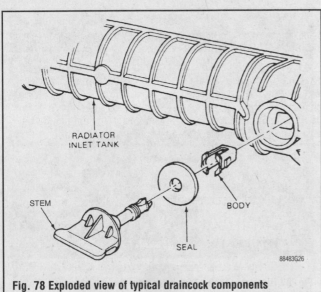

Fig. 78 Exploded view of typical draincock components

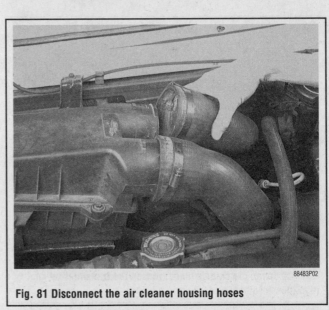

Fig. 81 Disconnect the air cleaner housing hoses

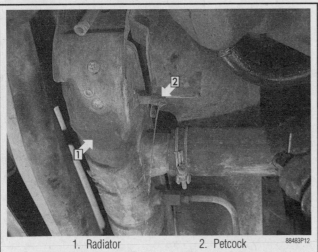

1. Radiator   2. Petcock

Fig. 79 Open the draincock and drain the coolant into a suitable container

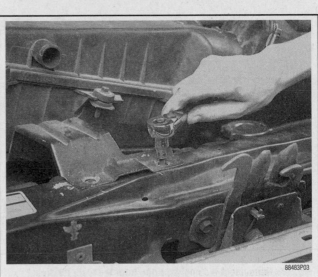

Fig. 82 Loosen the air cleaner housing retaining bolts . . .

Fig. 83 . . . and remove the housing from the engine compartment

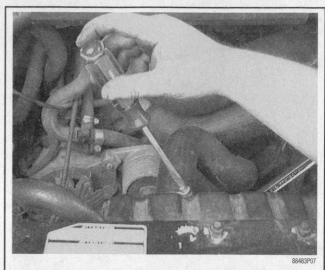

Fig. 86 Loosen the upper radiator hose clamp

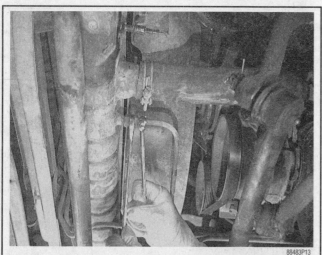

Fig. 84 Using a back-up wrench, loosen the transmission cooling lines

Fig. 87 Disconnect the upper hose from the radiator

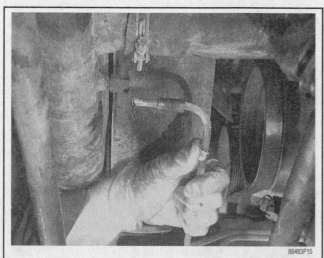

Fig. 85 Disconnect the cooling lines from the radiator, being careful not to kink them

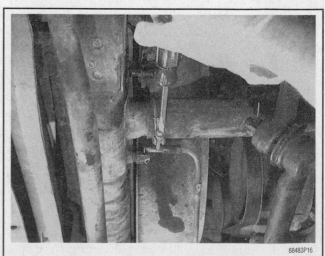

Fig. 88 Loosen the lower radiator hose clamp with a screwdriver

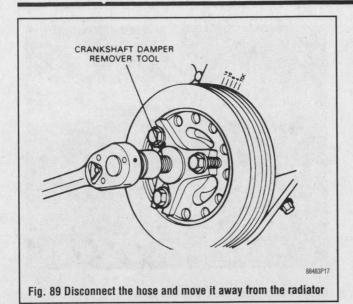

Fig. 89 Disconnect the hose and move it away from the radiator

Fig. 90 Loosen the radiator shroud mounting bolts

Fig. 91 Unfasten the radiator mounting bolts

Fig. 92 Position the shroud over the fan and remove the radiator

To install:

9. Install the radiator and tighten the retainers to 10–15 ft. lbs. (14–20 Nm).
10. Engage the automatic transmission cooling lines, if equipped.
11. Engage the upper and lower radiator hoses and tighten the clamps securely.
12. If equipped, connect the heated water bypass hose attached to the lower tank.
13. Position the shroud and tighten the retainers to 4–6 lbs. (5–8 Nm).
14. Connect the overflow tube from the recovery tank, if equipped.
15. Fill the cooling system and check for leaks.

Engine Fan and Fan Clutch

REMOVAL & INSTALLATION

4.9L Engine

♦ See Figures 93 and 94

1. Remove the fan shroud.
2. Remove one of the fan-to-clutch bolts, to access the clutch-to-hub nut.
3. Turn the large fan clutch-to-hub nut COUNTERCLOCKWISE to

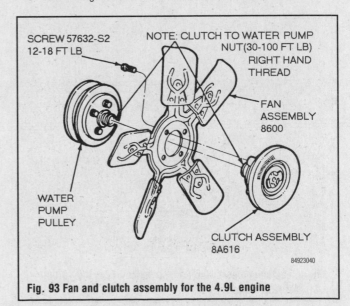

Fig. 93 Fan and clutch assembly for the 4.9L engine

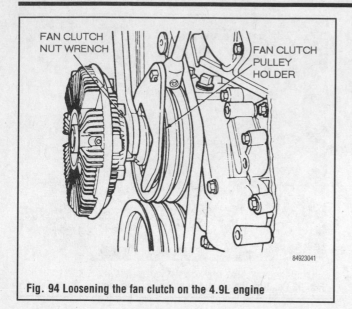

Fig. 94 Loosening the fan clutch on the 4.9L engine

Fig. 96 If necessary, remove the fan shroud

remove the fan and clutch from the hub. Use holding tool T84T-6312-C and nut wrench T84T-6312-D, or equivalent.

4. If the fan and clutch have to be separated, remove the remaining fan-to-clutch bolts.

To install:

5. Attach the fan to the clutch using all but one of the bolts. The bolts are tightened to 12–18 ft. lbs. (16–24 Nm).

6. Install the assembly on the hub and tighten the hub nut clockwise to 37–55 ft. lbs. (50–74 Nm).

7. Install and tighten the last fan-to-clutch bolt.

8. Install the shroud.

5.0L, 5.8L and 7.5L Engines

▶ See Figures 95, 96, 97 and 98

1. If you need the clearance, remove the fan shroud and, if necessary, the radiator.

2. Remove the four fan clutch-to-water pump hub bolts and lift off the fan/clutch assembly.

3. Remove the four fan-to-clutch bolts and separate the fan from the clutch.

4. Installation is the reverse of removal. Tighten all the bolts to 12–18 ft. lbs. (17–24 Nm).

Fig. 97 Remove the cooling fan-to-clutch bolts

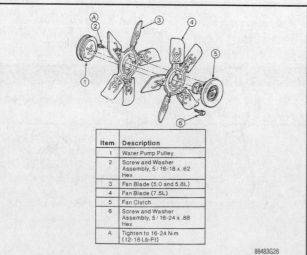

Item	Description
1	Water Pump Pulley
2	Screw and Washer Assembly, 5 / 16-18 x .62 Hex
3	Fan Blade (5.0 and 5.8L)
4	Fan Blade (7.5L)
5	Fan Clutch
6	Screw and Washer Assembly, 5 / 16-24 x .88 Hex
A	Tighten to 16-24 N·m (12-18 Lb-Ft)

Fig. 95 Exploded view of the fan and clutch assembly—5.0L, 5.8L and 7.5L engines

Fig. 98 Remove the clutch and fan assembly from the engine compartment

7.3L Diesel Engines

1989–94 MODELS

▶ **See Figure 99**

1. Remove the fan shroud.
2. Turn the large fan clutch-to-hub nut CLOCKWISE (left-handed threads) to remove the fan and clutch from the hub. There are 2 tools made for this purpose, holding tool T84T-6312-A and nut wrench T84T-6312-B.
3. Remove the fan and clutch assembly.
4. If the fan and clutch have to be separated, remove the fan-to-clutch bolts.

To install:
5. Attach the fan to the clutch. Tighten the bolts to 12–18 ft. lbs. (17–24 Nm).
6. Install the assembly on the hub and tighten the hub nut to a maximum of 89–118 ft. lbs. (120–160 Nm). Remember, the nut is left-hand threaded. Tighten it by turning it COUNTERCLOCKWISE.
7. Install the fan shroud.

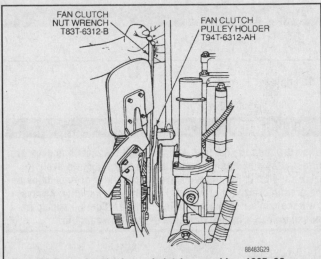

Fig. 100 Removing the fan and clutch assembly—1995–96 diesel engines

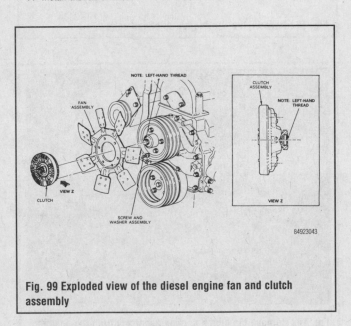

Fig. 99 Exploded view of the diesel engine fan and clutch assembly

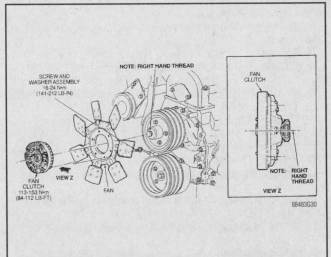

Fig. 101 Exploded view of the cooling fan and clutch assembly—1995–96 diesel engines

1995–96 MODELS

▶ **See Figures 100 and 101**

1. Remove the air cleaner assembly.
2. Partially drain the cooling system below the level of the upper radiator hose, then disconnect the hose.
3. Disconnect the reservoir hose from the radiator.

> ❈ **CAUTION**

The fan clutch nut is a right-hand thread and must be removed by turning it counterclockwise.

4. Turn the large fan clutch-to-hub nut COUNTERCLOCKWISE (right-handed threads) to remove the fan and clutch from the hub. There are 2 tools made for this purpose, holding tool T94T-6312-AH and nut wrench T83T-6312-B.
5. Loosen the fan shroud retainers and remove the shroud and the fan clutch assembly.
6. To separate the fan blade and clutch, loosen the retaining bolts.

To install:
7. Engage the fan blade to the clutch and tighten the bolts to 12–18 ft. lbs. (16–24 Nm).
8. Install the fan shroud and the fan clutch assembly.
9. Position the fan shroud and tighten the retainers.

> ❈ **CAUTION**

The fan clutch nut is a right-hand thread and must be installed by turning it clockwise.

10. Tighten the large fan clutch-to-hub nut CLOCKWISE (right-handed threads) to install the fan and clutch on the hub. There are 2 tools made for this purpose, holding tool T94T-6312-AH and nut wrench T83T-6312-B.
11. Connect the reservoir and upper radiator hose's to the radiator.
12. Refill and bleed the cooling system.
13. Install the air cleaner assembly, start the van and check for proper operation.

Water Pump

REMOVAL & INSTALLATION

4.9L Engine

1. Drain the cooling system.

> **✳✳ CAUTION**
>
> When draining the coolant, keep in mind that cats and dogs are attracted by ethylene glycol antifreeze and are quite likely to drink any that is left in an uncovered container or in puddles on the ground. This will prove fatal in sufficient quantity. Always drain the coolant into a sealable container. Coolant should be reused unless it is contaminated or several years old.

2. On 1989–90 models remove the alternator and, if equipped, air compressor belt.
3. Remove the drive belt.
4. If equipped, remove the wiring bracket.
5. Remove the clutch, and water pump pulley.
6. Disconnect the lower radiator hose, heater hose and if equipped, the radiator supply line from the water pump.
7. Loosen the retainers and remove the water pump and gasket.

To install:

8. Before installing the old water pump, clean the gasket mounting surfaces on the pump and on the cylinder block. If a new water pump is being installed, remove the any necessary fittings from the old pump and install it on the new one.
9. Coat the new gaskets with sealer on both sides and install the water pump. Tighten the mounting bolts to 12–18 ft. lbs. (17–24 Nm).
10. Connect the heater hose, radiator supply line (if equipped) and lower radiator hose to the water pump.
11. Install the water pump pulley and the fan clutch.
12. Install the drive belt.
13. On 1989–90 models install the alternator and if equipped, air compressor belt.
14. If equipped, install the wiring bracket and tighten the retainers to 6–10 ft. lbs. (8–13 Nm).
15. Fill the cooling system, start the van and check for leaks.

5.0L and 5.8L Engines

1989–95 MODELS

▶ See Figures 102 thru 112

1. Drain the cooling system.

> **✳✳ CAUTION**
>
> When draining the coolant, keep in mind that cats and dogs are attracted by ethylene glycol antifreeze and are quite likely to drink any that is left in an uncovered container or in puddles on the ground. This will prove fatal in sufficient quantity. Always drain the coolant into a sealable container. Coolant should be reused unless it is contaminated or several years old.

2. If necessary, remove the air cleaner assembly, intake duct and crankcase ventilation hose.
3. Remove the radiator.
4. Remove the drive belt, fan shroud, fan clutch and pulley.
5. Disconnect the heater hose, radiator hose and by-pass hose at the water pump.
6. Remove the A/C compressor/power steering pump bracket from the cylinder head and water pump water pump stud bolt after disengaging the A/C and power steering systems.
7. Remove the bolts securing the water pump to the front cover and remove the water pump and gasket.

Fig. 102 Remove the cooling fan-to-clutch bolts

Fig. 103 Remove the clutch and fan assembly from the engine compartment

Fig. 104 Remove the water pump pulley

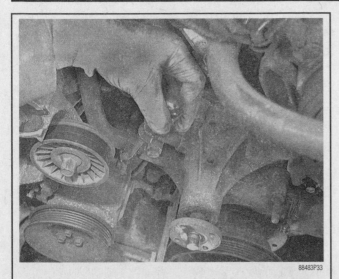

Fig. 105 Loosen the heater hose and bypass hose clamps . . .

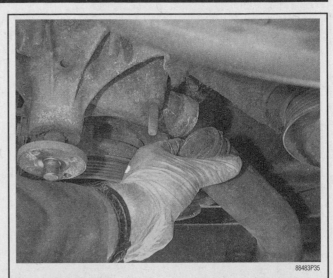

Fig. 108 Disconnect the radiator hose from the water pump

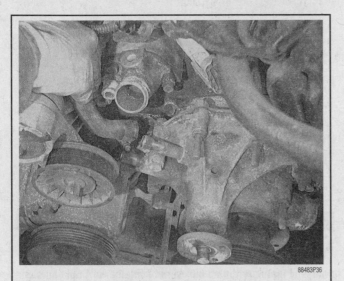

Fig. 106 . . . and disconnect the hoses from the pump

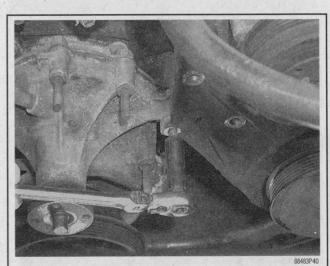

Fig. 109 Loosen the A/C compressor/power steering pump bracket-to-water pump retainers

Fig. 107 Loosen the lower radiator hose clamp

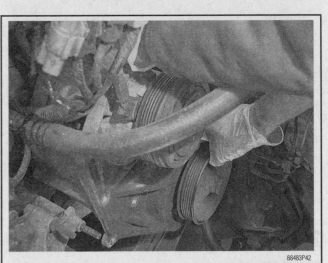

Fig. 110 Slide the bracket forward to disengage it from the studs on the pump

Fig. 111 Loosen the water pump mounting bolts

Fig. 112 Remove the water pump from the engine compartment

To install:

8. Clean the gasket mating surfaces.

9. If installing the old water pump, check it for damage

10. Coat a new gasket with sealer and install the water pump. Tighten the bolts to 15–21 ft. lbs. (20–28 Nm).

11. Connect the heater hose and by-pass hose at the water pump.

12. Connect the A/C and power steering pump accessories and bracket to the cylinder head and water pump stud.

13. Install the water pump pulley, fan shroud, fan clutch and drive belt.

14. Fill and bleed the cooling system.

15. If removed, install the air cleaner assembly, intake duct and crankcase ventilation hose.

1996 MODELS

1. Drain the cooling system.

✳✳ CAUTION

When draining the coolant, keep in mind that cats and dogs are attracted by ethylene glycol antifreeze and are quite likely to drink any that is left in an uncovered container or in puddles on

the ground. This will prove fatal in sufficient quantity. Always drain the coolant into a sealable container. Coolant should be reused unless it is contaminated or several years old.

2. If necessary, remove the air cleaner assembly, intake duct and crankcase ventilation hose.

3. Remove the radiator.

4. Disconnect the upper radiator hose from the engine.

5. Remove the drive belt.

6. Remove the fan shroud and fan clutch as an assembly.

7. Remove the water pump pulley.

8. Raise the van and support it with safety stands.

9. Disconnect the lower radiator hose from the water pump and the fuel line and the injection supply manifold.

10. Lower the van.

11. Remove the A/C compressor/power steering pump bracket from the cylinder head and water pump water pump stud bolt after disengaging the A/C and power steering systems.

12. Disconnect the heater hose and by-pass hose at the water pump.

13. Remove the bolts securing the water pump to the front cover and remove the water pump and gasket.

To install:

14. Clean the gasket mating surfaces.

15. If installing the old water pump, check it for damage

16. Coat a new gasket with sealer and install the water pump. Tighten the bolts to 15–21 ft. lbs. (20–28 Nm).

17. Connect the heater hose and by-pass hose at the water pump.

18. Connect the A/C and power steering pump accessories and bracket to the cylinder head and water pump stud.

19. Install the water pump pulley, fan shroud, fan clutch and drive belt.

20. Fill and bleed the cooling system.

21. If removed, install the air cleaner assembly, intake duct and crankcase ventilation hose.

7.5L Engines

1989–91 MODELS

1. Drain the cooling system.

✳✳ CAUTION

When draining the coolant, keep in mind that cats and dogs are attracted by ethylene glycol antifreeze and are quite likely to drink any that is left in an uncovered container or in puddles on the ground. This will prove fatal in sufficient quantity. Always drain the coolant into a sealable container. Coolant should be reused unless it is contaminated or several years old.

2. Loosen the bolts retaining the fan assembly to the water pump, then remove the fan and shroud.

3. Remove the power steering drive belts.

4. If equipped with A/C, loosen the compressor retaining bolts and set the compressor aside. DO NOT DISCONNECT THE REFRIGERANT LINES!

5. Loosen the A/C compressor and power steering bracket retainers and remove the bracket.

6. Remove the alternator and air pump drive belts.

7. If necessary, remove the alternator.

8. Remove the air pump and bracket.

9. Disengage the hose(s) from the pump.

10. Loosen the water pump retaining bolts, then remove the pump separator plate and gaskets.

To install:

11. Clean the old gasket material from the pump, front cover and the separator plate mating surfaces.

12. Coat a new gasket on both sides with water resistant sealer and install the water pump. Tighten the bolts to 12–18 ft. lbs. (16–24 Nm).

13. Install the water pump pulley.

14. Position the drive belts on their pulleys.

15. Connect the hoses to the water pump.

16. Install the A/C compressor bracket with the power steering pump in place.
17. Install the alternator and air pump bracket and tighten the retainers.
18. Install the air pump and the alternator.
19. Install the shroud and fan assembly. Tighten the fan retaining bolts to 12–18 ft. lbs. (16–24 Nm).
20. Adjust the tension on the drive belts.
21. Fill and bleed the cooling system.
22. Start the van and check for leaks.

1992–96 MODELS

▶ **See Figure 113**

1. Drain the cooling system.

✳✳ CAUTION

When draining the coolant, keep in mind that cats and dogs are attracted by ethylene glycol antifreeze and are quite likely to drink any that is left in an uncovered container or in puddles on the ground. This will prove fatal in sufficient quantity. Always drain the coolant into a sealable container. Coolant should be reused unless it is contaminated or several years old.

2. Remove the drive belts.
3. Loosen the fan shroud retainers.
4. Remove the fan blade from the fan clutch, then remove the fan and shroud.
5. Remove the fan clutch and water pump pulley.
6. Disengage any hoses from the water pump.
7. Loosen the retainers connecting the A/C compressor mounting bracket to the cylinder head and the water pump. Do not remove the compressor or power steering pump from the A/C compressor mounting bracket.
8. Remove the power steering pump bracket that connects the power steering pump to the left exhaust manifold.
9. Pull the A/C compressor forward to disengage the stud from the water pump.
10. Loosen the retainer attaching the alternator adjusting arm to the water pump.
11. Loosen the retainers engaging the alternator mounting bracket to the cylinder head, block and water pump.
12. Loosen the remaining water pump bolts, then remove the pump and separator plate (if equipped).
13. Discard the old gaskets.

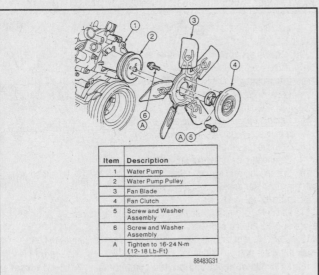

Item	Description
1	Water Pump
2	Water Pump Pulley
3	Fan Blade
4	Fan Clutch
5	Screw and Washer Assembly
6	Screw and Washer Assembly
A	Tighten to 16-24 N·m (12-18 Lb-Ft)

88483G31

Fig. 113 View of the water pump and related components

To install:
14. Clean the old gasket material from the pump, front cover and the separator plate mating surfaces.
15. Coat a new gasket on both sides with water resistant sealer and install the water pump. Tighten the bolts to 12–18 ft. lbs. (16–24 Nm).
16. Connect the hoses to the water pump.
17. Install the alternator mounting bracket to the cylinder head, block and water pump and tighten the retainers. Install the alternator adjusting arm to the water pump and tighten the retainers. Tighten the ⁷⁄₁₆ in. bolts to 40–53 ft. lbs. (53–71 Nm) and the ⅜ in. bolts to 30–40 ft. lbs. (40–53 Nm).
18. Install the A/C compressor bracket over the water pump stud and engage it to the cylinder head. Tighten the bolts to 40–53 ft. lbs. (53–71 Nm).
19. Install the nut to the water pump and tighten to 30–40 ft. lbs. (40–53 Nm).
20. Tighten the power steering pump bracket nuts to 30–40 ft. lbs. (40–53 Nm).
21. Install the water pump pulley and the fan clutch to the pump hub.
22. Engage the fan clutch to the blade. Tighten the pulley, clutch hub bolts and fan-to-fan hub bolts to 12–18 ft. lbs. (16–24 Nm).
23. Install the fan shroud and the drive belts.
24. Fill and bleed the cooling system.
25. Start the van and check for leaks.

7.3L Diesel Engines

1989–93 MODELS

▶ **See Figure 114**

1. Disconnect both negative battery cables.

✳✳ CAUTION

When draining the coolant, keep in mind that cats and dogs are attracted by ethylene glycol antifreeze and are quite likely to drink any that is left in an uncovered container or in puddles on the ground. This will prove fatal in sufficient quantity. Always drain the coolant into a sealable container. Coolant should be reused unless it is contaminated or several years old.

2. Drain the cooling system.
3. Remove the radiator shroud halves.
4. Remove the fan clutch and fan.

➡ **The fan clutch bolts are left-hand thread. Remove them by turning them CLOCKWISE.**

5. Remove the power steering pump and the A/C compressor belts.
6. Remove the vacuum pump drive and the alternator drive belts.
7. Remove the water pump pulley.
8. Disconnect the heater hose at the water pump.
9. If you're installing a new pump, remove the heater hose fitting from the old pump at this time.
10. Remove the alternator adjusting arm and bracket.
11. Unbolt the A/C compressor and position it out of the way. DO NOT DISCONNECT THE REFRIGERANT LINES!
12. Remove the A/C compressor brackets.
13. Unbolt the power steering pump and bracket and position it out of the way. DO NOT DISCONNECT THE POWER STEERING FLUID LINES!
14. Loosen the bolts attaching the water pump to the front cover and remove the pump.

To install:
15. Thoroughly clean the mating surfaces of the pump and front cover.
16. Using a new gasket, position the water pump into place on the front cover.

➡ **It is a good idea to coat the bolts with Aviation Permatex ™ No. 3 or equivalent before installation. After applying the sealant, it is best to install the bolts within a few minutes of application.**

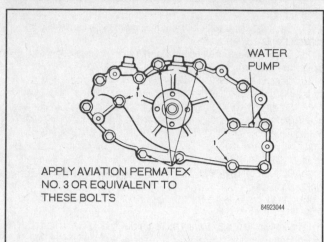

Fig. 114 Apply sealant to the areas indicated—1989–93 diesel engine

17. Install the attaching bolts ensuring the correct length bolts are in the correct length bolts. Tighten the bolts to 14 ft. lbs. (19 Nm).
18. Install the alternator adjusting arm bracket and tighten the retainers.
19. Install the water pump pulley.
20. Wrap the heater hose fitting threads with Teflon® tape and screw it into the water pump. Torque it to 12–18 ft. lbs. (17–24 Nm).
21. Connect the heater hose to the pump.
22. Install the power steering pump and bracket. Install the belt.
23. Install the A/C compressor bracket.
24. Install the A/C compressor. Install the belt.
25. Install the alternator adjusting arm and drive belt.
26. Install the vacuum pump drive belt.
27. Adjust all the drive belt(s).
28. Install the fan and clutch. Remember that the bolts are left-hand thread. Turn them COUNTERCLOCKWISE to tighten them. Tighten them to 113 ft. lbs. (153 Nm).
29. Install the fan shroud halves.
30. Fill and bleed the cooling system.
31. Connect both negative battery cables.
32. Start the engine and check for leaks.

1994 MODELS

1. Disconnect both negative battery cables.

❋❋ CAUTION

When draining the coolant, keep in mind that cats and dogs are attracted by ethylene glycol antifreeze and are quite likely to drink any that is left in an uncovered container or in puddles on the ground. This will prove fatal in sufficient quantity. Always drain the coolant into a sealable container. Coolant should be reused unless it is contaminated or several years old.

2. Drain the cooling system.
3. Remove the radiator shroud.
4. Remove the fan clutch and fan.

➡ The fan clutch bolts are left-hand thread. Remove them by turning them CLOCKWISE.

5. Remove the drive belt and the water pump pulley.
6. Disconnect the heater hose and fitting from the water pump
7. Loosen the retaining bolts and remove the water pump.
To install:
8. Thoroughly clean the mating surfaces of the pump and front cover.
9. Using a new gasket, position the water pump into place on the front cover.

➡ Coat the two top and bottom bolts with Aviation Permatex ™ No. 3 or equivalent before installation. After applying the sealant it is best to install the bolts within application.

10. Install the attaching bolts ensuring the correct length bolts are in the correct length bolts. Tighten the bolts to 14 ft. lbs. (19 Nm).
11. install the pulley and tighten the retainers.
12. Wrap the heater hose fitting threads with Teflon® tape and screw it into the water pump. Torque it to 12–18 ft. lbs. (17–24 Nm).
13. Connect the heater hose to the water pump and tighten the retainers.
14. Install the drive belt.
15. Install the fan and clutch. Remember that the bolts are left-hand threaded. Turn them COUNTERCLOCKWISE to tighten them. Tighten them to 40–120 ft. lbs. (54–163 Nm).
16. Install the fan shroud.
17. Fill and bleed the cooling system.
18. Connect the negative battery cables.
19. Start the engines and check for leaks.

1995–96 MODELS

▶ **See Figure 115**

1. Disconnect both negative battery cables.

❋❋ CAUTION

When draining the coolant, keep in mind that cats and dogs are attracted by ethylene glycol antifreeze and are quite likely to drink any that is left in an uncovered container or in puddles on the ground. This will prove fatal in sufficient quantity. Always drain the coolant into a sealable container. Coolant should be reused unless it is contaminated or several years old.

2. Partially drain the cooling system.
3. Remove the air cleaner housing assembly.
4. Remove the upper radiator hose and disconnect the reservoir hose at the radiator.
5. Remove the fan clutch and fan.

➡ The fan clutch bolts are right-hand thread. Remove them by turning them COUNTERCLOCKWISE.

6. Loosen the fan shroud retainers, then remove the shroud and fan clutch assembly as a unit.
7. remove the drive belt and remove the water pump pulley.
8. Disengage the Engine Coolant Temperature (ECT) sensor and, if necessary, remove the sensor.

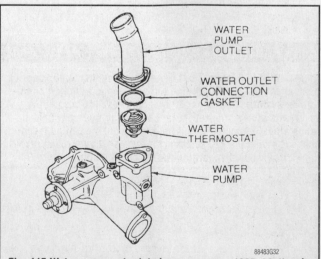

Fig. 115 Water pump and related components—1995–96 diesel engines

9. Loosen the water pump inlet bolts and then remove the inlet.

10. Loosen the retainers and remove the water pump.

11. Clean the gasket mating surfaces.

To install:

12. Install the water pump and gasket. Tighten the bolts to 15 ft. lbs. (20 Nm).

13. Install the water pump inlet and tighten the bolts to 15 ft. lbs. (20 Nm).

14. If removed, insole the ECT sensor. Engage the sensor electrical connection.

15. Connect the heater hose to the water pump and tighten the clamp.

16. Install the water pump pulley, finger-tighten the bolts, install the drive belt and then tighten the pulley bolts to 12–18 (17–24 Nm).

17. Install the fan shroud and the fan clutch assembly. Tighten the shroud retainers.

18. Install the fan and clutch. Remember that the bolts are right-hand thread. Turn them CLOCKWISF to tighten them.

19. Connect the reservoir hose to the radiator, install the upper radiator hose and tighten the clamps.

20. Install the air cleaner housing.

21. Fill and bleed the cooling system.

22. Start the van and check for leaks.

Cylinder Head

REMOVAL & INSTALLATION

4.9L Engine

▶ See Figure 116

1. Disconnect the negative battery cable.

2. Drain the cooling system and the crankcase.

❋❋ CAUTION

When draining the coolant, keep in mind that cats and dogs are attracted by ethylene glycol antifreeze and are quite likely to drink any that is left in an uncovered container or in puddles on the ground. This will prove fatal in sufficient quantity. Always drain the coolant into a sealable container. Coolant should be reused unless it is contaminated or several years old.

3. If applicable, remove the air cleaner outlet tube.

4. Remove the engine cover.

5. If applicable, remove the throttle body inlet tubes.

6. Disconnect the fuel line from the fuel pump or, from the fuel injection manifold.

❋❋ CAUTION

Please refer to Section 1 before discharging the compressor or disconnecting air conditioning lines. Damage to the air conditioning system or personal injury could result. Consult your local laws concerning refrigerant discharge and recycling. In many areas it may be illegal for anyone but a certified technician to service the A/C system. Always use an approved recovery station when discharging the air conditioning.

7. Remove the air conditioning compressor.

8. Remove the condenser.

9. Disconnect the heater hoses from the water pump and coolant outlet housing.

10. Remove the radiator.

11. Remove the engine fan and fan drive or drive belt idler bracket, the water pump pulley and the drive belt.

12. Disconnect the accelerator cable and retracting spring.

13. Disconnect the power brake hose at the manifold.

14. If equipped, disconnect the transmission kickdown rod on vans with automatic transmission.

15. Disconnect the muffler inlet pipe at the exhaust manifold(s). Pull the muffler inlet pipe down. Remove the gasket.

16. Disconnect the body ground strap and negative battery cable at the engine.

17. Disconnect the EEC or PCM wiring harness from all the sensors.

18. Tag and disconnect all remaining wiring from the head and related components.

19. Remove the alternator, leaving the wires connected and position it out of the way.

20. If equipped, remove the air pump and alternator/air pump bracket.

21. Remove the power steering pump and position it out of the way with the hoses still connected.

22. If the van is equipped with an air compressor, bleed the system, disconnect the two air pressure lines al the compressor.

23. Remove the A/C compressor from the bracket, then remove the power steering/A/C bracket.

24. If equipped, remove the upper intake manifold.

25. Loosen the coil bracket retainers and position the assembly aside.

26. Remove the valve cover.

27. Loosen the rocker arm bolts so they can be pivoted out of the way. Remove the pushrods in sequence so that they can be identified and reinstalled in their original positions.

28. Tag and disconnect the spark plug wires at the spark plugs.

29. Remove the cylinder head bolts and remove the cylinder head. Do not pry between the cylinder head and the block, as the gasket surfaces may be damaged.

30. If equipped, remove the secondary air injection manifold and check valve.

To install:

31. Clean the head and block gasket surfaces. If the cylinder head was removed for a gasket change, check the flatness of the cylinder head and block.

32. If equipped, install the secondary air injection manifold and check valve.

33. Position the gasket on the cylinder block.

34. Install a new gasket on the flange of the muffler inlet pipe.

35. Lift the cylinder head above the cylinder block and lower it into position using two head bolts installed through the head as guides.

36. Coat the threads of the cylinder head with a small amount of engine oil.

37. Install the bolts.

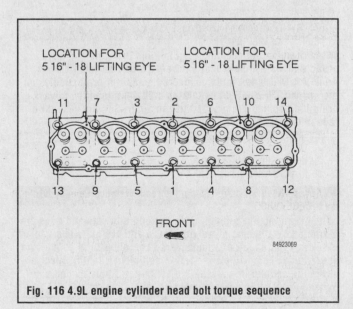

Fig. 116 4.9L engine cylinder head bolt torque sequence

38. For 1989–94 models, the cylinder head bolts are tightened in 3 progressive steps. Tighten them in the proper sequence as follows:
- Step 1: 50–55 ft. lbs. (68–75 Nm)
- Step 2: 60–65 ft. lbs. (81–88 Nm)
- Step 3: 70–85 ft. lbs. (95–115 Nm)

39. For 1995 models, tighten all bolts in numerical sequence in three steps:
- Step 1: 25–35 ft. lbs. (34–47 Nm)
- Step 2: 48–55 ft. lbs. (65–74 Nm)
- Step 3: Rotate all bolts an additional 80–100°

40. For 1996 models, tighten all bolts in numerical sequence in two steps:
- Step 1: 45–55 ft. lbs. (61–74 Nm)
- Step 2: Rotate all bolts an additional 80–100°

41. Apply multi-purpose grease to both ends of the pushrods and install them in their original positions.

42. Apply multi-purpose grease to both the fulcrum and seat and position the rocker arms on the valves and pushrods.

43. Adjust the valves. Refer to Section 1.

44. Install the valve cover.

45. Install the air compressor and bracket.

46. Install the power steering pump.

47. Install the air pump and bracket.

48. Install the alternator.

49. Connect all wiring at the head and related components.

50. Connect the EEC or PCM wiring harness to all the sensors.

51. Connect the muffler inlet pipe at the exhaust manifold.

52. Connect the engine ground strap and negative battery cable.

53. If equipped, connect the transmission kickdown rod on vans with an automatic transmission.

54. Connect the power brake hose at the manifold.

55. Connect the accelerator cable and retracting spring.

56. Install the water pump pulley, the engine fan and fan drive and the drive belt.

57. Install the radiator.

58. Connect the fuel line at the fuel pump or fuel injection manifold.

59. Connect the heater hoses at the water pump and coolant outlet housing.

60. Connect the negative battery cable.

61. Install the condenser.

62. Install the air conditioning compressor.

63. Have the system recharged by a qualified technician using an approved recovery/recycling station.

64. If equipped, install the throttle body inlet tubes.

65. Check that all hoses, tubes and wires are properly connected and fastened.

66. Fill and bleed the cooling system.

67. Add the correct amount and grade of engine oil.

68. On vans with automatic transmission, check the fluid level and add as necessary

69. If necessary, adjust the automatic transmission control linkage.

70. Install the engine cover.

71. Start the van and check for proper operation.

5.0L and 5.8L Engines

▶ See Figures 117 thru 123

Disconnect the negative battery cable.
1. Drain the cooling system.

✳✳ CAUTION

When draining the coolant, keep in mind that cats and dogs are attracted by ethylene glycol antifreeze and are quite likely to drink any that is left in an uncovered container or in puddles on the ground. This will prove fatal in sufficient quantity. Always drain the coolant into a sealable container. Coolant should be reused unless it is contaminated or several years old.

2. Remove the intake manifold(s) and throttle body as an assembly.
3. Remove the rocker arm cover(s).
4. If the right cylinder head is to be removed on 1989–90 models as follows:
 a. Remove the alternator and air pump mounting bracket with the accessories still attached.
 b. Swing the alternator down and out of the way.
 c. Remove the ignition coil and the air cleaner inlet duct from the left-hand cylinder head.
5. If the right cylinder head is to be removed on 1991–94 models as follows:
 a. Lift the tensioner and remove the drive belt.
 b. Loosen the alternator adjusting arm bolt and remove the alternator mounting bracket bolt and spacer.
 c. Swing the alternator down and out of the way. Remove the air cleaner inlet duct

If the left cylinder head is being removed, remove the air conditioning compressor/power steering bracket with accessories still attached and set them to one side. DO NOT DISCONNECT ANY LINES FROM EITHER COMPONENT!

✳✳ CAUTION

If the A/C compressor lines must be disconnected, please refer to Section 1 before discharging the compressor or disconnecting air conditioning lines. Damage to the air conditioning system or personal injury could result. Consult your local laws concerning refrigerant discharge and recycling. In many areas it may be illegal for anyone but a certified technician to service the A/C system. Always use an approved recovery station when discharging the air conditioning.

6. Remove the oil dipstick and tube. Remove the cruise control bracket.
7. Disconnect the exhaust manifold(s) from the muffler inlet pipe(s).
8. Loosen the rocker arm stud nuts so that the rocker arms can be rotated to the side. Remove the pushrods and identify them so that they can be reinstalled in their original positions.
9. Loosen the bolts holding the Thermactor® air supply manifold to the rear of the cylinder head, then disconnect the hose at the air pump.
10. Remove the hose, pump valve and air supply manifold as an assembly.
11. Remove the cylinder head bolts and lift the cylinder head from the block. Remove the discard the gasket.

Fig. 117 Unfasten the bolts holding the Thermactor® air supply manifold to the rear of the cylinder head

Fig. 118 Use a socket and breaker bar to loosen the cylinder head bolts

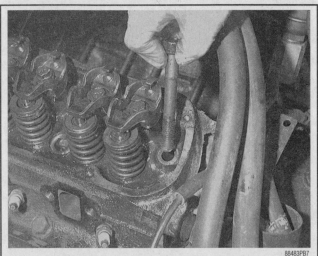

Fig. 119 Remove the old head bolts and discard them. Use only new bolts when installing the cylinder head

Fig. 120 Separate the head from the block and remove it from the engine compartment

To install:

12. Clean the cylinder head, intake manifold, the valve cover and the head gasket surfaces.

13. A specially treated composition head gasket is used. Do not apply sealer to a composition gasket. Position the new gasket over the locating dowels on the cylinder block. Then, position the cylinder head on the block and install the attaching bolts.

14. For 1989–91 models, the cylinder head bolts are tightened in progressive steps. Tighten all the bolts in the proper sequence to:

5.0L Engines
- Step 1: 55–65 ft. lbs. (75–88 Nm)
- Step 2: 66–72 ft. lbs. (89–97 Nm)

5.8L Engines
- Step 1: 85 ft. lbs. (115 Nm)
- Step 2: 95 ft. lbs. (129 Nm)
- Step 3: 105–112 ft. lbs. (142–151 Nm)

➡**All 1995–96 5.0L engines came with the flanged type of bolt only.**

15. For 1992–96 models, the cylinder head bolts are tightened in progressive steps. Tighten all the bolts in the proper sequence to:

Fig. 121 Use a gasket scraper to clean the cylinder head mating surfaces

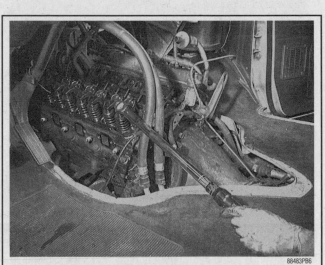

Fig. 122 Use a torque wrench to tighten the head bolts in the proper sequence to the correct specification

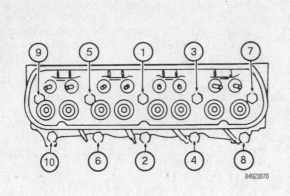

Fig. 123 Cylinder head bolt tightening sequence—5.0L, 5.8L and 7.5L engines

5.0L engines with FLANGED head bolts
- Step 1: 25–35 ft. lbs. (34–47 Nm)
- Step 2: 45–55 ft. lbs. (61–75 Nm)
- Step 3: Rotate all bolts an additional 85–95°

5.0L engines with HEX head bolts
- Step 1: 55–65 ft. lbs. (75–88 Nm)
- Step 2: 65–72 ft. lbs. (88–98 Nm)

5.8L engines
- Step 1: 95–105 ft. lbs. (129–142 Nm)
- Step 3: 105–112 ft. lbs. (142–151 Nm)

16. Clean the pushrods. Blow out the oil passage in the rods with compressed air. Check the pushrods for straightness by rolling them on a piece of glass. Never try to straighten a bent pushrod; always replace it.

17. Apply multi-purpose grease to the ends of the pushrods and install them in their original positions.

18. Apply multi-purpose grease to the rocker arms and their fulcrum seats and install the rocker arms. Adjust the valves.

19. Position a new gasket(s) on the muffler inlet pipe(s) as necessary. Connect the exhaust manifold(s) at the muffler inlet pipe(s).

20. If the right cylinder head was removed, install the secondary air injection pump (if equipped) and the alternator and air cleaner duct.

21. Install the ignition coil and air cleaner.

22. Install the drive belt.

23. If the left cylinder head was removed, install the power steering and A/C compressor with the accessories, to the front of the cylinder head.

24. Install the dipstick and cruise control bracket.

25. Clean the valve cover and the cylinder head gasket surfaces. Place the new gaskets in the covers, making sure that the tabs of the gasket engage the notches provided in the cover.

26. If the A/C system lines were disconnected, have the system recharged by a qualified technician using an approved recovery/recycling station

27. Install the intake manifold(s) and related parts. Install the secondary air injection manifold tube, unplug the check valve and connect the supply hose.

28. Fill and bleed the cooling system.

7.5L Engine

1. Disconnect the negative battery cable.
2. Drain the cooling system.

✳✳ CAUTION

When draining the coolant, keep in mind that cats and dogs are attracted by ethylene glycol antifreeze and are quite likely to drink any that is left in an uncovered container or in puddles on the ground. This will prove fatal in sufficient quantity. Always drain the coolant into a sealable container. Coolant should be reused unless it is contaminated or several years old.

3. Remove the upper and lower intake manifolds.
4. Disconnect the exhaust pipe from the exhaust manifold.
5. Remove the drive belts.
6. Remove the secondary air injection system and alternator.
Remove the air pump or alternator bracket from the cylinder head.

✳✳ CAUTION

If the A/C lines must be disconnected, please refer to Section 1 before discharging the compressor or disconnecting air conditioning lines. Damage to the air conditioning system or personal injury could result. Consult your local laws concerning refrigerant discharge and recycling. In many areas it may be illegal for anyone but a certified technician to service the A/C system. Always use an approved recovery station when discharging the air conditioning.

7. If possible, unbolt the A/C compressor and set it aside without disconnecting the hoses. if not remove the air conditioning compressor from the engine.

8. Remove the bolts securing the power steering reservoir/A/C compressor bracket from the cylinder head and water pump. Position the reservoir and bracket out of the way.

9. Remove the oil filler tube.

10. Remove the valve covers. Remove the rocker arm bolts, rocker arms, oil deflectors, fulcrums and pushrods in sequence so that they can be reinstalled in their original positions.

11. Remove the cylinder head bolts and lift the head and exhaust manifold off the engine. If necessary, pry at the forward corners of the cylinder head against the casting bosses provided on the cylinder block. Do not damage the gasket mating surfaces of the cylinder head and block by prying against them.

To install:

12. Remove all gasket material from the cylinder head and block. Clean all gasket material from the mating surfaces of the intake manifold. If the exhaust manifold was removed, clean the mating surfaces of the cylinder head and exhaust manifold. Apply a thin coat of graphite grease to the cylinder head exhaust port areas and install the exhaust manifold.

13. Position two long cylinder head bolts in the two rear lower bolt holes of the left cylinder head. Place a long cylinder head bolt in the rear lower bolt hole of the right cylinder head. Use rubber bands to keep the bolts in position until the cylinder heads are installed on the cylinder block.

14. Position new cylinder head gaskets on the cylinder block dowels. Do not apply sealer to the gaskets, heads, or block.

15. Place the cylinder heads on the block, guiding the exhaust manifold studs into the exhaust pipe connections. Install the remaining cylinder head bolts. The longer bolts go in the lower row of holes.

16. On 1989–93 models, tighten all the cylinder head attaching bolts in the proper sequence in three stages as follows:
- Step 1: 80–90 ft. lbs. (108–122 Nm)
- Step 2: 100–110 ft. lbs. (135–149 Nm)
- Step 3: 130–140 ft. lbs. (176–190 Nm).

➡**When this procedure is used, it is not necessary to retighten the heads after extended use.**

17. On 1994–96 models, tighten all the cylinder head attaching bolts in the proper sequence in three stages as follows:
- Step 1: 70–80 ft. lbs. (95–108 Nm)
- Step 2: 100–110 ft. lbs. (135–149 Nm)
- Step 3: 130–140 ft. lbs. (176–190 Nm).

➡**When this procedure is used, it is not necessary to retighten the heads after extended use.**

18. Make sure that the oil holes in the pushrods are open and install the pushrods in their original positions. Place a dab of Multi-purpose grease to the ends of the pushrods before installing them.

19. Lubricate and install the valve rockers. Make sure that the pushrods remain seated in their lifters.

20. Connect the exhaust pipes to the exhaust manifolds.

21. Install the intake manifold(s).

22. Check the valve clearance. Refer to Section 1.

23. Apply oil-resistant sealer to one side of the new valve cover gaskets and lay the cemented side in place in the valve cover. Install the covers.

24. Install the air conditioning compressor.

25. Install the power steering reservoir.

26. Install the alternator.

27. Install and adjust the drive belts.

28. Install the oil filler tube.

29. Fill and bleed the cooling system.

30. Connect the negative battery cable.

31. Start the engine and check for leaks.

32. If the A/C lines where disconnected to remove a system component, have the system evacuated and recharged by a qualified technician using an approved recovery/recycling station.

7.3L Diesel Engines

1989–94 MODELS

▶ See Figures 124 and 125

1. Disconnect both negative battery cables.

✷✷ CAUTION

When draining the coolant, keep in mind that cats and dogs are attracted by ethylene glycol antifreeze and are quite likely to drink any that is left in an uncovered container or in puddles on the ground. This will prove fatal in sufficient quantity. Always drain the coolant into a sealable container. Coolant should be reused unless it is contaminated or several years old.

2. Drain the cooling system and remove the radiator fan shroud.

3. Remove the radiator fan and clutch assembly using special tool T83T–6312–A and B, or equivalent.

➡This tool (T83T–6312–A and B) is available through Ford dealers and through many tool rental shops.

➡The fan clutch uses a left-hand thread and must be removed by turning the nut CLOCKWISE.

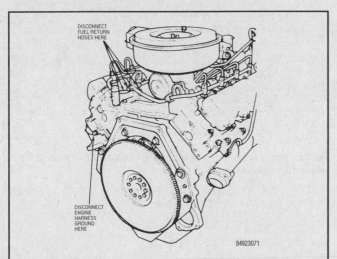

Fig. 124 Diesel fuel hose and engine ground harness connections

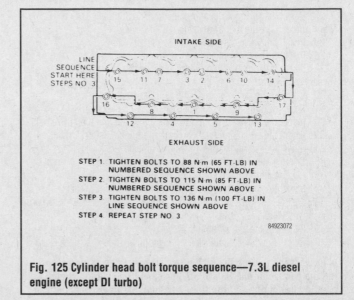

Fig. 125 Cylinder head bolt torque sequence—7.3L diesel engine (except DI turbo)

4. Label and disconnect the wiring from the alternator and fuel filter/heater/water separator.

5. Remove the adjusting bolts and pivot bolts from the alternator and the vacuum pump and remove both units.

6. If necessary, remove the power steering pump and bracket.

7. If necessary, unbolt the A/C compressor and set it aside.

8. If necessary, disconnect and cap the fuel lines.

9. Remove the heater hose from the cylinder head.

10. Remove the fuel injection pump as described in Section 5 under Diesel Fuel System.

11. Remove the intake manifold and valley cover.

12. Raise the van and support it with safety stands.

13. Disconnect the exhaust pipes from the exhaust manifolds.

14. Remove the clamp holding the engine oil dipstick tube in place and the bolt attaching the transmission oil dipstick to the cylinder head.

15. Lower the van.

16. Remove the engine oil dipstick tube and O-ring.

17. Remove the exhaust manifolds.

18. Remove the valve covers, rocker arms and pushrods. Keep the pushrods in order so they can be returned to their original positions.

19. Remove the nozzles and glow plugs as described in Section 5 under Diesel Fuel System.

20. Remove the cylinder head bolts and attach lifting eyes, using special tool T70P–6000 or equivalent, to each end of the cylinder heads.

21. Carefully lift the cylinder heads out of the engine compartment and remove the head gaskets.

➡The cylinder head pre-chambers may fall out of the heads upon removal.

To install:

22. Position the cylinder head gasket on the engine block with the silver stamped "This Side Up" facing the installer, then carefully lower the cylinder head in place.

➡Use care in installing the cylinder heads to prevent the pre-chambers from falling out into the cylinder bores.

23. Install the cylinder head bolt and torque in 4 steps using the sequence shown in the illustration.

➡Lubricate the threads and the mating surfaces of the bolt heads and washers with engine oil. Do not use anti-seize compound or grease.

24. Install the nozzles and glow plugs.

25. Dip the pushrod ends in clean engine oil and install the pushrods with the copper colored ends toward the rocker arms, making sure the pushrods are fully seated in the tappet pushrod seats.

26. Install the rocker arms and posts in their original positions. Apply Multi-purpose grease to the valve stem tips.

27. Install the valve covers.

28. Install the valley pan and the intake manifold.

29. Install the fuel injection pump as described in Section 5 under Diesel Fuel System.

30. Connect the heater hose to the cylinder head.

31. If removed, install the A/C compressor.

32. Install the fuel filter, alternator, vacuum pump and their drive belt(s).

33. Install the engine oil (with O-ring) and transmission dip stick.

34. Raise the van and support it with safety stands.

35. Connect the exhaust pipe to the exhaust manifolds.

36. Reconnect the alternator wiring harness.

37. Install the air cleaner. Connect both negative battery cables.

38. Ensure all electrical connections, hoses, clamps and tubes are properly connected and fastened.

39. Refill and bleed the cooling system.

40. Run the engine and check for fuel, coolant and exhaust leaks.

➡️If necessary, purge the high pressure fuel lines of air by loosening the connector one half to one turn and cranking the engine until a solid stream of fuel, free from any bubbles, flows from the connections.

41. Check the injection pump timing. Refer to Section 5 for these procedures.

42. Install the radiator fan and clutch assembly using special tools T83T–6312A and B or equivalent.

➡️The fan clutch uses a left-hand thread. Tighten by turning the nut COUNTERCLOCKWISE. Install the radiator fan shroud.

1995–96 MODELS—RIGHT CYLINDER HEAD

▶ See Figures 126 thru 131

1. Remove the engine from the van.
2. Disengage the vacuum hose from the right intake manifold.
3. Disengage both electrical harness connectors from the valve cover.
4. Remove the valve cover and gasket.
5. Remove the intake manifold covers.
6. Disengage the fuel injector electrical injectors.
7. Disengage and cap the fuel lines from the heads.
8. Loosen the banjo bolt from the fuel supply line at the fuel pump.
9. Remove the fuel supply assembly.
10. Disconnect the heater hose.
11. Loosen the dipstick tube bracket retainer at the right exhaust manifold.
12. Remove the rocker arms and pushrods.
13. Loosen the four inboard fuel injector hold-down bolts.
14. Remove the four outboard fuel injector hold-down bolts, retaining screws and four oil deflectors.

✳️ WARNING

Remove the oil drain plugs prior to removing the injectors or oil could enter the combustion chamber which could result in hydrostatic lock and severe engine damage.

15. Remove the oil rail drain plugs.
16. Remove the fuel injectors using Injector Remover No. T94T–9000–AH1, or equivalent. Position the tool's fulcrum beneath the fuel injector hold-down plate and over the edge of the cylinder head. Install the remover screw in the threaded hole of the fuel injector plate (see illustration). Tighten the screw to lift out the injector from its bore. Place the injector in a suitable protective sleeve such as Rotunda Injector Protective Sleeve, No. 014–00933–2, and set the injector in a suitable holding rack.

➡️During removal the injector tab (located above the fuel injector) must be bent completely flat and flush with the cowl and heat shield.

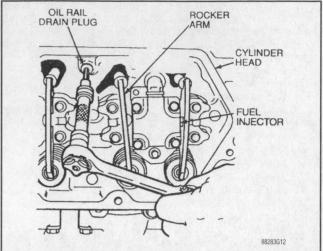

Fig. 126 Remove the oil rail drain plug as shown—7.3L DI turbo diesel engine

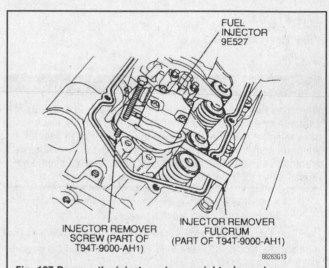

Fig. 127 Remove the injector using special tools as shown—7.3L DI turbo diesel engine

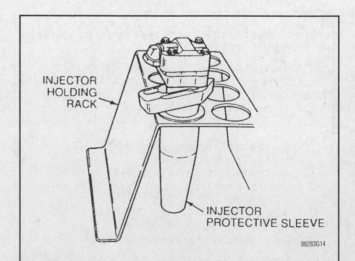

Fig. 128 Special fuel injector protection sleeve and holding rack—7.3L DI turbo diesel engine

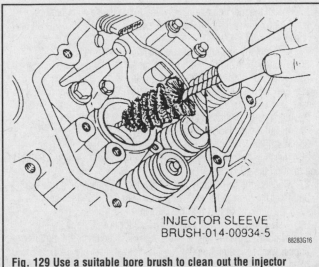

Fig. 129 Use a suitable bore brush to clean out the injector bores

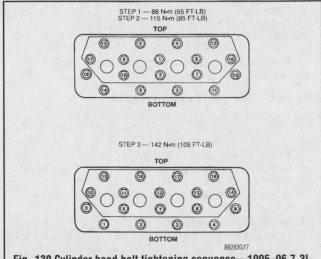

Fig. 130 Cylinder head bolt tightening sequence—1995–96 7.3L turbo diesel engine

17. Use a suitable vacuum tool, such as Rotunda Vacuum Pump, No. 021–00037, or equivalent to remove the oil and fuel left over in the injector bores.

18. Remove the four glow plugs.

19. Disconnect the high pressure oil pump supply line from the cylinder head.

20. Remove the grille opening reinforcement, headlamp assembly, radiator, oil reservoir and fuel filter assembly.

21. Remove the exhaust back pressure line.

22. Loosen the glow plug relay bracket retainers and disengage the ground wire.

23. Disconnect the fuel return line at the front of the cylinder head.

24. Loosen the cylinder head bolts.

25. Carefully lift the cylinder head out of the engine compartment and remove the head gaskets.

To install:

➡**To prepare a good seat for the fuel injector O-rings, use a suitable injector sleeve brush to clean any debris from the bore.**

26. Carefully clean the cylinder block and head mating surfaces.

27. Position the cylinder head gasket on the engine block and carefully lower the cylinder head in place.

28. Install the cylinder head bolt and torque in 3 steps using the sequence shown in the illustration.

➡**Lubricate the threads and the mating surfaces of the bolt heads and washers with engine oil.**

29. Connect the fuel return line to the cylinder head.

30. Install the glow plug relay bracket and ground wire, then tighten the retainers.

31. Install the exhaust back pressure line.

32. Install the high pressure fuel supply line and tighten the fitting to 19 ft. lbs. (26 Nm).

33. Connect the heater hose to the cylinder head.

34. Connect the manifold hoses.

35. Connect the fuel supply lines to the rear of the cylinder head.

36. Install the banjo bolt through the fuel line and into the pump. Tighten the pump to 40 ft. lbs. (55 Nm).

37. Coat the glow plugs with anti-seize compound and install them. Tighten the glow plugs to 14 ft. lbs. (19 Nm).

38. Install the fuel injectors using special tools as follows:

   a. Lubricate the injector O-rings with clean engine oil. Using new copper washers, carefully push the injectors square into the bore using hand pressure only to seat the O-rings.

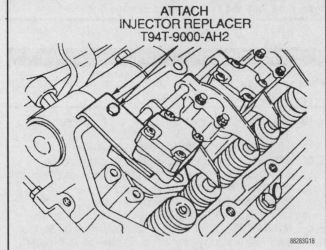

Fig. 131 Install the injectors using the special tool as shown— 7.3L DI turbo diesel engine

   b. Position the open end of Injector replacer, No. T94T–9000–AH2, or equivalent between the fuel injector body and injector hold-down plate, while positioning the opposite end of the tool over the edge of the cylinder head.

   c. Align the hole in the tool with the threaded hole in the cylinder head and install the bolt from the tool kit. Tighten the bolt to fully seat the injector, then remove the bolt and tool.

39. Install the oil rail drain plugs and tighten them to 53 inch lbs. (6 Nm).

40. Install the four outboard fuel injector hold-down bolts, the four oil deflectors and retaining screws. Tighten them to 120 inch lbs. (12 Nm).

41. Install the four inboard fuel injector hold-down bolts and tighten them to 120 inch lbs. (12 Nm).

42. Install the oil deflectors.

43. Turn the engine by hand until the timing mark is at the 11 o'clock position as viewed from the front.

44. Dip the pushrod ends in clean engine oil and install the pushrods with the copper colored ends toward the rocker arms, making sure the pushrods are fully seated in the tappet pushrod seats.

45. Install the rocker arms and posts in their original positions. Apply multi-purpose grease to the valve stem tips. Install the rocker arm posts, bolts and tighten to 27 ft. lbs. (37 Nm).

46. Install the valve cover gasket.
47. Connect the wiring to the fuel injectors and glow plugs.
48. Install the valve cover, tightening the bolts to 97 inch lbs. (11 Nm).
49. Connect both electrical harness connectors to the valve cover.
50. Connect the vacuum hose to the right intake valve manifold cover.
51. Install the engine in the van.

1995–96 MODELS—LEFT CYLINDER HEAD

▶ See Figures 126 thru 131

1. Remove the engine from the van.
2. Remove the wiring harness bracket.
3. Disengage the electrical connections from the valve cover gasket, then remove the valve cover.
4. Disengage the electrical connections from the fuel injectors and glow plugs.
5. Remove the valve cover gasket.
6. Remove the rocker arms and pushrods, KEEP EVERYTHING IN ORDER.
7. Remove the four inboard fuel injector hold-down bolts.

✶✶ WARNING

Remove the oil drain plugs prior to removing the injectors or oil could enter the combustion chamber which could result in hydrostatic lock and severe engine damage.

8. Remove the oil rail drain plugs.

✶✶ CAUTION

Make sure to retrieve the fuel injector copper washer, located at the tip of the injector during removal.

9. Remove the four outboard fuel injector hold-down bolts, retaining screws and four oil deflectors.
10. Remove the fuel injectors using Injector Remover No. T94T–9000–AH1, or equivalent. Position the tool's fulcrum beneath the fuel injector hold-down plate and over the edge of the cylinder head. Install the remover screw in the threaded hole of the fuel injector plate (see illustration). Tighten the screw to lift out the injector from its bore. Place the injector in a suitable protective sleeve such as Rotunda Injector Protective Sleeve, No. 014–00933–2, and set the injector in a suitable holding rack.
11. Use a suitable vacuum tool, such as Rotunda Vacuum Pump, No. 021–00037, or equivalent to remove the oil and fuel left over in the injector bores.
12. Remove the four glow plugs.
13. Disconnect the fuel supply lines from the rear of the cylinder head.
14. Remove the banjo bolt from the fuel line at the pump.
15. Disengage the oil line from the high pressure oil pump.
16. Disengage the electrical connection from the injection control pressure sensor.
17. Remove the high pressure oil supply line from the left cylinder head.
18. Lossen the fuel line nut from the intake manifold stud, then disconnect the fuel return line from the left cylinder head.
19. Loosen the fuel return line block screws at the front of the left cylinder head.
20. Remove the fuel line retaining clamp from the intake manifold cover.
21. Loosen the cylinder head bolts.
22. Remove the oil reservoir and fuel filter.
23. Remove the cylinder head and gasket.
To install:

➥**To prepare a good seat for the fuel injector O-rings, use a suitable injector sleeve brush to clean any debris from the bore.**

24. Carefully clean the cylinder block and head mating surfaces.
25. Position the cylinder head gasket on the engine block and carefully lower the cylinder head in place.
26. Install the cylinder head bolt and torque in 3 steps using the sequence shown in the illustration.

27. Install the fuel line retaining clamp to the intake manifold cover.
28. Tighten the fuel return line block screws at the front of the left cylinder head.
29. Connect the fuel return line to the left cylinder head.
30. Tighten the fuel line nut from the intake manifold stud.
31. Install the high pressure oil supply line to the left cylinder head.
32. Engage the electrical connection to the injection control pressure sensor.
33. Engage the oil line to the high pressure oil pump.
34. Install the manifold hoses.
35. Install the fuel supply line.
36. Install the banjo bolt through the fuel line into the pump. Tighten the bolt to 40 ft. lbs. (55 Nm).
37. Connect the fuel supply lines at the rear of the cylinder heads.
38. Coat the glow plugs with anti-seize compound and install them. Tighten the glow plugs to 14 ft. lbs. (19 Nm).
39. Install the fuel injectors using special tools as follows:
    a. Lubricate the injector O-rings with clean engine oil. Using new copper washers, carefully push the injectors square into the bore using hand pressure only to seat the O-rings.
    b. Position the open end of Injector replacer, No. T94T–9000–AH2, or equivalent between the fuel injector body and injector hold-down plate, while positioning the opposite end of the tool over the edge of the cylinder head.
    c. Align the hole in the tool with the threaded hole in the cylinder head and install the bolt from the tool kit. Tighten the bolt to fully seat the injector, then remove the bolt and tool.
40. Install the four outboard fuel injector hold-down bolts, the four oil deflectors and retaining screws. Tighten them to 120 inch lbs. (12 Nm).
41. Install the oil deflectors and tighten the bolts to 120 inch lbs. (12 Nm).
42. Install the oil rail drain plugs and tighten them to 53 inch lbs. (6 Nm).
43. Install the four inboard fuel injector hold-down bolts and tighten them to 120 inch lbs. (12 Nm).
44. Turn the engine over by hand until the timing mark is at the 11 o'clock position as viewed from the front.
45. Dip the pushrod ends in clean engine oil and install the pushrods with the copper colored ends toward the rocker arms, making sure the pushrods are fully seated in the tappet pushrod seats.
46. Install the rocker arms and posts in their original positions. Apply Multi-purpose grease to the valve stem tips. Install the rocker arm posts, bolts and tighten to 27 ft. lbs. (37 Nm).
47. Install the valve cover gasket.
48. Connect the wiring to the fuel injectors and glow plugs.
49. Install the valve cover, tightening the bolts to 97 inch lbs. (11 Nm).
50. Connect both electrical harness connectors to the valve cover.
51. Install the engine in the van.

Oil Pan

REMOVAL & INSTALLATION

4.9L Engines

1989–91 MODELS

▶ See Figure 132

1. Remove the engine cover.
2. Remove the air cleaner and disconnect the air inlet hoses from the throttle body.
3. If the van is equipped with A/C, have the system evacuated by a qualified technician using an approved recovery/recycling system, then remove the compressor.
4. Remove the EGR valve.
5. Drain the crankcase.

⚜ CAUTION

The EPA warns that prolonged contact with used engine oil may cause a number of skin disorders, including cancer! You should make every effort to minimize your exposure to used engine oil. Protective gloves should be worn when changing the oil. Wash your hands and any other exposed skin areas as soon as possible after exposure to used engine oil. Soap and water, or waterless hand cleaner should be used.

6. Drain the cooling system.

⚜ CAUTION

When draining the coolant, keep in mind that cats and dogs are attracted by ethylene glycol antifreeze and are quite likely to drink any that is left in an uncovered container or in puddles on the ground. This will prove fatal in sufficient quantity. Always drain the coolant into a sealable container. Coolant should be reused unless it is contaminated or several years old.

7. Remove the upper intake manifold and throttle body assembly.
8. Disconnect the Thermactor® inlet hose and remove the check valve.
9. Disconnect the upper radiator hose and remove the fan shroud.
10. If equipped with an automatic transmission, remove the fluid filler tube.
11. Loosen the exhaust pipe-to-manifold nuts.
12. Raise the van and support it with safety stands.
13. Disconnect the fuel pump inlet hose.
14. Loosen the front engine support retainers.
15. Disconnect the power steering return line clip from the front of the crossmember.
16. Disconnect the lower radiator hose and transmission cooler lines.
17. Remove the starter.
18. Raise the front of the engine with a jack and wood block and place a 3 in. (76mm) thick wood blocks under the front support mounts. Lower the engine and remove the transmission jack.
19. Remove the engine oil dipstick tube.
20. Remove the oil pan attaching bolts and lower the pan .
21. Remove the pan and gasket.

To install:

22. Clean the gasket surfaces of the oil pump, oil pan and cylinder block. Clean the seal grooves.
23. apply a pressure sensitive silicone adhesive to the block rails and front cover of the oil pan.

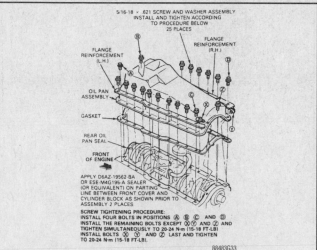

Fig. 132 Oil pan bolt tightening specifications—1989–91 4.9L engines

24. Apply a bead of silicone sealant to the parting line between the front cover and the block; also to the tapered ends of the rear seal portion of the gasket.
25. Install the gasket, clean the inlet tube and screen assembly and place it in the pan.
26. Install the pan and tighten the retainers to 144–216 ft. lbs. (16–24 Nm).
27. Install the dipstick tube, raise the engine and withdraw the wood block.
28. Install the front support retainers, starter and connect the fuel line.
29. Install the lower radiator hose and transmission cooler lines.
30. Install the power steering return line clip and lower the van.
31. Install the upper intake and throttle body assembly.
32. Install the EGR valve, connect the exhaust pipe to the manifold.
33. Install the Thermactor® check valve and connect the hose.
34. Install the fan shroud and connect the upper radiator hose.
35. Fill the cooling system.
36. If equipped with A/C, install the compressor and have the system recharged by a qualified technician using an approved recovery/recycling station.
37. Install a new oil filter and fill the crankcase with correct amount and grade of engine oil.
38. Start the van and check for leaks.
39. Install the air cleaner and inlet tubes.
40. Install the engine cover.

1992–96 MODELS

▶ **See Figure 133**

1. Remove the engine cover.
2. Remove the air cleaner and disconnect the air inlet hoses from the throttle body.
3. If equipped, loosen the idle air control valve retainers and set the valve aside, then cover the opening in the manifold with a clean shop towel.
4. Remove the fan shroud and rest it on the fan.
5. Remove the oil filler tube bracket and set it aside.
6. Drain the cooling system.

⚜ CAUTION

When draining the coolant, keep in mind that cats and dogs are attracted by ethylene glycol antifreeze and are quite likely to drink any that is left in an uncovered container or in puddles on the ground. This will prove fatal in sufficient quantity. Always drain the coolant into a sealable container. Coolant should be reused unless it is contaminated or several years old.

7. Remove the upper radiator hose.
8. If equipped, disconnect the auxiliary heater hoses from the cowl.
9. Raise the van and support it with safety stands.
10. Drain the crankcase and remove the oil filter.

⚜ CAUTION

The EPA warns that prolonged contact with used engine oil may cause a number of skin disorders, including cancer! You should make every effort to minimize your exposure to used engine oil. Protective gloves should be worn when changing the oil. Wash your hands and any other exposed skin areas as soon as possible after exposure to used engine oil. Soap and water, or waterless hand cleaner should be used.

11. Disconnect the lower radiator hose.
12. Disengage the starter motor and the oxygen sensor.
13. Loosen the front engine support retainers, then raise the engine with a jack and wood block and place a 3 in. (76mm) thick wood blocks under the front support mounts. Lower the engine and remove the transmission jack.
14. Remove the oil pan attaching bolts and lower the pan .

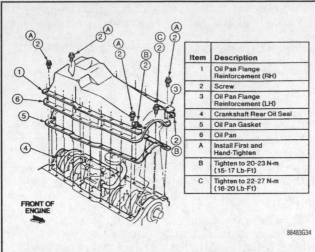

Item	Description
1	Oil Pan Flange Reinforcement (RH)
2	Screw
3	Oil Pan Flange Reinforcement (LH)
4	Crankshaft Rear Oil Seal
5	Oil Pan Gasket
6	Oil Pan
A	Install First and Hand-Tighten
B	Tighten to 20-23 N·m (15-17 Lb-Ft)
C	Tighten to 22-27 N·m (16-20 Lb-Ft)

FRONT OF ENGINE

88483G34

Fig. 133 Oil pan bolt tightening specifications—1992–96 4.9L engines

To install:

15. Clean the gasket surfaces of the oil pump, oil pan and cylinder block. Clean the seal grooves.

16. Apply a pressure sensitive silicone adhesive to the block rails and front cover of the oil pan.

17. Apply a bead of silicone sealant to the parting line between the front cover and the block. Also to the tapered ends of the rear seal portion of the gasket.

18. Install the gasket, clean the inlet tube and screen assembly and place it in the pan.

19. Install the pan and tighten the retainers to 12–18 ft. lbs. (16–24 Nm) on 1992–94 models or 15–17 ft. lbs. (20–23 Nm) on 1995–96 models, except retainer **C** (refer to the illustration), which is tightened to 16–20 ft. lbs. (21–27 Nm).

20. Raise the engine and withdraw the wood block.

21. Engage the starter motor and the oxygen sensor.

22. Connect the lower radiator hose, install a new oil filter and lower the van.

23. If equipped, connect the auxiliary heater hoses from the cowl.

24. Connect the upper radiator hose and install the fan shroud.

25. Install the idle air control valve and tighten the retainers.

26. Fill the radiator.

27. Fill the crankcase with the correct type and amount of engine oil.

28. Start the van and check for leaks.

29. Install the air cleaner and connect the air inlet hoses to the throttle body.

30. Install the engine cover.

5.0L and 5.8L Engines

1989–91 MODELS

▶ See Figure 134

1. Remove the engine cover.
2. Remove the air cleaner.
3. Drain the cooling system.

✻ CAUTION

When draining the coolant, keep in mind that cats and dogs are attracted by ethylene glycol antifreeze and are quite likely to drink any that is left in an uncovered container or in puddles on the ground. This will prove fatal in sufficient quantity. Always drain the coolant into a sealable container. Coolant should be reused unless it is contaminated or several years old.

4. Loosen the power steering and A/C compressor belts and brackets, then set them aside. Do not disconnect the lines.

5. Disconnect the upper radiator hose.

6. Remove the fan shroud and rest it on the fan.

7. Remove the oil filler tube retainers.

8. Raise the van and support it with safety stands.

9. If equipped, remove the splash shield from under the alternator.

10. Disconnect the transmission cooler lines (if equipped) and the lower radiator hose.

11. Disconnect the fuel line at the fuel rail.

12. Loosen the engine mount retainers.

13. Drain the crankcase.

✻ CAUTION

The EPA warns that prolonged contact with used engine oil may cause a number of skin disorders, including cancer! You should make every effort to minimize your exposure to used engine oil. Protective gloves should be worn when changing the oil. Wash your hands and any other exposed skin areas as soon as possible after exposure to used engine oil. Soap and water, or waterless hand cleaner should be used.

14. Remove the dipstick tube from the oil pan and disconnect the exhaust inlet pipe from the manifolds.

15. if equipped, remove the automatic transmission filler tube and dipstick.

16. Disconnect the transmission manual linkage.

17. Remove the center driveshaft support and the driveshaft.

18. Raise the engine with a jack and wood block at least 4 inches (102 mm).

19. Insert wooden blocks to support the engine.

20. Loosen the oil pan attaching bolts, then remove the pan.

To install:

21. Clean the gasket surfaces of the oil pump, oil pan and cylinder block.

22. Position new gaskets and seals on the block.

23. Install the pan and tighten the bolts to the indicated specifications.

24. Install the dipstick tube.

25. Install the driveshaft and support.

26. Connect the transmission manual linkage.

27. Install the muffler inlet pipe and the transmission filler tube.

28. Connect the lower radiator hose.

29. If equipped, connect the automatic transmission cooler lines and the fuel line to the fuel rail.

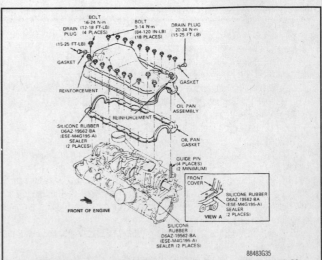

88483G35

Fig. 134 Tighten the oil pan bolts as indicated—1989–91 5.0L and 5.8L engines

30. Install the splash shield and lower the van.
31. Install the fan shroud and connect the upper radiator hose.
32. Install the power steering pump and A/C compressor assemblies and brackets.
33. Tighten the oil fillet tube retainers.
34. Install and adjust the drive belts.
35. Install the air cleaner and filler the crankcase with the proper type and amount of engine oil.
36. Fill the cooling system and install the engine cover.
37. Start the van and check for leaks.

1992–96 MODELS

▶ See Figure 135

1. Remove the engine cover.
2. Disconnect the negative battery cable.
3. Remove the air cleaner.
4. Drain the cooling system.

※※ CAUTION

When draining the coolant, keep in mind that cats and dogs are attracted by ethylene glycol antifreeze and are quite likely to drink any that is left in an uncovered container or in puddles on the ground. This will prove fatal in sufficient quantity. Always drain the coolant into a sealable container. Coolant should be reused unless it is contaminated or several years old.

5. Disconnect the upper radiator hose.
6. Remove the fan shroud and fan.
7. Remove the oil filler tube.
8. Disconnect the power steering hose from the steering gear.
9. Remove the oil dipstick and tube.
10. Disconnect the junction block from the engine.
   a. If equipped, disconnect the auxiliary heater hoses from the engine.
11. Remove the upper intake manifold.
12. Raise the van and support it with safety stands.
13. Drain the crankcase.

※※ CAUTION

The EPA warns that prolonged contact with used engine oil may cause a number of skin disorders, including cancer! You should make every effort to minimize your exposure to used engine oil. Protective gloves should be worn when changing the oil. Wash your hands and any other exposed skin areas as soon as possible after exposure to used engine oil. Soap and water, or waterless hand cleaner should be used.

14. Disconnect the exhaust pipe from the manifolds, pipe-to-muffler clamp and the muffler support bolt.
15. Disengage the oxygen sensor electrical connection, then remove the exhaust pipe and front catalytic converters.
16. Remove the four engine mount retaining nuts and the starter wiring clip.
17. Raise the engine with a jack and wood block at least 4 in. (102mm).
18. Insert wooden blocks to support the engine.
19. Loosen the oil pan attaching bolts, then remove the pan
To install:
20. Clean the gasket surfaces of the oil pump, oil pan and cylinder block.
21. On 5.8L engines, apply black silicone rubber F4AZ-19562-B or its equivalent on two places on the front cover, two places on the flange and two places on the gasket at the rear main bearing cap-to-block seam and place the gasket on the block.
22. On 5.0L engines, apply sealant WSE-M4G323-A3 to the areas indicated in the illustration.
23. Install the pan and tighten the bolts to the indicated specifications.
24. Install the starter wiring clip, remove the blocks and lower the engine.

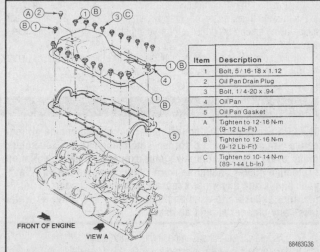

Item	Description
1	Bolt, 5 / 16-18 x 1.12
2	Oil Pan Drain Plug
3	Bolt, 1/ 4-20 x .94
4	Oil Pan
5	Oil Pan Gasket
A	Tighten to 12-16 N·m (9-12 Lb-Ft)
B	Tighten to 12-16 N·m (9-12 Lb-Ft)
C	Tighten to 10-14 N·m (89-144 Lb-In)

FRONT OF ENGINE   VIEW A

88483G36

Fig. 135 Oil pan bolts tightening specifications—1992–96 5.0L and 5.8L engines

25. Install the engine mount retainers.
26. With the aid of a helper, install the exhaust pipe and catalytic converters. Tighten the pipe-to-manifold nuts to 24–36 ft. lbs. (33–49 Nm).
27. Engage the oxygen sensor electrical connection and lower the van.
28. Install the upper intake manifold and if equipped, the auxiliary heater hose's.
29. Install the junction block, then the oil dipstick and tube.
30. Connect the power steering hose to the gear and install the oil filler tube.
31. Install the fan shroud and fan.
32. Install the upper radiator hose.
33. Install the air cleaner and filler the crankcase with the proper type and amount of engine oil.
34. Fill the cooling system and bleed the power steering system.
35. Install the engine cover and connect the negative battery cable.
36. Start the van and check for leaks.

7.5L Engines

1989–93 MODELS

1. Remove the engine cover.
2. Disconnect the battery ground cable.
3. Drain the cooling system.

※※ CAUTION

When draining the coolant, keep in mind that cats and dogs are attracted by ethylene glycol antifreeze and are quite likely to drink any that is left in an uncovered container or in puddles on the ground. This will prove fatal in sufficient quantity. Always drain the coolant into a sealable container. Coolant should be reused unless it is contaminated or several years old.

4. Remove the air intake tube and air cleaner assembly.
5. Disconnect the throttle and transmission linkage at the throttle body.
6. Disconnect the power brake vacuum line at the manifold.
7. Disconnect the fuel lines at the fuel rail.
8. Disconnect the air tubes at the throttle body.
9. Remove the radiator and fan.
10. Remove the front engine mount through-bolts.
11. Remove the power steering pump and position it out of the way without disconnecting the lines.
12. Remove the oil dipstick tube.

13. Position the air conditioner refrigerant hoses so that they are clear of the firewall. If necessary, have the system discharged by a qualified technician using an approved recovery/recycling station and remove the compressor.

14. Remove the upper intake manifold and throttle body as an assembly.

15. Raise the van and support it with safety stands.

16. Drain the crankcase. Remove the oil filter.

✳✳ CAUTION

The EPA warns that prolonged contact with used engine oil may cause a number of skin disorders, including cancer! You should make every effort to minimize your exposure to used engine oil. Protective gloves should be worn when changing the oil. Wash your hands and any other exposed skin areas as soon as possible after exposure to used engine oil. Soap and water, or waterless hand cleaner should be used.

17. Disconnect the exhaust pipe at the manifolds.

18. Disconnect the transmission linkages at the transmission.

19. Remove the driveshaft.

20. Remove the transmission fill tube.

21. Raise the engine with a jack placed under the crankshaft damper and a block of wood to act as a cushion. Raise the engine until the transmission contacts the underside of the floor. Place wood blocks under the engine supports. The engine **must** remain centralized at a point at least 4 in. (102mm) above the mounts, to remove the oil pan!

22. Loosen the oil pan attaching screws, then remove the pan.

To install:

23. Clean the gasket surfaces of the oil pan and cylinder block.

24. Apply a coating of gasket adhesive on the block mating surface and stick the 1-piece silicone gasket on the block.

25. Position the oil pan against the cylinder block and install the retaining bolts. Tighten all ¼ inch bolts to 7–9 ft. lbs. (10–12 Nm) and the 5⁄16 inch bolts to 8–11 ft. lbs. (11–15 Nm).

26. Lower the engine and bolt it in place.

27. Install the transmission fill tube.

28. Install the driveshaft.

29. Connect the transmission linkage at the transmission.

30. Connect the exhaust pipe at the manifolds.

31. Install the oil filter.

32. Install the upper intake manifold and throttle body.

33. Install the compressor or reposition the hoses. Have the system recharged by a qualified technician using an approved recovery/recycling station.

34. Install the oil dipstick tube.

35. Install the power steering pump.

36. Install the radiator and fan.

37. Connect the air tubes at the throttle body.

38. Connect the fuel lines at the fuel rail.

39. Connect the power brake vacuum line at the manifold.

40. Connect the throttle linkage at the throttle body.

41. Install the air intake tube and air cleaner assembly.

42. Fill and bleed the cooling system.

43. Fill the crankcase.

44. Connect the battery ground cable.

45. Install the engine cover.

1994–96 MODELS

▶ See Figure 136

1. Remove the engine cover.

2. Disconnect the battery ground cable.

3. Drain the cooling system.

✳✳ CAUTION

When draining the coolant, keep in mind that cats and dogs are attracted by ethylene glycol antifreeze and are quite likely to drink any that is left in an uncovered container or in puddles on the ground. This will prove fatal in sufficient quantity. Always drain the coolant into a sealable container. Coolant should be reused unless it is contaminated or several years old.

4. Remove the air intake tube and air cleaner assembly.

5. Remove the fan shroud, fan and water pump pulley.

6. Remove the upper intake manifold, then tag and disengage the vacuum hose's from the upper and lower intake manifolds.

7. Relieve the fuel system pressure and disengage the fuel supply and return lines.

8. Disconnect the both the radiator hose's and the transmission cooler lines from the radiator.

9. Unbolt the power steering pump and set it aside with the lines still attached.

10. Loosen the front engine mount retainers and the nuts attaching the oil level indicator tube to the exhaust manifold.

11. Loosen the filler pipe and bracket.

12. Rotate the lines at the rear of the A/C compressor down so that they clear the dash, then remove the compressor and set it aside with the lines still attached.

13. Raise the van and support it with jackstands.

14. Drain the oil and remove the oil bypass filter.

15. Disconnect the muffler inlet, then disconnect the transmission linkages from the transmission.

16. Remove the driveshaft assembly and the oil filler tube assembly.

17. Remove the oil level indicator and tube.

18. Raise the engine with a jack placed under the crankshaft damper and a block of wood to act as a cushion. Raise the engine until the transmission contacts the underside of the floor. Place wood blocks under the engine supports. The engine **must** remain centralized at a point at least 4 in. (102mm) above the mounts, to remove the oil pan!

19. Loosen the oil pan attaching retainers, then remove the pan.

To install:

20. Clean the gasket surfaces of the oil pan and cylinder block.

21. Apply a coating of gasket adhesive on the block mating surface and a bead of silicone rubber D6AZ-19562-AA or its equivalent, at the parting line of the front cover and cylinder block.

22. Install the gasket and the pan, then tighten the retainers to 8–12 ft. lbs. (11–16 Nm).

23. Raise the engine, remove the blocks and lower the engine.

24. Engage the oil level indicator tube to the oil pan and exhaust manifold.

25. Install the A/C compressor and ensure the lines are routed properly.

26. Install the engine support retainers and connect the transmission linkages.

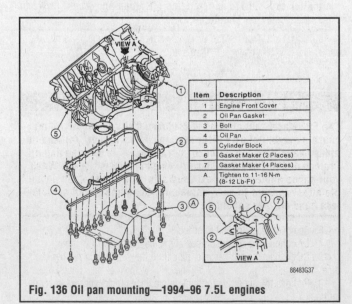

Item	Description
1	Engine Front Cover
2	Oil Pan Gasket
3	Bolt
4	Oil Pan
5	Cylinder Block
6	Gasket Maker (2 Places)
7	Gasket Maker (4 Places)
A	Tighten to 11-16 N·m (8- 12 Lb-Ft)

88483G37

Fig. 136 Oil pan mounting—1994–96 7.5L engines

27. Install the driveshaft assembly and the muffler inlet pipe assembly.
28. Install the oil bypass filter.
29. Lower the van, install the oil fill pipe, then tighten the oil level indicator-to-exhaust manifold nut.
30. Connect the transmission cooler lines and radiator hose's.
31. Install the water pump pulley, fan assembly and shroud.
32. Install the upper intake manifold.
33. Connect the vacuum lines to the intake manifolds.
34. install the power steering pump and drive belt.
35. Install the air cleaner and outlet tube.

➡When the battery is disconnected and reconnected, some abnormal drive systems may occur while the Powertrain Control Module (PCM) relearns the adaptive strategy. The van may need to be driven 10 miles or more for the strategy to be relearned.

36. Fill and bleed the cooling system and connect the negative battery cable.
37. Fill the crankcase with the proper amount and type of engine oil.
38. Start the van and check for leaks.

7.3L Diesel Engines

▶ See Figure 137

1. Disconnect both battery ground cables.
2. Remove the engine oil dipstick.
3. Remove the transmission oil dipstick.
4. Remove the air cleaner and cover the intake opening.
5. If equipped, remove the turbocharger.
6. Remove the fan and fan clutch.

➡The fan uses left-hand threads. Remove them by turning them clockwise.

7. Drain the cooling system.

❋❋ CAUTION

When draining the coolant, keep in mind that cats and dogs are attracted by ethylene glycol antifreeze and are quite likely to drink any that is left in an uncovered container or in puddles on the ground. This will prove fatal in sufficient quantity. Always drain the coolant into a sealable container. Coolant should be reused unless it is contaminated or several years old.

8. Disconnect the lower radiator hose.
9. Disconnect the power steering return hose and plug the line and pump.
10. Disconnect the alternator wiring harness.
11. Disconnect the fuel line heater connector from the alternator.
12. Raise and support the front end on jackstands.
13. On vans with automatic transmission, disconnect the transmission cooler lines at the radiator and plug them.
14. Disconnect and plug the fuel pump inlet line.
15. Drain the crankcase and remove the oil filter.

❋❋ CAUTION

The EPA warns that prolonged contact with used engine oil may cause a number of skin disorders, including cancer! You should make every effort to minimize your exposure to used engine oil. Protective gloves should be worn when changing the oil. Wash your hands and any other exposed skin areas as soon as possible after exposure to used engine oil. Soap and water, or waterless hand cleaner should be used.

16. Remove the engine oil filler tube.
17. Disconnect the exhaust pipes at the manifolds.
18. Disconnect the muffler inlet pipe from the muffler and remove the pipe.
19. Remove the upper inlet mounting stud from the right exhaust manifold.

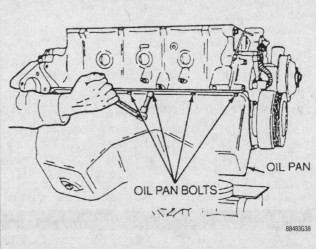

Fig. 137 Loosen the oil pan bolts, then remove the oil pan from the engine

20. Unbolt the engine from the No.1 crossmember.
21. Lower the vehicle.
22. Install lifting brackets on the front of the engine.
23. Raise the engine until the transmission contact the body.
24. Install wood blocks 2¾ in. (70mm) on the left side; 2 in. (50mm) on the right side, between the engine insulators and crossmember.
25. Lower the engine onto the blocks.
26. Raise and support the front end on jackstands.
27. Remove the flywheel inspection plate.
28. Position fuel pump inlet line No.1 rearward of the crossmember and position the oil cooler lines out of the way.
29. Remove the oil pan bolts.
30. Lower the oil pan.

➡The oil pan is sealed to the crankcase with RTV silicone sealant in place of a gasket. It may be necessary to separate the pan from the crankcase with a utility knife.

➡The crankshaft may have to be turned to allow the pan to clear the crankshaft throws.

31. Clean the pan and crankcase mating surfaces thoroughly.
To install:
32. Apply a ⅛ in. (3mm) bead of RTV silicone sealant to the pan mating surfaces, and a ¼ in. (6mm) bead on the front and rear covers and in the corners. You have 15 minutes within which to install the pan!
33. Install locating dowels (which you supply) into position as shown.
34. Position the pan on the engine and install the pan bolts loosely.
35. Remove the dowels.
36. Torque the pan bolts to 7 ft. lbs. (9 Nm) for ¼ in. (20 bolts); 14 ft. lbs. (18 Nm) for ⁵⁄₁₆ in. (18 bolts); 24 ft. lbs. (32 Nm) for ⅜ in. (16 bolts).
37. Install the flywheel inspection cover.
38. Lower the van.
39. Raise the engine and remove the wood blocks.
40. Lower the engine onto the crossmember and remove the lifting brackets.
41. Raise and support the front end on jackstands.
42. Torque the engine-to-crossmember nuts to 70 ft. lbs. (95 Nm).
43. Install the upper inlet pipe mounting stud.
44. Install the inlet pipe, using a new gasket.
45. Install the transmission oil filler tube, using a new gasket.
46. Install the oil pan drain plug.
47. Install a new oil filter.
48. Connect the fuel pump inlet line. Make sure that the clip is installed on the crossmember.
49. Connect the transmission cooler lines.

50. Lower the van.
51. Connect all wiring.
52. Connect the power steering return line.
53. Connect the lower radiator hose.
54. Install the fan and fan clutch.

➡**The fan uses left-hand threads. Install them by turning them counterclockwise.**

55. Remove the cover and install the air cleaner.
56. Install the dipsticks.
57. Fill the crankcase.
58. Fill and bleed the cooling system.
59. Fill the power steering reservoir.
60. Connect the batteries.
61. Run the engine and check for leaks.

Oil Pump

REMOVAL & INSTALLATION

Gasoline Engines

▶ **See Figure 138**

1. Remove the oil pan.
2. Rcmove the oil pump inlet tube and screen assembly.
3. Remove the oil pump attaching bolts and remove the oil pump gasket and intermediate driveshaft.
4. Before installing the oil pump, prime it by filling the inlet and outlet port with engine oil and rotating the shaft of the pump to distribute it.
5. Position the intermediate driveshaft into the distributor socket.
6. Position the new gasket on the pump body and insert the intermediate driveshaft into the pump body.

To install:

7. Install the pump and intermediate driveshaft as an assembly. Do not force the pump if it does not seal readily. The driveshaft may be misaligned with the distributor shaft. To align it, rotate the intermediate driveshaft into a new position.
8. Install the oil pump attaching bolts and tighten them to 10–12 ft. lbs. (14–20 Nm) on the 1989–94 six-cylinder engines, 12–18 ft. lbs. (16–24 Nm) on the 1995–96 six-cylinder engines, or 22–32 ft. lbs. (30–43 Nm) on the V8 engines.

Diesel Engines

1989–94 MODELS

1. Loosen the oil pan retainers and lower it so that it rests on the front crossmember.
2. Remove the oil pan and pickup tube retainers, then lower them into the oil pan.

➡**It may be necessary to rotate the crankshaft so that there is enough clearance to remove the pan.**

3. Remove the pan, then lift the pump assembly from the pan.

To install:

4. Before installing the oil pump, prime it by filling the inlet and outlet port with engine oil and rotating the shaft of the pump to distribute it.
5. Place the oil pump and pickup tube in the oil pan, then set the pan on the front crossmember.
6. Install the pump and pickup tube, then tighten the retainers.
7. Install the oil pan.

1995–96 MODELS

▶ **See Figures 139, 140 and 141**

1. Remove the radiator, then raise the van and support it with safety stands.
2. Remove the flywheel inspection cover.

➡**Use a breaker bar to prevent the crankshaft from crankshaft from turning.**

3. Remove the crankshaft pulley bolt, then remove the damper using a puller.
4. Loosen the oil pump housing retainers, then remove the oil pump body plate and square cut O-ring.
5. Remove the inner and outer gerotors.
6. Clean the assembly and inspect for damage.

To install:

7. Install the inner gerotor on the crankshaft.
8. Install the body plate, outer gerotor and the O-ring. Coat the gerotor pump liberally with oil.
9. Tighten the body plate retainers.

➡**When the crankshaft damper is removed, the front seal should be replaced.**

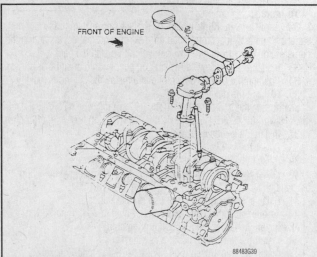

Fig. 138 Exploded view of a typical engine oil pump assembly— 5.0L engine shown; other gasoline engine pumps are similar

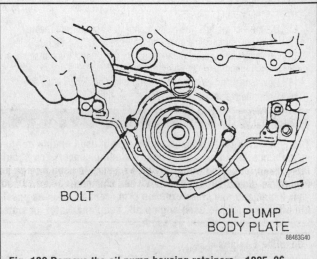

Fig. 139 Remove the oil pump housing retainers—1995–96 diesel engine

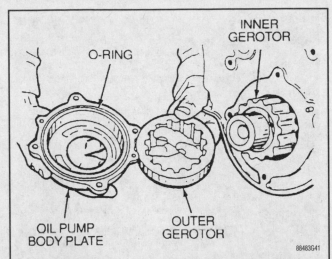

Fig. 140 Remove the body plate, then the inner and outer gerotors—1995–96 diesel engines

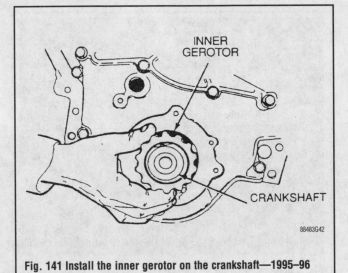

Fig. 141 Install the inner gerotor on the crankshaft—1995–96 diesel engines

10. Apply RTV sealant to the crankshaft keyway and then install the damper.

11. Install and tighten the pulley bolt to 212 ft. lbs. (287 Nm).

12. Remove the breaker bar and install the flywheel inspection cover.

13. Lower the van and install the radiator.

14. Install the fan and clutch assembly.

15. Check and refill the engine oil.

16. Start the van and check for proper operation.

Crankshaft Damper

REMOVAL & INSTALLATION

Gasoline Engines

▶ **See Figures 142 thru 149**

1. Remove the fan shroud, if required.
2. If necessary, drain the cooling system and remove the radiator.
3. Remove the drive belt from the pulley.

> ✸✸ **CAUTION**
>
> When draining the coolant, keep in mind that cats and dogs are attracted by ethylene glycol antifreeze and are quite likely to drink any that is left in an uncovered container or in puddles on the ground. This will prove fatal in sufficient quantity. Always drain the coolant into a sealable container. Coolant should be reused unless it is contaminated or several years old.

4. On those engines with a separate pulley, matchmark the pulley to its mount, then remove the retaining bolts to separate the pulley from the vibration damper.

5. Remove the vibration damper/pulley retaining bolt from the crankshaft end.

6. Using a puller, remove the damper/pulley from the crankshaft.

To install:

7. Align the key slot of the pulley hub to the crankshaft key, then install the damper, tightening the retaining hardware to specification.

8. Install the drive belt.

9. Install the radiator and fan shroud.

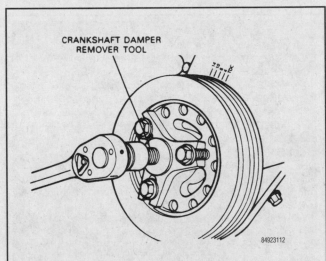

Fig. 142 Remove the crankshaft damper using a puller such as this one—4.9L engine shown

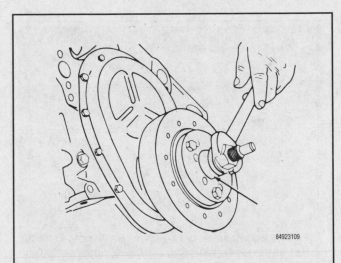

Fig. 143 The threaded rod portion of the puller tool can also be used to install the crankshaft damper on gasoline engines

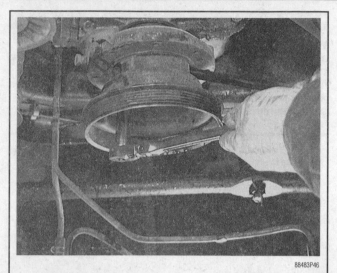

Fig. 144 Loosen the crankshaft pulley retaining bolts . . .

Fig. 145 . . . then remove the pulley

Fig. 146 Use a breaker bar and a socket to loosen the damper retaining bolt . . .

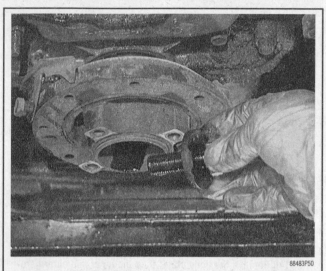

Fig. 147 . . . then unscrew the bolt by hand and set it aside

Fig. 148 Install a puller on the damper, following the tool manufacturer's instructions on the assembly and use of the equip-

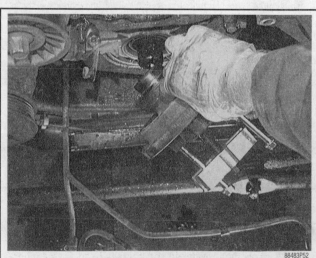

Fig. 149 Remove the puller and damper from the engine compartment

Diesel Engines

▶ See Figure 150

1. Drain the cooling system.
2. Remove the upper radiator hose.
3. Detach the coolant reservoir hose at the radiator.
4. Remove the fan and clutch assembly using Clutch Nut Wrench T83T–6312–B and Fan Clutch Pulley Holder T94T–6312–AH, or their equivalents. Turn the nut COUNTERCLOCKWISE, it is right-hand threaded. Rest the assembly in the fan shroud until the shroud is removed.
5. Remove the fan shroud and fan and clutch assembly.
6. Remove the radiator.
7. Raise the vehicle and safely support it with jackstands.
8. Remove the flywheel housing cover.
9. Using a breaker bar to prevent the crankshaft from rotating, remove the crankshaft pulley bolt and washer.
10. Remove the crankshaft vibration damper using a suitable puller.

To install:

11. Apply RTV sealant to the damper keyway, then drive on the damper using a suitable installation tool set.
12. Position a breaker bar to prevent the crankshaft from turning, then install the crankshaft pulley bolt and washer, tightening them to specification.
13. Install the radiator, the fan and clutch and fan shroud assembly.
14. Refill and bleed the cooling system.
15. Check the oil level and refill as necessary.

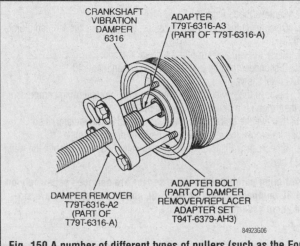

Fig. 150 A number of different types of pullers (such as the Ford tools shown), can be used to remove the damper on diesel engines

Timing Chain Cover and Seal

REMOVAL & INSTALLATION

5.0L and 5.8L Engines

1989–95 MODELS

▶ See Figures 151, 152, 153 and 154

1. Drain the cooling system and the crankcase.

✳✳ CAUTION

The EPA warns that prolonged contact with used engine oil may cause a number of skin disorders, including cancer! You should make every effort to minimize your exposure to used engine oil.

Protective gloves should be worn when changing the oil. Wash your hands and any other exposed skin areas as soon as possible after exposure to used engine oil. Soap and water, or waterless hand cleaner should be used.

2. Remove the radiator
3. Disconnect the lower radiator hose, then remove the fan, fan clutch and shroud.
4. Raise the van and support it with jackstands.
5. Disconnect the fuel line from the injection manifold.
6. Lower the van.
7. Remove the power steering pump and air conditioning compressor from their mounting brackets, if so equipped.
8. Remove the bolts holding the fan shroud to the radiator, if so equipped. Remove the fan, spacer, pulley and drive belt(s).
9. If necessary, disconnect the heater water hose and remove the water bypass tube.
10. Remove the crankshaft pulley from the crankshaft damper.
11. Remove the oil pan-to-cylinder front cover attaching bolts. Use a sharp, thin cutting blade to cut the oil pan gasket flush with the cylinder block. Remove the front cover and water pump as an assembly.
12. Discard the front cover gasket.

Fig. 151 Loosen the oil pan-to-front cover bolts

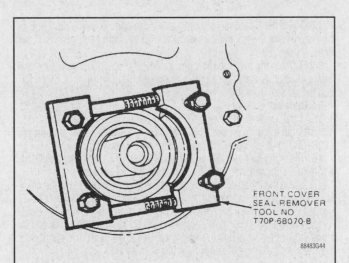

Fig. 152 Remove the front cover seal using tool T70P–6B070–B or equivalent

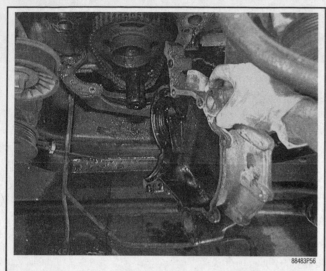

Fig. 153 Remove the timing chain cover from the van

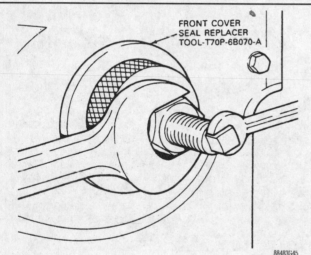

Fig. 154 Install the front cover seal using tool T70P–6B070–A or equivalent

13. Place the front seal removing tool (Ford part no. T70P–6B070–B or equivalent) into the front cover plate and over the front of the seal as shown in the illustration.

14. Tighten the two through-bolts to force the seal puller under the seal flange, then alternately tighten the four puller bolts a half-turn at a time to pull the oil seal from the cover.

To install:

15. Coat a new front cover oil seal with Lubriplate® or equivalent and place it onto the front oil seal alignment and installation tool (Ford part no. T70P–6B070–A or equivalent) as shown in the illustration.

16. Place the tool and the seal onto the end of the crankshaft and push it toward the engine until the seal starts into the front cover.

17. Place the installation screw, washer and nut onto the end of the crankshaft, then thread the screw into the crankshaft. Tighten the nut against the washer and tool to force the seal into the front cover plate. Remove the tool.

18. Apply Lubriplate® or equivalent to the oil seal rubbing surface of the vibration damper inner hub to prevent damage to the seal. Coat the front of the crankshaft with engine oil for damper installation.

19. Position the gasket on the front cover, then apply silicone rubber D6AZ-19562-AA or its equivalent to the oil pan and cylinder block junction.

20. Cut the pan gasket and position it on the front cover.

21. Install the front cover.

22. Line up the damper keyway with the key on the crankshaft, then install the damper onto the crankshaft. Install the cap screw and washer and tighten the screw to 80 ft. lbs. (108 Nm). Install the crankshaft pulley.

23. Connect the fuel lines.

24. Install the fan, pulley and drive belt(s).

25. Install the bolts holding the fan shroud to the radiator, if so equipped.

26. Install the power steering pump and air conditioning compressor.

27. Install the radiator.

28. Connect all hoses.

29. Fill the cooling system and the crankcase.

1996 MODELS

◗ See Figures 155 and 156

1. Drain the cooling system and the crankcase.

✳✳ CAUTION

The EPA warns that prolonged contact with used engine oil may cause a number of skin disorders, including cancer! You should make every effort to minimize your exposure to used engine oil. Protective gloves should be worn when changing the oil. Wash your hands and any other exposed skin areas as soon as possible after exposure to used engine oil. Soap and water, or waterless hand cleaner should be used.

2. Remove the radiator

3. Disconnect the lower radiator hose, then remove the fan, fan clutch and shroud.

4. Raise the van and support it with jackstands.

5. Disconnect the fuel line from the injection manifold.

6. Lower the van.

7. Remove the power steering pump and air conditioning compressor from their mounting brackets, if so equipped.

8. Remove the bolts holding the fan shroud to the radiator, if so equipped. Remove the fan, spacer, pulley and drive belt(s).

9. If necessary, disconnect the heater water hose and remove the water bypass tube.

➡The timing pointer and misfire sensor are serviced separately on the 5.8L engines, but not on the 5.0L engine, where they are serviced as an assembly.

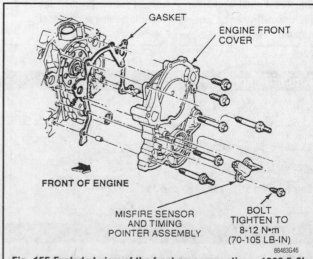

Fig. 155 Exploded view of the front cover mounting—1996 5.0L engine shown (5.8L similar)

10. Loosen the retainers and remove the timing pointer and misfire sensor.

11. Remove the crankshaft pulley from the crankshaft damper.

12. Remove the oil pan-to-cylinder front cover attaching bolts. Use a sharp, thin cutting blade to cut the oil pan gasket flush with the cylinder block. Remove the front cover and water pump as an assembly.

13. Discard the front cover gasket.

14. Use a suitable prytool to remove the front seal.

To install:

15. Coat a new front cover oil seal with Lubriplate® or equivalent and place it onto the front oil seal alignment and installation tool (Ford part no. T88T–6701–A or equivalent) as shown in the illustration. Place the tool and the seal onto the end of the crankshaft and push it toward the engine until the seal starts into the front cover.

16. Place the installation screw, washer and nut onto the end of the crankshaft, then thread the screw into the crankshaft. Tighten the nut against the washer and tool to force the seal into the front cover plate. Remove the tool.

17. Apply Lubriplate® or equivalent to the oil seal rubbing surface of the vibration damper inner hub to prevent damage to the seal. Coat the front of the crankshaft with engine oil for damper installation.

18. Position the gasket on the front cover, then apply silicone rubber F4AZ-19562-B or its equivalent to the oil pan and cylinder block junction.

19. Cut the pan gasket and position it on the front cover and oil pan.

20. Install the front cover.

21. On the 5.8L engines, finger-tighten the bolts in holes 3, 4, 6, 10, 12, 13 and 14, then tighten them to 70–120 inch lbs. (8–13 Nm).

22. On the 5.0L engine, install the bolts in holes 14 and 15 and tighten them to 70–120 inch lbs. (8–13 Nm).

23. Install the timing pointer and misfire sensor, then tighten the retainers to 70–105 inch lbs. (8–12 Nm).

24. Tighten the remaining bolts to 12–18 ft. lbs. (16–24 Nm).

25. Line up the damper keyway with the key on the crankshaft, then install the damper onto the crankshaft. Install the cap screw and washer and tighten the screw. Install the crankshaft pulley.

26. Connecvt the fuel lines.

27. Install the fan, pulley and drive belt(s).

28. Install the bolts holding the fan shroud to the radiator, if so equipped.

29. Install the power steering pump and air conditioning compressor.

30. Connect all hoses.

31. Fill the cooling system and the crankcase.

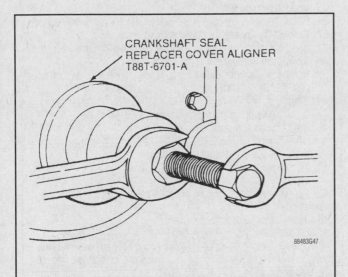

Fig. 156 Use tool T88T–6701–A or equivalent to install the seal

7.5L Engine

1989–91 MODELS

▶ See Figures 152 and 154

1. Drain the cooling system and crankcase.

> **❋❋ CAUTION**
>
> The EPA warns that prolonged contact with used engine oil may cause a number of skin disorders, including cancer! You should make every effort to minimize your exposure to used engine oil. Protective gloves should be worn when changing the oil. Wash your hands and any other exposed skin areas as soon as possible after exposure to used engine oil. Soap and water, or waterless hand cleaner should be used.

2. Remove the radiator shroud and fan.

3. Disconnect the upper and lower radiator hoses and the automatic transmission oil cooler lines from the radiator.

4. Remove the radiator upper support and remove the radiator.

5. If equipped, remove the alternator splash shield.

6. Loosen the alternator bolts, then remove the drive belt and alternator.

7. Remove the alternator bracket from the water pump.

8. Remove all drive belts and the water pump pulley.

9. Remove the air pump and A/C compressor and their brackets.

10. Remove the crankshaft pulley from the vibration damper. Remove the bolt and washer attaching the crankshaft damper and remove the damper with a puller.

11. Remove the Woodruff key from the crankshaft.

12. Loosen the bypass hose at the water pump and disconnect the heater return tube at the water pump.

13. Remove the bolts attaching the front cover to the cylinder block. Cut the oil pan seal flush with the cylinder block face with a thin knife blade prior to separating the cover from the cylinder block. Remove the cover and water pump as an assembly. Discard the front cover gasket and oil pan seal.

14. Place the front seal removing tool (Ford part no. T70P–6B070–A or equivalent) into the front cover plate and over the front of the seal.

15. Tighten the two through bolts to force the seal puller under the seal flange, then alternately tighten the four puller bolts a half turn at a time to pull the oil seal from the cover.

To install:

16. Coat a new front cover oil seal with Lubriplate® or equivalent and place it onto the front oil seal alignment and installation tool (Ford part no. T70P–6B070–A or equivalent). Place the tool and the seal onto the end of the crankshaft and push it toward the engine until the seal starts into the front cover.

17. Place the installation screw, washer and nut onto the end of the crankshaft, then thread the screw into the crankshaft. Tighten the nut against the washer and tool to force the seal into the front cover plate. Remove the tool.

18. Transfer the water pump if a new cover is going to be installed. Clean all of the gasket sealing surfaces on both the front cover and the cylinder block.

19. Coat the gasket surface of the oil pan with sealer. Cut and position the required sections of a new seal on the oil pan. Apply sealer to the corners.

20. Coat the gasket surfaces of the cylinder block and cover with sealer and position the new gasket on the block.

21. Position the front cover on the cylinder block. Use care not to damage the seal and gasket or misplace them.

22. Coat the front cover attaching screws with sealer and install them.

23. Install the Woodruff key from the crankshaft.

24. Install the damper.

25. Install the crankshaft pulley and water pump pulley.

26. Tighten the bypass hose at the water pump.

27. Connect the heater return tube at the water pump.

28. Install the compressor, air pump and brackets, if so equipped.

29. Install the drive belt(s).

30. Install the alternator and drive belt.
31. Install the radiator and upper support.
32. Connect the upper and lower radiator hoses and the automatic transmission oil cooler lines.
33. Install the radiator shroud and fan.
34. Fill the cooling system and crankcase.
Observe the following torque specifications:
- Front cover-to-cylinder block retainers: 15–21 ft. lbs. (17–24 Nm)
- Oil pan-to-cover bolts: 9–11 ft. lbs. (12–15 Nm)

1992–96 MODELS

▶ See Figure 157

1. Drain the cooling system and crankcase.

✳✳ CAUTION

The EPA warns that prolonged contact with used engine oil may cause a number of skin disorders, including cancer! You should make every effort to minimize your exposure to used engine oil. Protective gloves should be worn when changing the oil. Wash your hands and any other exposed skin areas as soon as possible after exposure to used engine oil. Soap and water, or waterless hand cleaner should be used.

2. Remove the alternator and power steering belts.
3. Remove the radiator shroud, fan and fan clutch.
4. Remove the water pump pulley.
5. Disconnect the upper and lower radiator hoses and the automatic transmission oil cooler lines from the radiator.
6. Remove the radiator upper support and the radiator.
7. If equipped, remove the alternator splash shield.
8. Loosen the alternator pivot and mounting bolts.
9. Remove the alternator
10. Remove the alternator adjusting bracket from the water pump.
11. Remove the air pump.
12. Remove the alternator and air pump bracket.
13. Remove the pulley from the power steering pump.
14. Remove the power steering pump brace.
15. Disconnect and cap the lines from the power steering pump, then remove the pump.
16. Remove the A/C compressor and the compressor/power steering pump bracket.
17. Remove the crankshaft pulley from the vibration damper. Remove the bolt and washer attaching the crankshaft damper and remove the damper with a puller.
18. Remove the Woodruff key from the crankshaft.
19. Loosen the by-pass hose at the water pump and disconnect the heater return tube at the water pump.
20. Remove the bolts attaching the front cover to the cylinder block. Cut the oil pan seal flush with the cylinder block face with a thin knife blade prior to separating the cover from the cylinder block. Remove the cover and water pump as an assembly. Discard the front cover gasket and oil pan seal.
21. Place the front seal removing tool (Ford part no. T70P–6B070–B or equivalent) into the front cover plate and over the front of the seal.
22. Tighten the two through bolts to force the seal puller under the seal flange, then alternately tighten the four puller bolts a half turn at a time to pull the oil seal from the cover.
To install:
23. Coat a new front cover oil seal with Lubriplate® or equivalent and place it onto the front oil seal alignment and installation tool (Ford part no. T70P–6B070–A or equivalent). Place the tool and the seal onto the end of the crankshaft and push it toward the engine until the seal starts into the front cover.
24. Place the installation screw, washer and nut onto the end of the crankshaft, then thread the screw into the crankshaft. Tighten the nut against the washer and tool to force the seal into the front cover plate. Remove the tool.

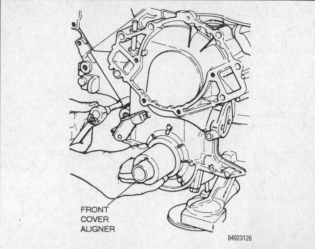

FRONT COVER ALIGNER

84923126

Fig. 157 Use tool T68P-6019-A or equivalent to install the cover—1992–96 7.5L engines

25. Transfer the water pump if a new cover is going to be installed. Clean all of the gasket sealing surfaces on both the front cover and the cylinder block.
26. Coat the gasket surface of the oil pan with sealer.
27. Coat the gasket surfaces of the cylinder block and cover with sealer and position the new gasket on the block.
28. Position the front cover on the cylinder block. Use care not to damage the seal and gasket or misplace them.

➡**It may be necessary to force the front cover downward to compress the oil pan seal in order to install the front cover attaching bolts. Use a prytool or drift to engage the cover screw holes through the cover and pry downward.**

29. While pushing in on the front cover aligner tool T68P-6019-A or its equivalent, tighten the oil pan-to-cover bolts to 70–105 inch lbs. (8–12 Nm).
30. Remove the tool and tighten the cover-to-cylinder block retainers to 12–18 ft. lbs. (17–24 Nm).
31. Install the Woodruff key from the crankshaft.
32. Install the damper.
33. Install the crankshaft pulley and water pump pulley.
34. Install the A/C compressor/power steering pump bracket and tighten the retainers to 30–33 ft. lbs. (40–45 Nm).
35. Install the compressor.
36. Install the power steering pump brace and tighten the retainers.
37. Connect the lines to the power steering pump.
38. Press the pulley onto the power steering pump and make sure the pulley hub is flush with the end of the pump shaft.
39. Install the alternator and air pump bracket, tighten the ⅜ inch bolts to 30–33 ft. lbs. (40–45 Nm) and the ⁷⁄₁₆ inch bolts to 41–52 ft. lbs. (50–70 Nm).
40. Install the air pump and tighten the bolts to 30–41 ft. lbs. (40–45 Nm).
41. Install the air pump adjusting bracket and tighten the bolts to 30–41 ft. lbs. (40–45 Nm).
42. Install the alternator and the drive belts.
43. Tighten the by-pass hose at the water pump.
44. Install the radiator and upper support.
45. Connect the upper and lower radiator hoses and the automatic transmission oil cooler lines.
46. Install the radiator shroud and fan.
47. Fill and bleed the cooling system.
48. Operate the engine at fast idle then shut off the engine. Check the coolant level and for oil leaks. Check and adjust the ignition timing according to the specification on the engine decal.
49. Install the air cleaner and intake duct assembly, including the crankcase ventilation hose.

Timing Gear Cover and Seal

REMOVAL & INSTALLATION

4.9L Engine

1989–93 MODELS

◗ See Figures 158 and 159

1. Drain the cooling system.

> ✳✳ **CAUTION**
>
> When draining the coolant, keep in mind that cats and dogs are attracted by ethylene glycol antifreeze and are quite likely to drink any that is left in an uncovered container or in puddles on the ground. This will prove fatal in sufficient quantity. Always drain the coolant into a sealable container. Coolant should be reused unless it is contaminated or several years old.

2. Raise the vehicle and drain the crankcase.

> ✳✳ **CAUTION**
>
> The EPA warns that prolonged contact with used engine oil may cause a number of skin disorders, including cancer! You should make every effort to minimize your exposure to used engine oil. Protective gloves should be worn when changing the oil. Wash your hands and any other exposed skin areas as soon as possible after exposure to used engine oil. Soap and water, or waterless hand cleaner should be used.

3. Remove the radiator.
4. Remove the drive belts.
5. Remove the power steering bracket bolts and swing the assembly aside.
6. Use a gear puller to remove the crankshaft pulley damper.
7. Remove the front oil pan and engine cover retaining bolts. Loosen the first six bolts one each side of the pan and lightly push the pan down so that it does not exert any force on the front cover and affect the seal alignment.
8. Place the front seal removing tool (Ford part no. T70P–6B070–B or equivalent) into the front cover plate and over the front of the seal.
9. Tighten the two through bolts to force the seal puller under the seal flange, then alternately tighten the four puller bolts a half turn at a time to pull the oil seal from the cover.

To install:

10. Coat a new front cover oil seal with clean engine oil or 50 weight oil only. and place it onto the front oil seal alignment and installation tool (Ford part no. T70P–6B070–A or equivalent). Place the tool and the seal onto the end of the crankshaft and push it toward the engine until the seal starts into the front cover.
11. Place the installation screw, washer and nut onto the end of the crankshaft, then thread the screw into the crankshaft. Tighten the nut against the washer and tool to force the seal into the front cover plate. Remove the tool.
12. Clean the cylinder front cover and the gasket surface of the cylinder block. Apply an oil-resistant sealer to the new front cover gasket and install the gasket onto the block.
13. Position the gasket on the front cover, then apply silicone rubber D6AZ-19562-AA or its equivalent to the oil pan and cylinder block junction.
14. Position the front cover assembly over the end of the crankshaft and against the cylinder block. Start, but do not tighten, the cover and pan attaching screws. Slide a front cover alignment tool (Ford part no.

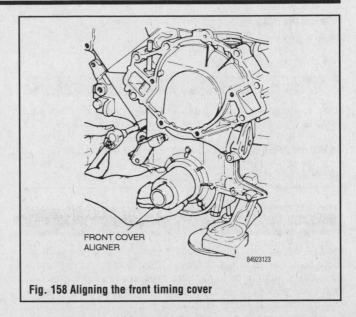

Fig. 158 Aligning the front timing cover

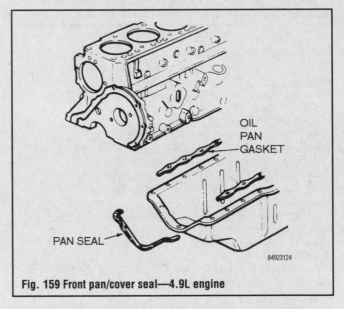

Fig. 159 Front pan/cover seal—4.9L engine

T61P–6019–B or equivalent) over the crank stub and into the seal bore of the cover. Tighten all oil pan attaching screws to 10–15 ft. lbs. (14–20 Nm) and the front cover screws to 10–15 ft. lbs. (14–20 Nm), tightening the oil pan screws first.

15. Lubricate the hub of the crankshaft damper pulley with clean engine oil or 50 weight oil to prevent damage to the seal during installation or on initial starting of the engine.
16. Install the crankshaft damper and pulley.
17. Install the fan belt, fan and pulley.
18. Install the radiator and shroud.
19. Install the splash shield and the automatic transmission oil cooling lines, if so equipped.
20. Fill the crankcase.
21. Connect the radiator upper hose at the coolant outlet elbow and install the two upper radiator retaining bolts.
22. Fill and bleed the cooling system.
23. Operate the engine at fast idle then shut off the engine. Check the coolant level and for oil leaks. Check and adjust the ignition timing according to the specification on the engine decal.

1994–96 MODELS

◗ See Figures 158 and 159

1. Drain the cooling system.

> ❄❄ **CAUTION**
>
> When draining the coolant, keep in mind that cats and dogs are attracted by ethylene glycol antifreeze and are quite likely to drink any that is left in an uncovered container or in puddles on the ground. This will prove fatal in sufficient quantity. Always drain the coolant into a sealable container. Coolant should be reused unless it is contaminated or several years old.

2. Raise the vehicle and drain the crankcase.

> ❄❄ **CAUTION**
>
> The EPA warns that prolonged contact with used engine oil may cause a number of skin disorders, including cancer! You should make every effort to minimize your exposure to used engine oil. Protective gloves should be worn when changing the oil. Wash your hands and any other exposed skin areas as soon as possible after exposure to used engine oil. Soap and water, or waterless hand cleaner should be used.

3. Remove the radiator.
4. Remove the drive belts.
5. Remove the power steering pump with the lines still attached and set it aside.
6. Have the A/C system evacuated by a qualified technician using an approved recovery/recycling station.
7. Remove the A/C compressor.
8. Remove the A/C and power steering pump bracket.
9. Use a gear puller to remove the crankshaft pulley damper.
10. Remove the front oil pan and engine cover retaining bolts. Loosen the first six bolts one each side of the pan and lightly push the pan down so that it does not exert any force on the front cover and effect the seal alignment.
11. Remove the cover.
12. Use a knife to cut the front cover gasket at the water pump and discard the gasket not retained by the pump.
13. Place the front seal removing tool (Ford part no. T70P–6B070–B or equivalent) into the front cover plate and over the front of the seal.
14. Tighten the two through bolts to force the seal puller under the seal flange, then alternately tighten the four puller bolts a half turn at a time to pull the oil seal from the cover.

To install:

15. Coat a new front cover oil seal with clean engine oil or 50 weight oil only, and place it onto the front oil seal alignment and installation tool (Ford part no. T70P–6B070–A or equivalent). Place the tool and the seal onto the end of the crankshaft and push it toward the engine until the seal starts into the front cover.
16. Place the installation screw, washer and nut onto the end of the crankshaft, then thread the screw into the crankshaft. Tighten the nut against the washer and tool to force the seal into the front cover plate. Remove the tool.
17. Clean the cylinder front cover and the gasket surface of the cylinder block. Apply an oil-resistant sealer to the new front cover gasket and install the gasket onto the block.
18. If the water pump was not removed, trim off the piece of gasket that would go under the pump.
19. Position the gasket on the front cover, then apply silicone rubber D6AZ-19562-AA or its equivalent to the oil pan and cylinder block junction.
20. Position the front cover assembly over the end of the crankshaft and against the cylinder block. Start, but do not tighten, the cover and pan attaching screws. Slide a front cover alignment tool (Ford part no. T61P–6019–B or equivalent) over the crank stub and into the seal bore of the cover. Tighten all oil pan attaching screws to 15–17 ft. lbs. (20–23 Nm) and the front cover screws to 13–18 ft. lbs. (17–24 Nm), tightening the oil pan screws first.

21. Lubricate the hub of the crankshaft damper pulley with clean engine oil or 50 weight oil to prevent damage to the seal during installation or on initial starting of the engine.
22. Install the crankshaft damper and pulley.
23. Install the fan belt, fan and pulley.
24. Install the power steering pump and A/C compressor bracket and units.
25. Have the system recharged by a qualified technician using an approved recovery/recycling station
26. Install the radiator and shroud.
27. Fill the crankcase.
28. Fill and bleed the cooling system.
29. Operate the engine at fast idle then shut off the engine. Check the coolant level and for oil leaks. Check and adjust the ignition timing according to the specification on the engine decal.

7.3L Diesel Engines

1989–94 MODELS

◗ See Figures 160 thru 167

1. Disconnect both negative battery cables. Drain the cooling system.

> ❄❄ **CAUTION**
>
> When draining the coolant, keep in mind that cats and dogs are attracted by ethylene glycol antifreeze and are quite likely to drink any that is left in an uncovered container or in puddles on the ground. This will prove fatal in sufficient quantity. Always drain the coolant into a sealable container. Coolant should be reused unless it is contaminated or several years old.

2. Remove the air cleaner and cover the air intake on the manifold with clean rags. Do not allow any foreign material to enter the intake.
3. On turbocharged models, remove the upper and lower air cleaner housing, then cap the compressor opening.
4. Remove the radiator fan shroud halves.
5. Remove the fan and fan clutch assembly. You will need a puller or Ford tool No. T83T–6312–A for this.

➡ The nut is a left-hand thread; remove by turning the nut CLOCKWISE.

6. Remove the water pump.
7. Remove the injection pump as described in Section 5 under Diesel Fuel System.

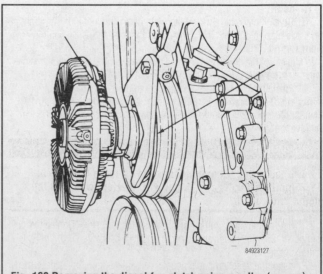

84923127

Fig. 160 Removing the diesel fan clutch using a puller (arrows)

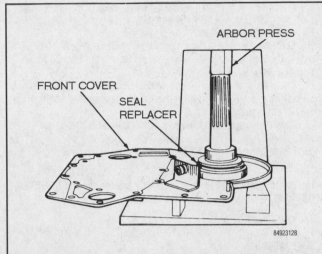

Fig. 161 Diesel front oil seal removal and installation using an arbor press

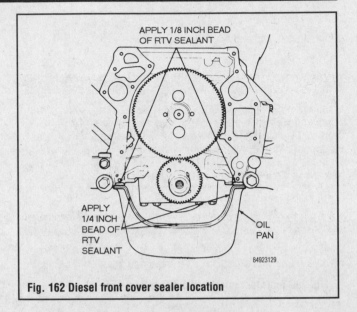

Fig. 162 Diesel front cover sealer location

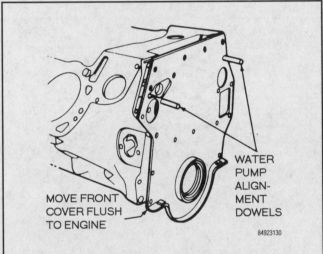

Fig. 163 Front cover installation on diesels, showing the alignment dowels

8. Jack up the van and safely support it with jackstands.

9. Remove the crankshaft pulley and vibration damper as described in this section.

10. Remove the engine ground cables at the front of the engine.

11. Remove the five bolts attaching the engine front cover to the engine block and oil pan.

12. Lower the van.

13. Remove the front cover.

➡Drive out the oil seal with an arbor press, drive handle T80T-4000-W and a 3¼ in. (82.5mm) diameter spacer.

To install:

14. Remove all old gasket material from the front cover, engine block, oil pan sealing surfaces and water pump surfaces.

15. Coat the new front oil seal with Lubriplate® or equivalent grease.

16. The new seal must be installed using a seal installation tool, Ford part no. T83T–6700–A, a suitable spacer and an arbor press. When the seal bottoms out on the front cover surface, it is installed at the proper depth.

17. Install alignment dowels into the engine block to align the front cover and gaskets. These can be made out of round stock. Apply a gasket sealer to the engine block sealing surfaces, then install the gaskets on the block.

18. Apply a ⅛ in. (3mm) bead of RTV sealer on the front of the engine block as shown in the illustration. Apply a ¼ in. (6mm) bead of RTV sealer on the oil pan as shown.

19. Install the front cover immediately after applying RTV sealer. The sealer will begin to cure and lose its effectiveness unless the cover is installed quickly.

20. Install the water pump gasket on the engine front cover. Apply RTV sealer to the four water pump bolts illustrated. Install the water pump and hand tighten all bolts.

❋❋ WARNING

The two top water pump bolts must be no more than 1¼ in. (31.75mm) long bolts any longer will interfere with (hit) the engine drive gears.

21. Tighten the water pump bolts to 19 ft. lbs. (25 Nm). Tighten the front cover bolts to specifications according to bolt size (see Torque Specifications chart).

22. Install the injection pump adapter and injection pump as described in Section 5 under Diesel Fuel System.

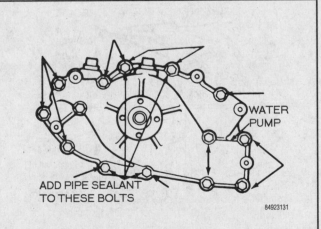

Fig. 164 Water pump-to-front cover installation on the diesel. The two top pump bolts must be no more than 1¼ in. (31.75mm) long

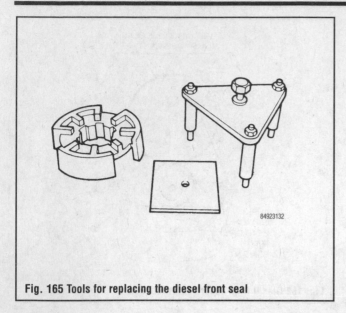

Fig. 165 Tools for replacing the diesel front seal

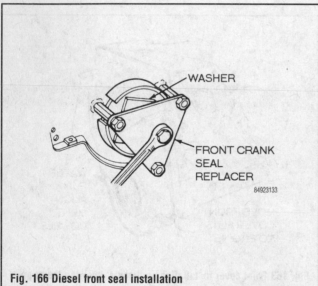

WASHER

FRONT CRANK
SEAL
REPLACER

Fig. 166 Diesel front seal installation

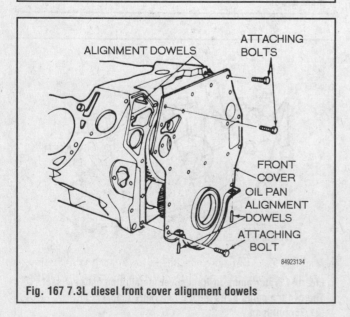

ALIGNMENT DOWELS

ATTACHING
BOLTS

FRONT
COVER

OIL PAN
ALIGNMENT
DOWELS

ATTACHING
BOLT

Fig. 167 7.3L diesel front cover alignment dowels

23. Install the heater hose fitting in the pump using pipe sealant and connect the heater hose to the water pump.

24. Jack up the van and safely support it with jackstands.

25. Lubricate the front of the crankshaft with clean engine oil. Apply RTV sealant to the engine side of the retaining bolt washer to prevent oil seepage past the keyway.

26. Install the crankshaft vibration damper using Ford Special tools T83T–6316B, or equivalent. Tighten the damper-to-crankshaft bolt to 90 ft. lbs. (122 Nm).

27. Install the crankshaft pulley and battery ground cables on the engine.

28. Lower the van and install the water pump pulley.

29. Install the fan and fan clutch assembly.

➡**The nut is a left-hand thread; install by turning the nut COUNTERCLOCKWISE.**

30. Install the drive belt(s)

31. Install the radiator fan shroud halves.

32. Install the air cleaner.

33. On turbocharged models, install the upper and lower air cleaner housing assembly.

34. Connect both negative battery cables.

35. Fill the cooling system.

SEAL—1995–96 MODELS

▶ **See Figures 168 and 169**

The crankshaft oil seal is removed with the front cover on the engine as follows:

1. Remove the crankshaft damper.

2. Using lube tube remover T86P-70001-A and impact slide hammer T59L-100-B, carefully remove the seal.

The crankshaft oil seal is installed as follows:

3. Coat the new seal with multi-purpose grease such as D0AZ-19584-AA or its equivalent.

➡**It may be necessary to rotate the front crank seal replacer T94T-6700-AH to align it with the crankshaft key.**

4. Install the seal by pressing it into place using front crank seal replacer T94T-6700-AH, thread adapter T94T-6379-AH3, driver sleeve T79T-6316-A4 (part of T79T-6316-A and driver puller screw T79T-6316-A1 (part of T79T-6316-A). Refer to the tool manufacturers instructions on the proper operation of these tools.

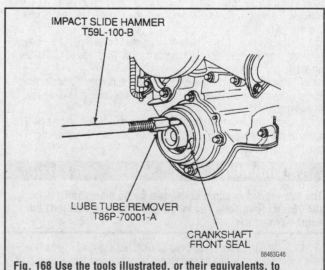

IMPACT SLIDE HAMMER
T59L-100-B

LUBE TUBE REMOVER
T86P-70001-A

CRANKSHAFT
FRONT SEAL

Fig. 168 Use the tools illustrated, or their equivalents, to remove the front crankshaft seal—1995–96 diesel engines

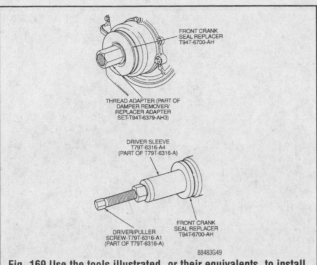

Fig. 169 Use the tools illustrated, or their equivalents, to install the front crankshaft seal—1995–96 diesel engines

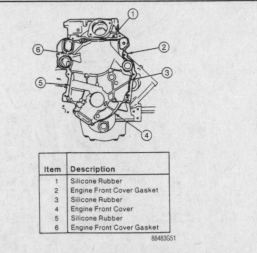

Item	Description
1	Silicone Rubber
2	Engine Front Cover Gasket
3	Silicone Rubber
4	Engine Front Cover
5	Silicone Rubber
6	Engine Front Cover Gasket

Fig. 171 Silicone rubber should be applied to the areas indicated

COVER—1995–96 MODELS

▶ See Figures 170 and 171

If the oil pan can be removed with the engine in the van, perform the water pump removal procedures and go on from there.

If the oil pan cannot be removed with the engine in the van the engine must be removed. The following procedure is written under the assumption that the engine is removed from the van.

1. Remove the engine from the van.
2. Remove the water pump and the crankshaft damper.
3. Remove the oil pan, oil pump screen cover and tube.
4. Loosen the front cover bolts, then remove the cover and gaskets.

To install:

5. Clean the gasket mating surfaces.
6. Install the two new engine front cover gaskets and apply silicone rubber D6AZ-19562-BA or its equivalent to the sealing grooves in the cover.
7. Install the cover and finger-tighten the bolts.
8. Install the water pump and tighten the cover retainers to 15 ft. lbs. (20 Nm).
9. Install the oil pump screen cover, tube and pan.

10. Install the crankshaft damper.
11. If the oil pan cannot be removed with the engine in the van and was removed, install the engine.

If the oil pan can be removed with van in the engine, perform the water pump installation procedure.

Timing Chain

REMOVAL & INSTALLATION

5.0L, 5.8L and 7.5L Engines

▶ See Figures 172 thru 177

1. Remove the front cover.
2. Turn the crankshaft until the timing marks on the sprockets are aligned vertically.
3. Remove the camshaft sprocket retainer and, if equipped, remove the fuel pump eccentric and washers.
4. Alternately slide both of the sprockets and timing chain off the crankshaft and camshaft until free of the engine.

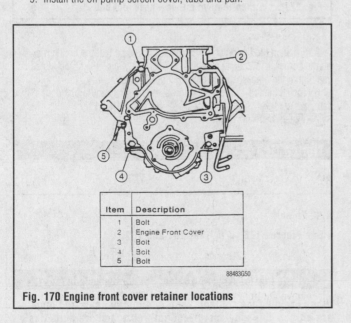

Item	Description
1	Bolt
2	Engine Front Cover
3	Bolt
4	Bolt
5	Bolt

Fig. 170 Engine front cover retainer locations

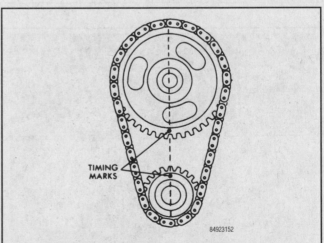

TIMING MARKS

Fig. 172 Make sure the timing marks are aligned as illustrated during removal and installation of the timing chain and sprockets on V8 gasoline engines

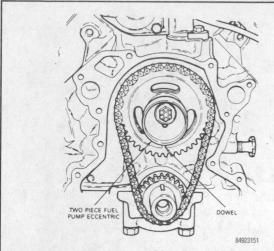

Fig. 173 Some V8 gasoline engines have a fuel pump eccentric located on the camshaft sprocket

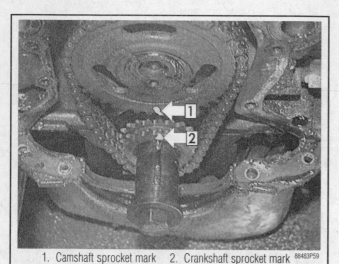

1. Camshaft sprocket mark   2. Crankshaft sprocket mark

Fig. 174 Make sure the timing marks on the sprockets are aligned dot-to-dot before removal

Fig. 175 Slide the sprockets off their shafts with the timing chain, and remove the assembly as a unit

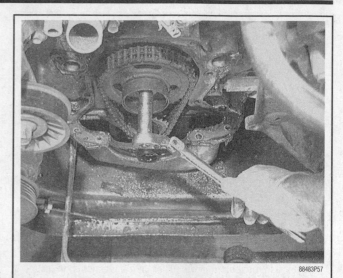

Fig. 176 Loosen the fuel pump eccentric retaining bolt . . .

Fig. 177 . . . then remove the eccentric and bolt

To install:

5. Position the timing chain on the sprockets so that the timing marks on the sprockets are aligned vertically. Alternately slide the sprockets and chain onto the crankshaft and camshaft sprockets.

6. Install the fuel pump eccentric washers and attaching bolt on the camshaft sprocket. Tighten to 40–45 ft. lbs. (54–61 Nm).

7. Install the front cover.

Timing Gears

REMOVAL & INSTALLATION

4.9L Engine

▶ See Figures 178, 179, 180, 181 and 182

1. Drain the cooling system and remove the front cover.

❊❊ CAUTION

When draining the coolant, keep in mind that cats and dogs are attracted by ethylene glycol antifreeze and are quite likely

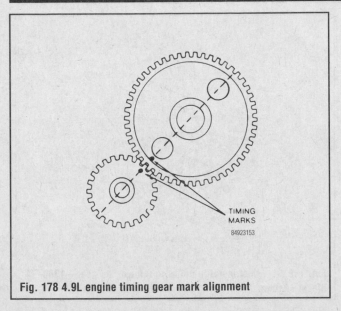

Fig. 178 4.9L engine timing gear mark alignment

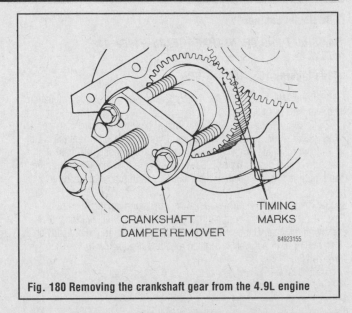

Fig. 180 Removing the crankshaft gear from the 4.9L engine

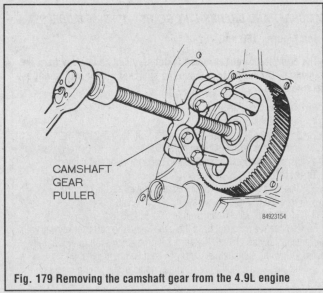

Fig. 179 Removing the camshaft gear from the 4.9L engine

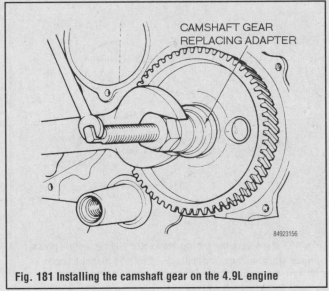

Fig. 181 Installing the camshaft gear on the 4.9L engine

to drink any that is left in an uncovered container or in puddles on the ground. This will prove fatal in sufficient quantity. Always drain the coolant into a sealable container. Coolant should be reused unless it is contaminated or several years old.

2. Crank the engine until the timing marks on the camshaft and crankshaft gears are aligned.

3. Use gear puller T82T-6256-A to remove the camshaft sprocket and use crankshaft damper removal tool T58P-6316-D to remove the crankshaft sprocket.

To install:

4. Before installing the timing gears, be sure that the key and spacer are properly installed. Align the gear key way with the key and install the gear on the camshaft. Be sure that the timing marks line up on the camshaft and the crankshaft gears and install the crankshaft gear.

5. Install the front cover and assemble the rest of the engine in the reverse order of disassembly. Fill the cooling system.

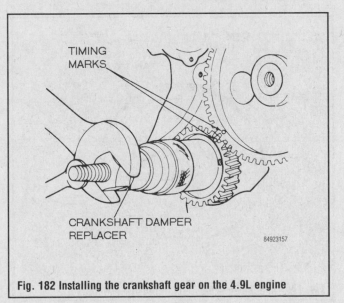

Fig. 182 Installing the crankshaft gear on the 4.9L engine

7.3L Diesel Engines

CAMSHAFT AND CRANKSHAFT GEARS—1989–94 MODELS

▶ **See Figures 183, 184 and 185**

1. Follow the procedures for timing gear cover removal and installation and remove the front cover.

2. To remove the crankshaft gear, install gear puller (Ford part) no. T83T–6316–A or equivalent and using a breaker bar to prevent the crankshaft from rotating, remove the crankshaft gear. To install the crankshaft gear use tool (Ford part) no. T83T–6316–B or equivalent while aligning the timing marks as shown in the illustration and press the gear into place.

3. The camshaft gear may be removed by taking out the Allen screw and installing a gear puller, Ford part no. T83T–6316–A or equivalent and removing the gear. The gear may be replaced by using tool (Ford part) no. T83T–6316–B or equivalent. Tighten the Allen head screw to 12–18 ft. lbs. (16–24 Nm).

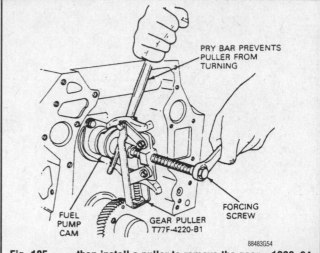

Fig. 185 . . . then install a puller to remove the gear—1989–94 diesel engines

CAMSHAFT AND CRANKSHAFT GEARS—1995–96 MODELS

▶ **See Figures 186 and 187**

➡The crankshaft gear sprocket is not serviced separately from the crankshaft. Do not try to remove the sprocket or you will damage the crankshaft.

Remove the camshaft sprocket as follows:
1. Remove the camshaft.
2. Use a press to remove the sprocket from the camshaft.
3. Remove the thrust plate and sprocket key.
4. Inspect the camshaft and related parts for wear and damage.

To install:
5. Clean the nose of the camshaft and install the thrust plate.
6. Place the key in the keyway on the camshaft.
7. Heat the sprocket in an oven to 500°F (260°C).
8. Remove the sprocket from the oven, align the sprocket keyway with the camshaft key and install the sprocket on the camshaft until it is fully seated. Allow the camshaft assembly to cool before installation
9. Install the camshaft in the engine and align the timing marks on the gears.

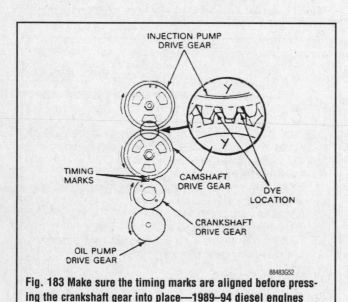

Fig. 183 Make sure the timing marks are aligned before pressing the crankshaft gear into place—1989–94 diesel engines

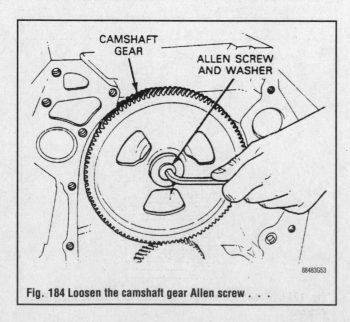

Fig. 184 Loosen the camshaft gear Allen screw . . .

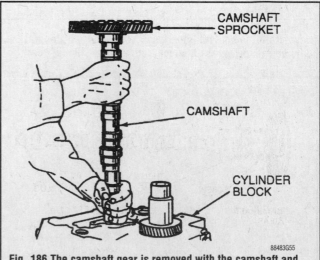

Fig. 186 The camshaft gear is removed with the camshaft and then pressed off—1995–96 diesel engines

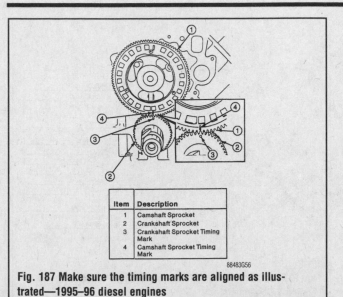

Fig. 187 Make sure the timing marks are aligned as illustrated—1995–96 diesel engines

Item	Description
1	Camshaft Sprocket
2	Crankshaft Sprocket
3	Crankshaft Sprocket Timing Mark
4	Camshaft Sprocket Timing Mark

88483G56

Camshaft, Bearings and Lifters

REMOVAL & INSTALLATION

Camshaft

4.9L ENGINE

▶ See Figure 188

1. Disconnect both negative battery cables. Drain the cooling system.

☀ CAUTION

When draining the coolant, keep in mind that cats and dogs are attracted by ethylene glycol antifreeze and are quite likely to drink any that is left in an uncovered container or in puddles on the ground. This will prove fatal in sufficient quantity. Always drain the coolant into a sealable container. Coolant should be reused unless it is contaminated or several years old.

2. Remove the grille if necessary.
3. Remove the radiator.
4. Have the A/C system evacuated by a qualified technician using an approved recovery/recycling station.
5. Remove the air conditioner condenser, and timing cover.
6. Disconnect the primary wire from the coil.
7. Remove the distributor
8. Align the timing marks.
9. Remove the rocker covers, and either remove the rocker arm shafts or loosen the rockers on their pivots and remove the pushrods. The pushrods must be reinstalled in their original positions.
10. Remove the valve lifters in sequence with a magnet. They must be replaced in their original positions.
11. loosen the camshaft thrust plate screws and the sprocket.
12. Remove the key, thrust plate and sprocket spacer.
13. Remove the camshaft very carefully to prevent nicking the bearings.
To install:
14. Oil the camshaft bearing journals and use Multi-purpose grease D0AZ-19584-AA or something similar on the lobes.
15. Assemble the key, spacer and thrust plate on the camshaft.
16. Align the gear keyway with the key and install the gear on the camshaft.
17. Install the camshaft, sprocket, and thrust plate, as an assembly making sure the sprocket marks are aligned.
18. Tighten down the thrust plate screws to 12–18 ft. lbs. (16–24 Nm). Make sure that the camshaft end-play is not excessive.
19. Install the lifters, pushrods and rocker arms. Perform the valve adjustment procedures outlined in Section 1.
20. Install the front cover.
21. Install the distributor. The rotor should be at the firing position for no. 1 cylinder, with the stator armature tooth exactly with the armature tooth before tightening the distributor hold-down clamp.
22. Install the condenser and the radiator.
23. Have the A/C system recharged by a qualified technician using an approved recovery/recycling station.
24. If removed, install the grille.
25. Fill and bleed the cooling system.
26. Fill the crankcase with the proper type and amount of engine oil.
27. Start the van and check for proper operation

5.0L AND 5.8L ENGINES

▶ See Figure 189

1. Remove the grille.
2. Remove the radiator.

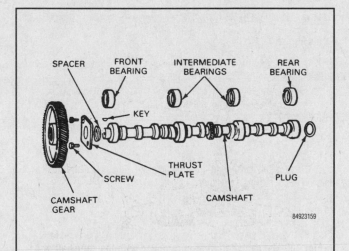

Fig. 188 Exploded view of the camshaft and related components used on 4.9L engines

84923159

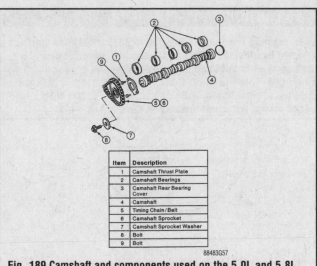

Item	Description
1	Camshaft Thrust Plate
2	Camshaft Bearings
3	Camshaft Rear Bearing Cover
4	Camshaft
5	Timing Chain/Belt
6	Camshaft Sprocket
7	Camshaft Sprocket Washer
8	Bolt
9	Bolt

88483G57

Fig. 189 Camshaft and components used on the 5.0L and 5.8L engines

3. Unbolt the A/C compressor and power steering pump assemblies and the bracket. Set them aside. Do not disconnect the lines to either unit.

4. Remove the distributor

5. Remove the front cover and timing chain.

6. Remove the intake manifold and throttle body as an assembly.

7. Remove the rocker covers, and either remove the rocker arm shafts or loosen the rockers on their pivots and remove the pushrods. The pushrods must be reinstalled in their original positions.

8. Remove the valve lifters in sequence with a magnet. They must be replaced in their original positions.

9. Remove the thrust plate.

10. Remove the camshaft very carefully to prevent nicking the lobes and bearings.

To install:

11. Oil the camshaft bearing journals and use Multi-purpose grease D0AZ-19584-AA or something similar on the lobes.

12. Carefully install the camshaft through the bearings.

13. Lubricate the thrust plate with engine oil and install it with the groove towards the block.

14. Lubricate the lifters and their bores with heavy duty engine oil, then install them in the bores they were removed from.

15. Lubricate the ends of the pushrods with multi-purpose grease and install them to their original positions.

16. Install the rocker arms.

17. Install the intake manifold and throttle body assembly.

18. Install the timing chain and front cover.

19. Perform the valve clearance procedure outlined in Section 1.

20. Install the rocker covers.

21. Install the distributor.

22. Install the A/C compressor and power steering pump bracket and assemblies.

23. Install the radiator.

24. Fill and bleed the cooling system.

25. change the oil.

26. Start the van, check and, if necessary, adjust the ignition timing.

27. Operate the van at fast idle until the proper operating temperature is reached, then check for leaks and if necessary, adjust the idle speed and mixture.

28. Install the grille.

7.5L ENGINE

▶ See Figure 190

1. Have the A/C system evacuated by a qualified technician using an approved recovery/recycling station.

2. Drain the cooling system.

❄❄ CAUTION

When draining the coolant, keep in mind that cats and dogs are attracted by ethylene glycol antifreeze and are quite likely to drink any that is left in an uncovered container or in puddles on the ground. This will prove fatal in sufficient quantity. Always drain the coolant into a sealable container. Coolant should be reused unless it is contaminated or several years old.

3. Remove the grille.

4. Remove the front cover, timing chain and sprockets.

5. Remove the intake manifold(s) and throttle body assembly.

6. Remove the valve covers.

7. Remove the rocker arm shafts or loosen the rockers on their pivots and remove the pushrods. The pushrods must be reinstalled in their original positions.

8. Remove the valve lifters in sequence with a magnet. They must be replaced in their original positions.

9. Remove the A/C condenser and set it aside.

10. Remove the camshaft very carefully to prevent nicking the lobes and bearings.

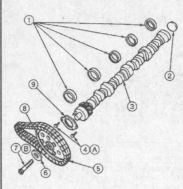

Item	Description
1	Camshaft Bearing
2	Camshaft Rear Bearing Cover
3	Camshaft
4	Bolt, 1/4-20 x 1/2, Self-Locking
5	Timing Chain
6	Camshaft Sprocket Washer
7	Bolt, 3/8-16 x 1.38
8	Camshaft Sprocket
9	Camshaft Thrust Plate
A	Tighten to 11-15 N·m (90-135 Lb-In)
B	Tighten to 54-68 N·m (40-50 Lb-Ft)

88483G58

Fig. 190 Exploded view of the camshaft and related components used on 7.5L engines

To install:

11. Oil the camshaft bearing journals and use Multi-purpose grease D0AZ-19584-AA or something similar on the lobes.

12. Carefully install the camshaft through the bearings.

13. Install the thrust plate.

14. Install the timing chain, sprockets and front cover.

15. Install the radiator and condenser.

16. Lubricate the lifters and their bores with heavy duty engine oil, then install them in the bores they were removed from.

17. Lubricate the ends of the pushrods with multi-purpose grease and install them to their original positions.

18. Install the rocker arms.

19. Perform the valve clearance procedure outlined in Section 1.

20. Install the rocker arm covers.

21. Install the intake manifold and throttle body assembly.

22. Install. the distributor.

23. Fill and bleed the cooling system.

24. Change the oil.

25. Start the van, check and if necessary adjust, the ignition timing.

26. Operate the van at fast idle until the proper operating temperature is reached, then check for leaks and if necessary, adjust the idle speed and mixture.

27. Install the grille.

1989–94 7.3L ENGINES

▶ See Figure 191

The manufacturer recommends that the engine be removed from the van for this procedure.

1. Remove the engine and place it on a suitable engine stand.

2. Remove the injection pump and adapter.

3. Remove the intake manifold and the front cover.

4. Remove the rocker arm shafts or loosen the rockers on their pivots and remove the pushrods. The pushrods must be reinstalled in their original positions.

5. Remove the valve lifters in sequence with a magnet. They must be replaced in their original positions.

6. Rotate the crankshaft until the timing marks on the sprockets (gears) are aligned.

7. Remove the fuel pump.

8. Remove the camshaft drive gear, fuel pump cam, spacer and the thrust plate.

9. Remove the camshaft very carefully to prevent nicking the lobes and bearings.

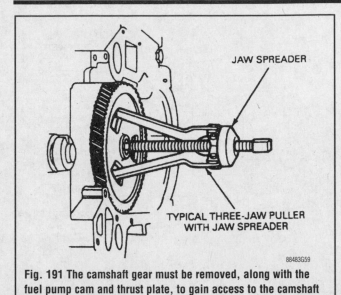

Fig. 191 The camshaft gear must be removed, along with the fuel pump cam and thrust plate, to gain access to the camshaft

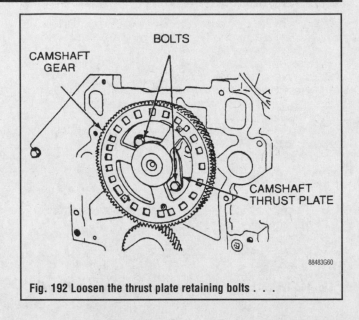

Fig. 192 Loosen the thrust plate retaining bolts . . .

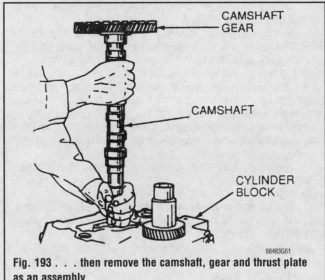

Fig. 193 . . . then remove the camshaft, gear and thrust plate as an assembly

To install:

10. Oil the camshaft bearing journals and use Multi-purpose grease D0AZ-19584-AA or something similar on the lobes.
11. Carefully install the camshaft through the bearings.
12. Install a new thrust plate.
13. Install the spacer and fuel pump cam against the camshaft thrust flange using a crank/cam and damper replacer tool T83T-6316-B or its equivalent.
14. Install the camshaft gear against the fuel pump cam making sure the timing mark is aligned with the mark on the crankshaft gear using a crank/cam and damper replacer tool T83T-6316-B or its equivalent.
15. Install the Allen screw and tighten it to 15 ft. lbs. (20 Nm).
16. Install the fuel pump.
17. Install a new crankshaft seal in the front cover.
18. Install the front cover.
19. Install the water pump and injection pump adapter.
20. Lubricate the tappets and their bores with engine oil, then install them in their original bores.
21. Install the tappet guides and their retainers.
22. Install the pushrods in their original bores making sure they are fully seated, with the copper colored end towards the rocker arms.
23. Install the rocker arms and valve covers.
24. Install the intake manifold and injection pump.
25. Install the engine in the van.

1995–96 7.3L ENGINES

▶ See Figures 192 and 193

The manufacturer recommends that the engine be removed from the van for this procedure.
1. Remove the engine and place it on a suitable engine stand.
2. Remove the front cover.
3. Remove the rocker arm shafts or loosen the rockers on their pivots and remove the pushrods. The pushrods must be reinstalled in their original positions.
4. Remove the valve lifters in sequence with a magnet. They must be replaced in their original positions.
5. Rotate the crankshaft until the timing marks on the sprockets (gears) are aligned.
6. Loosen the thrust plate retainers.
7. Remove the camshaft, sprocket and the thrust plate as an assembly.
8. Remove the camshaft very carefully to prevent nicking the lobes and bearings.

To install:

9. Lubricate the camshaft bearing journals with diesel engine oil and use Multi-purpose grease D0AZ-19584-AA or something similar on the lobes.
10. Carefully install the camshaft assembly through the bearings.
11. Tighten thrust plate retainers.
12. Install a new crankshaft seal in the front cover.
13. Install the front cover.
14. Lubricate the tappets and their bores with engine oil, then install them in their original bores.
15. Install the pushrods in their original bores making sure they are fully seated, with the copper colored end towards the rocker arms.
16. Install the rocker arms and valve covers.
17. Install the engine in the van.

Camshaft Bearings

▶ See Figure 194

1. Remove the engine following the procedures in this section and install it on a workstand.
2. Remove the camshaft, flywheel and crankshaft, following the appropriate procedures. Push the pistons to the top of the cylinder.

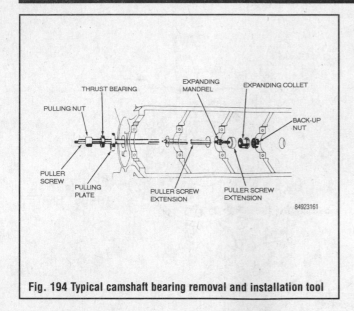

Fig. 194 Typical camshaft bearing removal and installation tool

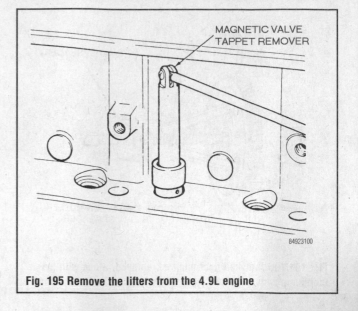

Fig. 195 Remove the lifters from the 4.9L engine

3. Remove the camshaft rear bearing bore plug. Remove the camshaft bearings with Tool T65L–6250–A or equivalent.

4. Select the proper size expanding collet and back-up nut and assemble on the mandrel. With the expanding collet collapsed, install the collet assembly in the camshaft bearing and tighten the back-up nut on the expanding mandrel until the collet fits the camshaft bearing.

5. Assemble the puller screw and extension (if necessary) and install on the expanding mandrel. Wrap a cloth around the threads of the puller screw to protect the front bearing or journal. Tighten the pulling nut against the thrust bearing and pulling plate to remove the camshaft bearing. Be sure to hold a wrench on the end of the puller screw to prevent it from turning.

6. To remove the front bearing, install the puller from the rear of the cylinder block.

To install:

7. Position the new bearings at the bearing bores, and press them in place with tool T65L–6250–A or equivalent. Be sure to center the pulling plate and puller screw to avoid damage to the bearing. Failure to use the correct expanding collet can cause severe bearing damage. Align the oil holes in the bearings with the oil holes in the cylinder block before pressing bearings into place.

➡**Be sure the front bearing is installed below the front face of the cylinder block on gasoline engines as follows:**

- 4.9L engines: 0.020–0.035 in. (0.51–0.89mm)
- 5.0L and 5.8L engines: 0.005–0.020 in. (0.127–0.508mm)
- 1989–90 7.5L engines: 0.040–0.060 (0.054–0.081mm)
- 1991–96 7.5L engines: 0.002–0.003 in. (0.051–0.762mm)

8. On diesel engines, make sure the bearing and bore oil holes are aligned.

9. Install the camshaft rear bearing bore plug.

10. Install the camshaft, crankshaft, flywheel and related parts, following the appropriate procedures.

11. Install the engine in the van, following procedures described earlier in this section.

Valve Lifters

4.9L ENGINE

♦ **See Figure 195**

1. Remove the upper intake manifold and throttle body assembly (see Section 5).

2. Remove the ignition coil and wires.

3. Remove the rocker arm cover.

4. Remove the spark plug wires.

5. Remove the distributor cap.

6. Remove the pushrod cover (engine side cover).

7. Loosen the rocker arm bolts until the pushrods can be removed. KEEP THE PUSHRODS IN ORDER, FOR INSTALLATION!

8. Using a magnetic lifter removal tool, remove the lifters. Wipe clean the exterior of each lifter as it's removed and mark it with an indelible marker, so that it can be installed in its original bore.

To install:

9. Coat the bottom surface of each lifter with multi-purpose grease and coat the rest of the lifter with clean engine oil.

10. Install each lifter in its original bore using the magnetic tool.

11. Coat each end of each pushrod with multi-purpose grease and install each in its original position. Make sure that each pushrod is properly seated in the lifter socket.

12. Engage the rocker arms with the pushrods and tighten the rocker arm bolts enough to hold the pushrods in place.

13. Adjust the valve clearance.

14. Install the pushrod cover (engine side cover).

15. Install the distributor cap.

16. Install the spark plug wires.

17. Install the rocker arm cover.

18. Install the ignition coil and wires.

19. Install the upper intake manifold and throttle body assembly (see Section 5).

5.0L and 5.8L Engines

♦ **See Figures 196, 197 and 198**

1. Remove the intake manifold.

2. Disconnect the secondary air injection (Thermactor®) air supply hose at the pump.

3. Remove the rocker arm covers.

4. Loosen the rocker arm fulcrum bolts until the rocker arms can be rotated off the pushrods.

5. Remove the pushrods and KEEP THEM IN ORDER FOR INSTALLATION.

6. Using a magnetic lifter removal tool, remove the lifters. Wipe clean the exterior of each lifter as it's removed and mark it with an indelible marker, so that it can be installed in its original bore.

To install:

7. Coat the bottom surface of each lifter with multi-purpose grease and coat the rest of the lifter with clean engine oil.

Fig. 196 Remove the pushrods, keeping them in order for installation

Fig. 197 Remove the lifters from their bores

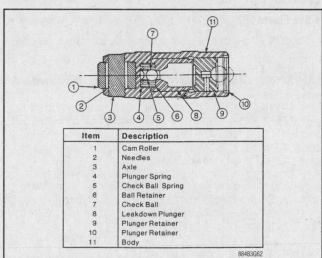

Item	Description
1	Cam Roller
2	Needles
3	Axle
4	Plunger Spring
5	Check Ball Spring
6	Ball Retainer
7	Check Ball
8	Leakdown Plunger
9	Plunger Retainer
10	Plunger Retainer
11	Body

Fig. 198 Exploded view of a roller tappet (lifter) which is used on some later model 5.0L and 5.8L engines

8. Install each lifter in its original bore using the magnetic tool.

9. Coat each end of each pushrod with multi-purpose grease and install each in its original position. Make sure that each pushrod is properly seated in the lifter socket.

10. Engage the rocker arms with the pushrods and tighten the rocker arm fulcrum bolts to 18–25 ft. lbs. (24–34 Nm). No valve adjustment should be necessary, however, if there is any question as to post-assembly collapsed lifter clearance, refer to the valve clearance procedure in Section 1.

11. Install the rocker arm covers.

12. Connect the secondary air injection (Thermactor®) air supply hose at the pump.

13. Install the intake manifold.

7.5L ENGINE

▶ See Figure 199

1. Remove the upper intake manifold.
2. Remove the rocker arm covers.
3. Loosen the rocker arm fulcrum bolts until the rocker arms can be rotated off the pushrods.
4. Remove the pushrods. KEEP THE PUSHRODS IN ORDER, FOR INSTALLATION!
5. Using a magnetic lifter removal tool, remove the lifters. Wipe clean the exterior of each lifter as it's removed and mark it with an indelible marker, so that it can be installed in its original bore.

To install:

6. Coat the bottom surface of each lifter with multi-purpose grease and coat the rest of the lifter with clean engine oil.
7. Install each lifter in it original bore using the magnetic tool.
8. Coat each end of each pushrod with multi-purpose grease and install each in its original position. Make sure that each pushrod is properly seated in the lifter socket.
9. Install the rocker arms.
10. Check the valve clearance as described in the valve clearance procedure in Section 1.
11. Install the intake manifold.
12. Install the rocker arm covers.

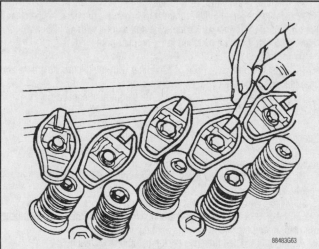
Fig. 199 Remove the pushrods and keep them in order so they can be installed in their original bores

7.3L ENGINE—1989–94 MODELS

▶ See Figure 200

1. Disconnect the negative battery cables and remove the engine cover.
2. Remove the air cleaner and install an intake manifold cover.
3. Disconnect the fuel inlet and return lines from the filter.

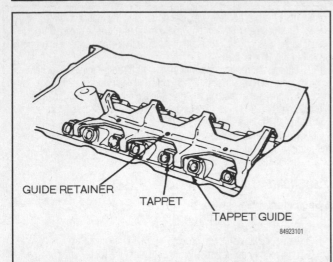

Fig. 200 Remove the tappet guide retainer to gain access to and remove the tappet—1989–94 diesel engines

4. Loosen the fuel filter bracket retainers, then remove the bracket and filter as an assembly.

5. Remove the injection pump.

6. Remove the glow plug harness and controller.

7. Move the engine wiring harness aside.

8. Disconnect the engine wiring harness from the left cylinder head.

9. Remove the intake manifold.

10. Remove the CDR tube and grommet from the valley pan.

11. Remove the valley pan strap from the front of the block.

12. Remove the valley pan drain plug and lift out the valley pan.

13. Remove the rocker arm covers.

14. Remove the rocker arms. KEEP THEM IN ORDER FOR INSTALLATION!

15. Remove the pushrods. KEEP THEM IN ORDER FOR INSTALLATION!

16. Remove the lifter guide retainer.

17. Using a magnetic lifter removal tool, remove the lifters. Wipe clean the exterior of each lifter as it's removed and mark it with an indelible marker, so that it can be installed in its original bore.

To install:

18. Coat the bottom surface of each lifter with multi-purpose grease and coat the rest of the lifter with clean engine oil.

19. Install each lifter in it original bore using the magnetic tool.

20. Install the lifter guide retainer.

21. Install the pushrods, copper colored end up, into their original locations, making sure that they are firmly seated in the lifters.

22. Coat the valve stem tips with multi-purpose grease and install the rocker arms and posts in their original positions.

23. Install all the rocker arms.

24. Install the rocker arm covers.

25. Clean all old RTV gasket material from the block and run a 1/8 in. (3mm) bead of new RTV gasket material at each end of the block. Within 15 minutes, install the valley pan. Install the pan drain plug.

26. Install the CDR tube, new grommet and new O-ring.

27. Connect the valley pan strap to the front of the block.

28. Install the intake manifold.

29. Install the engine wiring harness and connect the ground wire to the left cylinder head.

30. Install the glow plug harness and controller.

31. Install the fuel filter and bracket, then tighten the retainers.

32. Connect the fuel inlet and return lines to the filter.

33. Install the injection pump.

34. Install the air cleaner.

35. Connect the negative battery cables and install the engine cover.

36. Start the van and check for leaks.

37. If necessary, purge nozzle high pressure fuel lines of air by loosening the connector one half to one turn and cranking the engine until the bubble free air flows from the connection.

38. Retighten the connection.

7.3L ENGINE—1995–96 MODELS

◢ **See Figure 201**

1. Remove the cylinder head(s).

2. Remove the camshaft follower guide retainer screws and guide retainer.

3. Remove the camshaft follower guide.

4. Remove the tappet.

To install:

5. Lubricate the tappet with engine oil and install it in its original bore.

6. Install the camshaft follower guide, guide retainer and retainer screws.

7. Install the cylinder head(s).

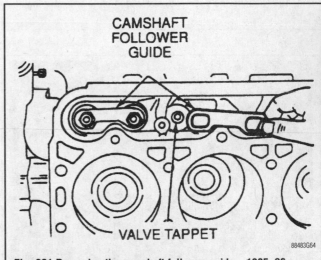

Fig. 201 Removing the camshaft follower guide—1995–96 diesel engines

INSPECTION

Camshaft

◢ **See Figure 202**

Check the lift of each lobe in consecutive order and make a note of the reading.

1. Remove valve cover(s).

2. Remove the rocker arm stud nut or fulcrum bolts, fulcrum seat and rocker arm.

3. Make sure the pushrod is in the valve tappet socket. Install a dial indicator with bracketry tool Tool-4201-C or equivalent, so that the actuating point of the indicator is in the push rod socket (or the indicator ball socket adapter tool 6565–AB is on the end of the push rod) and in the same plane as the push rod movement.

4. Disconnect the I terminal and the S terminal at the starter relay. Install an auxiliary starter switch between the battery and S terminals of the start relay. Crank the engine with the ignition switch off. Turn the crankshaft over until the tappet is on the base circle of the camshaft lobe. At this position, the push rod will be in its lowest position.

5. Zero the dial indicator. Continue to rotate the crankshaft slowly until the push rod is in the fully raised position.

6. Compare the total lift recorded on the dial indicator with the specification shown in the Engine Rebuilding chart.

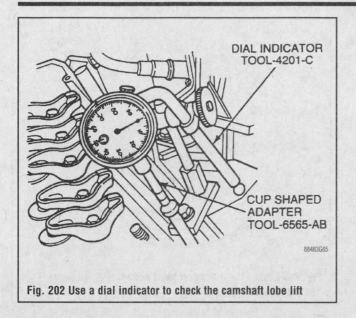

Fig. 202 Use a dial indicator to check the camshaft lobe lift

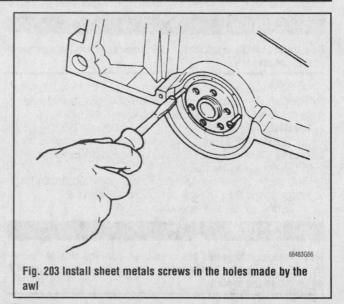

Fig. 203 Install sheet metals screws in the holes made by the awl

To check the accuracy of the original indicator reading, continue to rotate the crankshaft until the indicator reads zero. If the left on any lobe is below specified wear limits listed, the camshaft and the valve tappet operating on the worn lobe(s) must be replaced.

7. Install the dial indicator and auxiliary starter switch.

8. Install the rocker arm, fulcrum seat and stud nut or fulcrum bolts. Check the valve clearance, and adjust if required. (Refer to the procedure earlier in this section).

9. Install the valve cover(s).

Lifters

1. Throughly clean the lifter and its bore, then check for pitting, scoring or excessive wear.

2. On flat lifters, the bottom should be flat and not concaved.

3. If equipped with a roller, the roller should rotate freely without excessive play.

Rear Main Seal

REMOVAL & INSTALLATION

4.9L, 5.0L and 5.8L Engines

▶ See Figure 203

If the crankshaft rear oil seal replacement is the only operation being performed, it can be done in the vehicle as detailed in the following procedure. If the oil seal is being replaced in conjunction with a rear main bearing replacement, the engine must be removed from the vehicle and installed on a work stand.

1. Remove the transmission from the vehicle.

2. Loosen the flywheel retaining bolts, then remove the rear cap (main bearing) and the flywheel.

3. Use an awl to punch two holes in the crankshaft rear oil seal. Punch the holes on opposite sides of the crankshaft and just above the bearing cap to cylinder block split line.

4. Install a sheet metal screw in each hole. Use two small prybars to pry against both screws at the same time to remove the crankshaft rear oil seal. It may be necessary to place small blocks of wood against the cylinder block to provide a fulcrum point for the pry bars. Use caution throughout this procedure to avoid scratching or otherwise damaging the crankshaft oil seal surface.

5. Clean the oil seal recess in the cylinder block and main bearing cap.

To install:

6. Clean, inspect and polish the rear oil seal rubbing surface on the crankshaft. Coat the new oil seal and the crankshaft with a light film of engine oil. Start the seal in the recess with the seal lip facing forward and install it with a seal driver. Keep the tool straight with the centerline of the crankshaft and install the seal until the tool contacts the cylinder block surface. Remove the tool and inspect the seal to be sure it was not damaged during installation.

7. Position the flywheel on the crankshaft flange. Coat the threads of the flywheel attaching bolts with oil-resistant sealer and install the bolts. Tighten the bolts in sequence across from each other to 75–85 ft. lbs. (102–115 Nm).

8. Install the transmission, following the procedure in Section 7.

7.5L Engine

▶ See Figure 204

1. Raise the van and support it with safety stands.

2. Remove the oil pan.

3. Loosen all the crankshaft main bearing cap bolts and lower the crankshaft no more than 1/32 in. (0.7938mm).

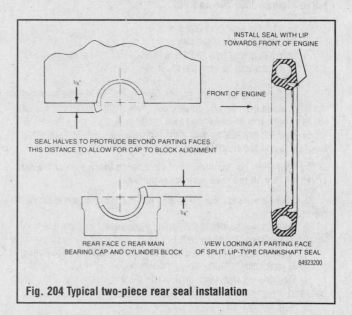

Fig. 204 Typical two-piece rear seal installation

❄❄ CAUTION

Be careful that the crankshaft sealing surfaces are not damaged in this process

4. Remove the rear main bearing cap and remove the seal. On the cylinder block half of the seal, use a seal removal tool, or install a small metal screw in one end of the seal and pull on the screw to remove the seal.

To install:

5. Clean the seal groove in the crankshaft main bearing cap and the block using a brush and a solvent such as metal surface cleaner F4AZ-19A536-RA or its equivalent.

6. Clean the areas where the sealer is to be applied later and dry the area thoroughly so that no solvent contacts the rear main seal.

7. Dip the seal halves in engine oil.

❄❄ CAUTION

Make sure no rubber has been removed from the outside diameter of the seal by the bottom edge of the groove. Do not allow oil to get on the sealer.

8. Install the upper half of the seal (cylinder block side) into its groove with the undercut side of the seal towards the front of the engine (with the tab side of the seal towards the rear face of the block), by rotating it on the seal journal until approximately ⅜ in. (9.525mm) protrudes below the parting surface.

9. Tighten all the crankshaft main bearing cap bolts, EXCEPT THE REAR MAIN BEARING, to 95–105 ft. lbs. (129–142 Nm).

10. Install the lower half of the seal in the rear crankshaft main bearing cap with the undercut side of the seal towards the front of the engine (with the tab side of the seal towards the rear face of the block), Allow the seal to protrude ⅜ in. (9.525mm) above the parting surface to mate with the upper half of the seal.

11. Apply a ¹⁄₁₆ in. (1.588mm) bead of gasket maker E2AZ-19562-B or its equivalent to the rear oil seal area of the block starting from the forward face of the return groove and overlaying the end of the wire seal retainer.

➡ **Do not allow the sealer to contact the inside diameter of the seal.**

12. Install the rear main cap and tighten the bolts to 95–105 ft. lbs. (129–142 Nm).

13. Install the pan. Refer to the appropriate procedures in this section.

7.3L Diesel Engines

1989–94 MODELS

◢ **See Figures 205, 206 and 207**

1. Remove the flywheel assemblies.
2. Remove the engine rear cover.
3. Using an arbor press and a 4⅛ in. (104.775mm) diameter spacer, press out the rear oil seal from the cover.

To install:

4. Clean the rear cover and engine block surfaces. Remove all traces of old RTV sealant from the oil pan and rear cover sealing surface by cleaning with a suitable solvent and drying thoroughly.

5. Coat the new rear oil seal with Lubriplate® or equivalent. Using an arbor press and spacer, install the new seal into the cover.

➡ **The seal must be installed from the engine block side of the rear cover, flush with the seal bore inner surface.**

6. Install a seal pilot, Ford part no. T83T–6701B or equivalent onto the crankshaft.

7. Apply gasket sealant to the engine block gasket surfaces and install the rear cover gasket to the engine.

8. Apply a ¼ in. (6mm) bead of RTV sealant onto the oil pan sealing surface, immediately after rear cover installation.

9. Push the rear cover into position on the engine and install the cover bolts and tighten them to 15 ft. lbs. (20 Nm).

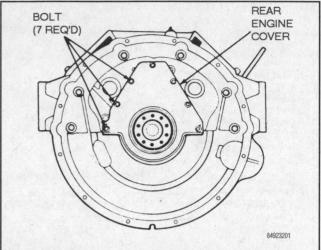

Fig. 205 Loosen the rear cover bolts and remove the cover— 1989–94 diesel engines

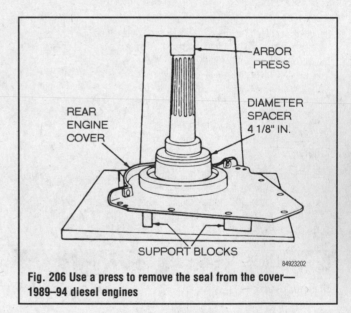

Fig. 206 Use a press to remove the seal from the cover— 1989–94 diesel engines

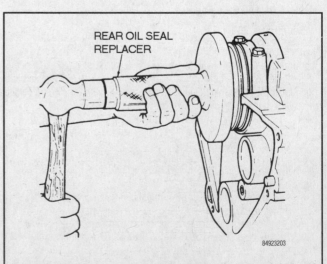

Fig. 207 A driver can be used to install the rear main seal— 1989–94 diesel engines

10. Position the flywheel on the crankshaft flange. Coat the threads of the flywheel attaching bolts with sealant and install the bolts and flexplate, if equipped. Tighten the bolts to specification, alternating across from each bolt.

1995–96 MODELS

◆ **See Figures 208, 209 and 210**

1. Remove the flywheel.
2. Loosen the crankshaft rear oil seal bolts and remove the seal.
3. Clean the seal mating surfaces.
4. If installing the old seal, inspect it for damage.
5. Using crankshaft wear ring removal tool T94T-6701-AH1, forcing screw T84T-7025-B, remover tube T77J-7025-B and wear ring remover sleeve T94T-6701-AH2 (refer to the illustration), or their equivalents, remove the wear ring.

To install:

6. Apply silicone sealant D6AZ-19562-BA, or equivalent, to the seal retaining ring and the seal retaining bolts.
7. using seal replacers T94T-6701-AH3 and T94T-AH4, driver sleeve T79T-6316-A4 (part of T79T-6316-A) and guide pins T94P-7000-P or their equivalents, install the wear ring and oil seal.
8. Install the seal retaining bolts and tighten them to specifications.
9. Remove the installation tools and install the flywheel.

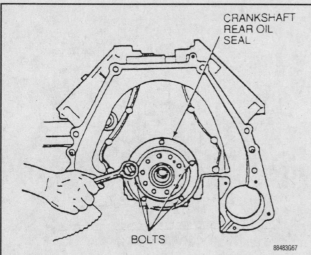

Fig. 208 Loosen the bolts and remove the rear cover—1995–96 diesel engines

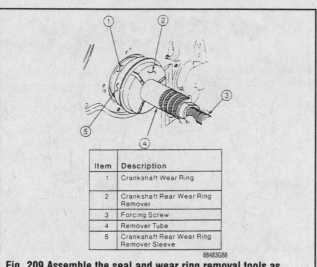

Item	Description
1	Crankshaft Wear Ring
2	Crankshaft Rear Wear Ring Remover
3	Forcing Screw
4	Remover Tube
5	Crankshaft Rear Wear Ring Remover Sleeve

Fig. 209 Assemble the seal and wear ring removal tools as shown, then remove the wear ring—1995–96 diesel engine

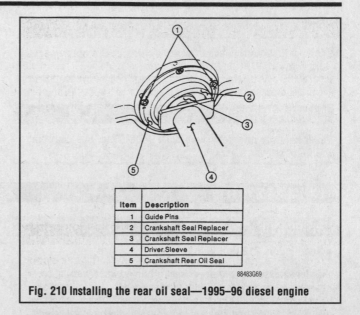

Item	Description
1	Guide Pins
2	Crankshaft Seal Replacer
3	Crankshaft Seal Replacer
4	Driver Sleeve
5	Crankshaft Rear Oil Seal

Fig. 210 Installing the rear oil seal—1995–96 diesel engine

Flywheel/Flexplate and Ring Gear

➡**Flexplate is the term for a flywheel mated with an automatic transmission.**

REMOVAL & INSTALLATION

All Engines

◆ **See Figure 211**

➡**The ring gear is replaceable only on engines mated with a manual transmission. Engines with automatic transmissions have ring gears which are welded to the flexplate.**

1. Remove the transmission.
2. Remove the clutch, if equipped, or torque converter from the flywheel. The flywheel bolts should be loosened a little at a time in a cross pattern to avoid warping the flywheel. On vans with manual transmissions, replace the pilot bearing in the end of the crankshaft if removing the flywheel.
3. The flywheel should be checked for cracks and glazing. It can be resurfaced by a machine shop.

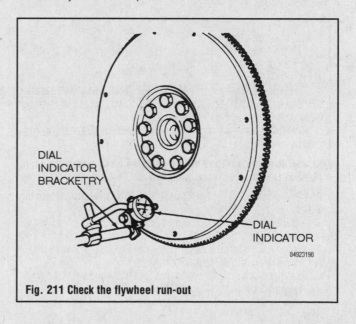

Fig. 211 Check the flywheel run-out

4. If the ring gear is to be replaced, drill a hole in the gear between two teeth, being careful not to contact the flywheel surface. Using a cold chisel at this point, crack the ring gear and remove it.

5. Polish the inner surface of the new ring gear and heat it in an oven to about 600°F (316°C). Quickly place the ring gear on the flywheel and tap it into place, making sure that it is fully seated.

✳✳ WARNING

Never heat the ring gear past 800°F (426°C), or the tempering will be destroyed.

EXHAUST SYSTEM

Inspection

◆ **See Figures 212 thru 218**

➡**Safety glasses should be worn at all times when working on or near the exhaust system. Older exhaust systems will almost always be covered with loose rust particles which will shower you when disturbed. These particles are more than a nuisance and could injure your eye.**

✳✳ CAUTION

Do NOT perform exhaust repairs or inspection with the engine or exhaust hot. Allow the system to cool completely before attempting any work. Exhaust systems are noted for sharp edges, flaking metal and rusted bolts. Gloves and eye protection are required. A healthy supply of penetrating oil and rags is highly recommended.

Your vehicle must be raised and supported safely to inspect the exhaust system properly. By placing 4 safety stands under the vehicle for support should provide enough room for you to slide under the vehicle and inspect the system completely. Start the inspection at the exhaust manifold or turbocharger pipe where the header pipe is attached and work your way to the back of the vehicle. On dual exhaust systems, remember to inspect both sides of the vehicle. Check the complete exhaust system for open seams, holes loose connections, or other deterioration which could permit exhaust fumes to seep into the passenger compartment. Inspect all mounting brackets and hangers for deterioration, some models may have rubber O-rings that can be overstretched and non-supportive.

6. Position the flywheel on the end of the crankshaft. Tighten the bolts a little at a time, in a cross pattern, to the torque figure shown in the Torque Specifications Chart.

7. Install the clutch or torque converter.

8. Install the transmission.

These components will need to be replaced if found. It has always been a practice to use a pointed tool to poke up into the exhaust system where the deterioration spots are to see whether or not they crumble. Some models may have heat shield covering certain parts of the exhaust system, it will be necessary to remove these shields to have the exhaust visible for inspection also.

Fig. 213 Check the muffler for rotted spot welds and seams

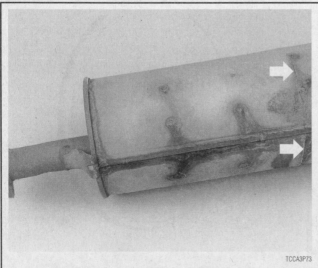

Fig. 212 Cracks in the muffler are a guaranteed leak

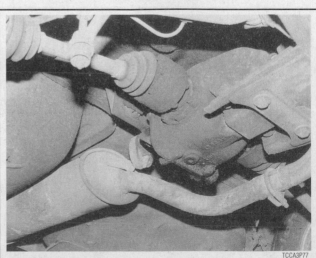

Fig. 214 Make sure the exhaust components are not contacting the body or suspension

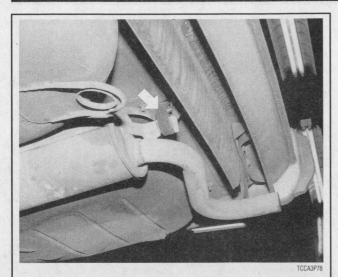

TCCA3P78

Fig. 215 Check for overstretched or torn exhaust hangers

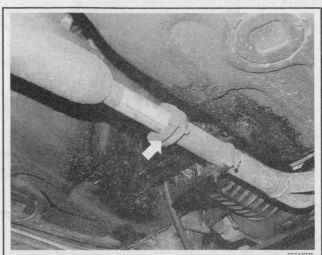

TCCA3P76

Fig. 218 Some systems, like this one, use large O-rings (donuts) in between the flanges

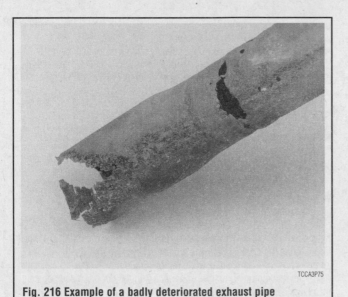

TCCA3P75

Fig. 216 Example of a badly deteriorated exhaust pipe

REPLACEMENT

▶ **See Figures 219 and 220**

There are basically two types of exhaust systems. One is the flange type where the component ends are attached with bolts and a gasket in-between. The other exhaust system is the slip joint type. These components slip into one another using clamps to retain them together.

✳✳ CAUTION

Allow the exhaust system to cool sufficiently before spraying a solvent exhaust fasteners. Some solvents are highly flammable and could ignite when sprayed on hot exhaust components.

Before removing any component of the exhaust system, ALWAYS squirt a liquid rust dissolving agent onto the fasteners for ease of removal. A lot of knuckle skin will be saved by following this rule. It may even be wise to spray the fasteners and allow them to sit overnight.

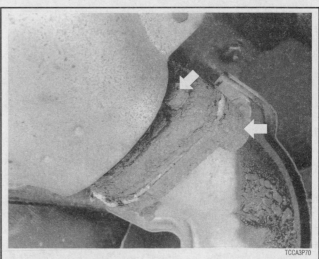

TCCA3P70

Fig. 219 Nuts and bolts will be extremely difficult to remove when deteriorated with rust

TCCA3P71

Fig. 217 Inspect flanges for gaskets that have deteriorated and need replacement

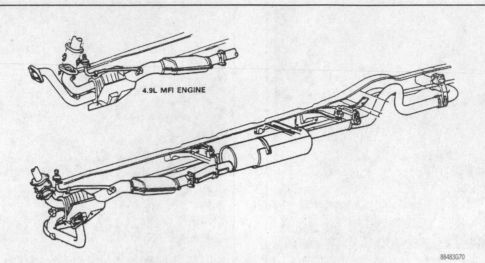

Fig. 220 Typical exhaust system used on E-150–350 vans under 8500 GVW with 4.9L and 5.8L engines

Flange Type

♦ See Figure 221

❊❊ CAUTION

Do NOT perform exhaust repairs or inspection with the engine or exhaust hot. Allow the system to cool completely before attempting any work. Exhaust systems are noted for sharp edges, flaking metal and rusted bolts. Gloves and eye protection are required. A healthy supply of penetrating oil and rags is highly recommended. Never spray liquid rust dissolving agent onto a hot exhaust component.

Before removing any component on a flange type system, ALWAYS squirt a liquid rust dissolving agent onto the fasteners for ease of removal. Start by unbolting the exhaust piece at both ends (if required). When unbolting the headpipe from the manifold, make sure that the bolts are free before trying to remove them. if you snap a stud in the exhaust manifold, the stud will have to be removed with a bolt extractor, which often means removal of the manifold itself. Next, disconnect the component from the mounting; slight twisting and turning may be required to remove the com-

ponent completely from the vehicle. You may need to tap on the component with a rubber mallet to loosen the component. If all else fails, use a hacksaw to separate the parts. An oxy-acetylene cutting torch may be faster but the sparks are DANGEROUS near the fuel tank, and at the very least, accidents could happen, resulting in damage to the under-vehicle parts, not to mention yourself.

Slip Joint Type

♦ See Figure 222

Before removing any component on the slip joint type exhaust system, ALWAYS squirt a liquid rust dissolving agent onto the fasteners for ease of removal. Start by unbolting the exhaust piece at both ends (if required). When unbolting the headpipe from the manifold, make sure that the bolts are free before trying to remove them. if you snap a stud in the exhaust manifold, the stud will have to be removed with a bolt extractor, which often means removal of the manifold itself. Next, remove the mounting U-bolts from around the exhaust pipe you are extracting from the vehicle. Don't be surprised if the U-bolts break while removing the nuts. Loosen the exhaust pipe from any mounting brackets retaining it to the floor pan and separate the components.

Fig. 221 Example of a flange type exhaust system joint

Fig. 222 Example of a common exhaust system slip joint

ENGINE RECONDITIONING

Determining Engine Condition

Anything that generates heat and/or friction will eventually burn or wear out (ie. a light bulb generates heat, therefore its life span is limited). With this in mind, a running engine generates tremendous amounts of both; friction is encountered by the moving and rotating parts inside the engine and heat is created by friction and combustion of the fuel. However, the engine has systems designed to help reduce the effects of heat and friction and provide added longevity. The oiling system reduces the amount of friction encountered by the moving parts inside the engine, while the cooling system reduces heat created by friction and combustion. If either system is not maintained, a break-down will be inevitable. Therefore, you can see how regular maintenance can affect the service life of your vehicle. If you do not drain, flush and refill your cooling system at the proper intervals, deposits will begin to accumulate in the radiator, thereby reducing the amount of heat it can extract from the coolant. The same applies to your oil and filter; if it is not changed often enough it becomes laden with contaminates and is unable to properly lubricate the engine. This increases friction and wear.

There are a number of methods for evaluating the condition of your engine. A compression test can reveal the condition of your pistons, piston rings, cylinder bores, head gasket(s), valves and valve seats. An oil pressure test can warn you of possible engine bearing, or oil pump failures. Excessive oil consumption, evidence of oil in the engine air intake area and/or bluish smoke from the tail pipe may indicate worn piston rings, worn valve guides and/or valve seals. As a general rule, an engine that uses no more than one quart of oil every 1000 miles is in good condition. Engines that use one quart of oil or more in less than 1000 miles should first be checked for oil leaks. If any oil leaks are present, have them fixed before determining how much oil is consumed by the engine, especially if blue smoke is not visible at the tail pipe.

COMPRESSION TEST

A noticeable lack of engine power, excessive oil consumption and/or poor fuel mileage measured over an extended period are all indicators of internal engine wear. Worn piston rings, scored or worn cylinder bores, blown head gaskets, sticking or burnt valves, and worn valve seats are all possible culprits. A check of each cylinder's compression will help locate the problem.

Gasoline Engines

▶ See Figure 223

➥A screw-in type compression gauge is more accurate than the type you simply hold against the spark plug hole. Although it takes slightly longer to use, it's worth the effort to obtain a more accurate reading.

1. Make sure that the proper amount and viscosity of engine oil is in the crankcase, then ensure the battery is fully charged.
2. Warm up the engine to normal operating temperature, then shut the engine **OFF**.
3. Disable the ignition system.
4. Label and disconnect all of the spark plug wires from the plugs.
5. Thoroughly clean the cylinder head area around the spark plug ports, then remove the spark plugs.
6. Set the throttle plate to the fully open (wide-open throttle) position. You can block the accelerator linkage open for this, or you can have an assistant fully depress the accelerator pedal.
7. Install a screw-in type compression gauge into the No. 1 spark plug hole until the fitting is snug.

✳✳ **WARNING**

Be careful not to crossthread the spark plug hole.

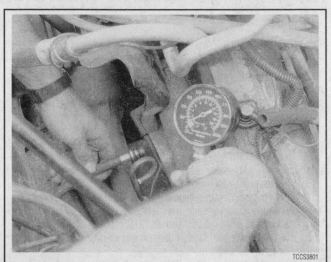

Fig. 223 A screw-in type compression gauge is more accurate and easier to use without an assistant

TCCS3801

8. According to the tool manufacturer's instructions, connect a remote starting switch to the starting circuit.
9. With the ignition switch in the **OFF** position, use the remote starting switch to crank the engine through at least five compression strokes (approximately 5 seconds of cranking) and record the highest reading on the gauge.
10. Repeat the test on each cylinder, cranking the engine approximately the same number of compression strokes and/or time as the first.
11. Compare the highest readings from each cylinder to that of the others. The indicated compression pressures are considered within specifications if the lowest reading cylinder is within 75 percent of the pressure recorded for the highest reading cylinder. For example, if your highest reading cylinder pressure was 150 psi (1034 kPa), then 75 percent of that would be 113 psi (779 kPa). So the lowest reading cylinder should be no less than 113 psi (779 kPa).
12. If a cylinder exhibits an unusually low compression reading, pour a tablespoon of clean engine oil into the cylinder through the spark plug hole and repeat the compression test. If the compression rises after adding oil, it means that the cylinder's piston rings and/or cylinder bore are damaged or worn. If the pressure remains low, the valves may not be seating properly (a valve job is needed), or the head gasket may be blown near that cylinder. If compression in any two adjacent cylinders is low, and if the addition of oil doesn't help raise compression, there is leakage past the head gasket. Oil and coolant in the combustion chamber, combined with blue or constant white smoke from the tail pipe, are symptoms of this problem. However, don't be alarmed by the normal white smoke emitted from the tail pipe during engine warm-up or from cold weather driving. There may be evidence of water droplets on the engine dipstick and/or oil droplets in the cooling system if a head gasket is blown.

Diesel Engines

Checking cylinder compression on diesel engines is basically the same procedure as on gasoline engines except for the following:
1. A special compression gauge adaptor suitable for diesel engines (because these engines have much greater compression pressures) must be used.
2. Remove the injector tubes and remove the injectors from each cylinder.

✳✳ **WARNING**

Do not forget to remove the washer underneath each injector. Otherwise, it may get lost when the engine is cranked.

3. When fitting the compression gauge adaptor to the cylinder head, make sure the bleeder of the gauge (if equipped) is closed.

4. When reinstalling the injector assemblies, install new washers underneath each injector.

OIL PRESSURE TEST

Check for proper oil pressure at the sending unit passage with an externally mounted mechanical oil pressure gauge (as opposed to relying on a factory installed dash-mounted gauge). A tachometer may also be needed, as some specifications may require running the engine at a specific rpm.

1. With the engine cold, locate and remove the oil pressure sending unit.

2. Following the manufacturerís instructions, connect a mechanical oil pressure gauge and, if necessary, a tachometer to the engine.

3. Start the engine and allow it to idle.

4. Check the oil pressure reading when cold and record the number. You may need to run the engine at a specified rpm, so check the specifications chart located earlier in this section.

5. Run the engine until normal operating temperature is reached (upper radiator hose will feel warm).

6. Check the oil pressure reading again with the engine hot and record the number. Turn the engine **OFF**.

7. Compare your hot oil pressure reading to that given in the chart. If the reading is low, check the cold pressure reading against the chart. If the cold pressure is well above the specification, and the hot reading was lower than the specification, you may have the wrong viscosity oil in the engine. Change the oil, making sure to use the proper grade and quantity, then repeat the test.

Low oil pressure readings could be attributed to internal component wear, pump related problems, a low oil level, or oil viscosity that is too low. High oil pressure readings could be caused by an overfilled crankcase, too high of an oil viscosity or a faulty pressure relief valve.

Buy or Rebuild?

Now that you have determined that your engine is worn out, you must make some decisions. The question of whether or not an engine is worth rebuilding is largely a subjective matter and one of personal worth. Is the engine a popular one, or is it an obsolete model? Are parts available? Will it get acceptable gas mileage once it is rebuilt? Is the vehicle itís being put into worth keeping? Would it be less expensive to buy a new engine, have your engine rebuilt by a pro, rebuild it yourself or buy a used engine from a salvage yard? Or would it be simpler and less expensive to buy another car? If you have considered all these matters and more, and have still decided to rebuild the engine, then it is time to decide how you will rebuild it.

➡**The editors at Chilton feel that most engine machining should be performed by a professional machine shop. Donít think of it as wasting money, rather, as an assurance that the job has been done right the first time. There are many expensive and specialized tools required to perform such tasks as boring and honing an engine block or having a valve job done on a cylinder head. Even inspecting the parts requires expensive micrometers and gauges to properly measure wear and clearances. Also, a machine shop can deliver to you clean, and ready to assemble parts, saving you time and aggravation. Your maximum savings will come from performing the removal, disassembly, assembly and installation of the engine and purchasing or renting only the tools required to perform the above tasks. Depending on the particular circumstances, you may save 40 to 60 percent of the cost doing these yourself.**

A complete rebuild or overhaul of an engine involves replacing all of the moving parts (pistons, rods, crankshaft, camshaft, etc.) with new ones and machining the non-moving wearing surfaces of the block and heads. Unfortunately, this may not be cost effective. For instance, your crankshaft may have been damaged or worn, but it can be machined undersize for a minimal fee.

So, as you can see, you can replace everything inside the engine, but, it is wiser to replace only those parts which are really needed, and, if possible, repair the more expensive ones. Later in this section, we will break the engine down into its two main components: the cylinder head and the engine block. We will discuss each component, and the recommended parts to replace during a rebuild on each.

Engine Overhaul Tips

Most engine overhaul procedures are fairly standard. In addition to specific parts replacement procedures and specifications for your individual engine, this section is also a guide to acceptable rebuilding procedures. Examples of standard rebuilding practice are given and should be used along with specific details concerning your particular engine.

Competent and accurate machine shop services will ensure maximum performance, reliability and engine life. In most instances it is more profitable for the do-it-yourself mechanic to remove, clean and inspect the component, buy the necessary parts and deliver these to a shop for actual machine work.

Much of the assembly work (crankshaft, bearings, piston rods, and other components) is well within the scope of the do-it-yourself mechanic's tools and abilities. You will have to decide for yourself the depth of involvement you desire in an engine repair or rebuild.

TOOLS

The tools required for an engine overhaul or parts replacement will depend on the depth of your involvement. With a few exceptions, they will be the tools found in a mechanic's tool kit (see Section 1 of this manual). More in-depth work will require some or all of the following:

- A dial indicator (reading in thousandths) mounted on a universal base
- Micrometers and telescope gauges
- Jaw and screw-type pullers
- Scraper
- Valve spring compressor
- Ring groove cleaner
- Piston ring expander and compressor
- Ridge reamer
- Cylinder hone or glaze breaker
- Plastigage®
- Engine stand

The use of most of these tools is illustrated in this section. Many can be rented for a one-time use from a local parts jobber or tool supply house specializing in automotive work.

Occasionally, the use of special tools is called for. See the information on Special Tools and the Safety Notice in the front of this book before substituting another tool.

OVERHAUL TIPS

Aluminum has become extremely popular for use in engines, due to its low weight. Observe the following precautions when handling aluminum parts:

- Never hot tank aluminum parts (the caustic hot tank solution will eat the aluminum.
- Remove all aluminum parts (identification tag, etc.) from engine parts prior to the tanking.
- Always coat threads lightly with engine oil or anti-seize compounds before installation, to prevent seizure.
- Never overtighten bolts or spark plugs especially in aluminum threads.

When assembling the engine, any parts that will be exposed to frictional contact must be prelubed to provide lubrication at initial start-up. Any product specifically formulated for this purpose can be used, but engine oil is not recommended as a prelube in most cases.

When semi-permanent (locked, but removable) installation of bolts or nuts is desired, threads should be cleaned and coated with Loctite® or another similar, commercial non-hardening sealant.

CLEANING

▶ **See Figures 224, 225, 226 and 227**

Before the engine and its components are inspected, they must be thoroughly cleaned. You will need to remove any engine varnish, oil sludge and/or carbon deposits from all of the components to insure an accurate inspection. A crack in the engine block or cylinder head can easily become overlooked if hidden by a layer of sludge or carbon.

Most of the cleaning process can be carried out with common hand tools and readily available solvents or solutions. Carbon deposits can be chipped away using a hammer and a hard wooden chisel. Old gasket material and varnish or sludge can usually be removed using a scraper and/or cleaning solvent. Extremely stubborn deposits may require the use of a power drill with a wire brush. If using a wire brush, use extreme care around any critical machined surfaces (such as the gasket surfaces, bearing saddles, cylinder bores, etc.). Use of a wire brush is NOT RECOMMENDED on any aluminum components. Always follow any safety recommendations given by the manufacturer of the tool and/or solvent. You should always wear eye protection during any cleaning process involving scraping, chipping or spraying of solvents.

An alternative to the mess and hassle of cleaning the parts yourself is to drop them off at a local garage or machine shop. They will, more than likely, have the necessary equipment to properly clean all of the parts for a nominal fee.

✳✳ CAUTION

Always wear eye protection during any cleaning process involving scraping, chipping or spraying of solvents.

Remove any oil galley plugs, freeze plugs and/or pressed-in bearings and carefully wash and degrease all of the engine components including the fasteners and bolts. Small parts such as the valves, springs, etc., should be placed in a metal basket and allowed to soak. Use pipe cleaner type brushes, and clean all passageways in the components. Use a ring expander and remove the rings from the pistons. Clean the piston ring grooves with a special tool or a piece of broken ring. Scrape the carbon off of the top of the piston. You should never use a wire brush on the pistons. After preparing all of the piston assemblies in this manner, wash and degrease them again.

✳✳ WARNING

Use extreme care when cleaning around the cylinder head valve seats. A mistake or slip may cost you a new seat.

When cleaning the cylinder head, remove carbon from the combustion chamber with the valves installed. This will avoid damaging the valve seats.

Fig. 224 Use a gasket scraper to remove the old gasket material from the mating surfaces

TCCS3132

Fig. 226 Clean the piston ring grooves using a ring groove cleaner tool, or . . .

TCCS3208

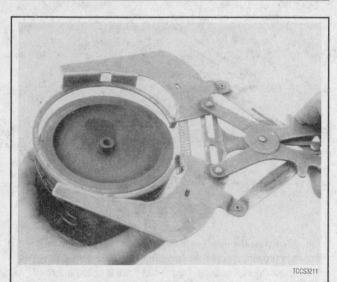

Fig. 225 Use a ring expander tool to remove the piston rings

TCCS3211

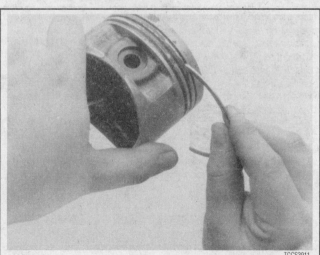

Fig. 227 . . . use a piece of an old ring to clean the grooves. Be careful, the ring can be quite sharp

TCCS3911

REPAIRING DAMAGED THREADS

▶ **See Figures 228, 229, 230, 231 and 232**

Several methods of repairing damaged threads are available. Heli-Coil® (shown here), Keenserts® and Microdot® are among the most widely used. All involve basically the same principle—drilling out stripped threads, tapping the hole and installing a prewound insert—making welding, plugging and oversize fasteners unnecessary.

Two types of thread repair inserts are usually supplied: a standard type for most inch coarse, inch fine, metric course and metric fine thread sizes and a spark lug type to fit most spark plug port sizes. Consult the individual tool manufacturer's catalog to determine exact applications. Typical thread repair kits will contain a selection of prewound threaded inserts, a tap (corresponding to the outside diameter threads of the insert) and an installation tool. Spark plug inserts usually differ because they require a tap equipped with pilot threads and a combined reamer/tap section. Most manufacturers also supply blister-packed thread repair inserts separately in addition to a master kit containing a variety of taps and inserts plus installation tools.

Before attempting to repair a threaded hole, remove any snapped, broken or damaged bolts or studs. Penetrating oil can be used to free frozen

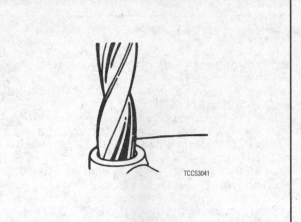

Fig. 230 Drill out the damaged threads with the specified size bit. Be sure to drill completely through the hole or to the bottom of a blind hole

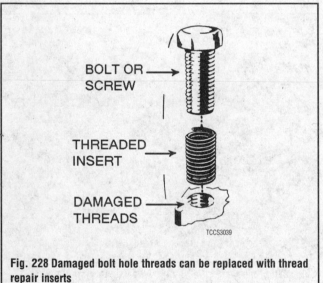

Fig. 228 Damaged bolt hole threads can be replaced with thread repair inserts

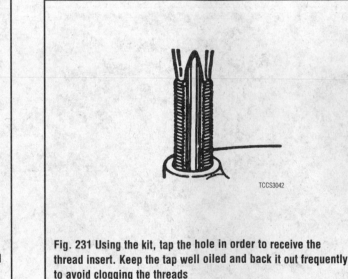

Fig. 231 Using the kit, tap the hole in order to receive the thread insert. Keep the tap well oiled and back it out frequently to avoid clogging the threads

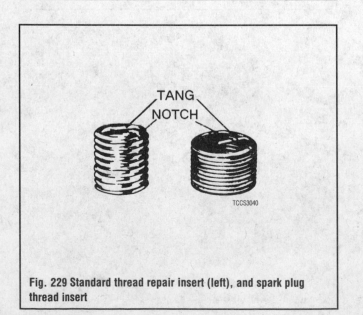

Fig. 229 Standard thread repair insert (left), and spark plug thread insert

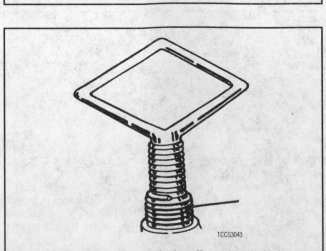

Fig. 232 Screw the insert onto the installer tool until the tang engages the slot. Thread the insert into the hole until it is ¼–½ turn below the top surface, then remove the tool and break off the tang using a punch

threads. The offending item can usually be removed with locking pliers or using a screw/stud extractor. After the hole is clear, the thread can be repaired, as shown in the series of accompanying illustrations and in the kit manufacturer's instructions.

Engine Preparation

To properly rebuild an engine, you must first remove it from the vehicle, then disassemble and diagnose it. Ideally you should place your engine on an engine stand. This affords you the best access to the engine components. Follow the manufacturer's directions for using the stand with your particular engine. Remove the flywheel or flexplate before installing the engine to the stand.

Now that you have the engine on a stand, and assuming that you have drained the oil and coolant from the engine, it's time to strip it of all but the necessary components. Before you start disassembling the engine, you may want to take a moment to draw some pictures, or fabricate some labels or containers to mark the locations of various components and the bolts and/or studs which fasten them. Modern day engines use a lot of little brackets and clips which hold wiring harnesses and such, and these holders are often mounted on studs and/or bolts that can be easily mixed up. The manufacturer spent a lot of time and money designing your vehicle, and they wouldn't have wasted any of it by haphazardly placing brackets, clips or fasteners on the vehicle. If it's present when you disassemble it, put it back when you assemble, you will regret not remembering that little bracket which holds a wire harness out of the path of a rotating part.

You should begin by unbolting any accessories still attached to the engine, such as the water pump, power steering pump, alternator, etc. Then, unfasten any manifolds (intake or exhaust) which were not removed during the engine removal procedure. Finally, remove any covers remaining on the engine such as the rocker arm, front or timing cover and oil pan. Some front covers may require the vibration damper and/or crank pulley to be removed beforehand. The idea is to reduce the engine to the bare necessities (cylinder head(s), valve train, engine block, crankshaft, pistons and connecting rods), plus any other 'in block' components such as oil pumps, balance shafts and auxiliary shafts.

Finally, remove the cylinder head(s) from the engine block and carefully place on a bench. Disassembly instructions for each component follow later in this section.

Cylinder Head

There are two basic types of cylinder heads used on today's automobiles: the Overhead Valve (OHV) and the Overhead Camshaft (OHC). The latter can also be broken down into two subgroups: the Single Overhead Camshaft (SOHC) and the Dual Overhead Camshaft (DOHC). Generally, if there is only a single camshaft on a head, it is just referred to as an OHC head. Also, an engine with a OHV cylinder head is also known as a pushrod engine.

Most cylinder heads these days are made of an aluminum alloy due to its light weight, durability and heat transfer qualities. However, cast iron was the material of choice in the past, and is still used on many vehicles today. Whether made from aluminum or iron, all cylinder heads have valves and seats. Some use two valves per cylinder, while the more hi-tech engines will utilize a multi-valve configuration using 3, 4 and even 5 valves per cylinder. When the valve contacts the seat, it does so on precision machined surfaces, which seals the combustion chamber. All cylinder heads have a valve guide for each valve. The guide centers the valve to the seat and allows it to move up and down within it. The clearance between the valve and guide can be critical. Too much clearance and the engine may consume oil, lose vacuum and/or damage the seat. Too little, and the valve can stick in the guide causing the engine to run poorly if at all, and possibly causing severe damage. The last component all cylinder heads have are valve springs. The spring holds the valve against its seat. It also returns the valve to this position when the valve has been opened by the valve train or camshaft. The spring is fastened to the valve by a retainer and valve locks (sometimes called keepers). Aluminum heads will also have a valve spring shim to keep the spring from wearing away the aluminum.

An ideal method of rebuilding the cylinder head would involve replacing all of the valves, guides, seats, springs, etc. with new ones. However, depending on how the engine was maintained, often this is not necessary. A major cause of valve, guide and seat wear is an improperly tuned engine. An engine that is running too rich, will often wash the lubricating oil out of the guide with gasoline, causing it to wear rapidly. Conversely, an engine which is running too lean will place higher combustion temperatures on the valves and seats allowing them to wear or even burn. Springs fall victim to the driving habits of the individual. A driver who often runs the engine rpm to the redline will wear out or break the springs faster then one that stays well below it. Unfortunately, mileage takes it toll on all of the parts. Generally, the valves, guides, springs and seats in a cylinder head can be machined and re-used, saving you money. However, if a valve is burnt, it may be wise to replace all of the valves, since they were all operating in the same environment. The same goes for any other component on the cylinder head. Think of it as an insurance policy against future problems related to that component.

Unfortunately, the only way to find out which components need replacing, is to disassemble and carefully check each piece. After the cylinder head(s) are disassembled, thoroughly clean all of the components.

DISASSEMBLY

▶ **See Figures 233 thru 238**

Before disassembling the cylinder head, you may want to fabricate some containers to hold the various parts, as some of them can be quite small (such as keepers) and easily lost. Also keeping yourself and the components organized will aid in assembly and reduce confusion. Where possible, try to maintain a components original location; this is especially important if there is not going to be any machine work performed on the components.

1. If you haven't already removed the rocker arms and/or shafts, do so now.
2. Position the head so that the springs are easily accessed.
3. Use a valve spring compressor tool, and relieve spring tension from the retainer.

➡**Due to engine varnish, the retainer may stick to the valve locks. A gentle tap with a hammer may help to break it loose.**

4. Remove the valve locks from the valve tip and/or retainer. A small magnet may help in removing the locks.
5. Lift the valve spring, tool and all, off of the valve stem.
6. If equipped, remove the valve seal. If the seal is difficult to remove with the valve in place, try removing the valve first, then the seal. Follow the steps below for valve removal.
7. Position the head to allow access for withdrawing the valve.

Fig. 233 When removing an OHV valve spring, use a compressor tool to relieve the tension from the retainer

Fig. 234 A small magnet will help in removal of the valve locks

Fig. 237 Removing an umbrella/positive type seal

Fig. 235 Be careful not to lose the small valve locks (keepers)

Fig. 238 Invert the cylinder head and withdraw the valve from the valve guide bore

Fig. 236 Remove the valve seal from the valve stem—O-ring type seal shown

→Cylinder heads that have seen a lot of miles and/or abuse may have mushroomed the valve lock grove and/or tip, causing difficulty in removal of the valve. If this has happened, use a metal file to carefully remove the high spots around the lock grooves and/or tip. Only file it enough to allow removal.

8. Remove the valve from the cylinder head.
9. If equipped, remove the valve spring shim. A small magnetic tool or screwdriver will aid in removal.
10. Repeat Steps 3 though 9 until all of the valves have been removed.

INSPECTION

Now that all of the cylinder head components are clean, itís time to inspect them for wear and/or damage. To accurately inspect them, you will need some specialized tools:

- A 0–1 inch micrometer for the valves
- A dial indicator or inside diameter gauge for the valve guides
- A spring pressure test gauge

If you do not have access to the proper tools, you may want to bring the components to a shop that does.

Valves

▶ **See Figures 239 and 240**

The first thing to inspect are the valve heads. Look closely at the head, margin and face for any cracks, excessive wear or burning. The margin is the best place to look for burning. It should have a squared edge with an even width all around the diameter. When a valve burns, the margin will look melted and the edges rounded. Also inspect the valve head for any signs of tulipping. This will show as a lifting of the edges or dishing in the center of the head and will usually not occur to all of the valves. All of the heads should look the same, any that seem dished more than others are probably bad. Next, inspect the valve lock grooves and valve tips. Check for any burrs around the lock grooves, especially if you had to file them to remove the valve. Valve tips should appear flat, although slight rounding with high mileage engines is normal. Slightly worn valve tips will need to be machined flat. Last, measure the valve stem diameter with the micrometer. Measure the area that rides within the guide, especially towards thc tip where most of the wear occurs. Take several measurements along its length and compare them to each other. Wear should be even along the length with little to no taper. If no minimum diameter is given in the specifications, then the stem should not read more than 0.001 in. (0.025mm) below the specification. Any valves that fail these inspections should be replaced.

Springs, Retainers and Valve Locks

▶ **See Figures 241 and 242**

The first thing to check is the most obvious, broken springs. Next check the free length and squareness of each spring. If applicable, insure to distinguish between intake and exhaust springs. Use a ruler and/or carpenters square to measure the length. A carpenters square should be used to check the springs for squareness. If a spring pressure test gauge is available, check each springs rating and compare to the specifications chart. Check the readings against the specifications given. Any springs that fail these inspections should be replaced.

The spring retainers rarely need replacing, however they should still be checked as a precaution. Inspect the spring mating surface and the valve lock retention area for any signs of excessive wear. Also check for any signs of cracking. Replace any retainers that are questionable.

Valve locks should be inspected for excessive wear on the outside contact area as well as on the inner notched surface. Any locks which appear worn or broken and its respective valve should be replaced.

Cylinder Head

There are several things to check on the cylinder head: valve guides, seats, cylinder head surface flatness, cracks and physical damage.

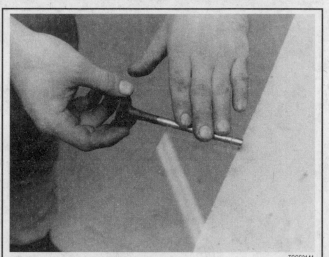

Fig. 239 Valve stems may be rolled on a flat surface to check for bends

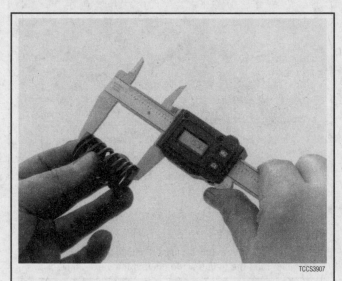

Fig. 241 Use a caliper to check the valve spring free-length

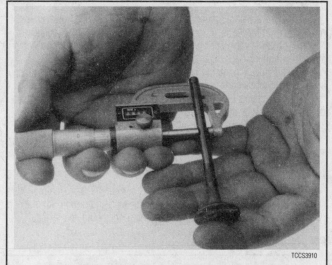

Fig. 240 Use a micrometer to check the valve stem diameter

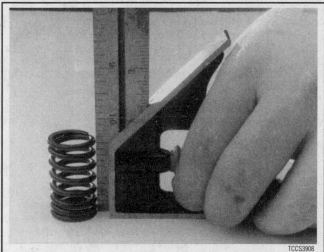

Fig. 242 Check the valve spring for squareness on a flat surface; a carpenter's square can be used

VALVE GUIDES

▶ See Figure 243

Now that you know the valves are good, you can use them to check the guides, although a new valve, if available, is preferred. Before you measure anything, look at the guides carefully and inspect them for any cracks, chips or breakage. Also if the guide is a removable style (as in most aluminum heads), check them for any looseness or evidence of movement. All of the guides should appear to be at the same height from the spring seat. If any seem lower (or higher) from another, the guide has moved. Mount a dial indicator onto the spring side of the cylinder head. Lightly oil the valve stem and insert it into the cylinder head. Position the dial indicator against the valve stem near the tip and zero the gauge. Grasp the valve stem and wiggle towards and away from the dial indicator and observe the readings. Mount the dial indicator 90 degrees from the initial point and zero the gauge and again take a reading. Compare the two readings for a out of round condition. Check the readings against the specifications given. An Inside Diameter (I.D.) gauge designed for valve guides will give you an accurate valve guide bore measurement. If the I.D. gauge is used, compare the readings with the specifications given. Any guides that fail these inspections should be replaced or machined.

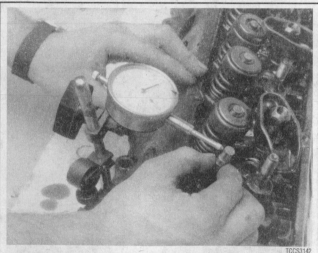

Fig. 243 A dial gauge may be used to check valve stem-to-guide clearance; read the gauge while moving the valve stem

VALVE SEATS

A visual inspection of the valve seats should show a slightly worn and pitted surface where the valve face contacts the seat. Inspect the seat carefully for severe pitting or cracks. Also, a seat that is badly worn will be recessed into the cylinder head. A severely worn or recessed seat may need to be replaced. All cracked seats must be replaced. A seat concentricity gauge, if available, should be used to check the seat run-out. If run-out exceeds specifications the seat must be machined (if no specification is given use 0.002 in. or 0.051mm).

CYLINDER HEAD SURFACE FLATNESS

▶ See Figures 244 and 245

After you have cleaned the gasket surface of the cylinder head of any old gasket material, check the head for flatness.

Place a straightedge across the gasket surface. Using feeler gauges, determine the clearance at the center of the straightedge and across the cylinder head at several points. Check along the centerline and diagonally on the head surface. If the warpage exceeds 0.003 in. (0.076mm) within a 6.0 in. (15.2cm) span, or 0.006 in. (0.152mm) over the total length of the head, the cylinder head must be resurfaced. After resurfacing the heads of a V-type engine, the intake manifold flange surface should be checked, and if necessary, milled proportionally to allow for the change in its mounting position.

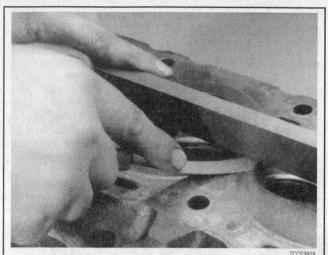

Fig. 244 Check the head for flatness across the center of the head surface using a straightedge and feeler gauge

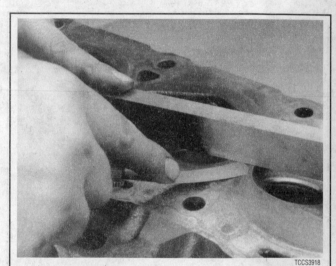

Fig. 245 Checks should also be made along both diagonals of the head surface

CRACKS AND PHYSICAL DAMAGE

Generally, cracks are limited to the combustion chamber, however, it is not uncommon for the head to crack in a spark plug hole, port, outside of the head or in the valve spring/rocker arm area. The first area to inspect is always the hottest: the exhaust seat/port area.

A visual inspection should be performed, but just because you don't see a crack does not mean it is not there. Some more reliable methods for inspecting for cracks include Magnaflux®, a magnetic process or Zyglo®, a dye penetrant. Magnaflux® is used only on ferrous metal (cast iron) heads. Zyglo® uses a spray on fluorescent mixture along with a black light to reveal the cracks. It is strongly recommended to have your cylinder head checked professionally for cracks, especially if the engine was known to have overheated and/or leaked or consumed coolant. Contact a local shop for availability and pricing of these services.

Physical damage is usually very evident. For example, a broken mounting ear from dropping the head or a bent or broken stud and/or bolt. All of these defects should be fixed or, if unrepairable, the head should be replaced.

REFINISHING & REPAIRING

Many of the procedures given for refinishing and repairing the cylinder head components must be performed by a machine shop. Certain steps, if the inspected part is not worn, can be performed yourself inexpensively. However, you spent a lot of time and effort so far, why risk trying to save a couple bucks if you might have to do it all over again?

Valves

Any valves that were not replaced should be refaced and the tips ground flat. Unless you have access to a valve grinding machine, this should be done by a machine shop. If the valves are in extremely good condition, as well as the valve seats and guides, they may be lapped in without performing machine work.

It is a recommended practice to lap the valves even after machine work has been performed and/or new valves have been purchased. This insures a positive seal between the valve and seat.

LAPPING THE VALVES

➡ Before lapping the valves to the seats, read the rest of the cylinder head section to insure that any related parts are in acceptable enough condition to continue.

➡ Before any valve seat machining and/or lapping can be performed, the guides must be within factory recommended specifications.

1. Invert the cylinder head.
2. Lightly lubricate the valve stems and insert them into the cylinder head in their numbered order.
3. Raise the valve from the seat and apply a small amount of fine lapping compound to the seat.
4. Moisten the suction head of a hand-lapping tool and attach it to the head of the valve.
5. Rotate the tool between the palms of both hands, changing the position of the valve on the valve seat and lifting the tool often to prevent grooving.
6. Lap the valve until a smooth, polished circle is evident on the valve and seat.
7. Remove the tool and the valve. Wipe away all traces of the grinding compound and store the valve to maintain its lapped location.

❄❄ WARNING

Do not get the valves out of order after they have been lapped. They must be put back with the same valve seat they were lapped with.

Springs, Retainers and Valve Locks

There is no repair or refinishing possible with the springs, retainers and valve locks. If they are found to be worn or defective, they must be replaced with new (or known good) parts.

Cylinder Head

Most refinishing procedures dealing with the cylinder head must be performed by a machine shop. Read the sections below and review your inspection data to determine whether or not machining is necessary.

VALVE GUIDE

➡ If any machining or replacements are made to the valve guides, the seats must be machined.

Unless the valve guides need machining or replacing, the only service to perform is to thoroughly clean them of any dirt or oil residue.

There are only two types of valve guides used on automobile engines: the replaceable-type (all aluminum heads) and the cast-in integral-type (most cast iron heads). There are four recommended methods for repairing worn guides.

- Knurling
- Inserts
- Reaming oversize
- Replacing

Knurling is a process in which metal is displaced and raised, thereby reducing clearance, giving a true center, and providing oil control. It is the least expensive way of repairing the valve guides. However, it is not necessarily the best, and in some cases, a knurled valve guide will not stand up for more than a short time. It requires a special knurlizer and precision reaming tools to obtain proper clearances. It would not be cost effective to purchase these tools, unless you plan on rebuilding several of the same cylinder head.

Installing a guide insert involves machining the guide to accept a bronze insert. One style is the coil-type which is installed into a threaded guide. Another is the thin-walled insert where the guide is reamed oversize to accept a split-sleeve insert. After the insert is installed, a special tool is then run through the guide to expand the insert, locking it to the guide. The insert is then reamed to the standard size for proper valve clearance.

Reaming for oversize valves restores normal clearances and provides a true valve seat. Most cast-in type guides can be reamed to accept an valve with an oversize stem. The cost factor for this can become quite high as you will need to purchase the reamer and new, oversize stem valves for all guides which were reamed. Oversizes are generally 0.003 to 0.030 in. (0.076 to 0.762mm), with 0.015 in. (0.381mm) being the most common.

To replace cast-in type valve guides, they must be drilled out, then reamed to accept replacement guides. This must be done on a fixture which will allow centering and leveling off of the original valve seat or guide, otherwise a serious guide-to-seat misalignment may occur making it impossible to properly machine the seat.

Replaceable-type guides are pressed into the cylinder head. A hammer and a stepped drift or punch may be used to install and remove the guides. Before removing the guides, measure the protrusion on the spring side of the head and record it for installation. Use the stepped drift to hammer out the old guide from the combustion chamber side of the head. When installing, determine whether or not the guide also seals a water jacket in the head, and if it does, use the recommended sealing agent. If there is no water jacket, grease the valve guide and its bore. Use the stepped drift, and hammer the new guide into the cylinder head from the spring side of the cylinder head. A stack of washers the same thickness as the measured protrusion may help the installation process.

VALVE SEATS

➡ Before any valve seat machining can be performed, the guides must be within factory recommended specifications.

➡ If any machining or replacements were made to the valve guides, the seats must be machined.

If the seats are in good condition, the valves can be lapped to the seats, and the cylinder head assembled. See the valves section for instructions on lapping.

If the valve seats are worn, cracked or damaged, they must be serviced by a machine shop. The valve seat must be perfectly centered to the valve guide, which requires very accurate machining.

CYLINDER HEAD SURFACE

If the cylinder head is warped, it must be machined flat. If the warpage is extremely severe, the head may need to be replaced. In some instances, it may be possible to straighten a warped head enough to allow machining. In either case, contact a professional machine shop for service.

CRACKS AND PHYSICAL DAMAGE

Certain cracks can be repaired in both cast iron and aluminum heads. For cast iron, a tapered threaded insert is installed along the length of the crack. Aluminum can also use the tapered inserts, however welding is the preferred method. Some physical damage can be repaired through brazing or welding. Contact a machine shop to get expert advice for your particular dilemma.

ASSEMBLY

The first step for any assembly job is to have a clean area in which to work. Next, thoroughly clean all of the parts and components that are to be assembled. Finally, place all of the components onto a suitable work space and, if necessary, arrange the parts to their respective positions.

1. Lightly lubricate the valve stems and insert all of the valves into the cylinder head. If possible, maintain their original locations.

2. If equipped, install any valve spring shims which were removed.

3. If equipped, install the new valve seals, keeping the following in mind:

- If the valve seal presses over the guide, lightly lubricate the outer guide surfaces.
- If the seal is an O-ring type, it is installed just after compressing the spring but before the valve locks.

4. Place the valve spring and retainer over the stem.

5. Position the spring compressor tool and compress the spring.

6. Assemble the valve locks to the stem.

7. Relieve the spring pressure slowly and insure that neither valve lock becomes dislodged by the retainer.

8. Remove the spring compressor tool.

9. Repeat Steps 2 through 8 until all of the springs have been installed.

Engine Block

GENERAL INFORMATION

A thorough overhaul or rebuild of an engine block would include replacing the pistons, rings, bearings, timing belt/chain assembly and oil pump. For OHV engines also include a new camshaft and lifters. The block would then have the cylinders bored and honed oversize (or if using removable cylinder sleeves, new sleeves installed) and the crankshaft would be cut undersize to provide new wearing surfaces and perfect clearances. However, your particular engine may not have everything worn out. What if only the piston rings have worn out and the clearances on everything else are still within factory specifications? Well, you could just replace the rings and put it back together, but this would be a very rare example. Chances are, if one component in your engine is worn, other components are sure to follow, and soon. At the very least, you should always replace the rings, bearings and oil pump. This is what is commonly called a ìfreshen upî.

Cylinder Ridge Removal

Because the top piston ring does not travel to the very top of the cylinder, a ridge is built up between the end of the travel and the top of the cylinder bore.

Pushing the piston and connecting rod assembly past the ridge can be difficult, and damage to the piston ring lands could occur. If the ridge is not removed before installing a new piston or not removed at all, piston ring breakage and piston damage may occur.

➡It is always recommended that you remove any cylinder ridges before removing the piston and connecting rod assemblies. If you know that new pistons are going to be installed and the engine block will be bored oversize, you may be able to forego this step. However, some ridges may actually prevent the assemblies from being removed, necessitating its removal.

There are several different types of ridge reamers on the market, none of which are inexpensive. Unless a great deal of engine rebuilding is anticipated, borrow or rent a reamer.

1. Turn the crankshaft until the piston is at the bottom of its travel.

2. Cover the head of the piston with a rag.

3. Follow the tool manufacturers instructions and cut away the ridge, exercising extreme care to avoid cutting too deeply.

4. Remove the ridge reamer, the rag and as many of the cuttings as possible. Continue until all of the cylinder ridges have been removed.

DISASSEMBLY

▶ See Figures 246 and 247

The engine disassembly instructions following assume that you have the engine mounted on an engine stand. If not, it is easiest to disassemble the engine on a bench or the floor with it resting on the bellhousing or trans-

mission mounting surface. You must be able to access the connecting rod fasteners and turn the crankshaft during disassembly. Also, all engine covers (timing, front, side, oil pan, whatever) should have already been removed. Engines which are seized or locked up may not be able to be completely disassembled, and a core (salvage yard) engine should be purchased.

If not done during the cylinder head removal, remove the pushrods and lifters, keeping them in order for assembly. Remove the timing gears and/or timing chain assembly, then remove the oil pump drive assembly and withdraw the camshaft from the engine block. Remove the oil pick-up and pump assembly. If equipped, remove any balance or auxiliary shafts. If necessary, remove the cylinder ridge from the top of the bore. See the cylinder ridge removal procedure earlier in this section.

Rotate the engine over so that the crankshaft is exposed. Use a number punch or scribe and mark each connecting rod with its respective cylinder number. The cylinder closest to the front of the engine is always number 1. However, depending on the engine placement, the front of the engine could either be the flywheel or damper/pulley end. Generally the front of the engine faces the front of the vehicle. Use a number punch or scribe and also mark the main bearing caps from front to rear with the front most cap being number 1 (if there are five caps, mark them 1 through 5, front to rear).

✳✳ WARNING

Take special care when pushing the connecting rod up from the crankshaft because the sharp threads of the rod bolts/studs will score the crankshaft journal. Insure that special plastic caps are installed over them, or cut two pieces of rubber hose to do the same.

Again, rotate the engine, this time to position the number one cylinder bore (head surface) up. Turn the crankshaft until the number one piston is at the bottom of its travel, this should allow the maximum access to its connecting rod. Remove the number one connecting rods fasteners and cap and place two lengths of rubber hose over the rod bolts/studs to protect the crankshaft from damage. Using a sturdy wooden dowel and a hammer, push the connecting rod up about 1 in. (25mm) from the crankshaft and remove the upper bearing insert. Continue pushing or tapping the connecting rod up until the piston rings are out of the cylinder bore. Remove the piston and rod by hand, put the upper half of the bearing insert back into the rod, install the cap with its bearing insert installed, and hand-tighten the cap fasteners. If the parts are kept in order in this manner, they will not get lost and you will be able to tell which bearings came form what cylinder if any problems are discovered and diagnosis is necessary. Remove all the other

TCCS3803

Fig. 246 Place rubber hose over the connecting rod studs to protect the crankshaft and cylinder bores from damage

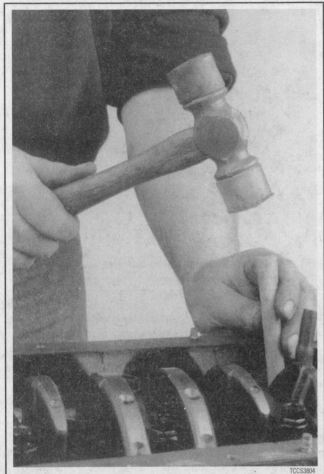

Fig. 247 Carefully tap the piston out of the bore using a wooden dowel

piston assemblies in the same manner. On V-style engines, remove all of the pistons from one bank, then reposition the engine with the other cylinder bank head surface up, and remove that banks piston assemblies.

The only remaining component in the engine block should now be the crankshaft. Loosen the main bearing caps evenly until the fasteners can be turned by hand, then remove them and the caps. Remove the crankshaft from the engine block. Thoroughly clean all of the components.

INSPECTION

Now that the engine block and all of its components are clean, itís time to inspect them for wear and/or damage. To accurately inspect them, you will need some specialized tools:

• Two or three separate micrometers to measure the pistons and crankshaft journals
• A dial indicator
• Telescoping gauges for the cylinder bores
• A rod alignment fixture to check for bent connecting rods

If you do not have access to the proper tools, you may want to bring the components to a shop that does.

Generally, you shouldnít expect cracks in the engine block or its components unless it was known to leak, consume or mix engine fluids, it was severely overheated, or there was evidence of bad bearings and/or crankshaft damage. A visual inspection should be performed on all of the components, but just because you donít see a crack does not mean it is not there. Some more reliable methods for inspecting for cracks include Magnaflux®, a magnetic process or Zyglo®, a dye penetrant. Magnaflux® is used only on ferrous metal (cast iron). Zyglo® uses a spray on fluorescent mix-

ture along with a black light to reveal the cracks. It is strongly recommended to have your engine block checked professionally for cracks, especially if the engine was known to have overheated and/or leaked or consumed coolant. Contact a local shop for availability and pricing of these services.

Engine Block

ENGINE BLOCK BEARING ALIGNMENT

Remove the main bearing caps and, if still installed, the main bearing inserts. Inspect all of the main bearing saddles and caps for damage, burrs or high spots. If damage is found, and it is caused from a spun main bearing, the block will need to be align-bored or, if severe enough, replacement. Any burrs or high spots should be carefully removed with a metal file.

Place a straightedge on the bearing saddles, in the engine block, along the centerline of the crankshaft. If any clearance exists between the straightedge and the saddles, the block must be align-bored.

Align-boring consists of machining the main bearing saddles and caps by means of a flycutter that runs through the bearing saddles.

DECK FLATNESS

The top of the engine block where the cylinder head mounts is called the deck. Insure that the deck surface is clean of dirt, carbon deposits and old gasket material. Place a straightedge across the surface of the deck along its centerline and, using feeler gauges, check the clearance along several points. Repeat the checking procedure with the straightedge placed along both diagonals of the deck surface. If the reading exceeds 0.003 in. (0.076mm) within a 6.0 in. (15.2cm) span, or 0.006 in. (0.152mm) over the total length of the deck, it must be machined.

CYLINDER BORES

▶ See Figure 248

The cylinder bores house the pistons and are slightly larger than the pistons themselves. A common piston-to-bore clearance is 0.0015–0.0025 in. (0.0381mm–0.0635mm). Inspect and measure the cylinder bores. The bore should be checked for out-of-roundness, taper and size. The results of this inspection will determine whether the cylinder can be used in its existing size and condition, or a rebore to the next oversize is required (or in the case of removable sleeves, have replacements installed).

The amount of cylinder wall wear is always greater at the top of the cylinder than at the bottom. This wear is known as taper. Any cylinder that has a taper of 0.0012 in. (0.305mm) or more, must be rebored. Measurements are taken at a number of positions in each cylinder: at the top, middle and bottom and at two points at each position; that is, at a point 90

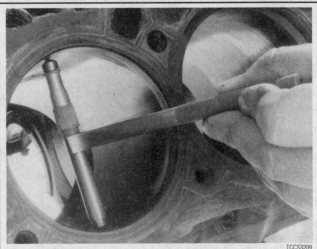

Fig. 248 Use a telescoping gauge to measure the cylinder bore diameter—take several readings within the same bore

degrees from the crankshaft centerline, as well as a point parallel to the crankshaft centerline. The measurements are made with either a special dial indicator or a telescopic gauge and micrometer. If the necessary precision tools to check the bore are not available, take the block to a machine shop and have them mike it. Also if you don't have the tools to check the cylinder bores, chances are you will not have the necessary devices to check the pistons, connecting rods and crankshaft. Take these components with you and save yourself an extra trip.

For our procedures, we will use a telescopic gauge and a micrometer. You will need one of each, with a measuring range which covers your cylinder bore size.

1. Position the telescopic gauge in the cylinder bore, loosen the gauges lock and allow it to expand.

➡ **Your first two readings will be at the top of the cylinder bore, then proceed to the middle and finally the bottom, making a total of six measurements.**

2. Hold the gauge square in the bore, 90 degrees from the crankshaft centerline, and gently tighten the lock. Tilt the gauge back to remove it from the bore.

3. Measure the gauge with the micrometer and record the reading.

4. Again, hold the gauge square in the bore, this time parallel to the crankshaft centerline, and gently tighten the lock. Again, you will tilt the gauge back to remove it from the bore.

5. Measure the gauge with the micrometer and record this reading. The difference between these two readings is the out-of-round measurement of the cylinder.

6. Repeat steps 1 through 5, each time going to the next lower position, until you reach the bottom of the cylinder. Then go to the next cylinder, and continue until all of the cylinders have been measured.

The difference between these measurements will tell you all about the wear in your cylinders. The measurements which were taken 90 degrees from the crankshaft centerline will always reflect the most wear. That is because at this position is where the engine power presses the piston against the cylinder bore the hardest. This is known as thrust wear. Take your top, 90 degree measurement and compare it to your bottom, 90 degree measurement. The difference between them is the taper. When you measure your pistons, you will compare these readings to your piston sizes and determine piston-to-wall clearance.

Crankshaft

Inspect the crankshaft for visible signs of wear or damage. All of the journals should be perfectly round and smooth. Slight scores are normal for a used crankshaft, but you should hardly feel them with your fingernail. When measuring the crankshaft with a micrometer, you will take readings at the front and rear of each journal, then turn the micrometer 90 degrees and take two more readings, front and rear. The difference between the front-to-rear readings is the journal taper and the first-to-90 degree reading is the out-of-round measurement. Generally, there should be no taper or out-of-roundness found, however, up to 0.0005 in. (0.0127mm) for either can be overlooked. Also, the readings should fall within the factory specifications for journal diameters.

If the crankshaft journals fall within specifications, it is recommended that it be polished before being returned to service. Polishing the crankshaft insures that any minor burrs or high spots are smoothed, thereby reducing the chance of scoring the new bearings.

Pistons and Connecting Rods

PISTONS

▶ **See Figure 249**

The piston should be visually inspected for any signs of cracking or burning (caused by hot spots or detonation), and scuffing or excessive wear on the skirts. The wristpin attaches the piston to the connecting rod. The piston should move freely on the wrist pin, both sliding and pivoting. Grasp the connecting rod securely, or mount it in a vise, and try to rock the

Fig. 249 Measure the piston's outer diameter, perpendicular to the wrist pin, with a micrometer

piston back and forth along the centerline of the wristpin. There should not be any excessive play evident between the piston and the pin. If there are C-clips retaining the pin in the piston then you have wrist pin bushings in the rods. There should not be any excessive play between the wrist pin and the rod bushing. Normal clearance for the wrist pin is approx. 0.001–0.002 in. (0.025mm–0.051mm).

Use a micrometer and measure the diameter of the piston, perpendicular to the wrist pin, on the skirt. Compare the reading to its original cylinder measurement obtained earlier. The difference between the two readings is the piston-to-wall clearance. If the clearance is within specifications, the piston may be used as is. If the piston is out of specification, but the bore is not, you will need a new piston. If both are out of specification, you will need the cylinder rebored and oversize pistons installed. Generally if two or more pistons/bores are out of specification, it is best to rebore the entire block and purchase a complete set of oversize pistons.

CONNECTING RODS

You should have the connecting rod checked for straightness at a machine shop. If the connecting rod is bent, it will unevenly wear the bearing and piston, as well as place greater stress on these components. Any bent or twisted connecting rods must be replaced. If the rods are straight and the wrist pin clearance is within specifications, then only the bearing end of the rod need be checked. Place the connecting rod into a vice, with the bearing inserts in place, install the cap to the rod and torque the fasteners to specifications. Use a telescoping gauge and carefully measure the inside diameter of the bearings. Compare this reading to the rods original crankshaft journal diameter measurement. The difference is the oil clearance. If the oil clearance is not within specifications, install new bearings in the rod and take another measurement. If the clearance is still out of specifications, and the crankshaft is not, the rod will need to be reconditioned by a machine shop.

➡ **You can also use Plastigage® to check the bearing clearances. The assembling section has complete instructions on its use.**

Camshaft

Inspect the camshaft and lifters/followers as described earlier in this section.

Bearings

All of the engine bearings should be visually inspected for wear and/or damage. The bearing should look evenly worn all around with no deep scores or pits. If the bearing is severely worn, scored, pitted or heat blued, then the bearing, and the components that use it, should be brought to a machine shop for inspection. Full-circle bearings (used on most camshafts, auxiliary shafts, balance shafts, etc.) require specialized tools for REMOVAL & INSTALLATION, and should be brought to a machine shop for service.

Oil Pump

➡The oil pump is responsible for providing constant lubrication to the whole engine and so it is recommended that a new oil pump be installed when rebuilding the engine.

Completely disassemble the oil pump and thoroughly clean all of the components. Inspect the oil pump gears and housing for wear and/or damage. Insure that the pressure relief valve operates properly and there is no binding or sticking due to varnish or debris. If all of the parts are in proper working condition, lubricate the gears and relief valve, and assemble the pump.

REFINISHING

◗ See Figure 250

Almost all engine block refinishing must be performed by a machine shop. If the cylinders are not to be rebored, then the cylinder glaze can be removed with a ball hone. When removing cylinder glaze with a ball hone, use a light or penetrating type oil to lubricate the hone. Do not allow the hone to run dry as this may cause excessive scoring of the cylinder bores and wear on the hone. If new pistons are required, they will need to be installed to the connecting rods. This should be performed by a machine shop as the pistons must be installed in the correct relationship to the rod or engine damage can occur.

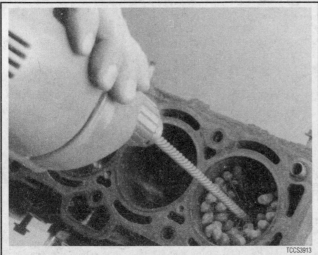

Fig. 250 Use a ball type cylinder hone to remove any glaze and provide a new surface for seating the piston rings

Pistons and Connecting Rods

◗ See Figure 251

Only pistons with the wrist pin retained by C-clips are serviceable by the home-mechanic. Press fit pistons require special presses and/or heaters to remove/install the connecting rod and should only be performed by a machine shop.

All pistons will have a mark indicating the direction to the front of the engine and the must be installed into the engine in that manner. Usually it is a notch or arrow on the top of the piston, or it may be the letter F cast or stamped into the piston.

ASSEMBLY

Before you begin assembling the engine, first give yourself a clean, dirt free work area. Next, clean every engine component again. The key to a good assembly is cleanliness.

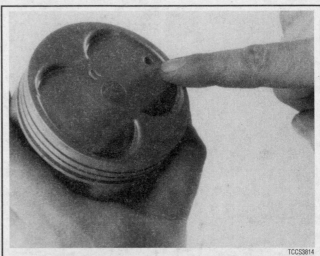

Fig. 251 Most pistons are marked to indicate positioning in the engine (usually a mark means the side facing the front)

Mount the engine block into the engine stand and wash it one last time using water and detergent (dishwashing detergent works well). While washing it, scrub the cylinder bores with a soft bristle brush and thoroughly clean all of the oil passages. Completely dry the engine and spray the entire assembly down with an anti-rust solution such as WD-40® or similar product. Take a clean lint-free rag and wipe up any excess anti-rust solution from the bores, bearing saddles, etc. Repeat the final cleaning process on the crankshaft. Replace any freeze or oil galley plugs which were removed during disassembly.

Crankshaft

◗ See Figures 252, 253, 254 and 255

1. Remove the main bearing inserts from the block and bearing caps.
2. If the crankshaft main bearing journals have been refinished to a definite undersize, install the correct undersize bearing. Be sure that the bearing inserts and bearing bores are clean. Foreign material under inserts will distort bearing and cause failure.
3. Place the upper main bearing inserts in bores with tang in slot.

➡The oil holes in the bearing inserts must be aligned with the oil holes in the cylinder block.

4. Install the lower main bearing inserts in bearing caps.
5. Clean the mating surfaces of block and rear main bearing cap.
6. Carefully lower the crankshaft into place. Be careful not to damage bearing surfaces.
7. Check the clearance of each main bearing by using the following procedure:
   a. Place a piece of Plastigage® or its equivalent, on bearing surface across full width of bearing cap and about ¼ in. off center.
   b. Install cap and tighten bolts to specifications. Do not turn crankshaft while Plastigage® is in place.
   c. Remove the cap. Using the supplied Plastigage® scale, check width of Plastigage® at widest point to get maximum clearance. Difference between readings is taper of journal.
   d. If clearance exceeds specified limits, try a 0.001 in. or 0.002 in. undersize bearing in combination with the standard bearing. Bearing clearance must be within specified limits. If standard and 0.002 in. undersize bearing does not bring clearance within desired limits, refinish crankshaft journal, then install undersize bearings.
8. After the bearings have been fitted, apply a light coat of engine oil to the journals and bearings. Install the rear main bearing cap. Install all bearing caps except the thrust bearing cap. Be sure that main bearing caps are installed in original locations. Tighten the bearing cap bolts to specifications.

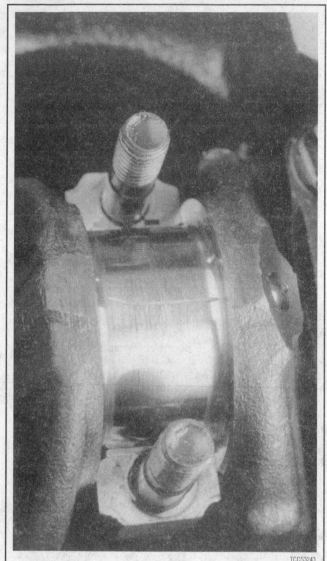

Fig. 252 Apply a strip of gauging material to the bearing journal, then install and torque the cap

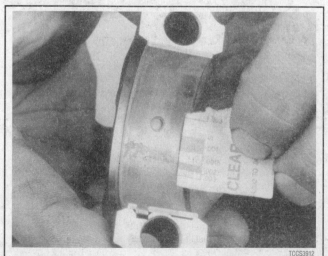

Fig. 253 After the cap is removed again, use the scale supplied with the gauging material to check the clearance

Fig. 254 A dial gauge may be used to check crankshaft end-play

Fig. 255 Carefully pry the crankshaft back and forth while reading the dial gauge for end-play

9. Install the thrust bearing cap with bolts finger-tight.

10. Pry the crankshaft forward against the thrust surface of upper half of bearing.

11. Hold the crankshaft forward and pry the thrust bearing cap to the rear. This aligns the thrust surfaces of both halves of the bearing.

12. Retain the forward pressure on the crankshaft. Tighten the cap bolts to specifications.

13. Measure the crankshaft end-play as follows:

   a. Mount a dial gauge to the engine block and position the tip of the gauge to read from the crankshaft end.

   b. Carefully pry the crankshaft toward the rear of the engine and hold it there while you zero the gauge.

   c. Carefully pry the crankshaft toward the front of the engine and read the gauge.

   d. Confirm that the reading is within specifications. If not, install a new thrust bearing and repeat the procedure. If the reading is still out of specifications with a new bearing, have a machine shop inspect the thrust surfaces of the crankshaft, and if possible, repair it.

14. Rotate the crankshaft so as to position the first rod journal to the bottom of its stroke.

15. Install the rear main seal.

Pistons and Connecting Rods

▶ **See Figures 256, 257, 258 and 259**

1. Before installing the piston/connecting rod assembly, oil the pistons, piston rings and the cylinder walls with light engine oil. Install connecting rod bolt protectors or rubber hose onto the connecting rod bolts/studs. Also perform the following:

   a. Select the proper ring set for the size cylinder bore.
   b. Position the ring in the bore in which it is going to be used.

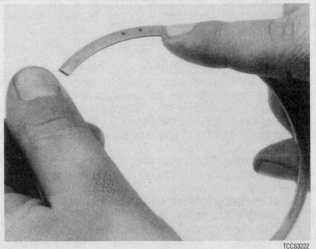

Fig. 258 Most rings are marked to show which side of the ring should face up when installed to the piston

Fig. 256 Checking the piston ring-to-ring groove side clearance using the ring and a feeler gauge

Fig. 259 Install the piston and rod assembly into the block using a ring compressor and the handle of a hammer

c. Push the ring down into the bore area where normal ring wear is not encountered.

d. Use the head of the piston to position the ring in the bore so that the ring is square with the cylinder wall. Use caution to avoid damage to the ring or cylinder bore.

e. Measure the gap between the ends of the ring with a feeler gauge. Ring gap in a worn cylinder is normally greater than specification. If the ring gap is greater than the specified limits, try an oversize ring set.

f. Check the ring side clearance of the compression rings with a feeler gauge inserted between the ring and its lower land according to specification. The gauge should slide freely around the entire ring circumference without binding. Any wear that occurs will form a step at the inner portion of the lower land. If the lower lands have high steps, the piston should be replaced.

2. Unless new pistons are installed, be sure to install the pistons in the cylinders from which they were removed. The numbers on the connecting rod and bearing cap must be on the same side when installed in the cylinder bore. If a connecting rod is ever transposed from one engine or cylinder to another, new bearings should be fitted and the connecting rod should be numbered to correspond with the new cylinder number. The notch on the piston head goes toward the front of the engine.

Fig. 257 The notch on the side of the bearing cap matches the tang on the bearing insert

3. Install all of the rod bearing inserts into the rods and caps.

4. Install the rings to the pistons. Install the oil control ring first, then the second compression ring and finally the top compression ring. Use a piston ring expander tool to aid in installation and to help reduce the chance of breakage.

5. Make sure the ring gaps are properly spaced around the circumference of the piston. Fit a piston ring compressor around the piston and slide the piston and connecting rod assembly down into the cylinder bore, pushing it in with the wooden hammer handle. Push the piston down until it is only slightly below the top of the cylinder bore. Guide the connecting rod onto the crankshaft bearing journal carefully, to avoid damaging the crankshaft.

6. Check the bearing clearance of all the rod bearings, fitting them to the crankshaft bearing journals. Follow the procedure in the crankshaft installation above.

7. After the bearings have been fitted, apply a light coating of assembly oil to the journals and bearings.

8. Turn the crankshaft until the appropriate bearing journal is at the bottom of its stroke, then push the piston assembly all the way down until the connecting rod bearing seats on the crankshaft journal. Be careful not to allow the bearing cap screws to strike the crankshaft bearing journals and damage them.

9. After the piston and connecting rod assemblies have been installed, check the connecting rod side clearance on each crankshaft journal.

10. Prime and install the oil pump and the oil pump intake tube.

11. Install the camshaft.

12. Install the lifters/followers into their bores.

13. Install the timing gears/chain assembly.

14. Install the cylinder head(s) using new gaskets.

15. Assemble the rest of the valve train (pushrods and rocker arms and/or shafts).

16. Install the cylinder head(s) using new gaskets.

17. Install the timing sprockets/gears and the belt/chain assemblies.

Install the timing cover(s) and oil pan. Refer to your notes and drawings made prior to disassembly and install all of the components that were removed. Install the engine into the vehicle.

Engine Start-up and Break-in

STARTING THE ENGINE

Now that the engine is installed and every wire and hose is properly connected, go back and double check that all coolant and vacuum hoses are connected. Check that you oil drain plug is installed and properly tightened. If not already done, install a new oil filter onto the engine. Fill the crankcase with the proper amount and grade of engine oil. Fill the cooling system with a 50/50 mixture of coolant/water.

1. Connect the vehicle battery.

2. Start the engine. Keep your eye on your oil pressure indicator; if it does not indicate oil pressure within 10 seconds of starting, turn the vehicle off.

❋❋ WARNING

Damage to the engine can result if it is allowed to run with no oil pressure. Check the engine oil level to make sure that it is full. Check for any leaks and if found, repair the leaks before continuing. If there is still no indication of oil pressure, you may need to prime the system.

3. Confirm that there are no fluid leaks (oil or other).

4. Allow the engine to reach normal operating temperature (the upper radiator hose will be hot to the touch).

5. If necessary, set the ignition timing.

6. Install any remaining components such as the air cleaner (if removed for ignition timing) or body panels which were removed.

BREAKING IT IN

Make the first miles on the new engine, easy ones. Vary the speed but do not accelerate hard. Most importantly, do not lug the engine, and avoid sustained high speeds until at least 100 miles. Check the engine oil and coolant levels frequently. Expect the engine to use a little oil until the rings seat. Change the oil and filter at 500 miles, 1500 miles, then every 3000 miles past that.

KEEP IT MAINTAINED

Now that you have just gone through all of that hard work, keep yourself from doing it all over again by thoroughly maintaining it. Not that you may not have maintained it before, heck you could have had one to two hundred thousand miles on it before doing this. However, you may have bought the vehicle used, and the previous owner did not keep up on maintenance. Which is why you just went through all of that hard work. See?

4.9L ENGINE SPECIFICATIONS

Description			English	Metric
Type			Inline Overhead Valve (OHV)	
Displacement			300 cu. in.	4.9 L (4917cc)
Number of Cylinders			6	
Bore			4.00 in.	1016mm
Stroke			3.98 in.	101.092mm
Compression ratio			8.8:1	
Cylinder Bore				
	Diameter		4.0000-4.0048 in.	101.6mm-101.72mm
	Out-of-round (max.)		0.015 in.	0.381mm
	Taper (max.)		0.10 in.	2.54mm
Pistons				
	Clearance to bore		0.0010-.0018 in. ①	0.025-0.045mm ①
	Diameter			
		Coded red	3.9982-3.9988 in.	101.55-101.56mm
		Coded blue	3.9994-4.0000 in.	101.58-101.60mm
		0.003 in. oversize	4.0008-4.0014 in.	101.62-101.63mm
Piston rings				
	End-gap			
		Top ring	0.010-0.020 in.	0.254-0.508mm
		Bottom ring	0.010-0.020 in.	0.254-0.508mm
		Oil ring	0.015-0.055 in.	0.381-1.397mm
	Side clearance			
		Top ring	0.0019-0.0036 in.	0.048-0.091mm
		Bottom ring	0.002-0.004 in.	0.050-0.101mm
		Oil ring	Snug	
	Ring width			
		Top ring	0.0774-.0781 in.	1.956-1.983mm
		Bottom ring	0.0770-0.0780 in.	1.955-1.981mm
Piston Pin				
	Length		3.150-3.170 in.	80.01-80.51mm
	Diameter			
		Standard	0.9749-0754 in.	24.76-1.915mm
		0.001 in. oversize	0.9760-0.9763 in.	24.790-24.798mm
		0.002 in. oversize	0.9770-0.9773 in.	24.815-24.823mm
Camshaft				
	Lobe lift			
		Intake	0.249-0.247 in.	6.32-6.27mm
		Exhaust	0.249-0.247 in.	6.32-6.27mm
	End-play		0.001-0.007 in.	0.025-0.017mm
	Service limit		0.009 in.	0.22mm
	Journal-to-bearing clearance		0.001-0.003 in.	0.025-0.076mm
	Journal diameter (standard)		2.017-2.018 in.	51.232-51.257mm
		No. 1:	2.017-2.018 in.	51.232-51.257mm
		No. 2:	2.017-2.018 in.	51.232-51.257mm
		No. 3:	2.017-2.018 in.	51.232-51.257mm
		No. 4:	2.017-2.018 in.	51.232-51.257mm

88483C23

4.9L ENGINE SPECIFICATIONS

Description	English	Metric
Camshaft (cont.)		
Bearing inside diameter	2.019-2.020 in.	51.283-51.308mm
No. 1:	2.019-2.020 in.	51.283-51.308mm
No. 2:	2.019-2.020 in.	51.283-51.308mm
No. 3:	2.019-2.020 in.	51.283-51.308mm
No. 4:	2.019-2.020 in.	51.283-51.308mm
Camshaft front bearing location:	0.020-0.035 in. ②	0.508-0.880mm ②
Crankshaft and flywheel		
Main bearing journal		
Diameter	2.3982-2.3990 in.	60.91-60.93mm
Runout (max.)	0.002 in	0.050mm
Taper (max.)	0.0005 in.	0.012mm
Thrust face runout (TIR max.)	0.001 in.	0.025mm
Bearing journal		
Length	1.1990-1.2010 in.	30.45-30.50mm
Connecting rod journal		
Diameter	2.1228-2.1236 in.	53.91-53.93mm
Taper	0.0006 in.	0.015mm
Crankshaft free end-play	0.004-0.008 in.	0.10-0.20mm
Flywheel		
Clutch face runout (assembled)	0.010 in.	0.254mm
Ring gear lateral runout (TIR)		
Man. trans	0.40 in	10.16mm
Auto.C94 trans	0.60 in.	15.24mm
Clutch face runout	0.010 in.	0.254mm
Crankshaft Bearings		
Connecting rod bearing-to-camshaft clearance		
Desired	0.0008-0.0015 in.	0.020-0.038mm
Allowable	0.0007-0.0024 in.	0.017-0.06mm
Bearing wall tickness (STD)	0.0752-0.0757 in.	1.91-1.92mm
Main bearing-to-crankshaft clearance		
Desired	0.0008-0.0015 in.	0.020-0.038mm
Allowable	0.0010-0.0028 in.	0.025-0.071mm
Bearing wall tickness (STD)	0.0951-0.0956 in.	2.41-2.42mm
Connecting rod		
Piston pin bore or bushing I.D.	0.9734-0.9742 in.	24.72-24.74mm
Rod bearing bore I.D.	2.2750-2.2758 in.	57.7-57.8mm
Rod length (center-to-center)	6.2082-6.2112 in.	157.6-157.7mm
Rod-to-crankshaft assembled side clearance	0.006-0.013 in. ③	0.15-0.33mm ③
Cylinder block		
Main bearing bore		
Diameter	2.5902-2.5910 in.	65.79-65.81mm
Distributor shaft bearing bore		
Diameter	0.5155-0.5165 in.	13.09-13.11mm
Head gasket surface		

4.9L ENGINE SPECIFICATIONS

Description	English	Metric
Cylinder block (cont.)		
Flatness	0.003 in. in any 6 in.	0.076mm in any 15.24 cm
Tappet bore		
Diameter	0.8752-0.8767	22.23-22.26mm
Cylinder head		
Valve guide bore		
Diameter	0.3433-0.3443 in.	8.71-8.74mm
Valve seat	0.3433-0.3443 in.	8.71-8.74mm
Width		
Intake	0.060-0.080 in.	1.524-2.032mm
Exhaust	0.070-0.090 in.	1.778-2.286mm
Angle	45 degrees	
Runout	0.002 in.	0.050mm
Gasket surface		
Flatness	0.006 in. in any 6 in.	0.15mm in any 15.24 cm
Valve rocker arm shaft, Push rods and Tappets		
Rocker arm ratio	1.61:1	
Pushrod runout	0.015 in.	0.38mm
Valve tappet or lifter		
Standard diameter	0.8740-0.8745 in.	22.19-22.21mm
Clearance to bore	0.0007-0.0027 in.	0.017-0.068mm
Collapsed tappet gap (clearance)		
Allowable	0.100-0.200 in.	2.54-5.08mm
Desired	0.125-0.175 in.	3.175-4.445mm
Valves Springs		
Intake	66-74 lbs. @ 1.640 in.④	30-33.6 kg @ 41.6mm
	166-184 lbs. @ 1.240 in.④	75-83kg @ 31.4mm
Exhaust	66-74 lbs. @ 1.640 in.④	30-33.6 kg @ 41.6mm
	166-184 lbs. @ 1.240 in ④	75-83kg @ 31.4mm
Free length		
Intake	1.96 in.	49.78mm
Exhaust	1.78 in.	45.21mm
Valves		
Stem-to-guide clearance		
Intake	0.010-0.027 in.	0.254-0.685mm
Exhaust	0.010-0.027 in.	0.254-0.685mm
Valve head diameter		
Intake	1.769-1.793 in.	44.93-45.54mm
Exhaust	1.551-1.569 in.	39.39-39.85mm
Valve face runout		
Max.	0.0020 in.	0.0508mm
Stem diameter		
Standard		
Intake	0.3416-0.3423 in.	8.66-8.69mm

88483C25

4.9L ENGINE SPECIFICATIONS

Description	English	Metric
Valves (cont.)		
Exhaust	0.3416-0.3423 in.	8.66-8.69mm
0.015 in. oversize		
Intake	0.3566-0.3573 in.	9.05-9.07mm
Exhaust	0.3566-0.3573 in.	9.05-9.07mm
0.030 in. oversize		
Intake	0.3716-0.3723 in.	9.44-9.45mm
Exhaust	0.3716-0.3723 in.	9.44-9.45mm
Oil Pump		
Relief valve spring pressure	20.6-22.6 lbs. @ 2.49 in.	9.3-10.2kg@63.2mm
Driveshaft-to-housing		
Clearance	0.0015-0.0030 in.	0.038-0.076mm
Relief valve-to-housing		
Clearance	0.0015-0.0030 in.	0.038-0.076mm
Rotor assembly		
End clearance (max.)	0.004 in.	0.101mm
Outer race-to-housing		
Clearance	0.01-0.013 in.	0.25-0.33mm
Oil capacity		
U.S quarts	5.0	
Imperial quarts	4.2	
Liters	4.7	
Inner-to-outer rotor tip		
Clearance (max.)	0.012 in. ⑤	0.30mm ⑤

TIR—Total Indicated Runout
① Rebuild specification only
② Distance in inches that front edge of bearing is installed
below the front face of the cylinder block
③ Service limit: 0.018 in. (0.45mm)

④ Compressed pressure @ specified height
⑤ With a feeler gauge inserted 1/2 inch minimum and rotor
removed from the housing

88483C26

5.0L ENGINE SPECIFICATIONS

Description					English	Metric
Type					V-8 Overhead valve (OHV)	
Displacement					302 cu. in.	5.0 L (4942cc)
Number of Cylinders					8	
Bore					4.00 in.	1016mm
Stroke					3.00 in.	76.2mm
Compression ratio					9.0:1	
Cylinder Bore						
	Diameter				4.0000-4.0052 in.	1.1.6mm-101.73mm
	Out-of-round (max.)				0.015 in.	0.381mm
	Taper (max.)				0.10 in.	2.54mm
Pistons						
	Clearance to bore				0.0013-0.0030 in.	0.033-0.07645mm
	Diameter					
		1989-90 models				
			Coded red		3.9991-3.9985 in.	101.57-101.56mm
			Coded blue		3.9990-4.0000 in.	101.57-101.60mm
			0.003 in. oversize		4.0008-4.0014 in.	101.62-101.63mm
		1991-96 models				
			Coded red		3.9989-3.9995 in.	101.57-101.58mm
			Coded blue		4.0001-4.0007 in.	101.60-101.61mm
			0.003 in. oversize		4.0013-4.0019 in.	101.63-101.64mm
Piston rings						
	End-gap					
		1989-92 models				
			Top ring		.010-0.020 in.	0.254-0.508mm
			Bottom ring		.010-0.020 in.	0.254-0.508mm
			Oil ring		0.015-0.055 in.	0.381-1.397mm
		1993-96 models				
			Top ring		.010-0.020 in.	0.254-0.508mm
			Bottom ring		.018-0.028 in.	0.457-0.711mm
			Oil ring		0.010-0.040 in.	0.254-1.016mm
	Side clearance					
		Top ring			0.0013-0.0033 in.	0.033-0.083mm
		Bottom ring			0.002-0.004 in.	0.050-0.101mm
		Oil ring			Snug	
	Ring width					
		Top ring			.0577-.0587 in.	1.465-1.490mm
		Bottom ring			.0577-.0587 in.	1.465-1.490mm
Piston Pin						
	Length				3.010-3.040 in.	76-454-77.21mm
	Diameter					
		Standard				
			1989-95 models		0.9119-0.9124 in.	23.16-23.17mm
			1996 models		0.9121-0.9122 in.	23.16-23.17mm
		0.001 in. oversize			0.9130-0.9133 in.	24.190-24.197mm
		0.002 in. oversize			0.9140-0.9143 in.	24.215-24.223mm

88483C18

5.0L ENGINE SPECIFICATIONS

Description	English	Metric
Camshaft		
Lobe lift		
1989-95 models		
Intake	0.2375 in.	6.03mm
Exhaust	0.2474 in.	6.28mm
1996 models		
Intake	0.2637 in.	6.69mm
Exhaust	0.2801 in.	7.11mm
End-play	0.001-0.007 in.	0.025-0.017mm
Service limit	0.009 in.	0.22mm
Journal-to-bearing clearance	0.001-0.003 in.	0.025-0.076mm
Journal diameter (standard)		
No. 1:	2.0805 in.	52.84mm
No. 2:	2.0655 in.	52.46mm
No. 3:	2.0505 in.	52.08mm
No. 4:	2.0355 in.	51.70mm
No. 5:	2.0205 in.	51.32mm
Bearing inside diameter		
No. 1:	2.0825 in.	52.89mm
No. 2:	2.0675 in.	52.51mm
No. 3:	2.0525 in.	52.13mm
No. 4:	2.0375 in.	51.75mm
No. 5:	2.0225 in.	51.37mm
Front bearing location	0.005-0.020 in. ①	0.127-0.508mm ①
Crankshaft and flywheel		
Main bearing journal		
Diameter	2.2482-2.2490 in.	57.10-5712mm
Runout (max.)	0.002 in	0.050mm
Taper (max.)	0.0005 in.	0.012mm
Thrust face runout (TIR max.)	0.001 in.	0.025mm
Bearing journal		
Length	1.137-1.139 in.	28.87-28.93mm
Connecting rod journal		
Diameter	2.1228-2.1236 in.	53.91-53.93mm
Taper	0.0006 in.	0.015mm
Crankshaft free end play	0.004-0.008 in.	0.10-0.20mm
Flywheel		
Clutch face runout (assembled)	0.010 in.	0.254mm
Ring gear lateral runout (TIR)		
Man. trans	0.40 in	10.16mm
Auto. trans	0.60 in.	15.24mm
Clutch face runout	0.010 in.	0.254mm
Crankshaft Bearings		
Connecting rod bearing-to-camshaft clearance		
Desired	0.0008-0.0015 in.	0.020-0.038mm
Allowable	0.0007-0.0024 in.	0.017-0.06mm

88483C19

5.0L ENGINE SPECIFICATIONS

Description	English	Metric
Crankshaft Bearings (cont.)		
Bearing wall thickness (STD)		
Standard	0.0572-0.0577 in.	14.53-14.55mm
0.002 in. undersize	0.0573-0.0578 in.	14.55-14.68mm
Main bearing-to-crankshaft clearance		
1989-95 models		
Desired	0.0008-0.0015 in.	0.020-0.038mm
No. 1 bearing	0.0001-0.0015 in.	0.025-0.038mm
All other bearings	0.0005-0.0015 in.	0.027-0.038mm
Allowable	0.0008-0.0026 in.	0.020-0.066mm
No. 1 bearing	0.0001-0.0020 in.	0.025-0.050mm
All other bearings	0.0005-0.0024 in.	0.0127-0.0609mm
1996 models		
Desired	0.0005-0.0015 in.	0.027-0.038mm
N0. 1 bearing	0.0001-0.0015 in.	0.025-0.038mm
All other bearings	0.0005-0.0015 in.	0.027-0.038mm
Allowable	0.0005-0.0024 in.	0.0127-0.0609mm
N0. 1 bearing	0.0001-0.0020 in.	0.025-0.050mm
All other bearings	0.0005-0.0024 in.	0.0127-0.0609mm
Bearing wall tickness		
Standard:	0.0957-0.0960 in.	2.430-2.438mm
No. 1 upper bearing	0.0961-0.0966 in.	2.4400-2.4500mm
All other bearings	0.0957-0.0962 in.	2.4300-2.4400mm
0.002 in.undersize:		
No. 1 bearing	0.0958-0.0962 in.	2.4330-2.4430
All other bearings	0.0958-0.0963 in.	2.4330-2.4460
Connecting rod		
Piston pin bore or bushing I.D.	0.9096-0.9112 in.	23.10-23.14mm
Rod bearing bore I.D.	2.2390-2.2398 in.	56.87-56.89mm
Rod length (center-to-center)	5.0885-5.0915 in.	129.24-1293234mm
Rod-to-crankshaft assembled side clearance	0.010-0.020 in. ②	0.254-0.508mm ②
Cylinder block		
Main bearing bore		
Diameter	2.4412-2.4420 in.	62.00-62.02mm
Distributor shaft bearing bore		
Diameter	0.4525-0.4541 in.	11.49-11.53mm
Head gasket surface		
Flatness	0.003 in. in any 6 in.	0.76mm in any 15.cmm
Tappet bore		
Diameter	0.8752-0.8767 in.	22.23-22.26mm

88483C20

5.0L ENGINE SPECIFICATIONS

Description	English	Metric
Cylinder head		
Valve guide bore		
Diameter		
Intake	0.3433-0.3443 in.	8.71-8.74mm
Exhaust	0.3433-0.3443 in.	8.71-8.74mm
Valve seat	0.3433-0.3443 in.	8.71-8.74mm
Width		
Intake	0.060-0.080 in.	1.524-2.032mm
Exhaust	0.060-0.080 in.	1.524-2.032mm
Angle	45 degrees	
Runout	0.002 in.	0.050mm
Gasket surface		
Flatness	0.003 in. in any 6 in.	0.76mm in any 15.cmm
Valve rocker arm shaft, Push rods and Tappets		
Rocker arm ratio		
1989-92 models	1.61:1	
1993-96 models	1.59:1	
Pushrod runout	0.015 in.	0.38mm
Valve tappet or lifter		
Standard diameter	0.8740-0.8745 in.	22.19-22.21mm
Clearance to bore	0.0007-0.0027 in.	0.017-0.068mm
Collapsed tappet gap (clearance)		
1989-92 models		
Allowable	0.071-0.193 in.	1.80-4.90mm
Desired	0.096-0.165 in.	2.438-4.191mm
1993-96 models		
Allowable	0.071-0.171 in. ③	1.80-4.34mm ③
Desired	0.091-0.15 in. ③	2.311-3.810mm ③
Valve spring compression		
Intake	74-82 lbs. @ 1.78 in. ③	33-39kg @ 45.21mm ③
	196-212 lbs. @ 1.36 in. ③	89.09-96.36kg @ 34.5mm ③
Exhaust	76-84lbs. @ 1.60 in. ③	34.54-38.18kg @ 40.64mm ③
	190-210 lbs. @ 1.20 in. ③	86.36-95.45kg @ 30.48mm ③
Free length		
1988-92 models		
Intake	2.04 in.	51.81mm
Exhaust	1.85 in.	46.99mm
1993-96 models		
Intake	2.06 in.	52.3mm
Exhaust	1.88 In.	47.75mm
Valves		
Stem-to-guide clearance		
Intake	0.010-0.027 in.	0.254-0.685mm
Exhaust	0.015-0.032 in.	0.038-0.081mm
Valve head diameter		
Intake	1.690-1.694 in.	42.92-43.02mm
Exhaust	1.439-1.436 in.	36.55-36.47mm

88483C21

5.0L ENGINE SPECIFICATIONS

Description	English	Metric
Valves (cont.)		
Valve face runout		
Max.	0.002 in.	0.050mm
Stem diameter		
Standard		
Intake	0.3416-0.3423 in.	8.66-8.69mm
Exhaust	0.3411-0.3418 in.	8.66-8.68mm
0.015 in. oversize		
Intake	0.3566-0.3573 in.	9.05-9.07mm
Exhaust	0.3561-0.3568 in.	9.04-9.06mm
0.030 in. oversize		
Intake	0.3716-0.3723 in.	9.44-9.45mm
Exhaust	0.3711-0.3718 in.	9.42-9.44mm
Oil Pump		
Relief valve spring pressure	10.6-12.2 lbs. @ 1.74in ④	4.8-5.5kg@44.1mm ④
Driveshaft-to-housing		
Clearance	0.0015-0.0030 in.	0.038-0.076mm
Relief valve-to-housing		
Clearance	0.0015-0.0030 in.	0.038-0.076mm
Rotor assembly		
End clearance (max.)	0.004 in.	0.101mm
Outer race-to-housing		
Clearance	0.01-0.013 in.	0.25-0.33mm
Oil capacity		
U.S quarts	5.0	
Imperial quarts	4.2	
Liters	4.7	

TIR—Total Indicated Runout

① Distance that front edge of bearing is installed
below the front face of the cylinder block

② Service limit: 0.023 in. (0.58mm)

③ Compressed pressure @ specified height

④ Compressed pressure @ specified length

88483C22

5.8L ENGINE SPECIFICATIONS

Description				English	Metric
Type				V-8 Overhead valve (OHV)	
Displacement				351 cu. in.	5.8 L (5766cc)
Number of Cylinders				8	
Bore				4.00 in.	1016mm
Stroke				3.50 in.	88.9mm
Compression ratio				8.8:1	
Cylinder Bore					
	Diameter			4.0000-4.0048 in.	1.1.60mm-101.72mm
	Out-of-round (max.)			0.015 in.	0.381mm
	Taper (max.)			0.10 in.	2.54mm
Pistons					
	Clearance to bore			0.0013-0.0030 in.	0.033-0.07645mm
	Diameter				
		Coded red		3.9978-3.9984 in.	101.54-101.56mm
		Coded blue		3.9990-4.9996 in.	101.57-101.96mm
		0.003 in. oversize		4.0002-4.0008 in.	101.60-101.62mm
Piston rings					
	End-gap				
		1989-92 models			
			Top ring	0.010-0.020 in.	0.254-0.508mm
			Bottom ring	0.010-0.020 in.	0.254-0.508mm
			Oil ring	0.015-0.055 in.	0.381-1.397mm
		1993-96 models			
			Top ring	0.010-0.020 in.	0.254-0.508mm
			Bottom ring	0.018-0.028 in.	0.457-0.711mm
			Oil ring	0.010-0.040 in.	0.254-1.016mm
	Side clearance				
		Top ring		0.0013-0.0033 in.	0.033-0.083mm
		Bottom ring		0.002-0.004 in.	0.050-0.101mm
		Oil ring		Snug	
	Ring width				
		Top ring		0.0577-.0587 in.	1.465-1.490mm
		Bottom ring		0.0577-.0587 in.	1.465-1.490mm
Piston Pin					
	Length			3.010-3.040 in.	76-454-77.21mm
	Diameter				
		Standard			
			1989-95 models	0.9119-0.9124 in.	23.16-23.17mm
			1996 models	0.9121-0.9122 in.	23.16-23.17mm
		0.001 in. oversize		0.9130-0.9133 in.	24.190-24.197mm
		0.002 in. oversize		0.9140-0.9143 in.	24.215-24.223mm

88483C09

5.8L ENGINE SPECIFICATIONS

Description	English	Metric
Camshaft		
Lobe lift		
1989-95 models		
Intake	0.2780 in.	7.06mm
Exhaust	0.2830 in.	7.18mm
1996 models		
Intake	0.2637 in.	6.69mm
Exhaust	0.2801 in.	7.11mm
End-play	0.001-0.007 in.	0.025-0.017mm
Service limit	0.009 in.	0.22mm
Journal-to-bearing clearance	0.001-0.003 in.	0.025-0.076mm
Journal diameter (standard)		
No. 1:	2.0815 in.	52.87mm
No. 2:	2.0655 in.	52.46mm
No. 3:	2.0515 in.	51.18mm
No. 4:	2.0365 in.	51.72mm
No. 5:	2.0215 in.	51.34mm
Bearing inside diameter		
No. 1:	2.0835 in.	52.92mm
No. 2:	2.0685 in.	52.54mm
No. 3:	2.0535 in.	52.15mm
No. 4:	2.0385 in.	51.77mm
No. 5:	2.0235 in.	51.39mm
Front bearing location	0.005-0.020 in. ①	0.127-0.508mm ①
Crankshaft and flywheel		
Main bearing journal		
Diameter	2.2994-3.0002 in.	76.18-76.20mm
Runout (max.)	0.002 in	0.050mm
Taper (max.)	0.0005 in.	0.012mm
Thrust face runout (TIR max.)	0.001 in.	0.025mm
Bearing journal		
Length	1.137-1.139 in.	28.87-28.93mm
Connecting rod journal		
Diameter	2.3103-2.3111 in.	53.6891-58.7019mm
Taper	0.0006 in.	0.015mm
Crankshaft free end play	0.004-0.008 in.	0.10-0.20mm
Flywheel		
Clutch face runout (assembled)	0.010 in.	0.254mm
Ring gear lateral runout (TIR)		
Man. trans	0.40 in	10.16mm
Auto. trans	0.60 in.	15.24mm
Clutch face runout	0.010 in.	0.254mm
Crankshaft Bearings		
Connecting rod bearing-to-camshaft clearance		
Desired	0.0008-0.0015 in.	0.020-0.038mm
Allowable	0.0008-0.0055 in.	0.020-0.063mm

88483C10

5.8L ENGINE SPECIFICATIONS

Description	English	Metric
Crankshaft Bearings (cont.)		
Bearing wall thickness		
Standard	0.0572-0.0577 in.	14.53-14.55mm
0.002 in. undersize	0.0573-0.0578 in.	14.55-14.68mm
Main bearing-to-crankshaft clearance		
Desired	0.0008-0.0015 in.	0.020-0.038mm
No. 1 bearing	0.0001-0.0015 in.	0.025-0.038mm
All other bearings	0.0005-0.0015 in.	0.027-0.038mm
Allowable	0.0008-0.0026 in.	0.020-0.066mm
No. 1 bearing	0.0001-0.0020 in.	0.025-0.050mm
All other bearings	0.0005-0.0024 in.	0.0127-0.0609mm
Bearing wall tickness		
Standard	0.0957-0.0960 in.	2.430-2.438mm
No. 1 upper bearing	0.0961-0.0966 in.	2.4400-2.4500mm
All other bearings	0.0957-0.0962 in.	2.4300-2.4400mm
0.002 in.undersize		
No. 1 bearing	0.0958-0.0962 in.	2.4330-2.4430
All other bearings	0.0958-0.0963 in.	2.4330-2.4460
Connecting rod		
Piston pin bore or bushing I.D.	0.9096-0.9112 in.	23.10-23.14mm
Rod bearing bore I.D.	2.4265-2.4273 in.	61.633-61.653mm
Rod length (center-to-center)	5.9545-5.9575 in.	151.24-151.321mm
Rod-to-crankshaft assembled side clearance	0.010-0.020 in. ②	0.254-0.508mm ②
Cylinder block		
Main bearing bore		
Diameter	3.1922-3.1930 in.	81.08-81.10mm
Distributor shaft bearing bore		
Diameter	0.5155-5170 in.	13.09-13.33mm
Head gasket surface		
Flatness	0.003 in. in any 6 in.	0.76mm in any 15.cm
Tappet bore		
Diameter	0.8752-0.8767 in.	22.23-22.26mm
Cylinder head		
Valve guide bore		
Diameter		
Intake	0.3433-0.3443 in.	8.71-8.74mm
Exhaust	0.3433-0.3443 in.	8.71-8.74mm
Valve seat		
Width		
Intake	0.060-0.080 in.	1.524-2.032mm
Exhaust	0.060-0.080 in.	1.524-2.032mm
Angle	45 degrees	
Runout	0.002 in.	0.050mm
Gasket surface		
Flatness	0.003 in. in any 6 in.	0.76mm in any 15.cmm

88483C11

5.8L ENGINE SPECIFICATIONS

Description	English	Metric
Valve rocker arm shaft, Push rods and Tappets		
Rocker arm ratio		
1989-92 models	1.61:1	
1993-96 models	1.59:1	
Pushrod runout	0.015 in.	0.38mm
Valve tappet or lifter		
Standard diameter	0.8740-0.8745 in.	22.19-22.21mm
Clearance to bore	0.0007-0.0027 in.	0.017-0.068mm
Collapsed tappet gap (clearance)		
1989-92 models		
Allowable	0.098-0.198 in.	2.337-4.876mm
Desired	0.123-0.173 in.	2.845-4.369mm
1993-96 models		
Allowable	0.071-0.171 in. ③	1.80-4.34mm ③
Desired	0.091-0.15 in. ③	2.311-3.810mm ③
Valve spring compression		
Intake	74-82 lbs.@1.78 in. ③	33-39kg@45.21mm ③
	196-212 lbs.@1.36 in. ③	89.09-96.36kg@34.5mm ③
Exhaust	76-84lbs.@1.60 in. ③	34.54-38.18kg@40.64mm ③
	190-210 lbs.@1.20 in. ③	86.36-95.45kg@30.48mm ③
Free length		
1988-92 models		
Intake	2.04 in.	51.81mm
Exhaust	1.85 in.	46.99mm
1993-96 models		
Intake	2.06 in.	52.3mm
Exhaust	1.88 in.	47.75mm
Valves		
Stem-to-guide clearance		
Intake	0.010-0.027 in.	0.254-0.685mm
Exhaust	0.015-0.032 in.	0.038-0.081mm
Valve head diameter		
Intake	1.770-1.794 in.	44.95-45.56mm
Exhaust	1.453-1.468 in.	36.90-37.28mm
Valve face runout		
Max.	0.002 in.	0.050mm
Stem diameter		
Standard		
Intake	0.3416-0.3423 in.	8.66-8.69mm
Exhaust	0.3411-0.3418 in.	8.66-8.68mm
0.015 in. oversize		
Intake	0.3566-0.3573 in.	9.05-9.07mm
Exhaust	0.3561-0.3568 in.	9.04-9.06mm
0.030 in. oversize		
Intake	0.3716-0.3723 in.	9.44-9.45mm
Exhaust	0.3711-0.3718 in.	9.42-9.44mm

88483C12

5.8L ENGINE SPECIFICATIONS

Description	English	Metric
Oil Pump		
Relief valve spring pressure	18.2-20.2 lbs. @ 2.49in ④	8.26-9.16kg@63.25mm ④
Driveshaft-to-housing		
Clearance	0.0015-0.0030 in.	0.038-0.076mm
Relief valve-to-housing		
Clearance	0.0015-0.0030 in.	0.038-0.076mm
Rotor assembly		
End clearance (max.)	0.004 in.	0.101mm
Outer race-to-housing		
Clearance	0.01-0.013 in.	0.25-0.33mm
Oil capacity		
U.S quarts	5.0	
Imperial quarts	4.2	
Liters	4.7	

TIR—Total Indicated Runout

① Distance that front edge of bearing is installed below the front face of the cylinder block

② Service limit: 0.023 in. (0.58mm)

③ Compressed pressure @ specified height

④ Compressed pressure @ specified length

88483C13

7.5L ENGINE SPECIFICATIONS

Description	English	Metric
Type	V-8 Overhead valve (OHV)	
Displacement	460 cu. in.	7.5 L (7536cc)
Number of Cylinders	8	
Bore	4.36 in.	101.7mm
Stroke	3.85 in.	97.7mm
Compression ratio	8.51	
Cylinder Block		
Cylinder bore		
Standard size	4.360-4.364 in.	110.744-110.846mm
Maximum out-of-round	0.0015 in.	0.0381mm
Maximum taper	0.01 in.	0.254mm
Main bearing		
Bore diameter	3.1922-3.1934 in.	81.082-81.112 mm
Distributor shaft bearing bore diameter	0.5160-0.5175 in.	13.106-13.145mm
Tappet bore diameter	0.8752-0.8767	22.230-22.690mm
Cylinder Head		
Combustion chamber volume	5.84-6.02 cid	95.70-98.70 cc
Valve guide bore diameter		
Intake	0.3433-0.3443 in.	8.719-8.745mm
Exhaust	0.3433-0.3443 in.	8.719-8.745mm
Valve seat		
Maximum runout	0.002 in.	0.00508mm
Angle	45 degrees	
Width		
Intake	0.060-0.080 in.	1.524-2.032mm
Exhaust	0.060-0.080 in.	1.524-2.032mm
Gasket surface flatness		
Overall	0.006 in.	0.1524mm
In any 6 in. (152.4mm)	0.003 in.	0.0762mm
Valve Rocker Arm Shaft, Pushrods and Tappets		
Rocker arm lift ratio to 11.73		
Pushrod runout TIR maximum	0.015 in.	0.381mm
Valve tappet or lifter		
Standard diameter	0.8740-0.8745 in.	22.1990-22.2120mm
Clearance to bore	0.0007-0.0027 in.	0.0178-0.0068mm
Service limit	0.005 in.	(0.127mm)
Hydraulic lifter leakdown rate	10 to 50 seconds for 1/16 travel	
Collapsed tappet gap		
Allowable	0.075-0.175 in.	1.905-4.445mm
Desired	0.100-0.150 in.	2.540-3.810mm
Valves		
Valve stem to guide clearance		
Intake and Exhaust	0.0010-.0027 in.	0.00254-0.0686mm
Valve head diameter		
Intake	1.965-1.989 in.	49.911-50.521mm
Exhaust	1.646-1.661 in.	41.808-42.189mm
Maximum valve face runout	0.002 in.	0.0508mm

88483C14

7.5L ENGINE SPECIFICATIONS

Description	English	Metric
Valve springs		
Valve springs		
Intake	76-84 lbs. @ 1.81 in. ①	34.47-38.10 kg @ 45.97mm ①
	218-240 lbs. @ 1.33 in. ①	98.89-108.86 kg. @ 33.78mm ①
Exhaust	76-84 lbs. @ 1.81 in. ①	34.47-38.10 kg @ 45.97mm ①
	218-240 lbs. @ 1.33 in. ①	98.89-108.86 kg. @ 33.78mm ①
Free length (approx.)		
Intake	2.06 in.	52.324 mm
Exhaust	2.06 in.	52.324 mm
Valve spring assembled height		
Intake	1.790-1.830 in.	45.466-46.482mm
Exhaust	1.790-1.830 in.	45.466-46.482mm
Valve spring out of square	5/64 (0.078) in.	1.98mm
Valve Stem Diameter		
Standard		
Intake	0.3415-0.3423 in.	8.68-8.69mm
Exhaust	0.3415-0.3423 in.	8.68-8.69mm
0.015 in. Oversize		
Intake	0.3565-0.3573 in.	9.06-9.08mm
Exhaust	0.3565-0.3573 in.	9.06-9.08mm
0.030 in. Oversize		
Intake	0.3715-0.3723 in.	9.44-9.46mm
Exhaust	0.3715-0.3723 in.	9.44-9.46mm
Crankshaft and Flywheel		
Main bearing journals		
Diameter	2.9994-3.0002 in. ②	76.1847-76.2051mm ②
TIR Maximum runout	0.002 in.	0.0508mm
Maximum out of round	0.0006 in.	0.01524mm
Thrust face runout TIR maximum	0.001 in.	0.0254mm
Maximum taper per inch/mm	0.0005 in.	0.0127mm
Thrust bearing journal length	1.124-1.126 in.	28.5496-28.6004mm
Connecting rod journal		
Diameter	2.4992-2.5000 in.	63.4797-63.5000mm
Taper	0.0006 in.	0.0152mm
Crankshaft free end-play	0.0040-0.0080 in.	0.1020-0.2030mm
Crankshaft Bearings		
Connecting rod bearing to crankshaft clearance selective fit		
Desired	0.0008-0.0015 in.	0.020-0.038mm
Allowable	0.0007-0.0025 in.	0.0178-0.0635mm
Bearing wall thickness		
Standard	0.0757-0.0762 in.	1.923-1.935mm
0.002 in. undersize	0.0767-0.0772 in.	1.948-1.961mm
Main bearing to crankshaft selective fit		
Desired	0.0008-0.0015 in.	0.020-0.038mm
Allowable	0.0008-0.0026 in.	0.0200-0.0660mm
Bearing wall thickness		
Standard	0.0955-0.0960 in.	2.426-2.38mm
0.002 in. undersize	0.0965-0.0970 in.	2.451-.2.464mm

88483C15

7.5L ENGINE SPECIFICATIONS

Description	English	Metric
Connecting rods		
Piston pin bore or bushing I.D.	1.0386-1.0393 in.	26.380-26.398mm
Rod bearing bore I.D.	2.2390-2.2398 in.	56.87-56.89mm
Connecting rod bore max. out of round	0.0004 in.	0.01016mm
Rod length center to center	6.6035-6.6065 in.	168.529-169.291mm
Connecting rod alignment maximum total difference		
Twist	0.024 in. ③	0.61mm ③
Bend	0.012 in. ③	0.3048mm ③
Rod to crankshaft assembled side clearance	0.010-0.020 in.	0.254-0.508mm
Service limit	0.023 in.	0.584mm
Pistons		
Diameter		
Coded red	4.3577-4.3583 in. ④	110.686-110.700mm ④
Coded blue	4.3589-4.3595 in. ④	110.716-110.731mm ④
0.003 in. oversize	4.3601-4.3607 in. ④	110.747-110.762mm ④
Piston to bore clearance selective fit	0.0022-0.0030 in.	0.056-0.076mm
Piston pin bore diameter	1.0401-1.0406 in.	26.419-26.431mm
Ring groove width compression		
Top and bottom	0.0805-0.0815 in.	2.045-2.070mm
Oil	0.188-0.189 in.	4.775-4.801mm
Piston pins		
Length	3.290-3.320 in.	83.566-84.328mm
Diameter		
Standard	1.0398-1.0403 in.	26.411-26.424mm
0.001 in. oversize	1.0410-1.0413 in.	26.441-26.449mm
Piston pin bore clearance (selective fit)	0.0002-0.0004 in.	0.005-0.010mm
Piston rings		
Ring width		
Top Compression	0.077-0.078 in.	1.956-.1981mm
Bottom compression	0.077-0.078 in.	1.956-.1981mm
Side clearance		
Top compression	0.0013-0.0033 in. ⑤	0.033-0.084mm ⑤
Bottom compression	0.0013-0.0033 in. ⑤	0.0330-0.0840mm ⑤
Oil	Snug	
Ring gap		
Top compression	0.010-0.020 in.	0.2540-0.5080mm
Bottom compression	0.010-0.020 in.	0.2540-0.5080mm
Oil (steel rail)	0.010-0.035 in.	0.2540-0.8890mm

88483C16

7.5L ENGINE SPECIFICATIONS

Description	English	Metric
Camshaft		
Lobe lift		
Intake	0.252 in. ⑤	6.4008mm ⑤
Exhaust	0.278 in. ⑤	7.0612mm ⑤
End-play		
Standard	0.001-0.006 in.	0.0254-0.1524mm
Maximum	0.009 in.	0.228mm
Camshaft journal to bearing clearance	0.001-0.003 in. ⑦	0.0254-0.076mm ⑦
Camshaft drive		
Journal diameter (standard)		
No. 1	2.1238-2.1248 in. ⑧	53.9445-53.9699mm ⑧
No. 2	2.1238-2.1248 in. ⑧	53.9445-53.9699mm ⑧
No. 3	2.1238-2.1248 in. ⑧	53.9445-53.9699mm ⑧
No. 4	2.1238-2.1248 in. ⑧	53.9445-53.9699mm ⑧
No. 5	2.1238-2.1248 in. ⑧	53.9445-53.9699mm ⑧
Bearing inside diameter		
No. 1	2.1258-2.1268 in. ⑧	53.9953-54.0207mm ⑧
No. 2	2.1258-2.1268 in. ⑧	53.9953-54.0207mm ⑧
No. 3	2.1258-2.1268 in. ⑧	53.9953-54.0207mm ⑧
No. 4	2.1258-2.1268 in. ⑧	53.9953-54.0207mm ⑧
No. 5	2.1258-2.1268 in. ⑧	53.9953-54.0207mm ⑧
Camshaft front bearing location	0.040-0.060 in. ⑨	1.0160-1.5240mm ⑨
Timing chain deflection (max.)	0.5 in.	12.7mm
Oil pump and oil capacity		
Relief valve spring pressure @ specified length	20.6 lbs.-22.6. @ 2.49 in.	9.35-10.26 kg @ 6.32mm
Driveshaft to housing clearance	0.0015-0.0030 in.	0.0381-0.076mm
Relief valve to housing clearance	0.0015-0.0030 in.	0.0381-0.076mm
Rotor assembly end clearance (max.)	0.0040 in.	0.100 mm
Outer race to housing clearance	0.0010-0.0130 in.	0.0254-0.3300mm
Engine oil capacity		
U.S. quarts	5.0	
Imperial quarts	4.2	
Litres	4.7	

① Compression @ specified height
② Service limit 0.005 in. (0.127mm)
③ Pin bushing and crankshaft bore must be parallel and in the same vertical plane with specified total difference when measured
   at the ends of an 8-inch long bar, 4 inches on each side of the rod ceneterline
④ Measured at the piston pin bore centerline at 90 degrees to the pin
⑤ Service limit 0.002 in. (0.0508mm) maximum increase in clearance
⑥ Maximum allowable lift loss 0.005 in. (0.127mm)
⑦ Service limit 0.006 in. (0.1524mm)
⑧ Camshaft journal runout 0.005 in. (0.127mm) TIR maximum
⑨ Distance in inches/millimeters that the front edge of the bearing is installed below the front face of the cylinder block

88483C17

1989-94 7.3L ENGINE SPECIFICATIONS

Description	English	Metric
Type		V-8 Overhead valve (OHV)
Displacement	444 cu. in.	7.3 L (7270cc)
Number of Cylinders		8
Bore		
1989-93 models	4.1095 in.	104.38mm
1994 models	4.11 in.	104.39mm
Stroke		
1989-93 models	4.1120 in.	104.44mm
1994 models	4.18 in.	106.17mm
Compression ratio		21.5
Cylinder Block		
Cylinder bore		
Standard size	4.1095-4.1115 in.	104.38-104.43mm
Maximum out-of-round	0.002 in.	0.0508mm
Maximum taper	0.002 in.	0.0508mm
Main bearing		
Bore diameter	3.3152-3.3162 in. ①	84.21-84.23mm ①
Head gasket surface flatness		
Overall	0.006 in.	0.1524mm
In any 6 in./(152.4mm)	0.003 in.	0.0762mm
Oversize		
0.010 (.254mm)	4.11425 in.	104.502mm
0.020 (.508mm)	4.12425 in.	104.756mm
0.030 (.762mm)	4.13425 in.	105.01mm
Cylinder Head		
Pre-chamber insert protrusion	-0.0025-to-0.0025 in.	-0.0635-to-0.0635mm
Valve guide bore diameter		
Intake	0.3736-0.3746 in.	9.489-9.515mm
Exhaust	0.3736-0.3746 in.	9.489-9.515mm
Valve seat width		
Intake	0.065-0.095 in. ②	1.651-2.413mm ②
Exhaust	0.065-0.095 in. ②	1.651-2.413mm ②
Maximum runout	0.002 in.	0.0051mm
Valve Rocker Arm Shaft, Pushrods and Tappets		
Rocker arm lift ratio to 1 1.59		
Pushrod runout TIR maximum	0.015 in.	0.381mm
Valve tappet or lifter		
Standard diameter	0.9209-0.9217 in.	23.391-23.411mm
Clearance to bore	0.0011-0.0034 in. ③	0.00279-0.00864mm ③
Hydraulic lifter leakdown rate	20 to 110 seconds for 0.125 in. (3.175mm) travel	
Collapsed tappet gap (clearance)	0.185 in.	4.699mm
Valves		
Valve stem to guide clearance		
Intake	0.0055 in.	0.14mm
Exhaust	0.0055 in.	0.14mm

88483C05

1989-94 7.3L ENGINE SPECIFICATIONS

Description	English	Metric
Valves (cont.)		
Valve face angle		
Intake	30 degrees	
Exhaust	37.5 degrees	
Maximum valve face runout	0.0015 in.	0.0381mm
Minimum value face margin		
Intake valves	0.112 in.	2.84mm
Exhaust valves	0.053 in.	1.35mm
Valve springs		
Valve spring		
Intake	80 lbs. @ 1.83 in. ④	36.29 kg. @ 46.48mm ④
Exhaust	80 lbs. @ 1.83 in. ④	36.29 kg. @ 46.48mm ④
Free length (approx.)		
Intake	1.925-2.225 in.	48.905-56.505mm
Exhaust	1.925-2.225 in.	48.905-56.505mm
Assembled height		
Intake	1.767 in.	44.8818mm
Exhaust	1.833 in.	46.5582mm
Valve spring out of square	5/64 (0.078) in.	1.900mm
Valve Stem Diameter		
Standard		
Intake	0.37165-0.37235 in.	9.4399-9.4577mm
Exhaust	0.37165-0.37235 in.	9.4399-9.4577mm
Valve head recession relative to deck surface		
Intake	0.042-0.054 in.	1.067-1.372mm
Exhaust	0.051-0.063 in.	1.29-1.60mm
Crankshaft and Flywheel		
Main bearing journals		
Diameter		
Standard	3.1228-3.1236 in.	79.319-79.340mm
Undersize		
0.01 in.	3.1128-3.1136 in.	79.065-79.085mm
0.02 in.	3.1028-3.1036 in.	78.811-78.831mm
0.03 in.	3.0928-3.0936 in.	78.557-78.577mm
TIR Maximum runout	0.002 in. ⑤	0.0508mm ⑤
Maximum out of round	0.0002 in.	0.00508mm
Thrust face runout TIR maximum	0.002 in.	0.0508mm
Taper (max.)	0.0005 in.	0.0127mm
Thrust bearing journal length	1.1325-1.1355 in.	28.766-28.842mm
Connecting rod journal		
Diameter		
Standard	2.4980-2.4990 in.	63.4492-63.4746mm
Undersize		
0.01 in.	2.488-2.489 in.	63.1952-63.2206mm
0.02 in.	2.478-2.479 in.	62.9412-62.9666mm
0.03 in.	2.468-2.469 in.	62.6872-62.7126mm
Taper (max.)	0.0006 in.	0.0152mm

1989-94 7.3L ENGINE SPECIFICATIONS

Description	English	Metric
Crankshaft and Flywheel (cont.)		
Crankshaft end-play	0.0025-0.0085 in.	0.00635-0.2159mm
Flywheel and ring gear runout	0.03 in.	0.762mm
Flywheel and ring gear concentricity	0.02 in.	0.508mm
Crankshaft Bearings		
Connecting rod bearing to crankshaft clearance selective fit		
Desired	0.0011-0.0026 in.	0.00279-0.0660mm
Allowable	0.0011-0.0036 in.	0.00279-0.09144mm
Main bearing to crankshaft selective fit		
Desired	0.0008-0.0036 in.	0.02032-0.09144mm
Allowable	0.0008-0.0046 in.	0.02032-0.11684mm
Connecting rods		
Piston pin bore or bushing I.D.	1.1105-1.1108 in.	28.2067-28.2143mm
Rod bearing bore I.D.	2.5001-2.5016 in. ⑥	63.5025-63.5406mm ⑥
Connecting rod bore max. out of round	0.0005 in.	0.0127mm
Connecting rod bore max. taper	0.0005 in.	0.0127mm
Connecting rod alignment maximum total difference		
Twist	0.002 in. ⑦	0.0508mm ⑦
Bend	0.002 in. ⑦	0.0508mm ⑦
Rod to crankshaft assembled side clearance	0.012-0.024 in.	0.3048-0.6096mm
Pistons		
Diameter		
Standard piston	4.1035-4.104 in. ⑧	104.2289-104.2416mm ⑧
Piston to bore clearance selective fit		
Bores 1-6	0.0055-0.0085 in.	0.1397-0.2159mm
Bores 7 and 8	0.0060-0.0085 in.	0.1524-0.2159mm
Piston pin bore diameter	1.1104-1.1106 in.	28.2042-28.2092mm
Piston height above crankcase	0.010-0.031 in.	0.254-0.787mm
Oversize		
0.01 in.	4.1138-4.1148 in.	104.491-104.516mm
0.02 in.	4.1238-4.1248 in.	104.745-104.770mm
0.03 in.	4.1338-4.1348 in.	104.999-105.024mm
Piston pins		
Length	2.692-2.702 in.	68.3768-68.6308mm
Diameter	1.1099-1.1101 in.	28.1915-28.1965mm
Ring end clearance	0.001-0.029 in.	0.0254-0.7366mm
To piston pin bore clearance (selective fit)	0.0003-0.0007 in.	0.00762-0.01778mm
To connecting rod bushing clearance	0.0004-0.0009 in.	0.0102-0.0229mm
Piston rings		
Diameter	4.11 in.	104.39mm
Side clearance		
Top compression	0.002-0.004 in. ⑨	0.0508mm ⑨
Bottom compression	0.002-0.004 in. ⑨	0.0508mm ⑨
Oil snug	0.001-0.003 in. ⑨	0.0254-0.0762mm ⑨
Ring gap		
Top compression	0.013-0.045 in.	0.3302-1.143mm
Bottom compression	0.060-0.085 in.	1.524-2.159mm
Oil		

88483C07

1989-94 7.3L ENGINE SPECIFICATIONS

Description			English	Metric
Piston rings (cont.)				
	Oversize			
		0.01 in.	4.12 in.	104.648mm
		0.02 in.	4.13 in.	104.902mm
		0.03 in.	4.14 in.	105.156mm
Camshaft				
	End-play		0.001-0.009 in.	0.0254-0.2286mm
	Camshaft journal to bearing clearance		0.0015-0.0035 in.	0.0381-0.0889mm
Camshaft drive				
	Bearing inside diameter			
		No. 1	2.1015-2.1025 in. ⑩	53.37-53.40mm ⑩
		No. 2	2.1015-2.1025 in. ⑩	53.37-53.40mm ⑩
		No. 3	2.1015-2.1025 in. ⑩	53.37-53.40mm ⑩
		No. 4	2.1015-2.1025 in. ⑩	53.37-53.40mm ⑩
		No. 5	2.1015-2.1025 in. ⑩	53.37-53.40mm ⑩
	Camshaft front bearing location		0.020-0.050 in.	0.508-1.270mm
	Gear backlash		0.0015-0.0130 in.	0.0381-0.3302mm
Oil pump, oil cooler and oil capacity				
	Oil pump pressures			
		Curb idle	10 psi	69 kPa
		3300 rpm	40-70 psi	276-483 kPa
	Engine oil capacity			
		U.S. quarts	9.0	
		Imperial quarts	9.7	
		Litres	8.5	
	Oil pump drive gear backlash		0.0056-0.010 in.	0.142-0.254mm

① With bearing caps tightened in place
② Valve seat angle intake 30 degrees, exhaust 37.5 degrees
③ Service limit 0.005 in. (0.127mm)
④ Compression pressure @ specified height
⑤ Service limit 0.005 in. (0.127mm)
⑥ With bearing caps tightened in place
⑦ Pin bushing and crankshaft bore must be parallel and in the same vertical plane with specified total difference when measured at the ends
of an 8-inch long bar, 4 inches on each side of the rod centerline
⑧ Measured at 90 degrees to the pin, at 1.25 in. (31.75mm) below the oil ring groove
⑨ Service limit 0.002 in. (0.0508mm) maximum increase in clearance
⑩ Distance in inches/millimeters that the front edge of the bearing is installed below the front face of the cylinder block

88483C08

1995-96 7.3L ENGINE SPECIFICATIONS

Description	English	Metric
Type	V-8 Overhead valve (OHV)	
Displacement	444 cu. in.	7.3 L (7270cc)
Number of Cylinders	8	
Bore	4.11 in.	104.39mm
Stroke	4.18 in.	106.17mm
Compression ratio	17.51	
Cylinder Block		
Cylinder bore		
Standard size	4.1096-4.1103 in.	104.384-104.402mm
Oversize		
0.010 (.254mm)	4.11425 in.	104.502mm
0.020 (.508mm)	4.12425 in.	104.756mm
0.030 (.762mm)	4.13425 in.	105.01
Maximum out-of-round	0.002 in.	0.0508mm
Maximum taper	0.002 in.	0.0508mm
Main bearing		
Bore diameter	3.3152-3.3162 in. ①	84.21-84.23mm ①
Head gasket surface flatness		
Overall	0.006 in.	0.1524mm
In any 6 in./(152.4mm)	0.003 in.	0.0762mm
Cylinder Head		
Valve guide bore diameter		
Intake	0.3141-0.3151 in.	7.978-8.004mm
Exhaust	0.3141-0.3151 in.	7.978-8.004mm
Valve seat width		
Intake	0.065-0.095 in.	1.651-2.413mm
Exhaust	0.065-0.095 in.	1.651-2.413mm
Maximum runout	0.002 in.	0.0051mm
Gasket surface flatness		
Overall	0.006 in.	0.1524mm
In any 6 in. (152.4mm)	0.003 in.	0.0762mm
Valve Rocker Arm Shaft, Pushrods and Tappets		
Pushrod runout TIR maximum	0.02 in.	0.5mm
Valve tappet or lifter		
Standard diameter	0.9209-0.9217 in.	23.391-23.411mm
Clearance to bore	0.0011-0.0034 in. ②	.00279-.00864mm ②
Hydraulic lifter leakdown rate	18 to 90 seconds for 0.125 in. (3.175mm) travel	
Collapsed tappet gap (clearance)	0.185 in.	4.699mm
Valves		
Valve stem to guide clearance		
Intake	0.0055 in.	0.1397mm
Exhaust	0.0055 in.	0.1397mm
Valve face angle		
Intake	30 degrees	
Exhaust	37.5 degrees	
Maximum valve face runout	0.002 in.	0.0508mm

88483C01

1995-96 7.3L ENGINE SPECIFICATIONS

Description	English	Metric
Valves (cont.)		
Minimum value face margin		
Intake valves	0.066 in.	1.6764mm
Exhaust valves	0.054 in.	1.3716mm
Valve springs		
Valve spring		
Intake	71-79 lbs. @ 1.833 in. ③	32.2-35.8 @ 46.56mm ③
Exhaust	71-79 lbs. @ 1.833 in. ③	32.2-35.8 @ 46.56mm ③
Free length (approx.)		
Intake	1.925-2.225 in.	48.905-56.505mm
Exhaust	1.925-2.225 in.	48.905-56.505mm
Assembled height		
Intake	1.767 in.	44.8818mm
Exhaust	1.833 in.	46.5582mm
Valve spring out of square (max.)	5/64 (0.078) in.	1.98
Valve Stem Diameter		
Standard	0.31185-0.31255 in.	7.921-7.939mm
Valve head recession relative to deck surface		
Intake	0.046-0.058 in.	1.168-1.473mm
Exhaust	0.052-0.064 in.	1.321-1.626mm
Crankshaft and Flywheel		
Main bearing journals		
Diameter		
Standard	3.1228-3.1236 in.	79.319-79.340mm
Undersize		
0.01 in.	3.1128-3.1136 in.	79.065-79.085mm
0.02 in.	3.1028-3.1036 in.	78.811-78.831mm
0.03 in.	3.0928-3.0936 in.	78.557-78.577mm
TIR Maximum runout	0.002 in. ④	0.0508mm ④
Maximum out of round	0.00022 in.	0.00508mm
Thrust face runout TIR maximum	0.001 in.	0.0254mm
Taper (max.)	0.0015 in.	0.0381mm
Thrust bearing journal width	1.1325-1.1355 in.	28.766-28.842mm
Connecting rod journal		
Diameter		
Standard	2.4980-2.4990 in.	63.4492-63.4746mm
Undersize		
0.01 in.	2.488-2.489 in.	63.1952-63.2206mm
0.02 in.	2.478-2.479 in.	62.9412-62.9666mm
0.03 in.	2.468-2.469 in.	62.6872-62.7126mm
Taper (max.)	0.00026 in.	0.0066mm
Crankshaft end-play	0.0025-0.0085 in.	0.063-0.216mm
Flywheel and ring gear runout	0.008 in.	0.2032mm
Flywheel and ring gear concentricity	0.008 in.	0.2032mm

88483C02

1995-96 7.3L ENGINE SPECIFICATIONS

Description	English	Metric
Crankshaft Bearings		
Connecting rod bearing to crankshaft clearance selective fit		
Desired	0.0015-0.0045 in.	0.0381-0.1140mm
Allowable	0.0011-0.0036 in.	0.0279-0.09144mm
Main bearing to crankshaft selective fit		
Desired	0.0018-0.0036 in.	0.0457-0.0914mm
Allowable	0.0018-0.0046 in.	0.0457-0.1168mm
Connecting rods		
Piston pin bushing bore I.D.	1.432-1.433 in.	36.373-36.398mm
Rod bearing bore I.D.	2.5005-2.5025 in. ⑤	63.513-63.564mm ⑤
Connecting rod bore max. out of round	0.0005 in.	0.0127mm
Connecting rod bore max. taper	0.0005 in.	0.0127mm
Connecting rod alignment maximum total difference		
Twist	0.002 in. ⑥	0.0508mm ⑥
Bend	0.002 in. ⑥	0.0508mm ⑥
Rod-to-crankshaft assembled side clearance	0.012-0.024 in.	0.3048-0.6096mm
Crankpin bearing bore diameter	2.6905-2.6915 in.	68.339-68.364mm
Pistons		
Diameter		
Standard piston	4.1045-4.1050 in. ⑦	104.2543-104.2670mm ⑦
Piston to bore clearance selective fit	0.0044-0.0057 in.	0.112-0.149mm
Piston pin bore diameter	1.3075-1.3095 in.	33.2105-33.2613mm
Piston height above crankcase	0.010-0.031 in.	0.254-0.787mm
Oversize		
0.01 in.	4.11475 in.	104.5146mm
0.02 in.	4.12475 in.	104.7686mm
0.03 in.	4.13475 in.	105.0226mm
Piston pins		
Length	2.99-3.00 in.	75.94-76.20mm
Diameter	1.3079-1.3081 in.	33.220-33.226mm
To piston pin bore clearance (selective fit)	0.0003-0.0007 in.	0.00762-0.01778mm
To connecting rod bushing clearance	0.0004-0.0009 in.	0.0102-0.0229mm
Piston rings		
Side clearance (2nd ring only)	0.002-0.004 in.	0.0508-0.1016mm
Ring gap		
Top compression	0.014-0.024 in.	0.35-0.61mm
Bottom compression	0.062-0.072 in.	1.57-1.83mm
Oil	0.012-0.024 in.	0.305-0.610mm
Oversize		
0.01 in.	4.12 in.	104.648mm
0.02 in.	4.13 in.	104.902mm
0.03 in.	4.14 in.	105.156mm
Exhaust manifold		
Maximum allowable warpage		
Between ports	0.005 in.	mm
Total	0.01 in.	0.25mm
Maximum allowable removal of material	0.01 in.	0.25mm

88483C03

1995-96 7.3L ENGINE SPECIFICATIONS

Description	English	Metric
Camshaft		
End-play	0.002-0.008 in.	0.051-0.203mm
Camshaft journal to bearing clearance	0.002-0.006 in. ⑧	0.051-0.165mm ⑧
Lobe lift		
Intake	0.2535 in.	6.439mm
Exhaust	0.2531 in.	6.429mm
Camshaft front bearing location	0.0020-0.0500 in.	0.508-1.270mm
Gear backlash	0.0055-0.010 in.	0.140-0.256mm
Camshaft drive		
Bearing inside diameter		
No. 1	2.102-2.105 in. ⑨	53.39-53.48mm ⑨
No. 2	2.102-2.105 in. ⑨	53.39-53.48mm ⑨
No. 3	2.102-2.105 in. ⑨	53.39-53.48mm ⑨
No. 4	2.102-2.105 in. ⑨	53.39-53.48mm ⑨
No. 5	2.102-2.105 in. ⑨	53.39-53.48mm ⑨
Camshaft front bearing location	0.020-0.050 in. ⑩	0.508-1.270mm ⑩
Gear backlash	0.0055-0.0100 in.	0.140-0.256mm
Oil pump, oil cooler and oil capacity		
Oil pump pressures		
Curb idle	10 psi	69 kPa
3300 rpm	40-70 psi	276-483 kPa
Engine oil capacity		
U.S. quarts	14.0	
Imperial quarts	11.6	
Litres	13.2	
Oil pump drive gear radial clearance	0.012-0.032 in.	0.305-0.813mm
Oil pump drive gear end clearance	0.001-0.003 in.	0.025-0.0762mm

① With bearing caps tightened in place

② Service limit 0.005 in. (0.127mm)

③ Compression pressure @ specified height

④ Service limit 0.005 in. (0.127mm)

⑤ With bearing caps tightened in place

⑥ Pin bushing and crankshaft bore must be parallel and in the same vertical plane with specified total difference when measured at the ends of an 8-inch long bar, 4 inches on each side of the rod centerline

⑦ Measured at 90 degrees to the pin, at 1.25 in. (31.75mm) below the oil ring groove

⑧ Service limit 0.002 in. (0.0508mm) maximum increase in clearance

⑨ Distance in inches/millimeters that the front edge of the bearing is installed below the front face of the cylinder block

⑩ All camshaft journals are 2.099-2.100 in. (53.315-53.340mm)

88483C04

TORQUE SPECIFICATIONS

Component	Ft. lbs.	Nm
Valve cover		
4.9L Engine		
1989-91 models	4-7	5-9
1992-96 models	70-124 inch lbs.	8-14
5.0L and 5.8L Engines		
1989-93 models	10-13	13-17
1994-96 models	11-14	16-20
7.5L Engines	9-11	12-15
7.3L Engine		
1989-94 models	6	8
1995-96 models	8	11
Rocker Arm bolts		
Gasoiline engines	18-25	24-34
Diesel Engines	20	27
Thermostat housing		
4.9L Engine	12-15	17-20
5.0L and 5.8L engine	12-18	17-24
7.5L engine	23-28	32-37
7.3L Diesel Engines		
1987-94 models	20	27
1995-96 models	15	20
Upper intake manifold		
4.9L engine		
1994-96 models		
Upper manifold studs	12-18	16-24
Upper intake manifold screws	22-32	30-43
EGR valve-to-exhaust manifold tube fittings	25-35	34-47
Secondary air bypass tube assembly nuts	8-12	11-16
EGR transducer retainers	12-18	16-24
5.0L, 5.8L and 7.5L Engines		
EGR transducer retainers		
5.0L engine	9-12	12-16
5.8L engine	12-18	16-24
Upper intake manifold bolts	12-18	16-24
Lower intake manifold		
5.0L, 5.8L and 7.5L engines		
Manifold bolts		
1989-93 models	23-35	32-33
1994-95 models		
First pass:	8	11
Second pass:	16	22
Final pass:	23-25	31-34
1996 models		
First pass:	5-10	7-14
Final pass:	23-35	31-34
7.3L Diesel Engines		
1989-94 models		
Intake manifold bolts	24	32
Fuel filter and bracket retainers	24-39	33-52
1995-96 models		
Intake manifold bolts	18	24

88483C30

TORQUE SPECIFICATIONS

Component	Ft. lbs.	Nm
Exhaust Manifold bolts		
5.0L and 5.8L Engines		
1989-95 models	18-24	25-33
1996 models	26-32	35-43
7.5L Engines		
1989-93 models	22-30	29-40
1994-96 models	38-48	52-65
7.3L Diesel engines		
1989-94 models	35	47
1995-96 models	45	61
Combination manifold bolts		
4.9L Engine		
1989-93 models		
Intake manifold-to-engine bolts	22-32	30-43
Intake manifold-to-exhaust manifolds nuts	22-32	30-43
1994-96 models		
Exhaust manifold bolts	22-32	30-43
Lower intake manifold bolts	22-32	30-43
Dual converter Y-pipe lockwashers and nuts	25-36	34-39
Turbocharger		
1994 Models		
Turbocharger retainers	30	40
Exhaust crossover pipe-to-left exhaust manifold retainers	25-36	34-46
Oil drain pedestal bolts	14	19
1995-96 models		
Turbocharger pedestal assembly-to-engine block	18	24
Turbocharger exhaust inlet pipes-to-exhaust manifolds bolts	36	49
Engine Fan and Fan Clutch		
4.9L Engine		
Fan-to-clutch bolts	12-18	16-24
Hub nut (clockwise)	37-55	50-74
5.0L, 5.8L and 7.5L Engines		
Fan-to-clutch bolts	12-18	16-24
7.3L Diesel Engines		
1989-94 models		
Fan-to-clutch bolts	12-18	16-24
Hub nut (counterclockwise)	89-118	120-160
1995-96 models		
Fan-to-clutch bolts	12-18	17-24
Hub nut (clockwise)	83-113	113-153
Water Pump		
4.9L Engine		
Water pump bolts	12-18	17-24
5.0L, 5.8L Engines		
Water pump bolts	15-21	20-28
7.5L Engines		
Water pump bolts	12-18	17-24
7.3L Diesel Engines		
1989-94 models		
Water pump bolts	14	19
1995-96 models		
Water pump	15	20

88483C31

TORQUE SPECIFICATIONS

Component	Ft. lbs.	Nm
Cylinder Head		
4.9L Engine		
1989-94 models		
Step 1:	50-55	68-75
Step 2:	60-65	81-88
Step 3:	70-85	95-115
1995 models		
Step 1:	25-35	34-47
Step 2:	48-55	65-74
Step 3:	Rotate all bolts an additional 80-100 degrees	
1996 models		
Step 1:	45-55	61-74
Step 2:	Rotate all bolts an additional 80-100 degrees	
5.0L and 5.8L Engines		
1989-91 models		
5.0L Engines		
Step 1:	55-65	75-88
Step 2:	66-72	89-97
5.8L Engines		
Step 1:	85	115
Step 2:	95	129
Step 3:	105-112	142-151
1992-96 models		
5.0L engines with FLANGED head bolts		
Step 1:	25-35	34-47
Step 2:	45-55	61-75
Step 3:	Rotate all bolts an additional 85-95 degrees	
5.0L engines with HEX head bolts		
Step 1:	55-65	75-88
Step 2:	65-72	88-98
5.8L engines		
Step 1:	95-105	129-142
Step 3:	105-112	142-151
7.5L Engine		
1989-93 models		
Step 1:	80-90	108-122
Step 2:	100-110	135-149
Step 3:	130-140	176-190
1994-96 models		
Step 1:	70-80	95-108
Step 2:	100-110	135-149
Step 3:	130-140	176-190
Oil Pan bolts		
4.9L Engines		
1989-91 Models	10-12	14-17
1992-94 models	12-18	16-24
95-96 models	15-17 ①	20-23 ①
5.0L and 5.8L Engines		
1989-91 models	9-11	13-14
1992-96 models	22-32	30-44

88483C32

TORQUE SPECIFICATIONS

Component	Ft. lbs.	Nm
Oil Pan bolts (cont.)		
7.5L Engines		
1989-93 models		
1/4 inch bolts	7-9	10-12
5/16 inch bolts	8-11	11-15
1994-96 models	70-105 inch. lbs.	8-12
7.3L Diesel Engines		
1/4 inch bolts	7	9
5/16 inch bolts	14	19
3/8 inch bolts	24	32
Oil Pump bolts		
4.9L engines		
1989-94	10-12	14-20
1995-96	12-18	16-24
V8 engines	22-32	30-43
Crankshaft Damper		
4.9L engine	130-150	177-203
5.0L, 5.8L and 7.5L engines	70-90	95-12
Diesel Engines	90	122
Timing Chain Cover and Seal		
5.0L and 5.8L Engines		
1989-95 models		
Cap screw and washer	80	108
1996 models		
Cover bolts	70-120 inch. lbs.	8-13
7.5L Engine		
1989-91 models		
Front cover-to-cylinder block retainers	15-21	17-24
Oil pan-to-cover bolts	9-11	12-14
1992-96 models		
Oil pan-to-cover bolts	70-105 inch. lbs.	8-12
Cover-to-cylinder block retainers	12-18	17-24
Timing Gear Cover and Seal		
4.9L Engine		
1989-93 models		
Oil pan screws	10-15	14-20
Front cover screws	10-15	14-20
1994-96 models		
Oil pan screws	15-17	20-23
Front cover screws	13-18	17-24
7.3L Diesel Engines		
1989-94 models		
1/4 inch	7	10
5/16 inch	14	19
3/8 inch	24	32
7/16 inch	38	51
1/2 inch	60	81
1995-96 models		
Cover retainers	15	20

88483C33

TORQUE SPECIFICATIONS

Component	Ft. lbs.	Nm
Camshaft		
4.9L Engines		
Thrust plate screws	12-18	16-24
7.3L Engine		
1989-94 models		
Allen screw	15	20
Rear Main Seal		
4.9L, 5.0L and 5.8L Engines		
Flywheel bolts	75-85	102-115
7.5L Engine		
Crankshaft main bearing cap bolts	95-105	129-142
Rear main cap bolts	95-105	129-142
7.3L Diesel Engines		
1989-94 Models		
Rear cover bolts	15	20
Flywheel-to-crankshaft bolts		
Gasoline engines	75-85	102-115
Diesel	47	64

① Except retainer C which is tightened to 16-20 ft. lbs. (21-27Nm)

Component	Ft. lbs.	Nm
Connecting Rod Cap Nuts		
4.9L and 5.8L Engines	40 to 45	
5.0L Engine	19 to 24	
7.3L Engine		
1994 and earlier (except Direct Injection Turbo)		
First step	38	
Second step	51	
1994 and 1995 (Direct Injection Turbo)		
First step	52	
Second step	80	
1996	70	
7.5L Engine	41 to 50	
Main Bearing Cap Bolts		
4.9L Engine	60 to 70	
5.8L and 7.5L Engines	95 to 105	
7.3L Engine		
First step	75	
Second step	90	

USING A VACUUM GAUGE

White needle = steady needle   *Dark needle = drifting needle*

The vacuum gauge is one of the most useful and easy-to-use diagnostic tools. It is inexpensive, easy to hook up, and provides valuable information about the condition of your engine.

Indication: Normal engine in good condition

Gauge reading: Steady, from 17–22 in./Hg.

Indication: Sticking valve or ignition miss

Gauge reading: Needle fluctuates from 15–20 in./Hg. at idle

Indication: Late ignition or valve timing, low compression, stuck throttle valve, leaking carburetor or manifold gasket.

Gauge reading: Low (15–20 in./Hg.) but steady

Indication: Improper carburetor adjustment, or minor intake leak at carburetor or manifold

NOTE: Bad fuel injector O-rings may also cause this reading.

Gauge reading: Drifting needle

Indication: Weak valve springs, worn valve stem guides, or leaky cylinder head gasket (vibrating excessively at all speeds).

NOTE: A plugged catalytic converter may also cause this reading.

Gauge reading: Needle fluctuates as engine speed increases

Indication: Burnt valve or improper valve clearance. The needle will drop when the defective valve operates.

Gauge reading: Steady needle, but drops regularly

Indication: Choked muffler or obstruction in system. Speed up the engine. Choked muffler will exhibit a slow drop of vacuum to zero.

Gauge reading: Gradual drop in reading at idle

Indication: Worn valve guides

Gauge reading: Needle vibrates excessively at idle, but steadies as engine speed increases

TCCS3C01

Troubleshooting Engine Mechanical Problems

Problem	Cause	Solution
External oil leaks	• Cylinder head cover RTV sealant broken or improperly seated	• Replace sealant; inspect cylinder head cover sealant flange and cylinder head sealant surface for distortion and cracks
	• Oil filler cap leaking or missing	• Replace cap
	• Oil filter gasket broken or improperly seated	• Replace oil filter
	• Oil pan side gasket broken, improperly seated or opening in RTV sealant	• Replace gasket or repair opening in sealant; inspect oil pan gasket flange for distortion
	• Oil pan front oil seal broken or improperly seated	• Replace seal; inspect timing case cover and oil pan seal flange for distortion
	• Oil pan rear oil seal broken or improperly seated	• Replace seal; inspect oil pan rear oil seal flange; inspect rear main bearing cap for cracks, plugged oil return channels, or distortion in seal groove
	• Timing case cover oil seal broken or improperly seated	• Replace seal
	• Excess oil pressure because of restricted PCV valve	• Replace PCV valve
	• Oil pan drain plug loose or has stripped threads	• Repair as necessary and tighten
	• Rear oil gallery plug loose	• Use appropriate sealant on gallery plug and tighten
	• Rear camshaft plug loose or improperly seated	• Seat camshaft plug or replace and seal, as necessary
Excessive oil consumption	• Oil level too high	• Drain oil to specified level
	• Oil with wrong viscosity being used	• Replace with specified oil
	• PCV valve stuck closed	• Replace PCV valve
	• Valve stem oil deflectors (or seals) are damaged, missing, or incorrect type	• Replace valve stem oil deflectors
	• Valve stems or valve guides worn	• Measure stem-to-guide clearance and repair as necessary
	• Poorly fitted or missing valve cover baffles	• Replace valve cover
	• Piston rings broken or missing	• Replace broken or missing rings
	• Scuffed piston	• Replace piston
	• Incorrect piston ring gap	• Measure ring gap, repair as necessary
	• Piston rings sticking or excessively loose in grooves	• Measure ring side clearance, repair as necessary
	• Compression rings installed upside down	• Repair as necessary
	• Cylinder walls worn, scored, or glazed	• Repair as necessary

TCCS3C02

Troubleshooting Engine Mechanical Problems

Problem	Cause	Solution
Excessive oil consumption (cont.)	• Piston ring gaps not properly staggered	• Repair as necessary
	• Excessive main or connecting rod bearing clearance	• Measure bearing clearance, repair as necessary
No oil pressure	• Low oil level	• Add oil to correct level
	• Oil pressure gauge, warning lamp or sending unit inaccurate	• Replace oil pressure gauge or warning lamp
	• Oil pump malfunction	• Replace oil pump
	• Oil pressure relief valve sticking	• Remove and inspect oil pressure relief valve assembly
	• Oil passages on pressure side of pump obstructed	• Inspect oil passages for obstruction
	• Oil pickup screen or tube obstructed	• Inspect oil pickup for obstruction
	• Loose oil inlet tube	• Tighten or seal inlet tube
Low oil pressure	• Low oil level	• Add oil to correct level
	• Inaccurate gauge, warning lamp or sending unit	• Replace oil pressure gauge or warning lamp
	• Oil excessively thin because of dilution, poor quality, or improper grade	• Drain and refill crankcase with recommended oil
	• Excessive oil temperature	• Correct cause of overheating engine
	• Oil pressure relief spring weak or sticking	• Remove and inspect oil pressure relief valve assembly
	• Oil inlet tube and screen assembly has restriction or air leak	• Remove and inspect oil inlet tube and screen assembly. (Fill inlet tube with lacquer thinner to locate leaks.)
	• Excessive oil pump clearance	• Measure clearances
	• Excessive main, rod, or camshaft bearing clearance	• Measure bearing clearances, repair as necessary
High oil pressure	• Improper oil viscosity	• Drain and refill crankcase with correct viscosity oil
	• Oil pressure gauge or sending unit inaccurate	• Replace oil pressure gauge
	• Oil pressure relief valve sticking closed	• Remove and inspect oil pressure relief valve assembly
Main bearing noise	• Insufficient oil supply	• Inspect for low oil level and low oil pressure
	• Main bearing clearance excessive	• Measure main bearing clearance, repair as necessary
	• Bearing insert missing	• Replace missing insert
	• Crankshaft end-play excessive	• Measure end-play, repair as necessary
	• Improperly tightened main bearing cap bolts	• Tighten bolts with specified torque
	• Loose flywheel or drive plate	• Tighten flywheel or drive plate attaching bolts
	• Loose or damaged vibration damper	• Repair as necessary

TCCS3C03

Troubleshooting Engine Mechanical Problems

Problem	Cause	Solution
Connecting rod bearing noise	• Insufficient oil supply	• Inspect for low oil level and low oil pressure
	• Carbon build-up on piston	• Remove carbon from piston crown
	• Bearing clearance excessive or bearing missing	• Measure clearance, repair as necessary
	• Crankshaft connecting rod journal out-of-round	• Measure journal dimensions, repair or replace as necessary
	• Misaligned connecting rod or cap	• Repair as necessary
	• Connecting rod bolts tightened improperly	• Tighten bolts with specified torque
Piston noise	• Piston-to-cylinder wall clearance excessive (scuffed piston)	• Measure clearance and examine piston
	• Cylinder walls excessively tapered or out-of-round	• Measure cylinder wall dimensions, rebore cylinder
	• Piston ring broken	• Replace all rings on piston
	• Loose or seized piston pin	• Measure piston-to-pin clearance, repair as necessary
	• Connecting rods misaligned	• Measure rod alignment, straighten or replace
	• Piston ring side clearance excessively loose or tight	• Measure ring side clearance, repair as necessary
	• Carbon build-up on piston is excessive	• Remove carbon from piston
Valve actuating component noise	• Insufficient oil supply	• Check for: (a) Low oil level (b) Low oil pressure (c) Wrong hydraulic tappets (d) Restricted oil gallery (e) Excessive tappet to bore clearance
	• Rocker arms or pivots worn	• Replace worn rocker arms or pivots
	• Foreign objects or chips in hydraulic tappets	• Clean tappets
	• Excessive tappet leak-down	• Replace valve tappet
	• Tappet face worn	• Replace tappet; inspect corresponding cam lobe for wear
	• Broken or cocked valve springs	• Properly seat cocked springs; replace broken springs
	• Stem-to-guide clearance excessive	• Measure stem-to-guide clearance, repair as required
	• Valve bent	• Replace valve
	• Loose rocker arms	• Check and repair as necessary
	• Valve seat runout excessive	• Regrind valve seat/valves
	• Missing valve lock	• Install valve lock
	• Excessive engine oil	• Correct oil level

TCCS3C04

Troubleshooting Engine Performance

Problem	Cause	Solution
Hard starting (engine cranks normally)	• Faulty engine control system component	• Repair or replace as necessary
	• Faulty fuel pump	• Replace fuel pump
	• Faulty fuel system component	• Repair or replace as necessary
	• Faulty ignition coil	• Test and replace as necessary
	• Improper spark plug gap	• Adjust gap
	• Incorrect ignition timing	• Adjust timing
	• Incorrect valve timing	• Check valve timing; repair as necessary
Rough idle or stalling	• Incorrect curb or fast idle speed	• Adjust curb or fast idle speed (If possible)
	• Incorrect ignition timing	• Adjust timing to specification
	• Improper feedback system operation	• Refer to Chapter 4
	• Faulty EGR valve operation	• Test EGR system and replace as necessary
	• Faulty PCV valve air flow	• Test PCV valve and replace as necessary
	• Faulty TAC vacuum motor or valve	• Repair as necessary
	• Air leak into manifold vacuum	• Inspect manifold vacuum connections and repair as necessary
	• Faulty distributor rotor or cap	• Replace rotor or cap (Distributor systems only)
	• Improperly seated valves	• Test cylinder compression, repair as necessary
	• Incorrect ignition wiring	• Inspect wiring and correct as necessary
	• Faulty ignition coil	• Test coil and replace as necessary
	• Restricted air vent or idle passages	• Clean passages
	• Restricted air cleaner	• Clean or replace air cleaner filter element
Faulty low-speed operation	• Restricted idle air vents and passages	• Clean air vents and passages
	• Restricted air cleaner	• Clean or replace air cleaner filter element
	• Faulty spark plugs	• Clean or replace spark plugs
	• Dirty, corroded, or loose ignition secondary circuit wire connections	• Clean or tighten secondary circuit wire connections
	• Improper feedback system operation	• Refer to Chapter 4
	• Faulty ignition coil high voltage wire	• Replace ignition coil high voltage wire (Distributor systems only)
	• Faulty distributor cap	• Replace cap (Distributor systems only)
Faulty acceleration	• Incorrect ignition timing	• Adjust timing
	• Faulty fuel system component	• Repair or replace as necessary
	• Faulty spark plug(s)	• Clean or replace spark plug(s)
	• Improperly seated valves	• Test cylinder compression, repair as necessary
	• Faulty ignition coil	• Test coil and replace as necessary

TCCS3C05

Troubleshooting Engine Performance

Problem	Cause	Solution
Faulty acceleration (cont.)	• Improper feedback system operation	• Refer to Chapter 4
Faulty high speed operation	• Incorrect ignition timing • Faulty advance mechanism	• Adjust timing (if possible) • Check advance mechanism and repair as necessary (Distributor systems only)
	• Low fuel pump volume • Wrong spark plug air gap or wrong plug	• Replace fuel pump • Adjust air gap or install correct plug
	• Partially restricted exhaust manifold, exhaust pipe, catalytic converter, muffler, or tailpipe	• Eliminate restriction
	• Restricted vacuum passages • Restricted air cleaner	• Clean passages • Cleaner or replace filter element as necessary
	• Faulty distributor rotor or cap	• Replace rotor or cap (Distributor systems only)
	• Faulty ignition coil • Improperly seated valve(s)	• Test coil and replace as necessary • Test cylinder compression, repair as necessary
	• Faulty valve spring(s)	• Inspect and test valve spring tension, replace as necessary
	• Incorrect valve timing	• Check valve timing and repair as necessary
	• Intake manifold restricted	• Remove restriction or replace manifold
	• Worn distributor shaft	• Replace shaft (Distributor systems only)
	• Improper feedback system operation	• Refer to Chapter 4
Misfire at all speeds	• Faulty spark plug(s) • Faulty spark plug wire(s) • Faulty distributor cap or rotor	• Clean or relace spark plug(s) • Replace as necessary • Replace cap or rotor (Distributor systems only)
	• Faulty ignition coil • Primary ignition circuit shorted or open intermittently • Improperly seated valve(s)	• Test coil and replace as necessary • Troubleshoot primary circuit and repair as necessary • Test cylinder compression, repair as necessary
	• Faulty hydraulic tappet(s) • Improper feedback system operation • Faulty valve spring(s)	• Clean or replace tappet(s) • Refer to Chapter 4 • Inspect and test valve spring tension, repair as necessary
	• Worn camshaft lobes • Air leak into manifold	• Replace camshaft • Check manifold vacuum and repair as necessary
	• Fuel pump volume or pressure low • Blown cylinder head gasket • Intake or exhaust manifold passage(s) restricted	• Replace fuel pump • Replace gasket • Pass chain through passage(s) and repair as necessary
Power not up to normal	• Incorrect ignition timing • Faulty distributor rotor	• Adjust timing • Replace rotor (Distributor systems only)

TCCS3C06

Troubleshooting Engine Performance

Problem	Cause	Solution
Power not up to normal (cont.)	• Incorrect spark plug gap	• Adjust gap
	• Faulty fuel pump	• Replace fuel pump
	• Faulty fuel pump	• Replace fuel pump
	• Incorrect valve timing	• Check valve timing and repair as necessary
	• Faulty ignition coil	• Test coil and replace as necessary
	• Faulty ignition wires	• Test wires and replace as necessary
	• Improperly seated valves	• Test cylinder compression and repair as necessary
	• Blown cylinder head gasket	• Replace gasket
	• Leaking piston rings	• Test compression and repair as necessary
	• Improper feedback system operation	• Refer to Chapter 4
Intake backfire	• Improper ignition timing	• Adjust timing
	• Defective EGR component	• Repair as necessary
	• Defective TAC vacuum motor or valve	• Repair as necessary
Exhaust backfire	• Air leak into manifold vacuum	• Check manifold vacuum and repair as necessary
	• Faulty air injection diverter valve	• Test diverter valve and replace as necessary
	• Exhaust leak	• Locate and eliminate leak
Ping or spark knock	• Incorrect ignition timing	• Adjust timing
	• Distributor advance malfunction	• Inspect advance mechanism and repair as necessary (Distributor systems only)
	• Excessive combustion chamber deposits	• Remove with combustion chamber cleaner
	• Air leak into manifold vacuum	• Check manifold vacuum and repair as necessary
	• Excessively high compression	• Test compression and repair as necessary
	• Fuel octane rating excessively low	• Try alternate fuel source
	• Sharp edges in combustion chamber	• Grind smooth
	• EGR valve not functioning properly	• Test EGR system and replace as necessary
Surging (at cruising to top speeds)	• Low fuel pump pressure or volume	• Replace fuel pump
	• Improper PCV valve air flow	• Test PCV valve and replace as necessary
	• Air leak into manifold vacuum	• Check manifold vacuum and repair as necessary
	• Incorrect spark advance	• Test and replace as necessary
	• Restricted fuel filter	• Replace fuel filter
	• Restricted air cleaner	• Clean or replace air cleaner filter element
	• EGR valve not functioning properly	• Test EGR system and replace as necessary
	• Improper feedback system operation	• Refer to Chapter 4

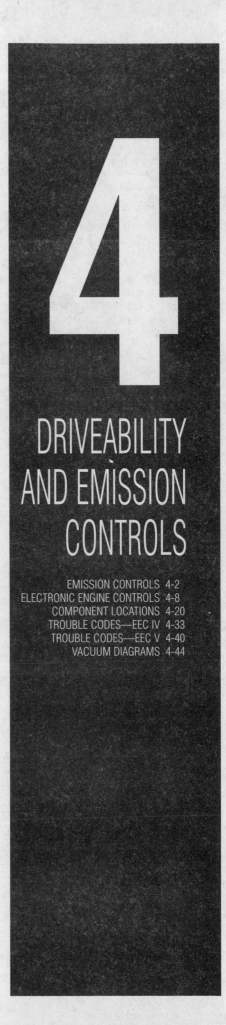

4

DRIVEABILITY AND EMISSION CONTROLS

EMISSION CONTROLS

Crankcase Ventilation System

OPERATION

▶ See Figure 1

The crankcase emission control equipment consists of a positive crankcase ventilation (PCV) valve, a closed oil filler cap and the hoses that connect this equipment.

When the engine is running, a small portion of the gases which are formed in the combustion chamber leak by the piston rings and enter the crankcase. Since these gases are under pressure they tend to escape from the crankcase and enter into the atmosphere. If these gases are allowed to remain in the crankcase for any length of time, they would contaminate the engine oil and cause sludge to build up. If the gases are allowed to escape into the atmosphere, they would pollute the air, as they contain unburned hydrocarbons. The crankcase emission control equipment recycles these gases back into the engine combustion chamber, where they are burned.

Crankcase gases are recycled in the following manner: While the engine is running, clean filtered air is drawn into the crankcase through the intake air filter and then through a hose leading to the oil filler cap. As the air passes through the crankcase it picks up the combustion gases and carries them out of the crankcase, up through the PCV valve and into the intake manifold. After they enter the intake manifold they are drawn into the combustion chamber and are burned.

The most critical component of the system is the PCV valve. This vacuum-controlled valve regulates the amount of gases which are recycled into the combustion chamber. At low engine speeds the valve is partially closed, limiting the flow of gases into the intake manifold. As engine speed increases, the valve opens to admit greater quantities of the gases into the intake manifold. If the valve should become blocked or plugged, the gases will be prevented from escaping the crankcase by the normal route. Since these gases are under pressure, they will find their own way out of the crankcase. This alternate route is usually a weak oil seal or gasket in the engine. As the gas escapes by the gasket, it also creates an oil leak. Besides causing oil leaks, a clogged PCV valve also allows these gases to remain in the crankcase for an extended period of time, promoting the formation of sludge in the engine.

The above explanation and the component testing procedure which follows applies to all of the gasoline engines installed in Ford vans, since all are equipped with PCV systems.

TESTING

▶ See Figure 2

With the engine running at idle, pull the PCV valve and hose from the valve rocker cover rubber grommet.

A hissing noise should be heard as air passes through the valve and a strong vacuum should be felt when you place a finger over the valve inlet if the valve is working properly. While you have your finger over the PCV valve inlet, check for vacuum leaks in the hose and at the connections.

When the PCV valve is removed from the engine, a metallic clicking noise should be heard when it is shaken. This indicates that the metal check ball inside the valve is still free and is not gummed up.

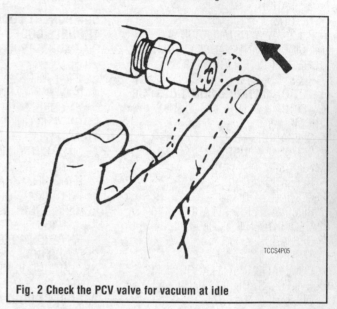

TCCS4P05

Fig. 2 Check the PCV valve for vacuum at idle

REMOVAL & INSTALLATION

Refer to Section 1 for this procedure.

Evaporative Emission Controls

OPERATION

Fuel vapors trapped in the sealed fuel tank are vented through the orifice vapor valve assembly in the top of the tank. The vapors leave the valve assembly through a single vapor line and continue to the carbon canister for storage until they are purged to the engine for burning.

Purging the carbon canister removes the fuel vapor stored in the carbon canister. The fuel vapor is purged via a CANister Purge (CANP) solenoid or vacuum controlled purge valve. Purging occurs when the engine is at normal operating temperature and off idle.

The evaporative emission control system consists of the following components: fuel vapor (charcoal) canister, fuel vapor Canister Purge (CANP) solenoids, the fuel tank and fuel tank filler pipe, vapor tube and fuel vapor hoses.

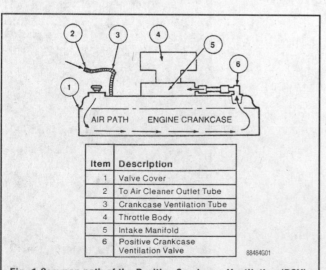

Item	Description
1	Valve Cover
2	To Air Cleaner Outlet Tube
3	Crankcase Ventilation Tube
4	Throttle Body
5	Intake Manifold
6	Positive Crankcase Ventilation Valve

88464G01

Fig. 1 Common path of the Positive Crankcase Ventilation (PCV) airflow

Fuel Vapor (Charcoal) Canister

▶ See Figure 3

➡ The fuel vapor canister is referred to as the evaporative emissions canister on 1995–97 models.

The fuel vapors from the fuel tank are stored in the fuel vapor canister until the vehicle is operated, at which time, the vapors will purge from the canister into the engine for consumption. The fuel vapor canister contains activated carbon, which absorbs the fuel vapor. The canister is located in the engine compartment or along the frame rail.

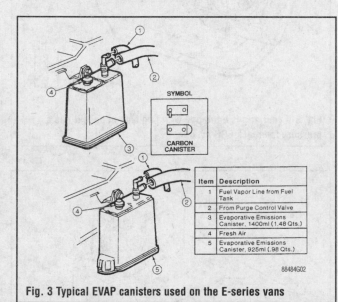

Fig. 3 Typical EVAP canisters used on the E-series vans

Item	Description
1	Fuel Vapor Line from Fuel Tank
2	From Purge Control Valve
3	Evaporative Emissions Canister, 1400ml (1.48 Qts.)
4	Fresh Air
5	Evaporative Emissions Canister, 925ml (.98 Qts.)

CANP Solenoid

The CANP solenoid is inline with the carbon canister and controls the flow of fuel vapors out of the canister. It is normally closed. When the engine is shut **OFF**, the vapors from the fuel tank flow into the canister. After the engine is started, the solenoid is engaged and opens, purging the vapors into the engine. With the solenoid open, vapors from the fuel tank are routed directly into the engine.

DIAGNOSIS & TESTING

CANP Solenoid

▶ See Figure 4

1991–1994 MODELS

1. Remove the CANP solenoid.
2. Using an external voltage source, apply 9–14 DC volts to the CANP solenoid electrical terminals. Then, use a hand-held vacuum pump and apply 9 in. Hg (16 kPa) vacuum to the manifold side nipple of the CANP solenoid.

   a. If the solenoid opens and allows air to freely pass through it, the solenoid is working properly.

   b. If the solenoid does not allow air to pass freely while energized, replace the solenoid with a new one.

1995–96 MODELS

▶ See Figure 4

1. Remove the CANP solenoid.
2. Using an external voltage source, apply 9–14 DC volts to the CANP

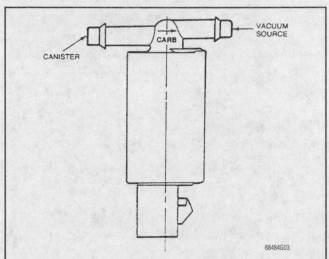

Fig. 4 Apply vacuum to the manifold (vacuum) side of the solenoid

solenoid electrical terminals. Then, use a hand-held vacuum pump and apply 16 in. Hg (53 kPa) vacuum to the manifold side nipple of the CANP solenoid.

   a. If the solenoid opens and allows air to freely pass through it, the solenoid is working properly.

   b. If the solenoid does not allow air to pass freely while energized, replace the solenoid with a new one.

REMOVAL & INSTALLATION

Canister

▶ See Figures 5, 6 and 7

1. Disconnect the hoses from the canister.
2. Loosen the canister-to-bracket retainers.
3. Remove the canister from the bracket and van.
4. Installation is the reverse of removal. Tighten the retainers to 44–62 inch lbs. (5–7 Nm).

Fig. 5 Unfasten the EVAP canister retaining bolts

Fig. 6 Slide the EVAP canister forward to gain access to the hoses

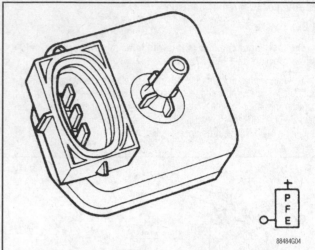

Fig. 8 If your van is equipped with this type of unit, it has a pressure feedback EGR system

Fig. 7 Disconnect the hoses and remove the canister

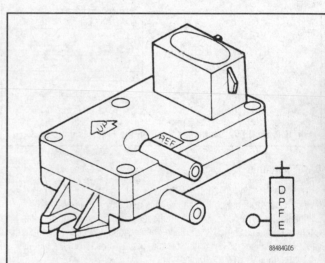

Fig. 9 If your van is equipped with this type of unit, it has a differential pressure feedback EGR system

Exhaust Gas Recirculation (EGR) System

OPERATION

♦ See Figures 8 and 9

The Exhaust Gas Recirculation (EGR) system is designed to reintroduce exhaust gas into the combustion chambers, thereby lowering combustion temperatures and reducing the formation of Oxides of Nitrogen (NO_x).

The amount of exhaust gas that is reintroduced into the combustion cycle is determined by several factors, such as: engine speed, engine vacuum, exhaust system backpressure, coolant temperature, throttle position. All EGR valves are vacuum operated. The EGR vacuum diagram for your particular vehicle is displayed on the Vehicle Emission Control Information (VECI) label.

The EGR system is a Pressure Feedback EGR (PFE) or Differential PFE (DPFE) system, controlled by the Powertrain Control Module (PCM) and composed of the following components: PFE or DPFE sensor (also referred to as the backpressure transducer), EGR Vacuum Regulator (EVR) solenoid, EGR valve, and assorted hoses and tubing.

COMPONENT TESTING

System Integrity Inspection

Check the EGR system hoses and connections for looseness, pinching, leaks, splitting, blockage, etc. Ensure that the EGR valve mounting bolts are not loose, or that the flange gasket is not damaged. If the system appears to be in good shape, proceed to the EGR vacuum test, otherwise repair the damaged components.

EGR System Vacuum Test

♦ See Figure 10

➡ The EVR solenoid has a constant internal leak; this is normal. There may be a small vacuum signal, however, it should be less than 1.0 in. Hg (3.4 kPa) of vacuum.

Start the engine and allow it to run until normal operating temperature is reached. With the engine running at idle, detach the vacuum supply hose from the EGR valve and install a vacuum gauge to the hose. The vacuum reading should be less than 1.0 in. Hg (3.4 kPa) of vacuum. If the vacuum is greater than that specified, the problem may lie with the EVR solenoid.

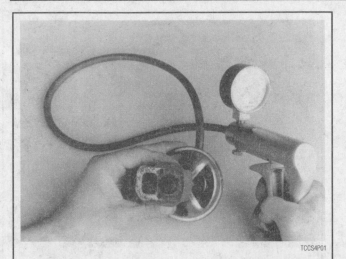

Fig. 10 Some EGR valves may be tested using a vacuum pump by watching for diaphragm movement

Fig. 11 Unplug the EGR valve electrical connection

EVR Solenoid Test

1. Remove the EVR solenoid.
2. Attempt to lightly blow air into the EVR solenoid.
   a. If air blows through the solenoid, replace the solenoid with a new one.
   b. If air does not pass freely through the solenoid, continue with the test.
3. Apply battery voltage (approximately 12 volts) and a ground to the EVR solenoid electrical terminals. Attempt to lightly blow air, once again, through the solenoid.
   a. If air does not pass through the solenoid, replace the solenoid with a new one.
   b. If air does not flow through the solenoid, the solenoid is OK.

EGR Valve Function Test

1. Install a tachometer on the engine, following the manufacturer's instructions.
2. Detach the engine wiring harness connector from the Idle Air Control (IAC) solenoid.
3. Disconnect and plug the vacuum supply hose from the EGR valve.
4. Start the engine, then apply the parking brake, block the rear wheels and position the transmission in Neutral.
5. Observe and note the idle speed.

➡️If the engine will not idle with the IAC solenoid disconnected, provide an air bypass to the engine by slightly opening the throttle plate or by creating an intake vacuum leak. Do not allow the idle speed to exceed typical idle rpm.

6. Using a hand-held vacuum pump, slowly apply 5–10 in. Hg (17–34 kPa) of vacuum to the EGR valve nipple.
   a. If the idle speed drops more than 100 rpm with the vacuum applied and returns to normal after the vacuum is removed, the EGR valve is OK.
   b. If the idle speed does not drop more than 100 rpm with the vacuum applied and return to normal after the vacuum is removed, inspect the EGR valve for a blockage; clean it if a blockage is found. Replace the EGR valve if no blockage is found, or if cleaning the valve does not remedy the malfunction.

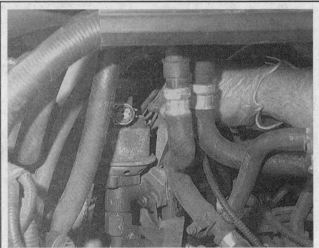

Fig. 12 Disconnect the vacuum hose from the valve

REMOVAL & INSTALLATION

EGR Valve

▶ See Figures 11 thru 17

1. Disconnect the negative battery cable.
2. If necessary, remove the air cleaner outlet tube.
3. Disconnect the EGR valve sensor wire at the valve.

Fig. 13 Unfasten the EGR valve-to-exhaust manifold tube nut . . .

Fig. 14 . . . and disconnect the line from the valve

Fig. 15 Loosen the EGR valve mounting bolts

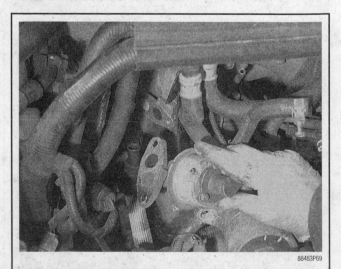
Fig. 16 Remove the EGR valve from the engine compartment

Fig. 17 Remove the EGR valve gasket AND REPLACE IT WITH A NEW ONE

4. Disconnect the EGR valve-to-exhaust manifold tube from the EGR valve.
5. Disconnect the vacuum line from the EGR valve.
6. Remove the mounting bolts and remove the EGR valve.
7. Remove any old gasket material from the engine mating area.

To install:

8. Install the EGR valve to the engine with a new gasket and tighten.
9. Attach the vacuum line to the valve.
10. Connect the sensor wiring.
11. Connect the EGR valve-to-exhaust manifold tube to the EGR valve.
12. If removed, install the air cleaner outlet tube.
13. Connect the negative battery cable.

Pressure Valve Sensor

1. Disengage the EGR valve sensor electrical connection.
2. Loosen the sensor retaining nuts.
3. Remove the sensor.
4. Installation is the reverse of removal.

Secondary Air Injection (AIR) System

OPERATION

▶ **See Figure 18**

The Secondary Air Injection (AIR) system is an electronically controlled system. The system diverts secondary air upstream to the exhaust manifold check valve or downstream to the rear section check valve and catalyst. The system will also dump secondary air into the atmosphere during some operating modes.

The air bypass valve is used to control the engine idle speed and is operated by the Electronic Engine Control (EEC) module.

The air bypass valve allows air to pass around the throttle plates and control:

- Cold engine fast idle
- Cold starting
- Dashpot operation
- Over-temperature idle boost
- Engine load correction

➡ **The air bypass valve is not serviceable and correction is by replacement only.**

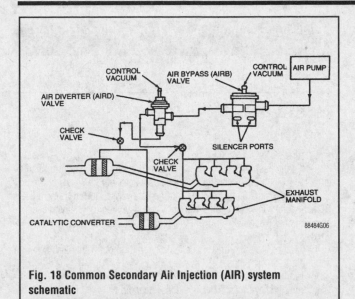

Fig. 18 Common Secondary Air Injection (AIR) system schematic

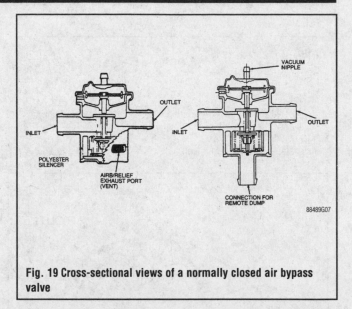

Fig. 19 Cross-sectional views of a normally closed air bypass valve

The catalytic converter, mounted in the van's exhaust system, is a muffler-shaped device containing a ceramic honeycomb shaped material coated with aluminum, and impregnated with catalytically active precious metals such as platinum, palladium and rhodium.

The catalyst's job is to reduce air pollutants by oxidizing hydrocarbons (HC) and carbon monoxide (CO). Catalysts containing palladium and rhodium also oxidize nitrous oxides (NOx).

On some vans, the catalyst is also fed by the secondary air system, via a small supply tube in the side of the catalyst.

No maintenance is possible on the converter, other than keeping the heat shield clear of flammable debris, such as leaves and twigs.

Other than external damage, the only significant damage possible to a converter is through the use of leaded gasoline, or by way of a too rich fuel/air mixture. Both of these problems will ruin the converter through contamination of the catalyst and will eventually plug the converter, causing loss of power and engine performance. When this occurs, the catalyst must be replaced.

For information on converter replacement (as well as other exhaust system components), refer to Section 3 of this manual.

TESTING

Normally Closed Air Bypass Valve Functional Test

◗ See Figure 19

1. Disconnect the air supply hose at the valve.
2. Run the engine to normal operating temperature.
3. Disconnect the vacuum line and make sure vacuum is present. If no vacuum is present, remove or bypass any restrictors or delay valves in the vacuum line.
4. Run the engine at 1500 rpm with the vacuum line connected. Air pump supply air should be heard and felt at the valve outlet.
5. With the engine still at 1500 rpm, disconnect the vacuum line. Air at the outlet should shut off or dramatically decrease. Air pump supply air should now be felt or heard at the silencer ports.
6. If the valve doesn't pass each of these tests, replace it.

Normally Open Air Bypass Valve Functional Test

1. Disconnect the air supply hose at the valve.
2. Run the engine to normal operating temperature.
3. Disconnect the vacuum lines from the valve.

4. Run the engine at 1500 rpm with the vacuum lines disconnected. Air pump supply air should be heard and felt at the valve outlet.
5. Shut off the engine. Using a spare length of vacuum hose, connect the vacuum nipple of the valve to direct manifold vacuum.
6. Run the engine at 1500 rpm. Air at the outlet should shut off or dramatically decrease. Air pump supply air should now be felt or heard at the silencer ports.
7. With the engine still in this mode, cap the vacuum vent. Accelerate the engine to 2,000 rpm and suddenly release the throttle. A momentary interruption of air pump supply air should be felt at the valve outlet.
8. If the valve doesn't pass each of these tests, replace it. Reconnect all lines.

Air Control Valve Functional Test

1. Run the engine to normal operating temperature, then increase the speed to 1500 rpm.
2. Disconnect the air supply hose at the valve inlet and verify that there is airflow present.
3. Reconnect the air supply hose.
4. Disconnect both air supply hoses.
5. Disconnect the vacuum hose from the valve.
6. With the engine running at 1500 rpm, airflow should be felt and heard at the outlet on the side of the valve, with no airflow heard or felt at the outlet opposite the vacuum nipple.
7. Shut off the engine.
8. Using a spare piece of vacuum hose, connect direct manifold vacuum to the valve's vacuum fitting. Airflow should be heard and felt at the outlet opposite the vacuum nipple, and no airflow should be present at the other outlet.
9. If the valve is not functioning properly, replace it.

Air Supply Pump Functional Check

1. Check and, if necessary, adjust the belt tension. Press at the midpoint of the belt's longest straight run. You should be able to depress the belt about ½ in. (13mm) at most.
2. Run the engine to normal operating temperature and let it idle.
3. Disconnect the air supply hose from the bypass control valve. If the pump is operating properly, airflow should be felt at the pump outlet. The flow should increase as you increase the engine speed. The pump is not serviceable and should be replaced if it is not functioning properly.

REMOVAL & INSTALLATION

Air Pump

▶ See Figure 20

1. Remove the drive belt.
2. Disconnect the hoses from the pump.
3. Loosen the pump retaining bolts and remove the pump from the engine compartment.
4. Installation is the reverse of removal.

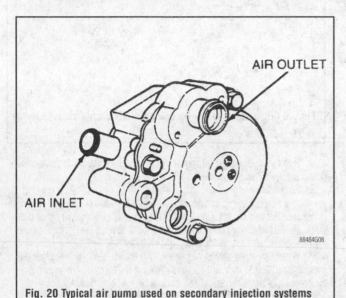

Fig. 20 Typical air pump used on secondary injection systems

RESETTING

1989–93 Models

▶ See Figure 21

1. Turn the key to the **OFF** position.
2. Lightly push a Phillips screwdriver through the 0.2 in. (5mm) diameter hole labeled RESET, and lightly press down and hold it.
3. While maintaining pressure with the screwdriver, turn the key to the **RUN** position. The EMW lamp will light and stay lit as long as you keep pressure on the screwdriver. Hold the screwdriver down for about 5 seconds.
4. Remove the screwdriver. The lamp should go out within 2–5 seconds. If not, repeat Steps 1–3.
5. Turn the key **OFF**.
6. Turn the key to the **RUN** position. The lamp will light for 2–5 seconds and then go out. If not, repeat the reset procedure.

➡**If the light comes on between 15,000 and 45,000 miles (24,155–72,464 km) or between 75,000 and 105,000 miles (120,773–169,082 km), you'll have to replace the 1000 hour pre-timed module.**

1994–96 Models

There is no reset procedure for these models. The light will reset itself once the problem is rectified.

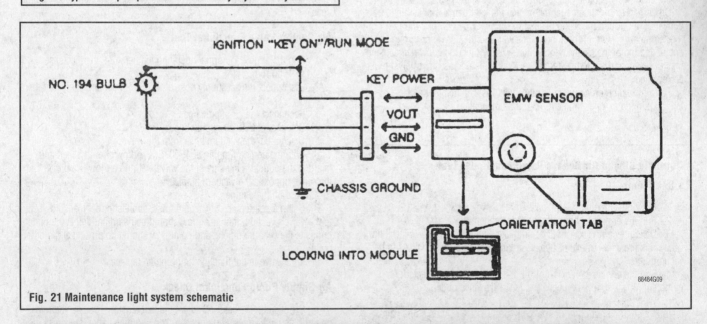

Fig. 21 Maintenance light system schematic

ELECTRONIC ENGINE CONTROLS

Powertrain Control Module (PCM)

OPERATION

▶ See Figure 22

➡**Most of the models covered by this manual employ the fourth generation Electronic Engine Control system, commonly designated EEC-IV,** to manage fuel, ignition and emissions on vehicle engines. Other models (depending on engine application), will be equipped with EEC-V.

The Powertrain Control Module (PCM) is responsible for the operation of the emission control devices, cooling fans, ignition and advance, and in some cases, automatic transmission functions. Because the EEC system oversees both the ignition timing and the fuel injector operation, a precise air/fuel ratio will be maintained under all operating conditions. The PCM is a microprocessor or small computer which receives electrical

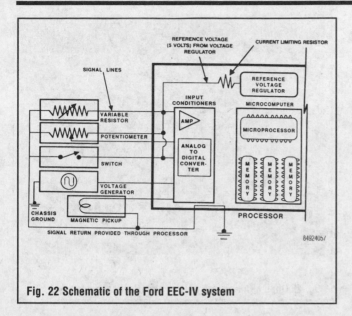

Fig. 22 Schematic of the Ford EEC-IV system

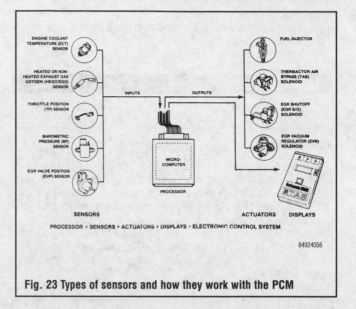

Fig. 23 Types of sensors and how they work with the PCM

inputs from several sensors, switches and relays on and around the engine.

➡ **PCM's for EEC-IV systems use a 60-pin connector. For the EEC-V PCM, a 104-pin connector is used.**

Based on combinations of these inputs, the PCM controls outputs to various devices concerned with engine operation and emissions. The engine control assembly relies on the signals to form a correct picture of current vehicle operation. If any of the input signals is incorrect, the PCM reacts to what ever picture is painted for it. For example, if the coolant temperature sensor is inaccurate and reads too low, the PCM may see a picture of the engine never warming up. Consequently, the engine settings will be maintained as if the engine were cold. Because so many inputs can affect one output, correct diagnostic procedures are essential on these systems.

The EEC system employs adaptive fuel logic. This process is used to compensate for normal wear and variability within the fuel system. Once the engine enters steady-state operation, the engine control assembly watches the oxygen sensor signal for a bias or tendency to run slightly rich or lean. If such a bias is detected, the adaptive logic corrects the fuel delivery to bring the air/fuel mixture towards a centered or 14.7:1 ratio. This compensating shift is stored in a non-volatile memory which is retained by battery power even with the ignition switched off. The correction factor is then available the next time the vehicle is operated.

The Powertrain Control Module (PCM) is usually located under the instrument panel or passenger's seat and is usually covered by a kick panel. A multi-pin connector links the PCM with all system components. The processor provides a continuous reference voltage to the B/MAP, EVP and TP sensors. EEC systems use a 5 volt reference signal. Different calibration information is used in different vehicle applications, such as California or Federal models. For this reason, careful identification of the engine, year, model and type of electronic control system is essential to ensure correct component replacement.

➡ **If the battery cable(s) is disconnected for longer than 5 minutes, the adaptive fuel factor will be lost. After repair it will be necessary to drive the truck at least 10 miles to allow the processor to relearn the correct factors. The driving period should include steady-throttle open road driving if possible. During the drive, the vehicle may exhibit driveability symptoms not noticed before. These symptoms should clear as the PCM computes the correction factor. The PCM will also store Code 19 indicating loss of power to the controller.**

Electronic Engine Control

♦ See Figure 23

The electronic engine control subsystem consists of the PCM and various sensors and actuators. The PCM reads inputs from engine sensors,

then outputs a voltage signal to various components (actuators) to control engine functions. The period of time that the injectors are energized ("ON" time or "pulse width") determines the amount of fuel delivered to each cylinder. The longer the pulse width, the richer the fuel mixture.

➡ **The operating reference voltage (Vref) between the PCM and its sensors and actuators is 5 volts. This allows these components to work during the crank operation even though the battery voltage drops.**

In order for the PCM to properly control engine operation, it must first receive current status reports on various operating conditions. The control unit constantly monitors crankshaft position, throttle plate position, engine coolant temperature, exhaust gas oxygen level, air intake volume and temperature, air conditioning (On/Off), spark knock and barometric pressure.

REMOVAL & INSTALLATION

♦ See Figure 24

The PCM is usually located in the left rear of the engine compartment, near the master cylinder.
1. Disconnect the negative battery cable.
2. Disconnect the module wiring leading to the unit.
3. Unscrew, then remove the control unit from the vehicle.

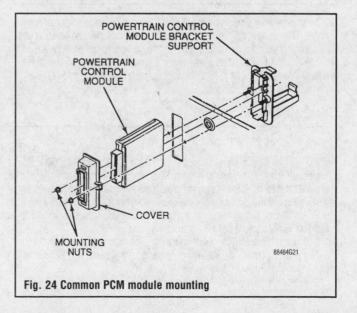

Fig. 24 Common PCM module mounting

To install:

4. Attach the module to the bracket, then screw in place.
5. Attach the wiring to the module.
6. Connect the negative battery cable.

Oxygen Sensor

OPERATION

▶ **See Figure 25**

An Oxygen Sensor (O2S) or heated Oxygen Sensor (HO2S) is used on all engines. The sensor is mounted in the right side exhaust manifold on some V8 engines, while other V8 engines use a sensor in both right and left manifolds. The sensor protrudes into the exhaust stream and monitors the oxygen content of the exhaust hoses. The difference between the oxygen content of the exhaust gases and that of the outside air generates a voltage signal to the PCM. The PCM monitors this voltage and, depending upon the value of the signal received, issues a command to adjust for a rich or a lean condition.

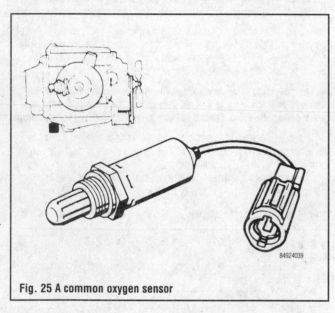

Fig. 25 A common oxygen sensor

TESTING

No attempt should ever be made to measure the voltage output of the sensor. The current drain of any conventional voltmeter would be such that it would permanently damage the sensor. No jumpers, test leads or any other electrical connections should ever be made to the sensor. Use these tools ONLY on the PCM side of the wiring harness connector AFTER disconnecting it from the sensor.

REMOVAL & INSTALLATION

▶ **See Figures 26, 27 and 28**

The oxygen sensor must be replaced every 30,000 miles (48,000 km). The sensor may be difficult to remove when the engine temperature is below 120°F (48°C). Excessive removal force may damage the threads in the exhaust manifold or pipe; follow the removal procedure carefully.

1. Locate the oxygen sensor. It protrudes from the exhaust manifold or pipe and looks somewhat like a spark plug.
2. Detach the electrical connector from the oxygen sensor.
3. Spray a commercial solvent onto the sensor threads and allow it to soak in for at least five minutes.
4. Carefully unscrew and remove the sensor.

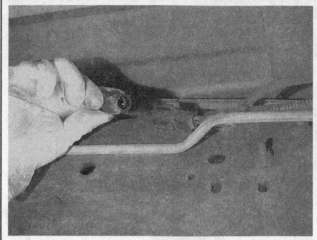

Fig. 26 Unplug the oxygen sensor electrical connector

1. Oxygen sensor

Fig. 27 Use a wrench to loosen the oxygen sensor and remove it from the exhaust pipe

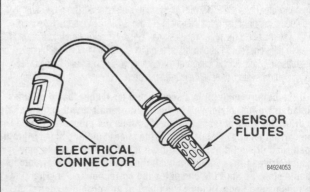

ELECTRICAL CONNECTOR

SENSOR FLUTES

Fig. 28 Do not allow contaminants such as grease, oil or anti-seize compound to contact the sensor prior to installation

To install:

5. Coat the new sensor's threads with anti-seize compound made for oxygen sensors. This is NOT a conventional anti-seize paste. The use of a regular compound may electrically insulate the sensor, rendering it inoperative. You must coat the threads with an electrically conductive anti-seize compound.

6. The proper installation torque is 30 ft. lbs. (42 Nm). Do NOT overtighten.

7. Reconnect the electrical connector. Be careful not to damage the connector.

Heated Oxygen Sensor

OPERATION

Heated oxygen sensors are located in the exhaust pipes below the exhaust manifolds. The sensors react with the oxygen in the exhaust gases and generates a voltage based on this reaction. A low voltage indicates too much oxygen or a lean condition, while a high voltage indicates not enough oxygen or a rich condition.

TESTING

OBD-I System

1. Disconnect the Oxygen Sensor (O_2S). Measure resistance between PWR and GND (heater) terminals of the sensor. If the reading is about 6 ohms at 68°F (20°C). the sensor's heater element is okay.

2. With the O_2S connected and engine running, measure voltage with DVOM between terminals HO2S and **SIG RTN** (GND) of the oxygen sensor connector. If the voltage readings are about equal to those in the table, the sensor is okay.

OBD-II System

✳✳ WARNING

Do not pierce the wires when testing this sensor; this can lead to wiring harness damage. Backprobe the connector to properly read the voltage of the HO2S.

1. Disconnect the HO2S.
2. Measure the resistance between PWR and GND terminals of the sensor. Resistance should be approximately 6 ohms at 68°F (20°C). If resistance is not within specification, the sensor's heater element is faulty.
3. With the HO2S connected and engine running, measure the voltage with a Digital Volt-Ohmmeter (DVOM) between terminals **HO2S** and **SIG RTN** (GND) of the oxygen sensor connector. Voltage should fluctuate between 0.01–1.1 volts. If voltage fluctuation is slow or voltage is not within specification, the sensor may be faulty.

REMOVAL & INSTALLATION

▶ **See Figure 29**

1. Disconnect the negative battery cable.
2. Raise and safely support the vehicle.
3. Disconnect the heated oxygen sensor from the engine control sensor wiring.

➥**If excessive force is needed to remove the sensors, lubricate the sensors with penetrating oil prior to removal.**

4. Remove the sensors from the Y pipe or left manifold with a sensor removal tool T94P-9472-A or equivalent.
To install:
5. Install the sensor in its correct location, tighten to 26–34 ft. lbs. (36–46 Nm).
6. Connect the sensor electrical wiring.

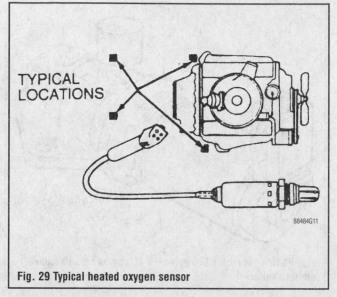

Fig. 29 Typical heated oxygen sensor

7. Lower the vehicle.
8. Connect the negative battery cable.

Idle Air Control (IAC) Valve

OPERATION

▶ **See Figures 30 and 31**

The Idle Air Control (IAC) valve controls the engine idle speed and dashpot functions. The valve is located on the throttle body. This valve allows air to bypass the throttle plate. The amount of air is determined by the Powertrain Control Module (PCM) and controlled by a duty cycle signal.

TESTING

OBD-I System

1. Make sure the ignition key is **OFF**.
2. Disconnect the air control valve.
3. Use an ohmmeter to measure the resistance between the terminals of the valve solenoid.

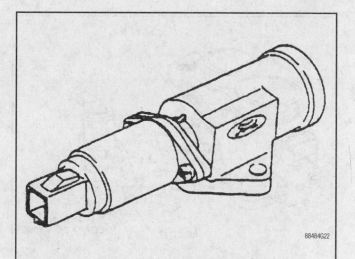

Fig. 30 Cleanable IAC valve—5.0L engine version shown, others similar

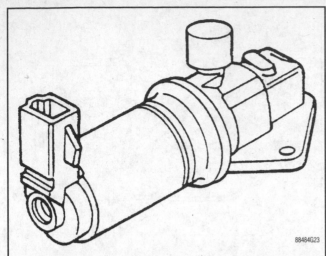

Fig. 31 Non-cleanable IAC valve—5.0L engine version shown, others similar

Fig. 33 Disengage the idle air control solenoid electrical connection

➡Due to the diode in the solenoid, place the ohmmeter positive lead on the VPWR pin and the negative lead on the ISC pin.

4. If the resistance is not 7–13 ohms, replace the air control valve.

OBD-II System

1. Turn the ignition switch to the **OFF** position.
2. Disconnect the wiring harness from the IAC valve .
3. Measure the resistance between the terminals of the valve.

➡Due to the diode in the solenoid, place the ohmmeter positive lead on the VPWR terminal and the negative lead on the ISC terminal.

4. Resistance should be 6–13 ohms.
5. If resistance is not within specification, the valve may be faulty.

REMOVAL & INSTALLATION

◆ See Figures 32, 33, 34 and 35

1. Disconnect the negative battery cable.
2. Disconnect the engine wiring to the IAC sensor.
3. Remove the two retaining screws for the valve.
4. Remove the IAC valve and discard of the old gasket.

Fig. 34 Loosen the idle control solenoid retaining screws

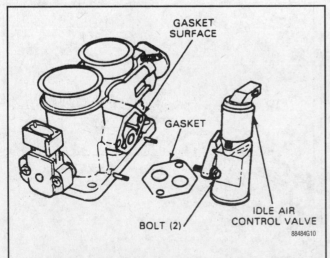

Fig. 32 Idle air control valve mounting—4.9L engine version shown, others similar

Fig. 35 Remove the idle air control solenoid from the throttle body

To install:

5. Clean the area of old gasket material.

6. Using a new gasket, attach the IAC valve to the engine. Tighten the retaining screws to 71–102 inch lbs. (8–12 Nm).

7. Connect the IAC valve wiring to the unit.

8. Connect the negative battery cable.

Engine Coolant Temperature (ECT) Sensor

OPERATION

▶ **See Figure 36**

The ECT sensor is located either in the heater supply tube at the rear of the engine, or in the lower intake manifold. The ECT sensor is a thermistor (changes resistance as temperature changes). The sensor detects the temperature of engine coolant and provides a corresponding signal to the PCM. From this signal, the PCM will modify the air/fuel ratio (mixture), idle speed, spark advance, EGR and canister purge control. When the engine coolant is cold, the ECT sensor signal causes the PCM to provide enrichment to the air/fuel ratio for good cold drive-away; as engine coolant warms up, the voltage will drop.

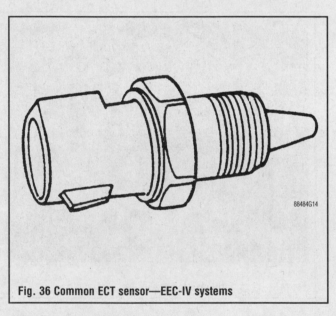

Fig. 36 Common ECT sensor—EEC-IV systems

TESTING

▶ **See Figures 37, 38, 39 and 40**

In-Vehicle

1. Disconnect the temperature sensor.

2. Connect an ohmmeter between the sensor terminals and set the ohmmeter scale on 200,000 ohms.

3. Measure the resistance with the engine off and cool and with the engine running and warmed up. Compare the resistance values obtained with the chart.

4. Replace the sensor if the readings are incorrect.

Out of Vehicle

1. Remove the sensor from the vehicle.

2. Immerse the tip of the sensor in container of water.

3. Connect a digital ohmmeter to the two terminals of the sensor.

4. Using a calibrated thermometer, compare the resistance of the sensor to the temperature of the water. Refer to the engine coolant sensor temperature vs. resistance illustration.

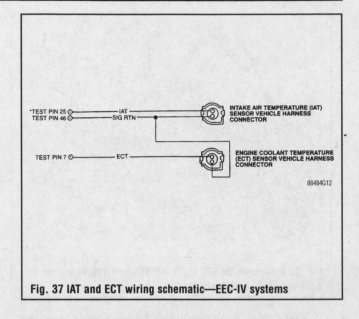

Fig. 37 IAT and ECT wiring schematic—EEC-IV systems

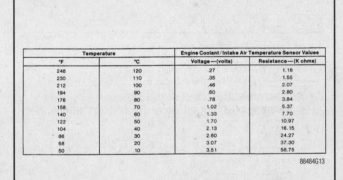

Temperature		Engine Coolant/Intake Air Temperature Sensor Values	
°F	°C	Voltage —(volts)	Resistance —(K ohms)
248	120	.27	1.18
230	110	.35	1.55
212	100	.46	2.07
194	90	.60	2.80
176	80	.78	3.84
158	70	1.02	5.37
140	60	1.33	7.70
122	50	1.70	10.97
104	40	2.13	16.15
86	30	2.60	24.27
68	20	3.07	37.30
50	10	3.51	58.75

Fig. 38 IAT and ECT temperature vs. resistance chart—EEC-IV and EEC-V systems

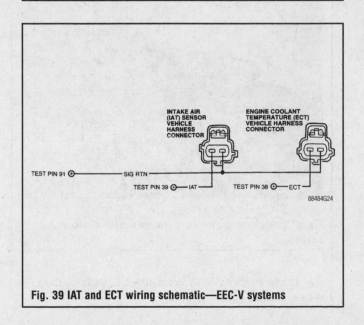

Fig. 39 IAT and ECT wiring schematic—EEC-V systems

Fig. 40 Submerge the end of the temperature sensor in cold or hot water and check resistance

5. Repeat the test at two other temperature points, heating or cooling the water as necessary.
6. If the sensor does not meet specification, it must be replaced.

REMOVAL & INSTALLATION

▶ **See Figures 41, 42 and 43**

1. Drain the engine cooling system slightly.
2. Disconnect the negative battery cable.
3. Detach the wiring connection from the sensor.
4. Unfasten its retainers and remove the coolant temperature sensor.
5. Clean the sensor area of any debris.

To install:

6. Install a new sensor. Tighten the retainers to 6–14 ft. lbs. (8–19 Nm).
7. Attach the sensor wiring to the unit.
8. Connect the negative battery cable.
9. Fill the engine cooling system with a 50/50 coolant water mixture.
10. Start the engine and top off the cooling system.

1. Coolant temperature sensor

Fig. 41 Unplug the coolant temperature sensor electrical connection

Fig. 42 Use a wrench to unfasten the coolant temperature sensor . . .

Fig. 43 . . . and remove the sensor from the engine

Intake Air Temperature (IAT) Sensor

OPERATION

The Intake Air Temperature (IAT) sensor changes the resistance in response to the intake air temperature. The sensor resistance decreases as the surrounding air temperature increases. This provides a signal to the PCM indicating the temperature of the incoming air intake.

TESTING

▶ **See Figure 38**

With ignition **OFF**, disconnect the IAT sensor. Measure the resistance across the sensor connector terminals. If the reading for a given temperature is about that shown in the table, the IAT sensor is okay.

REMOVAL & INSTALLATION

▶ **See Figure 44**

1. Disconnect the negative battery cable.
2. Disconnect the wiring to the IAT.
3. Remove the sensor from the intake manifold (MFI engines) or air cleaner/tube (SFI engines).

To install:

4. Clean the sensor area. Install the sensor into the intake manifold and tighten to 12–15 ft. lbs. (16–24 Nm) on MFI engines. Fasten the twist-lock part on SFI engines.
5. Attach the wiring to the unit.
6. Connect the negative battery cable.

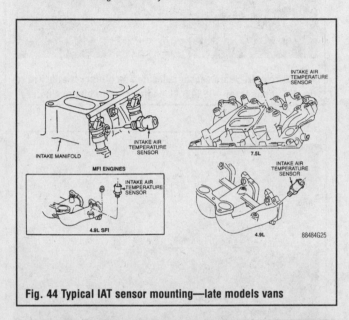

Fig. 44 Typical IAT sensor mounting—late models vans

Mass Air Flow (MAF) Sensor

OPERATION

The Mass Air Flow (MAF) sensor directly measures the mass of the air flowing into the engine. The sensor output is an analog signal ranging from about 0.5–5.0 volts. The signal is used by the PCM to calculate the injector pulse width. The sensing element is a thin platinum wire wound on a ceramic bobbin and coated with glass. This "hot wire" is maintained at 200°C above the ambient temperature as measured by a constant "cold wire". The MAF sensor is located in the outlet side of the air cleaner lid assembly.

TESTING

OBD-I System

1. Make sure the ignition key is **OFF**.
2. Connect Breakout Box T83L–50–EEC-IV or equivalent, to the PCM harness and connect the PCM.
3. Start the engine and let it idle.
4. Use a voltmeter to measure the voltage between test pin **50** of the Breakout Box and the battery negative post.
5. Replace the MAF sensor if the voltage is not 0.36–1.50 volts.

OBD-II System

▶ **See Figure 45**

1. Using a multimeter, check for voltage by backprobing the MAF sensor connector.

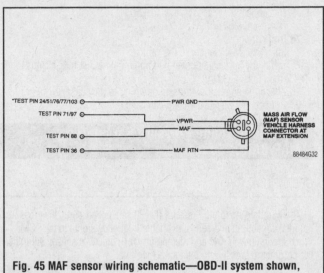

Fig. 45 MAF sensor wiring schematic—OBD-II system shown, others similar

2. With the engine running at idle, verify there is at least 10.5 volts between the VPWR and PWR GND terminals of the MAF sensor connector. If voltage is not within specification, check power and ground circuits and repair as necessary.
3. Check voltage between the MAF and MAF RTN terminals. Voltage should be approximately 0.34–1.96 volts. If voltage is not within specification, the sensor may be faulty.

REMOVAL & INSTALLATION

▶ **See Figure 46**

✲✲ CAUTION

The mass air flow sensor hot wire sensing element and housing are calibrated as a unit and must be serviced as a complete assembly. Do not damage the sensing element or possible failure of the sensor may occur.

1. Disconnect the negative battery cable.
2. Disconnect the air tube at the sensor.
3. Disconnect the engine control sensor wiring from the MAF sensor.

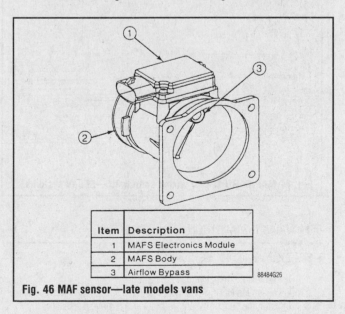

Item	Description
1	MAFS Electronics Module
2	MAFS Body
3	Airflow Bypass

Fig. 46 MAF sensor—late models vans

4. Disconnect the mass air flow sensor.
5. Remove the gasket.
To install:
6. Install the MAF sensor to the vehicle.
7. Install the air cleaner cover and tighten the outlet tube clamps to 12–22 inch lbs. (1–3 Nm).
8. Attach the engine control sensor wiring to the sensor.
9. Connect the negative battery cable.

Manifold Absolute Pressure/Barometric (MAP/BARO) Sensor

OPERATION

The Manifold Absolute Pressure (MAP) sensor measures the pressure in the intake manifold and sends a variable frequency signal to the PCM. When the ignition is **ON** and the engine **OFF**, the MAP sensor will indicate the barometric pressure in the intake manifold.

The barometric sensor signals the PCM of changes in atmospheric pressure and density to regulate calculated air flow into the engine. The MAP sensor monitors and signals the PCM of changes in intake manifold pressure which result from engine load, speed and atmospheric pressure changes.

TESTING

▶ **See Figure 47**

1. Connect jumper wires from the sensor connector to the wiring harness. This permits the engine to operate normally while you check the sensor.
2. Connect a Digital Volt Ohm Meter (DVOM) between the VREF and SIG RTN terminals of the MAP sensor harness connector. The voltage should be between 4–6 volts.
3. If the voltage is not within specification, check the VREF wiring and circuit.
4. Probe the SIGRTN and MAP/SIG RTN terminals with the DVOM.
5. Unplug the sensor vacuum hose and attach a vacuum testing pump to the sensor.
6. With the ignition **ON** and engine **OFF**, apply varying amounts of vacuum to the sensor and use the DVOM to measure voltage across terminals.
7. If the DVOM voltage reading varies with the varying vacuum, the sensor is functioning properly.

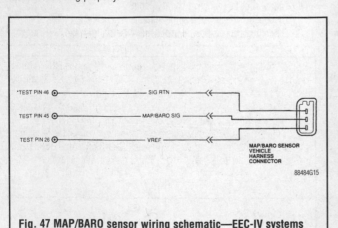

Fig. 47 MAP/BARO sensor wiring schematic—EEC-IV systems

REMOVAL & INSTALLATION

▶ **See Figures 48, 49, 50 and 51**

1. Disconnect the negative battery cable.
2. Disengage the electrical connector and the vacuum line from the sensor.
3. Unfasten the sensor mounting bolts and remove the sensor.

Fig. 48 The MAP/Baro sensor is located on a bracket attached to the A/C compressor—1989 5.0L engine shown, others similar

Fig. 49 Unplug the hoses and electrical connector from the MAP/Baro sensor

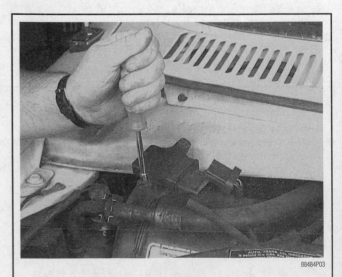

Fig. 50 Loosen the sensor retaining bolts . . .

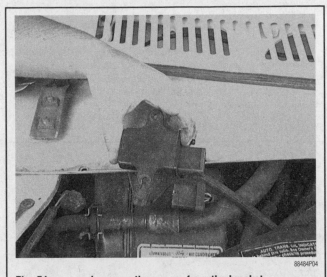

Fig. 51 . . . and remove the sensor from the bracket

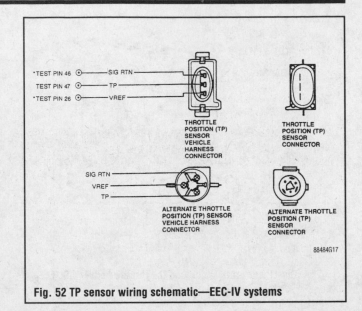

Fig. 52 TP sensor wiring schematic—EEC-IV systems

To install:
4. Install the sensor with the mounting bolts and tighten.
5. Attach the electrical wiring lead to the sensor.
6. Attach the vacuum line to the sensor.
7. Connect the negative battery cable.

Throttle Position (TP) Sensor

OPERATION

The Throttle Position (TP) sensor is a potentiometer that provides a signal to the PCM that is directly proportional to the throttle plate position. The TP sensor is mounted on the side of the throttle body and is connected to the throttle plate shaft.

The TP senses the throttle movement and position and transmits an appropriate electrical signal to the PCM. These signals are used by the PCM to adjust the air/fuel mixture, spark timing and EGR operation according to engine load at idle, part throttle, or full throttle. The TP sensor has 2 versions, an adjustable and a non-adjustable; the difference being elongated mounting holes that allow the rotary sensor to be turned slightly to adjust the output voltage. The rotary TP sensor with round mounting holes are not adjustable.

TESTING

♦ See Figures 52 and 53

1. Disconnect the negative battery cable.
2. Disconnect the wiring harness from the sensor.
3. Check resistance between terminals TP and VREF, on the TP sensor.

➡Do not measure the wiring harness connector terminals, rather the terminals on the sensor itself.

4. Slowly rotate the throttle shaft and monitor the ohmmeter for a continuous, steady change in resistance. Any sudden jumps, or irregularities (such as jumping back and forth) in resistance indicates a malfunctioning sensor.
5. Reconnect the negative battery cable.

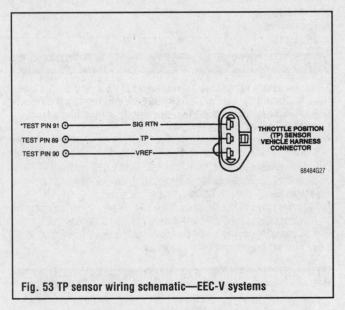

Fig. 53 TP sensor wiring schematic—EEC-V systems

6. Check sensor signal voltage between the TP and SIG RTN terminals. Turn the ignition switch **ON** and using the DVOM on voltmeter function, measure the voltage. The specification is 0.17–0.40 volts.
7. If the voltage is outside the standard value or if it does not change smoothly, inspect the circuit wiring and/or replace the TP sensor.
8. With ignition **OFF**, disconnect the TP sensor connector. Measure voltage between sensor connector terminals **SIG RTN** and **VREF**. The voltage reading should be 4.0–6.0 volts. If not, replace the sensor.

REMOVAL & INSTALLATION

♦ See Figure 54

1. Disconnect the TP sensor wiring harness.
2. On 5.0L and 5.8L engines, it may be necessary to remove the throttle body. On all other engines, proceed to the next step.
3. Disconnect the wiring from the sensor.

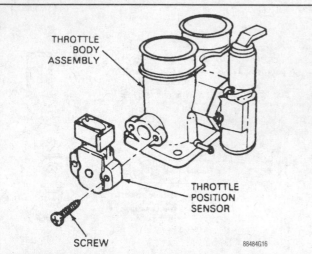

Fig. 54 The TP sensor is located on the throttle body—4.9L EEC-IV system, others similar

4. Matchmark the TP sensor and throttle body. Remove the 2 retaining screws and the sensor.
To install:

※ WARNING

Slide the rotary tangs into position over the throttle shaft blade, then rotate the TP sensor CLOCKWISE only to the installed position. Failure to follow this step may result in high idle speeds for 5.0L and 5.8L engines.

5. On 5.0L and 5.8L engines, position the TP sensor so that the pigtail points toward the IAC valve.
6. Secure the TP sensor to the throttle body with the retaining screws. Tighten to 18–27 inch lbs. (2–3 Nm) on 4.9L engines or 11–16 inch lbs. (1.2–1.8 Nm) on 5.0L/5.8L engines.
7. If applicable, install the throttle body.
8. Connect the wiring.
9. Connect the negative battery cable.

Camshaft Position (CMP) Sensor

The Camshaft Position (CMP) sensor is found on late model diesel engines. The sensor is a Hall effect switch that generates a digital frequency while windows in a target wheel pass through its magnetic field, allowing the engine to detect engine speed and position. Refer to the component location illustration in this section for the sensor location.

TESTING

1. Turn the ignition key **ON** but do not start the engine.
2. Using a high impedance Digital Volt Ohmmeter (DVOM), backprobe the CMP sensor's light blue wire with the negative lead and the dark green wire with the positive lead.
3. Place the correct size socket on the crankshaft damper bolt, then use a breaker bar to turn the engine SLOWLY and observe the voltage reading.
4. The voltage should fluctuate between 0 and 5 volts.
5. If the voltage does not fluctuate, backprobe the brown wire with a white stripe with the positive lead of the DVOM and connect the negative lead to a good known ground. If the voltage is not 5 volts, check the wire for damage.
6. Backprobe the brown wire with a white stripe with the positive lead of the DVOM and connect the negative lead to the light blue wire. If the voltage is not 5 volts, check the light blue wire for damage.
7. If 5 volts is present at both the light blue and brown with white striped wires, the sensor may be defective.

REMOVAL & INSTALLATION

1. Disconnect the camshaft position sensor wiring.
2. Remove the bolt, then the camshaft position sensor.
To install:
3. Install the CMP sensor and bolt in place.
4. Engage the wiring connector.

Knock Sensor (KS)

OPERATION

◆ See Figure 55

This sensor is used on some 4.9L engines. The KS detects engine vibrations caused by preignition or detonation and provides information to the PCM, which then retards the timing to eliminate detonation.

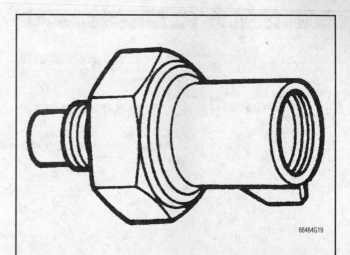

Fig. 55 The knock sensor detects engine vibration such as preignition; such information is used by the PCM to adjust timing

TESTING

◆ See Figure 56

1. With ignition **ON** and engine **OFF**, measure voltage between KS connector terminals. If voltage reading is 2.4–2.6V, the circuit between the ECM and KS is okay.
2. With engine running at idle and 3000 rpm, measure voltage using a DVOM on the AC setting between the KS terminals. If the AC voltage reading increases as the rpm increases, the sensor is okay.

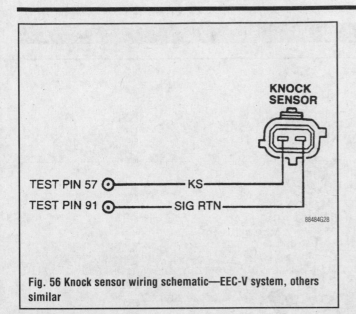

Fig. 56 Knock sensor wiring schematic—EEC-V system, others similar

REMOVAL & INSTALLATION

1. Disconnect the negative battery cable.
2. Disconnect the wiring from the sensor.
3. Remove the sensor from the cylinder block.

To install:

4. Attach the KS to the cylinder block.
5. Attach the electrical connector to the sensor.
6. Connect the negative battery cable.

EGR Valve Position (EVP) Sensor

OPERATION

The Exhaust Gas Recirculation (EGR) Valve Position (EVP) system uses an electronic EGR valve to control the flow of exhaust gases. The Engine Control Module (ECM) monitors the flow by means of an EVP sensor and regulates the electronic EGR valve accordingly. The valve is operated by a vacuum signal from the EGR Vacuum Regulator (EVR) solenoid which actuates the valve diaphragm.

As the supply vacuum overcomes the spring load, the diaphragm is actuated. This lifts the pintle off its seat and allows exhaust gases to flow. The amount of flow is proportional to the pintle position. The EVP sensor, mounted on the valve, sends an electronic signal representing pintle position to the ECM.

TESTING

▶ **See Figure 57**

1. Disconnect the EVP sensor connector. With the ignition **ON** and the engine **OFF**, measure the voltage between **VREF** and **SIG RTN** terminals of EVP sensor harness connector. If the voltage is 4.0–6.0V, the power circuits to the sensor are okay.
2. Reconnect the EVP sensor. With the ignition **ON** and the engine **OFF**, measure the voltage between EVP sensor terminals EVP and **SIG RTN**. If the voltage reading is 0.67V or less, the sensor is okay.

REMOVAL & INSTALLATION

1. Disconnect the negative battery cable.
2. Disconnect the wiring from the sensor.
3. Remove the sensor mounting nuts and remove the sensor from the EGR valve.

To install:

4. Attach the sensor to the EGR valve and tighten the mounting nuts.
5. Connect the sensor electrical lead to the sensor.
6. Connect the negative battery cable.

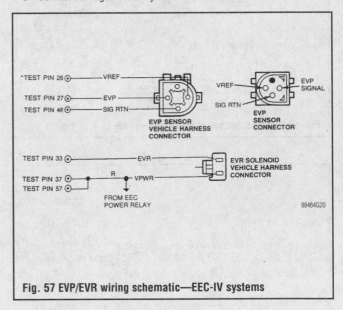

Fig. 57 EVP/EVR wiring schematic—EEC-IV systems

COMPONENT LOCATIONS

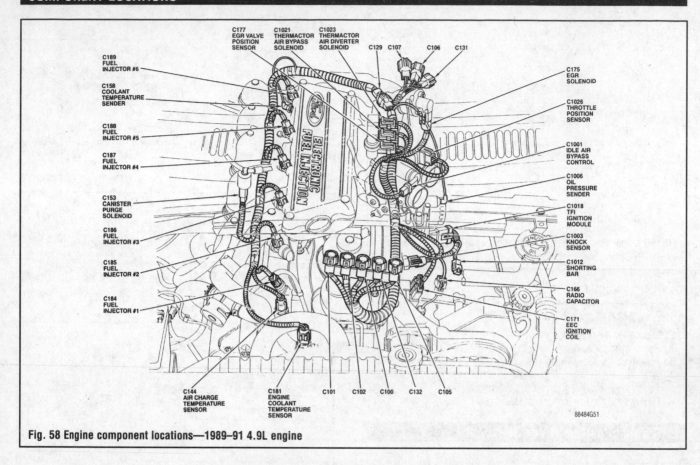

Fig. 58 Engine component locations—1989–91 4.9L engine

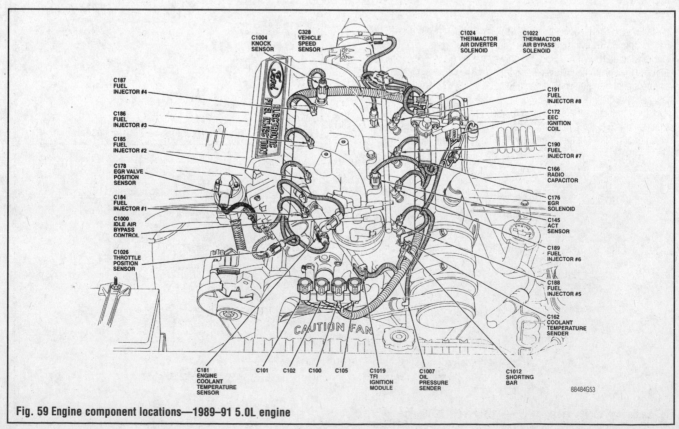

Fig. 59 Engine component locations—1989–91 5.0L engine

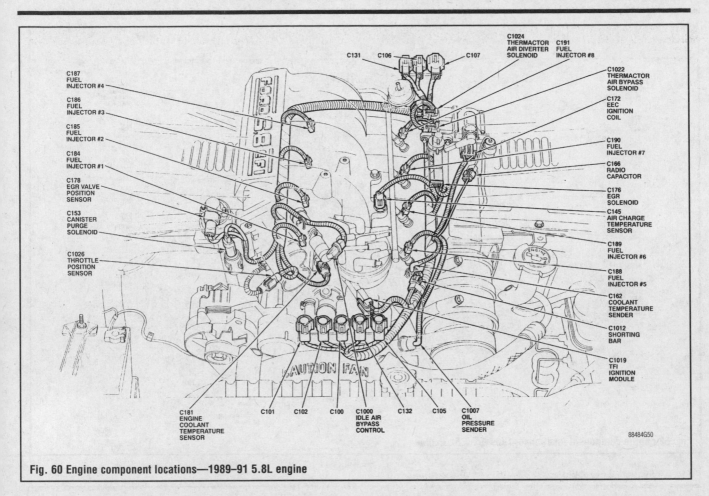

Fig. 60 Engine component locations—1989-91 5.8L engine

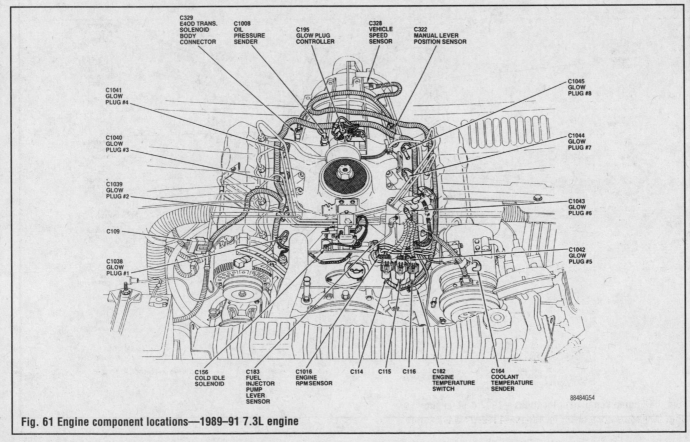

Fig. 61 Engine component locations—1989-91 7.3L engine

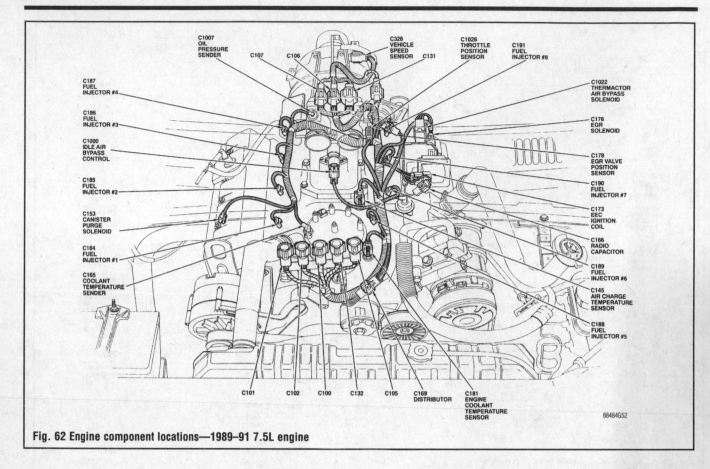

Fig. 62 Engine component locations—1989–91 7.5L engine

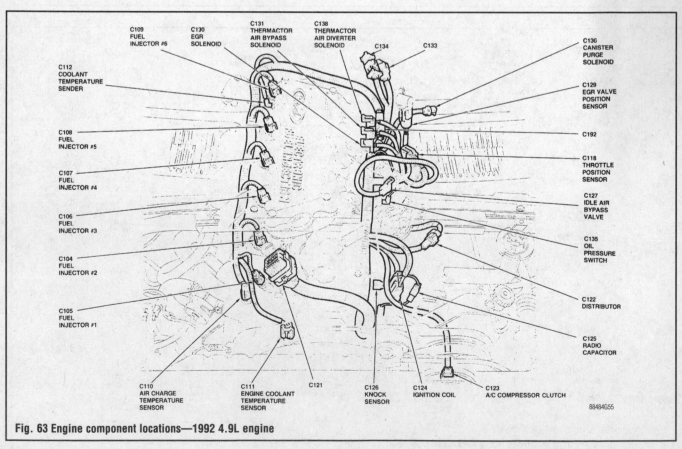

Fig. 63 Engine component locations—1992 4.9L engine

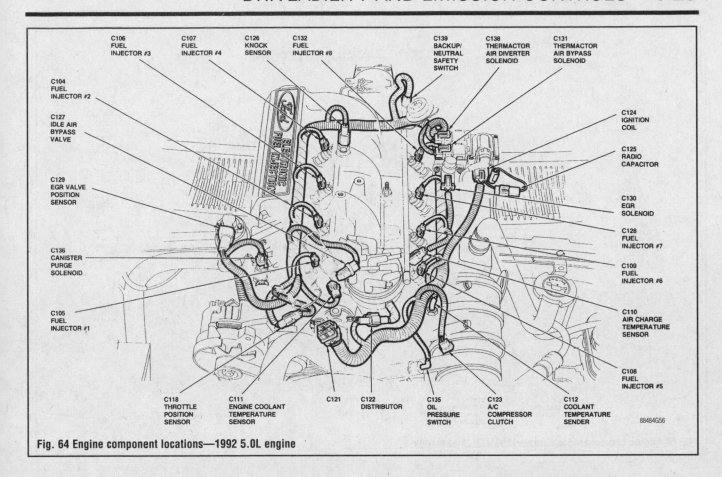

Fig. 64 Engine component locations—1992 5.0L engine

C106 FUEL INJECTOR #3
C107 FUEL INJECTOR #4
C126 KNOCK SENSOR
C132 FUEL INJECTOR #8
C139 BACKUP/NEUTRAL SAFETY SWITCH
C138 THERMACTOR AIR DIVERTER SOLENOID
C131 THERMACTOR AIR BYPASS SOLENOID
C104 FUEL INJECTOR #2
C127 IDLE AIR BYPASS VALVE
C129 EGR VALVE POSITION SENSOR
C136 CANISTER PURGE SOLENOID
C105 FUEL INJECTOR #1
C124 IGNITION COIL
C125 RADIO CAPACITOR
C130 EGR SOLENOID
C128 FUEL INJECTOR #7
C109 FUEL INJECTOR #6
C110 AIR CHARGE TEMPERATURE SENSOR
C108 FUEL INJECTOR #5
C118 THROTTLE POSITION SENSOR
C111 ENGINE COOLANT TEMPERATURE SENSOR
C121
C122 DISTRIBUTOR
C135 OIL PRESSURE SWITCH
C123 A/C COMPRESSOR CLUTCH
C112 COOLANT TEMPERATURE SENDER
88484G56

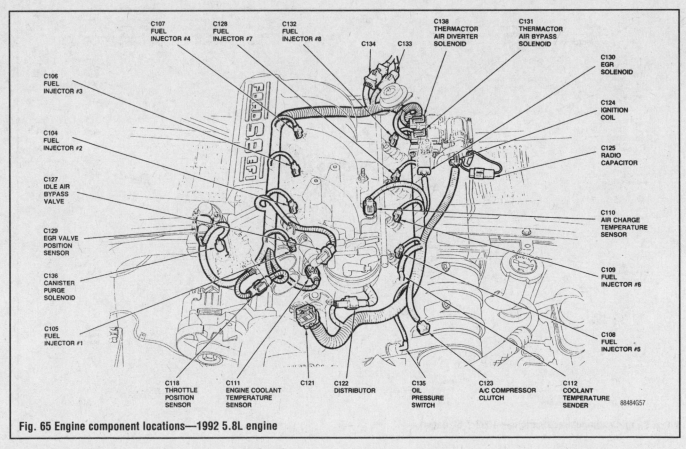

Fig. 65 Engine component locations—1992 5.8L engine

C107 FUEL INJECTOR #4
C128 FUEL INJECTOR #7
C132 FUEL INJECTOR #8
C134 C133
C138 THERMACTOR AIR DIVERTER SOLENOID
C131 THERMACTOR AIR BYPASS SOLENOID
C106 FUEL INJECTOR #3
C104 FUEL INJECTOR #2
C127 IDLE AIR BYPASS VALVE
C129 EGR VALVE POSITION SENSOR
C136 CANISTER PURGE SOLENOID
C105 FUEL INJECTOR #1
C130 EGR SOLENOID
C124 IGNITION COIL
C125 RADIO CAPACITOR
C110 AIR CHARGE TEMPERATURE SENSOR
C109 FUEL INJECTOR #6
C108 FUEL INJECTOR #5
C118 THROTTLE POSITION SENSOR
C111 ENGINE COOLANT TEMPERATURE SENSOR
C121
C122 DISTRIBUTOR
C135 OIL PRESSURE SWITCH
C123 A/C COMPRESSOR CLUTCH
C112 COOLANT TEMPERATURE SENDER
88484G57

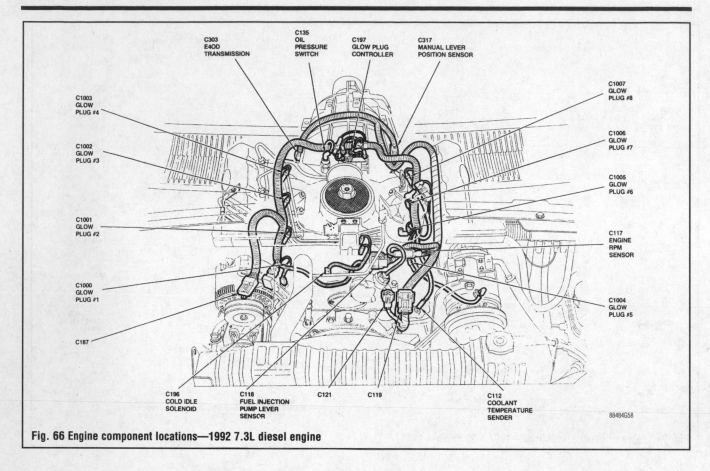

Fig. 66 Engine component locations—1992 7.3L diesel engine

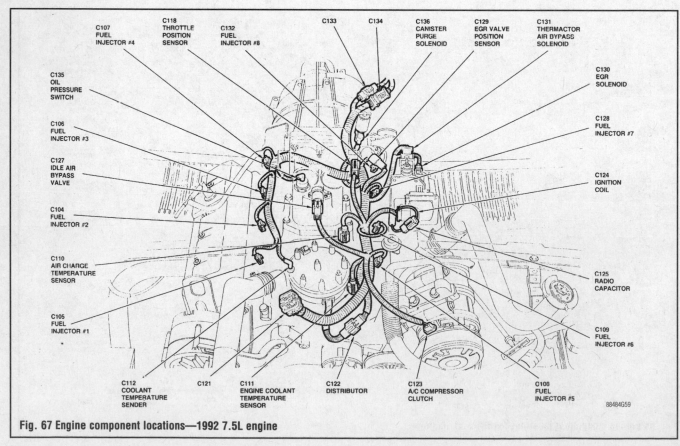

Fig. 67 Engine component locations—1992 7.5L engine

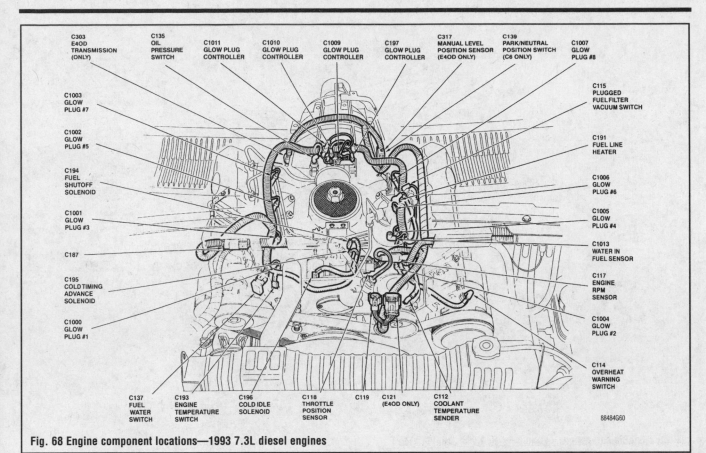

C303
E4OD
TRANSMISSION
(ONLY)

C135
OIL
PRESSURE
SWITCH

C1011
GLOW PLUG
CONTROLLER

C1010
GLOW PLUG
CONTROLLER

C1009
GLOW PLUG
CONTROLLER

C197
GLOW PLUG
CONTROLLER

C317
MANUAL LEVEL
POSITION SENSOR
(E4OD ONLY)

C139
PARK/NEUTRAL
POSITION SWITCH
(C6 ONLY)

C1007
GLOW
PLUG #8

C1003
GLOW
PLUG #7

C1002
GLOW
PLUG #5

C194
FUEL
SHUTOFF
SOLENOID

C1001
GLOW
PLUG #3

C187

C195
COLD TIMING
ADVANCE
SOLENOID

C1000
GLOW
PLUG #1

C115
PLUGGED
FUEL FILTER
VACUUM SWITCH

C191
FUEL LINE
HEATER

C1006
GLOW
PLUG #6

C1005
GLOW
PLUG #4

C1013
WATER IN
FUEL SENSOR

C117
ENGINE
RPM
SENSOR

C1004
GLOW
PLUG #2

C114
OVERHEAT
WARNING
SWITCH

C137
FUEL
WATER
SWITCH

C193
ENGINE
TEMPERATURE
SWITCH

C196
COLD IDLE
SOLENOID

C118
THROTTLE
POSITION
SENSOR

C119

C121
(E4OD ONLY)

C112
COOLANT
TEMPERATURE
SENDER

88484G60

Fig. 68 Engine component locations—1993 7.3L diesel engines

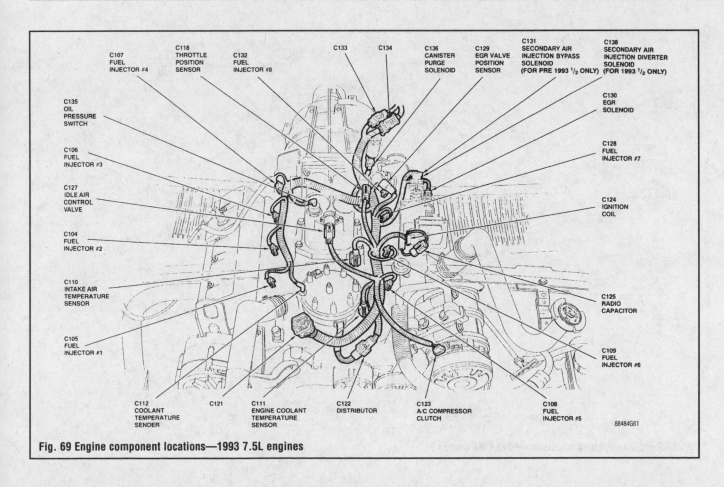

C107
FUEL
INJECTOR #4

C118
THROTTLE
POSITION
SENSOR

C132
FUEL
INJECTOR #8

C133

C134

C136
CANISTER
PURGE
SOLENOID

C129
EGR VALVE
POSITION
SENSOR

C131
SECONDARY AIR
INJECTION BYPASS
SOLENOID
(FOR PRE 1993 1/2 ONLY)

C138
SECONDARY AIR
INJECTION DIVERTER
SOLENOID
(FOR 1993 1/2 ONLY)

C135
OIL
PRESSURE
SWITCH

C106
FUEL
INJECTOR #3

C127
IDLE AIR
CONTROL
VALVE

C104
FUEL
INJECTOR #2

C110
INTAKE AIR
TEMPERATURE
SENSOR

C105
FUEL
INJECTOR #1

C130
EGR
SOLENOID

C128
FUEL
INJECTOR #7

C124
IGNITION
COIL

C125
RADIO
CAPACITOR

C109
FUEL
INJECTOR #6

C112
COOLANT
TEMPERATURE
SENDER

C121

C111
ENGINE COOLANT
TEMPERATURE
SENSOR

C122
DISTRIBUTOR

C123
A/C COMPRESSOR
CLUTCH

C108
FUEL
INJECTOR #5

88484G61

Fig. 69 Engine component locations—1993 7.5L engines

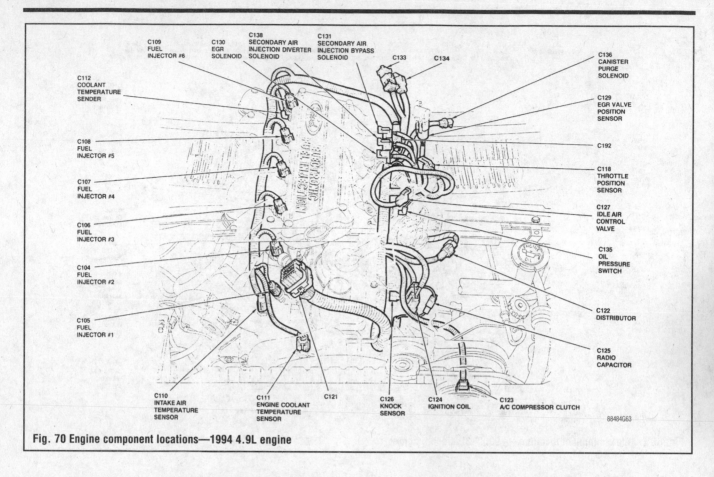

Fig. 70 Engine component locations—1994 4.9L engine

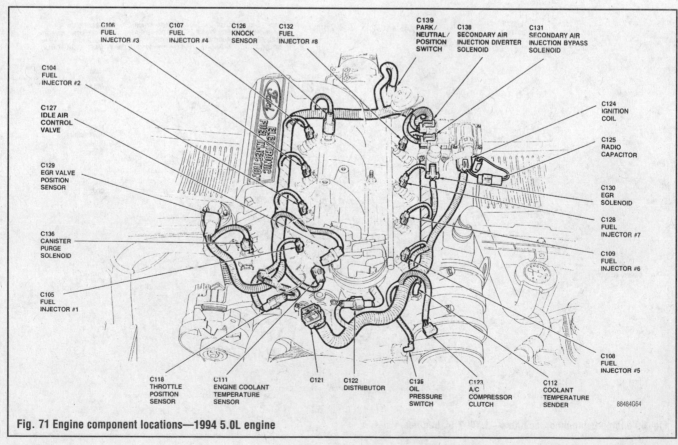

Fig. 71 Engine component locations—1994 5.0L engine

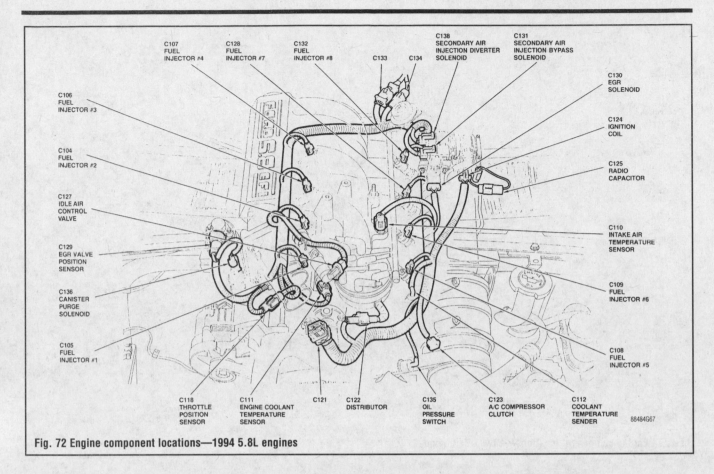

C107 FUEL INJECTOR #4
C128 FUEL INJECTOR #7
C132 FUEL INJECTOR #8
C133
C134
C138 SECONDARY AIR INJECTION DIVERTER SOLENOID
C131 SECONDARY AIR INJECTION BYPASS SOLENOID
C130 EGR SOLENOID
C106 FUEL INJECTOR #3
C124 IGNITION COIL
C104 FUEL INJECTOR #2
C125 RADIO CAPACITOR
C127 IDLE AIR CONTROL VALVE
C129 EGR VALVE POSITION SENSOR
C110 INTAKE AIR TEMPERATURE SENSOR
C136 CANISTER PURGE SOLENOID
C109 FUEL INJECTOR #6
C105 FUEL INJECTOR #1
C108 FUEL INJECTOR #5
C118 THROTTLE POSITION SENSOR
C111 ENGINE COOLANT TEMPERATURE SENSOR
C121
C122 DISTRIBUTOR
C135 OIL PRESSURE SWITCH
C123 A/C COMPRESSOR CLUTCH
C112 COOLANT TEMPERATURE SENDER
88484G67

Fig. 72 Engine component locations—1994 5.8L engines

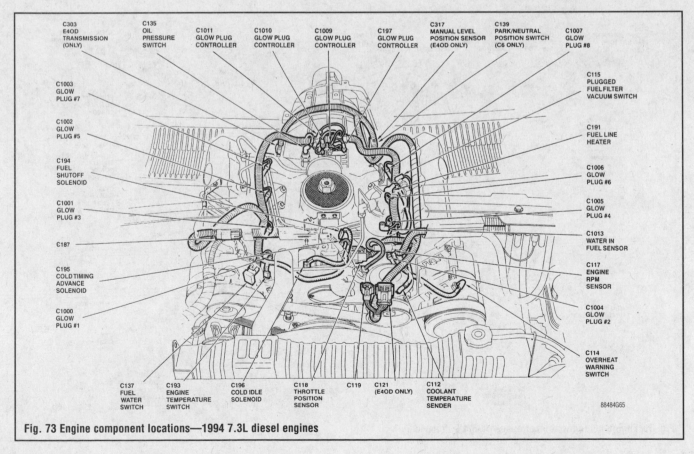

C303 E4OD TRANSMISSION (ONLY)
C135 OIL PRESSURE SWITCH
C1011 GLOW PLUG CONTROLLER
C1010 GLOW PLUG CONTROLLER
C1009 GLOW PLUG CONTROLLER
C197 GLOW PLUG CONTROLLER
C317 MANUAL LEVEL POSITION SENSOR (E4OD ONLY)
C139 PARK/NEUTRAL POSITION SWITCH (C6 ONLY)
C1007 GLOW PLUG #8
C1003 GLOW PLUG #7
C115 PLUGGED FUEL FILTER VACUUM SWITCH
C1002 GLOW PLUG #5
C191 FUEL LINE HEATER
C194 FUEL SHUTOFF SOLENOID
C1006 GLOW PLUG #6
C1001 GLOW PLUG #3
C1005 GLOW PLUG #4
C187
C1013 WATER IN FUEL SENSOR
C195 COLD TIMING ADVANCE SOLENOID
C117 ENGINE RPM SENSOR
C1000 GLOW PLUG #1
C1004 GLOW PLUG #2
C114 OVERHEAT WARNING SWITCH
C137 FUEL WATER SWITCH
C193 ENGINE TEMPERATURE SWITCH
C196 COLD IDLE SOLENOID
C118 THROTTLE POSITION SENSOR
C119
C121 (E4OD ONLY)
C112 COOLANT TEMPERATURE SENDER
88484G65

Fig. 73 Engine component locations—1994 7.3L diesel engines

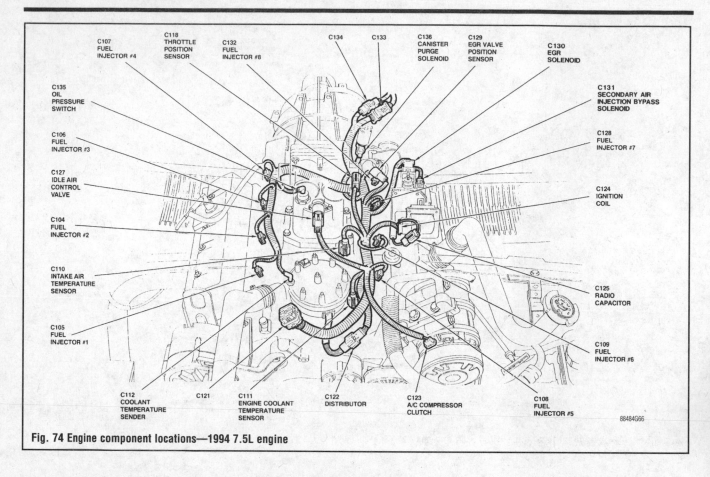

Fig. 74 Engine component locations—1994 7.5L engine

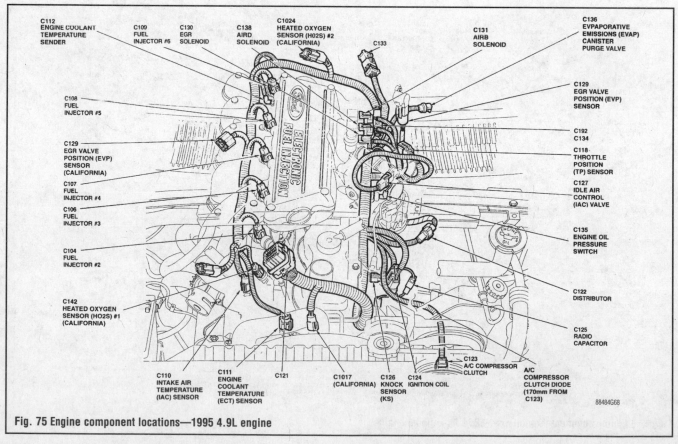

Fig. 75 Engine component locations—1995 4.9L engine

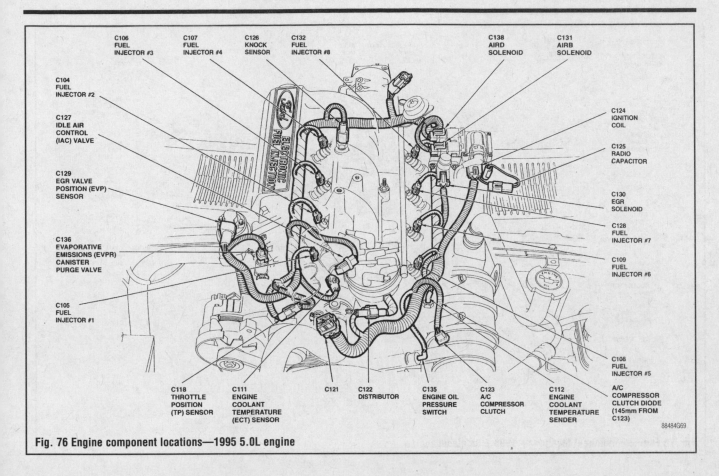

Fig. 76 Engine component locations—1995 5.0L engine

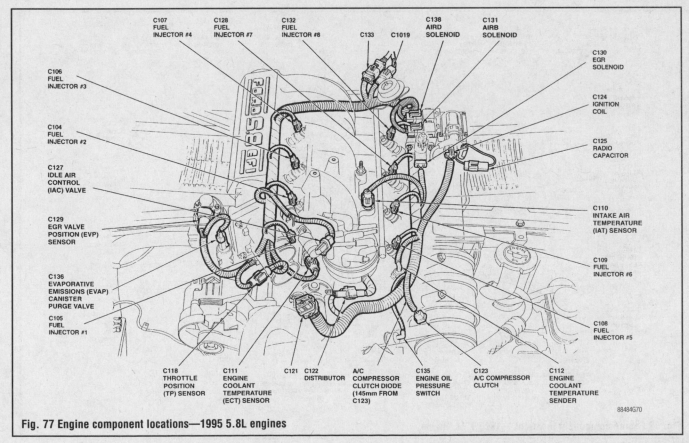

Fig. 77 Engine component locations—1995 5.8L engines

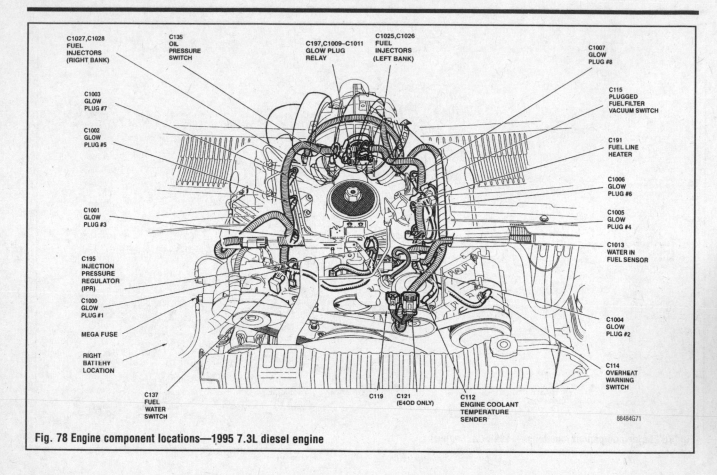

Fig. 78 Engine component locations—1995 7.3L diesel engine

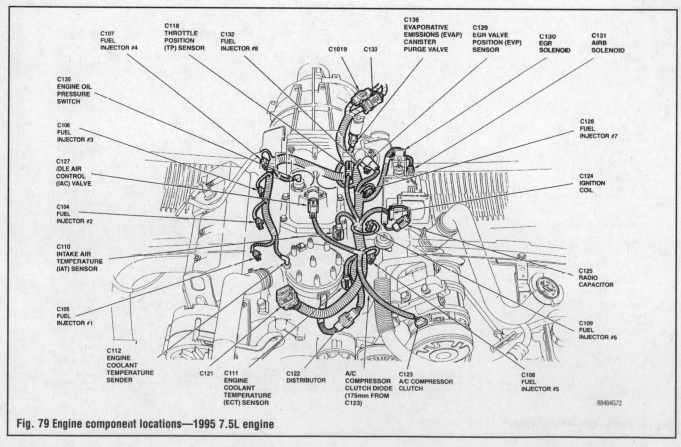

Fig. 79 Engine component locations—1995 7.5L engine

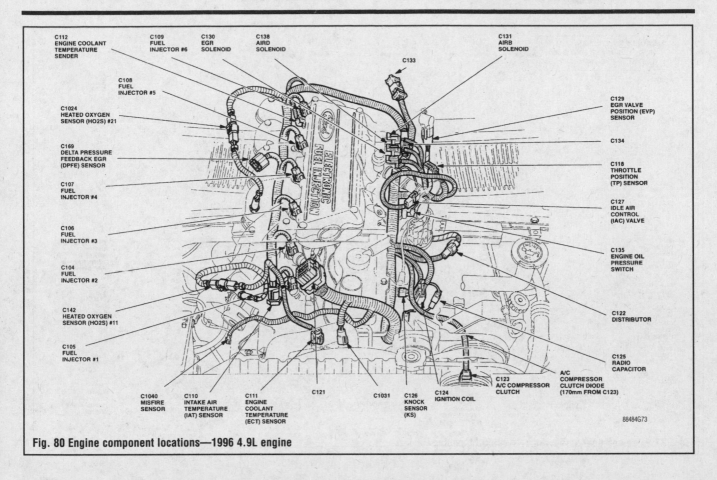

Fig. 80 Engine component locations—1996 4.9L engine

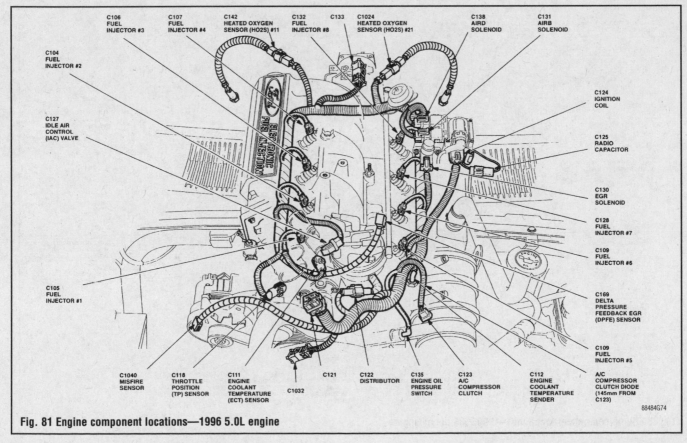

Fig. 81 Engine component locations—1996 5.0L engine

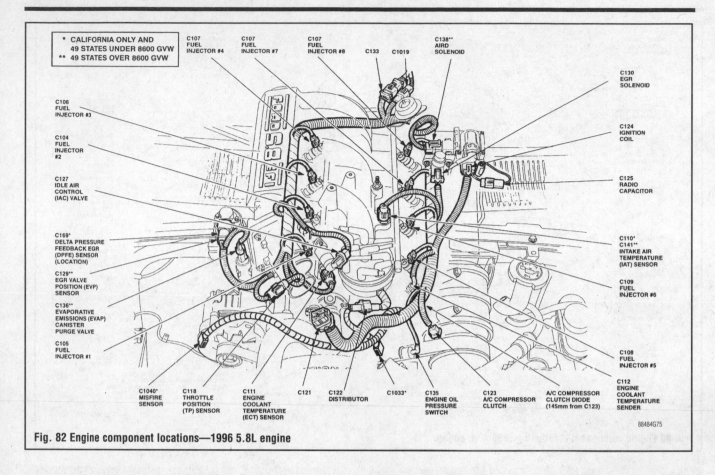

Fig. 82 Engine component locations—1996 5.8L engine

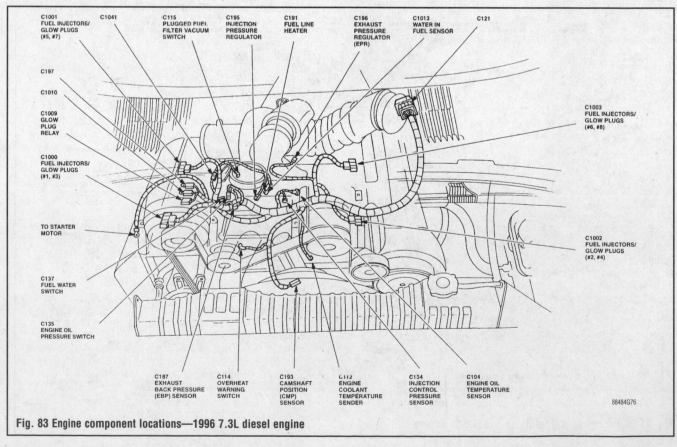

Fig. 83 Engine component locations—1996 7.3L diesel engine

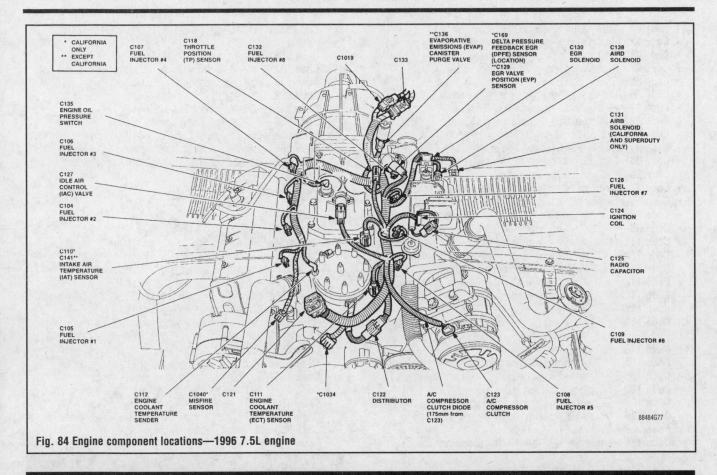

* CALIFORNIA
  ONLY
** EXCEPT
   CALIFORNIA

C107 FUEL INJECTOR #4

C118 THROTTLE POSITION (TP) SENSOR

C132 FUEL INJECTOR #8

C1019

C133

**C136 EVAPORATIVE EMISSIONS (EVAP) CANISTER PURGE VALVE

*C169 DELTA PRESSURE FEEDBACK EGR (DPFE) SENSOR (LOCATION) **C129 EGR VALVE POSITION (EVP) SENSOR

C130 EGR SOLENOID

C138 AIRD SOLENOID

C135 ENGINE OIL PRESSURE SWITCH

C106 FUEL INJECTOR #3

C127 IDLE AIR CONTROL (IAC) VALVE

C104 FUEL INJECTOR #2

C110* C141** INTAKE AIR TEMPERATURE (IAT) SENSOR

C105 FUEL INJECTOR #1

C131 AIRB SOLENOID (CALIFORNIA AND SUPERDUTY ONLY)

C128 FUEL INJECTOR #7

C124 IGNITION COIL

C125 RADIO CAPACITOR

C109 FUEL INJECTOR #6

C112 ENGINE COOLANT TEMPERATURE SENDER

C1040* MISFIRE SENSOR

C121

C111 ENGINE COOLANT TEMPERATURE (ECT) SENSOR

*C1034

C122 DISTRIBUTOR

A/C COMPRESSOR CLUTCH DIODE (175mm from C123)

C123 A/C COMPRESSOR CLUTCH

C108 FUEL INJECTOR #5

88484G77

Fig. 84 Engine component locations—1996 7.5L engine

TROUBLE CODES—EEC-IV

Diagnostic Trouble Codes (DTC)

* **Code 11**—System passes
* **Code 12**—RPM unable to reach upper test limit
* **Code 13**—RPM unable to reach lower test limit
* **Code 14**—Pip circuit failure
* **Code 15**—PCM read only memory test failed
* **Code 15**—PCM keep alive memory test failed
* **Code 16**—IDM signal not received
* **Code 18**—SPOUT circuit open or spark angle word failure
* **Code 18**—IDM circuit failure or SPOUT circuit grounded
* **Code 19**—Failure in PCM internal voltage
* **Code 21**—ECT out of self-test range
* **Code 22**—BP sensor out of self-test range
* **Code 22**—BP sensor or MAP out of range
* **Code 23**—TP sensor out of self-test range
* **Code 24**—ACT sensor out of self-test range
* **Code 25**—Knock not sensed during dynamic test
* **Code 26**—VAF/MAF out of self-test range
* **Code 26**—TOT out of self-test range
* **Code 26**—TOT sensor out of self-test range (E-400)
* **Code 28**—Loss of IDM, right side
* **Code 29**—Insufficient input from vehicle speed sensor
* **Code 31**—PFE, EVP or EVR circuit below minimum voltage
* **Code 32**—EVP voltage below closed limit
* **Code 33**—EGR valve opening not detected
* **Code 34**—EVP voltage above closed limit
* **Code 35**—PFE or EVP circuit above closed limit
* **Code 41**—HEGO sensor circuit indicates system lean
* **Code 41**—No HEGO switching detected
* **Code 42**—HEGO sensor circuit indicates system rich
* **Code 44**—Thermactor air system inoperative–right side

* **Code 45**—Thermactor air upstream during self-test
* **Code 45**—Coil 1, 2 or 3 failure
* **Code 46**—Thermactor air not bypassed during self-test
* **Code 47**—4WD switch closed (E40D)
* **Code 48**—Loss of IDM, left side
* **Code 49**—1–2 shift error (E40D)
* **Code 51**—ECT/ACT reads −40°F or circuit open
* **Code 52**—Power steering pressure switch circuit open
* **Code 52**—Power steering pressure switch always open or closed
* **Code 53**—TP circuit above maximum voltage
* **Code 54**—ACT sensor circuit open
* **Code 56**—VAF or MAF circuit above maximum voltage
* **Code 56**—TOT reads −40°F or circuit open (E40D)
* **Code 59**—2–3 shift error (E40D)
* **Code 61**—ECT reads 254°F or circuit grounded
* **Code 63**—TP circuit below minimum voltage
* **Code 64**—ACT sensor grounded or input reads 254°F
* **Code 65**—Overdrive cancel switch open, no change seen (E40D)
* **Code 66**—MAF sensor input below minimum voltage
* **Code 66**—TOT grounded or reads 290°F (E40D)
* **Code 67**—Neutral/drive switch open or A/C on
* **Code 67**—Clutch switch circuit failure
* **Code 67**—MLP sensor out of range or A/C on (E40D)
* **Code 69**—3–4 shift error
* **Code 72**—Insufficient MAF/MAP change during dynamic test
* **Code 73**—Insufficient TP change during dynamic test
* **Code 74**—Brake on/off switch failure or not actuated
* **Code 77**—Operator error
* **Code 79**—A/C on during self-test
* **Code 79**—A/C or defrost on during self-test
* **Code 81**—Air management 2 circuit failure
* **Code 82**—Air management 1 circuit failure

- **Code 84**—EGR vacuum solenoid circuit failure
- **Code 85**—Canister purge solenoid circuit failure
- **Code 86**—Shift solenoid circuit failure
- **Code 87**—Fuel pump primary circuit failure
- **Code 88**—Loss of dual plug input control
- **Code 89**—Converter clutch solenoid circuit failure
- **Code 91**—Shift solenoid 1 circuit failure (E40D)
- **Code 92**—Shift solenoid 2 circuit failure (E40D)
- **Code 93**—Coast clutch solenoid circuit failure (E40D)
- **Code 94**—Converter clutch solenoid circuit failure (E40D)
- **Code 95**—Fuel pump secondary circuit failure— PCM to ground
- **Code 96**—Fuel pump secondary circuit failure—battery to PCM
- **Code 97**—Overdrive cancel indicator light—circuit failure(E40D)
- **Code 98**—Electronic pressure control driver open in PCM (E40D)
- **Code 98**—Hard fault present
- **Code 99**—Electronic pressure control circuit failure (E40D)
- **Code 111**—System pass
- **Code 112**—ACT sensor circuit grounded or reads 254° F
- **Code 113**—ACT sensor circuit open or reads -40° F
- **Code 114**—ACT outside test limits during KOEO or KOER tests
- **Code 116**—ECT outside test limits during KOEO or KOER tests
- **Code 117**—ECT sensor circuit grounded
- **Code 117**—ECT sensor circuit below minimum voltage or reads 254°F
- **Code 118**—ECT sensor circuit open
- **Code 118**—ECT sensor circuit below maximum voltage or reads -40°F
- **Code 121**—Closed throttle voltage higher or lower than expected
- **Code 122**—TP sensor circuit below minimum voltage
- **Code 123**—TP sensor circuit below maximum voltage
- **Code 126**—BP or MAP sensor higher or lower than expected
- **Code 128**—MAP vacuum circuit failure
- **Code 129**—Insufficient MAF or MAP change during dynamic responded test
- **Code 144**—No HEGO switching detected
- **Code 167**—Insufficient TP change during dynamic response test
- **Code 171**—Fuel system at adaptive limit, HEGO unable to switch
- **Code 172**—HEGO shows system always lean
- **Code 173**—HEGO shows system always rich
- **Code 174**—HEGO switching time is slow
- **Code 179**—Fuel at lean adaptive limit at part throttle; system rich
- **Code 181**—Fuel at rich adaptive limit at part throttle; system lean
- **Code 182**—Fuel at lean adaptive limit at idle; system rich
- **Code 183**—Fuel at rich adaptive limit at idle; system lean
- **Code 211**—PIP circuit fault
- **Code 212**—Loss of IDM input to PCM or SPOUT circuit grounded
- **Code 213**—SPOUT circuit open
- **Code 224**—Erratic IDM input to processor
- **Code 225**—Knocked not sensed during dynamic response test
- **Code 311**—Thermactor air system inoperative
- **Code 312**—Thermactor air upstream during self-test
- **Code 313**—Thermactor air not bypassed during self-test
- **Code 327**—EVP or DPFE circuit below minimum voltage
- **Code 328**—EGR closed voltage higher than expected
- **Code 332**—Insufficient EGR flow detected
- **Code 334**—EGR closed voltage higher than expected
- **Code 337**—EVP or DPFE circuit above maximum voltage
- **Code 411**—Cannot control rpm during KOER low rpm check
- **Code 412**—Cannot control rpm during KOER high rpm check
- **Code 452**—Insufficient input from vehicle speed sensor
- **Code 511**—EEC processor ROM test failed
- **Code 512**—EEC processor Keep Alive Memory test failed
- **Code 513**—Failure in EEC processor internal voltage
- **Code 519**—Power steering pressure switch circuit open
- **Code 521**—Power steering pressure switch did not change state
- **Code 525**—Vehicle in gear or A/C on during self-test
- **Code 536**—Brake on/off circuit failure, switch not actuated during KOER test

- **Code 538**—Insufficient RPM change during KOER dynamic response test
- **Code 538**—Operator error
- **Code 542**—Fuel pump secondary circuit failure: PCM to ground
- **Code 543**—Fuel pump secondary circuit failure: Battery to PCM
- **Code 552**—Air management 1 circuit failure
- **Code 553**—Air management 2 circuit failure
- **Code 556**—Fuel pump primary circuit failure
- **Code 558**—EGR vacuum regulator circuit failure
- **Code 565**—Canister purge circuit failure
- **Code 569**—Canister purge 2 circuit failure
- **Code 617**—1–2 shift error (E40D)
- **Code 618**—2–3 shift error (E40D)
- **Code 619**—3–4 shift error (E40D)
- **Code 621**—Shift solenoid 1 circuit failure
- **Code 622**—Shift solenoid 2 circuit failure
- **Code 624**—EPC solenoid or driver circuit failure
- **Code 625**—EPC driver open in PCM
- **Code 626**—Coast clutch solenoid circuit failure (E40D)
- **Code 627**—Converter clutch solenoid circuit failure (E40D)
- **Code 628**—Converter clutch error (E40D)
- **Code 629**—Converter clutch control circuit failure
- **Code 631**—Overdrive cancel indicator light circuit failure
- **Code 632**—Overdrive cancel switch not changing states (E40D)
- **Code 633**—4WD switch is closed
- **Code 634**—MLP sensor voltage out of self-test range, A/C on
- **Code 636**—TOT sensor voltage out of self-test range
- **Code 637**—TOT sensor circuit above maximum voltage
- **Code 638**—TOT sensor circuit below minimum voltage
- **Code 654**—MLP sensor not in park position
- **Code 998**—Hard fault present

General Information

POWERTRAIN CONTROL MODULE

One part of the PCM is devoted to monitoring both input and output functions within the system. This ability forms the core of the self-diagnostic system. If a problem is detected within a circuit, the controller will recognize the fault, assign it an identification code, and store the code in a memory section. Depending on the year and model, the fault code(s) may be represented by two or three-digit numbers. The stored code(s) may be retrieved during diagnosis.

While the EEC-IV system is capable of recognizing many internal faults, certain faults will not be recognized. Because the computer system sees only electrical signals, it cannot sense or react to mechanical or vacuum faults affecting engine operation. Some of these faults may affect another component which will set a code. For example, the PCM monitors the output signal to the fuel injectors, but cannot detect a partially clogged injector. As long as the output driver responds correctly, the computer will read the system as functioning correctly. However, the improper flow of fuel may result in a lean mixture. This would, in turn, be detected by the oxygen sensor and noticed as a constantly lean signal by the PCM. Once the signal falls outside the pre-programmed limits, the engine control assembly would notice the fault and set an identification code.

Failure Mode Effects Management (FMEM)

The PCM contains back-up programs which allow the engine to operate if a sensor signal is lost. If a sensor input is seen to be out of range— either high or low—the FMEM program is used. The processor substitutes a fixed value for the missing sensor signal. The engine will continue to operate, although performance and driveability may be noticeably reduced. This function of the controller is sometimes referred to as the limp-in or fail-safe mode. If the missing sensor signal is restored, the FMEM system immediately returns the system to normal operation. The dashboard warning lamp will be lit when FMEM is in effect.

Diagnostic Link Connector (DLC)

▶ See Figure 85

The DLC is located on the left-hand side of the engine compartment.

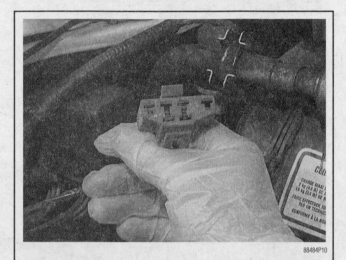

Fig. 85 The DLC is usually located in the engine compartment on the passenger side of the van

Hardware Limited Operation Strategy (HLOS)

This mode is only used if the fault is too extreme for the FMEM circuit to handle. In this mode, the processor has ceased all computation and control; the entire system is run on fixed values. The vehicle may be operated but performance and driveability will be greatly reduced. The fixed or default settings provide minimal calibration; allowing the vehicle to be carefully driven in for service. The dashboard warning lamp will be lit when HLOS is engaged. Codes cannot be read while the system is operating in this mode.

MALFUNCTION INDICATOR LAMP (MIL)

The CHECK ENGINE or SERVICE ENGINE SOON dashboard warning lamp is referred to as the Malfunction Indicator Lamp (MIL). The lamp is connected to the engine control assembly and will alert the driver to certain malfunctions within the EEC-IV system. When the lamp is lit, the PCM has detected a fault and stored an identity code in memory. The engine control system will usually enter either FMEM or HLOS mode and driveability will be impaired.

The light will stay on as long as the fault causing it is present. Should the fault self-correct, the MIL will extinguish but the stored code will remain in memory.

Under normal operating conditions, the MIL should light briefly when the ignition key is turned **ON**. As soon as the PCM receives a signal that the engine is cranking, the lamp will be extinguished. The dash warning lamp should remain out during the entire operating cycle.

HAND-HELD SCAN TOOLS

▶ See Figures 86, 87 and 88

Although stored codes may be read through the flashing of the CHECK ENGINE or SERVICE ENGINE SOON lamp, the use of hand-held scan tools such as Ford's Self-Test Automatic Readout (STAR) tester or the second generation SUPER STAR II tester or their equivalent is highly recommended. There are many manufacturers of these tools; the purchaser must be certain that the tool is proper for the intended use.

Fig. 86 Among other features, a scan tool combines many standard testers into a single device for quick and accurate diagnosis

Fig. 87 Inexpensive scan tools, such as this Auto Xray®, are available to interface with your Ford vehicle

Fig. 88 When using a scan tool, make sure to follow all of the manufacturer's instructions carefully to ensure proper diagnosis

The scan tool allows any stored faults to be read from the engine controller memory. Use of the scan tool provides additional data during troubleshooting, but does not eliminate the use of the charts. The scan tool makes collecting information easier, but the data must be correctly interpreted by an operator familiar with the system.

ELECTRICAL TOOLS

▶ **See Figures 90, 91, 92 and 93**

The most commonly required electrical diagnostic tool is the Digital Multimeter, allowing voltage, ohmage (resistance) and amperage to be read by one instrument. Many of the diagnostic charts require the use of a volt or ohmmeter during diagnosis.

The multimeter must be a high impedance unit, with 10 megohms of impedance in the voltmeter. This type of meter will not place an additional load on the circuit it is testing; this is extremely important in low voltage circuits. The multimeter must be of high quality in all respects. It should be handled carefully and protected from impact or damage. Replace the batteries frequently in the unit.

Additionally, an analog (needle type) voltmeter may be used to read stored fault codes if the STAR tester is not available. The codes are transmitted as visible needle sweeps on the face of the instrument.

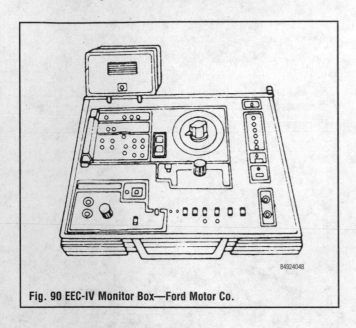

Fig. 90 EEC-IV Monitor Box—Ford Motor Co.

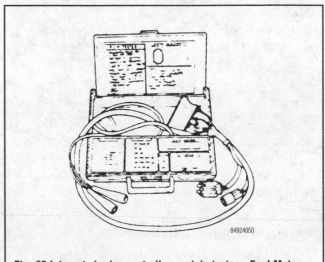

Fig. 92 Integrated relay controller module tester—Ford Motor Co.

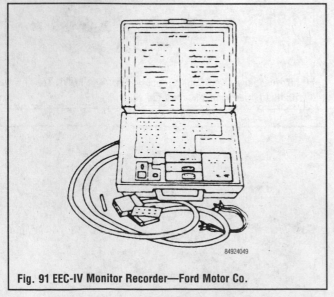

Fig. 91 EEC-IV Monitor Recorder—Ford Motor Co.

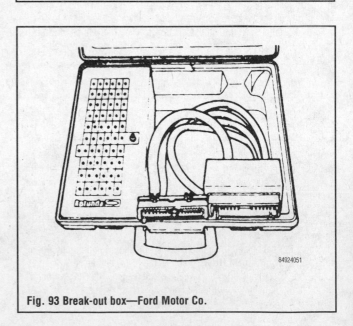

Fig. 93 Break-out box—Ford Motor Co.

Almost all diagnostic procedures will require the use of a Breakout Box, a device which connects into the EEC-IV harness and provides testing ports for the 60 wires in the harness. Direct testing of the harness connectors at the terminals or by backprobing is not recommended; damage to the wiring and terminals is almost certain to occur.

Other necessary tools include a quality tachometer with inductive (clip-on) pickup, a fuel pressure gauge with system adapters and a vacuum gauge with an auxiliary source of vacuum.

Reading Codes

Diagnosis of a driveability problem requires attention to detail and following the diagnostic procedures in the correct order. Resist the temptation to begin extensive testing before completing the preliminary diagnostic steps. The preliminary or visual inspection must be completed in detail before diagnosis begins. In many cases this will shorten diagnostic time and often cure the problem without electronic testing.

VISUAL INSPECTION

This is possibly the most critical step of diagnosis. A detailed examination of all connectors, wiring and vacuum hoses can often lead to a repair without further diagnosis. Performance of this step relies on the skill of the technician performing it; a careful inspector will check the undersides of hoses as well as the integrity of hard-to-reach hoses blocked by the air cleaner or other components. Wiring should be checked carefully for any sign of strain, burning, crimping or terminal pull-out from a connector.

Checking connectors at components or in harnesses is required; usually, pushing them together will reveal a loose fit. Pay particular attention to ground circuits, making sure they are not loose or corroded. Remember to inspect connectors and hose fittings at components not mounted on the engine, such as the evaporative canister or relays mounted on the fender aprons. Any component or wiring in the vicinity of a fluid leak or spillage should be given extra attention during inspection.

Additionally, inspect maintenance items such as belt condition and tension, battery charge and condition and the radiator cap carefully. Any of these very simple items may affect the system enough to set a fault.

ELECTRONIC TESTING

If a code was set before a problem self-corrected (such as a momentarily loose connector), the code will be erased if the problem does not reoccur within 80 warm-up cycles. Codes will be output and displayed as numbers on the hand-held scan tool, such as 23. If the codes are being read through the dashboard warning lamp, the codes will be displayed as groups of flashes separated by pauses. Code 23 would be shown as two flashes, a pause and three more flashes. A longer pause will occur between codes. If the codes are being read on an analog voltmeter, the needle sweeps indicate the code digits in the same manner as the lamp flashes.

In all cases, the codes 11 or 111 are used to indicate PASS during testing. Note that the PASS code may appear, followed by other stored codes. These are codes from the continuous memory and may indicate intermittent faults, even though the system does not presently contain the fault. The PASS designation only indicates that the system passes all internal tests at the moment.

Key On Engine Off (KOEO) Test

▶ **See Figures 94, 95 and 96**

1. Connect the scan tool to the self-test connectors. Make certain the test button is unlatched or up.
2. Start the engine and run it until normal operating temperature is reached.
3. Turn the engine **OFF** for 10 seconds.
4. Activate the test button on the STAR tester.
5. Turn the ignition switch **ON** but do not start the engine. For vehicles with 4.9L engines, depress the clutch during the entire test. For vehicles with the 7.3L diesel engine, hold the accelerator to the floor during the test.

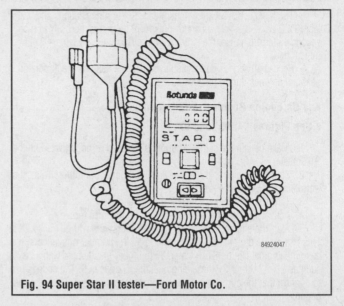

Fig. 94 Super Star II tester—Ford Motor Co.

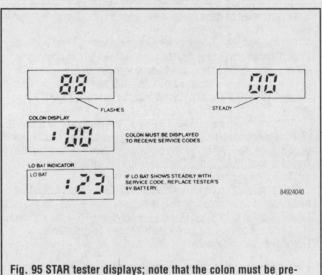

Fig. 95 STAR tester displays; note that the colon must be present before codes can be received

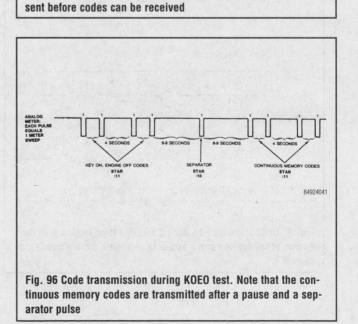

Fig. 96 Code transmission during KOEO test. Note that the continuous memory codes are transmitted after a pause and a separator pulse

6. The KOEO codes will be transmitted. Six to nine seconds after the last KOEO code, a single separator pulse will be transmitted. Six to nine seconds after this pulse, the codes from the Continuous Memory will be transmitted.

7. Record all service codes displayed. Do not depress the throttle on gasoline engines during the test.

Key On Engine Running (KOER) Test

◗ See Figures 94, 95, and 97

1. Make certain the self-test button is released or de-activated on the STAR tester.

2. Start the engine and run it at 2000 rpm for two minutes. This action warms up the oxygen sensor.

3. Turn the ignition switch **OFF** for 10 seconds.

4. Activate or latch the self-test button on the scan tool.

5. Start the engine. The engine identification code will be transmitted. This is a single digit number representing ½ the number of cylinders in a gasoline engine. On the STAR tester, this number may appear with a zero, such as 20 = 2. For 7.3L diesel engines, the ID code is 5. The code is used to confirm that the correct processor is installed and that the self-test has begun.

6. If the vehicle is equipped with a Brake On/Off (BOO) switch, the brake pedal must be depressed and released after the ID code is transmitted.

7. If the vehicle is equipped with a Power Steering Pressure Switch (PSPS), the steering wheel must be turned at least ½ turn and released within 2 seconds after the engine ID code is transmitted.

8. If the vehicle is equipped with the E4OD transmission, the Overdrive Cancel Switch (OCS) must be cycled after the engine ID code is transmitted.

9. Certain Ford vehicles will display a Dynamic Response code 6–20 seconds after the engine ID code. This will appear as one pulse on a meter or as a 10 on the STAR tester. When this code appears, briefly take the engine to wide open throttle. This allows the system to test the throttle position, MAF and MAP sensors.

10. All relevant codes will be displayed and should be recorded. Remember that the codes refer only to faults present during this test cycle. Codes stored in Continuous Memory are not displayed in this test mode.

11. Do not depress the throttle during testing unless a dynamic response code is displayed.

Reading Codes With Analog Voltmeter

◗ See Figures 98 and 99

In the absence of a scan tool, an analog voltmeter may be used to retrieve stored fault codes. Set the meter range to read DC 0–15 volts. Connect the + lead of the meter to the battery positive terminal and connect the − lead of the meter to the self-test output pin of the diagnostic connector.

Follow the directions given previously for performing the KOEO and KOER tests. To activate the tests, use a jumper wire to connect the signal return pin on the diagnostic connector to the self-test input connector. The self-test input line is the separate wire and connector with or near the diagnostic connector.

The codes will be transmitted as groups of needle sweeps. This method may be used to read either 2 or 3-digit codes. The Continuous Memory codes are separated from the KOEO codes by 6 seconds, a single sweep and another 6 second delay.

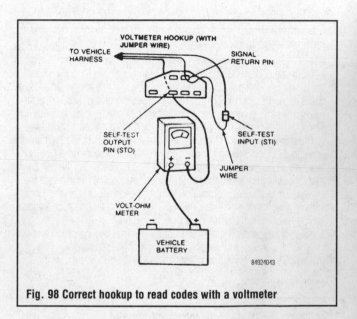

Fig. 98 Correct hookup to read codes with a voltmeter

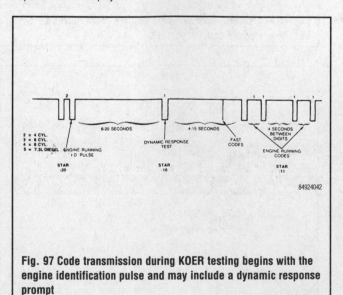

Fig. 97 Code transmission during KOER testing begins with the engine identification pulse and may include a dynamic response prompt

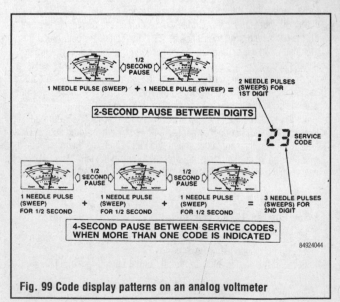

Fig. 99 Code display patterns on an analog voltmeter

Reading Codes With MIL

▶ **See Figures 100 and 101**

The Malfunction Indicator Lamp on the dashboard may also be used to retrieve the stored codes. This method displays only the stored codes and does not allow for any system investigation.

Follow the directions given previously for performing the KOEO and KOER tests. To activate the tests, use a jumper wire to connect the signal return pin on the diagnostic connector to the self-test input connector. The self-test input line is the separate wire and connector with or near the diagnostic connector.

Codes are transmitted by place value with a pause between the digits; Code 32 would be sent as 3 flashes, a pause and 2 flashes. A slightly longer pause divides codes from each other. Be ready to count and record codes; the only way to repeat a code is to re-cycle the system. This method may be used to read either 2 or 3-digit codes. The Continuous Memory codes are separated from the KOEO codes by 6 seconds, a single flash and another 6 second delay.

To perform the KOER test:

1. Hold in all 3 buttons, start the engine and release the buttons.
2. Press the SELECT or GAUGE SELECT button 3 times. The message **dealer 4** should appear at the bottom of the message panel.

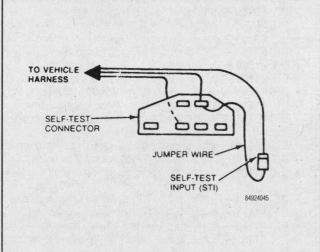

Fig. 100 Only a jumper wire is needed to read codes through the MIL or the message center

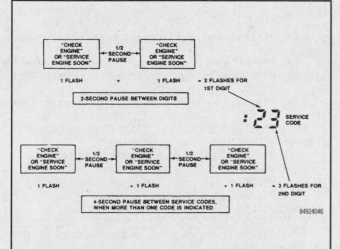

Fig. 101 Code display pattern using the dashboard warning lamp

3. Initiate the test by using a jumper wire to connect the signal return pin on the diagnostic connector to the self-test input connector. The self-test input line is the separate wire and connector with or near the diagnostic connector.
4. The stored codes will be output to the vehicle display.
5. To exit the test, turn the ignition switch **OFF** and disconnect the jumper wire.

Other Test Modes

CONTINUOUS MONITOR OR WIGGLE TEST

Once entered, this mode allows the operator to attempt to recreate intermittent faults by wiggling or tapping components, wiring or connectors. The test may be performed during either KOEO or KOER procedures. The test requires the use of either an analog voltmeter or a hand-held scan tool.

To enter the continuous monitor mode during KOEO testing, turn the ignition switch **ON**. Activate the test, wait 10 seconds, then deactivate and reactivate the test; the system will enter the continuous monitor mode. Tap, move or wiggle the harness, component or connector suspected of causing the problem; if a fault is detected, the code will store in the memory. When the fault occurs, the dash warning lamp will illuminate, the STAR tester will light a red indicator (and possibly beep) and the analog meter needle will sweep once.

To enter this mode in the KOER test:

1. Start the engine and run it at 2000 rpm for two minutes. This action warms up the oxygen sensor.
2. Turn the ignition switch **OFF** for 10 seconds.
3. Start the engine.
4. Activate the test, wait 10 seconds, then deactivate and reactivate the test; the system will enter the continuous monitor mode.
5. Tap, move or wiggle the harness, component or connector suspected of causing the problem; if a fault is detected, the code will store in the memory.
6. When the fault occurs, the dash warning lamp will illuminate, the STAR tester will light a red indicator (and possibly beep) and the analog meter needle will sweep once.

OUTPUT STATE CHECK

This testing mode allows the operator to energize and de-energize most of the outputs controlled by the EEC-IV system. Many of the outputs may be checked at the component by listening for a click or feeling the item move or engage by a hand placed on the case. To enter this check:

1. Enter the KOEO test mode.
2. When all codes have been transmitted, depress the accelerator all the way to the floor and release it.
3. The output actuators are now all ON. Depressing the throttle pedal to the floor again switches the all the actuator outputs OFF.
4. This test may be performed as often as necessary, switching between ON and OFF by depressing the throttle.
5. Exit the test by turning the ignition switch **OFF**, disconnecting the jumper at the diagnostic connector or releasing the test button on the scan tool.

Clearing Codes

CONTINUOUS MEMORY CODES

These codes are retained in memory for 80 warm-up cycles. To clear the codes for the purposes of testing or confirming repair, perform the KOEO test. When the fault codes begin to be displayed, de-activate the test by either disconnecting the jumper wire (meter, MIL or message center) or releasing the test button on the hand scanner. Stopping the test during code transmission will erase the Continuous Memory. Do not disconnect the negative battery cable to clear these codes; the Keep Alive memory will be cleared and a new code, 19, will be stored for loss of PCM power.

KEEP ALIVE MEMORY

The Keep Alive Memory (KAM) contains the adaptive factors used by the processor to compensate for component tolerances and wear. It should not be routinely cleared during diagnosis. If an emissions related part is replaced during repair, the KAM must be cleared. Failure to clear the KAM may cause severe driveability problems since the correction factor for the old component will be applied to the new component.

To clear the Keep Alive Memory, disconnect the negative battery cable for at least 5 minutes. After the memory is cleared and the battery reconnected, the vehicle must be driven at least 10 miles (16 km) so that the processor may relearn the needed correction factors. The distance to be driven depends on the engine and vehicle, but all drives should include steady-throttle cruise on open roads. Certain driveability problems may be noted during the drive because the adaptive factors are not yet functioning.

TROUBLE CODES—EEC-V

Diagnostic Trouble Codes (DTC)

- DTC **P0102**—Mass Air Flow (MAF) Sensor circuit low input
- DTC **P0103**—Mass Air Flow (MAF) Sensor circuit high input
- DTC **P0112**—Intake Air Temperature (IAT) Sensor circuit low input
- DTC **P0113**—Intake Air Temperature (IAT) Sensor high input
- DTC **P0117**—Engine Coolant Temperature (ECT) low input
- DTC **P0118**—Engine Coolant Temperature (ECT) Sensor circuit high input
- DTC **P0122**—Throttle Position (TP) Sensor circuit low input
- DTC **P0123**—Throttle Position (TP) Sensor high input
- DTC **P0125**—Insufficient coolant temperature to enter closed loop fuel control
- DTC **P0132**—Upstream Heated Oxygen Sensor (HO2S 11) circuit high voltage (Bank #1)
- DTC **P0135**—Heated Oxygen Sensor Heater (HTR 11) circuit malfunction
- DTC **P0138**—Downstream Heated Oxygen Sensor (HO2S 12) circuit high voltage (Bank #1)
- DTC **P0140**—Heated Oxygen Sensor (HO2S 12) circuit no activity detected (Bank #1)
- DTC **P0141**—Heated Oxygen Sensor Heater (HTR 12) circuit malfunction
- DTC **P0152**—Upstream Heated Oxygen Sensor (HO2S 21) circuit high voltage (Bank #2)
- DTC **P0155**—Heated Oxygen Sensor Heater (HTR 21) circuit malfunction
- DTC **P0158**—Downstream Heated Oxygen Sensor (HO2S 22) circuit high voltage (Bank #2)
- DTC **P0160**—Heated Oxygen Sensor (HO2S 12) circuit no activity detected (Bank #2)
- DTC **P0161**—Heated Oxygen Sensor Heater (HTR 22) circuit malfunction
- DTC **P0171**—System (adaptive fuel) too lean (Bank #1)
- DTC **P0172**—System (adaptive fuel) too lean (Bank #1)
- DTC **P0174**—System (adaptive fuel) too lean (Bank #1)
- DTC **P0175**—System (adaptive fuel) too lean (Bank #1)
- DTC **P0300**—Random misfire detected
- DTC **P0301**—Cylinder #1 misfire detected
- DTC **P0302**—Cylinder #2 misfire detected
- DTC **P0303**—Cylinder #3 misfire detected
- DTC **P0304**—Cylinder #4 misfire detected
- DTC **P0305**—Cylinder #5 misfire detected
- DTC **P0306**—Cylinder #6 misfire detected
- DTC **P0307**—Cylinder #7 misfire detected
- DTC **P0308**—Cylinder #8 misfire detected
- DTC **P0320**—Ignition engine speed (Profile Ignition Pickup or PIP) input circuit malfunction
- DTC **P0340**—Camshaft Position (CMP) sensor circuit malfunction (CID)
- DTC **P0402**—Exhaust Gas Recirculation (EGR) excess flow detected (valve open at idle)
- DTC **P0420**—Catalyst system efficiency below threshold (Bank #1)
- DTC **P0430**—Catalyst system efficiency below threshold (Bank #2)
- DTC **P0443**—Evaporative emission control system Canister Purge (CANP) Control Valve circuit malfunction

- DTC **P0500**—Vehicle Speed Sensor (VSS) malfunction
- DTC **P0505**—Idle Air Control (IAC) system malfunction
- DTC **P0605**—Powertrain Control Module (PCM)—Read Only Memory (ROM) test error
- DTC **P0703**—Brake On/Off (BOO) switch input malfunction
- DTC **P0707**—Manual Lever Position (MLP) sensor circuit low input
- DTC **P0708**—Manual Lever Position (MLP) sensor circuit high input
- DTC **P0720**—Output Shaft Speed (OSS) sensor circuit malfunction
- DTC **P0741**—Torque Converter Clutch (TCC) system incorrect mechanical performance
- DTC **P0743**—Torque Converter Clutch (TCC) system electrical failure
- DTC **P0750**—Shift Solenoid #1 (SS1) circuit malfunction
- DTC **P0751**—Shift Solenoid #1 (SS1) performance
- DTC **P0755**—Shift Solenoid #2 (SS2) circuit malfunction
- DTC **P0756**—Shift Solenoid #2 (SS2) performance
- DTC **P1000**—OBD II Monitor Testing not complete
- DTC **P1100**—Mass Air Flow (MAF) sensor intermittent
- DTC **P1101**—Mass Air Flow (MAF) sensor out of Self-Test range
- DTC **P1112**—Intake Air Temperature (IAT) sensor intermittent
- DTC **P1116**—Engine Coolant Temperature (ECT) sensor out of Self-Test range
- DTC **P1117**—Engine Coolant Temperature (ECT) sensor intermittent
- DTC **P1120**—Throttle Position (TP) sensor out of range low
- DTC **P1121**—Throttle Position (TP) sensor inconsistent with MAF sensor
- DTC **P1124**—Throttle Position (TP) sensor out of Self-Test range
- DTC **P1125**—Throttle Position (TP) sensor circuit intermittent
- DTC **P1130**—Lack of HO2S 11 switch, adaptive fuel at limit
- DTC **P1131**—Lack of HO2S 11 switch, sensor indicates lean (Bank #1)
- DTC **P1132**—Lack of HO2S 11 switch, sensor indicates rich (Bank #1)
- DTC **P1137**—Lack of HO2S 12 switch, sensor indicates lean (Bank #1)
- DTC **P1138**—Lack of HO2S 12 switch, sensor indicates rich (Bank #1)
- DTC **P1150**—Lack of HO2S 21 switch, adaptive fuel at limit
- DTC **P1151**—Lack of HO2S 21 switch, sensor indicates lean (Bank #2)
- DTC **P1152**—Lack of HO2S 21 switch, sensor indicates rich (Bank #2)
- DTC **P1157**—Lack of HO2S 22 switch, sensor indicates lean (Bank #2)
- DTC **P1158**—Lack of HO2S 22 switch, sensor indicates rich (Bank #2)
- DTC **P1351**—Ignition Diagnostic Monitor (IDM) circuit input malfunction
- DTC **P1352**—Ignition coil A primary circuit malfunction
- DTC **P1353**—Ignition coil B primary circuit malfunction
- DTC **P1354**—Ignition coil C primary circuit malfunction
- DTC **P1355**—Ignition coil D primary circuit malfunction
- DTC **P1364**—Ignition coil primary circuit malfunction
- DTC **P1390**—Octane Adjust (OCT ADJ) out of Self-Test range
- DTC **P1400**—Differential Pressure Feedback Electronic (DPFE) sensor circuit low voltage detected
- DTC **P1401**—Differential Pressure Feedback Electronic (DPFE) sensor circuit high voltage detected

- DTC **P1403**—Differential Pressure Feedback Electronic (DPFE) sensor hoses reversed
- DTC **P1405**—Differential Pressure Feedback Electronic (DPFE) sensor upstream hose off or plugged
- DTC **P1406**—Differential Pressure Feedback Electronic (DPFE) sensor downstream hose off or plugged
- DTC **P1407**—Exhaust Gas Recirculation (EGR) no flow detected (valve stuck closed or inoperative)
- DTC **P1408**—Exhaust Gas Recirculation (EGR) flow out of Self-Test range
- DTC **P1473**—Fan Secondary High with fan(s) off
- DTC **P1474**—Low Fan Control primary circuit malfunction
- DTC **P1479**—High Fan Control primary circuit malfunction
- DTC **P1480**—Fan Secondary low with low fan on
- DTC **P1481**—Fan Secondary low with high fan on
- DTC **P1500**—Vehicle Speed Sensor (VSS) circuit intermittent
- DTC **P1505**—Idle Air Control (IAC) system at adaptive clip
- DTC **P1605**—Powertrain Control Module (PCM)—Keep Alive Memory (KAM) test error
- DTC **P1703**—Brake On/Off (BOO) switch out of Self-Test range
- DTC **P1705**—Manual Lever Position (MLP) sensor out of Self-Test range
- DTC **P1711**—Transmission Fluid Temperature (TFT) sensor out of Self-Test range
- DTC **P1742**—Torque Converter Clutch (TCC) solenoid mechanically failed (turns MIL on)
- DTC **P1743**—Torque Converter Clutch (TCC) solenoid mechanically failed (turns TCIL on)
- DTC **P1744**—Torque Converter Clutch (TCC) system mechanically stuck in off position
- DTC **P1746**—Electronic Pressure Control (EPC) solenoid circuit low input (open circuit)
- DTC **P1747**—Electronic Pressure Control (EPC) solenoid circuit high input (short circuit)
- DTC **P1751**—Shift Solenoid #1 (SS1) performance
- DTC **P1756**—Shift Solenoid #2 (SS2) performance
- DTC **P1780**—Transmission Control Switch (TCS) circuit out of Self-Test range

General Information

ON-BOARD DIAGNOSTICS (OBD) II

➡**Most vehicles covered by this manual employ the fourth generation Electronic Engine Control system, commonly designated EEC-IV, to manage fuel, ignition and emissions on vehicle engines. However, all 1995–96 diesel engines and some 1996 gasoline engines (depending on engine application), are equipped with EEC-V.**

Ford developed the EEC-V system in response to the increased diagnostic requirements for the California Air Resource Board. The regulations developed by the Environmental Protection Agency are designated as the OBD II system.

The On Board Diagnostics (OBD) II system is similar to the OBD I system, but not identical. The OBD I requires that the Malfunction Indicator Lamp (MIL) illuminates to inform the driver when an emissions component or monitored system fails. The MIL also lights up to indicate when the Powertrain Control Module (PCM) is operating in Hardware Limited Operation Strategy (HLOS).

The EEC-V is an evolutionary development from the EEC-IV. None of the components involved are actually new, only the applications have changed.

The only component that has been added is another heated Oxygen sensor (HO$_2$S located behind the catalyst. These downstream sensors are called the Catalyst Monitor Sensors (CMS). This means that there are four sensors on models so equipped, instead of two.

POWERTRAIN CONTROL MODULE (PCM)

➡**PCM's for EEC-IV systems use a 60-pin connector. For the EEC-V PCM, a 104-pin connector is used.**

As with the EEC-IV system, the PCM is given responsibility for the operation of the emission control devices, cooling fans, ignition and advance and in some cases, automatic transmission functions. Because the EEC system oversees both the ignition timing and the fuel injector operation, a precise air/fuel ratio will be maintained under all operating conditions. The PCM is a microprocessor or small computer which receives electrical inputs from several sensors, switches and relays on and around the engine.

Based on combinations of these inputs, the PCM controls outputs to various devices concerned with engine operation and emissions. The engine control assembly relies on the signals to form a correct picture of current vehicle operation. If any of the input signals is incorrect, the PCM reacts to what ever picture is painted for it. For example, if the coolant temperature sensor is inaccurate and reads too low, the PCM may see a picture of the engine never warming up. Consequently, the engine settings will be maintained as if the engine were cold. Because so many inputs can affect one output, correct diagnostic procedures are essential on these systems.

One part of the PCM is devoted to monitoring both input and output functions within the system. This ability forms the core of the self-diagnostic system. If a problem is detected within a circuit, the controller will recognize the fault, assign it an identification code, and store the code in a memory section. The fault codes may be retrieved during diagnosis.

While the EEC system is capable of recognizing many internal faults, certain faults will not be recognized. Because the computer system sees only electrical signals, it cannot sense or react to mechanical or vacuum faults affecting engine operation. Some of these faults may affect another component which will set a code. For example, the PCM monitors the output signal to the fuel injectors, but cannot detect a partially clogged injector. As long as the output driver responds correctly, the computer will read the system as functioning correctly. However, the improper flow of fuel may result in a lean mixture. This would, in turn, be detected by the oxygen sensor and noticed as a constantly lean signal by the PCM. Once the signal falls outside the pre-programmed limits, the engine control assembly would notice the fault and set an identification code.

Additionally, the EEC system employs adaptive fuel logic. This process is used to compensate for normal wear and variability within the fuel system. Once the engine enters steady-state operation, the engine control assembly watches the oxygen sensor signal for a bias or tendency to run slightly rich or lean. If such a bias is detected, the adaptive logic corrects the fuel delivery to bring the air/fuel mixture towards a centered or 14.7:1 ratio. This compensating shift is stored in a non-volatile memory which is retained by battery power even with the ignition switched off. The correction factor is then available the next time the vehicle is operated.

➡**If the battery cable(s) is disconnected for longer than 5 minutes, the adaptive fuel factor will be lost. After repair it will be necessary to drive the car at least 10 miles (16 km) to allow the processor to relearn the correct factors. The driving period should include steady-throttle open road driving if possible. During the drive, the vehicle may exhibit driveability symptoms not noticed before. These symptoms should clear as the PCM computes the correction factor.**

Failure Mode Effects Management (FMEM)

The engine controller assembly contains back-up programs which allow the engine to operate if a sensor signal is lost. If a sensor input is seen to be out of range—either high or low—the FMEM program is used. The processor substitutes a fixed value for the missing sensor signal. The engine will continue to operate, although performance and driveability may be noticeably reduced. This function of the controller is sometimes referred to as the limp-in or fail-safe mode. If the missing sensor signal is restored, the FMEM system immediately returns the system to normal operation. The dashboard warning lamp will be lit when FMEM is in effect.

Hardware Limited Operation Strategy (HLOS)

This mode is only used if the fault is too extreme for the FMEM circuit to handle. In this mode, the processor has ceased all computation and control; the entire system is run on fixed values. The vehicle may be operated but performance and driveability will be greatly reduced. The fixed or default settings provide minimal calibration, allowing the vehicle to be carefully driven in for service. The dashboard warning lamp will be lit when HLOS is engaged. Codes cannot be read while the system is operating in this mode.

Data Link Connector (DLC)

The DLC for the EEC-V system is located in the left hand side of the passenger's compartment of the vehicle, attached to the instrument panel, and is accessible from the driver's seat.

The DLC is rectangular in design and capable of allowing access to 16 terminals. The connector has keying features that allow easy connection. The test equipment and the DLC have a latching feature to ensure a good mated connection.

Reading Codes

▶ **See Figures 102 thru 107**

The EEC-V (OBD II) codes differ from the 2 or 3-digit codes of the (former) EEC-IV system in that they are accompanied by a letter prefix before a 4-digit number. Example: P0102 would indicate a Mass Air Flow (MAF) Sensor circuit (low input).

➡ **The number of digits used in the OBD II codes, along with the letter prefix makes flash diagnosis all but impossible, so no provision has been made in OBD II systems to read codes in any other way than with a scan tool.**

When diagnosing the OBD II EEC-V system, the New Generation Star (NGS) tester or generic scan tool may be used to retrieve codes, view the system operating specifications or test the system components. There are also several other pieces of equipment which may be used for diagnosis purposes.

- Vacuum pressure gauge and pump
- Tach/Dwell Volt/Ohmmeter tester
- 104-pin Breakout Box
- Multimeter with a 10 megaohm impedance
- Distributorless ignition system tester
- Constant control relay modular tester

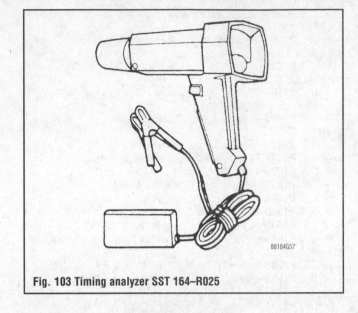

Fig. 103 Timing analyzer SST 164–R025

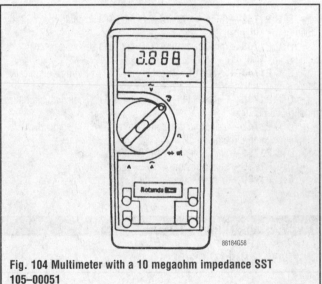

Fig. 104 Multimeter with a 10 megaohm impedance SST 105–00051

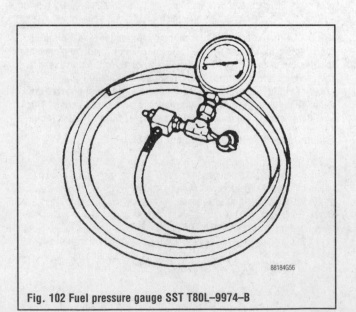

Fig. 102 Fuel pressure gauge SST T80L–9974–B

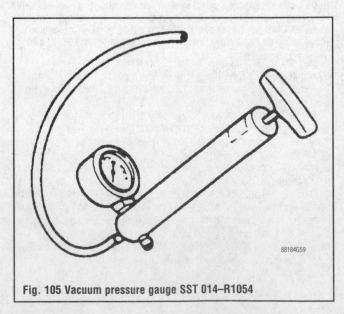

Fig. 105 Vacuum pressure gauge SST 014–R1054

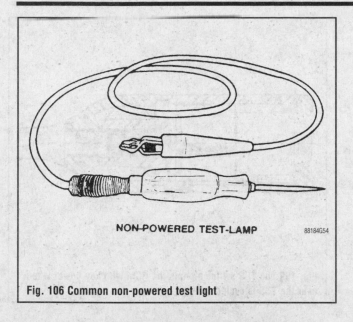

Fig. 106 Common non-powered test light

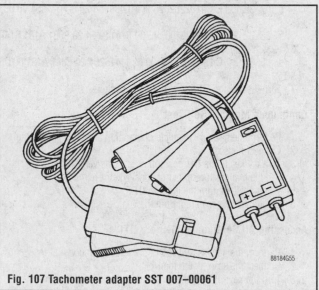

Fig. 107 Tachometer adapter SST 007–00061

- Tachometer adapter
- Fuel pressure gauge
- Timing light
- Test light (non-powered)

Clearing Codes

PCM RESET

The PCM reset mode allows the scan tool to clear any emission related diagnostic information from the PCM. When resetting the PCM, a DTC P1000 will be stored until all OBD II system monitors or components have been tested to satisfy a trip without any other faults occurring.

The following items occur when the PCM Reset is performed:
- The DTC is cleared
- The freeze frame data is cleared
- The oxygen sensor test data is cleared
- The status of the OBD II system monitors is reset
- A DTC P1000 code is set

PCM fault codes may be cleared by using the scan tool or disconnecting the negative battery cable for a minimum of 15 seconds.

KEEP ALIVE MEMORY (KAM) RESET

The Keep Alive Memory (KAM) contains the adaptive factors used by the processor to compensate for component tolerances and wear. It should not be routinely cleared during diagnosis. If and emissions related part is replaced during repair, the KAM must be cleared. Failure to clear the KAM may cause severe driveability problems, since the correction factor for the old component will be applied to the new component.

To clear the KAM disconnect the negative battery cable for at least 5 minuets. After the memory is cleared and the battery is reconnected, the vehicle must be driven a couple of miles so that the PCM may relearn the needed correction factors. The distance to be driven depends on the engine and vehicle, but all drives should include steady throttle cruise on the open roads. Certain driveability problems may be noted during the drive because the adaptive factors are not yet functioning.

Test Equipment

▶ **See Figure 108**

The Ford EEC-V system will requires the use of a 104-pin Break Out Box (BOB) to be used for diagnosis. The 104-pin BOB is used to test circuits exactly as the 60-pin BOB is used on the EEC-IV system. Another piece of test equipment is the STAR (NSG) tester. This tester may be used on OBD I also.

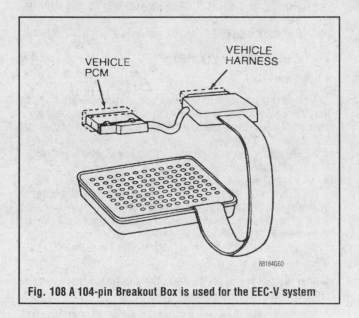

Fig. 108 A 104-pin Breakout Box is used for the EEC-V system

TESTING

These test procedures listed below are for a generic scan tool in the enhanced diagnostic test mode. Only the manufacturer has the STAR tool. Your local jobber should have a generic tool available.

When performing these tests, always do a visual check and preparation of the vehicle first.
- Inspect the air cleaner and inlet ducting.
- Check all of the engine hoses for damages, leaks, cracks, proper routing etc.
- Check the EEC system wiring harness for good connections, bent or broken pins, corrosion, loose wiring etc.
- Check the engine coolant for proper levels and mixture.
- Check the PCM, sensors and actuators for any damages.
- Check the transmission fluid level and quality.
- Make any necessary repairs before proceeding with testing.
- Check the vehicle for safety such as the parking brake must be on. Wheels blocked, etc.

- Turn off all lights, radios, blower switches etc.
- Bring the engine up to operating temperature before running a quick test.

Key On Engine Off (KOEO)

A series of characters must be entered into the scan tool to perform this test. The codes are listed below and must be entered as such to perform the test correctly. See the manufacture of the scan tool for any additional instructions.

1. Perform the necessary vehicle preparation and visual inspection.
2. Connect the scan tool to the DLC.
3. Turn the ignition to the **ON** position but DO NOT start the engine.
4. Verify that the scan tool is connected and communicating correctly by entering the OBD II system readiness test. All scan tools are required to automatically enter this test once communication is established between the tool and the PCM.
5. Enter the following strings of information to initiate the KOEO self-test.
6. Enter the four strings separately and in the order shown. All of the string ID numbers must match in the order shown:

    a. 04, 31, 21, C4 103381, 9E 00 445443287329 20 8042 20 8062 20 8082 A851 FF, 2E

    b. 03, 32, 22FF, C4 10220202, 9E 00 434E54 20 8061 A961 00 04, EA

    c. 02, 32, 21, C4 10328100, 9E 00 574149 54 20 8081 A181 61 03, 5E

    d. 01, 32, 21, C4 103181, 9E 00 53544155254 20 8081 A 181 00 02, 54

7. Turn the ignition **OFF** to end the test cycle.

Key On Engine Running (KOER)

▶ **See Figure 109**

A series of characters must be entered into the scan tool to perform this test. The codes are listed below and must be entered as such to perform the test correctly. See the manufacture of the scan tool for any additional instructions.

1. Perform the necessary vehicle preparation and visual inspection.
2. Connect the scan tool to the DLC.
3. Turn the ignition to the **ON** position and start the engine.
4. Verify that the scan tool is connected and communicating correctly by entering the OBD II system readiness test. All scan tools are required to automatically enter this test once communication is established between the tool and the PCM.
5. Enter the following strings of information to initiate the KOEO self-test.

➡ **After the test begins, cycle BOO, 4X4 and Transmission Control (TCS) switches, if equipped.**

6. Enter the four strings separately and in the order shown. All of the string ID numbers must match in the order shown:

    a. 08, 31, 21, C4103382, 9E 00 445443287329 20 8042 20 8062 20 8082 A851 FF, 33

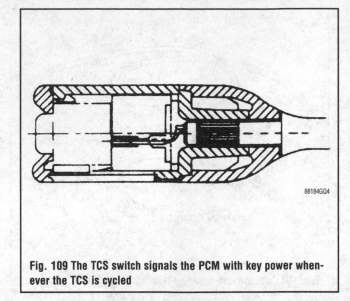

Fig. 109 The TCS switch signals the PCM with key power whenever the TCS is cycled

    b. 07, 32, 22FF, C410220202, 9E 00 434E54 20 8061 A961 00 08, F2

    c. 06, 32, 21, C4 10328200, 9E 00 574149 54 20 8081 A181 61 07, 67

    d. 05, 32, 21, C4 103182, 9E 00 5354415254 20 8081 A181 00 06, 5D

7. Turn the ignition **OFF** to end the test cycle.

Continuous Memory Self-Test

1. Perform the necessary vehicle preparation and visual inspection.
2. Connect the scan tool to the DLC.
3. Turn the key to the **ON** position or start the vehicle.
4. See the manufacturer's instructions to retrieve the DTC's.
5. When finished, turn the ignition **OFF**.
6. Disconnect the scan tool from the vehicle.

Accessing All Continuous Memory DTC's

1. Perform the necessary vehicle preparation and visual inspection.
2. Connect the scan tool to the DLC.
3. Turn the key to the **ON** position or start the vehicle. This may depend on the pinpoint manual instructions for the type of data requested.
4. Verify the tool is connected properly and communicating.
5. Enter the following string of characters to retrieve all the continuous DTC's (DTC CNT):

- 09, 2C, 21, C4 10 13,, 9E 00 44 54 43 20 43 4E 54 20 8B 44, B2

6. The scan tool will display all the continuous DTC's.

VACUUM DIAGRAMS

Following are vacuum diagrams for most of the engine and emissions package combinations covered by this manual. Because vacuum circuits will vary based on various engine and vehicle options, always refer first to the vehicle emission control information label, if present. Should the label be missing, or should vehicle be equipped with a different engine from the vehicle's original equipment, refer to the diagrams below for the same or similar configuration.

If you wish to obtain a replacement emissions label, most manufacturers make the labels available for purchase. The labels can usually be ordered from a local dealer.

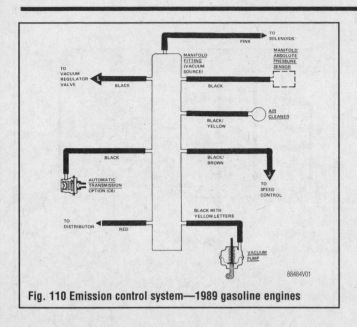

Fig. 110 Emission control system—1989 gasoline engines

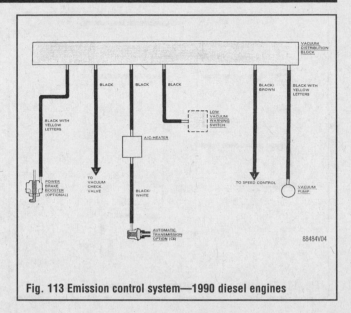

Fig. 113 Emission control system—1990 diesel engines

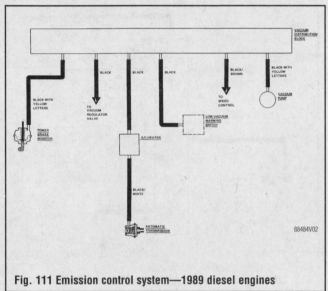

Fig. 111 Emission control system—1989 diesel engines

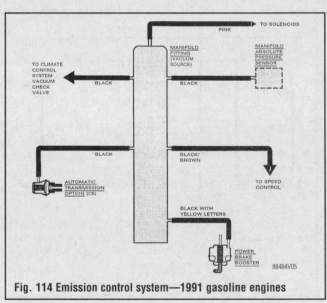

Fig. 114 Emission control system—1991 gasoline engines

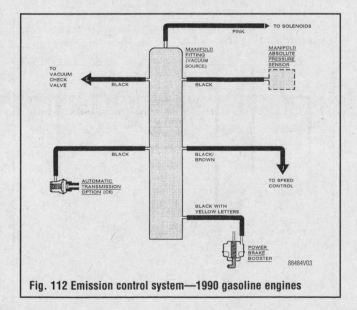

Fig. 112 Emission control system—1990 gasoline engines

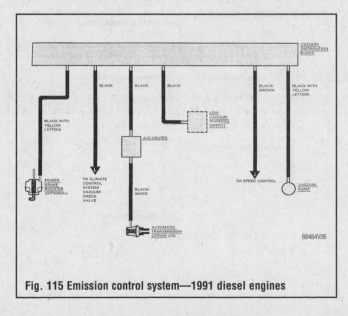

Fig. 115 Emission control system—1991 diesel engines

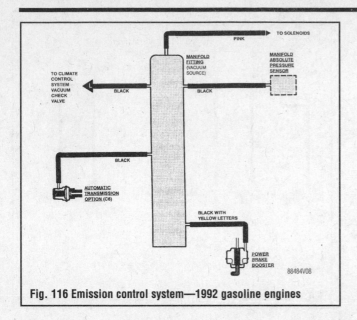

Fig. 116 Emission control system—1992 gasoline engines

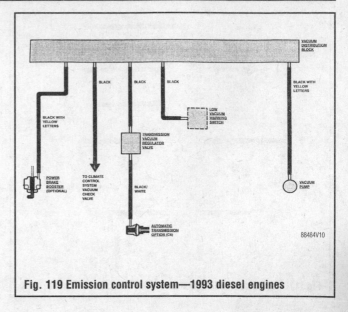

Fig. 119 Emission control system—1993 diesel engines

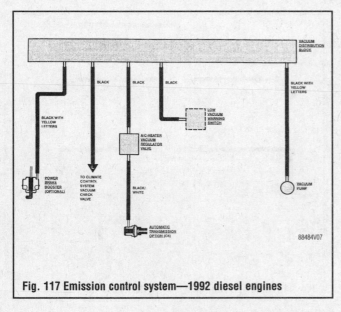

Fig. 117 Emission control system—1992 diesel engines

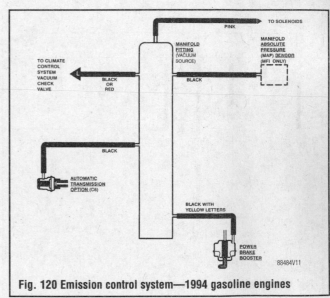

Fig. 120 Emission control system—1994 gasoline engines

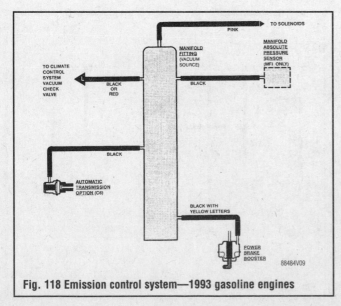

Fig. 118 Emission control system—1993 gasoline engines

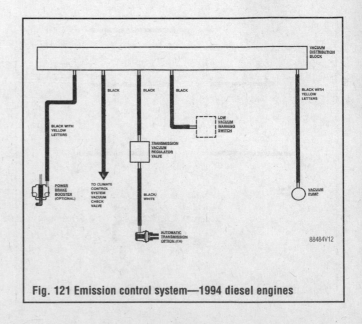

Fig. 121 Emission control system—1994 diesel engines

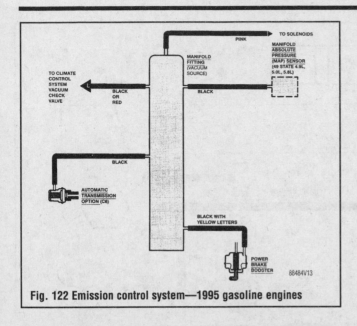

Fig. 122 Emission control system—1995 gasoline engines

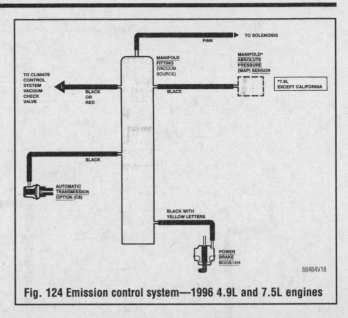

Fig. 124 Emission control system—1996 4.9L and 7.5L engines

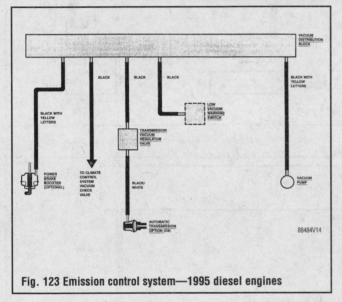

Fig. 123 Emission control system—1995 diesel engines

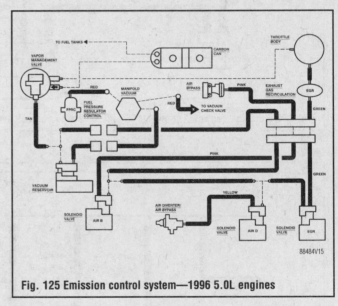

Fig. 125 Emission control system—1996 5.0L engines

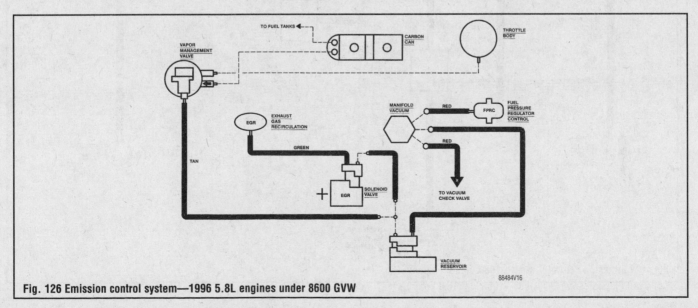

Fig. 126 Emission control system—1996 5.8L engines under 8600 GVW

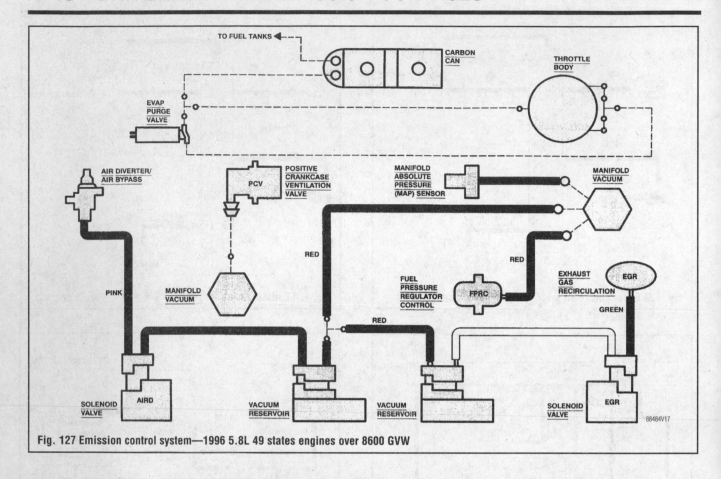

Fig. 127 Emission control system—1996 5.8L 49 states engines over 8600 GVW

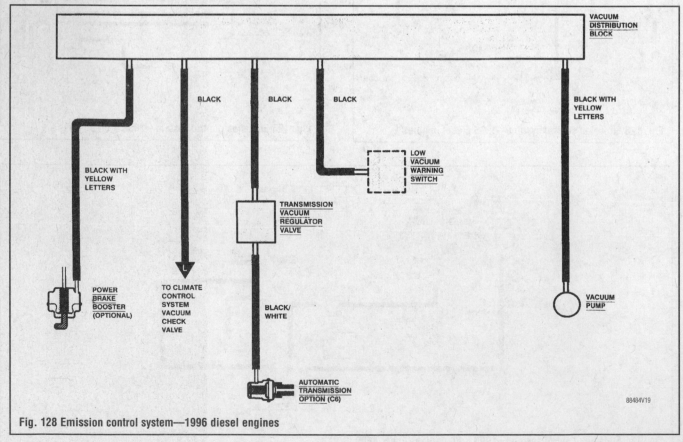

Fig. 128 Emission control system—1996 diesel engines

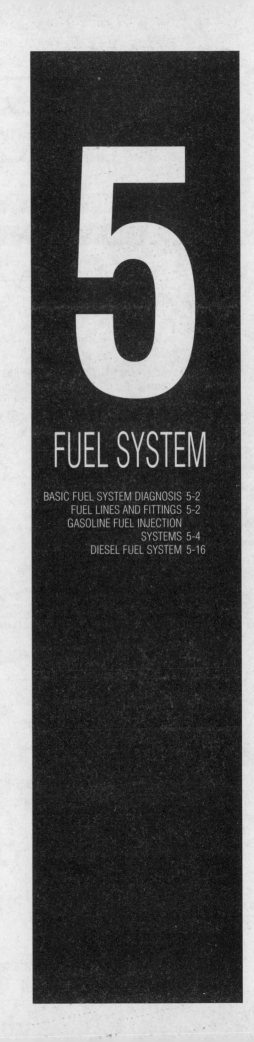

5

FUEL SYSTEM

BASIC FUEL SYSTEM DIAGNOSIS

When there is a problem starting or driving a vehicle, two of the most important checks involve the ignition and the fuel systems. The questions most mechanics attempt to answer first, "is there spark?" and "is there fuel?" will often lead to solving most basic problems. For ignition system diagnosis and testing, please refer to the information on engine electrical components and ignition systems found earlier in this manual. If the ignition system checks out (there is spark), then you must determine if the fuel system is operating properly (is there fuel?).

FUEL LINES AND FITTINGS

Quick-Connect Line Fittings

REMOVAL & INSTALLATION

The fuel system, depending on model year of the vehicle, may be equipped with push type connectors or spring lock couplings. When removing the fuel lines on these vehicles, it will be necessary to use Fuel Line Coupling Disconnect Tool D87L–9280–A or–B, or equivalent.

➡Quick-Connect (push) type fittings must be disconnected using proper procedures or the fitting may be damaged. Two types of retainers are used on the push connect fittings. Line sizes of ⅜ in. and ⁵⁄₁₆ in. use a hairpin clip retainer. ¼ in. line connectors use a Duck bill clip retainer.

Push Connect (Steel) Fittings

▸ **See Figures 1, 2, 3 and 4**

1. Relieve the fuel system pressure.
2. Open the safety clip and fit tools T90T-9550-B (⁵⁄₁₆ in.) or T90T-9550-C (⅜ in.) to the coupling so that the tool enters the female fitting.
3. Push the tool into the female fitting so that it releases the retaining fingers from the male tube end.
4. Pull the fittings apart and remove the tool.
5. Inspect the lines and fittings for damage.
To install:
6. Push the two ends of the fittings together until an audible click is heard.
7. Pull on the fitting to make sure that it is properly connected.
8. Lock the assembly with a safety clip, start the van and check for leaks

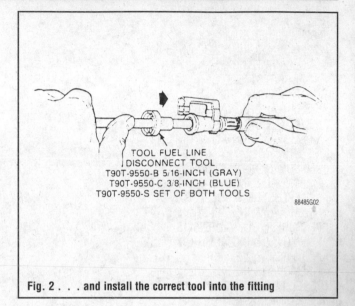

Fig. 2 . . . and install the correct tool into the fitting

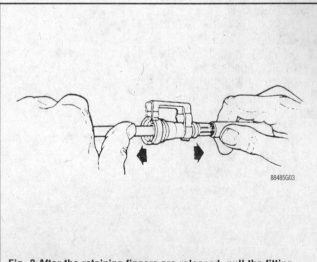

Fig. 3 After the retaining fingers are released, pull the fitting and tube apart

Spring Lock Couplings

▸ **See Figures 5, 6, 7, 8 and 9**

If the fuel system is equipped with spring lock couplings, remove the retaining clip from the spring lock coupling by hand only. Do not use any sharp tool or screwdriver, as it may damage the spring lock coupling.
1. Relieve the fuel system pressure.
2. Twist the fitting to free it from any adhesion at the O-ring seals.

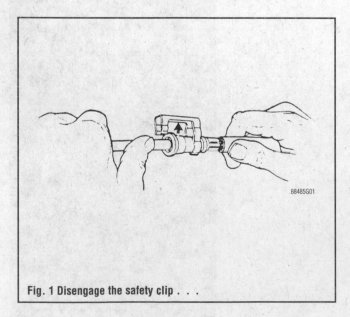

Fig. 1 Disengage the safety clip . . .

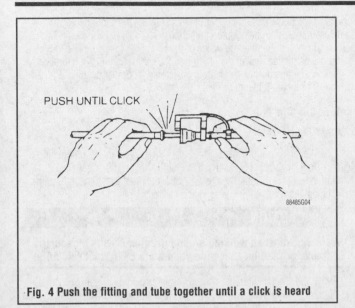
Fig. 4 Push the fitting and tube together until a click is heard

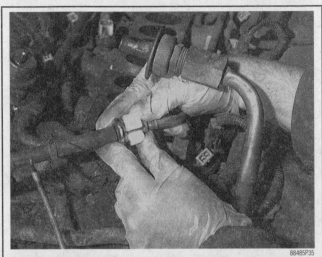
Fig. 7 Push the tool into the cage so that it expands the garter spring

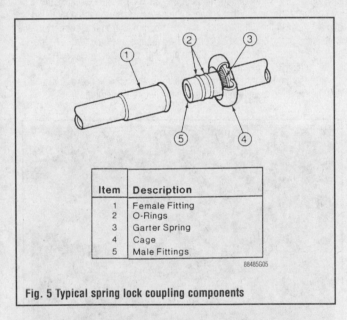

Item	Description
1	Female Fitting
2	O-Rings
3	Garter Spring
4	Cage
5	Male Fittings

Fig. 5 Typical spring lock coupling components

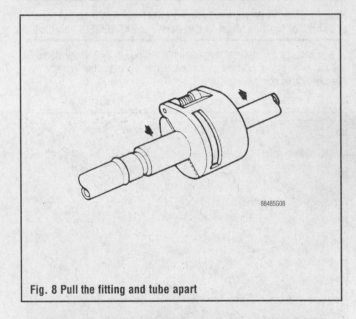
Fig. 8 Pull the fitting and tube apart

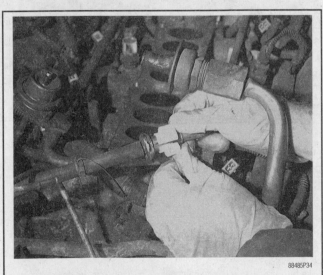
Fig. 6 Install the proper disconnection tool on the fitting

Fig. 9 Separate the fuel line couplings

➡Inspect the condition of the O-ring seals and replace them with the correct parts, if necessary.

3. Fit Spring Lock Coupling Tool T81P–19623–G1/G2 or equivalent to the coupling.

4. Close the tool and push it into the open side of the cage to expand the garter spring and release the female fitting.

5. After the garter spring is expanded, pull the fitting and tube apart.

6. Remove the tool from the disconnected coupling.

To install:

7. Lubricate the O-rings with refrigerant oil and insert the white indicator ring into the cage of the male fitting.

8. Push the couplings together with a slight twisting motion until the white indicator ring pops free.

Hairpin Clip

▶ **See Figure 10**

1. Clean all dirt and/or grease from the fittings. Spread the two clip legs about an ⅛ in. each to disengage from the fitting and pull the clip outward from the fitting. Use finger pressure only, do not use any tools.

❄❄ CAUTION

Never smoke when working around gasoline! Avoid all sources of sparks or ignition. Gasoline vapors are EXTREMELY volatile!

2. Grasp the fittings and hose assembly and pull away from the steel line. Twist the fitting and hose assembly slightly while pulling, if necessary, when a sticking condition exists.

3. Inspect the hairpin clip for damage, replace the clip if necessary. Reinstall the clip in position on the fitting.

4. Inspect the fitting and inside of the connector to ensure freedom of dirt or obstruction. Install the fitting into the connector and push together. A click will be heard when the hairpin snaps into its proper position. Pull on the line to insure full engagement.

Duck Bill Clip

▶ **See Figure 11**

1. A special tool is available for Ford for removing the retaining clip (Ford Tool No. T82L–9500–AH). If the tool is not available, see Step 2. Align the slot on the push connector disconnect tool with either tab on the retaining clip. Pull the line from the connector.

❄❄ CAUTION

Never smoke when working around gasoline! Avoid all sources of sparks or ignition. Gasoline vapors are EXTREMELY volatile!

2. If the special clip tool is not available, use a pair of narrow 6 in. (152mm) locking pliers with a jaw width of 0.2 in. (5mm) or less. Align the jaws of the pliers with the openings of the fitting case and compress the part of the retaining clip that engages the case. Compressing the retaining clip will release the fitting, which may then be pulled from the connector. Both sides of the clip must be compressed at the same time to disengage.

3. Inspect the retaining clip, fitting end and connector. Replace the clip if any damage is apparent.

4. Push the line into the steel connector until a click is heard, indicating that the clip is in place. Pull on the line to check engagement.

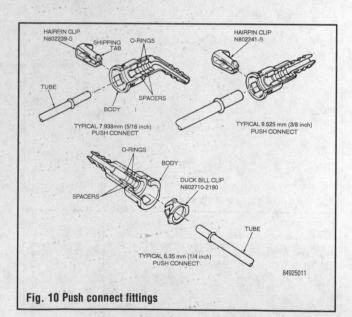

Fig. 10 Push connect fittings

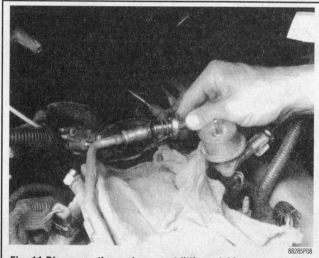

Fig. 11 Disengage the push connect fittings, taking care not to bend the lines

GASOLINE FUEL INJECTION SYSTEMS

General Information

➡**Both the Multi-port Fuel Injection (MFI) and Sequential Fuel Injection (SFI) systems are types of "multi-point" fuel injection. While Ford Motor Co. has changed terminology for many of its fuel system components, in many cases the technology has remained the same. For purposes of uniformity, the latest names of components will generally be used in this manual.**

The Multi-port Fuel Injection (MFI) and Sequential Fuel Injection (SFI) sub-systems include a high pressure inline electric fuel pump, a low-pressure tank-mounted fuel pump, fuel charging manifold, pressure regulator, fuel filter, and both solid and flexible fuel lines. The fuel charging manifold includes 6 or 8 electronically controlled fuel injectors, each mounted directly above an intake port in the lower intake manifold. On the 6-cylinder MFI system, the injectors are energized in two banks of three injectors, 1–3–5 in one bank and 2–4–6 in the other. One bank will spray once every crankshaft revolution, delivering a predetermined quantity of fuel into the intake air stream. On the V8 MFI engines, the injectors are energized in 2 banks of 4, once each crankshaft revolution. On the SFI engines, each fuel injector is energized once every other crankshaft revolution in sequence with the engine firing order.

The fuel pressure regulator maintains a constant pressure drop across the injector nozzles. The regulator is referenced to intake manifold vacuum and is connected parallel to the fuel injectors and positioned on the far end of the fuel rail. Any excess fuel supplied by the pump passes through the regulator and is returned to the fuel tank via a return line.

The fuel pressure regulator is a diaphragm operated relief valve in which the inside of the diaphragm senses fuel pressure and the other side senses manifold vacuum. Normal fuel pressure is established by a spring preload applied to the diaphragm. Control of the fuel system is maintained through the EEC power relay and the EEC-IV or EEC-V control unit, although electrical power is routed through the fuel pump relay and an inertia switch. The fuel pump relay is normally located on a bracket somewhere above the Powertrain Control Module (PCM) and the inertia switch is located in the cab. The in-line fuel pump is usually mounted on a bracket at the fuel tank, or on a frame rail. Tank-mounted pumps can be either high or low-pressure, depending on the model.

The inertia switch opens the power circuit to the fuel pump in the event of a collision. Once tripped, the switch must be reset manually by pushing the reset button on the assembly. Check that the inertia switch is reset before diagnosing power supply problems to the fuel pump circuit.

Relieving Fuel System Pressure

1. Disengage the electrical connection to either the fuel pump relay, inertia switch or in-line fuel pump.
2. Crank the engine for ten seconds.

➡The engine may start and run for a short time. If it does crank the engine for another 5 seconds after the engine stalls.

3. Engage the electrical connector that was disconnected in Step 1.
4. Disconnect the negative battery cable.

Electric Fuel Pump

REMOVAL & INSTALLATION

In-Tank Pump

▶ See Figures 12, 13, 14, 15 and 16

The electric fuel pump used in these models is located in the fuel tank and is removed as a unit with the fuel sender.

1. Release the fuel system pressure. Disconnect the negative battery cable.
2. Remove the fuel tank.

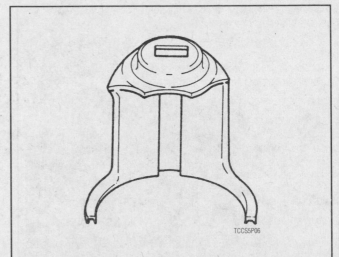

Fig. 13 A special tool is usually available to remove or install the fuel pump locking cam

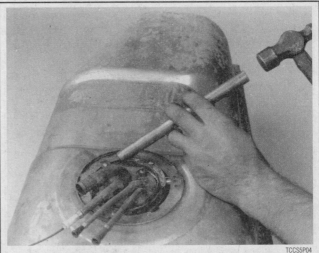

Fig. 14 A brass drift and a hammer can be used to loosen the fuel pump locking cam

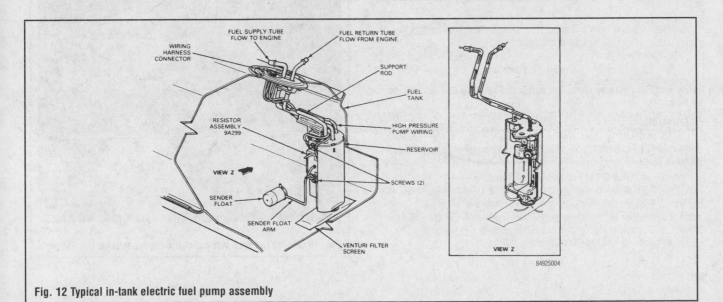

Fig. 12 Typical in-tank electric fuel pump assembly

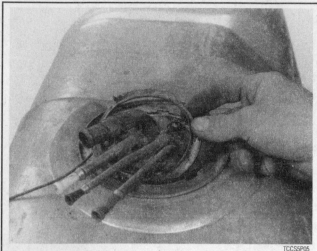

Fig. 15 Once the locking cam is released, it can be removed to free the fuel pump

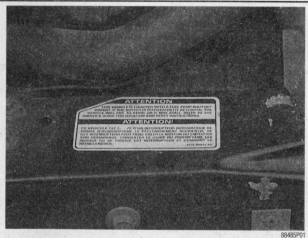

Fig. 16 The fuel system may be equipped with a cut-off switch; refer to underhood labels or your owner's manual for more information

3. Place the tank on a workbench and clean the dirt from around the pump/sender assembly locking ring area.

   a. Turn the locking ring counterclockwise to remove it.

4. Lift out the fuel pump and sending unit. Discard the gasket.

➡On E-series cutaway vans, the pump and sending unit is retained by bolts.

To install:

5. Clean the pump mounting flange and put a light coating of grease meeting Ford specification ESA-M1C75-B or its equivalent to hold the new gasket in place.

6. Place a new gasket in position in the groove in the tank.

7. Place the sending unit/fuel pump assembly in the tank, indexing the tabs with the slots in the tank. Make sure the gasket stays in place.

8. Hold the assembly in place and tighten the locking ring clockwise.

9. Connect the fuel lines and wiring.

10. Install the fuel tank.

External Pump

♦ See Figures 17 thru 23

1. Depressurize the fuel system.
2. Disconnect the negative battery cable.
3. Disengage the pump electrical connections.

❊❊ CAUTION

Never smoke when working around gasoline! Avoid all sources of sparks or ignition. Gasoline vapors are EXTREMELY volatile!

4. Raise and support the rear of the vehicle on jackstands.
5. Disconnect the inlet and outlet fuel lines.
6. Remove the pump from the mounting bracket.

To install:

7. Make sure the pump is indexed correctly in the mounting bracket insulator and tighten the retainers.

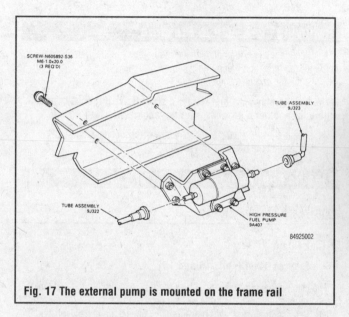

Fig. 17 The external pump is mounted on the frame rail

Fig. 18 Unplug the fuel pump electrical connections

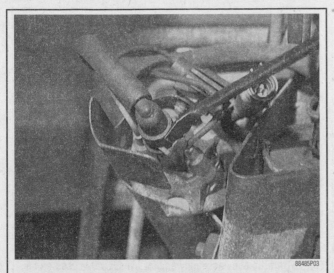

Fig. 19 Use a prytool to disengage the fuel line retaining clip

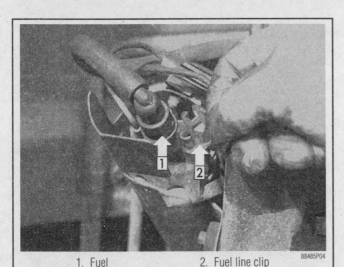

1. Fuel   2. Fuel line clip

Fig. 20 After the clip is loosened, grasp it and pull it from the line

Fig. 21 Unfasten the pump to bracket retainers

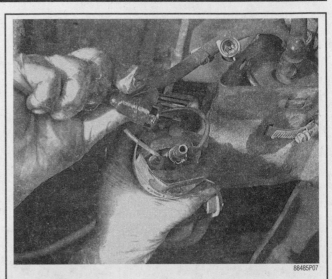

Fig. 22 Disconnect the front fuel line from the pump

Fig. 23 Slide the pump out to gain access to the rear fuel line and disconnect it in the same manner as the front

8. Engage the fuel lines.
9. Lower the van.
10. Connect the negative battery cable and check for leaks.

VOLUME TEST

1. Operate the engine at the specified idle rpm.

✳✳ CAUTION

Never smoke when working around gasoline! Avoid all sources of sparks or ignition. Gasoline vapors are EXTREMELY volatile!

2. Open the hose restrictor and catch the fuel in the container while observing the time it takes to pump 1 pint. 1 pint should be pumped in 20 seconds. If the pump does not pump to specifications, check for proper fuel tank venting or a restriction in the fuel line leading from the fuel tank to the carburetor before replacing the fuel pump.

GAUGE TEST

▶ **See Figure 24**

1. Connect a fuel gauge to the pressure test point (shrader valve) on the fuel rail.
2. With key **ON** engine **OFF** the readings should be as follows:
- 1989–94 4.9L engines: 50–60 PSI (345–415 kPa)
- 1989–94 5.0L, 5.8L and 7.5L engines: 35–45 PSI (240–310 kPa)
- 1995–96 all engines: 35–45 PSI (240–310 kPa)
3. With key **ON** engine **ON** the readings should be as follows:
- 1989–94 4.9L engines: 45–60 PSI (310–415 kPa)
- 1989–94 5.0L, 5.8L and 7.5L engines: 30–45 PSI (210–310 kPa)
- 1995–96 all engines: 30–45 PSI (210–310 kPa)

Fig. 24 Fuel pressure can be checked using an inexpensive pressure/vacuum gauge

TCCS4P04

Throttle Body

REMOVAL & INSTALLATION

4.9L Engines

1989–94 MODELS

▶ **See Figure 25**

1. Relieve the fuel system pressure.
2. Disconnect the negative battery cable and remove the air cleaner and outlet tube.
3. Disengage the throttle position sensor and air by-pass valve connectors.
4. Disconnect the throttle linkage shield, cable and the speed control cable.

➡ Use a prytool positioned close to the ball stud when removing the throttle cable from the ball stud. Do not remove the cable by hand, as doing so may damage the cable.

5. Disconnect the air intake hose.

✳✳ CAUTION

Never smoke when working around gasoline! Avoid all sources of sparks or ignition. Gasoline vapors are EXTREMELY volatile!

6. Disconnect the harness from the purge ports of the throttle body.
7. Remove the four throttle body mounting nuts and carefully separate the air throttle body from the upper intake manifold.

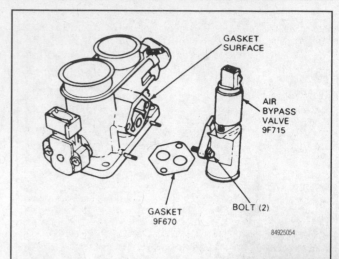

Fig. 25 Throttle body assembly and air bypass valve used on the 4.9L engine

8. Remove and discard the mounting gasket. Clean all mounting surfaces using care not to damage the gasket surfaces of the throttle body and manifold. Do not allow any material to drop into the intake manifold.
   To install:
9. Install a new gasket and the throttle body. Tighten the mounting nuts to 12–18 ft. lbs. (16–24 Nm).
10. Engage the throttle position sensor and air by-pass valve or idle air control valve connectors.
11. Connect the harness to the purge ports of the throttle body.
12. Connect the throttle linkage and cables.
13. Install the air cleaner assembly and connect the negative battery cable.

1995–96 MODELS

1. Relieve the fuel system pressure.
2. Disconnect the negative battery cable and remove the air cleaner assembly.
3. Disengage the throttle position sensor and idle air control valve connectors.
4. Remove the accelerator cable splash shield.
5. Disconnect the accelerator cable, transmission kickdown cable and the speed control cable.

➡ Use a prytool positioned close to the ball stud when removing the accelerator cable from the ball stud. Do not remove the cable by hand, as doing so may damage the cable.

6. Disconnect the air pump hoses from the throttle body.
7. Disengage the main emission vacuum control connector.

✳✳ CAUTION

Never smoke when working around gasoline! Avoid all sources of sparks or ignition. Gasoline vapors are EXTREMELY volatile!

8. Remove the four throttle body mounting nuts and carefully separate the air throttle body from the upper intake manifold.
9. Remove and discard the mounting gasket. Clean all mounting surfaces using care not to damage the gasket surfaces of the throttle body and manifold. Do not allow any material to drop into the intake manifold.
   To install:
10. Install a new gasket and the throttle body. Tighten the mounting nuts to 14–20 ft. lbs. (19–20 Nm).
11. Engage the throttle position sensor idle air control valve connectors.
12. Engage the main emission vacuum control connector.

13. Connect the accelerator cable, transmission kickdown cable and the speed control cable.

14. Install the accelerator cable splash shield.

15. Install the air cleaner assembly and connect the negative battery cable.

5.0L and 5.8L Engines

▶ **See Figures 26 thru 37**

1. Relieve the fuel system pressure.

2. Disconnect the negative battery cable and remove the air cleaner assembly.

3. Disengage the throttle position sensor and idle air control valve connectors.

4. Disconnect the accelerator cable and on models equipped with and C6 automatic transmission the transmission linkage.

➡**Use a prytool positioned close to the ball stud when removing the accelerator cable from the ball stud. Do not remove the cable by hand as it may damage it.**

5. Tag and disconnect the coolant and vacuum lines from the throttle body as necessary.

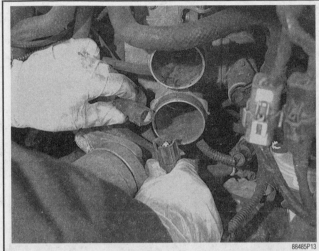

Fig. 28 Disengage the throttle position sensor electrical connection

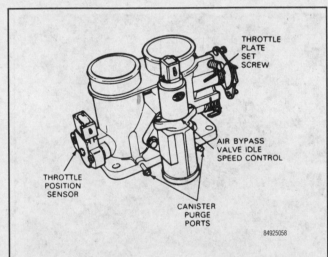

Fig. 26 Throttle body assembly, including throttle position sensor and air bypass valve—5.0L and 5.8L engines

Fig. 29 Loosen the hose clamps . . .

Fig. 27 Unplug the idle air control valve electrical connection

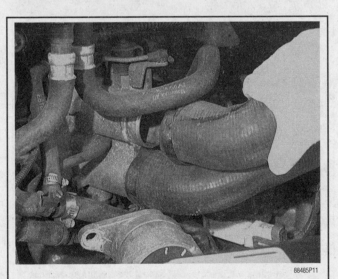

Fig. 30 . . . and disconnect the hoses from the throttle body

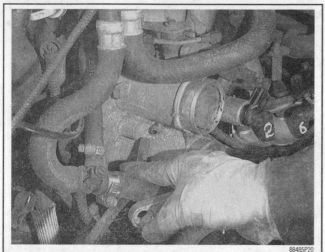

Fig. 31 Make sure all vacuum hoses are tagged and disconnected

Fig. 34 Disconnect the lower coolant lines

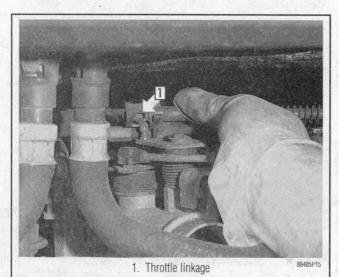

1. Throttle linkage

Fig. 32 Disconnect the throttle linkage from the ball stud

Fig. 35 Unfasten the throttle body mounting bolts

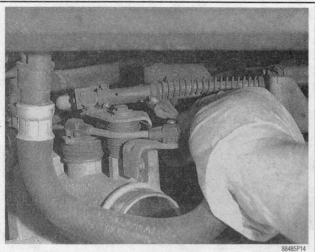

Fig. 33 On equipped models, disconnect the transmission linkage

Fig. 36 Remove the throttle body from the engine compartment

Fig. 37 Use a scraper to clean the throttle body mating surfaces

6. Remove the four throttle body mounting nuts and carefully separate the air throttle body from the upper intake manifold.

7. Remove and discard the mounting gasket. Clean all mounting surfaces using care not to damage the gasket surfaces of the throttle body and manifold. Do not allow any material to drop into the intake manifold.

To install:

8. Install a new gasket and the throttle body. Tighten the mounting nuts to 12–18 ft. lbs. (16–24 Nm).

9. Connect the coolant and vacuum lines to the throttle body.

10. Engage the throttle position sensor idle air control valve connectors.

11. Connect the accelerator cable and transmission linkage.

12. Install the air cleaner assembly and connect the negative battery cable.

7.5L Engine

◗ See Figure 38

1. Relieve the fuel system pressure.

2. Disconnect the throttle cable from the throttle ball.

3. If equipped, disconnect the automatic transmission linkage from the throttle body.

4. Tag and disengage all wires and hoses.

5. Remove the four throttle body mounting nuts and carefully separate the air throttle body from the upper intake manifold.

6. Remove and discard the mounting gasket. Clean all mounting surfaces using care not to damage the gasket surfaces of the throttle body and manifold. Do not allow any material to drop into the intake manifold.

To install:

7. Install a new gasket and the throttle body. Tighten the mounting nuts to 12–18 ft. lbs. (16–24 Nm).

8. Engage all wiring and hoses.

9. Connect all cables and linkages.

Fuel Injectors

REMOVAL & INSTALLATION

◗ See Figures 39, 40, 41, 42 and 43

1. Relieve the fuel system pressure.

2. On all except early model 7.5L engines, remove the upper intake manifold assembly.

3. Remove the fuel rail.

4. Disengage the electrical connections from the injectors.

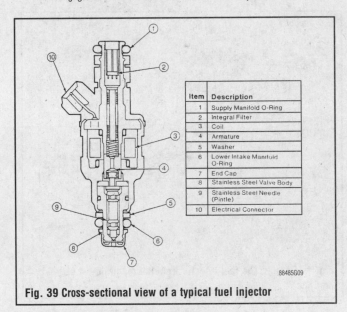

Item	Description
1	Supply Manifold O-Ring
2	Integral Filter
3	Coil
4	Armature
5	Washer
6	Lower Intake Manifold O-Ring
7	End Cap
8	Stainless Steel Valve Body
9	Stainless Steel Needle (Pintle)
10	Electrical Connector

Fig. 39 Cross-sectional view of a typical fuel injector

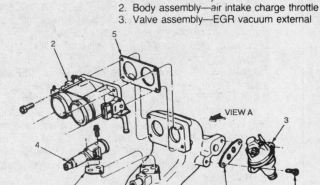
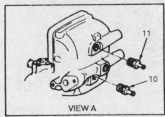

1. Manifold assembly—intake
2. Body assembly—air intake charge throttle
3. Valve assembly—EGR vacuum external
4. Valve assembly—throttle air bypass
5. Gasket—air charge control intake manifold
6. Gasket—EGR valve
7. Gasket—air bypass valve
8. Bolt 5/16 × 1.5 hex head UBS (6 reqd)
9. Bolt M6 × 25mm hex head UBS (2 reqd)
10. Connector 3/8" hose × 3/8" external pipe
11. Connector 3/8" hose × 3/8" external pipe
12. Connector 1/4" hose × 3/8" external pipe

VIEW A

Fig. 38 Exploded view of a throttle body and upper intake manifold assembly on 7.5L engines

Fig. 40 Unplug the injector's electrical connections

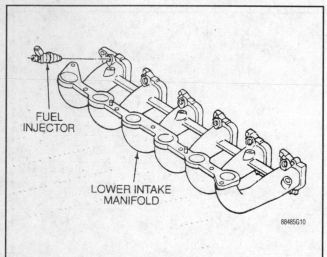

Fig. 41 Remove the fuel injector from the manifold—4.9L engines

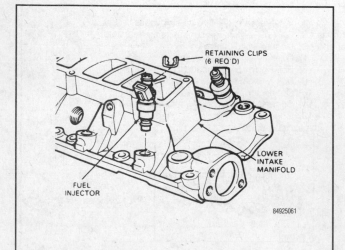

Fig. 42 Pull the injector from the bore in the intake manifold— 5.0L and 5.8L engines

Fig. 43 Rock the injector back and forth to remove it from the fuel rail

> **CAUTION**
>
> Never smoke when working around gasoline! Avoid all sources of sparks or ignition. Gasoline vapors are EXTREMELY volatile!

5. Pull upward on the injector body while gently rocking it from side-to-side.

6. Inspect the O-rings on the injector for any sign of leakage or damage. Replace any suspected O-rings.

7. Inspect the plastic cap at the top of each injector and replace it if any sign of deterioration is noticed.

To install:

8. Lubricate the O-rings with clean engine oil ONLY!

9. Install the injectors in the manifold by pushing them in with a gentle rocking motion.

10. Connect the electrical wiring.

11. Install the fuel rail.

12. If removed, install the upper intake manifold.

TESTING

Fuel Injector Pressure Test

▶ See Figures 44, 45 and 46

1. Connect pressure gauge T80L–9974–A, or equivalent, to the fuel pressure test fitting. Detach the coil connector from the coil. Disconnect the electrical lead from one injector and pressurize the fuel system. Disable the fuel pump by disconnecting the inertia switch or the fuel pump relay and observe the pressure gauge reading.

2. Crank the engine for 2 seconds. Turn the ignition **OFF** and wait 5 seconds, then observe the pressure drop. If the pressure drop is 2–16 psi (14–110 kPa), the injector is operating properly. Reconnect the injector, activate the fuel pump, then repeat the procedure for the other injectors.

3. If the pressure drop is less than 2 psi (14 kPa) or more than 16 psi (110 kPa), switch the electrical connectors on injectors and repeat the test. If the pressure drop is still incorrect, replace the disconnected injector with one of the same color code, then reconnect both injectors properly and repeat the test.

4. Disconnect and plug the vacuum hose at EGR valve. It may be necessary to disconnect the idle air control valve and use the throttle body stop screw to set the engine speed. Start and run the engine at 1,800 rpm (2,000 rpm on 1984 and later models). Disconnect the left injector electrical connector. Note the rpm after the engine stabilizes (around 1,200 rpm). Reconnect the injector and allow the engine to return to high idle.

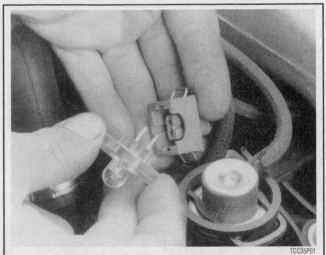

Fig. 44 A noid light can be attached to the fuel injector harness in order to test for injector pulse

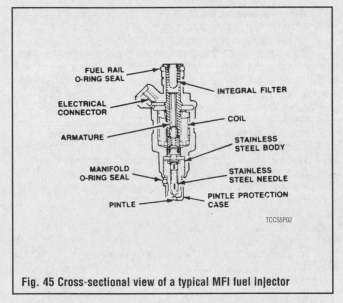

Fig. 45 Cross-sectional view of a typical MFI fuel injector

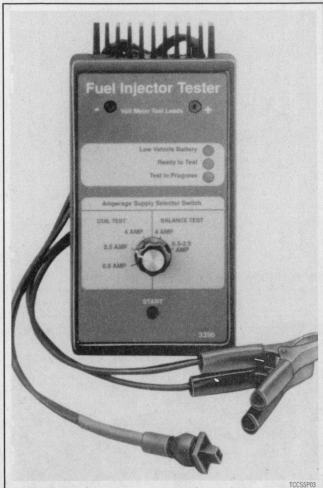

Fig. 46 Fuel injector testers can be purchased or sometimes rented

5. Perform the same procedure for the right injector. Note the difference between the rpm readings of the left and right injectors. If the difference is 100 rpm or less, check the oxygen sensor. If the difference is more than 100 rpm, replace both injectors.

Fuel Supply Manifold

REMOVAL & INSTALLATION

▶ See Figures 47, 48, 49, 50 and 51

❋❋ CAUTION

Never smoke when working around gasoline! Avoid all sources of sparks or ignition. Gasoline vapors are EXTREMELY volatile!

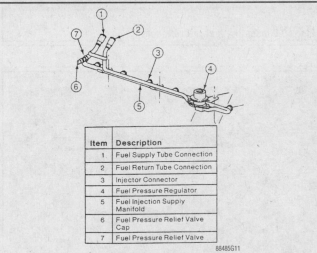

Item	Description
1	Fuel Supply Tube Connection
2	Fuel Return Tube Connection
3	Injector Connector
4	Fuel Pressure Regulator
5	Fuel Injection Supply Manifold
6	Fuel Pressure Relief Valve Cap
7	Fuel Pressure Relief Valve

Fig. 47 Fuel supply manifold and related components—4.9L engines

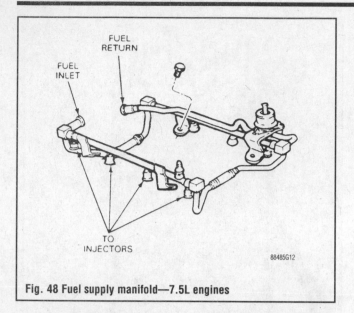

Fig. 48 Fuel supply manifold—7.5L engines

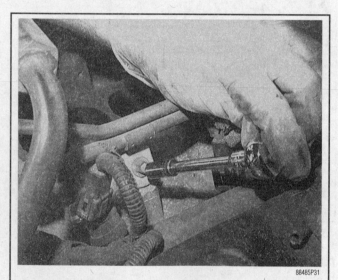

Fig. 49 Loosen the fuel rail retainers

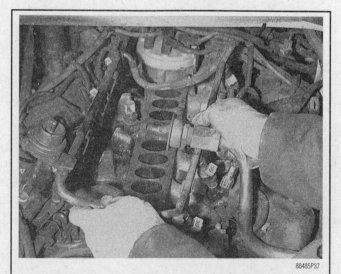

Fig. 50 Remove the fuel rail from the intake manifold

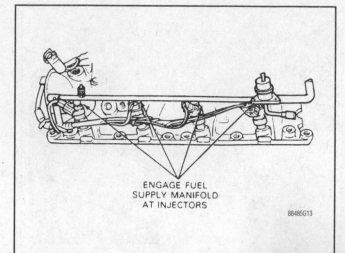

Fig. 51 Make sure the fuel supply manifold is firmly engaged to the injectors

1. Relieve fuel system pressure.
2. Disconnect the negative battery cable.
3. Remove the upper intake manifold assembly.
4. Tag and disengage any vacuum lines and electrical connections that will hinder fuel supply manifold removal.
5. Disengage the fuel lines from the manifold.
6. Remove the fuel supply manifold retaining bolts. Carefully disengage the manifold from the fuel injectors and remove the manifold.

To install:

7. Make sure the injector caps are clean and free of contamination.
8. Place the fuel supply manifold over each injector and seat the injectors into the manifold. Make sure the caps are seated firmly.
9. Tighten the fuel supply manifold retaining bolts as follows:
   - 1989–96 4.9L engines: 70–105 inch lbs. (8–12 Nm).
   - 1989–92 5.0L, 5.8L and 7.5L engines: 15–22 ft. lbs. (less than)20–30 Nm).
   - 1993–96 5.0L, 5.8L and 7.5L engines: 70–106 inch lbs. (8–12 Nm)
10. Engage the fuel lines and any wiring and vacuum lines disconnected during removal.
11. Install the upper intake manifold assembly.
12. Connect the negative battery cable.
13. Start the van and check for leaks.

Fuel Pressure Regulator

REMOVAL & INSTALLATION

▶ See Figures 52, 53, 54 and 55

1. Relieve the fuel system pressure.

❋❋ CAUTION

Never smoke when working around gasoline! Avoid all sources of sparks or ignition. Gasoline vapors are EXTREMELY volatile!

2. Disconnect the vacuum line at the regulator.
3. Remove the Allen or socket head screws from the regulator housing.

➡In some cases, the factory bent the fuel line over one of the screws making it difficult to remove with an Allen wrench. A pair of pliers may have to be used to break the screw loose so it can be unthreaded by hand.

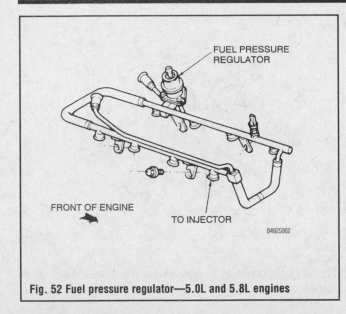

Fig. 52 Fuel pressure regulator—5.0L and 5.8L engines

Fig. 53 Disconnect the vacuum line from the fuel pressure regulator

Fig. 54 Loosen the fuel pressure regulator retainers . . .

Fig. 55 . . . then remove the regulator from the fuel rail

4. Remove the regulator, seal and O-rings.
5. Clean the gasket mating surfaces.
6. Inspect the regulator O-ring for signs of deterioration or damage. Discard the gasket.

To install:

7. Lubricate the O-ring with clean engine oil ONLY!
8. Make sure that the mounting surfaces are clean.
9. Using a new gasket, install the regulator. Tighten the retaining screws to 27–44 inch lbs. (3–3 Nm).
10. Connect the vacuum line.

Pressure Relief Valve

REMOVAL & INSTALLATION

▶ **See Figure 56**

This procedure applies to all 4.9L engines and 1995–96 5.0L and 5.8L engines only.

1. Relieve the fuel system pressure.

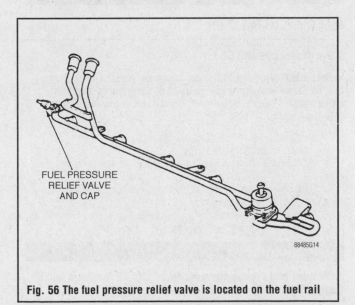

Fig. 56 The fuel pressure relief valve is located on the fuel rail

✳✳ CAUTION

Never smoke when working around gasoline! Avoid all sources of sparks or ignition. Gasoline vapors are EXTREMELY volatile!

2. Unscrew the valve from the fuel line.
3. When installing the valve, tighten it to 48–84 inch lbs. (5–9 Nm)
4. Tighten the cap to 5 inch lbs. (0.56 Nm).

Air Bypass Valve

REMOVAL & INSTALLATION

▸ See Figures 57 and 58

This procedure applies to 1989–93 models only.
1. Disconnect the wiring at the valve.

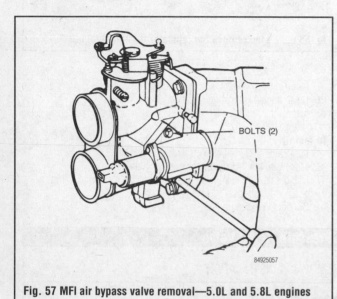

Fig. 57 MFI air bypass valve removal—5.0L and 5.8L engines

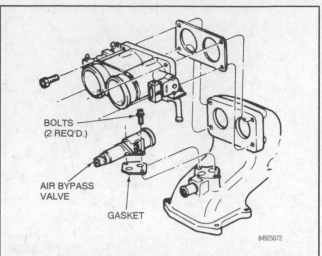

Fig. 58 Exploded view of air bypass valve mounting—7.5L engine

✳✳ CAUTION

Never smoke when working around gasoline! Avoid all sources of sparks or ignition. Gasoline vapors are EXTREMELY volatile!

2. Remove the retainers and lift off the valve.
3. Discard the gasket and clean and inspect the mating surfaces.
4. Install the valve with a new gasket, tightening the retainers to 102 inch lbs. (11.5 Nm). Connect the wiring.

DIESEL FUEL SYSTEM

Injection Lines

REMOVAL & INSTALLATION

▸ See Figures 59 and 60

➡Before removing any fuel lines, clean the exterior with clean fuel oil, or solvent to prevent entry of dirt into the fuel system when the fuel lines are removed. If available, blow dry with compressed air.

1. Disconnect the battery ground cables from both batteries.
2. Remove the engine cover.
3. Remove the air cleaner and cap intake manifold opening with clean rags.
4. Disconnect the accelerator cable and speed control cable, if so equipped, from the injection pump.
5. Remove the accelerator cable bracket from the intake manifold and position out of the way with cable(s) attached.

✳ WARNING

To prevent fuel system contamination, cap all fuel lines and fittings.

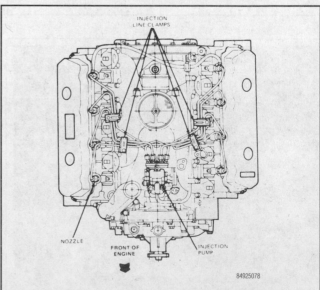

Fig. 59 Diesel engine injection line clamps; injection lines also shown

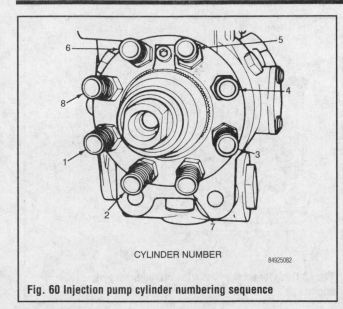

Fig. 60 Injection pump cylinder numbering sequence

6. Disconnect the fuel line from the fuel filter to injection pump and cap all fittings.

7. Disconnect and cap the nozzle fuel lines at nozzles.

8. Remove the fuel line clamps from the fuel lines to be removed.

9. Remove and cap the injection pump inlet elbow.

10. Remove and cap the inlet fitting adapter.

11. Remove the injection nozzle lines, one at a time, from the injection pump using Tool T83T–9396–A, or equivalent.

➡Fuel lines must be removed following this sequence: 5–6–4–8–3–1–7–2. Install caps on the end of each fuel line and pump fitting as the line is disconnected and identify each fuel line accordingly.

To install:

12. Install fuel lines on injection pump, one at a time, and tighten to 22 ft. lbs. (30 Nm).

➡Fuel lines must be installed in the following sequence: 2–7–1–3–8–4–6–5.

13. Clean the old sealant from the injection pump elbow, using clean solvent, and dry thoroughly.

14. Apply a light coating of pipe sealant on the elbow threads.

15. Connect the lines and connect them to 22 ft. lbs. (30 Nm).

16. Connect the fuel line from the filter and tighten to 22 ft. lbs. (30 Nm).

17. Install the line retaining clamps and the accelerator and speed control cable.

18. Remove the intake manifold cover.

19. Install the air cleaner and the engine cover.

20. Connect the negative battery cables.

➡On newer model vehicles when the battery is disconnected it may cause some abnormal drive symptoms until the Powertrain Control Module (PCM) relearns its adaptive strategy. The vehicle may need to be driven 10 miles or more for the PCM to relearn its strategy.

21. Start the van and check for leaks.

Injectors

REMOVAL & INSTALLATION

1989–94 Engines

▶ See Figures 61 and 62

➡Before removing the nozzle assemblies, clean the exterior of each nozzle assembly and the surrounding area with clean fuel oil or solvent to prevent entry of dirt into the engine when nozzle assemblies are removed. Also, clean the fuel inlet and fuel leak-off piping connections. Blow dry with compressed air.

1. Remove the fuel line retaining clamp(s) from the injection lines.

2. Disconnect the fuel injection lines and fuel leak-off tees from each injector and position out of the way. Cap the open ends of the fuel injectors with protective caps to prevent dirt from entering.

3. Remove the injectors by turning them counterclockwise. Pull the assembly with the copper washer attached from the engine. Cover the nozzle spray tips with plastic caps.

➡Remove the copper injector nozzle gasket from the nozzle bore with special tool, T71P–19703–C, or equivalent, whenever the gasket does not come out with the injector.

4. Place the injector assemblies in a fabricated holder as they are removed from the heads. The holder should be marked with numbers corresponding to the cylinder numbering of the engine.

To install:

5. Thoroughly clean the injector bore in cylinder head with nozzle special tool T83T–9527–A or an equivalent nozzle seat cleaner. Make certain that no small particles of metal or carbon remain on the seating surface. Blow out the particles with compressed air.

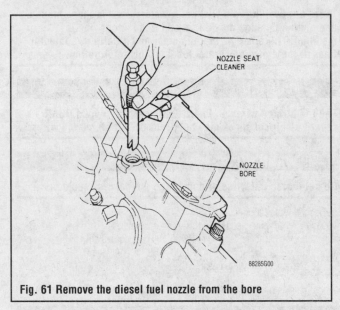

Fig. 61 Remove the diesel fuel nozzle from the bore

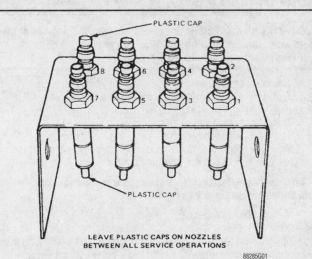

Fig. 62 Fabricate a holder like the one shown to organize the diesel fuel nozzles

6. Remove the protective cap and install a new copper gasket on the nozzle tip with a small dab of grease.

➡**Anti-seize compound or equivalent should be used on injectors threads to aid in installation and future removal.**

7. Install the injector assembly into the cylinder head and tighten to 33 ft. lbs. (45 Nm).

8. Remove the protective caps from injectors and fuel lines.

9. Connect the high pressure fuel lines and tighten them with a flare nut wrench.

10. Install the leak-off tees to the nozzle assemblies.

➡**Install two new O-ring seals for each fuel return tee.**

11. Install the fuel line retainer clamps.
12. Start the engine and check for leaks.

1995–96 Engines

RIGHT SIDE

♦ **See Figures 63, 64, 65 and 66**

> ※※ **WARNING**
>
> There are two different types of injectors used in these models and engine damage may be caused if the wrong one is installed. There is a 49 state injector and a California injector. Consult the emission control label for this information.

> ※※ **CAUTION**
>
> The red-striped wires on the DI Turbo carry 115 volts DC. A severe electrical shock may be given. Do not pierce the wires.

> ※※ **WARNING**
>
> Do not pierce the wires or damage to the harness could occur.

Special tools required:
- Slide Hammer, No. T50T–100–A, or equivalent
- Injector Remover, No. T94T–9000–AH1, or equivalent
- Injector Replacer, No. T94T–9000–AH2, or equivalent
1. Remove the engine cover.
2. Remove the valve cover.
3. Disengage the fuel injector electrical connector.

> ※※ **WARNING**
>
> Remove the oil drain plugs prior to removing the injectors or oil could enter the combustion chamber which could result in hydrostatic lock and severe engine damage.

4. Remove the oil rail drain plugs.
5. Remove the retaining screw and oil deflector. The shoulder bolt on the inboard side of the fuel injector does not require removal.
6. Remove the outboard fuel injector retaining bolt.
7. Remove the front body bolts.
8. Raise the right side of the van body until the injectors are sufficiently clear of all obstructions and can be removed without damage to the O-rings.

➡**Make sure the injector O-rings and copper washer are removed from the bores after injector removal.**

9. Remove the fuel injector using Injector Remover No. T94T–9000–AH1, or equivalent. Position the tool's fulcrum beneath the fuel injector hold-down plate and over the edge of the cylinder head. Install the remover screw in the threaded hole of the fuel injector plate (see illustration). Tighten the screw to lift out the injector from its bore. Place the injector in a suitable protective sleeve such as Rotunda Injector Protective Sleeve, No. 014–00933–2, and set the injector in a suitable holding rack.

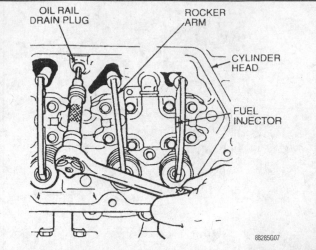

Fig. 63 Don't forget to remove the oil rail drain plug—1994–96 engines

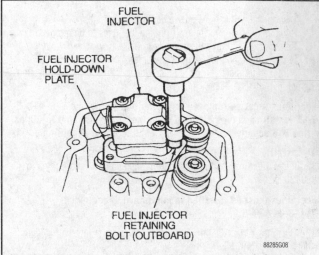

Fig. 64 Remove the outboard fuel injector retaining bolt as shown—1995–96 engines

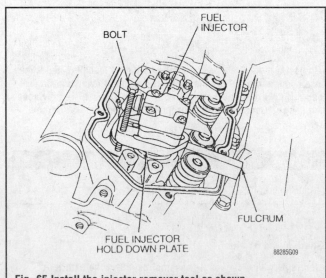

Fig. 65 Install the injector remover tool as shown

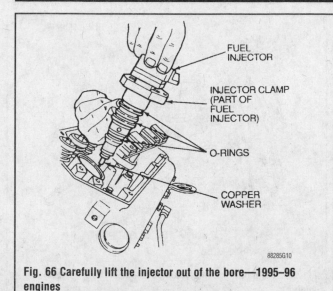

Fig. 66 Carefully lift the injector out of the bore—1995–96 engines

10. Remove the fuel injector sleeves, if required. Insert the Injector Sleeve Tap Plug, 014–00934–3 into the injector sleeve to prevent debris from entering the combustion chamber. Insert Injector Sleeve Tap Pilot into the fuel injector sleeve and tighten 1–1 ½ turns. Attach Slide Hammer T50T–100–A to the Injector Sleeve Tap 014–00934–1 and 014–00934–2 Injector Sleeve Tap Pilot and remove the fuel injector sleeve from the bore.

11. Use Rotunda Injector Sleeve Brush 104–00934–A, or equivalent to clean the injector bore of any sealant residue. Make sure to remove any debris.

To install:

12. If removed, install the fuel injector sleeves using Rotunda Sleeve Replacer, No. 014–00934–4, or equivalent. Apply Threadlock, No. 262–E2FZ–19554–B, or equivalent to the fuel injector sleeves as shown (see illustration). Using a rubber mallet, tap on the tool to seat the injector bore. Remove the tool and remove any residue sealant.

13. Clean the fuel injector sleeve using a suitable sleeve brush set. Clean any debris from the sleeve.

14. Clean the injector bore with a lint-free shop towel.

15. Install the fuel injectors using special tools as follows:

   a. Lubricate the injectors with clean engine oil. Using new copper washers, carefully push the injectors square into the bore using hand pressure only to seat the O-rings.

   b. Position the open end of Injector Replacer, No. T94T–9000–AH2, or equivalent between the fuel injector body and injector hold-down plate, while positioning the opposite end of the tool over the edge of the cylinder head.

   c. Align the hole in the tool with the threaded hole in the cylinder head and install the bolt from the tool kit. Tighten the bolt to fully seat the injector, then remove the bolt and tool.

16. Install the outer half of the heater distribution box and retaining hardware (for No. 4 injector only).

17. Install the oil deflector and bolt. Tighten the bolt to 108 inch lbs. (12 Nm).

18. Install the fuel rail drain plug, tightening it to 96 inch lbs. (11 Nm).

19. Install the oil rail drain plug, tightening it to 53 inch lbs. (6 Nm).

20. Lower the right side of the body and tighten the front body bolts to 44–66 ft. lbs. (60–81 Nm).

21. Connect the fuel injector wiring harness.

22. Install the valve cover.

23. Install the engine cover.

LEFT SIDE

1. Remove the engine cover.
2. Remove the valve cover.
3. Disengage the fuel injector electrical connector.

⁂⁂ WARNING

Remove the oil drain plugs prior to removing the injectors or oil could enter the combustion chamber which could result in hydrostatic lock and severe engine damage.

4. Remove the oil rail drain plugs.

5. Remove the retaining screw and oil deflector. The shoulder bolt on the inboard side of the fuel injector does not require removal.

6. Remove the outboard fuel injector retaining bolt.

7. Remove the fuel injector using Injector Remover No. T94T–9670–AH1, or equivalent. Position the tool's fulcrum beneath the fuel injector hold-down plate and over the edge of the cylinder head. Install the remover screw in the threaded hole of the fuel injector plate (see illustration). Tighten the screw to lift out the injector from its bore. Place the injector in a suitable protective sleeve such as Rotunda Injector Protective Sleeve, No. 014–00933–2, and set the injector in a suitable holding rack.

8. Remove the fuel injector sleeves, if required. Insert the Injector Sleeve Tap Plug, 014–00934–3 into the injector sleeve to prevent debris from entering the combustion chamber. Insert Injector Sleeve Tap Pilot into the fuel injector sleeve and tighten 1–1 ½ turns. Attach Slide Hammer T50T–100–A to the Injector Sleeve Tap 014–00934–1 and 014–00934–2 Injector Sleeve Tap Pilot and remove the fuel injector sleeve from the bore.

9. Use Rotunda Injector Sleeve Brush 104–00934–A, or equivalent to clean the injector bore of any sealant residue. Make sure to remove any debris.

To install:

10. If removed, install the fuel injector sleeves using Rotunda Sleeve Replacer, No. 014–00934–4, or equivalent. Apply Threadlock, No. 262–E2FZ–19554–B, or equivalent to the fuel injector sleeves as shown (see illustration). Using a rubber mallet, tap on the tool to seat the injector bore. Remove the tool and remove any residue sealant.

11. Clean the fuel injector sleeve using a suitable sleeve brush set. Clean any debris from the sleeve.

12. Clean the injector bore with a lint-free shop towel.

13. Install the fuel injectors using special tools as follows:

   a. Lubricate the injectors with clean engine oil. Using new copper washers, carefully push the injectors square into the bore using hand pressure only to seat the O-rings.

   b. Position the open end of Injector Replacer, No. T94T–9000–AH2, or equivalent between the fuel injector body and injector hold-down plate, while positioning the opposite end of the tool over the edge of the cylinder head.

   c. Align the hole in the tool with the threaded hole in the cylinder head and install the bolt from the tool kit. Tighten the bolt to fully seat the injector, then remove the bolt and tool.

14. Install the outer half of the heater distribution box and retaining hardware (for No. 4 injector only).

15. Install the oil deflector and bolt. Tighten the bolt to 108 inch lbs. (12 Nm).

16. Install the fuel rail drain plug, tightening it to 96 inch lbs. (11 Nm).

17. Install the oil rail drain plug, tightening it to 53 inch lbs. (6 Nm).

18. Connect the fuel injector wiring harness.

19. Install the valve cover.

Fuel Supply Pump

REMOVAL & INSTALLATION

1989–94 Engines

▶ See Figure 67

1. Loosen the threaded connections with the proper size wrench (a flare nut wrench is preferred) and retighten snugly. Do not remove the lines at this time.

2. Loosen the mounting bolts, one to two turns. Apply force with your hand to loosen the fuel pump if the gasket is stuck. Rotate the engine by

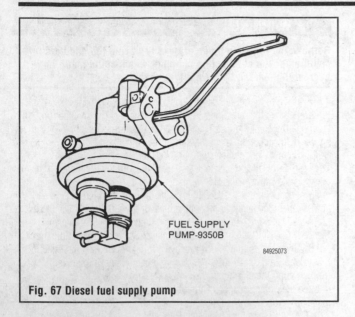

Fig. 67 Diesel fuel supply pump

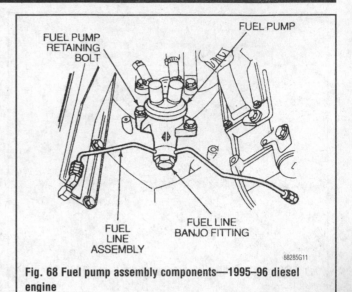

Fig. 68 Fuel pump assembly components—1995–96 diesel engine

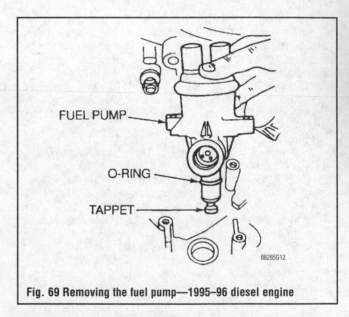

Fig. 69 Removing the fuel pump—1995–96 diesel engine

nudging the starter, until the fuel pump cam lobe is at the low position. At this position, spring tension against the fuel pump bolts will be greatly reduced.

3. Disconnect the fuel supply pump inlet, outlet and fuel return line.

⁑ CAUTION

Use care to prevent combustion of the spilled fuel.

4. Remove the fuel pump attaching bolts and remove the pump and gasket. Discard the old gasket.

5. Remove the remaining fuel pump gasket material from the engine and from the fuel pump if you are reinstalling the old pump. Make sure both mounting surfaces are clean.

To install:

6. Install the attaching bolts into the fuel supply pump and install a new gasket on the bolts. Position the fuel pump onto the mounting pad. Turn the attaching bolts alternately and evenly and tighten the bolts to the 19–27 ft. lbs. (26–37 Nm).

➡ **The cam must be at its low position before attempting to install the fuel supply pump. If it is difficult to start the mounting bolts, remove the pump and reinstall with a lever on the bottom side of the cam.**

7. Install the fuel outlet line. Start the fitting by hand to avoid crossthreading.

8. Tighten the line to 15–18 ft. lbs. (20–24 Nm).

9. Install the inlet line and the fuel return line.

10. Start the engine and observe all connections for fuel leaks for two minutes.

11. Stop the engine and check all fuel supply pump fuel line connections. Check for oil leaks at the pump mounting pad.

1995–96 Engines

▶ **See Figures 68 and 69**

1. Remove the turbocharger assembly.
2. Remove the fuel line banjo bolt at the pump.
3. Remove the fuel line fittings at the rear of the cylinder heads.
4. Remove the fuel lines assembly.
5. Loosen the three hose clamps at the fuel pump fittings.
6. Disconnect the water drain hose at the fuel filter.
7. Disconnect the filter and position it forward.

8. Remove the fuel pump retaining bolts, then lift the pump out of the crankcase bore.

9. Remove the fuel pump tappet from the crankcase bore.

To install:

10. Rotate the engine so the fuel pump eccentric is on the base circle.

11. Install the fuel pump tappet in the base of the fuel pump.

12. Replace the O-ring on the fuel pump base.

13. Install the fuel pump and tighten the bolts to 19–27 ft. lbs. (26–37 Nm).

14. Install the fuel filter and connect the water drain hose.

15. Connect the three fuel hoses at the front of the fuel pump.

16. Tighten the fuel line clamps and install the fuel filter retaining bolts.

17. Install the fuel line assembly and new seal rings at the rear of the pump.

18. Loosely install the fuel line fittings at the rear of the cylinder heads.

19. Install the fuel line banjo fitting at the pump. Tighten the bolt to 18 ft. lbs. (24 Nm).

20. Tighten the fuel line fittings.

21. Install the turbocharger assembly.

Injection Pump

REMOVAL & INSTALLATION

▶ **See Figures 70 thru 75**

1. Disconnect the negative battery cables.
2. Remove the engine cover.
3. If necessary, remove the engine oil filler neck.
4. If equipped, remove the adapter housing cover plate.
5. Remove the bolts attaching injection pump to drive gear.

⁑ WARNING

Before removing the fuel lines, clean the exterior with clean fuel oil or solvent to prevent entry of dirt into the engine when the fuel lines are removed. Also, do not wash or steam clean engine while engine is running. Serious damage to injection pump could occur.

6. Disengage the electrical connectors to the injection pump.

7. Remove the fast idle solenoid bracket assembly to provide access to the injection pump mounting nuts.
8. Disconnect the accelerator cable and speed control cable from throttle lever, if so equipped.
9. Remove the air cleaner and install clean rags to prevent dirt from entering the intake manifold.
10. Remove the accelerator cable bracket, with cables attached, from the intake manifold and position out of the way.

➡ **All fuel lines and fittings must be capped using Fuel System Protective Cap Set T83T–9395–A or equivalent, to prevent fuel contamination.**

11. Disconnect the lines from the fuel filter.
12. Remove the fuel filter-to-injection pump fuel line and cap the fittings.
13. Remove and cap the injection pump inlet elbow and the injection pump fitting adapter.
14. Remove the fuel return line on the injection pump, then rotate out of the way, and cap all fittings.

➡ **It is not necessary to remove injection lines from the injection pump. If lines are to be removed, loosen the injection line fittings at the injection pump before removing it from engine.**

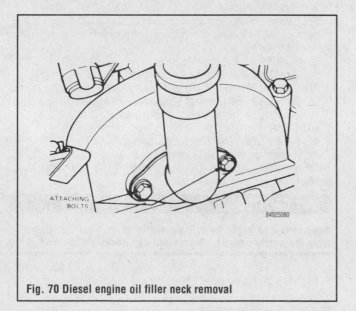

Fig. 70 Diesel engine oil filler neck removal

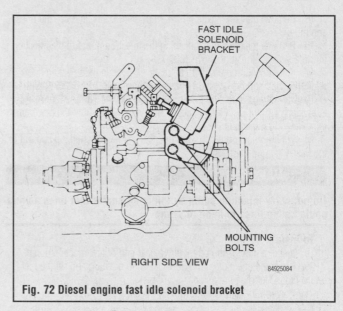

Fig. 72 Diesel engine fast idle solenoid bracket

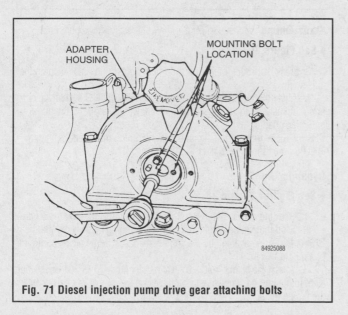

Fig. 71 Diesel injection pump drive gear attaching bolts

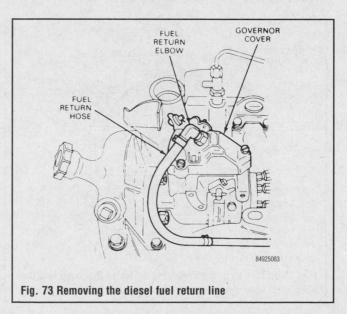

Fig. 73 Removing the diesel fuel return line

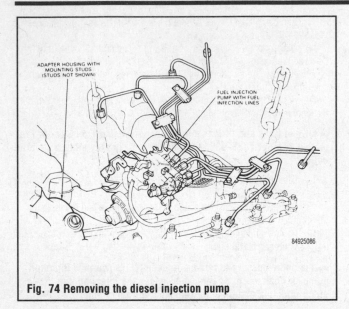

Fig. 74 Removing the diesel injection pump

15. Remove the fuel injection lines from the nozzles, and cap the lines and nozzles.

16. Remove the three nuts attaching the injection pump to the injection pump adapter using Tool T86T–9000–B.

17. If the injection pump is to be replaced, loosen the injection line retaining clips and the injection nozzle fuel lines with Tool T83T–9396–A and cap all fittings at this time with protective cap set T83T–9395–A or equivalent. Do not install the injection nozzle fuel lines until the new pump is installed in the engine.

18. Lift the injection pump, with the nozzle lines attached, up and out of the passenger compartment.

☀☀ WARNING

Do not carry injection pump by injection nozzle fuel lines as this could cause lines to bend or crimp.

To install:

19. Install a new O-ring on the drive gear end of the injection pump.

20. Move the injection pump down and into position and set the fuel return crossover pipe in position.

21. Position the alignment dowel on injection pump into the alignment hole on drive gear.

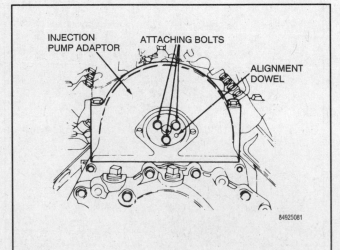

Fig. 75 Be sure to fit the alignment dowel on the pump into the hole in the drive gear

22. Install the bolts attaching the injection pump to drive gear and tighten to 26 ft. lbs. (35 Nm).

23. Install the nuts attaching injection pump to adapter. Align scribe lines on the injection pump flange and the injection pump adapter and tighten to 26 ft. lbs. (35 Nm).

24. If the injection nozzle fuel lines were removed from the injection pump install at this time, refer to the Injection Lines installation procedure in this section.

25. Remove the caps from nozzles and the fuel lines and install the fuel line nuts on the nozzles and tighten to 22 ft. lbs. (30 Nm).

26. Connect the fuel return line to injection pump and tighten the nuts to 22 ft. lbs. (30 Nm).

27. Install the injection pump fitting adapter with a new O-ring.

28. Clean the old sealant from the injection pump elbow threads, using clean solvent, and dry thoroughly. Apply a light coating of pipe sealant to the elbow threads.

29. Install the elbow in the injection pump adapter and tighten to a minimum of 72 inch lbs. (8 Nm). Then tighten further, if necessary, to align the elbow with the injection pump fuel inlet line, but do not exceed 360 degrees of rotation or 10 ft. lbs. (13 Nm).

30. Remove the caps and connect the fuel filter-to-injection pump fuel line.

31. Connect all lines to the filter assembly

32. Install the accelerator cable bracket on the intake manifold.

33. Remove the rags from the intake manifold and install the air cleaner.

34. Connect the accelerator and speed control cable, if so equipped, to the throttle lever.

35. Install the fast idle solenoid bracket assembly.

36. Install the electrical connectors on injection pump.

37. Clean the injection pump adapter and oil filler neck sealing surfaces.

38. Apply a ⅛ in. (3mm) bead of RTV sealant on the adapter housing grooves.

39. Install the oil filler neck and tighten the bolts.

40. Connect the battery ground cables to both batteries.

41. Run the engine and check for fuel leaks.

42. If necessary, purge high pressure fuel lines of air by loosening connector one half to one turn and cranking engine until solid fuel, free from bubbles flows from connection.

☀☀ CAUTION

Keep eyes and hands away from nozzle spray. Fuel spraying from the nozzle under high pressure can penetrate the skin.

43. Check and adjust injection pump timing as described in this section.

44. Install the engine cover.

INJECTION TIMING

Static Timing

▶ See Figure 76

1. Break the torque of the injection pump mounting nuts (keeping the nuts snug).

2. Rotate the injection pump using Tool T83–9000–C or equivalent to bring the mark on the pump into alignment with the mark on the pump mounting adapter.

3. Visually recheck the alignment of the timing marks and tighten the injection pump mounting nuts.

Dynamic Timing

▶ See Figures 77 and 78

1. Start the engine and bring it up to normal operating temperature.

2. Stop the engine and install a dynamic timing meter, Rotunda 078–00200 or equivalent, by placing the magnetic probe pick-up into the probe hole.

3. Attach the clamp from timing meter adapter 078-00201 or its equivalent to the line pressure sensor on the No. 4 injector nozzle and connect to the timing meter.

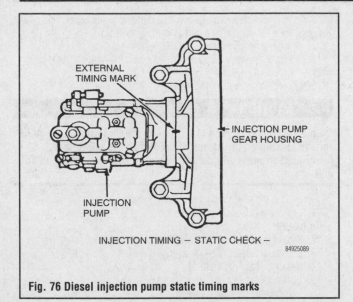

Fig. 76 Diesel injection pump static timing marks

EXTERNAL
TIMING MARK

INJECTION PUMP
GEAR HOUSING

INJECTION
PUMP

INJECTION TIMING – STATIC CHECK –

84925089

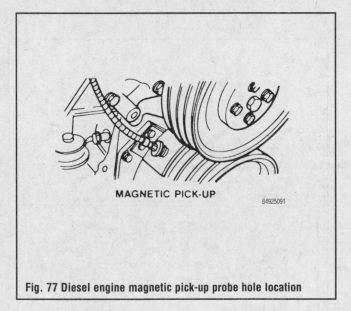

MAGNETIC PICK-UP

84925091

Fig. 77 Diesel engine magnetic pick-up probe hole location

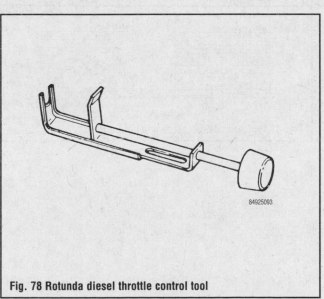

84925093

Fig. 78 Rotunda diesel throttle control tool

4. Connect the dynamic timing meter to the battery and adjust the off-set of the meter to minus 20 degrees.

5. Set the transmission in neutral and raise the rear wheels off the ground. Using Rotunda D83T–9000-E or equivalent throttle control tool, set the engine speed to 2000 rpm with no accessory load. Observe the injection timing on the dynamic timing meter.

6. The timing should be 8.5 degrees BTDC at 2000 rpm.

7. Apply battery voltage to the cold start advance solenoid and adjust the timing so that it stays at 2000 rpm as this may advance timing. The timing should be advanced 1 degree. If not replace the fuel injection pump top cover assembly.

8. If the dynamic timing is not within plug or minus 2 degrees of specification, then the injection pump timing will require adjustment.

9. Turn the engine **OFF**. Note the timing mark alignment.

10. Remove the fast idle bracket and solenoid from the pump.

11. Loosen the injection pump-to-adapter nuts.

12. Rotate the injection pump clockwise (when viewed from the front of the engine) to retard or counterclockwise to advance the timing. Two degrees of dynamic timing equals approximately 0.030 in. (0.76mm) of timing mark movement.

13. Start the engine and recheck the timing. If the timing is not within plus or minus 1 degree of specification, repeat Steps 8 through 12.

14. Turn the engine **OFF**. Remove the dynamic timing equipment.

15. Install the fast idle bracket and solenoid.

Glow Plugs

TESTING

▶ **See Figure 79**

1. Turn the ignition **OFF**.

2. Disconnect the leads from the glow plug.

3. Connect a test lamp between the battery positive terminal and the glow plug. There should be continuity and the light should go on.

4. If the light does not go on the plug is faulty and should be replaced.

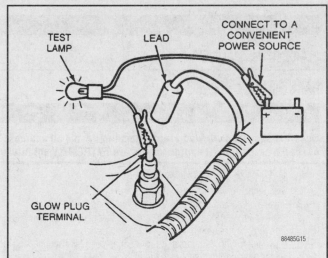

TEST
LAMP

LEAD

CONNECT TO A
CONVENIENT
POWER SOURCE

GLOW PLUG
TERMINAL

88485G15

Fig. 79 Connect a test light as illustrated to check the glow plug continuity

REMOVAL & INSTALLATION

▶ **See Figure 80**

❊❊ CAUTION

The red-striped wires on the 1995–96 DI Turbo engine carry 115 volts DC. A severe electrical shock may be given. Do not pierce the wires.

1. Make sure the ignition switch is **OFF**.
2. For 1994–96 engines, remove the valve cover.
3. Disconnect the wire connector from the glow plug.
4. Using a 10mm deep socket, with enough clearance as to not break or bend the wiring connector, unscrew the glow plug from the manifold.

To install:

5. Place anti-seize on the threads of the glow plug and screw it into the manifold.
6. Tighten the glow plug to 12 ft. lbs. (16 Nm).
7. Plug the wiring connector.
8. Connect the negative battery cable.
9. For 1995–96 engines, install the valve cover.

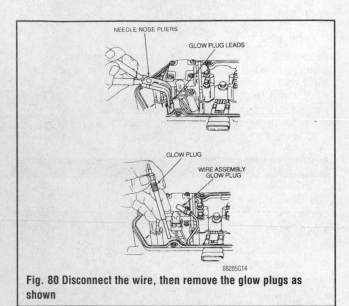

Fig. 80 Disconnect the wire, then remove the glow plugs as shown

Fuel Tank

REMOVAL & INSTALLATION

▶ **See Figure 81**

✳✳ CAUTION

Never smoke when working around gasoline! Avoid all sources of sparks or ignition. Gasoline vapors are EXTREMELY volatile!

1. Depressurize the fuel system.
2. Disconnect the battery ground cable(s).
3. Raise the van and support it with safety stands.
4. Drain the fuel from the tank into a suitable container by siphoning through the filler cap opening.
5. On vehicles with dual tanks, drain the fuel tanks by disconnecting the connector hoses, then disconnect the battery ground cable.

6. Disconnect the fuel gauge sending unit and pump wires, if possible. This may have to wait until the tank is partially lowered.
7. Disconnect the fuel and vacuum lines.
8. Position a piece of wood and a jack under the tank and support its weight.
9. Loosen the filler tube retainers.

✳✳ CAUTION

On the E-series 55 gallon tank, loosen the strap nuts enough to relieve tension on the straps. If the tension is not relieved, lower support arms will deform upward making installation difficult.

10. Loosen the tank strap retainers and lower the straps.
11. Lower the jack and remove the tank.

To install:

12. Place the tank on the jack and raise it into position.
13. Engage the straps and tighten the retainers.
14. Install the filler tube retainers.
15. Connect the fuel and vacuum lines.
16. Engage the electrical connections.
17. Lower the van and connect the battery cable(s).
18. Pour fuel in the tank, start the van and check for leaks.

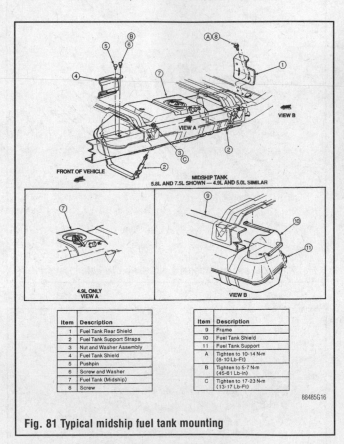

Item	Description
1	Fuel Tank Rear Shield
2	Fuel Tank Support Straps
3	Nut and Washer Assembly
4	Fuel Tank Shield
5	Pushpin
6	Screw and Washer
7	Fuel Tank (Midship)
8	Screw

Item	Description
9	Frame
10	Fuel Tank Shield
11	Fuel Tank Support
A	Tighten to 10-14 N·m (8-10 Lb-Ft)
B	Tighten to 5-7 N·m (45-61 Lb-In)
C	Tighten to 17-23 N·m (13-17 Lb-Ft)

Fig. 81 Typical midship fuel tank mounting

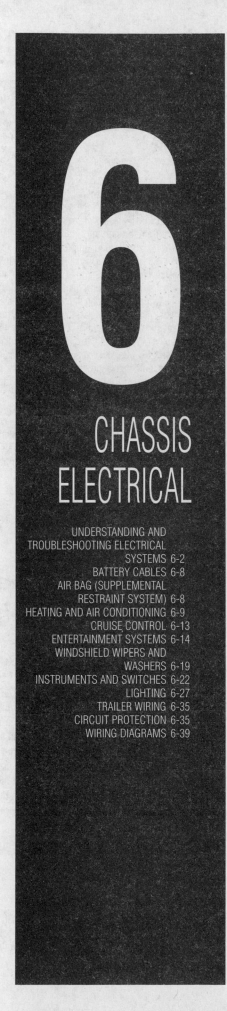

6

CHASSIS
ELECTRICAL

UNDERSTANDING AND TROUBLESHOOTING ELECTRICAL SYSTEMS

Basic Electrical Theory

▶ See Figure 1

For any 12 volt, negative ground, electrical system to operate, the electricity must travel in a complete circuit. This simply means that current (power) from the positive terminal (+) of the battery must eventually return to the negative terminal (-) of the battery. Along the way, this current will travel through wires, fuses, switches and components. If, for any reason, the flow of current through the circuit is interrupted, the component fed by that circuit will cease to function properly.

Perhaps the easiest way to visualize a circuit is to think of connecting a light bulb (with two wires attached to it) to the battery—one wire attached to the negative (-) terminal of the battery and the other wire to the positive (+) terminal. With the two wires touching the battery terminals, the circuit would be complete and the light bulb would illuminate. Electricity would follow a path from the battery to the bulb and back to the battery. It's easy to see that with longer wires on our light bulb, it could be mounted anywhere. Further, one wire could be fitted with a switch so that the light could be turned on and off.

The normal automotive circuit differs from this simple example in two ways. First, instead of having a return wire from the bulb to the battery, the current travels through the chassis of the vehicle. Since the negative (-) battery cable is attached to the chassis and the chassis is made of electrically conductive metal, the chassis of the vehicle can serve as a ground wire to complete the circuit. Secondly, most automotive circuits contain multiple components which receive power from a single circuit. This lessens the amount of wire needed to power components on the vehicle.

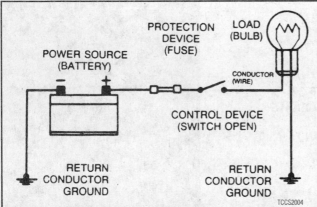

Fig. 1 This example illustrates a simple circuit. When the switch is closed, power from the positive (+) battery terminal flows through the fuse and the switch, and then to the light bulb. The light illuminates and the circuit is completed through the ground wire back to the negative (-) battery terminal. In reality, the two ground points shown in the illustration are attached to the metal chassis of the vehicle, which completes the circuit back to the battery

Electrical Components

POWER SOURCE

The power source for 12 volt automotive electrical systems is the battery. In most modern vehicles, the battery is a lead/acid electrochemical device consisting of six 2 volt subsections (cells) connected in series, so that the unit is capable of producing approximately 12 volts of electrical pressure. Each subsection consists of a series of positive and negative plates held a short distance apart in a solution of sulfuric acid and water.

The two types of plates are of dissimilar metals. This sets up a chemical reaction, and it is this reaction which produces current flow from the battery when its positive and negative terminals are connected to an electrical load. The power removed from the battery is replaced by the alternator, which forces electrons back through the battery, reversing the normal flow, and restoring the battery to its original chemical state.

GROUND

Two types of grounds are used in automotive electric circuits. Direct ground components are grounded through their mounting points. All other components use some sort of ground wire which is attached to the body or chassis of the vehicle. The electrical current runs through the chassis of the vehicle and returns to the battery through the ground (-) cable; if you look, you'll see that the battery ground cable connects between the battery and the body or chassis of the vehicle.

➡**It should be noted that a good percentage of electrical problems can be traced to bad grounds.**

PROTECTIVE DEVICES

▶ See Figure 2

It is possible for large surges of current to pass through the electrical system of your vehicle. If this surge of current were to reach the load in the circuit, it could burn it out or severely damage it. To prevent this, fuses, circuit breakers and/or fusible links are connected into the supply wires of the electrical system. These items are nothing more than a built-in weak spot in the system. When an abnormal amount of current flows through the system, these protective devices work as follows to protect the circuit:

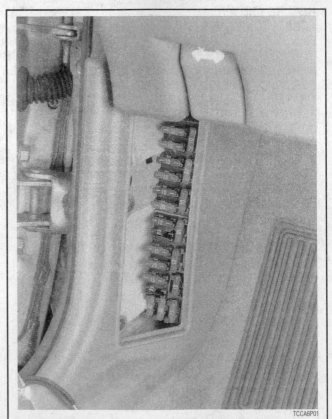

Fig. 2 Most vehicles use one or more fuse panels. This one is located in the driver's side kick panel

• Fuse—when an excessive electrical current passes through a fuse, the fuse "blows" (the conductor melts) and opens the circuit, preventing the passage of current.

• Circuit Breaker—a circuit breaker is basically a self-repairing fuse. It will open the circuit in the same fashion as a fuse, but when the surge subsides, the circuit breaker can be reset and does not need replacement.

• Fusible Link—a fusible link (fuse link or main link) is a short length of special, Hypalon high temperature insulated wire that acts as a fuse. When an excessive electrical current passes through a fusible link, the thin gauge wire inside the link melts, creating an intentional open to protect the circuit. To repair the circuit, the link must be replaced. Some newer type fusible links are housed in plug-in modules, which are simply replaced like a fuse, while older type fusible links must be cut and spliced if they melt. Since this link is very early in the electrical path, it's the first place to look if nothing on the vehicle works, but the battery seems to be charged and is properly connected.

✳✳ CAUTION

Always replace fuses, circuit breakers and fusible links with identically rated components. Under no circumstances should a component of higher or lower amperage rating be substituted.

SWITCHES & RELAYS

▶ See Figures 3 and 4

Switches are used in electrical circuits to control the passage of current. The most common use is to open and close circuits between the battery and the various electric devices in the system. Switches are rated according to the amount of amperage they can handle. If a sufficient amperage rated switch is not used in a circuit, the switch could overload and cause damage.

Some electrical components which require a large amount of current to operate use a special switch called a relay. Since these circuits carry a large amount of current, the thickness of the wire in the circuit is also greater. If this large wire were connected from the load to the control switch on the dashboard, the switch would have to carry the high amperage load and the dash would be twice as large to accommodate the increased size of the wiring harness. To prevent these problems, a relay is used.

Relays are composed of a coil and a switch. These two components are linked together so that when one operates, the other operates at the same time. The large wires in the circuit are connected from the battery to one side of the relay switch and from the opposite side of the relay switch to the load. Most relays are normally open, preventing current from passing through the circuit. Additional, smaller wires are connected from the relay coil to the control switch for the circuit and from the opposite side of the relay coil to ground. When the control switch is turned on, it grounds the smaller wire to

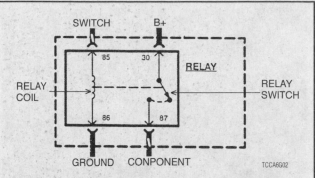

Fig. 4 Relays are composed of a coil and a switch. These two components are linked together so that when one operates, the other operates at the same time. The large wires in the circuit are connected from the battery to one side of the relay switch (B+) and from the opposite side of the relay switch to the load (component). Smaller wires are connected from the relay coil to the control switch for the circuit and from the opposite side of the relay coil to ground

the relay coil, causing the coil to operate. The coil pulls the relay switch closed, sending power to the component without routing it through the inside of the vehicle. Some common circuits which may use relays are the horn, headlights, starter, electric fuel pump and rear window defogger systems.

LOAD

Every complete circuit must include a "load" (something to use the electricity coming from the source). Without this load, the battery would attempt to deliver its entire power supply from one pole to another. The electricity would take a short cut to ground and cause a great amount of damage to other components in the circuit by developing a tremendous amount of heat. This condition could develop sufficient heat to melt the insulation on all the surrounding wires and reduce a multiple wire cable to a lump of plastic and copper.

WIRING & HARNESSES

▶ See Figures 5 and 6

The average automobile contains about ½ mile of wiring, with hundreds of individual connections. To protect the many wires from damage and to keep them from becoming a confusing tangle, they are organized into bundles,

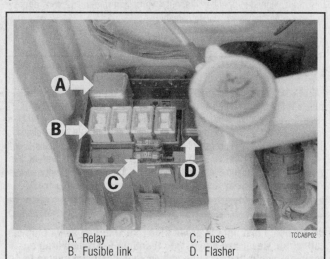

A. Relay   C. Fuse
B. Fusible link   D. Flasher

Fig. 3 The underhood fuse and relay panel usually contains fuses, relays, flashers and fusible links

Fig. 5 Hard shell (left) and weatherproof (right) connectors have replaceable terminals

Fig. 6 Weatherproof connectors are most commonly used in the engine compartment or where the connector is exposed to the elements

enclosed in plastic or taped together and called wiring harnesses. Different harnesses serve different parts of the vehicle. Individual wires are color coded to help trace them through a harness where sections are hidden from view.

Automotive wiring or circuit conductors can be either single strand wire, multi-strand wire or printed circuitry. Single strand wire has a solid metal core and is usually used inside such components as alternators, motors, relays and other devices. Multi-strand wire has a core made of many small strands of wire twisted together into a single conductor. Most of the wiring in an automotive electrical system is made up of multi-strand wire, either as a single conductor or grouped together in a harness. All wiring is color coded on the insulator, either as a solid color or as a colored wire with an identification stripe. A printed circuit is a thin film of copper or other conductor that is printed on an insulator backing. Occasionally, a printed circuit is sandwiched between two sheets of plastic for more protection and flexibility. A complete printed circuit, consisting of conductors, insulating material and connectors for lamps or other components is called a printed circuit board. Printed circuitry is used in place of individual wires or harnesses in places where space is limited, such as behind instrument panels.

Since automotive electrical systems are very sensitive to changes in resistance, the selection of properly sized wires is critical when systems are repaired. A loose or corroded connection or a replacement wire that is too small for the circuit will add extra resistance and an additional voltage drop to the circuit.

The wire gauge number is an expression of the cross-section area of the conductor. The most common system for expressing wire size is the American Wire Gauge (AWG) system. As gauge number increases, area decreases and the wire becomes smaller. An 18 gauge wire is smaller than a 4 gauge wire. A wire with a higher gauge number will carry less current than a wire with a lower gauge number. Gauge wire size refers to the size of the strands of the conductor, not the size of the complete wire. It is possible, therefore, to have two wires of the same gauge with different diameters because one may have thicker insulation than the other.

12 volt automotive electrical systems generally use 10, 12, 14, 16 and 18 gauge wire. Main power distribution circuits and larger accessories usually use 10 and 12 gauge wire. Battery cables are usually 4 or 6 gauge, although 1 and 2 gauge wires are occasionally used.

It is essential to understand how a circuit works before trying to figure out why it doesn't. An electrical schematic shows the electrical current paths when a circuit is operating properly. Schematics break the entire electrical system down into individual circuits. In a schematic, no attempt is made to represent wiring and components as they physically appear on the vehicle; switches and other components are shown as simply as possible. Face views of harness connectors show the cavity or terminal locations in all multi-pin connectors to help locate test points.

Test Equipment

Pinpointing the exact cause of trouble in an electrical circuit is most times accomplished by the use of special test equipment. The following describes different types of commonly used test equipment and briefly explains how to use them in diagnosis. In addition to the information covered below, the tool manufacturer's instructions booklet (provided with the tester) should be read and clearly understood before attempting any test procedures.

JUMPER WIRES

✳✳ CAUTION

Never use jumper wires made from a thinner gauge wire than the circuit being tested. If the jumper wire is of too small a gauge, it may overheat and possibly melt. Never use jumpers to bypass high resistance loads in a circuit. Bypassing resistances, in effect, creates a short circuit. This may, in turn, cause damage and fire. Jumper wires should only be used to bypass lengths of wire.

Jumper wires are simple, yet extremely valuable, pieces of test equipment. They are basically test wires which are used to bypass sections of a circuit. Although jumper wires can be purchased, they are usually fabricated from lengths of standard automotive wire and whatever type of connector (alligator clip, spade connector or pin connector) that is required for the particular application being tested. In cramped, hard-to-reach areas, it is advisable to have insulated boots over the jumper wire terminals in order to prevent accidental grounding. It is also advisable to include a standard automotive fuse in any jumper wire. This is commonly referred to as a "fused jumper". By inserting an in-line fuse holder between a set of test leads, a fused jumper wire can be used for bypassing open circuits. Use a 5 amp fuse to provide protection against voltage spikes.

Jumper wires are used primarily to locate open electrical circuits, on either the ground (-) side of the circuit or on the power (+) side. If an electrical component fails to operate, connect the jumper wire between the component and a good ground. If the component operates only with the jumper installed, the ground circuit is open. If the ground circuit is good, but the component does not operate, the circuit between the power feed and component may be open. By moving the jumper wire successively back from the component toward the power source, you can isolate the area of the circuit where the open is located. When the component stops functioning, or the power is cut off, the open is in the segment of wire between the jumper and the point previously tested.

You can sometimes connect the jumper wire directly from the battery to the "hot" terminal of the component, but first make sure the component uses 12 volts in operation. Some electrical components, such as fuel injectors, are designed to operate on about 4 volts, and running 12 volts directly to these components will cause damage.

TEST LIGHTS

▶ See Figure 7

The test light is used to check circuits and components while electrical current is flowing through them. It is used for voltage and ground tests. To use a 12 volt test light, connect the ground clip to a good ground and probe wherever necessary with the pick. The test light will illuminate when voltage is detected. This does not necessarily mean that 12 volts (or any particular amount of voltage) is present; it only means that some voltage is present. It is advisable before using the test light to touch its ground clip and probe across the battery posts or terminals to make sure the light is operating properly.

✳✳ WARNING

Do not use a test light to probe electronic ignition spark plug or coil wires. Never use a pick-type test light to probe wiring on computer controlled systems unless specifically instructed to do so. Any wire insulation that is pierced by the test light probe should be taped and sealed with silicone after testing.

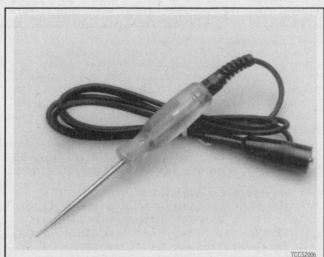

Fig. 7 A 12 volt test light is used to detect the presence of voltage in a circuit

Like the jumper wire, the 12 volt test light is used to isolate opens in circuits. But, whereas the jumper wire is used to bypass the open to operate the load, the 12 volt test light is used to locate the presence of voltage in a circuit. If the test light illuminates, there is power up to that point in the circuit; if the test light does not illuminate, there is an open circuit (no power). Move the test light in successive steps back toward the power source until the light in the handle illuminates. The open is between the probe and a point which was previously probed.

The self-powered test light is similar in design to the 12 volt test light, but contains a 1.5 volt penlight battery in the handle. It is most often used in place of a multimeter to check for open or short circuits when power is isolated from the circuit (continuity test).

The battery in a self-powered test light does not provide much current. A weak battery may not provide enough power to illuminate the test light even when a complete circuit is made (especially if there is high resistance in the circuit). Always make sure that the test battery is strong. To check the battery, briefly touch the ground clip to the probe; if the light glows brightly, the battery is strong enough for testing.

➡A self-powered test light should not be used on any computer controlled system or component. The small amount of electricity transmitted by the test light is enough to damage many electronic automotive components.

MULTIMETERS

Multimeters are an extremely useful tool for troubleshooting electrical problems. They can be purchased in either analog or digital form and have a price range to suit any budget. A multimeter is a voltmeter, ammeter and ohmmeter (along with other features) combined into one instrument. It is often used when testing solid state circuits because of its high input impedance (usually 10 megaohms or more). A brief description of the multimeter main test functions follows:

• Voltmeter—the voltmeter is used to measure voltage at any point in a circuit, or to measure the voltage drop across any part of a circuit. Voltmeters usually have various scales and a selector switch to allow the reading of different voltage ranges. The voltmeter has a positive and a negative lead. To avoid damage to the meter, always connect the negative lead to the negative (-) side of the circuit (to ground or nearest the ground side of the circuit) and connect the positive lead to the positive (+) side of the circuit (to the power source or the nearest power source). Note that the negative voltmeter lead will always be black and that the positive voltmeter will always be some color other than black (usually red).

• Ohmmeter—the ohmmeter is designed to read resistance (measured in ohms) in a circuit or component. All ohmmeters will have a selector switch which permits the measurement of different ranges of resistance (usually the selector switch allows the multiplication of the meter reading by 10, 100, 1,000 and 10,000). Since the meters are powered by an internal battery, the ohmmeter can be used as a self-powered test light. When the ohmmeter is connected, current from the ohmmeter flows through the circuit or component being tested. Since the ohmmeter's internal resistance and voltage are known values, the amount of current flow through the meter depends on the resistance of the circuit or component being tested. The ohmmeter can also be used to perform a continuity test for suspected open circuits. In using the meter for making continuity checks, do not be concerned with the actual resistance readings. Zero resistance, or any ohm reading, indicates continuity in the circuit. Infinite resistance indicates an opening in the circuit. A high resistance reading where there should be none indicates a problem in the circuit. Checks for short circuits are made in the same manner as checks for open circuits, except that the circuit must be isolated from both power and normal ground. Infinite resistance indicates no continuity to ground, while zero resistance indicates a dead short to ground.

✳✳ WARNING

Never use an ohmmeter to check the resistance of a component or wire while there is voltage applied to the circuit.

• Ammeter—an ammeter measures the amount of current flowing through a circuit in units called amperes or amps. At normal operating voltage, most circuits have a characteristic amount of amperes, called "current draw" which can be measured using an ammeter. By referring to a specified current draw rating, then measuring the amperes and comparing the two values, one can determine what is happening within the circuit to aid in diagnosis. An open circuit, for example, will not allow any current to flow, so the ammeter reading will be zero. A damaged component or circuit will have an increased current draw, so the reading will be high. The ammeter is always connected in series with the circuit being tested. All of the current that normally flows through the circuit must also flow through the ammeter; if there is any other path for the current to follow, the ammeter reading will not be accurate. The ammeter itself has very little resistance to current flow and, therefore, will not affect the circuit, but it will measure current draw only when the circuit is closed and electricity is flowing. Excessive current draw can blow fuses and drain the battery, while a reduced current draw can cause motors to run slowly, lights to dim and other components to not operate properly.

Troubleshooting

When diagnosing a specific problem, organized troubleshooting is a must. The complexity of a modern automotive vehicle demands that you approach any problem in a logical, organized manner. There are certain troubleshooting techniques which are standard:

• Establish when the problem occurs. Does the problem appear only under certain conditions? Were there any noises, odors or other unusual symptoms?

• Isolate the problem area. To do this, make some simple tests and observations, then eliminate the systems that are working properly. Check for obvious problems, such as broken wires and loose or dirty connections. Always check the obvious before assuming something complicated is the cause.

• Test for problems systematically to determine the cause once the problem area is isolated. Are all the components functioning properly? Is there power going to electrical switches and motors. Performing careful, systematic checks will often turn up most causes on the first inspection, without wasting time checking components that have little or no relationship to the problem.

• Test all repairs after the work is done to make sure that the problem is fixed. Some causes can be traced to more than one component, so a careful verification of repair work is important in order to pick up additional malfunctions that may cause a problem to reappear or a different problem to arise. A blown fuse, for example, is a simple problem that may require more than another fuse to repair. If you don't look for a problem that caused a fuse to blow, a shorted wire (for example) may go undetected.

Experience has shown that most problems tend to be the result of a fairly simple and obvious cause, such as loose or corroded connectors, bad grounds or damaged wire insulation which causes a short. This makes careful visual inspection of components during testing essential to quick and accurate troubleshooting.

Testing

OPEN CIRCUITS

♦ See Figure 8

1. Isolate the circuit from power and ground.
2. Connect the self-powered test light or ohmmeter ground clip to a good ground and probe sections of the circuit sequentially.
3. If the light is out or there is infinite resistance, the open is between the probe and the circuit ground.
4. If the light is on or the meter shows continuity, the open Is between the probe and end of the circuit toward the power source.

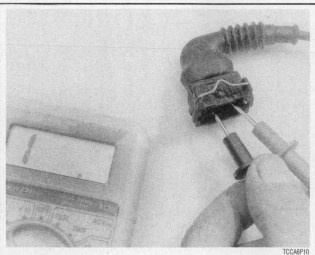

Fig. 8 The infinite reading on this multimeter (1 .) indicates that the circuit is open

SHORT CIRCUITS

➡ **Never use a self-powered test light to perform checks for opens or shorts when power is applied to the electrical system under test. The 12 volt vehicle power will quickly burn out the light bulb in the test light.**

1. Isolate the circuit from power and ground.
2. Connect the self-powered test light or ohmmeter ground clip to a good ground and probe any easy-to-reach test point in the circuit.
3. If the light comes on or there is continuity, there is a short somewhere in the circuit.
4. To isolate the short, probe a test point at either end of the isolated circuit (the light should be on or the meter should indicate continuity).
5. Leave the test light probe engaged and sequentially open connectors or switches, remove parts, etc. until the light goes out or continuity is broken.
6. When the light goes out, the short is between the last two circuit components which were opened.

VOLTAGE

♦ See Figures 9 and 10

This test determines voltage available from the battery and should be the first step in any electrical troubleshooting procedure. Many electrical problems, especially on computer controlled systems, can be caused by a low state of charge in the battery. Excessive corrosion at the battery cable terminals can cause poor contact that will prevent proper charging and full battery current flow.

1. Set the voltmeter selector switch to the 20V position.
2. Connect the multimeter negative lead to the battery's negative (-) post or terminal and the positive lead to the battery's positive (+) post or terminal.
3. Turn the ignition switch **ON** to provide a load.
4. A well charged battery should register over 12 volts. If the meter reads below 11.5 volts, the battery power may be insufficient to operate the electrical system properly.

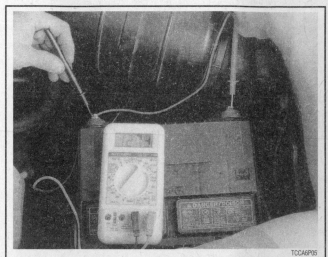

Fig. 9 Using a multimeter to check battery voltage. This battery is fully charged

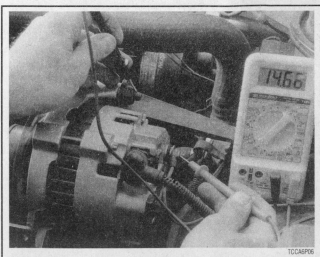

Fig. 10 Testing voltage output between the alternator's BAT terminal and ground. This voltage reading is normal

VOLTAGE DROP

▶ **See Figure 11**

When current flows through a load, the voltage beyond the load drops. This voltage drop is due to the resistance created by the load and also by small resistances created by corrosion at the connectors and damaged insulation on the wires. The maximum allowable voltage drop under load is critical, especially if there is more than one load in the circuit, since all voltage drops are cumulative.

1. Set the voltmeter selector switch to the 20 volt position.
2. Connect the multimeter negative lead to a good ground.
3. Operate the circuit and check the voltage prior to the first component (load).
4. There should be little or no voltage drop in the circuit prior to the first component. If a voltage drop exists, the wire or connectors in the circuit are suspect.
5. While operating the first component in the circuit, probe the ground side of the component with the positive meter lead and observe the voltage readings. A small voltage drop should be noticed. This voltage drop is caused by the resistance of the component.
6. Repeat the test for each component (load) down the circuit.
7. If a large voltage drop is noticed, the preceding component, wire or connector is suspect.

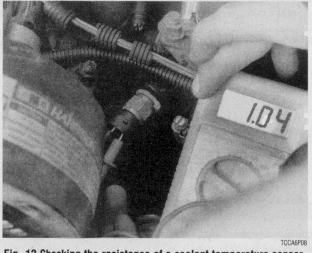

Fig. 12 Checking the resistance of a coolant temperature sensor with an ohmmeter. Reading is 1.04 kilohms

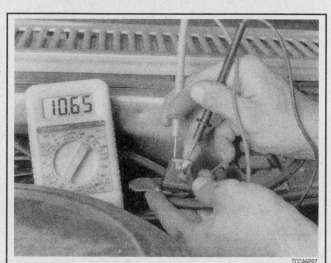

Fig. 11 This voltage drop test revealed high resistance (low voltage) in the circuit

RESISTANCE

▶ **See Figures 12 and 13**

❊❊ WARNING

Never use an ohmmeter with power applied to the circuit. The ohmmeter is designed to operate on its own power supply. The normal 12 volt automotive electrical system current could damage the meter!

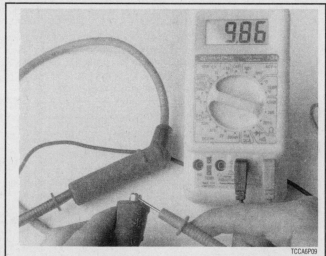

Fig. 13 Spark plug wires can be checked for excessive resistance using an ohmmeter

1. Isolate the circuit from the vehicle's power source.
2. Ensure that the ignition key is **OFF** when disconnecting any components or the battery.
3. Where necessary, also isolate at least one side of the circuit to be checked, in order to avoid reading parallel resistances. Parallel circuit resistances will always give a lower reading than the actual resistance of either of the branches.
4. Connect the meter leads to both sides of the circuit (wire or component) and read the actual measured ohms on the meter scale. Make sure the selector switch is set to the proper ohm scale for the circuit being tested, to avoid misreading the ohmmeter test value.

BATTERY CABLES

Disconnecting the Cables

When working on any electrical component on the vehicle, it is always a good idea to disconnect the negative (-) battery cable. This will prevent potential damage to many sensitive electrical components such as the Engine Control Module (ECM), radio, alternator, etc.

➡ **Any time you disengage the battery cables, it is recommended that you disconnect the negative (-) battery cable first. This will prevent your accidentally grounding the positive (+) terminal to the body of the vehicle when disconnecting it, thereby preventing damage to the above mentioned components.**

Before you disconnect the cable(s), first turn the ignition to the **OFF** position. This will prevent a draw on the battery which could cause arcing (electricity trying to ground itself to the body of a vehicle, just like a spark plug jumping the gap) and, of course, damaging some components such as the alternator diodes.

When the battery cable(s) are reconnected (negative cable last), be sure to check that your lights, windshield wipers and other electrically operated safety components are all working correctly. If your vehicle contains an Electronically Tuned Radio (ETR), don't forget to also reset your radio stations. Ditto for the clock.

AIR BAG (SUPPLEMENTAL RESTRAINT SYSTEM)

General Information

▶ **See Figure 14**

The Supplemental Restraint System (SRS) is designed to operate in frontal or front angled collisions. The system will activate in a crash with severe frontal deceleration, more severe than hitting a parked vehicle of similar size and weight at 28 mph (45 km/h). The system will sense the severity of the crash rather than vehicle speed so some frontal collisions at speeds above 28 mph (45 km/h) may not be severe enough to require inflation.

The SRS is designed to provide increased collision protection for the driver in addition to that provided by the three-point seat belt system.

Seat belt use is necessary to receive the full advantages of the SRS.

The system may use some or all of the following components:
- Electrical system
- Air bag module
- Diagnostic monitor
- Air bag indicator
- Tone generator
- Primary and Safing sensors

The SRS system must be disarmed before any repair or replacement procedures are performed on the steering wheel, steering column or any SRS system components.

Follow all service precautions carefully and completely as any deviation could cause serious injury or death.

SERVICE PRECAUTIONS

✳✳ CAUTION

Always wear safety glasses when servicing an air bag vehicle and handling the air bag to avoid possible injury.

- Carry a live air bag with the bag and trim cover pointed away from your body.
- Place a live air bag on a bench or other surface with the trim cover up, away from the surface.
- After deployment, the air bag surface may contain deposits of sodium hydroxide. This is a product of the gas generant combustion that is irritating to the skin.
- Wash your hands immediately with a mild soap after handling a deployed air bag.
- You can only replace, NOT service the crash sensors, sliding contact, diagnostic monitor and air bag modules.
- If the air bag module has a discolored or damaged trim cover deployment door it must be replaced. Do not attempt to paint it, any paint applied may damage the cover material. This could affect the air bag performance during deployment, which could cause personal injury.
- Never probe the connectors on the air bags. This may result in air bag deployment.
- All component replacement must be done with the negative battery

cable disconnected for a minimum of one minute before service or replacement is attempted.

DISARMING THE SYSTEM

1. Disconnect the negative and then the positive battery cables.
2. Wait one minute. This is the time required for back-up power supply to be depleted from the air bag diagnostic monitor.

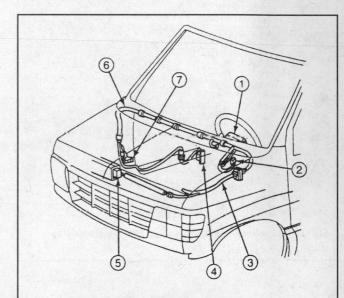

Item	Description
1	Driver Side Air Bag Module
2	Air Bag Diagnostic Monitor
3	Headlamp Dash Panel Junction Wire
4	Center Air Bag Sensor and Bracket
5	Front Air Bag Sensor and Bracket
6	Engine Control Sensor Wiring
7	Air Bag Safing Sensor — Center (Rod Support)

88486G19

Fig. 14 Supplemental Restraint System (SRS) component locations

ARMING THE SYSTEM

1. Connect the positive and then the negative battery cables.
2. Turn the ignition switch from **OFF** to **RUN** and visually monitor the air bag warning indicator. The light will illuminate continuously for approximately 6 seconds and then turn off. If a fault occurs, the air bag indicator will either fail to light, remain lighted continuously or flash. The flashing may not occur until approximately 30 seconds after the ignition switch has been turned from **OFF** to **RUN**. This is the time needed for the air bag diagnostic monitor to complete testing the system. If the air bag indicator is inoperative, an air bag system fault exists, a tone will sound in a pattern of 5 sets of 5 beeps. If this occurs, the air bag indicator will need to be serviced.

HEATING AND AIR CONDITIONING

Blower Motor

REMOVAL & INSTALLATION

▶ **See Figures 15, 16, 17, 18 and 19**

1. Disengage the wiring connector and the vent tube from the motor.
2. Remove the mounting retainers and lift the blower from the case.

➡ **Align the flat spot on the motor mounting plate with the accumulator to provide clearance with the accumulator.**

To install:

3. Install the motor and tighten the retainers.
4. Engage the electrical connections and the vent tube to the motor.

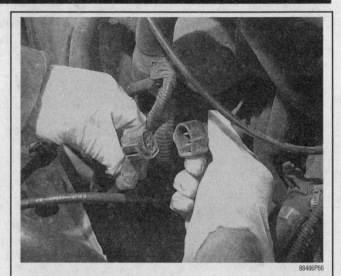

Fig. 16 Unplug the blower motor electrical connection . . .

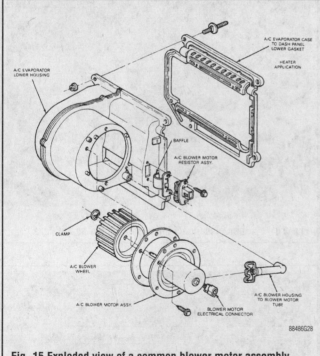

Fig. 15 Exploded view of a common blower motor assembly

Fig. 17 . . . and detach the vent tube

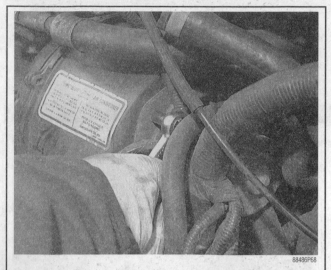

Fig. 18 Loosen the blower motor-to-housing retainers

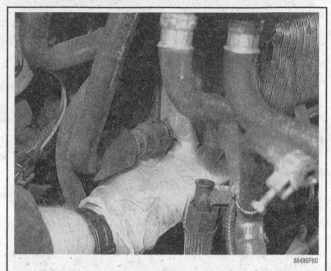

Fig. 20 Disengage the heater hose locking tabs . . .

Fig. 19 Slide the blower motor from the housing and remove it from the van

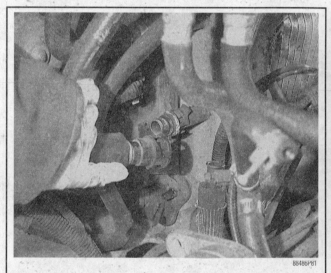

Fig. 21 . . . then disconnect the hose from the heater core

Heater Core

REMOVAL & INSTALLATION

1989–93 Models

▶ See Figures 20 thru 28

1. Drain the cooling system.

❄❄ CAUTION

When draining the coolant, keep in mind that cats and dogs are attracted by ethylene glycol antifreeze, and are quite likely to drink any that is left in an uncovered container or in puddles on the ground. This will prove fatal in sufficient quantity. Always drain the coolant into a sealable container. Coolant should be reused unless it is contaminated or several years old.

2. Disconnect the heater hoses at the core tubes in the engine compartment.

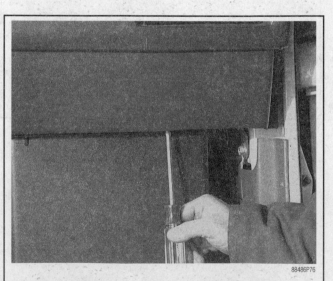

Fig. 22 Loosen the heater core trim panel retaining screws

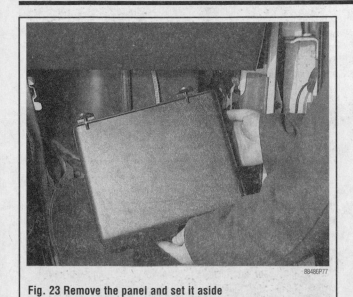

Fig. 23 Remove the panel and set it aside

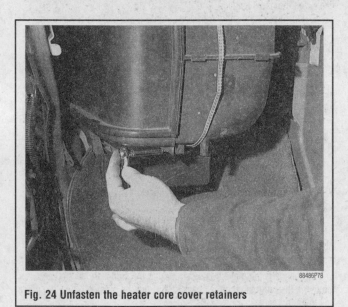

Fig. 24 Unfasten the heater core cover retainers

Fig. 25 Remove the cover to gain access to the heater core

Fig. 26 Loosen the heater core retainers . . .

Fig. 27 . . . and, if necessary, remove the bracket from the case

Fig. 28 Remove the heater core and seal from its housing

3. Remove the instrument panel lower trim panel
4. Remove the heater core cover from the left side of the heater case (4 screws).
5. Remove the core retainers and, if necessary, the bracket from the case.
6. Lift out the heater core and seal.

To install:
7. Install the seal and heater core.
8. Install the heater cover and screws.
9. Install the lower trim panel.
10. Connect the heater hoses and fill the cooling system.
11. Fill the cooling system. Disconnect the heater outlet hose at the water pump until coolant begins to escape (this will bleed the system), then reconnect the hose.

1994–96 Models

▶ **See Figure 29**

1. Use quick disconnect tool T85T-18539-AH to disengage the water hoses from the core, then plug the hoses.
2. Remove the lower left-hand trim panel by unsnapping it.
3. Loosen the core cover screws from both sides of the case.
4. Remove the core and seal.

To install:
5. Install the seal and core.
6. Install the cover and tighten the retainers.
7. Install lower trim panel.
8. Connect the hoses and fill the cooling system.
9. Fill the cooling system. Disconnect the heater outlet hose at the water pump until coolant begins to escape and this will bleed the system.

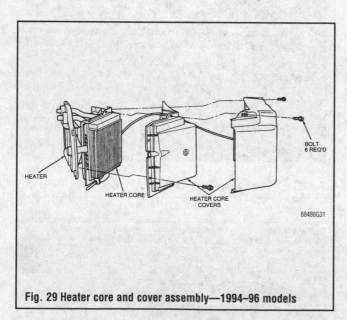

Fig. 29 Heater core and cover assembly—1994–96 models

Air Conditioning Components

REMOVAL & INSTALLATION

Repair or service of air conditioning components is not covered by this manual, because of the risk of personal injury or death, and because of the legal ramifications of servicing these components without the proper EPA certification and experience. Cost, personal injury or death, environmental damage, and legal considerations (such as the fact that it is a federal crime to vent refrigerant into the atmosphere), dictate that the A/C components on your vehicle should be serviced only by a Motor Vehicle Air Conditioning (MVAC) trained, and EPA certified automotive technician.

➡ **If your vehicle's A/C system uses R-12 refrigerant and is in need of recharging, the A/C system can be converted over to R-134a refrigerant (less environmentally harmful and expensive). Refer to Section 1 for additional information on R-12 to R-134a conversions, and for additional considerations dealing with your vehicle's A/C system.**

Control Cables

REMOVAL & INSTALLATION

1. Remove the control panel from the instrument panel.
2. Disengage the glove box by squeezing the side with the stop and removing the pin retaining the check strap from the outside. Allow the glove box to hang free.
3. Working through the glove box opening, remove the temperature control cable housing from the clip on the top of the plenum by depressing the tab and pulling the cable rearward.
4. Using a pair of needlenose pliers and working from the bottom, release the cable snap-in flag.
5. Rotate the control panel face 90 degrees upward and disconnect the cable. Set the panel aside.
6. Disconnect the cable from the cam on the top of the plenum and remove the cable.

To install:
7. Feed the wire loops of the cable through the control panel opening and connect the loop end of the cable to the cam assembly.

➡ **Make sure the wire loop coil is up and that the cable is routed under the hold-down on the cam assembly.**

8. Engage the cable to the temperature control lever on the control assembly.
9. Snap the flag into the top of the of the control assembly bracket.
10. Working through the glove box opening, route the cable so that it is not kinked or have any sharp bends.
11. Adjust the cable if necessary and check operation by actuating the control lever.
12. Install the control panel and glove box assemblies.

ADJUSTMENT

1. Disengage the glove box by squeezing the side with the stop and removing the pin retaining the check strap from the outside. Allow the glove box to hang free.
2. Working through the glove box opening, remove the cable jacket from the metal attaching clip on top of the plenum by depressing the clip tab and pull the cable rearward.

➡ **The cable end should remain attached to the cam and/or crank arm.**

3. Place the control lever **COOL** and hold it there.
4. With the cable end attached to the door cam, push gently on the cable jacket to seat the blend door. Keep pushing until resistance is felt.
5. Install the cable into the clip by pushing the cable jacket into the clip until it snaps into place.
6. Operate the system and make sure it is working properly.
7. Install the glove box assembly.

Control Panel

REMOVAL & INSTALLATION

▶ **See Figure 30**

1. Remove the trim appliqué.
2. Remove the control panel retaining screws.

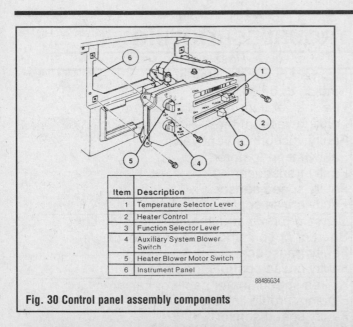

Item	Description
1	Temperature Selector Lever
2	Heater Control
3	Function Selector Lever
4	Auxiliary System Blower Switch
5	Heater Blower Motor Switch
6	Instrument Panel

88486G34

Fig. 30 Control panel assembly components

3. Slowly pull the control unit from the instrument panel.

4. Disengage the electrical connectors, vacuum lines and light bulb.

5. If equipped, with a control cable disconnect as follows:

a. Using needlenosed pliers to depress the tabs. The cable S-bend is removed by rotating the cable wire 90 degrees to the lever.

6. If equipped, disconnect the temperature control module, remove the push-on air conditioner plenum vacuum clips from the control and the harness from the control panel.

7. Remove the control panel.

To install:

8. If equipped, install the temperature control module, vacuum harness and engage the clips.

9. If equipped, connect the control cable.

10. Connect the electrical connectors, vacuum lines and light bulb.

11. Install the panel retaining screws.

12. Install the trim appliqué.

CRUISE CONTROL

When activated by the driver, the cruise control system is designed to maintain vehicle road speed without requiring further input from the accelerator pedal. To activate the system, the engine must be running and the van speed must be greater than 30 mph (48 km/h).

Vacuum Controlled Systems

▶ See Figure 31

The vacuum controlled cruise control system consists of the following components:
- Control switches
- Servo (throttle actuator)
- Speed sensor
- Clutch switch (manual transmissions)
- Stop light switch
- Vacuum dump valve
- Amplifier assembly

The throttle actuator is mounted in the engine compartment and is connected to the throttle linkage with an actuator cable. The speed control amplifier regulates the throttle actuator to keep the requested speed. When the brake pedal is depressed, an electrical signal from the stop light switch returns the system to stand-by mode. The vacuum dump valve also mechanically releases the vacuum in the throttle actuator, thus releasing the throttle independently of the amplifier control. This feature is used as a safety backup.

Electronic Systems

The electronic cruise control system consists of the following components:
- Control switches
- Servo/control unit (throttle actuator)
- Speed sensor
- Stop light and deactivator switches

The throttle actuator/control unit is mounted in the engine compartment and is connected to the throttle linkage with an actuator cable. The control unit regulates the throttle actuator to keep the requested speed. When the brake pedal is depressed, an electrical signal from the stop light and deactivator switches return the system to stand-by mode. This system operates independently of engine vacuum, therefore no vacuum lines are required.

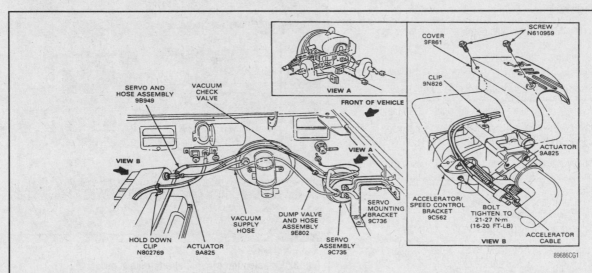

Fig. 31 Vacuum controlled cruise control system components

CRUISE CONTROL TROUBLESHOOTING

Problem	Possible Cause
Will not hold proper speed	Incorrect cable adjustment Binding throttle linkage Leaking vacuum servo diaphragm Leaking vacuum tank Faulty vacuum or vent valve Faulty stepper motor Faulty transducer Faulty speed sensor Faulty cruise control module
Cruise intermittently cuts out	Clutch or brake switch adjustment too tight Short or open in the cruise control circuit Faulty transducer Faulty cruise control module
Vehicle surges	Kinked speedometer cable or casing Binding throttle linkage Faulty speed sensor Faulty cruise control module
Cruise control inoperative	Blown fuse Short or open in the cruise control circuit Faulty brake or clutch switch Leaking vacuum circuit Faulty cruise control switch Faulty stepper motor Faulty transducer Faulty speed sensor Faulty cruise control module

Note: Use this chart as a guide. Not all systems will use the components listed.

TCCA6C01

ENTERTAINMENT SYSTEMS

Radio Receiver/Tape Player/CD Player

REMOVAL & INSTALLATION

1989–91 Models

▶ **See Figures 32 thru 38**

This sound system may contain a cassette player and is removed as an assembly.
1. Disconnect the negative battery cable.
2. Remove the heater and air conditioning control knobs. Remove the cigarette lighter.
3. Remove the radio knobs and discs.
4. If so equipped, snap out the name plate at the right side to remove the panel attaching screw.
5. Remove the five finish panel screws.
6. Very carefully pry out the cluster panel in two places.
7. If equipped with an access panel on the dashboard, loosen the screws and remove the panel to gain access to the electrical connections and rear radio retainers.
8. Detach the antenna lead and speaker wires.
9. Remove the four front radio attaching screws.
10. Disengage the electrical connections and remove the radio.
To install:
11. Engage the electrical connectors, antenna and speaker wires.
12. Install the radio and tighten the retaining screws.

13. Install the finish panel and tighten the screws.
14. If equipped, install the name plate by snapping it into place.
15. Install the cigarette lighter, radio knobs and discs.
16. Install the heater and air conditioning knobs.
17. Connect the negative battery cable.

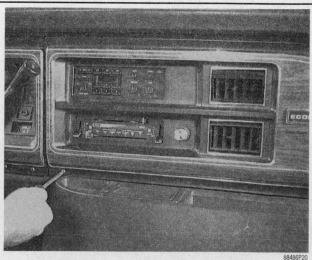

88486P20

Fig. 32 Unfasten the trim panel retaining screws . . .

Fig. 33 . . . then pull the trim panel forward to access the radio . . .

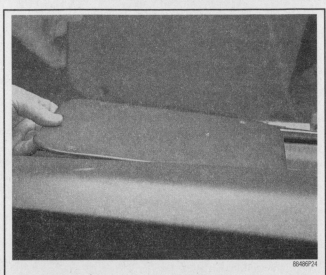

Fig. 36 Remove the panel and set it aside

Fig. 34 . . . and disengage the lighter's electrical connections

Fig. 37 Loosen the rear radio bracket retainers

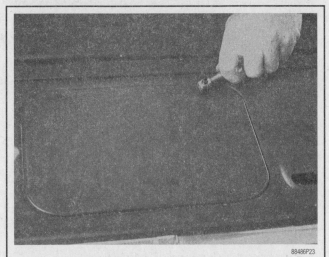

Fig. 35 If equipped with an access panel, loosen the retaining screws

Fig. 38 Unplug the radio electrical connections from the rear of the unit

1992–94 Models

▶ See Figure 39

This sound system may contain a cassette player or a CD player, and is removed as an assembly.

1. Disconnect the negative battery cable.
2. Remove the ashtray and the two air conditioning vents.
3. Remove the headlight knob.
4. Remove the two lower finish panels.
5. Remove the ashtray support and cigarette lighter.
6. Remove the steering column lower shroud trim panel.
7. Use a prytool to pop out the instrument cluster finish panel at two locations, being careful not to scratch or damage the instrument panel.
8. Insert radio removal tool T87P-19061-A or its equivalent into the radio face plate and press it in 1 in. (25.4mm) to release the retaining clips.
9. While flexing the tool outward (away from the radio), pull the radio out from the instrument panel using the tool as a handle.
10. Disengage the electrical connections and the antenna.

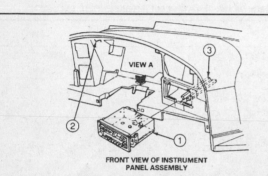

FRONT VIEW OF INSTRUMENT PANEL ASSEMBLY

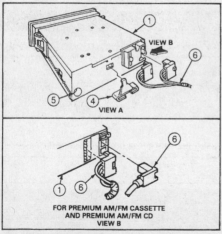

VIEW A

FOR PREMIUM AM/FM CASSETTE AND PREMIUM AM/FM CD VIEW B

Item	Description
1	Radio Chassis
2	Instrument Panel
3	Mounting Bracket
4	Radio Support
6	Main Wiring
7	Radio Antenna Lead In Cable
8	Holding Bracket (Part of 18806)

88486G27

Fig. 39 Sectional views of the radio mounting and electrical connections—1992–94 models (1995–96 models similar)

To install:

11. Engage the electrical connections and the antenna.
12. Install the radio and push it into place until the holding brackets engage.
13. Install the instrument cluster trim panel and the steering column lower shroud finish panel.
14. Install the cigarette lighter and ashtray support.
15. Install the two lower trim panels.
16. Install headlight control knob, two A/C vents and the ashtray.
17. Connect the negative battery cable, then check the radio and antenna for proper operation.

1995–96 Models

▶ See Figure 39

This sound system may contain a compact disc player, which is removed with the radio assembly as a unit.

1. Disconnect the negative battery cable.
2. Remove the left-hand rim molding by unsnapping it.
3. Open the ashtray, loosen the retaining screw and remove the center strap molding.
4. Loosen the screws at the front of the ashtray drawer and let it hang.
5. Remove the cigarette lighter element assembly.
6. Remove the headlamp switch knob and shaft, then unscrew the bezel.

➡To remove the headlight knob, insert a hooked tool into the knob to depress the spring then pull it off the shaft.

7. Loosen the screws and remove the steering column opening cover.
8. Loosen the instrument panel finish trim screws and pull it away from the dash and disconnect the lighter.
9. Insert radio removal tool T87P-19061-A or its equivalent into the radio face plate and press it in 1 in. (25mm) to release the retaining clips.
10. While flexing the tool outward (away from the radio), pull the radio out from the instrument panel using the tool as a handle.
11. Disengage the electrical connections and the antenna.

To install:

12. Engage the electrical connections and the antenna.
13. Install the radio and push it into place until the holding brackets engage.
14. Engage the cigarette lighter electrical connection, install the instrument panel finish trim and tighten the screws.
15. Install the steering column opening cover and tighten the screws.
16. Install the headlight switch knob on the shaft and press it in until it engages the spring.
17. Install the shaft and bezel.
18. Install the lighter element assembly.
19. Install the ashtray drawer and tighten the screws.
20. Install the center strap molding, tighten the screw and close the ashtray.
21. Install the left-hand rim molding by snapping it into place.
22. Connect the negative battery cable, then check the radio and antenna for proper operation.

➡On newer model vehicles when the battery is disconnected it may cause some abnormal drive symptoms until the Powertrain Control Module (PCM) relearns its adaptive strategy. The vehicle may need to be driven 10 miles or more for the PCM to relearn its strategy.

Amplifier

REMOVAL & INSTALLATION

1989–93 Models

1. Remove the speaker cover and retaining screws from the center of the instrument panel.
2. Disengage the amplifier wiring harness connector from the right-hand side of the instrument panel.
3. Loosen the retaining buts and remove the amplifier.
4. Installation is the reverse of removal.

1994–96 Models

▶ See Figure 40

1. Remove the right front cowl trim panel.
2. Disengage the electrical connections from the amplifier.
3. Loosen the screws and remove the amplifier.
4. Installation is the reverse of removal.

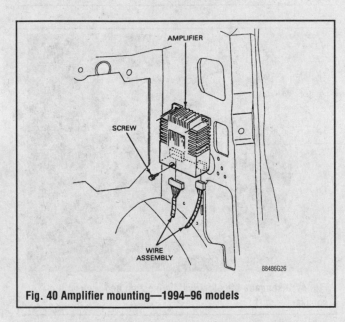

Fig. 40 Amplifier mounting—1994–96 models

Speakers

REMOVAL & INSTALLATION

Instrument Panel Mounted

1989–91 MODELS

▶ See Figure 41

1. Loosen the screws attaching the grille and speaker assembly to the instrument panel.
2. Pull the speaker forward and disengage the electrical connections from the speaker.
3. Loosen the nuts and separate the grille from the speaker.

To install:
4. Engage the grille to the speaker and tighten the nuts.
5. Engage the electrical connections, install the speaker and fasten the screws that attach the speaker assembly to the instrument panel.

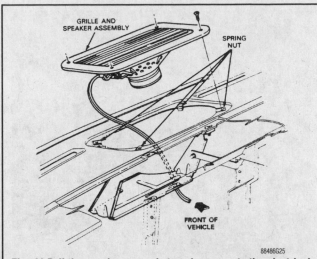

Fig. 41 Pull the speaker upwards to gain access to the electrical connection—1989–91 instrument panel mounted speaker

Door Mounted

1989–91 MODELS

▶ See Figures 42 thru 47

1. Loosen the screws attaching the speaker and grille to the door panel.
2. Pull the speaker forward and disengage the electrical connector from the rear of the speaker.
3. Remove the speaker assembly.

❋ CAUTION

Never operate the radio with the speakers disconnected.

To install:
4. Engage the electrical connection to the rear of the speaker.
5. Install the speaker and grille assembly and tighten the screws.

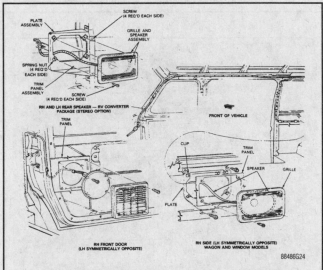

Fig. 42 Front and rear door speaker systems—1989–91 models

Fig. 43 Remove the speaker grille retainers . . .

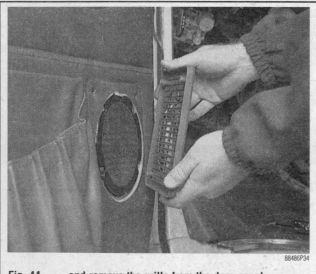

Fig. 44 . . . and remove the grille from the door panel

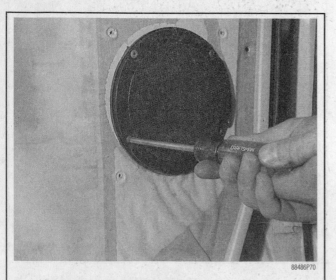

Fig. 45 Unfasten the speaker-to-door screws

Fig. 46 Slide the speaker forward until you can gain access to the electrical connection

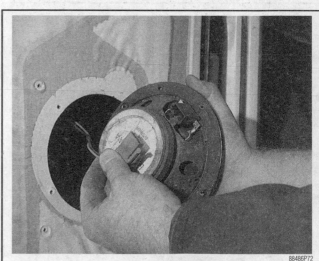

Fig. 47 Disengage the electrical connection and remove the speaker

1992–96 MODELS

▶ See Figures 48 and 49

1. Remove the door trim panel (for details, refer to Section 10).
2. Loosen the speaker-to-door attaching screws (front door) or speaker-to-bracket attaching screws (rear door).
3. Pull the speaker forward, disengage the electrical connection and remove the speaker assembly.

✳✳ CAUTION

Never operate the radio with the speakers disconnected.

To install:
4. Engage the speaker electrical connection.
5. Install the speaker in position and tighten the attaching screws.
6. Install the trim panel.

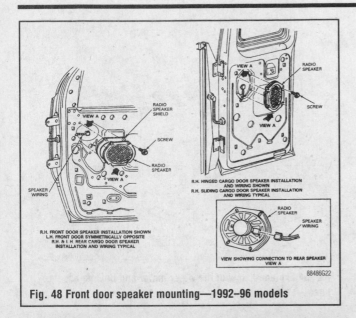

Fig. 48 Front door speaker mounting—1992–96 models

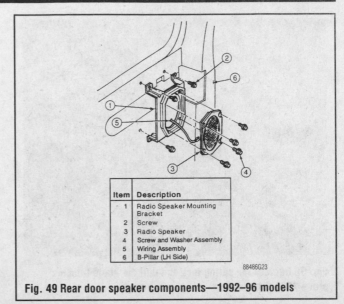

Item	Description
1	Radio Speaker Mounting Bracket
2	Screw
3	Radio Speaker
4	Screw and Washer Assembly
5	Wiring Assembly
6	B-Pillar (LH Side)

Fig. 49 Rear door speaker components—1992–96 models

WINDSHIELD WIPERS AND WASHERS

Windshield Wiper Blade and Arm

REMOVAL & INSTALLATION

▶ **See Figures 50, 51, 52 and 53**

Remove and install the wiper arm assembly as follows:
1. Disconnect the washer hose.
2. Raise the blade off the windshield and move the side latch away from the pivot shaft.
3. Pull the wiper arm off of the pivot shaft.
4. Make sure the arm is in the correct position and push it onto the pivot shaft.
5. Raise the blade off the windshield and push the side latch into the lock.

➡**After the blade has been lowered, if it does not touch the windshield properly, the latch is not properly engaged.**

Remove and install the wiper blade on 1989–94 models as follows:
6. Place the arm in a position that will help facilitate blade removal.
7. Press on the spring lock and pull the blade from the pin.
8. Install the blade on the pin until the spring lock engages, then gently pull on the blade assembly to ensure it is properly attached to the pin.

Remove and install the wiper blade on 1995–96 models as follows:
9. Place the wiper arm on an up position on the windshield.
10. Push the release pin and pull the wiper blade from the pivot arm.
11. Install the wiper blade assembly by pushing the assembly onto the pivot arm, until the lock tab engages.

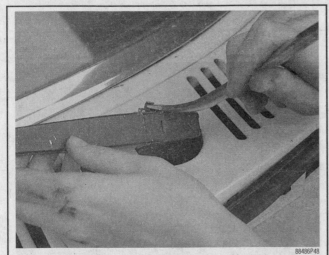

Fig. 50 Use a prytool to move the latch away from the pivot shaft to remove the wiper arm

Fig. 51 If not done previously, disconnect the washer hose and remove the wiper arm

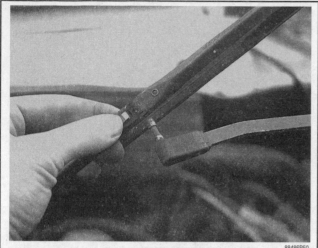

Fig. 52 Depress the spring lock and pull the blade from the arm—1989–94 models

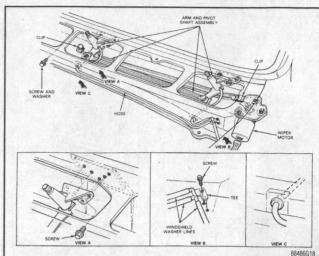

Fig. 54 Exploded view of the wiper motor and linkage assemblies—1989–91 models

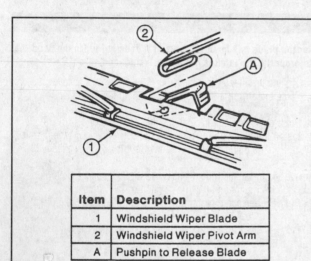

Item	Description
1	Windshield Wiper Blade
2	Windshield Wiper Pivot Arm
A	Pushpin to Release Blade

Fig. 53 Push the blade assembly onto the pivot arm to install—1995–96 models

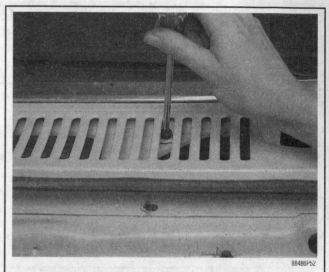

Fig. 55 Loosen the cowl panel retaining screws

Windshield Wiper Motor

REMOVAL & INSTALLATION

1989–91 Models

▶ See Figures 54 thru 59

1. Disconnect the negative battery cable.
2. Remove the fuse panel and bracket.
3. Disconnect the motor wiring.
4. Remove the wiper arms.
5. Remove the outer air intake cowl.
6. Remove the motor linkage clip and disengage the linkage from the wiper drive.
7. Remove the motor mounting bolts and lift out the motor.
8. Transfer the motor drive arm if a new motor is being installed.

To install:

9. Make sure the motor is in the PARK position and install it.
10. Connect the linkage.
11. Connect the wiring.

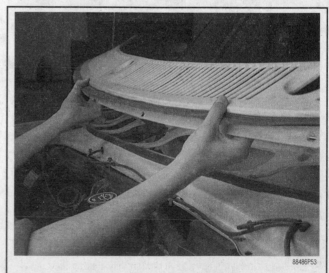

Fig. 56 Remove the cowl panel and set it aside

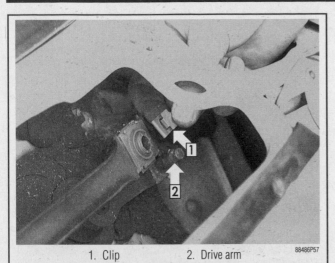

| 1. Clip | 2. Drive arm |

88486P57

Fig. 57 Remove the clip and separate the linkage from the motor drive arm

88486P58

Fig. 58 To gain access to the motor upper mounting bolt, it may be necessary to remove the headlight switch trim panel

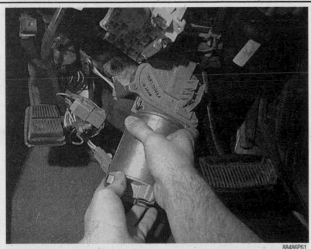

88486P61

Fig. 59 After the bolts have been unfastened, unplug the electrical connection and remove the motor

12. Install the cowl panel.
13. Install the wiper arms.
14. Install the fuse panel and bracket.
15. Check the motor operation.

1992–94 Models

▶ See Figure 60

1. Disconnect the negative battery cable.
2. Remove the wiper arm and blade assembly.
3. Remove the cowl vent grilles and seals and disconnect the washer hoses.
4. If necessary, disconnect the washer jets from the left cowl vent by pressing the latch tab at the outlet of the jet.
5. Disengage the wiper motor electrical connections.
6. Loosen the wiper motor retaining bolts.
7. Remove the outer air inlet cowl.
8. Remove the clip that retains the motor drive arm to the linkage mounting arm and pivot shaft assembly.
9. Remove the wiper motor.

To install:

➡ The motor arm must be 180 degrees for 1992 models and 165 degrees for 1993–94 models from the PARK position during installation.

10. Install the clip into the bearing and with the motor arm in the proper position (see note), listen for an audible snap as the clip engages.
11. Install the motor retaining bolts and tighten them to 60–85 inch lbs. (6.7–9.5 Nm).
12. Engage the electrical connections and cycle the motor to the **PARK** position. To cycle the motor, simply turn the wiper switch and ignition **ON** until it reaches the desired position and turn the ignition and the wiper switch **OFF**.
13. Install the washer jets, vent grilles and seals.
14. Install the wiper arm and blade assemblies.
15. Connect the negative battery cable and check for proper operation.

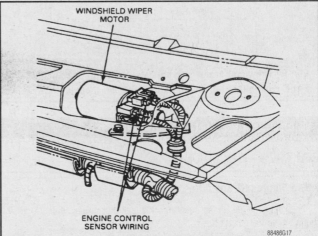

WINDSHIELD WIPER MOTOR

ENGINE CONTROL SENSOR WIRING

88486G17

Fig. 60 Disengage the electrical connections such as the engine control sensor before removing the wiper motor—1992–94 models

1995–96 Models

▶ See Figure 61

1. Disconnect the negative battery cable.
2. Remove the wiper arm and blade assembly.
3. Remove the cowl vent grilles and seals and disconnect the washer hoses.
4. Disengage the engine control sensor connectors from the motor.

5. Remove wiper adapter and connecting arm clip.
6. Loosen the wiper motor retaining bolts.
7. Remove the wiper motor.

To install:

➡**The motor arm must be 141 degrees from PARK during installation.**

8. Install the clip into the bearing and with the motor arm in the proper position (see note), listen for an audible snap as the clip engages.
9. Install the motor retaining bolts and tighten them to 60–85 in. lbs. (6.7–9.5 Nm).
10. Engage the engine sensor electrical connections and cycle the motor to the **PARK** position. To cycle the motor, simply turn the wiper switch and ignition **ON** until it reaches the desired position and turn the ignition and the wiper switch **OFF**.
11. Install the vent grilles and seals.
12. Install the wiper arm and blade assemblies.
13. Connect the negative battery cable and check for proper operation.

➡**On newer model vehicles when the battery is disconnected it may cause some abnormal drive symptoms until the Powertrain Control Module (PCM) relearns its adaptive strategy. The vehicle may need to be driven 10 miles or more for the PCM to relearn its strategy.**

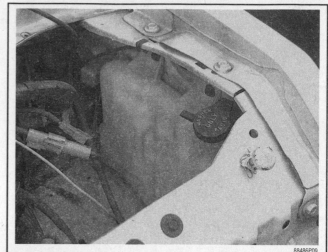

Fig. 62 The windshield washer reservoir is usually located on the firewall

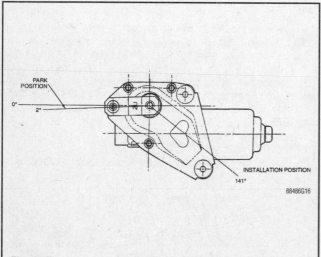

Fig. 61 The wiper motor arm must be 141 degrees from the PARK position during installation—1995–96 models

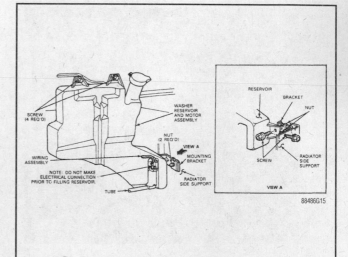

Fig. 63 Windshield washer reservoir and pump assembly—models with gasoline engine shown

Windshield Washer Motor

REMOVAL & INSTALLATION

▶ **See Figures 62 and 63**

1. Disengage the washer reservoir hoses and electrical connections, then remove the reservoir.

2. Use a small bladed prytool to pry out the pump, while being careful not to damage the housing.
3. Remove the one-piece seal/filter and inspect it for wear and damage.

To install:

4. Insert the seal, then lubricate the inside diameter of the seal with soapy solution and insert the pump until its firmly seated.
5. Engage the hoses and electrical connections and install the reservoir.
6. Refill the system and check for proper operation and leaks.

INSTRUMENTS AND SWITCHES

Precautions

▶ **See Figure 64**

Electronic modules, such as instrument clusters, powertrain controls and sound systems are sensitive to static electricity and can be damaged by Electro Static Discharge (ESD) which are below the levels that you can hear "snap" or detect on your skin. A detectable snap or shock of static electricity is in the 3,000 volt range. Some of these modules can be damaged by a charge of as little as 100 volts.

The following are some basic safeguards to avoid static electrical damage:
• Leave the replacement module in its original packing until you are ready to install it.
• Avoid touching the module connector pins
• Avoid placing the module on a non-conductive surface
• Use a commercially available static protection kit. These kits contain such things as grounding cords and conductive mats.

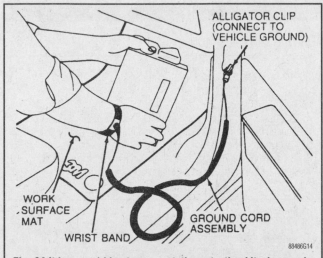

Fig. 64 It is a good idea to use a static protection kit when working on many of the electrically controlled devices in your van

Fig. 66 Loosen the instrument cluster-to-panel retaining screws

Instrument Cluster

REMOVAL & INSTALLATION

1989–91 Models

▶ **See Figures 65, 66 and 67**

1. Disconnect the battery ground cable.
2. Remove the instrument cluster finish panels, if equipped.
3. Remove the seven instrument cluster-to-panel retaining screws.
4. Position the cluster slightly away from the panel for access to the back of the cluster to disconnect the speedometer.

If there is not sufficient access to disengage the speedometer cable form the speedometer, it may be necessary to remove the speedometer cable at the transmission and pull the cable through the cowl, to allow room to reach the speedometer quick disconnect.

5. Disengage the harness connector plug from the printed circuit board and remove the cluster assembly from the instrument panel.

To install:

6. Apply an approximately ³⁄₁₆ in. (4.8mm) diameter ball of silicone dielectric compound in the drive hole of the speedometer head.

Fig. 67 Slide the instrument cluster forward, then reach behind it and disconnect the speedometer cable

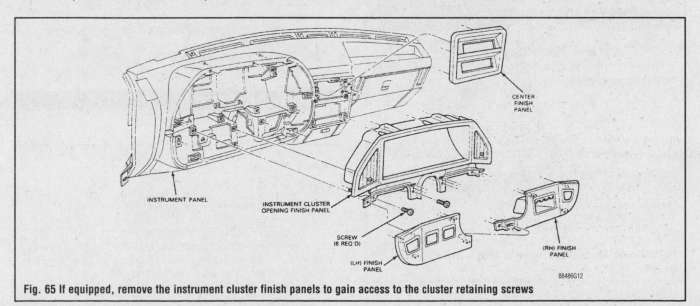

Fig. 65 If equipped, remove the instrument cluster finish panels to gain access to the cluster retaining screws

7. Position the cluster near its opening in the instrument panel.

8. Engage the harness connector plug to the printed circuit board.

9. Connect the speedometer cable (quick disconnect) to the speedometer head.

10. Connect the speedometer cable and housing assembly to the transmission (if removed).

11. Install the seven instrument cluster-to-panel retaining screws and connect the battery ground cable.

12. Check the operation of all gauges, lights, and signals.

1992–96 Models

▶ **See Figure 68**

1. Disconnect the negative battery cable.

2. Remove the cluster opening finish panels.

3. Remove the transmission selector cable loop from the ball stud on the shift lever.

4. Loosen the thumb wheel bracket screw and disengage the bracket from the steering column tube.

5. Loosen the four instrument cluster-to-instrument panel screws.

6. Pull the cluster out of the panel first and rest it on the steering column tube.

7. Disengage the electrical connections from the rear of the cluster and remove the cluster.

To install:

8. Engage the cluster electrical connections.

9. Position the cluster in the instrument panel and engage the locator pins.

10. Install cluster retaining screws.

11. Place the transmission selector cable loop on the ball stud on the shift lever.

12. Position the thumb wheel bracket on the right side of the steering column tube and tighten the screw.

13. Adjust the transmission lever as necessary.

14. Install the cluster finish panels.

15. Connect the negative battery cable and check for proper operation.

➡️**On newer model vehicles when the battery is disconnected it may cause some abnormal drive symptoms until the Powertrain Control Module (PCM) relearns its adaptive strategy. The vehicle may need to be driven 10 miles or more for the PCM to relearn its strategy.**

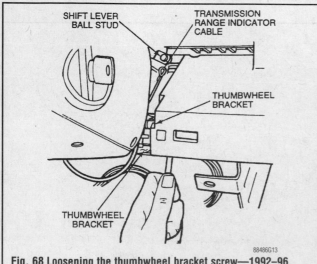

Fig. 68 Loosening the thumbwheel bracket screw—1992–96 models

SHIFT LEVER BALL STUD

TRANSMISSION RANGE INDICATOR CABLE

THUMBWHEEL BRACKET

THUMBWHEEL BRACKET

88486G13

Gauges

REMOVAL & INSTALLATION

1989–92 Models

▶ **See Figure 69**

1. Disconnect the negative battery cable.

2. Loosen the screws retaining the cluster lens and cluster mask to the cluster backplate.

3. Loosen the gauge retainers and remove the gauge.

4. Installation is the reverse of removal.

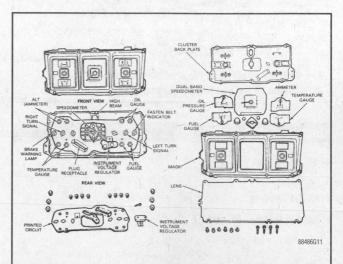

Fig. 69 Rear and exploded views of the instrument cluster assembly and component locations—1989–92 models

1993–96 Models

1. Disconnect the negative battery cable.

2. Loosen the screws retaining the cluster main lens and cluster mask to the cluster backplate.

3. Remove the main lens and cluster mask.

4. Disengage the gauge-to-backplate retaining clips, then grasp the outside edges of the gauge and remove it by lifting.

To install:

5. Install the gauge on the backplate and make sure the retaining clips are properly engaged.

6. Install the lens and cluster mask, then tighten the screws.

7. Connect the negative battery cable and check for proper operation.

Windshield Wiper Switch

REMOVAL & INSTALLATION

1989–91 Models

▶ **See Figure 70**

1. Disconnect the negative battery cable.

2. Remove the windshield wiper switch knob.

3. Remove the ignition switch bezel.

4. Remove the headlamp switch knob and shaft by pulling the switch to the headlamp **ON** position then depress the button on top of the switch and pull the knob and shaft out of the headlamp switch.

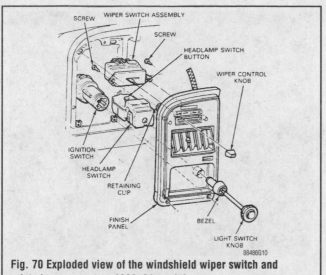

Fig. 70 Exploded view of the windshield wiper switch and related components—1989–91 models

Fig. 71 Remove the trim panel screws

5. Remove the two screws at the bottom of the finish panel. Then, carefully pry the two upper retainers away from the instrument panel assembly.
6. Disengage the connector from the wiper switch.
7. Remove the wiper switch attaching screws and remove the switch.
To install:
8. Install the switch and tighten the screws.
9. Engage the wiper switch electrical connection.
10. Install the ignition switch and bezel.
11. Install the headlight switch.
12. Install the wiper switch knob.
13. Install the finish panel and screws.
14. Connect the negative battery cable and check for proper operation.

1992–96 Models

The wiper switch on these models is part of the multi-function switch located on the steering column. For details concerning removal and installation of this component, please refer to Section 8 of this manual.

Headlight Switch

REMOVAL & INSTALLATION

1989–91 Models

▶ **See Figures 71 thru 77**

1. Disconnect the negative battery cable.
2. Remove the trim panel.
3. Remove the headlamp control knob and shaft by pressing the knob release button on the switch housing, with the knob in the full **ON** position.
4. Pull the knob and shaft assembly out of the switch.
5. Unscrew the mounting nut or bezel.
6. Remove the switch, then unplug the wiring connector from the switch.
To install:
7. Engage the wiring connector to the headlamp switch, position the switch in the instrument panel, and install the bezel and mounting nut.
8. Install the bezel or retaining nut.
9. Install the knob and shaft assembly by inserting it all the way into the switch until a distinct click is heard. In some instances it may be necessary to rotate the shaft slightly until it engages the switch contact carrier.
10. Connect the negative battery cable.

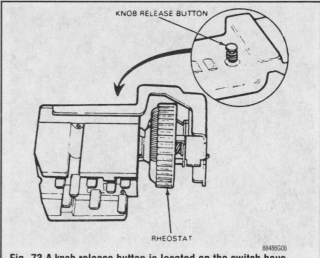

Fig. 72 Slide the assembly forward to gain access to the rear of the switch

Fig. 73 A knob release button is located on the switch housing—1989–91 models

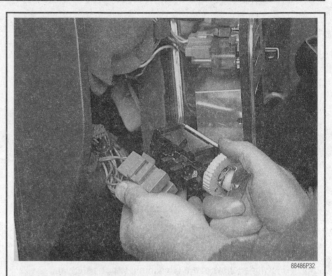

Fig. 74 While pressing the knob release button, remove the knob and shaft

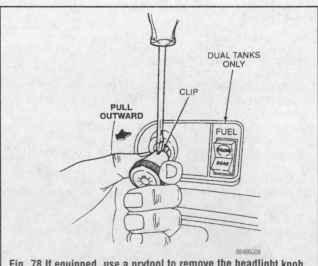

Fig. 77 Unplug the electrical connection and remove the switch

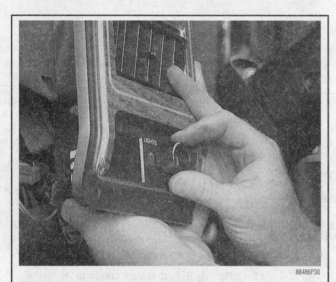

Fig. 75 Unscrew the bezel assembly

1992–96 Models

▶ **See Figure 78**

1. Disconnect the negative battery cable.
2. Remove the engine cover.
3. Pull out the ashtray drawer, loosen the screws retaining the ashtray drawer retainer and remove the retainer.
4. Unsnap and remove the center and left snap-on molding from the steering column.
5. Remove the cigarette lighter element.
6. Remove the headlight switch knob by inserting a small screwdriver onto the retaining clip to release it (if equipped) and pulling the knob off the shaft.
7. Unscrew the bezel.
8. Loosen the steering column opening cover and remove the cover.
9. Remove the steering column opening lower reinforcement.
10. Loosen the screws retaining the instrument cluster finish panel and pull the cluster away from the instrument panel by disengaging the snap-in retainers and wiring.
11. Remove the headlamp control knob and shaft by pressing the knob release button on the switch housing, with the knob in the full **ON** position.

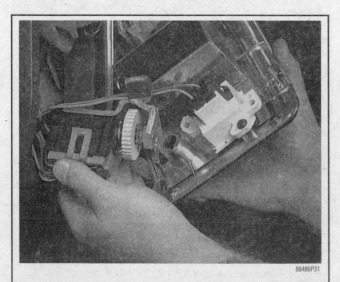

Fig. 76 Separate the switch from its mounting on the trim piece

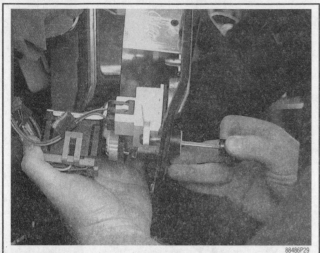

Fig. 78 If equipped, use a prytool to remove the headlight knob retaining clip—1992–96 models

12. Pull the knob and shaft assembly out of the switch and unscrew the mounting or bezel nut.

13. Remove the switch, then remove the wiring connector from the switch.

To install:

14. Engage the wiring connector to the headlamp switch, position the switch in the instrument panel, and install the bezel and mounting nut.

15. Install the knob and shaft assembly by inserting it all the way into the switch until a distinct click is heard. In some instances, it may be necessary to rotate the shaft slightly until it engages the switch contact carrier.

16. Install the cluster finish panel.

17. Install the steering column opening reinforcement and cover.

18. Install the headlight switch bezel, clip and knob.

19. Install the cigarette lighter element.

20. Install the center and left snap-on molding to the steering column.

21. Install the ashtray retainer and screws.

22. Install the engine cover, connect the negative battery cable and check for proper operation.

Back-up Light Switch

REMOVAL & INSTALLATION

Manual Transmission

▶ See Figure 79

The switch is located on the driver's side of the transmission assembly and is not adjustable.

1. Place the transmission in **PARK**.
2. Disengage the electrical connection from the switch.
3. Unscrew and remove the switch.
4. Installation is the reverse of removal.

LIGHTING

Headlights

REMOVAL & INSTALLATION

1989–91 Models

▶ See Figures 80 thru 85

1. Loosen or remove the headlight retaining ring by rotating it counterclockwise or remove the headlight trim piece. Do not disturb the adjusting screw settings.

2. Pull the headlight bulb forward and disconnect the wiring assembly plug from the bulb.

To install:

3. Connect the wiring assembly plug to the new bulb. Place the bulb in position, making sure that the locating tabs of the bulb are fitted in the positioning slots.

4. Install the headlight retaining ring.

5. Place the headlight trim ring or door into position, and install the retaining screws.

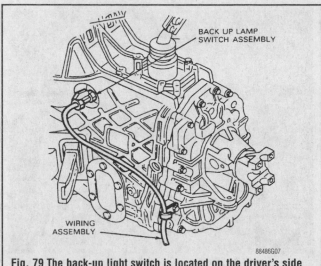

Fig. 79 The back-up light switch is located on the driver's side of the transmission

Automatic Transmission

The back-up light switch, also known as the park/neutral safety switch or transmission range selector switch, operates the back-up lights on models with automatic transmissions. Refer to Section 7 of this manual for the removal and installation of this component.

Ignition Switch

REMOVAL & INSTALLATION

The ignition switch is mounted on the steering column. For removal and installation of this component, please refer to the Steering portion of Section 8 in this manual.

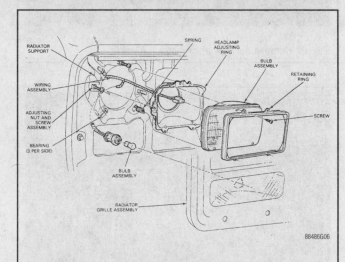

Fig. 80 Exploded view of the headlight assembly—1989–91 models

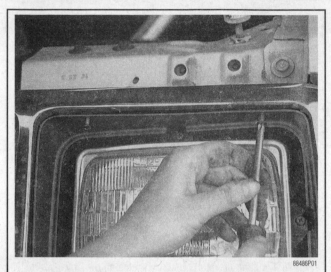

Fig. 81 Loosen the headlight trim piece retaining screws

Fig. 82 Remove the trim piece and set it aside

Fig. 83 Loosen the retaining ring screws. Do not touch the adjusting screws

Fig. 84 While supporting the bulb assembly, remove the retaining ring

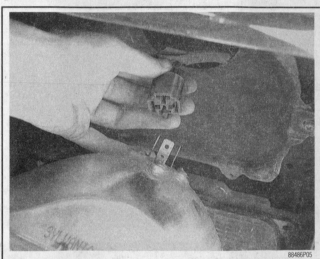

Fig. 85 Slide the bulb assembly forward and unplug the electrical connection

1992–96 Models

HI-SERIES

▶ See Figure 86

❊❊ WARNING

The halogen bulb contains gas which is under pressure. The glass may shatter if the bulb is scratched or dropped. Grasp the bulb by its plastic base and not by the glass.

1. Turn the headlight switch **OFF**.
2. Open the hood and locate the bulb which is in the rear of the headlamp body.
3. Bend back and lift up on the two black tabs retaining while holding the lamp to the van.
4. Disengage the electrical connection by grasping the wires and snapping the connector rearward.
5. Remove the bulb retaining ring by rotating it counterclockwise (when viewed from the rear) about ⅛ of a turn and sliding the ring off the base.
6. Remove the bulb by pulling it straight back out.

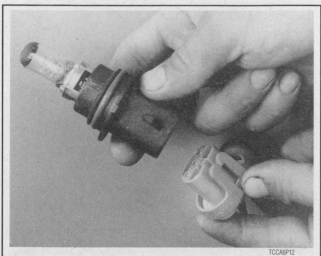

Fig. 86 Carefully pull the halogen headlight bulb from its socket. If applicable, release the retaining clip

To Install:

❋❋ WARNING

Do not touch the glass bulb with your fingers. Oil from your fingers can severely shorten the life of the bulb. If necessary, wipe off any dirt or oil from the bulb with rubbing alcohol before completing installation.

7. Insert the bulb into the socket with the flat side of the base facing forward. Turn the base slightly to the left or right, if necessary to align grooves in the forward part of the base with the locating tabs inside the socket.

8. When the tabs are aligned, push the bulb into the socket until the mounting face on the base contacts the rear face of the socket.

➡**Bulbs No. 9004 and 9007 are similar, but not interchangeable.**

9. Install the retaining ring and rotate it clockwise. A stop will be felt when the ring is full engaged.

10. Engage the electrical connector by pushing it on until it snaps and locks into position.

11. Install the lamp in the grille and engage the two black locking tabs.

12. Turn the lights **ON** to check for proper operation.

LO-SERIES

1. Loosen the screws retaining the headlight door, then pull forward and up to disengage the lower locating tabs.

2. Loosen the retaining screws and remove the retaining ring. Do not touch the adjusting screws.

3. Pull the headlight assembly forward, disengage the wiring and remove the bulb.

To install:

4. Engage the electrical connector, install the bulb and tighten the screws.

5. Install the retaining ring and screws.

6. Install the headlight door and tighten the screws.

Signal and Marker Lights

REMOVAL & INSTALLATION

◗ **See Figure 87**

Turn Signal and Brake Lights

◗ **See Figures 88 thru 93**

1. Depending on the vehicle and bulb application, either unscrew and remove the lens or disengage the bulb and socket assembly from the rear of the lens housing.

2. To remove a light bulb with retaining pins from its socket, grasp the bulb, then gently depress and twist it ⅛ turn counterclockwise, and pull it from the socket.

3. On other models, simply pull the bulb from the socket.

To install:

4. On models equipped, install the bulb into the socket by simply pushing it into the socket.

5. Before installing a light bulb into the socket, ensure that all electrical contact surfaces are free of corrosion or dirt.

➡**Before installing the light bulb, note the positions of the two retaining pins on the bulb. They will likely be at different heights on the bulb, to ensure that the bulb is installed correctly. If, when installing the bulb, it does not turn easily, do not force it. Remove the bulb and rotate it 180 degrees from its former position, then reinsert it into the bulb socket.**

6. Insert the light bulb into the socket and, while depressing the bulb, twist it ⅛ turn clockwise until the two pins on the light bulb are properly engaged in the socket.

7. To ensure that the replacement bulb functions properly, activate the applicable switch to illuminate the bulb which was just replaced. If the replacement light bulb does not illuminate, either it too is faulty or there is a problem in the bulb circuit or switch. Correct if necessary.

8. If applicable, install the socket and bulb assembly into the rear of the lens housing; otherwise, install the lens over the bulb.

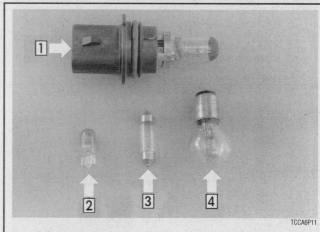

1. Halogen headlight bulb
2. Side marker light bulb
3. Dome light bulb
4. Turn signal/brake light bulb

Fig. 87 Examples of various types of automotive light bulbs

Fig. 88 Unfasten the turn signal lens retaining screws

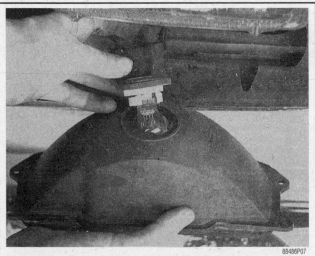

Fig. 89 Move the lens forward to disengage the bulb and socket assembly

Fig. 90 Pull the turn signal bulb from the socket and replace it with a new one

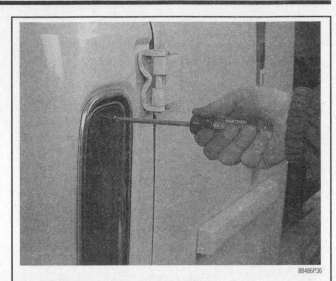

Fig. 91 Remove the brake light lens screws

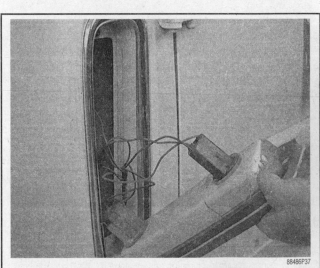

Fig. 92 Move the lens away from the body of the van so you can reach the bulb sockets

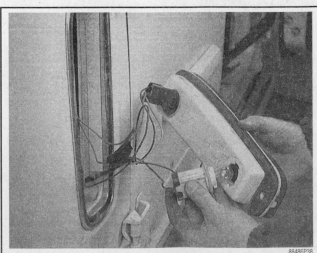

Fig. 93 Turn the sockets to disengage the locking tabs from the brake light lens

Side Marker Light

♦ **See Figures 94, 95 and 96**

1. Disengage the bulb and socket assembly from the lens housing.
2. Gently grasp the light bulb and pull it straight out of the socket.

To install:

3. Before installing the light bulb into the socket, ensure that all electrical contact surfaces are free of corrosion or dirt.
4. Line up the base of the light bulb with the socket, then insert the light bulb into the socket until it is fully seated.
5. To ensure that the replacement bulb functions properly, activate the applicable switch to illuminate the bulb which was just replaced. If the replacement light bulb does not illuminate, either it too is faulty or there is a problem in the bulb circuit or switch. Correct as necessary.
6. Install the socket and bulb assembly into the lens housing.

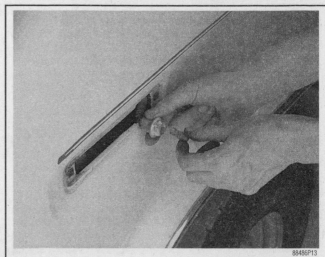

Fig. 96 Simply pull this side marker light bulb straight from its socket

Dome Light

♦ **See Figures 97 and 98**

1. Using a small prytool, carefully remove the cover lens from the lamp assembly.
2. Remove the bulb from its retaining clip contacts. If the bulb has tapered ends, gently depress the spring clip/metal contact and disengage the light bulb, then pull it free of the two metal contacts.

To install:

3. Before installing the light bulb into the metal contacts, ensure that all electrical conducting surfaces are free of corrosion or dirt.
4. Position the bulb between the two metal contacts. If the contacts have small holes, be sure that the tapered ends of the bulb are situated in them.
5. To ensure that the replacement bulb functions properly, activate the applicable switch to illuminate the bulb which was just replaced. If the replacement light bulb does not illuminate, either it is faulty or there is a problem in the bulb circuit or switch. Correct as necessary.
6. Install the cover lens until its retaining tabs are properly engaged.

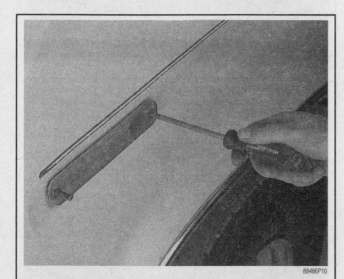

Fig. 94 Loosen the lens retaining screws

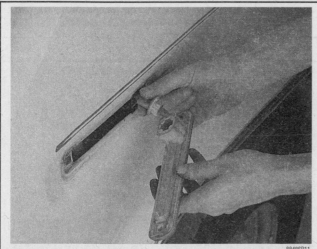

Fig. 95 Pull the lens forward and disconnect the socket by turning until the locking tabs disengage

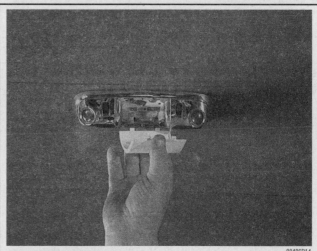

Fig. 97 Gently squeeze the lens cover until the tabs disengage and remove the cover

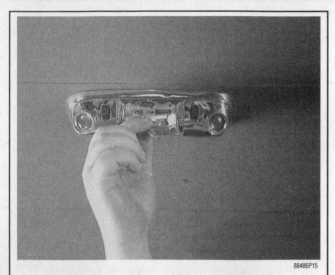

Fig. 98 Disconnect the bulb from the retaining clip contacts

Fig. 100 Remove the housing from the headliner

Map Lamp

▶ **See Figures 99, 100, 101 and 102**

1. Loosen the screws, then remove the housing.
2. Open the access panel at the back of the housing.
3. Grasp the bulb, then gently depress and twist it ⅛ turn counterclockwise, and pull it from the socket.

To install:

4. Before installing a light bulb into the socket, ensure that all electrical contact surfaces are free of corrosion or dirt.

➡ **Before installing the light bulb, note the positions of the two retaining pins on the bulb. They will likely be at different heights on the bulb, to ensure that the bulb is installed correctly. If, when installing the bulb, it does not turn easily, do not force it. Remove the bulb and rotate it 180 degrees from its former position, then reinsert it into the bulb socket.**

5. Insert the light bulb into the socket and, while depressing the bulb, twist it ⅛ turn clockwise until the two pins on the light bulb are properly engaged in the socket.

6. To ensure that the replacement bulb functions properly, activate the applicable switch to illuminate the bulb which was just replaced.

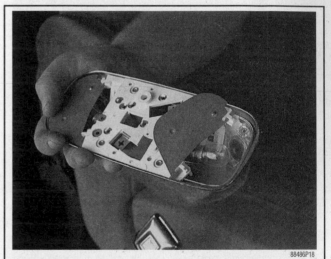

Fig. 101 Open the flap on the back of the housing to gain access to the bulb

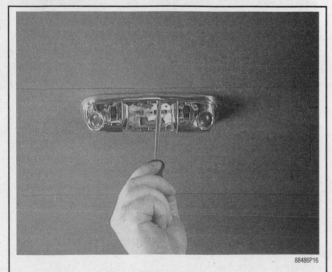

Fig. 99 Loosen the dome light housing screws

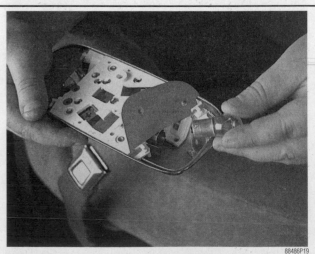

Fig. 102 Grasp the bulb, then gently depress and twist it ⅛ turn counterclockwise, and pull it from the socket

If the replacement light bulb does not illuminate, either it too is faulty or there is a problem in the bulb circuit or switch. Correct if necessary.

7. Install the housing and fasten the screws

Cargo Lamps

1. Loosen the screws and remove the lens.
2. Twist the bulb out of the socket and remove the bulb.
3. Installation is the reverse of removal.

License Plate Lamp

1989–94 MODELS

▶ See Figures 103, 104 and 105

1. Loosen the two plastic screws retaining the lamp(s).
2. Pull the lamp out of the housing and bracket.
3. Remove the lamp socket from the lamp assembly housing by twisting it counterclockwise.
4. Remove the bulb from the socket.
5. Installation is the reverse of removal.

Fig. 104 Loosen the lamp housing screws

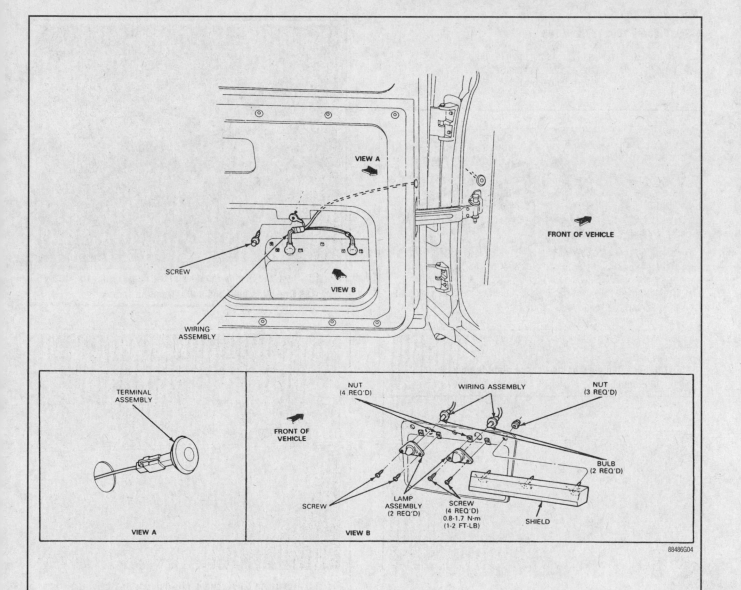

Fig. 103 License plate lamp assembly—1989–94 models

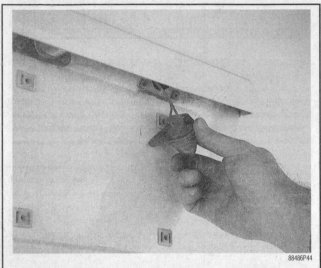

Fig. 105 Pull the housing down to gain access to the socket

Fig. 107 Turn the socket assembly until the tabs disengage and you are able to separate it from the housing

1995–96 MODELS

◗ See Figures 106, 107 and 108

1. Loosen the two plastic screws retaining the bulb.
2. Pull the bulb from the housing and bracket.
3. Installation is the reverse of removal.

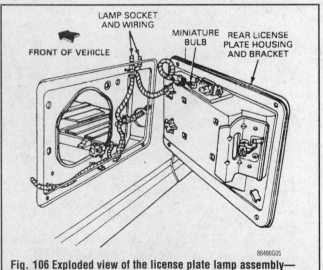

Fig. 106 Exploded view of the license plate lamp assembly—1995–96 models

Fig. 108 Grasp the bulb and pull it from the socket

TRAILER WIRING

Wiring the vehicle for towing is fairly easy. There are a number of good wiring kits available and these should be used, rather than trying to design your own.

All trailers will need brake lights and turn signals as well as tail lights and side marker lights. Most areas require extra marker lights for overwide trailers. Also, most areas have recently required back-up lights for trailers, and most trailer manufacturers have been building trailers with back-up lights for several years.

Additionally, some Class I, most Class II and just about all Class III trailers will have electric brakes. Add to this number an accessories wire, to operate trailer internal equipment or to charge the trailer's battery, and you can have as many as seven wires in the harness.

Determine the equipment on your trailer and buy the wiring kit necessary. The kit will contain all the wires needed, plus a plug adapter set which includes the female plug, mounted on the bumper or hitch, and the male plug, wired into, or plugged into the trailer harness.

When installing the kit, follow the manufacturer's instructions. The color coding of the wires is usually standard throughout the industry. One point to note: some domestic vehicles, and most imported vehicles, have separate turn signals. On most domestic vehicles, the brake lights and rear turn signals operate with the same bulb. For those vehicles without separate turn signals, you can purchase an isolation unit so that the brake lights won't blink whenever the turn signals are operated. The isolation units are simple and quick to install.

One, final point, the best kits are those with a spring loaded cover on the vehicle mounted socket. This cover prevents dirt and moisture from corroding the terminals. Never let the vehicle socket hang loosely; always mount it securely to the bumper or hitch.

CIRCUIT PROTECTION

Fuses

▶ **See Figures 109 and 110**

The fuse panel is located on a bracket on the driver's side of the instrument panel or, on some RV models, it is located on a bracket attached to the brake pedal.

If a fuse blows, the cause should be investigated and corrected before the installation of a new fuse. This, however, is easier to say than to do. Because each fuse protects a limited number of components, your job is narrowed down somewhat. Begin your investigation by looking for obvious fraying, loose connections, breaks in insulation, etc. Use the techniques outlined at the beginning of this section. Electrical problems are almost always a real headache to solve, but if you are patient and persistent, and approach the problem logically (that is, don't start replacing electrical components randomly), you will eventually find the solution.

Each fuse block uses miniature fuses (normally plug-in blade terminal-type for these vehicles) which are designed for increased circuit protection and greater reliability. The compact plug-in or blade terminal design allows for fingertip removal and replacement.

Although most fuses are interchangeable in size, the amperage values are not. Should you install a fuse with too high a value, damaging current could be allowed to destroy the component you were attempting to protect by using a fuse in the first place. The plug-in type fuses have a volt number molded on them and are color coded for easy identification. Be sure to only replace a fuse with the proper amperage rated substitute.

A blown fuse can easily be checked by visual inspection or by testing for continuity.

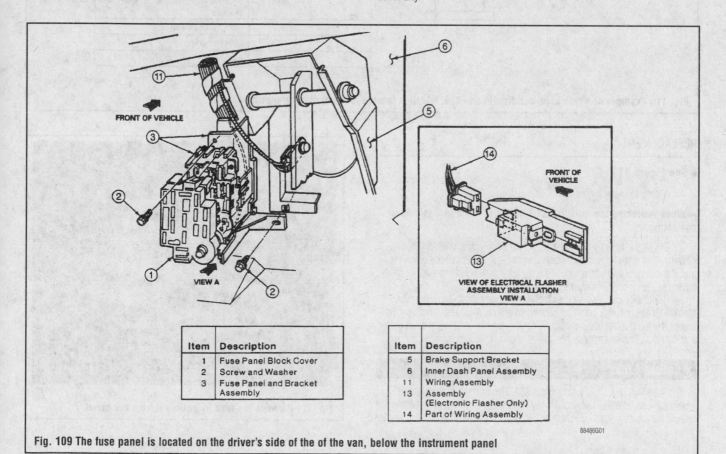

Item	Description
1	Fuse Panel Block Cover
2	Screw and Washer
3	Fuse Panel and Bracket Assembly

Item	Description
5	Brake Support Bracket
6	Inner Dash Panel Assembly
11	Wiring Assembly
13	Assembly (Electronic Flasher Only)
14	Part of Wiring Assembly

88486G01

Fig. 109 The fuse panel is located on the driver's side of the of the van, below the instrument panel

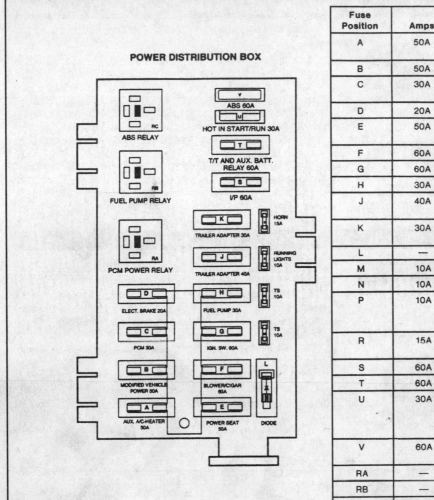

POWER DISTRIBUTION BOX

ABS RELAY — RC

ABS 60A

HOT IN START/RUN 30A

FUEL PUMP RELAY — RB

T/T AND AUX. BATT. RELAY 60A

I/P 60A

PCM POWER RELAY — RA

TRAILER ADAPTER 30A — K

HORN 15A

TRAILER ADAPTER 40A — J

RUNNING LIGHTS 10A

ELECT. BRAKE 20A — D

FUEL PUMP 30A — H

TS 10A

PCM 30A — C

IGN. SW. 60A — G

TS 10A

MODIFIED VEHICLE POWER 50A — B

BLOWER/CIGAR 60A — F

L

AUX. A/C-HEATER 50A — A

POWER SEAT 50A — E

DIODE

Fuse Position	Amps	Circuits Protected
A	50A	Aux. A/C — Heater, Remote Keyless Entry Module*
B	50A	Modified Vehicle Power*
C	30A	Powertrain Control Module (PCM), PCM Power Relay
D	20A	Electronic Brake*
E	50A	Power Seats, Power Lumbar Seats
F	60A	Blower Motor, Cigar
G	60A	Ignition Switch
H	30A	Fuel Pump, Fuel Pump Relay
J	40A	Trailer Adapter Battery Feed, Trailer Battery Charger Relay*
K	30A	Trailer Backup Lamp Relay, Trailer Running Lamp Relay*
L	—	Plug-in Diode
M	10A	Trailer RH Turn / Stop Lamp
N	10A	Trailer LH Turn / Stop Lamp
P	10A	Class I Trailer Running Lamps Class II Trailer Running Lamp Relay
R	15A	DRL Module, Horn Relay, Hood Lamp
S	60A	Headlamp Switch, IP
T	60A	Trailer Adapter, Aux. Battery*
U	30A	Ignition System, Instrument Cluster, PIA Engine (Diesel Only), PCM Power Relay, ABS Power Relay, 4WABS Relay
V	60A	ABS Valve, Pump Motor, 4WABS Module
RA	—	PCM Power Relay
RB	—	Fuel Pump Relay
RC	—	ABS Relay

* Optional.

88486G02

Fig. 110 Example of a typical power distribution box, which is located in the engine compartment

REPLACEMENT

▶ See Figure 111

1. Locate the fuse for the circuit in question.

➡**When replacing the fuse, DO NOT use one with a higher amperage rating.**

2. Check the fuse by pulling it from the fuse block and observing the element. If it is broken, install a replacement fuse the same amperage rating. If the fuse blows again, check the circuit for a short to ground or faulty device in the circuit protected by the fuse.

3. Continuity can also be checked with the fuse installed in the fuse block with the use of a test light connected across the 2 test points on the end of the fuse. If the test light lights, replace the fuse. Check the circuit for a short to ground or faulty device in the circuit protected by the fuse.

Fusible Links

The fuse link is a short length of special, Hypalon (high temperature) insulated wire, integral with the engine compartment wiring harness and should not be confused with standard wire. It is several wire gauges smaller

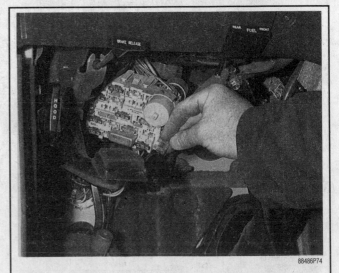

88486P74

Fig. 111 Remove the fuse by pulling it from the panel

WIRING DIAGRAMS

INDEX OF WIRING DIAGRAMS

DIAGRAM 1   SAMPLE DIAGRAM: HOW TO READ & INTERPRET WIRING DIAGRAMS

DIAGRAM 2   WIRING DIAGRAM SYMBOLS

DIAGRAM 3   1989- 9 4.9L ENGINE SCHEMATIC

DIAGRAM 4   1991 4 L ENGINE SCHEMATIC

DIAGRAM 5   1992-9 4.9L & 1995 4.9L (Federal) ENGINE SCHEMATIC

DIAGRAM 6   1995 4.9 (California) ENGINE SCHEMATIC

DIAGRAM 7   1996 4.9 ENGINE SCHEMATIC

DIAGRAM 8   1989 5.0L 5.8L & 7.5L ENGINE SCHEMATICS

DIAGRAM 9   1990-91 5 L ENGINE SCHEMATICS

DIAGRAM 10   1992 5.0L NGINE SCHEMATIC

DIAGRAM 11   1993-95 5.0 ENGINE SCHEMATIC

DIAGRAM 12   1996 5.0L E INE SCHEMATIC

DIAGRAM 13   1990-91 5.8L NGINE SCHEMATICS

DIAGRAM 14   1992-94 5.8L 995 5.8L (Federal), 1996 (Federal over 8600 GVW) 5.8L 1994-95 7.5L 996 7.5L (Federal) ENGINE SCHEMATIC

DIAGRAM 15   1995 (CALIFO IA) 5.8L ENGINE SCHEMATIC

DIAGRAM 16   1996 (Federal der 8600 GVW & California) 5.8L & 1996 7.5L (California) ENGINE SCHE ATIC

DIAGRAM 17   1989-94 7.3L DI EL ENGINE SCHEMATICS

DIAGRAM 18   1995-96 7.3L TU O DIESEL ENGINE SCHEMATIC

DIAGRAM 19   1990-91 7.5L EN NE SCHEMATICS

DIAGRAM 20   1992-93 7.5L EN IE SCHEMATICS

DIAGRAM 21   1989-91 CHASSIS ASOLINE) SCHEMATICS

DIAGRAM 22   1992-96 CHASSIS SOLINE) SCHEMATICS

DIAGRAM 23   1989-91 CHASSIS (EL) SCHEMATICS

DIAGRAM 24   1992-96 CHASSIS (L) SCHEMATICS

DIAGRAM 25   1989-91 CHASSIS S ATICS

DIAGRAM 26   1992-96 CHASSIS SC TICS

DIAGRAM 27   1989-96 CHASSIS SC TICS

88486W01

SAMPLE DIAGRAM: HOW TO READ & INTERPRET WIRING DIAGRAMS

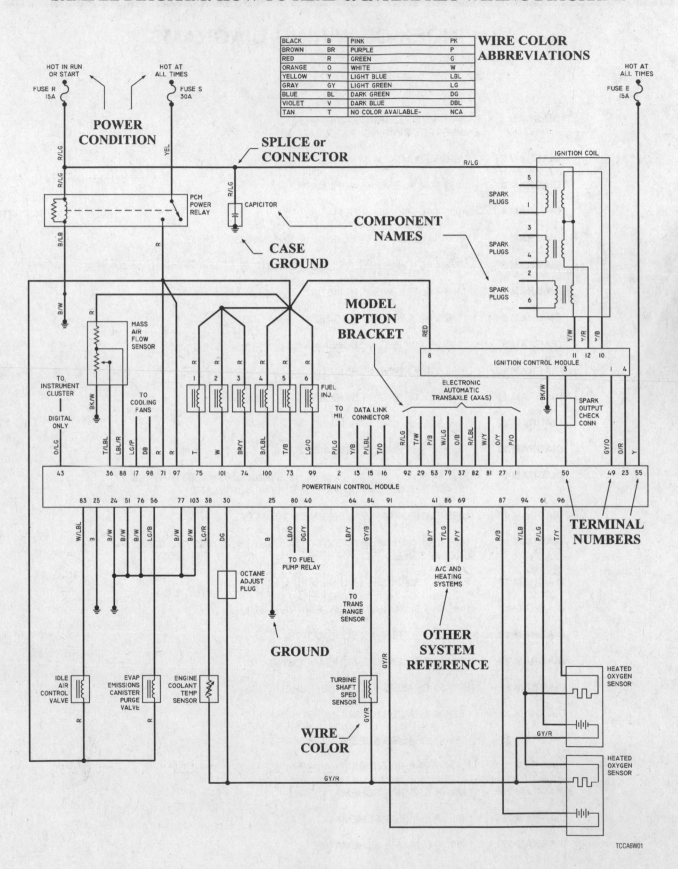

DIAGRAM 1

WIRING DIAGRAM SYMBOLS

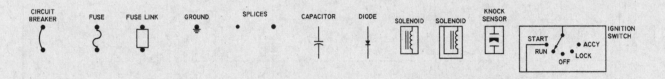

CIRCUIT BREAKER   FUSE   FUSE LINK   GROUND   SPLICES   CAPACITOR   DIODE   SOLENOID   SOLENOID   KNOCK SENSOR   IGNITION SWITCH

START   RUN   OFF   LOCK   ACCY

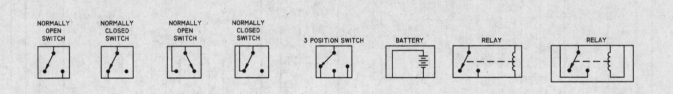

NORMALLY OPEN SWITCH   NORMALLY CLOSED SWITCH   NORMALLY OPEN SWITCH   NORMALLY CLOSED SWITCH   3 POSITION SWITCH   BATTERY   RELAY   RELAY

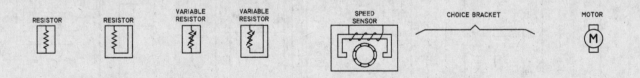

RESISTOR   RESISTOR   VARIABLE RESISTOR   VARIABLE RESISTOR   SPEED SENSOR   CHOICE BRACKET   MOTOR

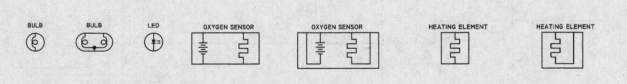

BULB   BULB   LED   OXYGEN SENSOR   OXYGEN SENSOR   HEATING ELEMENT   HEATING ELEMENT

DIAGRAM 2

TCCA6W02

1989-90 4.9L ENGINE SCHEMATIC

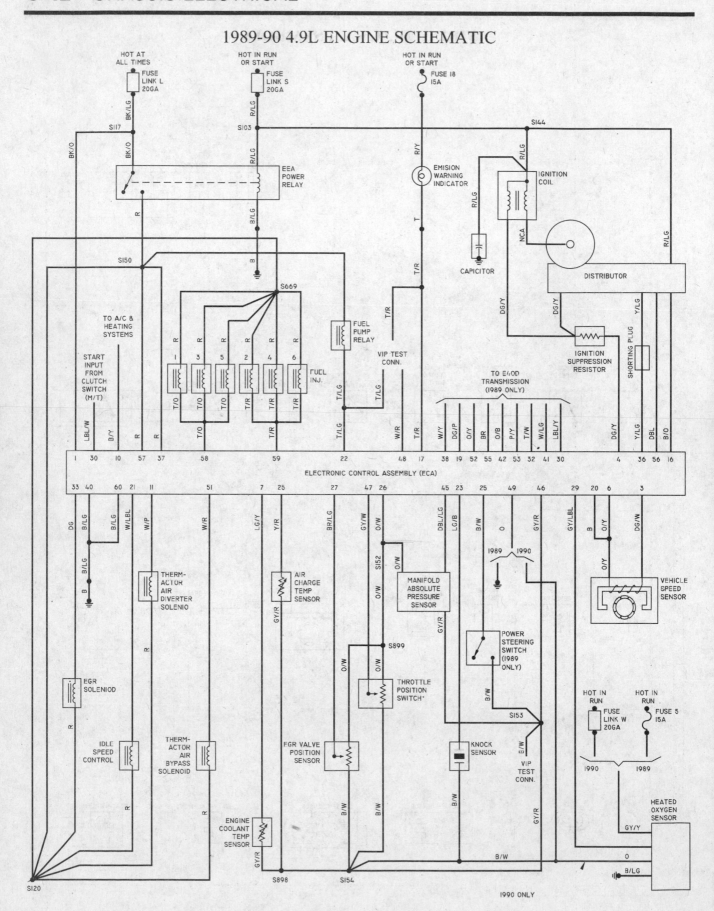

DIAGRAM 3

88486E07

1991 4.9L ENGINE SCHEMATIC

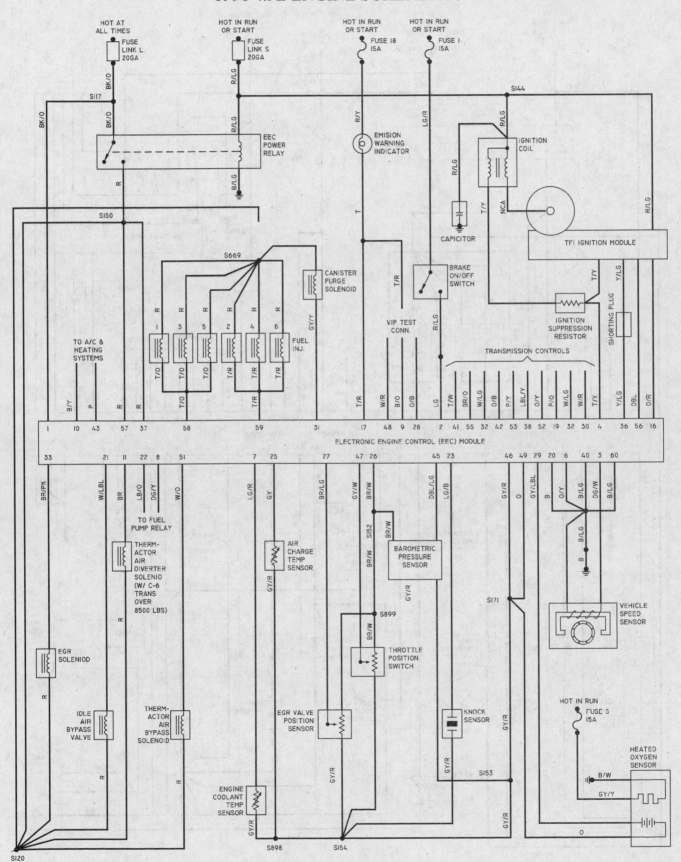

DIAGRAM 4

88486E06

1992-94 4.9L & 1995 4.9L (FEDERAL) ENGINE SCHEMATIC

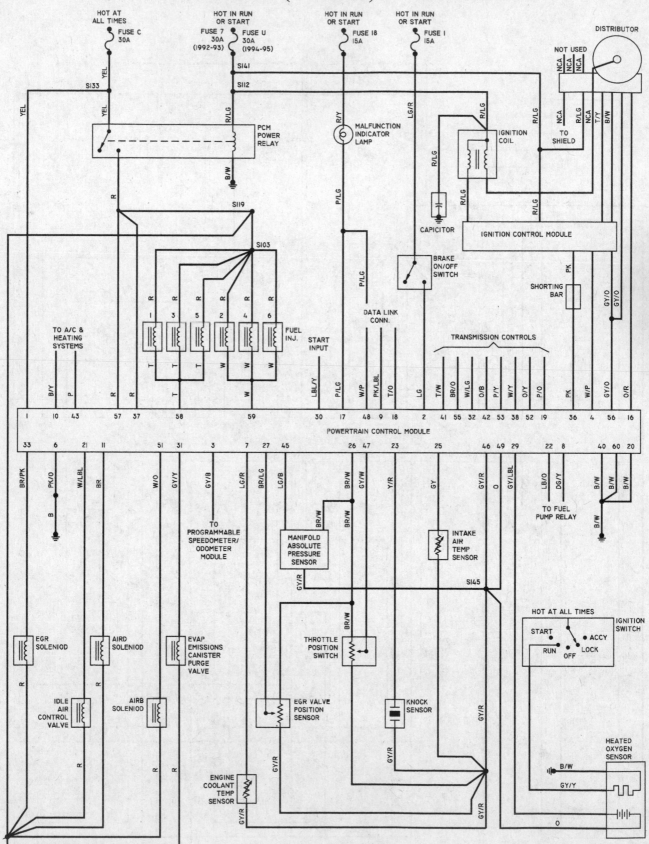

DIAGRAM 5

88486E05

1995 4.9L (CALIFORNIA) ENGINE SCHEMATIC

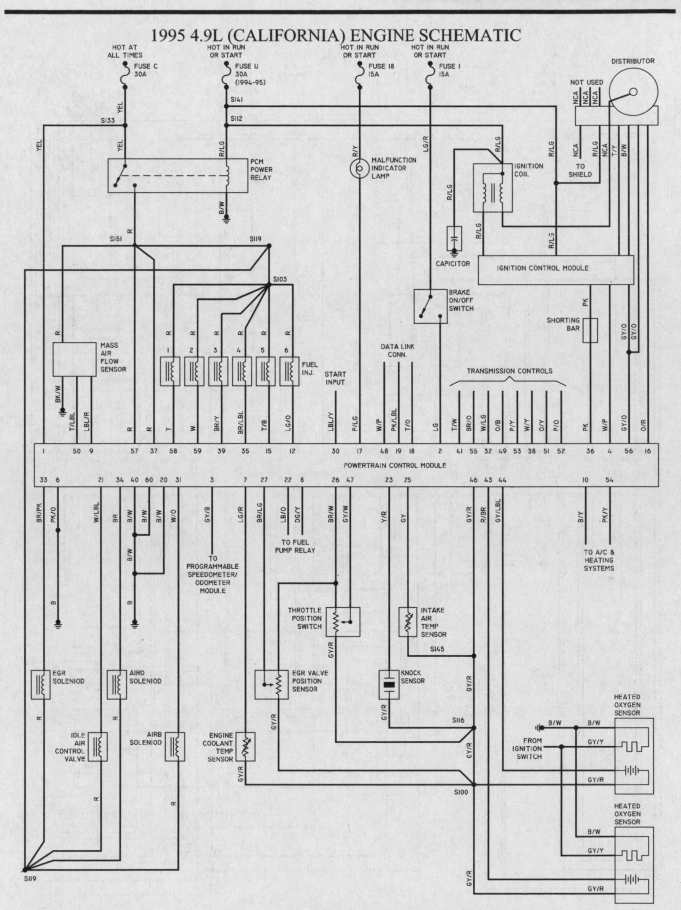

DIAGRAM 6

88486E04

1996 4.9L ENGINE SCHEMATIC

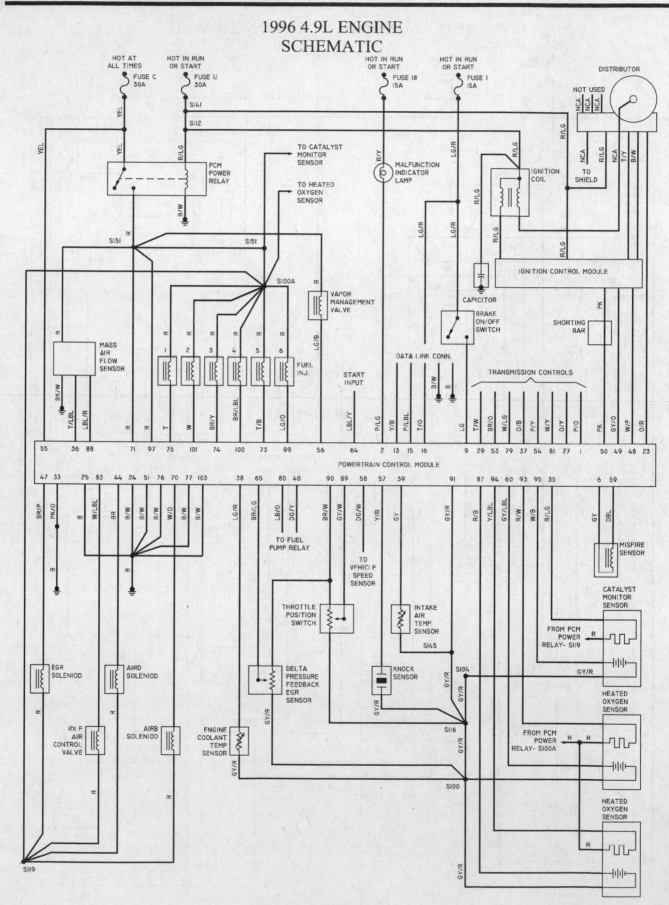

DIAGRAM 7

88486E03

1989 5.0L & 5.8L & 7.5L ENGINE SCHEMATICS

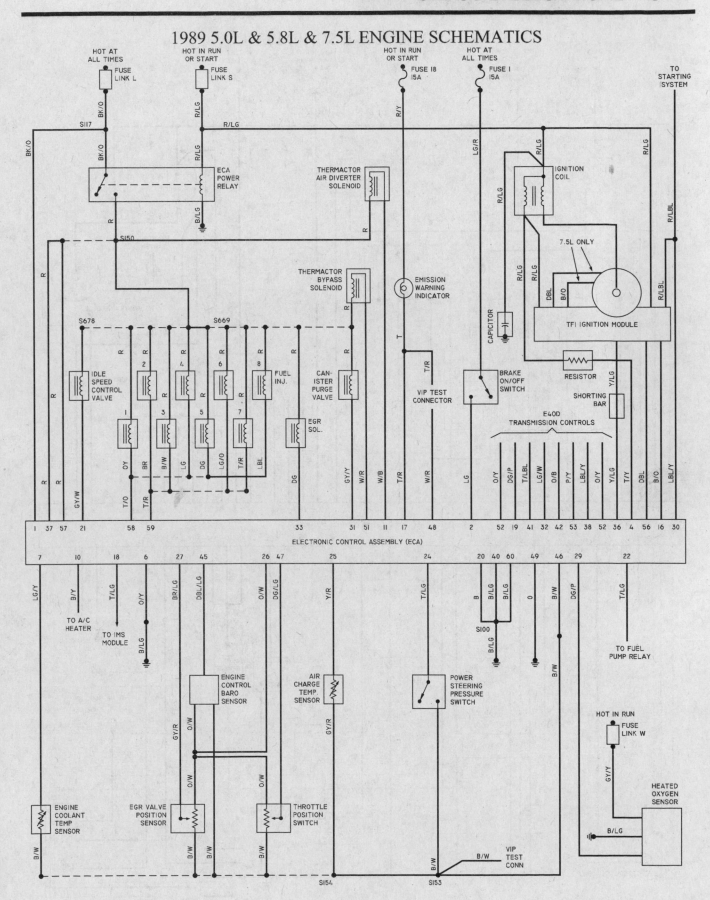

DIAGRAM 8

88486E14

1990-91 5.0L ENGINE SCHEMATICS

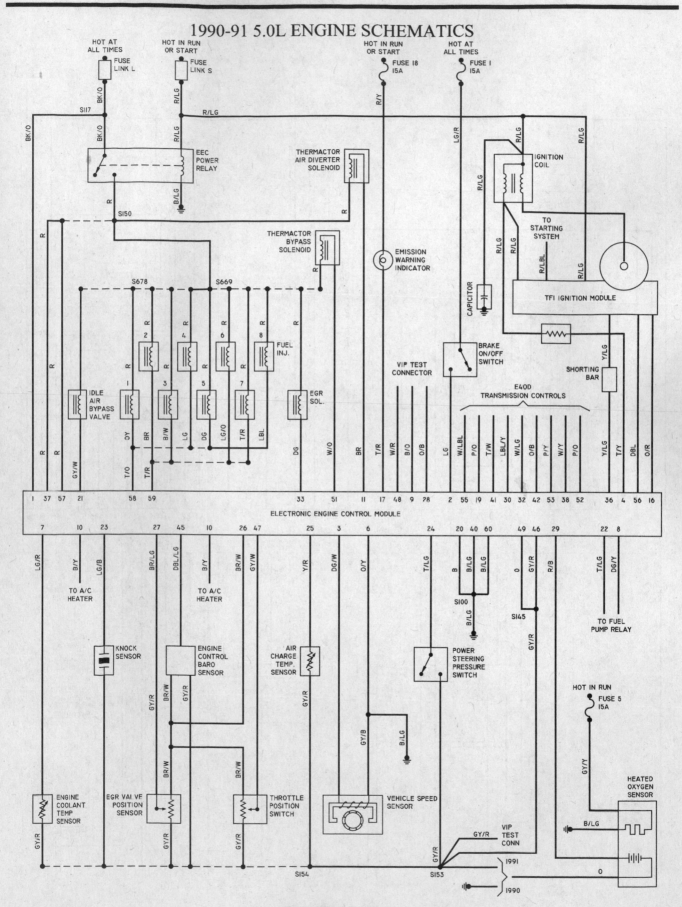

DIAGRAM 9

88486E13

1996 5.0L ENGINE SCHEMATIC

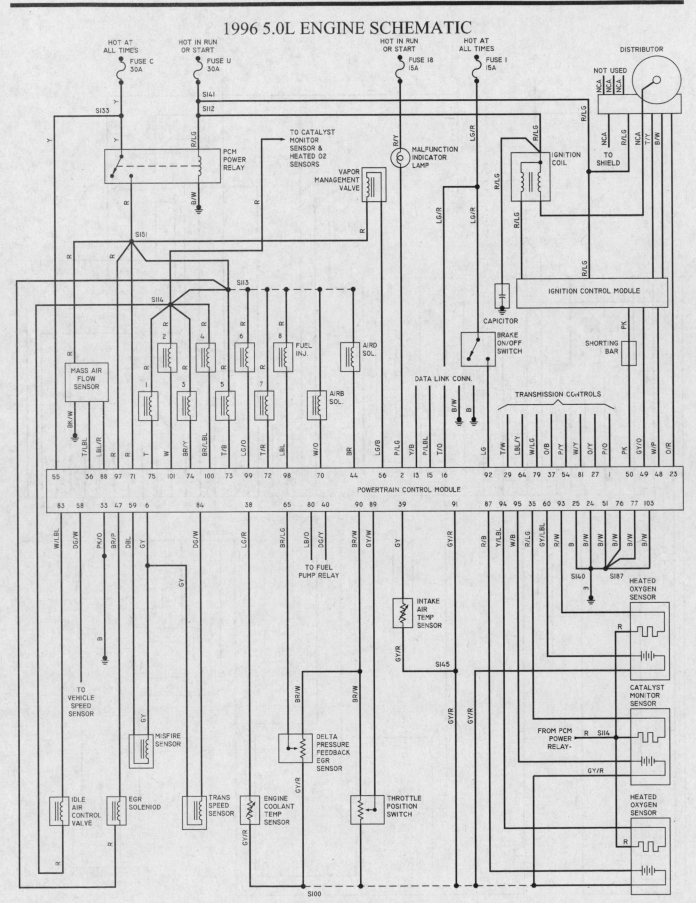

DIAGRAM 12

88486E10

1990-91 5.8L ENGINE SCHEMATICS

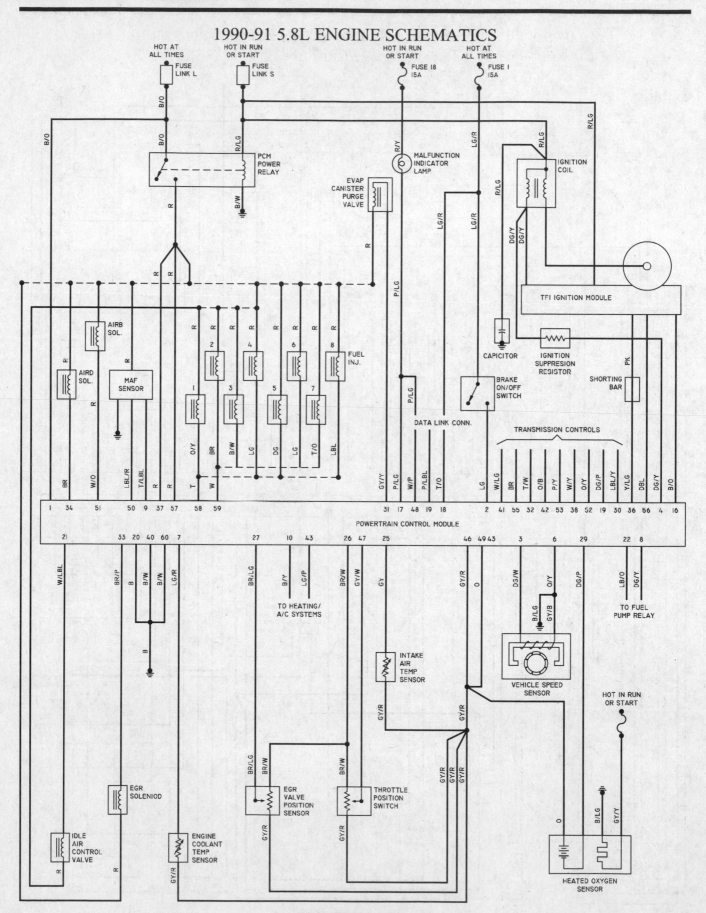

DIAGRAM 13

88486E16

1992-94 5.8L, 1995 5.8L (Federal) & 1996 (Federal over 8600 GVW) 5.8L
1994-95 7.5L & 1996 7.5L (Federal) ENGINE SCHEMATIC

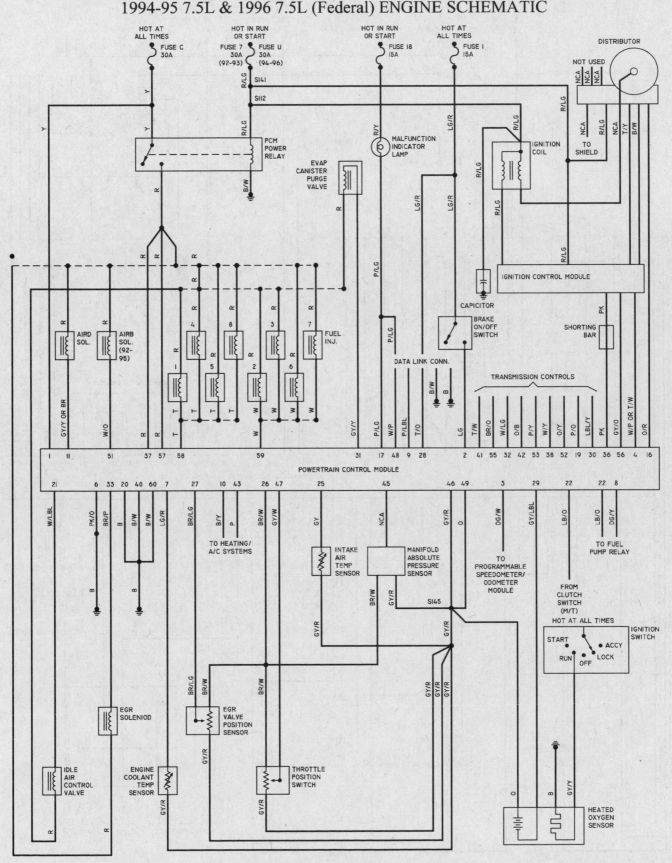

DIAGRAM 14

88486E09

1995 (CALIFORNIA) 5.8L ENGINE SCHEMATIC

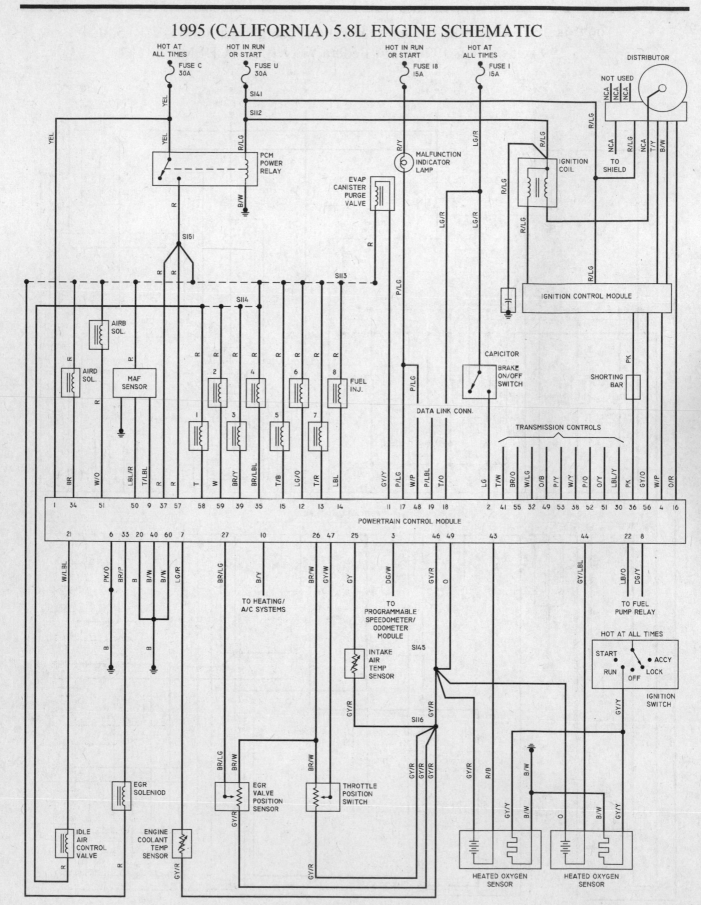

DIAGRAM 15

88486E15

1996 (Federal under 8600 GVW & California) 5.8L & 1996 7.5L (California)
ENGINE SCHEMATIC

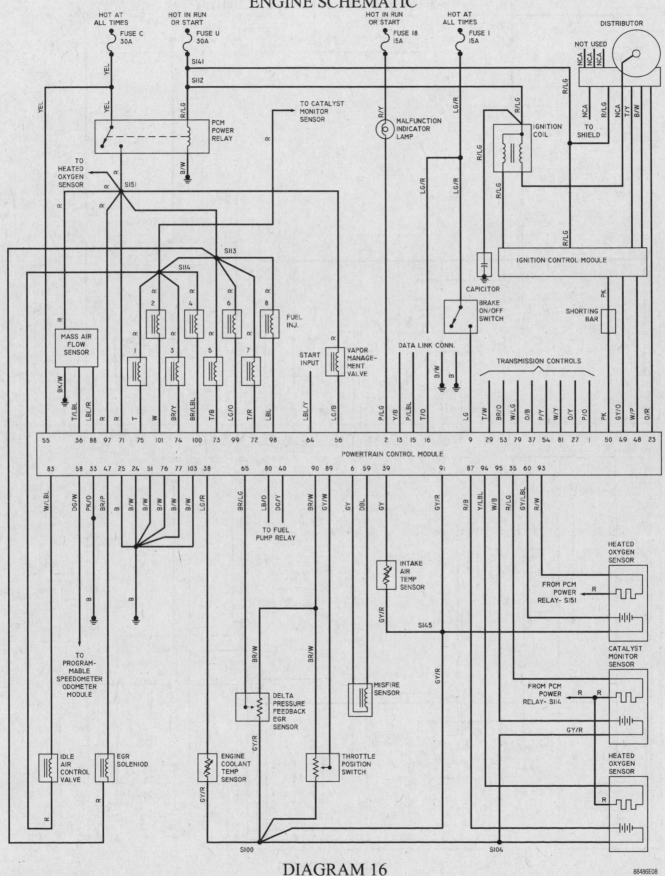

DIAGRAM 16

88486E08

1989-94 7.3L DIESEL ENGINE SCHEMATICS
1993-94 7.3L DIESEL 8 CYLINDER

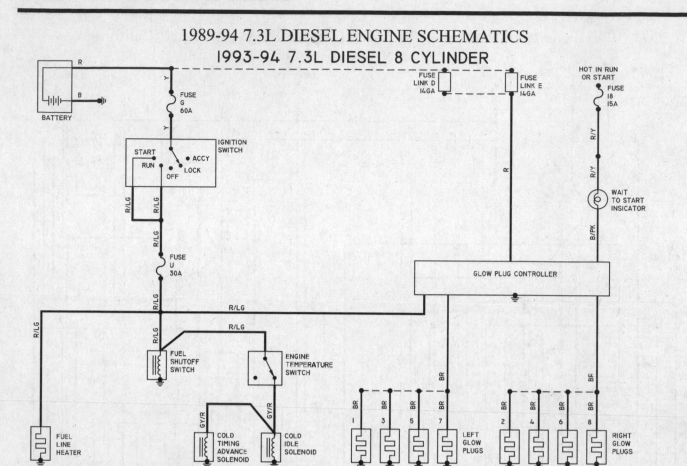

1989-92 7.3L DIESEL 8 CYLINDER

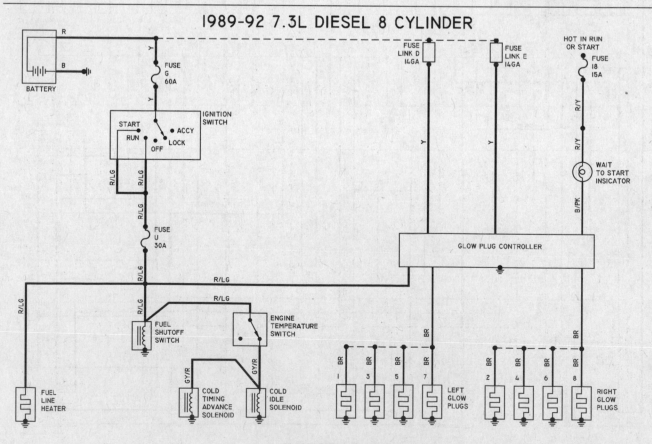

DIAGRAM 17

88486E02

1995-96 7.3L TURBO DIESEL ENGINE SCHEMATIC

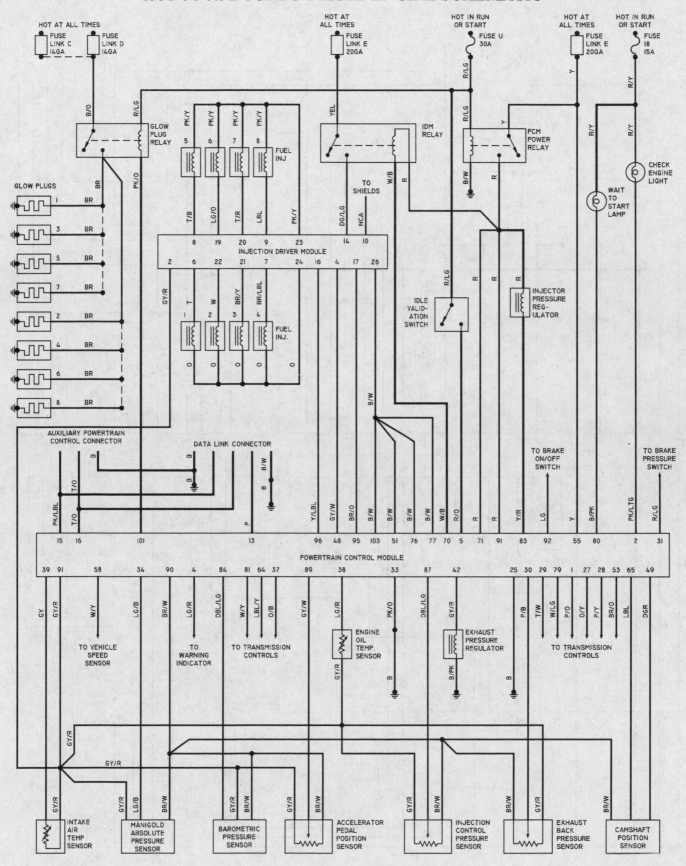

DIAGRAM 18

88486E01

1990-91 7.5L ENGINE SCHEMATICS

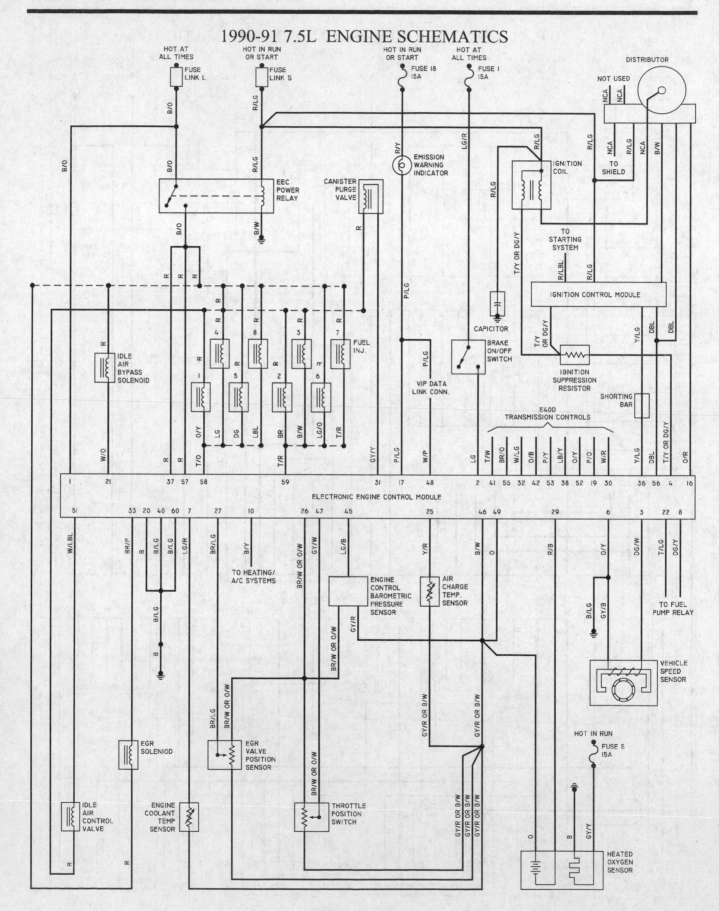

DIAGRAM 19

88486E19

1992-93 7.5L ENGINE SCHEMATICS

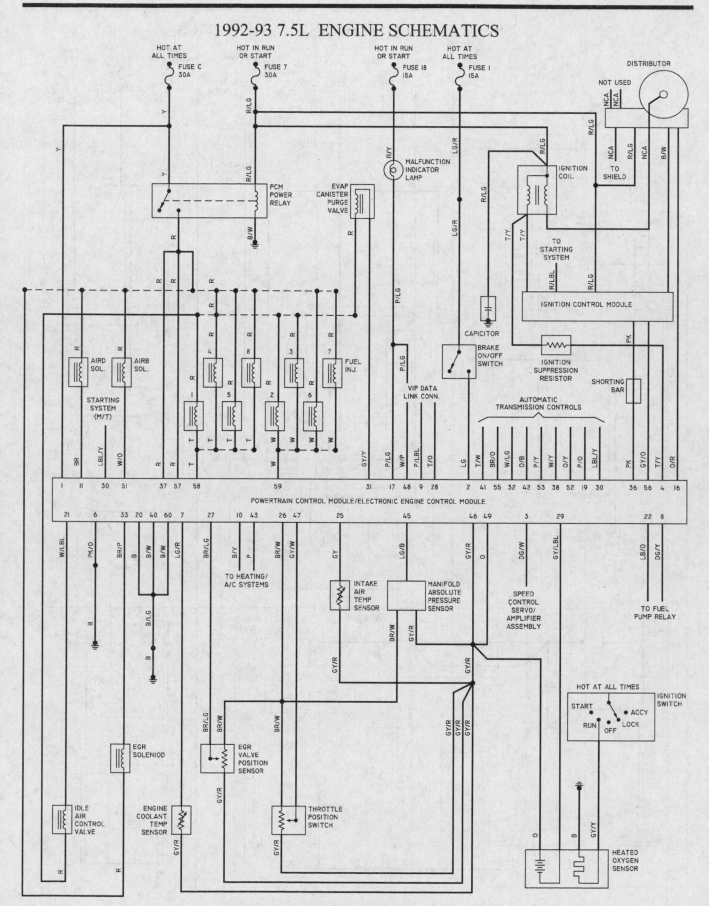

DIAGRAM 20

88486E18

1989-91 CHASSIS (GASOLINE) SCHEMATICS

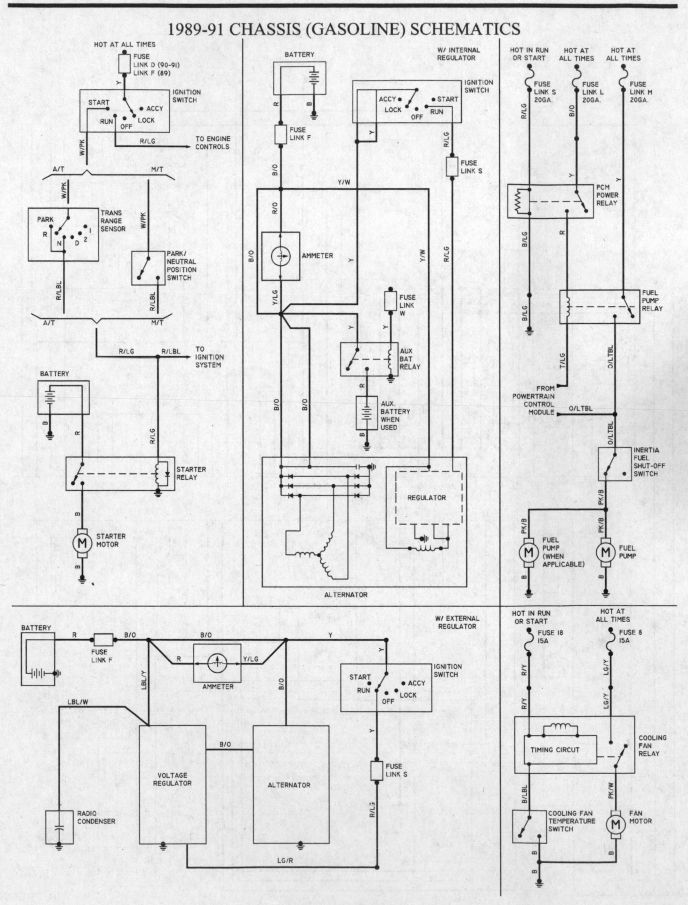

DIAGRAM 21

88486B01

1992-96 CHASSIS (GASOLINE) SCHEMATICS

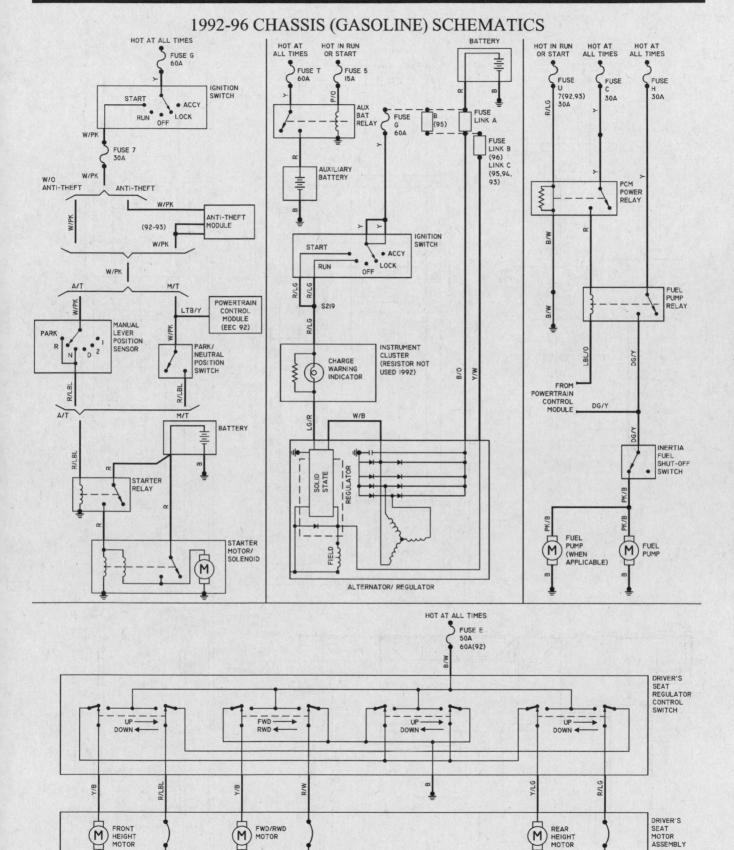

DIAGRAM 22

88486B02

1989-91 CHASSIS (DIESEL) SCHEMATICS

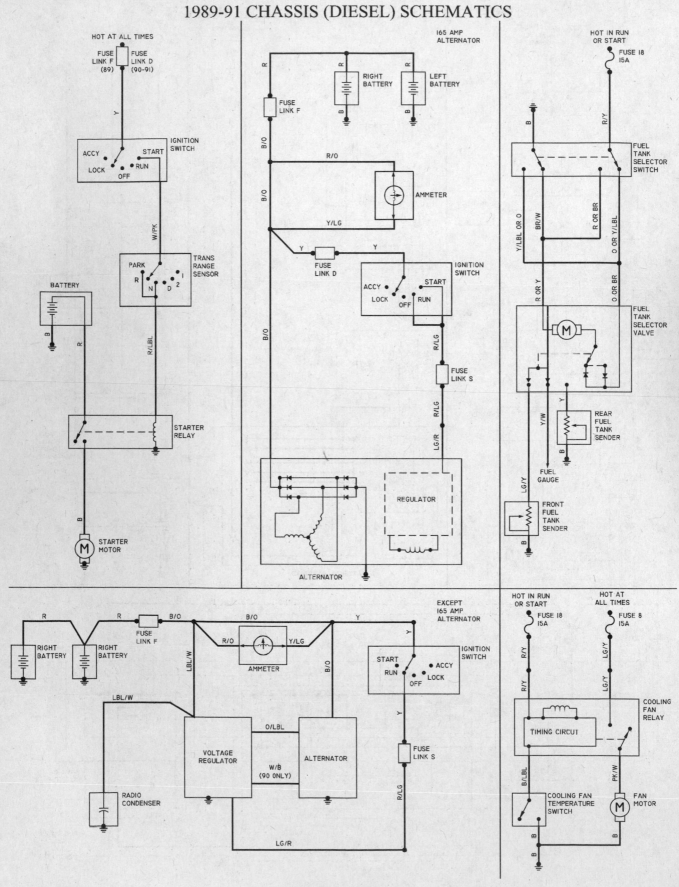

DIAGRAM 23

88486B04

1992-96 CHASSIS (DIESEL) SCHEMATICS

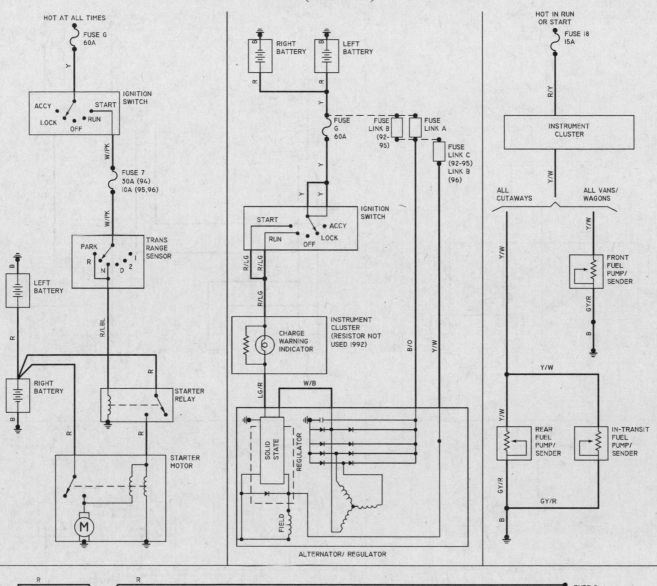

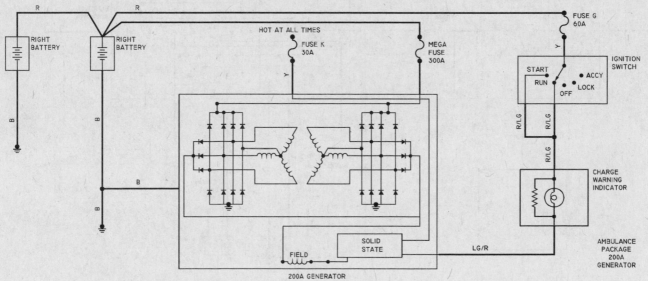

DIAGRAM 24

88486B05

1989-91 CHASSIS SCHEMATICS

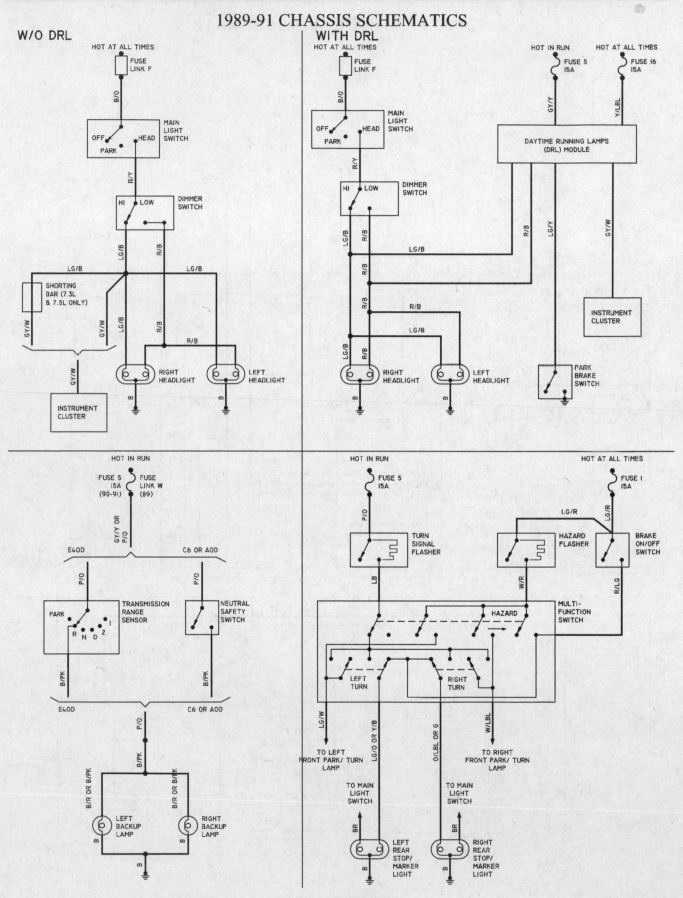

DIAGRAM 25

88486B03

1992-96 CHASSIS SCHEMATICS

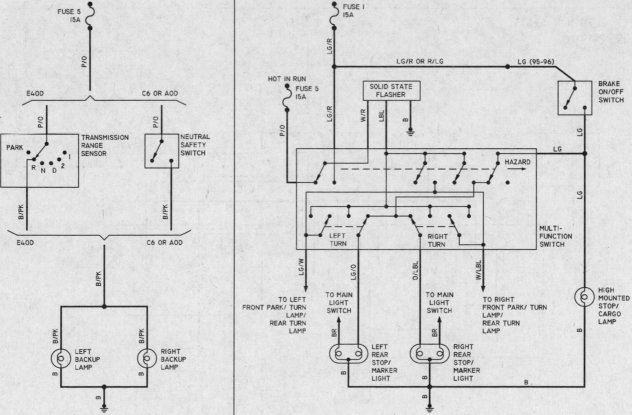

DIAGRAM 26

88486B06

1989-96 CHASSIS SCHEMATICS

EXTERIOR LAMPS
1989-1991

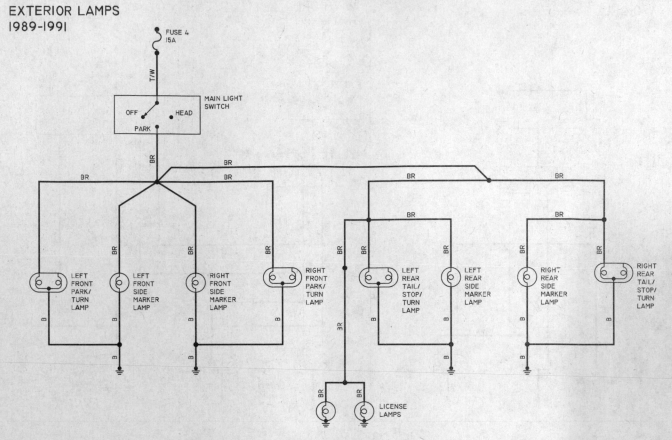

EXTERIOR LAMPS
1992-1996

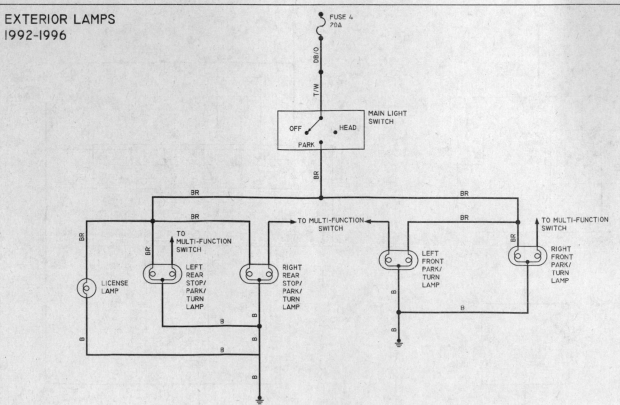

DIAGRAM 27

88486B07

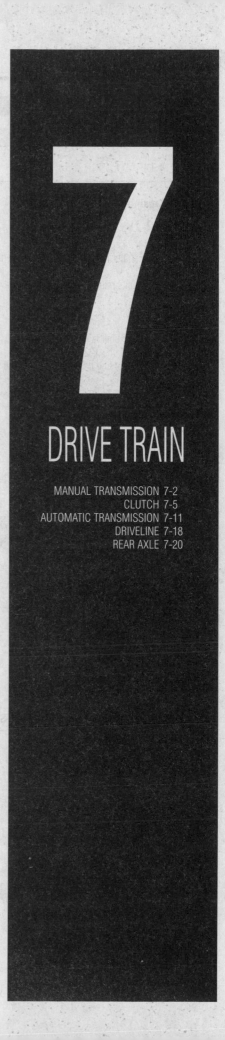

7
DRIVE TRAIN

MANUAL TRANSMISSION

Shift Handle

REMOVAL & INSTALLATION

S5-42 ZF Transmission

▶ **See Figure 1**

1. Disconnect the negative battery cable.
2. Remove the shifter boot and bezel assembly from the transmission opening cover.
3. Remove the bolts retaining the upper shift lever to the lower shift lever.
4. Loosen the Allen head bolts and remove the upper shift lever.

To install:

5. Install the upper shift lever to the lower lever and install the retaining bolts. Tighten 16–24 ft. lbs. (22–33 Nm).
6. Install shifter boot and bezel assembly to the transmission opening cover.
7. Install the Allen head bolts.
8. Install the shift ball on the upper shifter if removed.
9. Connect the negative battery cable.

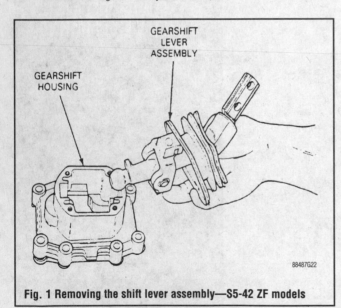

Fig. 1 Removing the shift lever assembly—S5-42 ZF models

Mazda M50D 5-Speed Transmission

▶ **See Figures 2 thru 8**

1. Disconnect the negative battery cable.
2. Shift the transmission into **Neutral**.
3. Remove the carpet or floor mats.
4. Remove the shifter boot retainer screws and slide the boot up the shift lever shaft.
5. Remove the shift lever retaining bolt locknut.
6. Remove the shift lever retaining bolt by placing the locknut on the opposite end of the bolt and tightening to loosen the bolt.
7. The shifter may be removed either by removing the bolt retaining the shifter to the shifter stub and then pulling the shifter off or by removing the screws retaining the shifter to the shift housing and remove the shifter and boot assembly.

To install:

8. If shifter was removed from the shifter stub shaft, install the retaining bolt in the shift lever hole so that the flat aligns with the mating flat on the transmission stub shaft. Push the bolt fully into position. Install the nut and tighten to 12–18 ft. lbs. (16–24 Nm).
9. If the shifter and stub shaft were removed together, position the shifter lever into the shift housing aligning the end of the shifter with the slot in the transmission. Install the retaining screws and tighten to 6–8 ft. lbs. (8–11 Nm).
10. Slide the gearshift boot and sound deadening material into position on the gearshift lever and housing, then install the retaining screws.
11. Install the Isolator pan assembly. Install the floor pan cover and floor carpet it removed.
12. Connect the negative battery cable.

Fig. 2 Removing the shifter boot retaining screws

Fig. 3 Pull the boot up over the shift lever, exposing the sound deadening material

Fig. 4 Examine the condition of the boot and sound deadening material

Fig. 5 If removing the shift lever from the stub shaft, install and tighten the locknut from the opposite side

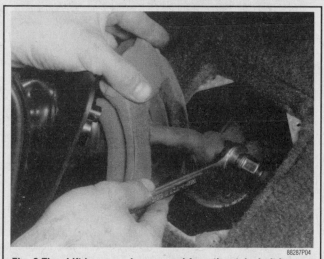

Fig. 6 The shift lever can be removed from the stub shaft by removing the shift lever-to-stub shaft bolt

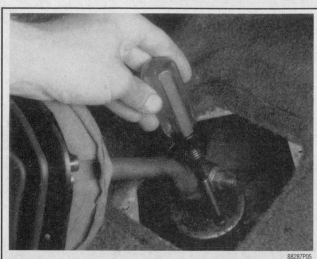

Fig. 7 To remove the shift lever and stub shaft together, remove the shift dust cover retaining screws

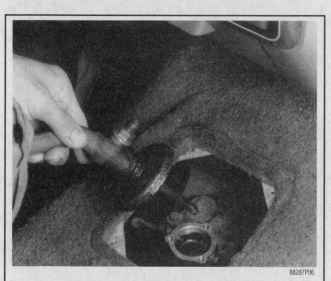

Fig. 8 Removing the shift lever assembly with the stub shaft

Back-up Light Switch

Refer to Section 6 in this manual for the Back-up Light Switch removal and installation procedure for manual transmissions.

Extension Housing Seal

REMOVAL & INSTALLATION

▶ **See Figures 9, 10, 11, 12 and 13**

The extension housing seal is located at the rear of the transmission case.
1. Raise and support the vehicle safely.
2. Drain the transmission of lubricant.
3. Matchmark the driveshaft to the yoke for reassembly and remove the driveshaft.
4. On the Mazda M50D transmission, remove the old seal using a seal puller or appropriate prytool.
5. On the S5-42 ZF transmission remove the seal as follows:
   a. Use a chisel to bend back the tab on the output flange locknut.
   b. Attach companion flange holding tool T78P-4851-A or its equivalent to the transmission output flange.

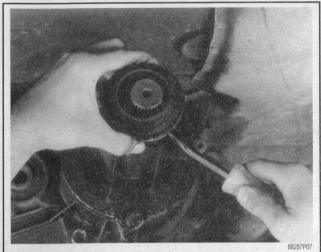

Fig. 9 Removing the extension housing seal with a prytool—Mazda M50D transmission

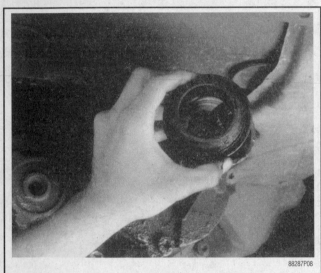

Fig. 10 Always replace the old seal with a new one

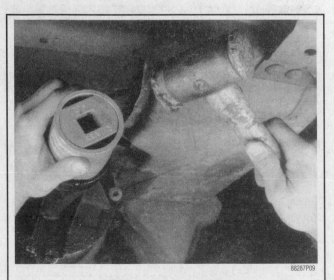

Fig. 11 Using a seal driver and mallet, install the new seal

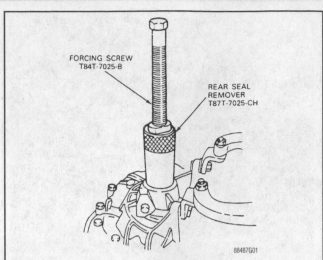

FORCING SCREW
T84T-7025-B

REAR SEAL
REMOVER
T87T-7025-CH

Fig. 12 Use the proper tools to remove the rear oil seal—S5-42 ZF models

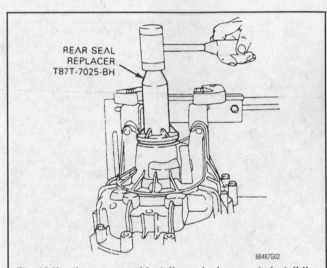

REAR SEAL
REPLACER
T87T-7025-BH

Fig. 13 Use the proper seal installer and a hammer to install the rear oil seal—S5-42 ZF models

c. Loosen the hex nut that holds the output flange to the mainshaft using socket T87T-7025-AH or its equivalent, then remove the tool after loosening the nut.

d. Remove the output flange from the mainshaft.

e. Remove the old seal using a seal remover T87T-7025-CH and forcing screw T84T-7025-B or their equivalents. Refer to the tool set-up illustration.

To install:

6. On the Mazda M50D transmission, install the new seal as follows:

a. Install a new seal with oil drain hole facing downward, coated with sealing compound, using an appropriate seal installation tool such as T61L-7657-A or its equivalent.

7. On the S5-42 ZF transmission, install the seal as follows:

a. Using an appropriate seal installation tool such as T87T-77025-BH or its equivalent and a hammer, install the new seal.

b. Install the output flange.

c. Attach companion flange holding tool T78P-4851-A or its equivalent to the transmission output flange.

d. Tighten the hex nut that holds the output flange to the mainshaft to 184 ft. lbs. (250 Nm), using socket T87T-7025-AH or its equivalent, then remove the tool after tightening the nut.

e. Use a chisel to bend over the tab on the output flange locknut.

8. Install the driveshaft, making certain to align the matchmarks.
9. Fill the transmission to the level of the fill plug hole. Install the plug and lower the vehicle.

Manual Transmission Assembly

REMOVAL & INSTALLATION

✳✳ CAUTION

The clutch driven disc may contain asbestos, which has been determined to be a cancer causing agent. Never clean clutch surfaces with compressed air! Avoid inhaling any dust from any clutch surface! When cleaning clutch surfaces, use a commercially available brake cleaning fluid.

1. Place the transmission in Neutral.
2. Remove the shift lever.
3. Disconnect the speedometer cable.
4. Disconnect the back-up switch wire.
5. Place a drain pan under the case and drain the case through the drain plug.
6. Position a transmission jack under the case and safety-chain the case to the jack.
7. Remove the driveshaft.

8. Disconnect the clutch linkage.
9. Remove the transmission rear insulator and lower retainer.
10. Unbolt and remove the crossmember.
11. Remove the transmission-to-engine block bolts.
12. Roll the transmission rearward until the input shaft clears, lower the jack and remove the transmission.
   To install:
13. Install 2 guide studs into the lower bolt holes.
14. Raise the transmission until the input shaft splines are aligned with the clutch disc splines. The clutch release bearing and hub must be properly positioned in the release lever fork.
15. Roll the transmission forward and into position.
16. Install the bolts and tighten them to 50 ft. lbs. (64 Nm). Remove the guide studs and install and tighten the 2 remaining bolts.
17. Install the crossmember and tighten the bolts to 55 ft. lbs. (74 Nm).
18. Install the transmission rear insulator and lower retainer. Tighten the bolts to 60 ft. lbs. (81 Nm).
19. Connect the clutch linkage.
20. Install the driveshaft.
21. Remove the transmission jack.
22. Fill the transmission.
23. Connect the back-up switch wire.
24. Connect the speedometer cable.
25. Lower the van.
26. Install the shift handle.

CLUTCH

REMOVAL & INSTALLATION

▶ **See Figures 14 thru 29**

1. Raise and support the van on jackstands.
2. On vans with the externally mounted slave cylinder, remove the clutch slave cylinder. On vans with an internally mounted slave cylinder, disconnect the quick-disconnect coupling with a spring coupling tool such as T88T-70522-A.
3. Remove the transmission, as described earlier in this section.
4. On gasoline engine models, except the 7.5L engine, remove the starter. Remove the flywheel housing attaching bolts and remove the housing. On diesel engine models and the 7.5L gasoline engine, remove the cover and then remove the release lever and bearing from the clutch housing. To remove the release lever:

a. Remove the dust boot.
b. Push the release lever forward to compress the slave cylinder.
c. Remove the slave cylinder by prying on the steel clip to free the tangs while pulling the cylinder clear.
d. Remove the release lever by pulling it outward.
5. Mark the pressure plate and cover assembly and the flywheel so that they can be reinstalled in the same relative position.
6. Loosen the pressure plate and cover attaching bolts evenly in a staggered sequence a turn at time until the pressure plate springs are relieved of their tension. Remove the attaching bolts.
7. Remove the pressure plate and cover assembly and the clutch disc from the flywheel.
8. Inspect the flywheel for wear, damage and flatness.

Fig. 14 Typical clutch alignment tool—note how the splines match the transmission's input shaft

Fig. 15 Loosen and remove the clutch and pressure plate bolts evenly, a little at a time . . .

Fig. 16 . . . then carefully remove the clutch and pressure plate assembly from the flywheel

To install:

9. Position the clutch disc on the flywheel so that an aligning tool or spare transmission mainshaft can enter the clutch pilot bearing and align the disc.

10. When reinstalling the original pressure plate and cover assembly, align the assembly and flywheel according to the marks made during removal. Position the pressure plate and cover assembly on the flywheel, align the pressure plate and disc, and install the retaining bolts. Tighten the bolts in an alternating sequence a few turns at a time until the proper torque is reached:

- 10 in. clutch: 15–20 ft. lbs. (20–27 Nm)
- 11 in. clutch: 20–29 ft. lbs. (27–39 Nm)

11. Remove the tool used to align the clutch disc.

12. With the clutch fully released, apply a light coat of grease on the sides of the driving lugs.

13. Position the clutch release bearing and the bearing hub on the release lever. Install the release lever on the fulcrum in the flywheel housing. Apply a light coating of grease to the release lever fingers and the fulcrum. Fill the groove of the release bearing hub with grease.

14. If the flywheel housing has been removed, position it against the rear engine cover plate and install the attaching bolts and tighten them to 40–50 ft. lbs. (54–68 Nm).

15. Install the starter motor, if removed.

16. Install the transmission.

17. Install the slave cylinder and bleed the system.

Fig. 17 Check across the flywheel surface—it should be flat

Fig. 18 If necessary, lock the flywheel in place and remove the retaining bolts . . .

Fig. 19 . . . then remove the flywheel from the crankshaft, in order to replace it or have it machined

Fig. 20 Upon installation, it is usually a good idea to apply a threadlocking compound to the flywheel bolts

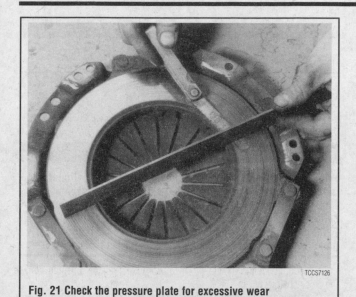

Fig. 21 Check the pressure plate for excessive wear

Fig. 24 Clutch plate installed with the arbor in place

Fig. 22 Be sure that the flywheel surface is clean, before installing the clutch

Fig. 25 Clutch plate and pressure plate installed with the alignment arbor in place

Fig. 23 Install a clutch alignment arbor, to align the clutch assembly during installation

Fig. 26 The pressure plate-to-flywheel bolt holes should align

Fig. 27 You may want to use a threadlocking compound on the clutch assembly bolts

Fig. 28 Install the clutch assembly bolts and tighten in steps, using an X pattern

Fig. 29 Be sure to use a torque wrench to tighten all bolts

Slave Cylinder

REMOVAL & INSTALLATION

Externally Mounted

There are 2 types of slave cylinders used: an internally mounted (in the bell housing) and an externally mounted type.

❈❈ WARNING

Prior to any service requiring removal of the slave cylinder on models with an externally mounted slave cylinder, such as transmission and/or clutch housing removal, the clutch master cylinder pushrod must be disconnected from the clutch pedal. Failure to do this may damage the slave cylinder if the clutch pedal is depressed while the slave cylinder is disconnected.

1. From inside the vehicle, pry the pushrod and retainer bushing from the cross shaft lever pin.
2. Disconnect the interlock switch connector plug.
3. Remove the 2 retaining nuts and support bracket connecting the clutch reservoir and master cylinder assembly to the firewall.
4. From the engine compartment, first note the clutch tube routing to the slave cylinder, then remove the attaching hardware for the hydraulic tube retaining clips.
5. From the engine compartment, remove the clutch reservoir and master cylinder assembly from the firewall.
6. On 7.3L diesel and 7.5L gasoline engine vehicles, use a suitable prytool and lift the 2 retaining tabs of the slave cylinder retaining bracket. Disengage the tabs from the bell housing lugs and then slide outward and remove.
7. On 4.9L, 5.0 and 5.8L engine vehicles, depress the release ring on the tube quick disconnect and gently pull the connector free of the concentric slave cylinder fitting.
8. Remove the clutch hydraulic system from the vehicle.

To install:

9. Position the clutch fluid reservoir and master cylinder assembly into the firewall from inside the cab install the 2 nuts.
10. Correctly route the hydraulic tubing and sleeve cylinder to the transmission bell housing.

➡**Care must be taken during routing of the nylon line to keep away from the engine exhaust system.**

11. Reinstall the clutch tube retaining clips.

➡**Before installing external type slave cylinders, perform the clutch system bleeding procedure.**

12. On 7.3L diesel and 7.5L gasoline engine vehicles, install the slave cylinder by pushing the slave cylinder pushrod into the cylinder. Engage the pushrod into the release lever and slide the slave cylinder into the bell housing lugs. Seat the cylinder into the recess in the lugs.
13. On 4.9L, 5.0 and 5.8L engine vehicles, push the tube quick disconnect back onto the concentric slave cylinder fitting.

➡**When installing a new hydraulic system, the external slave cylinder used on 7.3L diesel and 7.5L gas engine vehicles, contains a shipping strap that pre-positions the pushrod for installation and also provides a bearing insert. When installation of the slave cylinder is completed, the first actuation of the clutch pedal will beak the shipping strap and give normal system operation.**

Internally Mounted

♦ See Figures 30 thru 35

This type slave cylinder is internally located inside the bell housing on the transmission input shaft. Removal of the transmission is required in order to replace it.

1. Disconnect the negative battery cable.
2. Disconnect the fluid coupling at the transmission, using the clutch coupling removal tool T88T-70522-A or equivalent. Slide the white plastic sleeve toward the slave cylinder while applying a slight tug on the tube.

→**If the special coupling tool is not available, the fluid coupling can be uncoupled by using a flat-bladed tool. Carefully pressing in around the coupling while applying a slight tug on the tube.**

3. Remove the transmission assembly, as described earlier in this section.
4. Remove the slave cylinder-to-transmission retaining bolts.
5. Remove the slave cylinder from the transmission input shaft.

To install:

6. Fit the slave cylinder over the transmission input shaft with the bleed screws and coupling facing the left side of the transmission.
7. Install the slave cylinder retaining bolts. Tighten to 14–19 ft. lbs. (19–26 Nm).
8. Install the transmission.
9. Connect the coupling to the slave cylinder.
10. Properly bleed the hydraulic system.
11. Connect the negative battery cable.

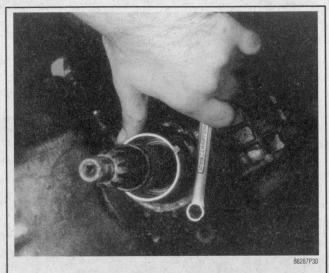

88287P30

Fig. 32 Removing the concentric slave cylinder attaching bolts

88287P28

Fig. 30 View of the concentric slave cylinder and throwout bearing assembly

88287P31

Fig. 33 Removing the concentric slave cylinder from the bell housing

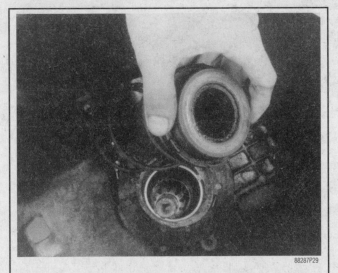

88287P29

Fig. 31 Removing the throwout bearing from the slave cylinder

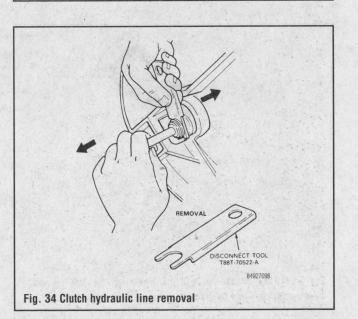

REMOVAL

DISCONNECT TOOL
T88T-70522-A

84927098

Fig. 34 Clutch hydraulic line removal

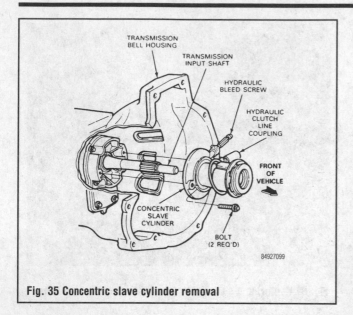

Fig. 35 Concentric slave cylinder removal

HYDRAULIC SYSTEM BLEEDING

Externally Mounted Slave Cylinder

▶ See Figure 36

1. Clean the reservoir cap and the slave cylinder connection.
2. Remove the slave cylinder from the housing.
3. Using a 3/32 in. punch, drive out the pin that holds the tube in place.
4. Remove the tube from the slave cylinder and place the end of the tube in a container.
5. Hold the slave cylinder so that the connector port is at the highest point, by tipping it about 30° from horizontal. Fill the cylinder with DOT 3 brake fluid through the port. It may be necessary to rock the cylinder or slightly depress the pushrod to expel all the air.

❊ WARNING

Pushing too hard on the pushrod will spurt fluid from the port!

Fig. 36 Fill the cylinder with DOT 3 brake fluid through the port on an external slave cylinder

6. When all air is expelled (no more bubble are seen), install the slave cylinder.

➡ **Some fluid will be expelled during installation as the pushrod is depressed.**

7. Remove the reservoir cap. Some fluid will run out of the tube end into the container. Pour fluid into the reservoir until a steady stream of fluid runs out of the tube and the reservoir is filled. Quickly install the diaphragm and cap. The flow should stop.
8. Connect the tube and install the pin. Check the fluid level.
9. Check the clutch operation.

Internally Mounted Slave Cylinder

▶ See Figures 37, 38, 39, 40 and 41

➡ **With the quick-disconnect coupling, no air should enter the system when the coupling is disconnected. However, if air should somehow enter the system, it must be bled.**

1. Remove the reservoir cap and diaphragm. Fill the reservoir with DOT 3 brake fluid.

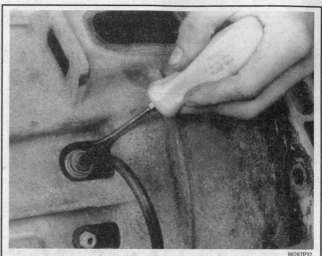

Fig. 37 If a special coupling tool is not available, the fluid coupling can be detached with a flat-bladed tool

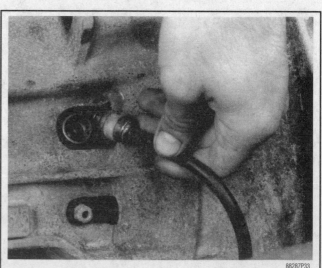

Fig. 38 Gently pull the fluid hose from the fitting

2. Connect a piece of rubber tubing to the slave cylinder bleed screw. Place the other end in a container.

3. Loosen the bleed screw. Gravity will force fluid from the master cylinder to flow down to the slave cylinder, forcing air out of the bleed screw. When a steady stream with no bubbles flows out, the system is bled. Close the bleed screw.

➡**Check periodically to make sure the master cylinder reservoir doesn't run dry.**

4. Add fluid to fill the master cylinder reservoir.

5. Fully depress the clutch pedal. Release it as quickly as possible. Pause for 2 seconds. Repeat this procedure 10 times.

6. Check the fluid level. Refill it if necessary. It should be kept full.

7. Repeat Steps 5 and 6 five more times.

8. Install the diaphragm and cap.

9. Have an assistant hold the pedal to the floor while you crack the bleed screw (not too far—just far enough to expel any trapped air). Close the bleed screw, then release the pedal.

10. Check and, if necessary, fill the reservoir.

Fig. 40 Use a box wrench to bleed the concentric slave cylinder at bleeder valve

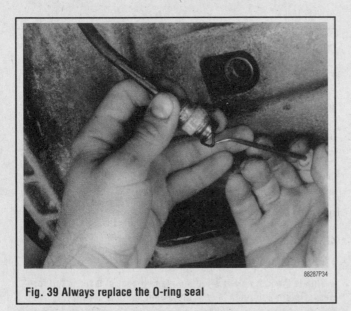

Fig. 39 Always replace the O-ring seal

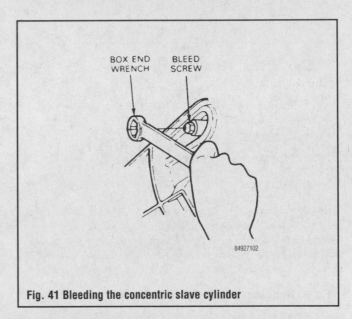

Fig. 41 Bleeding the concentric slave cylinder

AUTOMATIC TRANSMISSION

Neutral Safety/Back-up Light Switch

This is a combination switch which controls both the Neutral Safety and Back-up Lamp circuits.

REMOVAL & INSTALLATION

C6 Transmission

▶ **See Figure 42**

1. Disconnect the negative battery cable.

2. Raise and safely support the vehicle on jackstands.

3. Remove the downshift linkage rod return spring at the low-reverse servo cover.

4. Coat the outer lever attaching nut with penetrating oil. Remove the nut and lever.

5. Remove the 2 switch attaching bolts, disconnect the wiring at the connectors and remove the switch.

6. Installation is the reverse of removal. Adjust the switch and tighten the bolts to 55–75 inch lbs. (6.2–8.5 Nm).

7. Remove the jackstands and lower the vehicle.

8. Connect the negative battery cable.

AOD Transmission

▶ **See Figure 43**

1. Disconnect the negative battery cable.

2. Raise and safely support the vehicle on jackstands.

3. Disconnect the wiring from the switch.

4. Using a deep socket, unscrew the switch.

5. Installation is the reverse of removal. Tighten the switch to 10 ft. lbs. (14 Nm).

6. Remove the jackstands and lower the vehicle.

7. Connect the negative battery cable.

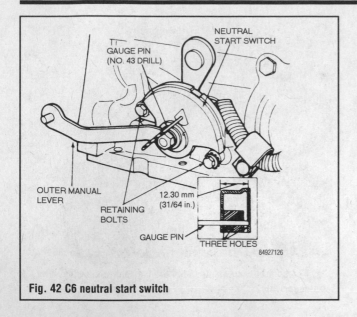

Fig. 42 C6 neutral start switch

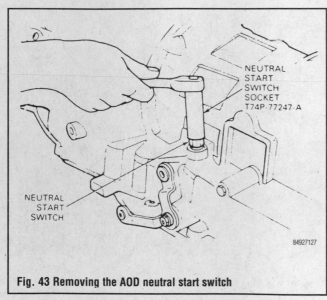

Fig. 43 Removing the AOD neutral start switch

4R70W Transmission

▶ **See Figure 44**

As of 1994, the neutral safety switch is referred to as a Manual Lever Position (MLP) sensor.
1. Disconnect the negative battery cable.
2. Raise and safely support the vehicle on jackstands.
3. Disengage the harness connector from the MLP sensor.
4. Remove the 2 sensor attaching bolts and remove the sensor.
To install:
5. Install the MLP sensor and install retaining bolts. Do not tighten, the sensor requires adjustment.
6. Adjust the MLP sensor then tighten attaching screws to 80–100 inch lbs. (9–11 Nm).
7. Remove the jackstands and lower the vehicle.
8. Connect the negative battery cable.

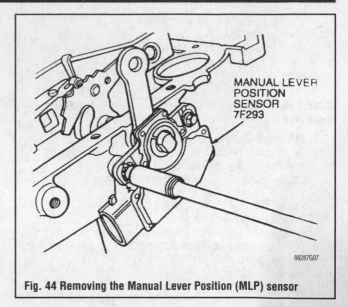

Fig. 44 Removing the Manual Lever Position (MLP) sensor

ADJUSTMENT

C6 Transmission

▶ **See Figure 42**

1. Hold the steering column transmission selector lever against the **Neutral** stop.
2. Move the sliding block assembly on the neutral switch to the **Neutral** position and insert a 0.091 in. (2.3mm) gauge pin in the alignment hole on the terminal side of the switch.
3. Move the switch assembly housing so that the sliding block contacts the actuating pin lever. Secure the switch to the outer tube of the steering column and remove the gauge pin.
4. Check the operation of the switch. The engine should only start in **Neutral** and **Park**.

4R70W Transmission

▶ **See Figure 45**

➡**Park is the last detent when the manual control lever is full forward. Return 2 detents toward the output shaft for Neutral.**

1. Position the manual control lever in **Neutral**.
2. Insert Gear Position Sensor Adjuster tool T93P-700 10-A or equivalent, into the slots.
3. Align all 3 slots on the MLP sensor with 3 tabs on the tool.
4. Tighten the attaching screws to 80–100 inch lbs. (9–11 Nm).

Vacuum Modulator

REMOVAL & INSTALLATION

C6 Transmission

▶ **See Figure 46**

1. Disconnect the vacuum hose at the unit.
2. Remove the bracket bolt, bracket and if equipped, the heat shield.
3. Pull the vacuum unit from the transmission.

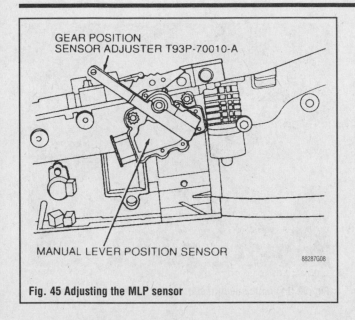

Fig. 45 Adjusting the MLP sensor

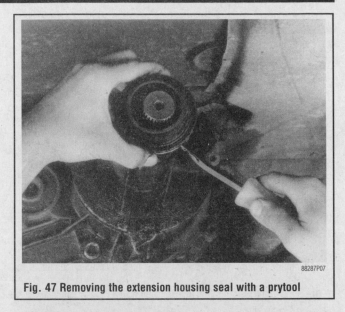

Fig. 47 Removing the extension housing seal with a prytool

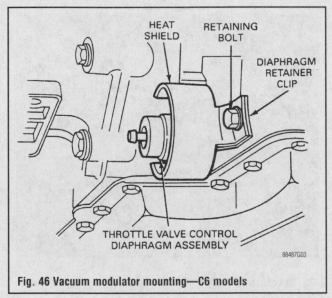

Fig. 46 Vacuum modulator mounting—C6 models

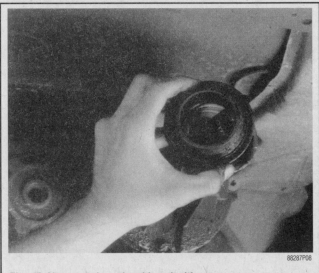

Fig. 48 Always replace the old seal with a new one

4. Installation is the reverse of removal. Tighten the bolt to 12–16 ft. lbs. (16–22 Nm). Connect the vacuum hose.

Extension Housing Seal

REMOVAL & INSTALLATION

▶ See Figures 47, 48 and 49

The extension seal is located at the rear of the transmission case.
1. Raise and support the vehicle safely.
2. Drain the transmission of lubricant.
3. Matchmark the driveshaft to the yoke for reassembly and remove the driveshaft.
4. Remove the old seal using a seal puller or appropriate prytool.
To install:
5. Install a new seal, coated with sealing compound, using an appropriate seal installation tool. Tool T61L-7657-A or B or equivalents are recommended.
6. Install the driveshaft, making certain to align the matchmark.
7. Fill the transmission to the proper level of the fill plug hole. Install the plug and lower the vehicle.

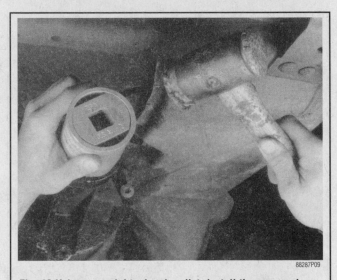

Fig. 49 Using a special tool and mallet, install the new seal

Automatic Transmission Assembly

REMOVAL & INSTALLATION

▶ **See Figures 50 thru 61**

1. Disconnect the negative battery cable.
2. Remove the engine cover and loosen the bell housing-to-engine bolts.
3. Tag and disengage any wires, hoses or lines that would interfere with transmission removal.
4. Raise the van and support it with safety stands.
5. Drain the transmission fluid.
6. Remove the torque converter cover and, if applicable, loosen the converter drain plug and drain the fluid. After the fluid has drained, replace the plug.
7. Matchmark and remove the driveshaft.
8. Remove the starter assembly.
9. Tag and disengage all linkages, wires, fluid filler tubes, coolant lines and cables.
10. Support the weight of the transmission with a transmission jack.

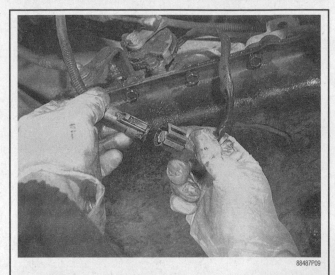

Fig. 52 Unplug the neutral start switch electrical connector

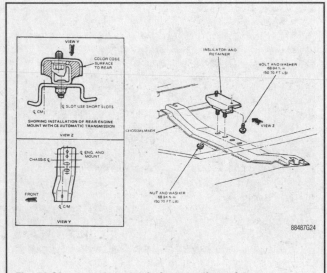

Fig. 50 C6 automatic transmission mounting points

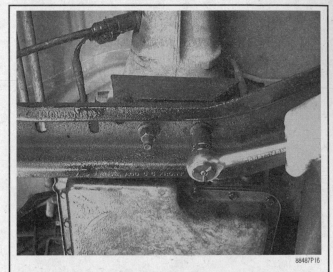

Fig. 53 Loosen the two transmission rear mounting support bolts

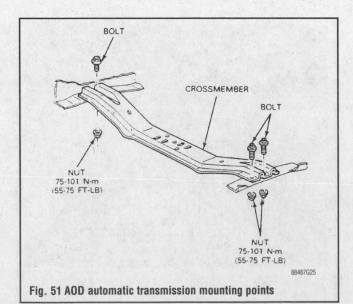

Fig. 51 AOD automatic transmission mounting points

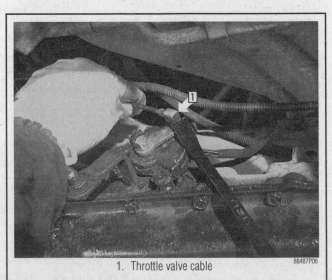

1. Throttle valve cable

Fig. 54 Disconnect the throttle valve linkage from the lever

Fig. 55 Use a pick to disengage the speedometer retaining clip

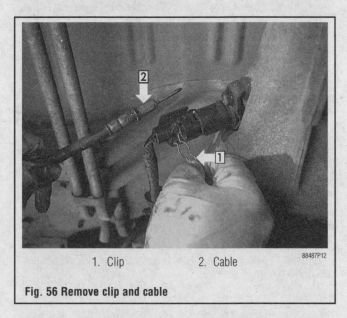

1. Clip   2. Cable

Fig. 56 Remove clip and cable

Fig. 57 Unscrew the cable from the transmission housing

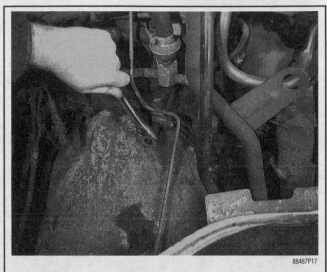

Fig. 58 Remove the transmission-to-engine attaching bolts

11. Loosen the transmission-to-crossmember bolts and, if necessary, remove the crossmember.

12. Loosen the transmission-to-engine bolts

13. Move the transmission away from the engine. Lower the jack and remove the converter and transmission assembly from under the vehicle.

To install:

14. Installation is the reverse of removal. Please note the following important steps:

15. On AOD, 4R70W and C6 transmissions, position the converter on the transmission, making sure the converter drive flats are fully engaged in the pump gear.

16. On E40D transmissions, install Torque Converter Handles T81P-7902-C or equivalent at the 12 o'clock and 6 o'clock positions. Install the converter, then push and rotate the converter until it bottoms out. Check the seating of the converter by placing a straightedge across the converter and bell housing. There must be a gap between the converter and straightedge. Remove the handles.

17. With the converter properly installed, place the transmission on the jack. Secure the transmission on the jack with the chain.

18. Rotate the converter until the studs and drain plug are in alignment with their holes in the flywheel.

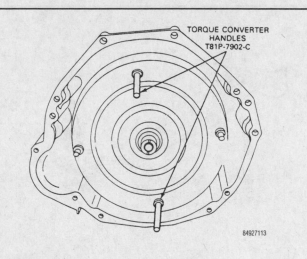

Fig. 59 Installation of the torque converter trandles on the E40D transmission

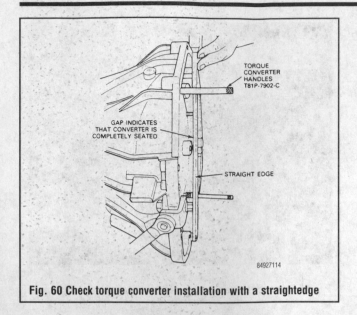

Fig. 60 Check torque converter installation with a straightedge

19. Move the converter and transmission assembly forward into position, taking care not to damage the flywheel and the converter pilot. The converter must rest squarely against the flywheel. This indicates that the converter pilot is not binding on the engine crankshaft.

20. On C6 transmissions, perform the following steps:

   a. Install the converter housing-to-engine attaching bolts and tighten them to 65 ft. lbs. (87 Nm) on diesel engine models, or to 50 ft. lbs. (67 Nm) for gasoline engine vans.

   b. Position the engine rear support and insulator assembly above the crossmember. Install the rear support/insulator assembly-to-extension housing bolts and tighten them to 70 ft. lbs. (94 Nm).

   c. Secure the engine rear support and insulator assembly to the crossmember and tighten the bolts to 80 ft. lbs. (108 Nm).

   d. Tighten the converter-to-flywheel nuts to 30 ft. lbs. (40 Nm).

21. On AOD transmissions, perform the following steps:

   a. Position the crossmember on the side supports. Tighten the bolts to 55 ft. lbs. (74 Nm). Position the rear mount on the crossmember and install the attaching nuts to 90 ft. lbs. (122 Nm).

   b. Secure the rear support to the extension housing and tighten the bolts to 80 ft. lbs. (108 Nm).

22. On E40D transmissions, perform the following steps:

   a. Install the 6 converter housing-to-cylinder block attaching bolts. Snug them alternately and evenly, then tighten them alternately and evenly to 38–52 ft. lbs. (51–70 Nm) for gasoline engine vehicles, or to 49–66 ft. lbs. (66–90 Nm) for diesel engine models.

   b. Install the rear mount-to-crossmember attaching nuts and the two crossmember-to-frame attaching bolts. Tighten the nuts and bolts to 50 ft. lbs. (68 Nm).

   c. Install the converter-to-flywheel attaching nuts. Place a wrench on the crankshaft pulley attaching bolt to turn the converter to gain access to the nuts. Tighten the nuts to 20–30 ft. lbs. (27–41 Nm).

23. On 4R70W transmissions perform the following steps:

   a. Before the torque converter is bolted to the flywheel, a check should be made to ensure that the torque converter is properly seated. The torque converter should move freely with respect to the flywheel. Grasp the torque converter stud. Movement back and forth should result in a metallic "clank" noise if the converter is properly seated. If the torque converter will not move, the transmission must be removed and the torque converter repositioned so that the impeller hub is properly engaged in the pump gear.

   b. Install the converter-to-flywheel retaining bolts and the converter housing-to-engine attaching bolts. Tighten the bolts to 40–50 ft. lbs. (54–68 Nm).

   c. Connect the oil cooler lines to the right side of transmission case. Tighten to 15–19 ft. lbs. (20–26 Nm).

24. Remove the jackstands and lower the vehicle.

25. Connect the negative battery cable.

26. Fill the transmission with approved transmission fluid. Road test the vehicle.

Adjustments

INTERMEDIATE BAND

C6 Transmission

▶ See Figure 62

➡ Intermediate band adjustment is possible only on the C6 transmission.

1. Raise the van on a hoist or jackstands.

2. Clean all dirt away from the band adjusting screw. Remove and discard the locknut.

3. Install a new locknut and tighten the adjusting screw to 10 ft. lbs. (13 Nm).

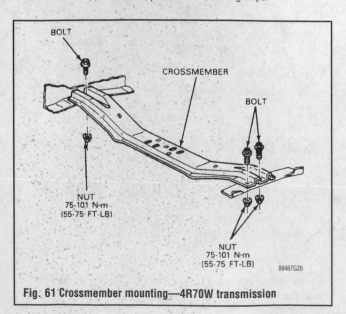

Fig. 61 Crossmember mounting—4R70W transmission

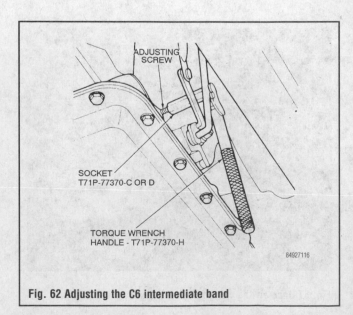

Fig. 62 Adjusting the C6 intermediate band

4. Back off the adjusting screw exactly 1½ turns.

5. Hold the adjusting screw from turning and tighten the locknut to 35–40 ft. lbs. (47–54 Nm).

6. Remove the jackstands and lower the vehicle.

SHIFT LINKAGE

◆ **See Figures 63, 64 and 65**

Shift Rod

1. With the engine stopped, place the transmission selector lever at the steering column in the D position for the C6 or the D overdrive position for the AOD and E4OD, and hold the lever against the stop by hanging an 8 lb. weight from the lever handle.

2. Loosen the shift rod adjusting nut at the transmission lever.

3. Shift the manual lever at the transmission to the **D** position, two detents from the rear.

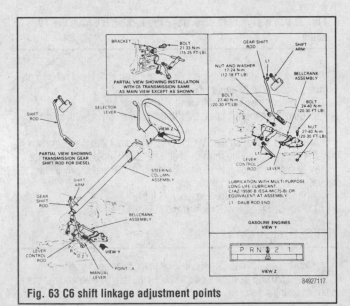

Fig. 63 C6 shift linkage adjustment points

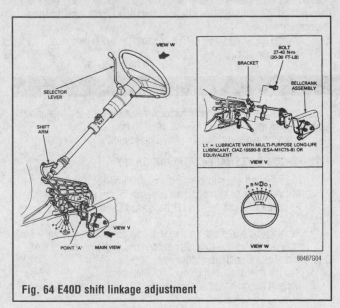

Fig. 64 E40D shift linkage adjustment

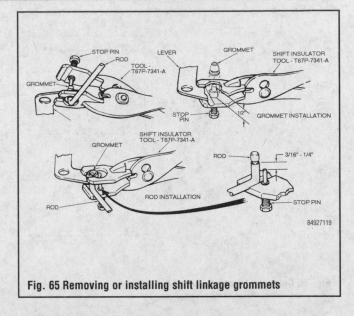

Fig. 65 Removing or installing shift linkage grommets

4. With the selector lever and transmission manual lever in the D or D overdrive position, tighten the adjusting nut to 12–18 ft. lbs. (16–24 Nm). Do not allow the rod or shift lever to move while tightening the nut. Remove the weight.

5. Check the operation of the shift linkage.

Shift Cable

1. With the engine stopped, place the transmission selector lever at the steering column in the D position for the C6 or the D overdrive position for the, 4R70W and E4OD.

2. Hang a 3 lb. (1.4 kg) weight on the end of the shift lever.

3. Pry the end of the shift cable from the transmission control lever ball stud.

4. Unlock the adjuster body, release the lock tab on the top side of the cable by pushing down on the 2 tangs.

5. Check to be sure the cable moves freely without binding.

6. Move the lever on the transmission all the way rearward and then 3 detent positions forward.

7. Holding the cable end fitting, push the cable rearward until the end fitting lines up with the manual control lever ball stud.

8. Push up on the lock tab to lock the adjuster body in the correctly adjusted position. Be sure the locator tab is properly seated in the bracket.

9. Make certain the shift cable is clipped to the floor pan at the white cable mark and the cable is routed into the tunnel.

10. Adjust the shift indicator pointer while the transmission is still in the overdrive position.

11. Remove the weight and check the control lever in all shift positions.

THROTTLE VALVE LINKAGE

AOD Transmission

WITH ENGINE OFF

◆ **See Figures 66, 67 and 68**

1. Set the parking brake and put the selector lever in **Neutral**.

2. Remove the protective cover from the cable.

3. Make sure that the throttle lever is at the idle stop. If it isn't, check for binding or interference. NEVER ATTEMPT TO ADJUST THE IDLE STOP!

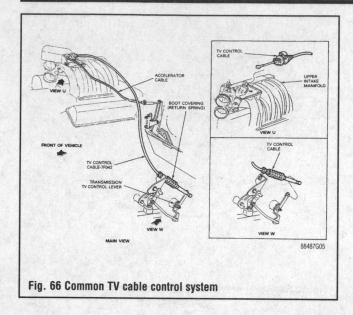

Fig. 66 Common TV cable control system

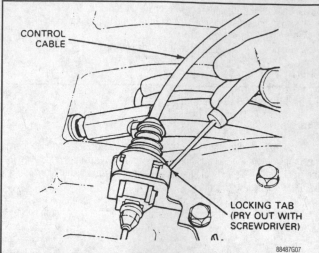

Fig. 68 Use a prytool to disengage the locking tab from the TV cable

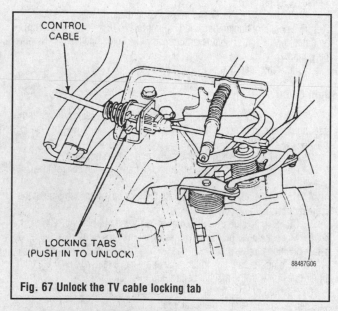

Fig. 67 Unlock the TV cable locking tab

4. Make sure that the cable is free of sharp bends or is not rubbing on anything throughout its entire length.

5. Lubricate the TV lever ball stud with chassis lube.

6. Unlock the locking tab at the throttle body by prying with a small screwdriver.

7. Install a spring on the TV control lever, to hold it in the rearmost travel position. The spring must exert at least 10 lbs. of force on the lever.

8. Rotate the transmission outer TV lever 10–30° and slowly allow it to return.

9. Push down on the locking tab until flush.

10. Remove the retaining spring from the lever.

THROTTLE KICKDOWN LINKAGE

1. Move the carburetor throttle linkage to the wide open position.

2. Insert a 0.060 in. thick spacer between the throttle lever and the kickdown adjusting screw.

3. Rotate the transmission kickdown lever until the lever engages the transmission internal stop. Do not use the kickdown rod to turn the transmission lever.

4. Turn the adjusting screw until it contacts the 0.060 in. spacer.

5. Remove the spacer.

DRIVELINE

Driveshaft

REMOVAL & INSTALLATION

Single Type U-Joint

ONE-PIECE DRIVESHAFT

♦ See Figures 69, 70, 71, 72 and 73

1. Raise the van and support it with safety stands.

2. Matchmark the driveshaft yoke and axle pinion flange.

3. Remove the U-bolt nuts and U-bolts attaching the yoke to the axle flange.

4. Separate the yoke from the flange. It may be necessary to pry it free with a small prybar. Immediately after separation, wrap tape around the U-joint caps to keep them from falling off.

5. Slip the driveshaft off the transmission splines.

6. Installation is the reverse of removal. Align the yoke-to-flange matchmarks. Tighten the U-bolt nuts to 15 ft. lbs. (20 Nm).

7. Lower the van and check for proper operation.

TWO-PIECE DRIVESHAFT/COUPLING SHAFT

1. Raise the van and support it with safety stands.

2. Matchmark the relationship of the driveshaft U-joint and axle joint flange.

3. Remove the U-bolt nuts and U-bolts attaching the yoke to the axle flange.

4. Separate the yoke from the flange. It may be necessary to pry it free with a small prybar. Immediately after separation, wrap tape around the U-joint caps to keep them from falling off.

5. Slip the driveshaft off the coupling shaft splines.

6. Support the driveshaft and loosen the two center bearing bolts.

7. Remove the center bearing.

8. Slide the coupling shaft from the transmission shaft splines.

9. Clean all parts and check for damage. Do not remove the blue plastic coating from the male splines.

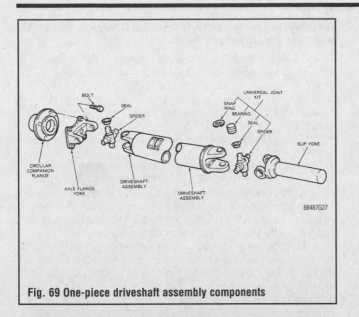

Fig. 69 One-piece driveshaft assembly components

Fig. 72 Separate the driveshaft from the axle flange

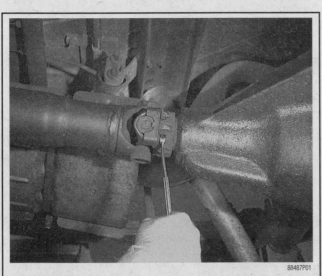

Fig. 70 Loosen the driveshaft U-bolt nuts

Fig. 73 Slide the driveshaft towards the rear of the van to disconnect it from the transmission splines

10. Coat the splines with chassis lube.
11. Install the front of the shaft to the transmission.
12. Install the center bearing and tighten the bolts to 39–54 Nm) ft. lbs. (53–73 Nm).
13. Align the yoke-to-flange matchmarks.
14. Engage the rear of the driveshaft to the rear axle and tighten the U-bolt nuts to:

- 5/16 in.-18: 8–15 ft. lbs. (11–20 Nm)
- 3/8 in.-18: 17–26 ft. lbs. (24–35 Nm)
- 7/16 In.-20: 30–40 ft. lbs. (41–54 Nm)

15. Lower the van and check for proper operation.

U-JOINT REPLACEMENT

▶ **See Figures 74 and 75**

1. Remove the driveshaft from the vehicle and place it in a vise, being careful not to damage it.
2. Remove the snaprings which retain the bearings in the flange and in the driveshaft.
3. Remove the driveshaft tube from the vise and position the U-joint in the vise with a socket smaller than the bearing cap on one side and a socket larger than the bearing cap on the other side.

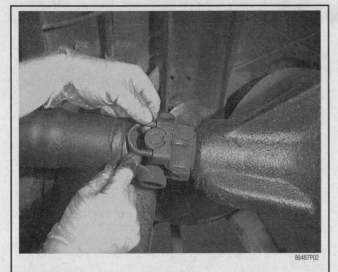

Fig. 71 Remove the nuts and U-bolt

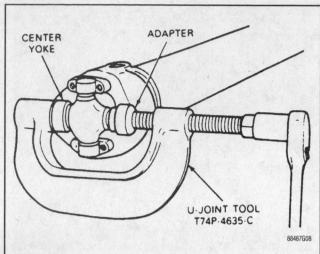

CENTER YOKE   ADAPTER

U-JOINT TOOL
T74P-4635-C

88487G08

Fig. 74 Use the U-joint removal tool to press the bearing from the yoke

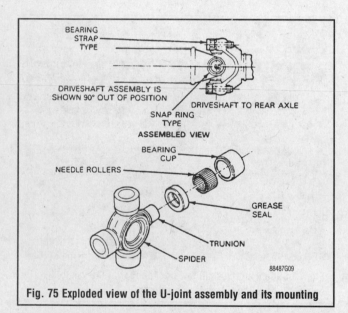

BEARING STRAP TYPE

DRIVESHAFT ASSEMBLY IS SHOWN 90° OUT OF POSITION

DRIVESHAFT TO REAR AXLE

SNAP RING TYPE

ASSEMBLED VIEW

BEARING CUP

NEEDLE ROLLERS

GREASE SEAL

TRUNION

SPIDER

88487G09

Fig. 75 Exploded view of the U-joint assembly and its mounting

REAR AXLE

Axle Shaft, Bearing and Seal

REMOVAL & INSTALLATION

▶ See Figures 76, 77 and 78

Ford 8.8 in. (223.5mm) Ring Gear Integral Carrier

1. Raise and safely support the vehicle on jackstands.
2. Remove the wheels from the brake drums.
3. Place a drain pan under the housing and drain the lubricant by loosening the housing cover.
4. Remove the locks securing the brake drums to the axle shaft flanges and remove the drums.
5. Remove the housing cover and gasket.
6. Remove the side gear pinion shaft lockbolt and the side gear pinion shaft.

➡**A U-joint tool can be purchased from your local parts store but a socket and vise are just as effective.**

4. Slowly tighten the jaws of the vise so that the smaller socket forces the U-joint spider and the opposite bearing into the larger socket.
5. Remove the other side of the spider in the same manner (if applicable) and remove the spider assembly from the driveshaft. Discard the spider assemblies.
6. Clean all foreign matter from the yoke areas at the end of the driveshaft(s).
7. Start the new spider and one of the bearing cap assemblies into a yoke by positioning the yoke in a vise with the spider positioned in place with one of the bearing cap assemblies positioned over one of the holes in the yoke. Slowly close the vise, pressing the bearing cap assembly in the yoke. Press the cap in far enough so that the retaining snapring can be installed. Use the smaller socket to recess the bearing cap.
8. Open the vise and position the opposite bearing cap assembly over the proper hole in the yoke with the socket that is smaller than the diameter of the bearing cap located on the cap. Slowly close the vise, pressing the bearing cap into the hole in the yoke with the socket. Make sure that the spider assembly is in line with the bearing cap as it is pressed in. Press the bearing cap in far enough so that the retaining snapring can be installed.
9. Install all remaining U-joints in the same manner.
10. Install the driveshaft and grease the new U-joints.

Center Bearing

REMOVAL & INSTALLATION

1. Remove the driveshafts.
2. Remove the two center support bearing attaching bolts and remove the assembly from the vehicle.
3. Do not immerse the sealed bearing in any type of cleaning fluid. Wipe the bearing and cushion clean with a cloth dampened with cleaning fluid.
4. Check the bearing for wear or rough action by rotating the inner race while holding the outer race. If wear or roughness is evident, replace the bearing. Examine the rubber cushion for evidence of hardening, cracking, or deterioration. Replace it if it is damaged in any way.
5. Place the bearing in the rubber support and the rubber support in the U-shaped support and install the bearing in the reverse order of removal. Tighten the bearing to support bracket fasteners.

7. Push the axle shafts inward and remove the C-locks from the inner end of the axle shafts. Temporarily replace the shaft and lockbolt to retain the differential gears in position.
8. Remove the axle shafts with a slide hammer. Be sure the seal is not damaged by the splines on the axle shaft.
9. Remove the bearing and oil seal from the housing. Both the seal and bearing can be removed with a slide hammer.
To install:
10. Two types of bearings are used on some axles, one requiring a press fit and the other a loose fit. A loose fitting bearing does not necessarily indicate excessive wear.
11. Inspect the axle shaft housing and axle shafts for burrs or other irregularities. Replace any work or damaged parts. A light yellow color on the bearing journal of the axle shaft is normal, and does not require replacement of the axle shaft. Slight pitting and wear is also normal.
12. Lightly coat the wheel bearing rollers with axle lubricant. Install the bearings in the axle housing until the bearing seats firmly against the shoulder.

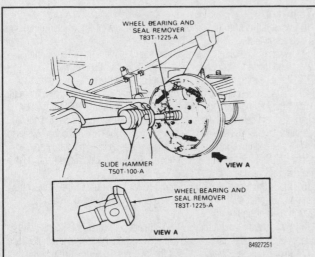

Fig. 76 Removing the rear axle bearing and seal—Ford 8.8 in. axle

13. Wipe all lubricant from the oil seal bore, before installing the seal.

14. Inspect the original seals for wear. If necessary, these may be replaced with new seals, which are prepacked with lubricant and do not require soaking.

15. Install the oil seal.

16. Remove the lockbolt and pinion shaft. Carefully slide the axle shafts into place. Be careful that you do not damage the seal with the splined end of the axle shaft. Engage the splined end of the shaft with the differential side gears.

17. Install the axle shaft C-locks on the inner end of the axle shafts and seat the C-locks in the counterbore of the differential side gears.

18. Rotate the differential pinion gears until the differential pinion shaft can be installed. Install the differential pinion shaft lockbolt. Tighten to 15–22 ft. lbs. (20–30 Nm).

19. Install the brake drum on the axle shaft flange.

20. Install the wheel and tire on the brake drum and tighten the attaching nuts.

21. Clean the gasket surface of the rear housing and install a new cover gasket and the housing cover. Some covers do not use a gasket. On these models, apply a bead of silicone sealer on the gasket surface. The bead should run inside of the bolt holes.

22. Raise the rear axle so that it is in the running position. Add the amount of specified lubricant to bring the lubricant level to ½ in. (12.7mm) below the filler hole.

Dana Axles

❋❋ CAUTION

New Dual Rear Wheel models have flat-faced lug nut replacing the old cone-shaped lug nuts. NEVER replace these new nuts with the older design! Never replace the newer designed wheels with older design wheels! The newer wheels have lug holes with special shoulders to accommodate the newly designed lug nuts.

FULL FLOATING AXLE

♦ See Figures 79 thru 84

The wheel bearings on full floating rear axles are packed with wheel bearing grease. Axle lubricant can also flow into the wheel hubs and bearings, however, wheel bearing grease is the primary lubricant. The wheel bearing grease provides lubrication until the axle lubricant reaches the bearings during normal operation.

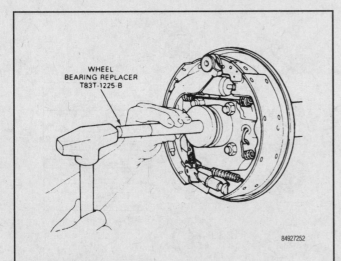

Fig. 77 Installing the rear axle bearing using a driver and a hammer—Ford 8.8 in. axle

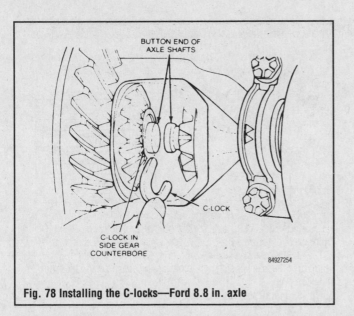

Fig. 78 Installing the C-locks—Ford 8.8 in. axle

Fig. 79 Use a heavy duty wheel dolly to remove the weight from the bearings

1. Set the parking brake and loosen, but do not remove, the axle shaft bolts.

2. Raise the rear wheels off the floor and place jackstands under the rear axle housing so that the axle is parallel with the floor. Release the parking brake and back of the rear brake adjustment.

3. Remove the axle shaft bolts and lockwashers. They should not be re-used.

4. Place a heavy duty wheel dolly under the wheels and raise them so that all weight is off the wheel bearings.

5. Remove the brake drum or caliper.

6. Remove the axle shaft and gasket(s).

7. Using a special hub nut wrench, remove the hub nut.

➡**Verify the thread direction before proceeding. Typically, the hub nut on the right spindle has a right-hand thread, while the one on the left spindle has a left-hand thread. If so, they will be marked RH and LH. If neither side is marked, chances are they both have a right-hand thread. NEVER use an impact wrench on the hub nut!**

8. Remove the outer bearing cone and pull the wheel straight off the axle.

9. With a brass drift which will just clear the outer bearing cup, drive the inner bearing cone and inner seal out of the wheel hub.

To install:

10. Wash all the old grease or axle lubricant out of the wheel hub, using a suitable solvent.

11. Wash the bearing cups and rollers and inspect them for pitting, galling, and uneven wear patterns. Inspect the roller for end wear.

12. If the bearing cups are to be replaced, drive them out with a brass drift. Install the new cups with a block of wood and hammer or press them in.

13. If the bearing cups are properly seated, a 0.0015 in. (0.038mm) feeler gauge will not fit between the cup and the wheel hub. The gauge should not fit beneath the cup. Check several places to make sure the cups are squarely seated.

14. Pack each bearing cone and roller with a bearing packer or in the manner outlined for the wheel bearings in Section 1. Use a multi-purpose wheel bearing grease.

15. Place the inner bearing cone and roller assembly in the wheel hub. Install a new inner seal in the hub with a seal installation tool such as T75T-1175-B or equivalent.

16. Wrap the threads of the spindle with tape and carefully slide the hub straight on the spindle. Take care to avoid damaging the seal! Remove the tape.

17. Install the outer bearing. Start the hub nut, making sure that the hub tab is engaged with the keyway prior to threading.

18. Tighten the nut to 65–75 ft. lbs. (88–102 Nm) while rotating the wheel. DO NOT use an impact wrench!

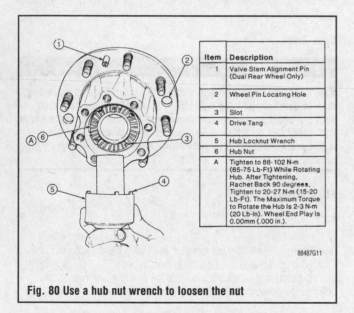

Item	Description
1	Valve Stem Alignment Pin (Dual Rear Wheel Only)
2	Wheel Pin Locating Hole
3	Slot
4	Drive Tang
5	Hub Locknut Wrench
6	Hub Nut
A	Tighten to 88-102 N·m (65-75 Lb-Ft) While Rotating Hub. After Tightening, Ratchet Back 90 degrees, Tighten to 20-27 N·m (15-20 Lb-Ft). The Maximum Torque to Rotate the Hub is 2-3 N·m (20 Lb-In). Wheel End Play is 0.00mm (.000 in.).

88487G11

Fig. 80 Use a hub nut wrench to loosen the nut

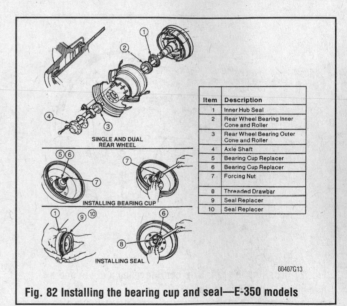

SINGLE AND DUAL REAR WHEEL

INSTALLING BEARING CUP

INSTALLING SEAL

Item	Description
1	Inner Hub Seal
2	Rear Wheel Bearing Inner Cone and Roller
3	Rear Wheel Bearing Outer Cone and Roller
4	Axle Shaft
5	Bearing Cup Replacer
6	Bearing Cup Replacer
7	Forcing Nut
8	Threaded Drawbar
9	Seal Replacer
10	Seal Replacer

00407G13

Fig. 82 Installing the bearing cup and seal—E-350 models

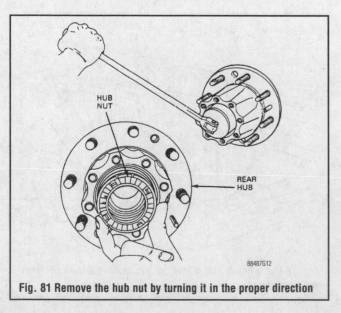

HUB NUT

REAR HUB

88487G12

Fig. 81 Remove the hub nut by turning it in the proper direction

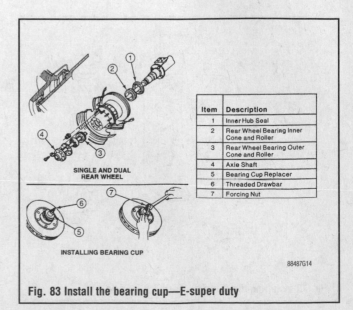

SINGLE AND DUAL REAR WHEEL

INSTALLING BEARING CUP

Item	Description
1	Inner Hub Seal
2	Rear Wheel Bearing Inner Cone and Roller
3	Rear Wheel Bearing Outer Cone and Roller
4	Axle Shaft
5	Bearing Cup Replacer
6	Threaded Drawbar
7	Forcing Nut

88487G14

Fig. 83 Install the bearing cup—E-super duty

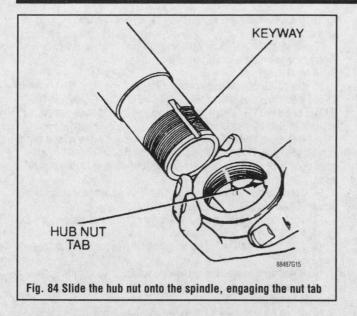

Fig. 84 Slide the hub nut onto the spindle, engaging the nut tab

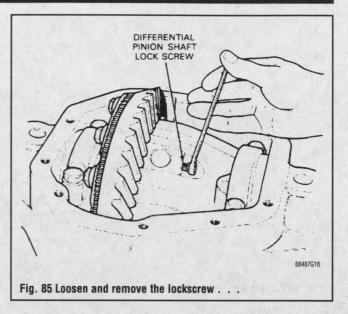

Fig. 85 Loosen and remove the lockscrew . . .

➡The hub will ratchet as torque is applied. This ratcheting can be avoided by using Ford tool No. T88T-4252-A. Avoiding ratcheting will give more even bearing preloads.

19. Back off (loosen) the adjusting nut 90° (¼ turn). Then, tighten it to 15–20 ft. lbs. (20–27 Nm).
20. Using a dial indicator, check end-play of the hub. No end-play is permitted.
21. Clean the hub bolt holes thoroughly. Replace the hub if any cracks are found around the holes or if the threads in the holes are in any way damaged.
22. Install the axle shaft, new flange gasket, lockwashers and new shaft retaining bolts. Coat the bolt threads with thread adhesive. Tighten them snugly, but not completely.
23. Install the brake drum or caliper.
24. Install the wheels.
25. Lower the van to the ground.
26. Tighten the wheel lug nuts.
27. Tighten the axle shaft bolts to 41–55 ft. lbs. (55–75 Nm) on 1989–92 models, 65–85 ft. lbs. (88–115 Nm) on 1993 models, or 90–120 ft. lbs. on 1994 models.
28. On 1995–96 models, tighten the axle shaft bolts to 90–120 ft. lbs. (122–163 Nm) for E-350 models, or to 83–113 ft. lbs. (113–153 Nm) for E-super duty models.

SEMI-FLOATING AXLE

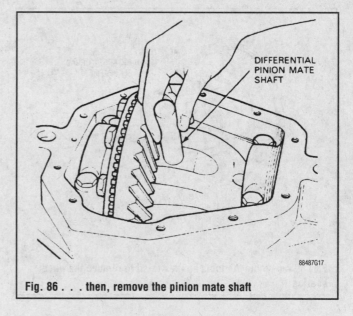

Fig. 86 . . . then, remove the pinion mate shaft

▶ See Figures 85 thru 90

1. Raise the van and support it with jackstands.
2. Remove the wheel and brake drum.
3. Drain the lubricant from the axle.
4. Remove the rear axle cover.
5. Remove the lockscrew.

➡The lockscrew will either be a Loctite treated lockscrew with a ⁵⁄₃₂ in. hexagram head (which must not be reused) or a torque prevailing 12-point drive head lockscrew (which may be reused up to four times).

6. Lift out pinion mate shaft.
7. Push the flanged end of the axle shaft towards the center and remove the C-clip.
8. Pull the axle shaft from the tube, while being careful not to damage the seals.
9. Remove and discard the oil seal.
10. Pull the bearing from the tube using puller T81P-1104-C, adapters T81P-1104-B (course thread) or D81T-1104-A (fine thread) and rear wheel bearing remover, T81T-1225-A or their equivalents.

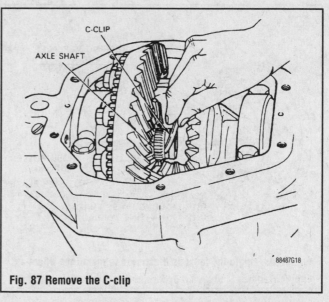

Fig. 87 Remove the C-clip

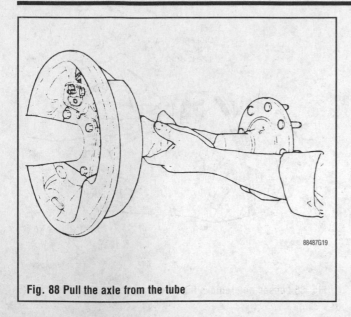

Fig. 88 Pull the axle from the tube

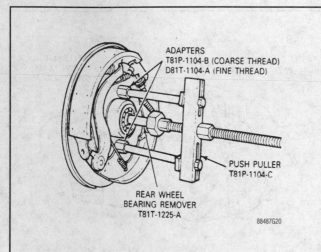

ADAPTERS
T81P-1104-B (COARSE THREAD)
D81T-1104-A (FINE THREAD)

PUSH PULLER
T81P-1104-C

REAR WHEEL
BEARING REMOVER
T81T-1225-A

88487G20

Fig. 89 Assemble the tools as illustrated to remove the wheel bearing

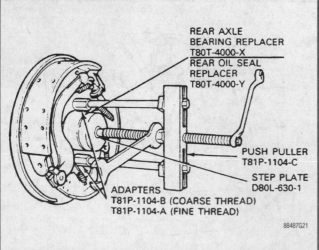

REAR AXLE
BEARING REPLACER
T80T-4000-X
REAR OIL SEAL
REPLACER
T80T-4000-Y

PUSH PULLER
T81P-1104-C

STEP PLATE
D80L-630-1

ADAPTERS
T81P-1104-B (COARSE THREAD)
T81P-1104-A (FINE THREAD)

88487G21

Fig. 90 Assemble the tools as illustrated to install the wheel bearing

11. Clean the bearing bore with metal cleaning solvent and wipe the area clean and dry.

12. Check the bearing bore for nicks and burrs. Wipe the bore with emery cloth to ensure a smooth surface.

To install:

13. Coat the bearing with differential lube.

14. Install the bearing using push-puller T81P-1104-C, adapters T81P-1104-B or D81T-1104-A, step plate D80L-630-1 and rear axle bearing replacer T80T-4000-X or their equivalents.

15. Make sure the bearing is not cocked and install a new oil seal using push-puller T81P-1104-C, adapters T81P-1104-B or D81T-1104-A, step plate D80L-630-1 and rear oil seal replacer T80T-4000-W or their equivalents.

16. Lubricate the cavity between the seal lips with a long life lubricant such as C1AZ-19590-BA or equivalent.

17. Push the axle into the tube making sure the splined end engages the gears.

18. Push the flanged end of the axle shaft towards the center and install the C-clip.

19. Install the pinion mate shaft making sure the shaft is lined up with the lockscrew hole in the case and the pinion side gear washers are installed correctly.

20. Install the lockscrew and tighten it to 20–25 ft. lbs. (27–34 Nm).

21. Install the rear axle cover.

22. After one hour, fill the carrier with the specified amount of axle fluid.

23. Install the brake drum and wheel.

24. Lower the van and road teat.

Pinion Seal

REMOVAL & INSTALLATION

Ford 8.8 in. (223.5mm) Ring Gear Integral Carrier Axle

▸ **See Figures 91 and 92**

➡ **A torque wrench capable of at least 225 ft. lbs. (305 Nm) is required for pinion seal installation.**

1. Raise and safely support the vehicle with jackstands under the frame rails. Allow the axle to drop to rebound position for working clearance.

2. Remove the rear wheels and brake drums. No drag must be present on the axle.

3. Mark the companion flanges and U-joints for correct reinstallation position.

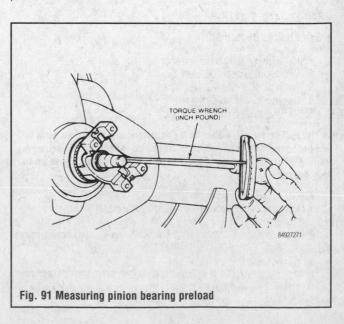

TORQUE WRENCH
(INCH POUND)

84927271

Fig. 91 Measuring pinion bearing preload

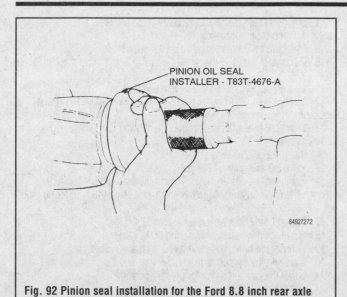

PINION OIL SEAL
INSTALLER - T83T-4676-A

84927272

Fig. 92 Pinion seal installation for the Ford 8.8 inch rear axle

4. Remove the driveshaft.

5. Using an inch pound torque wrench and socket on the pinion yoke nut measure the amount of torque needed to maintain differential rotation through several clockwise revolutions. Record the measurement.

6. Use a suitable tool to hold the companion flange. Remove the pinion nut.

7. Place a drain pan under the differential, clean the area around the seal, and mark the yoke-to-pinion relation.

8. Use a 2-jawed puller to remove the pinion.

9. Remove the seal with a small prybar.

To install:

10. Thoroughly clean the oil seal bore.

➡If you are not absolutely certain of the proper seal installation depth, the proper seal driver must be used. If the seal is misaligned or damaged during installation, it must be removed and a new seal installed.

11. Drive the new seal into place with a seal driver such as T83T–4676–A. Coat the seal lip with clean, waterproof wheel bearing grease.

12. Coat the splines with a small amount of wheel bearing grease and install the yoke, aligning the matchmarks. Never hammer the yoke onto the pinion!

13. Install a NEW nut on the pinion.

14. Hold the yoke with a holding tool. Tighten the pinion nut to at least 160 ft. lbs. (217 Nm), taking frequent turning torque readings until the original preload reading is attained. If the original preload reading, that you noted before disassembly, is lower than the specified reading of 8–14 inch lbs. (0.9–1.6 Nm) for used bearings; 16–29 inch lbs. (1.8–3,3 Nm) for new bearings, keep tightening the pinion nut until the specified reading is reached. If the original preload reading is higher than the specified values, tighten the nut just until the original reading is reached.

✴✴ WARNING

Under no circumstances should the nut be backed off to reduce the preload reading! If the preload is exceeded, the yoke and bearing must be removed and a new collapsible spacer must be installed. The entire process of preload adjustment must be repeated.

15. Install the driveshaft using the matchmarks. Tighten the nuts to 15 ft. lbs. (20 Nm).

Dana 60

➡**A torque wrench capable of at least 300 ft. lbs. (406 Nm) is required for pinion seal installation.**

1. Raise and support the van on jackstands.

2. Allow the axle to hang freely.

3. Matchmark and disconnect the driveshaft from the axle.

4. Using a tool such as T75T–4851–B, or equivalent, hold the pinion flange while removing the pinion nut.

5. Using a puller, remove the pinion flange.

6. Use a puller to remove the seal, or punch the seal out using a pin punch.

7. Thoroughly clean the seal bore and make sure that it is not damaged in any way. Coat the sealing edge of the new seal with a small amount of 80W/90 oil and drive the seal into the housing using a seal driver.

8. Coat the inside of the pinion flange with clean 80W/90 oil and install the flange onto the pinion shaft.

9. Install the nut on the pinion shaft and tighten it to 250–300 ft. lbs. (338–406 Nm).

10. Connect the driveshaft.

Dana 80

➡**A torque wrench capable of at least 500 ft. lbs. (677 Nm) is required for pinion seal installation.**

1. Raise and safely support the vehicle with jackstands under the frame rails.

2. Mark the companion flanges and U-joints for correct reinstallation position.

3. Remove the driveshaft.

4. Use a suitable tool to hold the companion flange. Remove the pinion nut.

5. Place a drain pan under the differential, clean the area around the seal, and mark the yoke-to-pinion relation.

6. Use a 2-jawed puller to remove the pinion flange.

7. Remove the seal with a small prybar.

8. Thoroughly clean the oil seal bore.

➡If you are not absolutely certain of the proper seal installation depth, the proper seal driver must be used. If the seal is misaligned or damaged during installation, it must be removed and a new seal installed.

9. Coat the new oil seal with gear lubricant. Install the seal using oil seal driver T83T–4676–A.. After the seal is installed, make sure that the seal garter spring has not become dislodged. If it has, remove and replace the seal.

10. Install the yoke, using flange replacer tool D81T–4858–A if necessary to draw the yoke into place.

11. Install a new pinion nut and washer. Tighten the nut to 440–500 ft. lbs. (597–677 Nm) for model 80 and 220–280 ft. lbs. (298–379 Nm)) for 60 or 70 models.

12. Connect the driveshaft.

Axle Housing

REMOVAL & INSTALLATION

Ford 8.8 in. (223.5mm) Ring Gear Integral Carrier

1. Disconnect the shock absorbers from the rear axle.

2. Loosen the axle shaft nuts.

3. Raise and support the rear end on jackstands placed under the frame.

4. Remove the rear wheels.

5. Disconnect the rear stabilizer bar.

6. Disconnect the brake hose at the frame.

7. Disconnect the parking brake cable at the equalizer and remove the cables from the support brackets.

8. Matchmark the driveshaft-to-axle flange position.

9. Disconnect the driveshaft from the rear axle and move it out of the way.

10. Take up the weight of the axle with a floor jack.

11. Remove the nuts from the spring U-bolts and remove the spring seat caps.

12. Lower the axle and roll it from under the van.

13. Installation is the reverse of removal. Tighten the spring U-bolt nuts to 160 ft. lbs. Bleed the brake system.

Dana Axles

1. Disconnect the shock absorbers from the rear axle.
2. Loosen the rear axle shaft nuts.
3. Raise and support the rear end on jackstands placed under the frame.
4. Remove the rear wheels.
5. Remove the shock absorbers.
6. Disconnect the rear stabilizer bar.
7. Disconnect the brake hose at the frame.

8. Disconnect the parking brake cable at the equalizer and remove the cables from the support brackets.

9. Matchmark the driveshaft-to-axle flange position.

10. Disconnect the driveshaft from the rear axle and move it out of the way.

11. Take up the weight of the axle with a floor jack.

12. Remove the nuts from the spring U-bolts and remove the spring seat caps.

13. Lower the axle and roll it from under the van.

To install:

14. Roll the axle under the van.

15. Raise the axle with a floor jack.

16. Install the U-bolts and nuts. Tighten the nuts to 110–160 ft. lbs. (150–217 Nm) for 60 and 70 models and 109 ft. lbs. (148 Nm) for 80 models.

17. Connect the shock absorbers and stabilizer bar.

18. Install the drive shaft and parking brake cable.

19. Connect the brake hose and bleed the brake system.

20. If drained, fill the rear axle with the specified fluid.

21. Lower the van and check for proper operation.

TORQUE SPECIFICATIONS

System	Component	Ft. Lbs.	Nm
Manual Transmission			
Shift Handle			
S5-42 and ZF			
	Upper shift lever-to-lower lever bolts	16-24	22-33
Mazda M50D 5-Speed			
	Shift lever bolt and nut	12-18	16-24
Extension Housing Seal			
S5-42 ZF Models			
	Output flange-to-mainshaft hex nut	184	250
Transmission			
	Transmission-to-engine bolts	50	64
	Crossmember bolts	55	74
	Rear insulator bolts	60	81
Clutch			
10 inch clutch			
	Retaining bolts	15-20	20-27
11 inch clutch			
	Retaining bolts	20-29	27-39
	Flywheel housing bolts	40-50	54-68
Slave Cylinder			
Internaly Mounted			
	Slave cylinder bolts	14-19	19-26
Automatic Transmission			
Neutral Safety/Back-up Light Switch			
C6 transmission			
	Switch retaining bolts	55-75 inch lbs	6.2-8.5
AOD transmission			
	Switch retaining bolts	10	14
4R70W transmission			
	Manual Lever Position sensor screws	80-100 inch lbs.	9-11
Vacuum Modulator			
	Bracket bolt	12-16	16-22
C6 transmission			
	Converter housing-to-engine bolts—Gasoline engines	50	67
	Converter housing-to-engine boltsDiesel engines	65	87
	Insulator assembly-to-extension housing bolts	70	94
	Engine rear support and insulator-to-crossmember bolts	80	108
	Converter-to-flywheel nuts	30	40
AOD transmission			
	Crossmember bolts	55	74
	Rear mount nuts	90	122
	Rear support-to-extension housing bolts	80	108
E4OD transmission			
	Converter housing-to-cylinder block bolts		
	Gasoline engines	38-52	51-70
	Diesel engines	49-66	66-90
	Rear mount-to-crossmember attaching nuts	50	68
	Crossmember-to-frame bolts	50	68
	Converter-to-flywheel nuts	20-30	27-41
4R70W transmission			
	Converter-to-flywheel bolts	40-50	50-68
	Converter housing-to-engine bolts	40-50	50-68
	Oil cooler lines	15-19	20-26

TORQUE SPECIFICATIONS

System	Component	Ft. Lbs.	Nm
Driveline			
	Driveshaft		
	One piece driveshaft		
	U-bolt nuts	15	20
	Two piece driveshaft		
	Center bearing bolts	39-54	53-73
	U-bolt nuts		
	5/16 inch x 18	8-15	11-20
	3/8 inch x18	17-26	24-35
	7/16 inch x 20	30-40	41-54
Rear axle			
	Ford 8.8 in. (223.5mm) Ring Gear		
	Differential pinion shaft lockbolt	15-22	20-29
	Pinion nut	160	217
	Driveshaft nuts 15 20		
	Dana Axles		
	Hub nut	65-75	88-101
	Adjusting nut	15-20	20-27
	Axle shaft bolts	70-85	94-115
	Full floating axle		
	Hub nut	65-75	88-102
	Adjusting nut	15-20	20-27
	Axle shaft bolts		
	1989-92 models	41-55	55-75
	1993 models	65-85	88-115
	1994 models	90-120	122-163
	1995-96 E-350 models	90-120	122-163
	1995-96 E-super duty models	83-113	113-153
	Semi floating axle		
	Lockscrew	20-25	27-34
	Dana 60		
	Pinion shaft nut	250-300	338-406
	Dana 70 and 80		
	Pinion nut		
	Model 80	440-500	597-677
	Model 70	220-280	298-379
	Axle Housing		
	Ford 8.8 in. (223.5mm) Ring Gear		
	Spring U-bolt nuts	160	216
	Dana Axles		
	U-bolt nuts		
	60 and 70 models	110-160	150-217
	80 models	109	148

88487C02

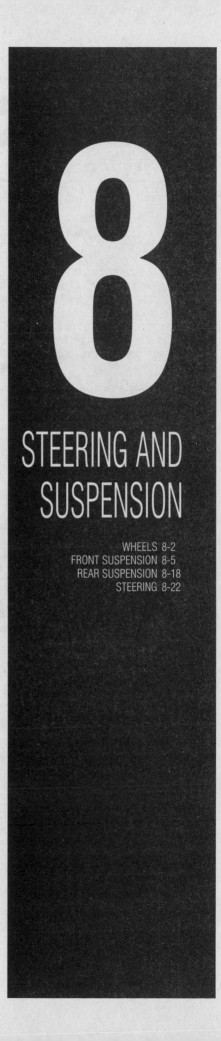

8

STEERING AND SUSPENSION

WHEELS

Wheels

REMOVAL & INSTALLATION

◗ **See Figures 1 thru 7**

1. Park the vehicle on a level surface.
2. Remove the jack, tire iron and, if necessary, the spare tire from their storage compartments.
3. Check the owner's manual or refer to Section 1 of this manual for the jacking points on your vehicle. Then, place the jack in the proper position.
4. If equipped with lug nut trim caps, remove them by either unscrewing or pulling them off the lug nuts, as appropriate. Consult the owner's manual, if necessary.
5. If equipped with a wheel cover or hub cap, insert the tapered end of the tire iron in the groove and pry off the cover.
6. Apply the parking brake and block the diagonally opposite wheel with a wheel chock or two.

➡ Wheel chocks may be purchased at your local auto parts store, or a block of wood cut into wedges may be used. If possible, keep one or two of the chocks in your tire storage compartment, in case any of the tires has to be removed on the side of the road.

7. If equipped with an automatic transmission, place the selector lever in **P** or Park; with a manual transmission, place the shifter in Reverse.
8. With the tires still on the ground, use the tire iron/wrench to break the lug nuts loose.

➡ If a nut is stuck, never use heat to loosen it or damage to the wheel and bearings may occur. If the nuts are seized, one or two heavy hammer blows directly on the end of the bolt usually loosens the rust. Be careful, as continued pounding will likely damage the brake drum or rotor.

9. Using the jack, raise the vehicle until the tire is clear of the ground. Support the vehicle safely using jackstands.
10. Remove the lug nuts, then remove the tire and wheel assembly.

TCCA8P00

Fig. 1 Place the jack at the proper lifting point on your vehicle

TCCA8P02

Fig. 3 With the vehicle still on the ground, break the lug nuts loose using the wrench end of the tire iron

TCCA8P01

Fig. 2 Before jacking the vehicle, block the diagonally opposite wheel with one or, preferably, two chocks

TCCA8P03

Fig. 4 After the lug nuts have been loosened, raise the vehicle using the jack until the tire is clear of the ground

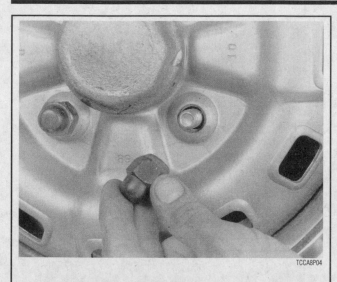

Fig. 5 Remove the lug nuts from the studs

Fig. 6 Remove the wheel and tire assembly from the vehicle

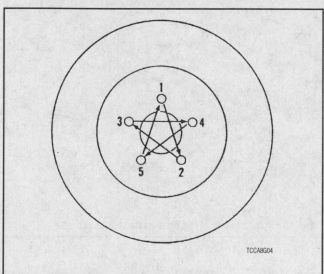

Fig. 7 Typical wheel lug tightening sequence

To install:

11. Make sure the wheel and hub mating surfaces, as well as the wheel lug studs, are clean and free of all foreign material. Always remove rust from the wheel mounting surface and the brake rotor or drum. Failure to do so may cause the lug nuts to loosen in service.

12. Install the tire and wheel assembly and hand-tighten the lug nuts.

13. Using the tire wrench, tighten all the lug nuts, in a crisscross pattern, until they are snug.

14. Raise the vehicle and withdraw the jackstand, then lower the vehicle.

15. Using a torque wrench, tighten the lug nuts in a crisscross pattern to the following specifications:

- 1989–95 E-150 models: 100 ft. lbs. (135 Nm)
- 1989–95 E-250 and 350 models: 140 ft. lbs. (190 Nm)
- 1996 E-150 models: 74–133 ft. lbs. (100–180 Nm)
- 1996 E-250 and 350 models: 126–170 ft. lbs. (170–230 Nm)

16. Check your owner's manual or refer to Section 1 of this manual for the proper tightening sequence.

✳✳ WARNING

Do not overtighten the lug nuts, as this may cause the wheel studs to stretch or the brake disc (rotor) to warp.

17. If so equipped, install the wheel cover or hub cap. Make sure the valve stem protrudes through the proper opening before tapping the wheel cover into position.

18. If equipped, install the lug nut trim caps by pushing them or screwing them on, as applicable.

19. Remove the jack from under the vehicle, and place the jack and tire iron/wrench in their storage compartments. Remove the wheel chock(s).

20. If you have removed a flat or damaged tire, place it in the storage compartment of the vehicle and take it to your local repair station to have it fixed or replaced as soon as possible.

INSPECTION

Inspect the tires for lacerations, puncture marks, nails and other sharp objects. Repair or replace as necessary. Also check the tires for treadwear and air pressure as outlined in Section 1 of the manual.

Check the wheel assemblies for dents, cracks, rust and metal fatigue. Repair or replace as necessary.

Wheel Lug Studs

REMOVAL & INSTALLATION

With Disc Brakes

♦ See Figures 8, 9 and 10

1. Raise and support the appropriate end of the vehicle safely using jackstands, then remove the wheel.

2. Remove the brake pads and caliper. Support the caliper aside using wire or a coat hanger. For details, please refer to Section 9 of this manual.

3. Remove the outer wheel bearing and lift off the rotor. For details on wheel bearing removal, installation and adjustment, please refer to Section 1 of this manual.

4. Properly support the rotor using press bars, then drive the stud out using an arbor press.

➡If a press is not available, CAREFULLY drive the old stud out using a blunt drift. MAKE SURE the rotor is properly and evenly supported or it may be damaged.

To install:

5. Clean the stud hole with a wire brush and start the new stud with a hammer and drift pin. Do not use any lubricant or thread sealer.

6. Finish installing the stud with the press.

➡️If a press is not available, start the lug stud through the bore in the hub, then position about 4 flat washers over the stud and thread the lug nut. Hold the hub/rotor while tightening the lug nut, and the stud should be drawn into position. **MAKE SURE THE STUD IS FULLY SEATED,** then remove the lug nut and washers.

7. Install the rotor and adjust the wheel bearings.

8. Install the brake caliper and pads.

9. Install the wheel, then remove the jackstands and carefully lower the vehicle.

10. Tighten the lug nuts to the proper torque.

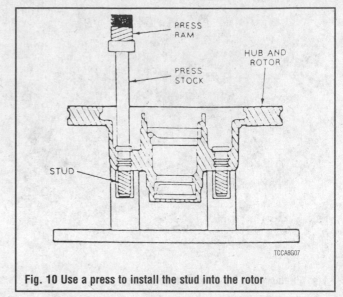

Fig. 10 Use a press to install the stud into the rotor

With Drum Brakes

▶ **See Figures 11, 12 and 13**

1. Raise the vehicle and safely support it with jackstands, then remove the wheel.

2. Remove the brake drum.

3. If necessary to provide clearance, remove the brake shoes, as outlined in Section 9 of this manual.

4. Using a large C-clamp and socket, press the stud from the axle flange.

5. Coat the serrated part of the stud with liquid soap and place it into the hole.

To install:

6. Position about 4 flat washers over the stud and thread the lug nut. Hold the flange while tightening the lug nut, and the stud should be drawn

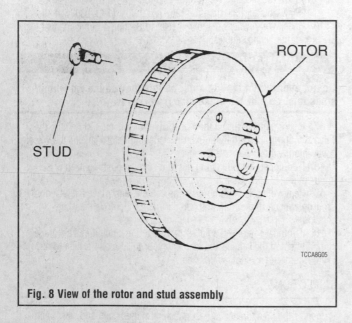

Fig. 8 View of the rotor and stud assembly

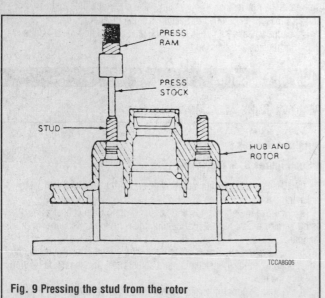

Fig. 9 Pressing the stud from the rotor

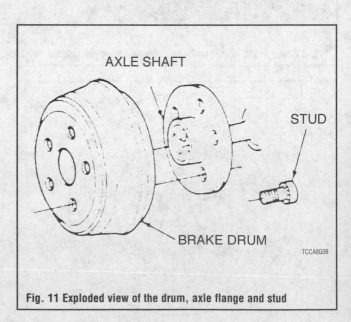

Fig. 11 Exploded view of the drum, axle flange and stud

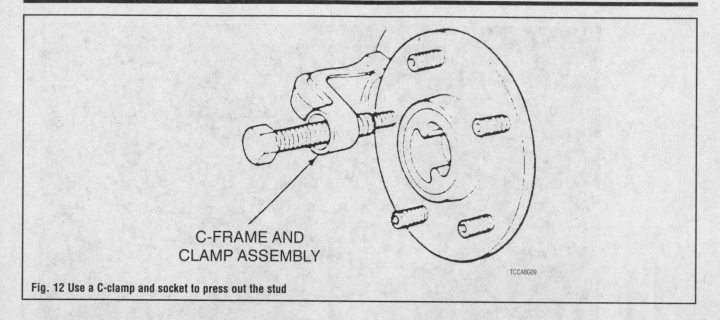

Fig. 12 Use a C-clamp and socket to press out the stud

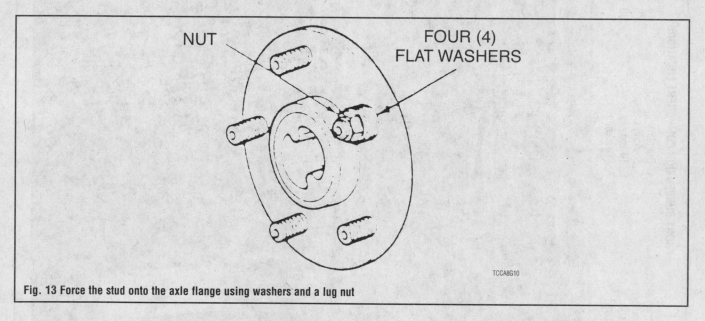

Fig. 13 Force the stud onto the axle flange using washers and a lug nut

into position. MAKE SURE THE STUD IS FULLY SEATED, then remove the lug nut and washers.

    7. If applicable, install the brake shoes.

    8. Install the brake drum.

    9. Install the wheel, then remove the jackstands and carefully lower the vehicle.

    10. Tighten the lug nuts to the proper torque.

FRONT SUSPENSION

▶ **See Figures 14 and 15**

    These vans use two I-beam type front axles; one for each wheel. One end of each axle is attached to the spindle and a radius arm, and the other end is attached to a frame pivot bracket on the opposite side of the van. Coil spring are used and are mounted between the frame spring pocket and the axle.

FRONT SUSPENSION COMPONENT LOCATIONS

1. Spring and shock
   absorber
2. Stabilizer bar
3. Tie rod
4. Drag link
5. Steering knuckle
6. Tie rod end
7. Pitman arm
8. Stabilizer link
9. I-beam
10. Trailing arm

88488P17

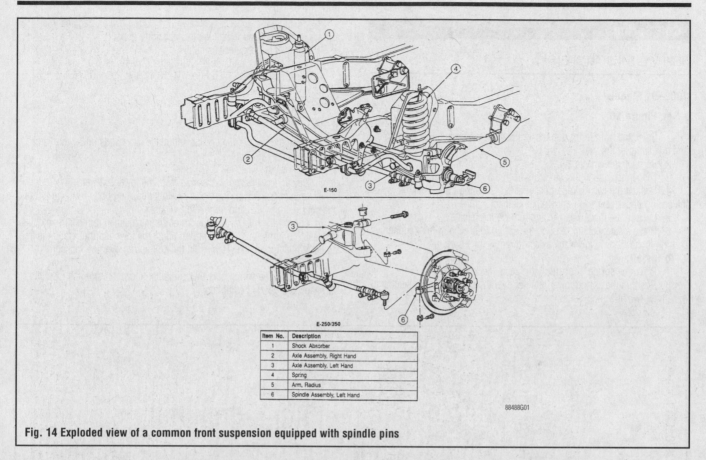

Item No.	Description
1	Shock Absorber
2	Axle Assembly, Right Hand
3	Axle Assembly, Left Hand
4	Spring
5	Arm, Radius
6	Spindle Assembly, Left Hand

88488G01

Fig. 14 Exploded view of a common front suspension equipped with spindle pins

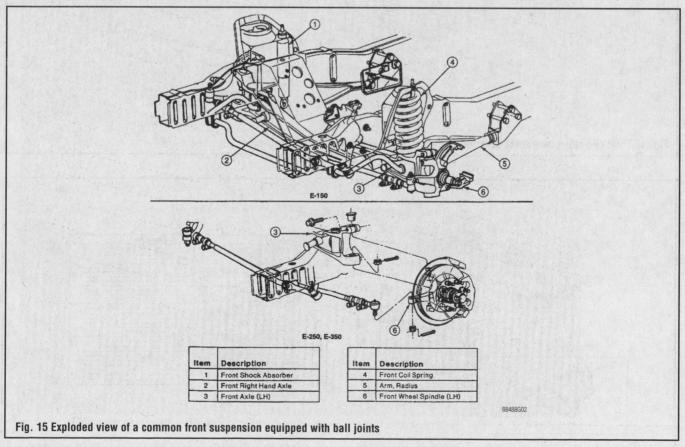

Item	Description		Item	Description
1	Front Shock Absorber		4	Front Coil Spring
2	Front Right Hand Axle		5	Arm, Radius
3	Front Axle (LH)		6	Front Wheel Spindle (LH)

88488G02

Fig. 15 Exploded view of a common front suspension equipped with ball joints

Coil Springs

REMOVAL & INSTALLATION

1989–91 Models

♦ See Figure 16

1. Raise the front of the vehicle and place jackstands under the frame and a jack under the axle.
2. Remove the wheels.
3. Disconnect the shock absorber from the lower bracket.
4. Loosen the two spring upper retainer attaching bolts from the top of the spring upper seat and remove the retainer.
5. Loosen the lower retainer and remove the retainer.
6. Place a safety chain through the spring to prevent it from suddenly coming loose. Slowly lower the axle and remove the spring.

To install:

7. Place the spring in position and raise the front axle.
8. Position the spring lower retainer over the stud and lower seat, and install the two attaching bolts.

9. Position the upper retainer over the spring coil and against the spring upper seat, and install the two attaching bolts.
10. Tighten the retainers as follows:
   - Upper retaining bolts to 20–30 ft. lbs. (28–40 Nm).
   - Lower retainer attaching nuts: 70–100 ft. lbs. (95–135 Nm).

1992–96 Models

♦ See Figure 17

1. Raise the front of the vehicle and place jackstands under the frame and a jack under the axle.
2. Remove the wheels.
3. Disconnect the shock absorber from the lower bracket.
4. Loosen the two spring upper retainer attaching bolts from the top of the spring upper seat and remove the retainer.
5. Loosen the nut holding the lower spring retainer, radius arm and axle at least four turns, push the joint bolt up so the lower spring retainer is free to tip. While tipping the retainer, lift the coil spring over the retainer.

To install:

6. Position the spring over lower retainer and make sure the insulator's **D** shape is properly positioned.

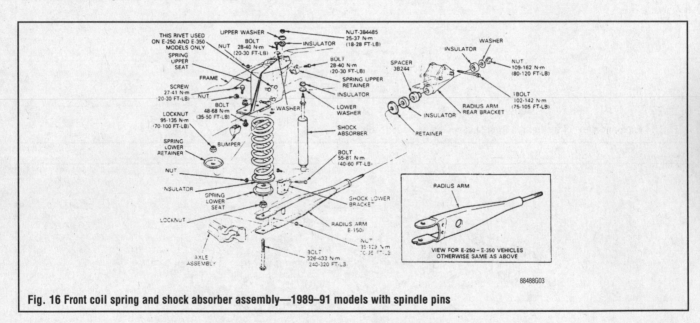

Fig. 16 Front coil spring and shock absorber assembly—1989–91 models with spindle pins

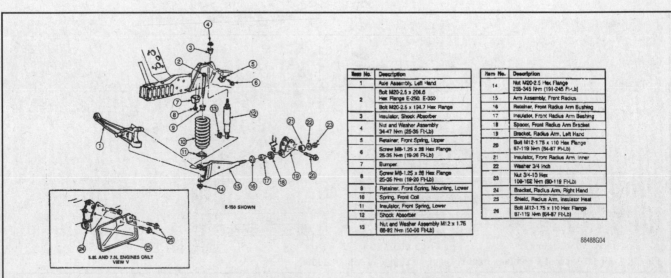

Item No.	Description
1	Axle Assembly, Left Hand
2	Bolt M20-2.5 x 206.8 Hex Flange E-250, E-350
	Bolt M20-2.5 x 194.7 Hex Flange
3	Insulator, Shock Absorber
4	Nut and Washer Assembly 34-47 Nm (25-35 Ft-Lb)
5	Retainer, Front Spring, Upper
6	Screw M8-1.25 x 28 Hex Flange 25-35 Nm (19-26 Ft-Lb)
7	Bumper
8	Screw M8-1.25 x 28 Hex Flange 25-35 Nm (19-26 Ft-Lb)
9	Retainer, Front Spring, Mounting, Lower
10	Spring, Front Coil
11	Insulator, Front Spring, Lower
12	Shock Absorber
13	Nut and Washer Assembly M12 x 1.75 68-92 Nm (50-68 Ft-Lb)

Item No.	Description
14	Nut M20-2.5 Hex Flange 255-345 Nm (191-245 Ft-Lb)
15	Arm Assembly, Front Radius
16	Retainer, Front Radius Arm Bushing
17	Insulator, Front Radius Arm Bushing
18	Spacer, Front Radius Arm Bracket
19	Bracket, Radius Arm, Left Hand
20	Bolt M12-1.75 x 110 Hex Flange 87-119 Nm (64-87 Ft-Lb)
21	Insulator, Front Radius Arm, Inner
22	Washer 3/4 Inch
23	Nut 3/4-10 Hex 108-162 Nm (80-119 Ft-Lb)
24	Bracket, Radius Arm, Right Hand
25	Shield, Radius Arm, Insulator Heat
26	Bolt M12-1.75 x 110 Hex Flange 87-119 Nm (64-87 Ft-Lb)

Fig. 17 Exploded view of the front coil spring and shock absorber assembly—1992–96 models

7. Position the upper retainer over the spring coil and against the spring upper seat, and install the two attaching bolts.

8. Tighten the retainers as follows:
- Upper retaining bolts to 19–26 ft. lbs. (25–35 Nm)
- Lower retainer attaching nuts: 191–245 ft. lbs. (255–345 Nm)

Shock Absorbers

REMOVAL & INSTALLATION

▶ **See Figures 18, 19 and 20**

1. Raise the van and support it with safety stands.
2. Use a wrench inserted from the rear side of the spring upper seat, and hold the shock absorber upper nut.
3. Loosen the stud by turning the hex on the exposed (lower) part of the stud and remove the nut.
4. Loosen and remove the lower shock absorber bolt and nut.
5. Remove the shock absorber.

To install:

When installing a new shock absorber, use new rubber bushings. Position the shock absorber on the mounting brackets with the stud end at the top.

Fig. 18 Insert a wrench from the rear side of upper seat to hold the nut, then loosen the nut by turning the hex head fastener

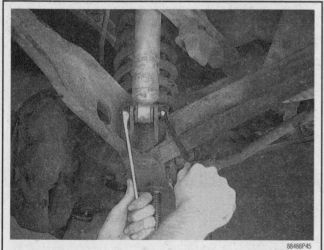

Fig. 19 Unfasten the lower shock absorber mounting nut and bolt using a back-up wrench

Fig. 20 Detach the shock absorber from the bracket and remove it from the van

6. While holding the nut tighten the hex head fastener to 18–28 ft. lbs. (25–37 Nm) on 1989–91 models and 25–35 ft. lbs. (34–47 Nm) on 1992–96 models.

7. Install the bolt and nut and tighten to 40–60 ft. lbs. (55–81 Nm) on 1989–91 models and 50–68 ft. lbs. (68–92 Nm) on 1992–96 models.

TESTING

▶ **See Figure 21**

The purpose of the shock absorber is simply to limit the motion of the spring during compression and rebound cycles. If the vehicle is not equipped with these motion dampers, the up and down motion would multiply until the vehicle was alternately trying to leap off the ground and to pound itself into the pavement.

Countrary to popular rumor, the shocks do not affect the ride height of the vehicle. This is controlled by other suspension components such as springs and tires. Worn shock absorbers can affect handling; if the front of the vehicle is rising or falling excessively, the "footprint" of the tires changes on the pavement and steering is affected.

The simplest test of the shock absorber is simply push down on one corner of the unladen vehicle and release it. Observe the motion of the body as it is released. In most cases, it will come up beyond it original rest position, dip back below it and settle quickly to rest. This shows that the

Fig. 21 When fluid is seeping out of the shock absorber, it's time to replace it

damper is controlling the spring action. Any tendency to excessive pitch (up-and-down) motion or failure to return to rest within 2–3 cycles is a sign of poor function within the shock absorber. Oil-filled shocks may have a light film of oil around the seal, resulting from normal breathing and air exchange. This should NOT be taken as a sign of failure, but any sign of thick or running oil definitely indicates failure. Gas filled shocks may also show some film at the shaft; if the gas has leaked out, the shock will have almost no resistance to motion.

While each shock absorber can be replaced individually, it is recommended that they be changed as a pair (both front or both rear) to maintain equal response on both sides of the vehicle. Chances are quite good that if one has failed, its mate is weak also.

Front Wheel Spindle Pins

REMOVAL & INSTALLATION

▶ **See Figures 22 and 23**

Some models use a spindle pin instead of traditional ball joint assemblies. If your van is equipped with these components, refer to the following procedures for removal and installation of the pins and bushings.

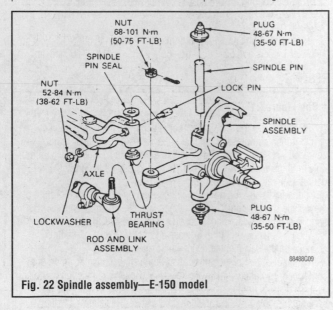

Fig. 22 Spindle assembly—E-150 model

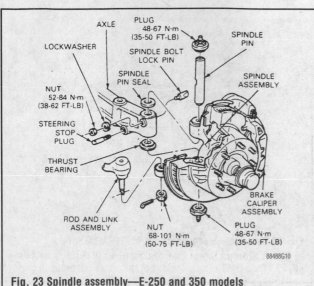

Fig. 23 Spindle assembly—E-250 and 350 models

1. Jack up the front of the van and safely support it with jackstands.
2. Remove the wheels.
3. Remove the front brake caliper assembly and hold it out of the way with a piece of wire. Do not disconnect the brake line.
4. Remove the brake rotor from the spindle.
5. Remove the inner bearing cone and seal. Discard the seal, as you'll be fitting a new one during installation.
6. Remove the brake dust shield.
7. Disconnect the steering linkage from the spindle arm by removing the cotter pin and nut, then using a tie rod end removal tool.
8. On motorhome and commercial stripped chassis models, disconnect the drag link from the steering arm using a tie rod end removal tool.
9. Remove the nuts and lockwasher from the lock pin, then remove the lock pin.
10. Remove the spindle pin plugs, then drive the spindle out from the top of the axle.
11. Remove the spindle and thrust bearing.
12. Remove the pin seal.

To install:

➡**Always use new cotter pins. When aligning the cotter pin holes, never back off the nut; always advance the nut until the holes align.**

13. Make sure that the spindle pin holes are clean and free from burrs and nicks.
14. Lightly coat the bore with chassis lube.
15. Install a new spindle pin seal with the metal backing facing upwards towards the bushing into the spindle by gently pushing it into position.
16. Install a new lower thrust bearing with the lip facing down towards the lower bushing. Press the bearing in until it is firmly seated against the surface of the spindle.
17. Lightly coat the bushing surfaces with grease and position the spindle on the axle.
18. Install the spindle pin with the **T** which is stamped on one end at the top and the notch in the pin is aligned with the lock pin hole in the axle.
19. Insert the pin through the bushings and axle from the top until the spindle pin notch and axle lock pin hole are in line.
20. Install the lock pin with the threads pointing forward and the wedge groove facing the spindle pin notch.
21. Drive the lock pin into position and install the lockwasher and nut. Tighten the nut to 40–60 ft. lbs. (54–81 Nm).
22. Install the spindle pin plugs into the threads at the top and bottom of the spindle and tighten the plugs to 35–50 ft. lbs. (48–67 Nm).
23. Lubricate the spindle pins and bushings with chassis lube through both fittings until grease is visible seeping past the upper seal and thrust bearing slip joint. If grease does not appear at the top and bottom points, the spindle is installed incorrectly and rapid deterioration of the spindle components will result.
24. Install the brake dust shield.
25. Pack the inner and outer bearing cone with a quality wheel bearing grease by hand, working the grease through the cage behind the roller.
26. Install the inner bearing cone and seal. Install the hub and rotor on the spindle.
27. Install the outer bearing cone, washer, and nut. Adjust the bearing end-play and install the nut retainer, cotter pin and dust cap.
28. Install the brake caliper. connect the steering linkage to the spindle. Tighten the nut to 70–100 ft. lbs. (95–135 Nm) and advance the nut as far necessary to install the cotter pin.
29. Install the wheels. Lower the van and adjust toe if necessary.

Spindle Bushings

REPLACEMENT

▶ **See Figures 24, 25, 26, 27 and 28**

1. Remove the spindle.
2. On E-150, use the following tools:

- Reamer T53T-3110-DA
- Remover/Installer/Driver D82T-3110-G
- Driver Handle D82T-3110-C
3. On E-250/350, use the following tools:
- Reamer D82T-3110-A
- Remover/Installer/Driver D82T-3110-B
- Driver Handle D82T-3110-C

➡**Each side of the Remover/Installer/Driver is marked with a T or B. Use the side with the T to install the top spindle bushing; the side with the B to install the bottom spindle bushing.**

4. Remove and discard the seal from the bottom of the upper bushing bore.

5. Remove and install the top spindle bushing:
   a. Install the driver handle through the bottom bore.
   b. Position a new bushing on the **T** side stamping of the driver.
   c. The bushing must be installed so that the open end grooves will face outward when installed.
   d. Position the new bushing and driver over the old bushing, insert the handle into the driver and drive the old bushing out while driving the new bushing in. Drive until the tool is seated.

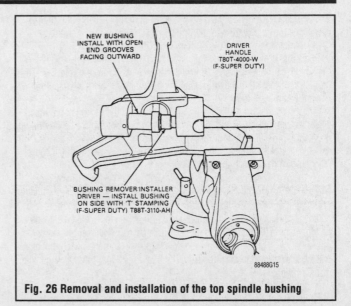

Fig. 26 Removal and installation of the top spindle bushing

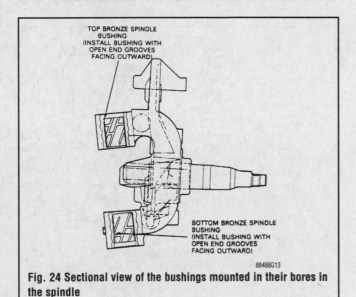

Fig. 24 Sectional view of the bushings mounted in their bores in the spindle

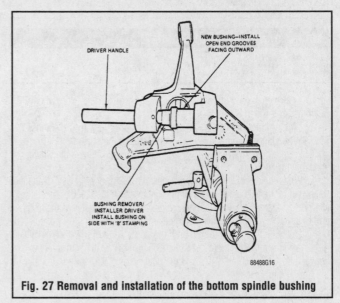

Fig. 27 Removal and installation of the bottom spindle bushing

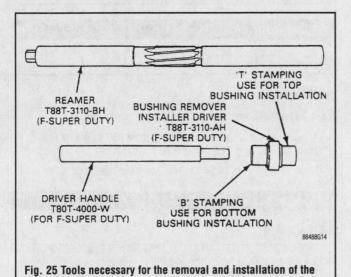

Fig. 25 Tools necessary for the removal and installation of the bushings

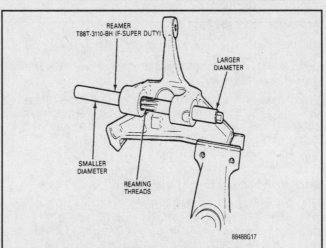

Fig. 28 Ream the new bushings to 0.001–0.003 in. (0.025–0.076mm) larger than the diameter of the new spindle pin

e. The bushing will then be seated to the proper depth of 0.080 in. (2mm) from the bottom of the upper spindle boss.

6. Remove and install the bottom spindle bushing:

a. Insert the driver handle through the top bushing bore.

b. Position a new bushing on the **B** side stamping of the driver. The bushing must be installed so that the open end grooves will face outward when installed.

c. Position the new bushing and driver over the old bushing, insert the handle into the driver and drive the old bushing out while driving the new bushing in. Drive until the tool is seated.

d. The bushing will then be seated to the proper depth of 0.130 in. (3.30mm) from the bottom of the upper spindle boss.

7. Ream the new bushings to 0.001–0.003 in. (0.025–0.076mm) larger than the diameter of the new spindle pin. Ream the top bushings first. Insert the smaller end of the reamer through the top bore and into the bottom bore until the threads are in position in the top bushing. Turn the tool until the threads exit the top bushing. Ream the bottom bushing. The larger diameter portion of the tool will act as a pilot in the top bushing to properly ream the bottom bushing.

8. Clean all metal shavings from the bushings. Coat the bushings with chassis lube.

9. Install a new seal on the driver on the side with the **T** stamping. Install the handle into the driver and push the seal into position in the bottom of the top bushing bore.

Upper and Lower Ball Joints

INSPECTION

1. Before an inspection of the ball joints, make sure the front wheel bearings are properly packed and adjusted.

2. Jack up the front of the van and safely support it with jackstands, placing the stands under the I-beam axle, beneath the spring.

3. Have a helper grab the lower edge of the tire and move the wheel assembly in and out.

4. While the wheel is being moved, observe the lower spindle arm and the lower part of the axle jaw (the end of the axle to which the spindle assembly attaches). If there is 1/32 in. (0.8mm) or greater movement between the lower part of the axle jaw and the lower spindle arm, the lower ball must be replaced.

5. To check upper ball joints, grab the upper edge of the tire and move the wheel in and out. If there is 1/32 in. (0.8mm) or greater movement between the upper spindle arm and the upper part of the jaw, the upper ball joint must be replaced.

REMOVAL & INSTALLATION

▶ **See Figures 29 and 30**

1. Remove the wheel spindle and ball joint assembly from the axle.

➡**The lower ball joint must always be removed first. DO NOT heat the ball joint or spindle!**

2. Remove the snapring from the ball joints. Assemble the C-frame assembly T74P–4635–C and receiver cup D81T–3010–A, or equivalents, on the upper ball joint. Turn the forcing screw clockwise until the ball joint is removed from the axle.

3. Repeat Step 2 on the upper ball joint.

To install:

➡**The upper ball joint must be installed first.**

4. To install the lower ball joint, assemble the C-frame with ball joint receiver cup D81T–3010–A5 and installation cup D81T–3010–A1, and turn the forcing screw clockwise until the ball joint is seated. DO NOT heat the ball joint to aid in installation!

5. Install the snapring onto the ball joint.

6. Install the lower ball joint in the same manner as the upper ball joint.

7. Install the spindle assembly.

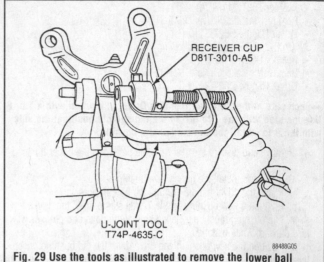

Fig. 29 Use the tools as illustrated to remove the lower ball joint

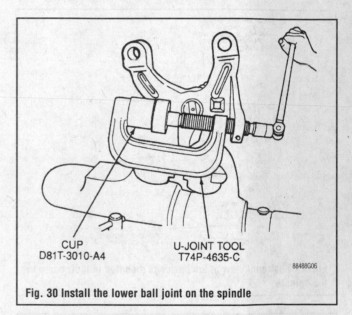

Fig. 30 Install the lower ball joint on the spindle

Radius Arm

REMOVAL & INSTALLATION

1989–94 Models

▶ **See Figures 16 and 17**

➡**A torque wrench with a capacity of at least 350 ft. lbs. (474 Nm) is necessary, along with other special tools, for this procedure.**

1. Raise the front of the vehicle and place safety stands under the frame and a jack under the axle. Remove the wheels.

2. If equipped, disconnect the stabilizer bar at the link.

3. Disconnect the lower end of the shock absorber from the radius arm bracket.

4. Remove the coil spring.

5. Remove the spring lower seat and shim from the radius arm. Then, remove the bolt and nut which attach the radius arm to the axle.

6. Remove the cotter pin, nut and washer from the radius arm rear attachment.

7. Remove the bushing from the radius arm and remove the radius arm from the vehicle.

8. Remove the inner bushing from the radius arm.

To install:

9. Position the radius arm to the axle and install the bolt and nut finger-tight.

10. Install the inner bushing on the radius arm and position the arm to the frame bracket.

11. Install the bushing, washer, and attaching nut. Tighten the nut to 120 ft. lbs. (163 Nm) and install the cotter pin.

12. Tighten the radius arm-to-axle bolt to 240–320 ft. lbs. (326–433 Nm).

13. Install the spring seat and insulator on the radius arm so that the hole in the seat fits over the arm-to-axle nut.

14. Install the spring.

15. Connect the shock absorber. Tighten the nut and bolt to 40–60 ft. lbs. (55–81 Nm).

16. Install the wheels and lower the van.

1995–96 Models

♦ See Figure 17

1. Raise the front of the vehicle and place safety stands under the frame and a jack under the axle. Remove the wheels.

2. If equipped, disconnect the stabilizer bar at the link.

3. Disconnect the lower end of the shock absorber from the radius arm bracket.

4. Remove the coil spring.

5. Remove the spring insulator and seat from the radius arm.

6. Loosen the radius arm-to-axle bolt and nut.

7. Remove the radius arm from the van.

8. Remove the spacer inner insulator and retainer from the radius arm stud.

9. Inspect the inner insulator for heat distortion and replace if damaged.

To install:

10. Position the radius arm to the axle, slide the lower spring retainer and insulator onto the attaching bolt.

11. Install the attaching bolt from the top through the arm and axle, then finger-tighten the nut.

12. Install the retainer and inner insulator on the radius arm stud, then install the stud through the rear bracket.

13. Install the retainer, inner insulator and spacer on the arm stud, then insert the stud through the arm rear bracket.

14. Install the other insulator, washer and nut on the arm stud.

15. Tighten the nut on the radius arm-to-axle bolt to 188–254 ft. lbs. (255–345 Nm).

16. Install the spring lower seat and insulator on the radius arm so that the hole in the seat fits over the arm-to-axle nut.

17. Install the spring.

18. Connect the shock absorber. Tighten the nut and bolt to 50–68 ft. lbs. (68–92 Nm).

19. Install the caliper.

20. Install the wheels and lower the van.

Stabilizer Bar

REMOVAL & INSTALLATION

1989–91 Models

♦ See Figure 31

1. Raise and support the front end on jackstands.

2. Disconnect the right and left stabilizer bar ends from the link assembly.

3. Disconnect the retainer bolts and remove the stabilizer bar.

4. Disconnect the stabilizer link assemblies by loosening the right and left locknuts from their respective brackets on the I-beams.

To install:

5. Connect the left and right stabilizer links to their brackets by sliding the bolt with the washer through the link, the I-beam bracket hole and toward the inside of the frame rail. Tighten the locknut to 40–60 ft. lbs. (55–81 Nm).

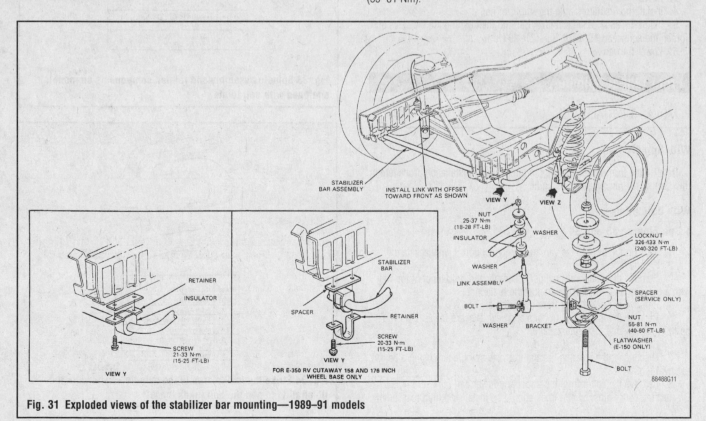

Fig. 31 Exploded views of the stabilizer bar mounting—1989–91 models

➡The link must be installed with the bend facing forward.

6. Connect the stabilizer bar to the frame rails and tighten the retainers to 18–28 ft. lbs. (25–37 Nm).

1992–96 Models

◆ **See Figure 32**

1. Raise the van and support it with safety stands.
2. Loosen the screws at the retaining brackets.
3. Remove the stabilizer bar by pulling it out of both axles.

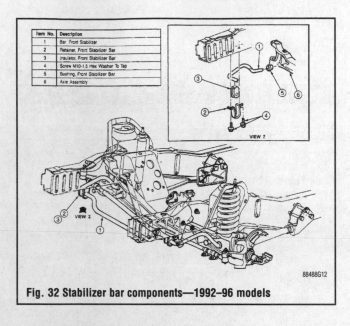

Item No.	Description
1	Bar, Front Stabilizer
2	Retainer, Front Stabilizer Bar
3	Insulator, Front Stabilizer Bar
4	Screw M10-1.5 Hex Washer To Tap
5	Bushing, Front Stabilizer Bar
6	Axle Assembly

88488G12

Fig. 32 Stabilizer bar components—1992–96 models

To install:

4. Install the insulators onto the stabilizer bar.
5. Insert the ends of the stabilizer bar into the bushings in the axles and tighten the screws to 15–21 ft. lbs. (21–29 Nm).
6. Lower the van.

Front Wheel Spindle

REMOVAL & INSTALLATION

With Spindle Pin

Refer to the front wheel spindle pin removal and installation procedure in this section for removal of the spindle.

With Ball Joints

◆ **See Figures 33 and 34**

1. Jack up the front of the van and safely support it with jackstands.
2. Remove the wheels.
3. Remove the front brake caliper assembly and hold it out of the way with a piece of wire. Do not disconnect the brake line.
4. Remove the brake rotor from the spindle.
5. Remove the inner bearing cone and seal. Discard the seal, as you'll be fitting a new one during installation.
6. Remove the brake dust shield.
7. Disconnect the steering linkage from the spindle arm using a tie rod removal tool.
8. Remove the cotter from the upper and lower ball joint stud nuts. Discard the cotter pins, as new ones should be installed during reassembly.

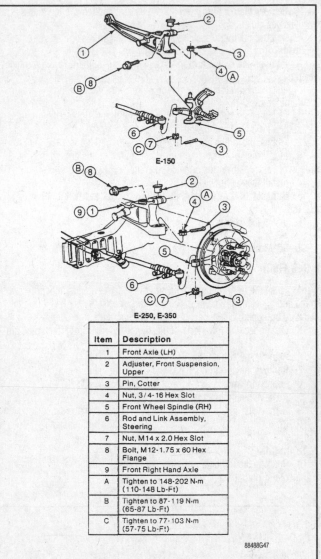

E-150

E-250, E-350

Item	Description
1	Front Axle (LH)
2	Adjuster, Front Suspension, Upper
3	Pin, Cotter
4	Nut, 3/4-16 Hex Slot
5	Front Wheel Spindle (RH)
6	Rod and Link Assembly, Steering
7	Nut, M14 x 2.0 Hex Slot
8	Bolt, M12-1.75 x 60 Hex Flange
9	Front Right Hand Axle
A	Tighten to 148-202 N·m (110-148 Lb-Ft)
B	Tighten to 87-119 N·m (65-87 Lb-Ft)
C	Tighten to 77-103 N·m (57-75 Lb-Ft)

88488G47

Fig. 33 Spindle assembly and related components on models equipped with ball joints

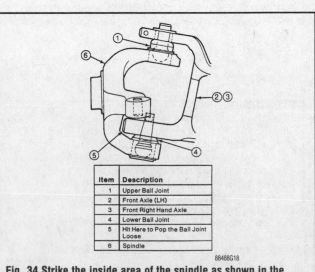

Item	Description
1	Upper Ball Joint
2	Front Axle (LH)
3	Front Right Hand Axle
4	Lower Ball Joint
5	Hit Here to Pop the Ball Joint Loose
6	Spindle

88488G18

Fig. 34 Strike the inside area of the spindle as shown in the illustration to pop the ball joints loose

9. Remove the upper ball joint nut and loosen the lower ball joint nut to the end of the threads.

10. Strike the inside area or the spindle as shown in the illustration to pop the ball joints loose from the spindle.

❋❋ WARNING

Do not use a forked ball joint removal tool to separate the ball joints as this will damage the seal and ball joint socket.

11. Remove the nut. Remove the spindle.

To install:

➡Before reassembly, be advised that new cotter pins should be used on the ball joints, and that new bearing seal(s) should also be used. Also, make sure the upper and lower ball joint seals are in place.

12. Place the spindle over the ball joints.

13. Install the nuts on the lower ball joint stud and partially tighten to 35 ft. lbs. (47 Nm). Turn the castellated nut until you are able to install the cotter pin.

14. Install the camber adapter in the upper spindle over the upper ball joint stud. Be sure the adapter is aligned properly.

➡If camber adjustment is necessary special adapters must be installed.

15. Install the nut on the upper ball joint stud. Hold the camber adapter with a wrench to keep the ball stud from turning. If the ball stud turns, tap the adapter deeper into the spindle. Tighten the nut to 109–149 ft. lbs. (148–202 Nm) and continue tightening the castellated nut until it lines up with the hole in the stud. Install the cotter pin.

16. Tighten the lower nut to 109–149 ft. lbs. (148–202 Nm). Advance the nut to install a new cotter pin.

17. Install the brake dust shield.

18. Pack the inner and outer bearing cone with a quality wheel bearing grease by hand, working the grease through the cage behind the roller.

19. Install the inner bearing cone and seal. Install the hub and rotor on the spindle.

20. Install the outer bearing cone, washer, and nut. Adjust the bearing end-play and install the nut retainer, cotter pin and dust cap.

21. Install the brake caliper. connect the steering linkage to the spindle. Tighten the nut to 52–74 ft. lbs. (70–100 Nm) and advance the nut as far necessary to install the cotter pin.

22. Install the wheels. Lower the van and adjust toe-in if necessary.

Front Wheel Bearings

PRECAUTIONS

Before handling the bearings, there are a few things that you should remember to do and not to do.

DO the following:
• Remove all outside dirt from the housing before exposing the bearing.
• Treat a used bearing as gently as you would a new one.
• Work with clean tools in clean surroundings.
• Use clean, dry canvas gloves, or at least clean, dry hands.
• Clean solvents and flushing fluids are a must.
• Use clean paper when laying out the bearings to dry.
• Protect disassembled bearings from rust and dirt. Cover them up.
• Use clean rags to wipe bearings.
• Keep the bearings in oil-proof paper when they are to be stored or are not in use.
• Clean the inside of the housing before replacing the bearing.

DO NOT do the following:
• Do not work in dirty surroundings.
• Do not use dirty, chipped or damaged tools.
• Do not work on wooden work benches or use wooden mallets.
• Do not handle bearings with dirty or moist hands.
• Do not use gasoline for cleaning; use a safe solvent.
• Do not spin-dry bearings with compressed air. They will be damaged.
• Do not spin dirty bearings.
• Do not use cotton waste or dirty cloths to wipe bearings.
• Do not scratch or nick bearing surfaces.
• Do not allow the bearing to come in contact with dirt or rust at any time.

REMOVAL & INSTALLATION

▶ See Figures 35, 36, 37 and 38

❋❋ WARNING

Before proceeding with any work on the front wheel bearings, read the precautions listed at the beginning of this section.

1. Raise and support the front end on jackstands.

2. Remove the wheel cover. Remove the wheel.

3. Remove the caliper from the disc and wire it to the underbody to prevent damage to the brake hose. Refer to Section 9.

4. Remove the grease cap from the hub. Then, remove the cotter pin, nut lock, adjusting nut and flat washer from the spindle. Remove the outer bearing assembly from the hub.

5. Pull the hub and disc assembly off the wheel spindle.

6. Remove and discard the old grease retainer. Remove the inner bearing cone and roller assembly from the hub.

7. Clean all grease from the inner and outer bearing cups with solvent. Inspect the cups for pits, scratches, or excessive wear. If the cups are damaged, remove them with a drift.

8. Clean the inner and outer cone and roller assemblies with solvent and shake them dry. If the cone and roller assemblies show excessive wear or damage, replace them with the bearing cups as a unit.

9. Clean the spindle and the inside of the hub with solvent to thoroughly remove all old grease.

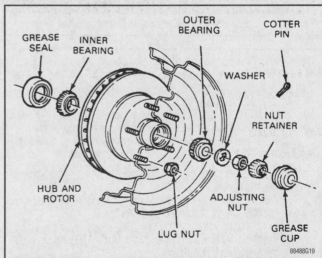

Fig. 35 Typical front wheel bearing assembly—E-150 shown, others similar

Fig. 36 Use a prytool to loosen the grease seal . . .

Fig. 38 Remove the inner bearing and roller cone from the hub

Fig. 37 . . . then remove the grease seal from the hub

10. Covering the spindle with a clean cloth, brush all loose dirt and dust from the brake assembly. Remove the cloth carefully so as to not get dirt on the spindle.

11. If the inner and/or outer bearing cups were removed, install the replacement cups on the hub. Be sure that the cups seat properly in the hub.

12. It is imperative that all old grease be removed from the bearings and surrounding surfaces before repacking. The new lithium-based grease is not compatible with the sodium base grease used in the past.

13. Install the hub and disc on the wheel spindle. To prevent damage to the grease retainer and spindle threads, keep the hub centered on the spindle.

14. Install the outer bearing cone and roller assembly and the flat washer on the spindle. Install the adjusting nut.

15. Adjust the wheel bearings by tightening the adjusting nut to 17–25 ft. lbs. (23–38 Nm) with the wheel rotating to seat the bearing. Then back off the adjusting nut ½ turn. Retighten the adjusting nut to 10–15 inch lbs.

(1.1–1.7 Nm). Install the locknut so that the castellations are aligned with the cotter pin hole. Install the cotter pin. Bend the ends of the cotter pin around the castellations of the locknut to prevent interference with the radio static collector in the grease cap. Install the grease cap.

➡**New bolts MUST be used when servicing floating caliper units. The upper bolt must be tightened first. For caliper service see Section 9.**

16. Install the wheels.
17. Install the wheel cover.

Wheel Alignment

If the tires are worn unevenly, if the vehicle is not stable on the highway or if the handling seems uneven in spirited driving, the wheel alignment should be checked. If an alignment problem is suspected, first check for improper tire inflation and other possible causes. These can be worn suspension or steering components, accident damage or even unmatched tires. If any worn or damaged components are found, they must be replaced before the wheels can be properly aligned. Wheel alignment requires very expensive equipment and involves minute adjustments which must be accurate; it should only be performed by a trained technician. Take your vehicle to a properly equipped shop.

Following is a description of the alignment angles which are adjustable on most vehicles and how they affect vehicle handling. Although these angles can apply to both the front and rear wheels, usually only the front suspension is adjustable.

CASTER

▶ See Figure 39

Looking at a vehicle from the side, caster angle describes the steering axis rather than a wheel angle. The steering knuckle is attached to a control arm or strut at the top and a control arm at the bottom. The wheel pivots around the line between these points to steer the vehicle. When the upper point is tilted back, this is described as positive caster. Having a positive caster tends to make the wheels self-centering, increasing directional stability. Excessive positive caster makes the wheels hard to steer, while an uneven caster will cause a pull to one side. Overloading the vehicle or sagging rear springs will affect caster, as will raising the rear of the vehicle. If the rear of the vehicle is lower than normal, the caster becomes more positive.

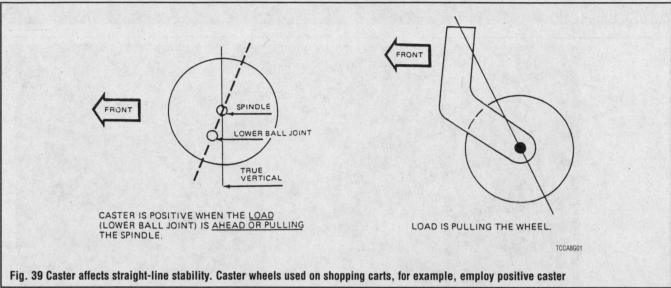

Fig. 39 Caster affects straight-line stability. Caster wheels used on shopping carts, for example, employ positive caster

CAMBER

♦ See Figure 40

Looking from the front of the vehicle, camber is the inward or outward tilt of the top of wheels. When the tops of the wheels are tilted in, this is negative camber; if they are tilted out, it is positive. In a turn, a slight amount of negative camber helps maximize contact of the tire with the road. However, too much negative camber compromises straight-line stability, increases bump steer and torque steer.

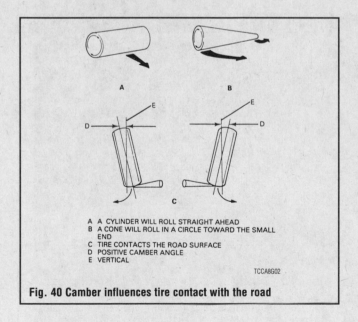

Fig. 40 Camber influences tire contact with the road

TOE

♦ See Figure 41

Looking down at the wheels from above the vehicle, toe angle is the distance between the front of the wheels, relative to the distance between the back of the wheels. If the wheels are closer at the front, they are said to be toed-in or to have negative toe. A small amount of negative toe enhances directional stability and provides a smoother ride on the highway.

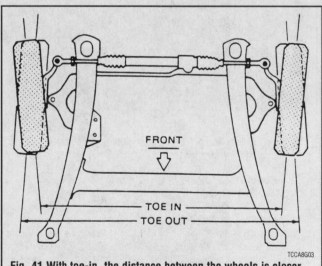

Fig. 41 With toe-in, the distance between the wheels is closer at the front than at the rear

REAR SUSPENSION

REAR SUSPENSION COMPONENT LOCATIONS

1. Rear shock absorber
2. Shock absorber lower mounting bracket
3. Axle housing
4. Leaf springs
5. Spring U-bolts

88488P18

Semi-elliptic, leaf type springs are used at the rear axle. The front end of the spring is attached to a spring bracket on the frame side member. The rear end of the spring is attached to the bracket on the frame side member with a shackle. Each spring is attached to the axle with two U-bolts. A spacer is located between the spring and the axle on some applications to obtain a level ride position.

Springs

REMOVAL & INSTALLATION

1989–91 Models

E-150 MODELS

1. Raise the rear of the van and support it with safety stands.
2. Support the weight of the rear axle with a floor jack.
3. Disconnect the lower end of the rear shock absorber from the axle.
4. Loosen the two U-bolts and remove the plate.
5. Lower the axle and loosen the upper and lower rear shackle bolts.
6. Pull the rear shackle assembly from the bracket and spring.
7. Loose the nut and bolt that retains the front end of the spring, then remove the spring from the shackle bracket.
To install:
8. Engage the front eye of the spring to the front bracket and finger-tighten the bolt and nut.
9. Engage the rear end of the spring to the rear shackle assembly and install the upper bolt, then install the lower bolt through the spring shackle bracket.
10. Assemble the spring center bolt in the pilot hole in the axle and install the plate.
11. Install the U-bolts and finger-tighten the nuts.
12. Raise the axle with the floor jack an d connect the lower end of the shock absorber to the axle.
13. Tighten the bolts and nuts to the following specifications:
• Leaf spring-to-front bracket nut and bolt: 150–204 ft. lbs. (204–276 Nm)
• Leaf spring-to-rear bracket nut and bolt: 74–107 ft. lbs. (101–145 Nm)
• Rear shackle-to-frame nut and bolt: 74–107 ft. lbs. (101–145 Nm)
• Leaf spring-to-axle U-bolt nut: 74–107 ft. lbs. (101–145 Nm)

E-250 AND 350 MODELS

▶ See Figure 42

1. Raise the rear of the van and support it with safety stands.
2. Support the weight of the rear axle with a floor jack.
3. Disconnect the lower end of the rear shock absorber from the axle.
4. Loosen the two U-bolts and remove the plate.
5. Lower the axle and remove the spring front bolt from the hanger.
6. Loosen the retaining bolts from the rear of the spring.
7. Remove the spring and shackle.
To install:
8. Engage the upper edge of the shackle to the spring and install the bolt.
9. Engage the front of the spring to the bracket and install the bolt.
10. Connect the spring and shackle to the rear bracket and install the bolts
11. Install the U-bolt plate over the nut o the center bolt.
12. Raise the axle with the floor jack , then assemble the spring center bolt in the pilot hole in the axle and install the plate.

Fig. 42 Loosen the rear spring U-bolt nuts

13. Install the U-bolts and finger-tighten the nuts.
14. Connect the lower end of the shock absorber to the axle.
15. Tighten the bolts and nuts to the following specifications:
• Leaf spring-to-front bracket nut and bolt: 150–204 ft. lbs. (204–276 Nm)
• Leaf spring-to-rear bracket nut and bolt: 74–107 ft. lbs. (101–145 Nm)
• Rear shackle-to-frame nut and bolt: 74–107 ft. lbs. (101–145 Nm)
• Leaf spring-to-axle U-bolt nut on E-250 light duty models: 74–107 ft. lbs. (101–145 Nm)
• Leaf spring-to-axle U-bolt nut on standard duty E-250 and 350 models: 150–180 ft. lbs. (204–244 Nm)

1992–96 Models

▶ See Figure 43

1. Raise the rear of the van and support it with safety stands.
2. Support the weight of the rear axle with a floor jack.
3. Disconnect the lower end of the rear shock absorber from the axle.
4. Loosen the two U-bolts and remove the plate.
5. Lower the axle and remove the spring front bolt from the hanger.
6. Loosen the rear shackle-to-frame retaining bolts.
7. Remove the spring and shackle from the van.
8. Remove the shackle from the spring.
To install:
9. Engage the upper edge of the shackle to the spring and install the bolt.
10. Engage the front of the spring to the bracket and install the bolt.
11. Connect the spring and shackle to the rear bracket and install the bolts
12. Install the U-bolt plate over the nut of the center bolt.
13. Raise the axle with the floor jack , then assemble the spring center bolt in the pilot hole in the axle and install the plate.
14. Install the U-bolts and finger-tighten the nuts.
15. Connect the lower end of the shock absorber to the axle.
16. Tighten the bolts and nuts to the following specifications:
• Leaf spring-to-front bracket bolt on E-150 models: 110–137 ft. lbs. (150–185 Nm)
• Leaf spring-to-front bracket bolt on E-250 and 350 models: 240–290 ft. lbs. (325–393 Nm)

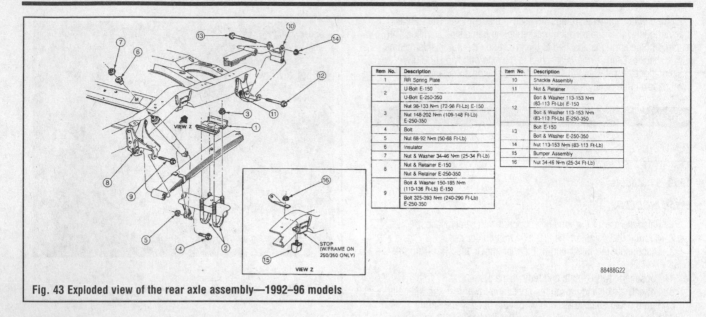

Fig. 43 Exploded view of the rear axle assembly—1992–96 models

Item No.	Description
1	RR Spring Plate
2	U-Bolt E-150
	U-Bolt E-250-350
3	Nut 98-133 N·m (72-98 Ft-Lb) E-150
	Nut 148-202 N·m (109-148 Ft-Lb) E-250-350
4	Bolt
5	Nut 68-92 N·m (50-68 Ft-Lb)
6	Insulator
7	Nut & Washer 34-46 N·m (25-34 Ft-Lb)
8	Nut & Retainer E-150
	Nut & Retainer E-250-350
9	Bolt & Washer 150-185 N·m (110-136 Ft-Lb) E-150
	Bolt 325-393 N·m (240-290 Ft-Lb) E-250-350

Item No.	Description
10	Shackle Assembly
11	Nut & Retainer
12	Bolt & Washer 113-153 N·m (83-113 Ft-Lb) E-150
	Bolt & Washer 113-153 N·m (83-113 Ft-Lb) E-250-350
13	Bolt E-150
	Bolt & Washer E-250-350
14	Nut 113-153 N·m (83-113 Ft-Lb)
15	Bumper Assembly
16	Nut 34-46 N·m (25-34 Ft-Lb)

• Leaf spring-to-rear shackle nut and bolt: 153–207 ft. lbs. (113–253 Nm)

• Leaf spring-to-axle U-bolt nut on E-150 models: 72–98 ft. lbs. (98–133 Nm)

• Leaf spring-to-axle U-bolt nut on E-250 and 350 models: 109–149 ft. lbs. (148–202 Nm)

Shock Absorbers

REMOVAL & INSTALLATION

◆ **See Figures 44, 45 and 46**

1. Raise and support the rear end on jackstands.
2. Remove the bolt and nut from the lower end of the shock absorber. Swing the lower end away from the bracket.

3. If necessary, use a back-up wrench on the upper shock stud to prevent rotation, then remove the upper mounting nut and washer.

To install:

4. Attach the upper end first, then the lower end; don't tighten the nuts yet. If you are installing new gas shocks, attach the upper end loosely, aim the lower end at its bracket and cut the strap holding the shock compressed. Once extended, these shocks are very difficult to compress by hand!

➡A back-up wrench may be necessary to hold the upper shock stud so that upper mounting nut can be tightened.

5. Attach the upper and lower ends of the shock absorbers.
6. Tighten the retainers on 1989–91 models as follows:
• Upper mount nut: 25–35 ft. lbs. (33–47 Nm)
• Lower mount nut and bolt: 52–74 ft. lbs. (70–100 Nm)
7. Tighten the retainers on 1992–96 models as follows:
• Upper mount nut: 26–33 ft. lbs. (35–44 Nm)
• Lower mount nut and bolt: 51–67 ft. lbs. (68–92 Nm)

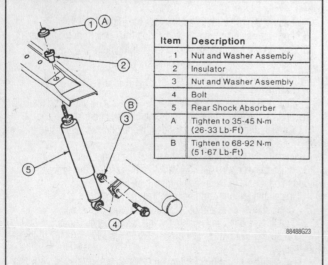

Item	Description
1	Nut and Washer Assembly
2	Insulator
3	Nut and Washer Assembly
4	Bolt
5	Rear Shock Absorber
A	Tighten to 35-45 N·m (26-33 Lb-Ft)
B	Tighten to 68-92 N·m (51-67 Lb-Ft)

Fig. 44 Exploded view of the rear shock absorber mounting

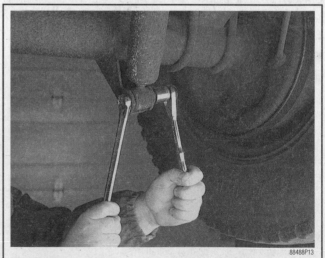

Fig. 45 Using a back-up wrench, loosen the lower shock absorber nut and bolt

Fig. 46 Unfasten the mounting nut from the upper stud and remove the shock absorber

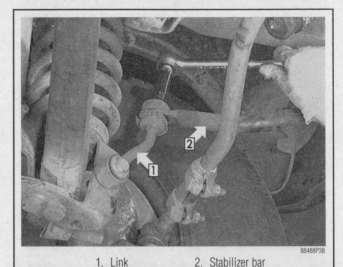

1. Link   2. Stabilizer bar

Fig. 48 Loosen the nut from the stabilizer bar link

TESTING

Refer to the Shock Absorber testing procedure under the Front Suspension portion of this section.

Stabilizer Bar

REMOVAL & INSTALLATION

▶ **See Figures 47 thru 52**

1. Loosen the nut from the lower end of the stabilizer bar link.
2. Remove the outer washer and insulator, then disconnect the rear stabilizer bar from the stabilizer bar link.
3. Remove the inner insulators and washers.
4. Disconnect the stabilizer bar link from the frame after loosening the nuts and bolts.
5. Loosen the bolts which retain the U-bolts to the axle.
6. Remove the stabilizer bar.
To install:
7. Install the stabilizer bar.

Fig. 49 Remove the nut and washer assemblies and set them aside

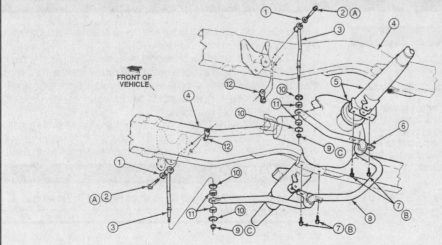

Item	Description
1	Flatwasher
2	Bolt
3	Stabilizer Bar Link
4	Frame
5	Rear Axle
6	Rear Stabilizer Bar Retainer
7	Bolt
8	Rear Stabilizer Bar
9	Nut
10	Washer
11	Insulator
12	Nut
A	Tighten to 55-85 N·m (41-63 Lb-Ft)
B	Tighten to 34-46 N·m (25-34 Lb-Ft)
C	Tighten to 24-31 N·m (18-23 Lb-Ft)

Fig. 47 Exploded view of the rear stabilizer bar components and mounting—1996 models

Fig. 50 Loosen the stabilizer bar-to-frame retainers and remove the bar

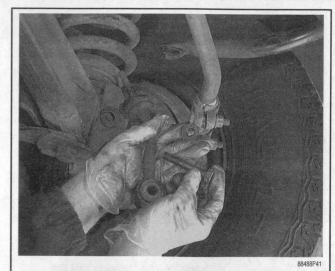

Fig. 52 . . . then remove the links from the van

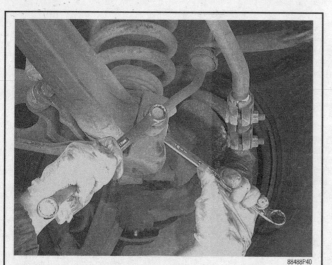

Fig. 51 To remove the links, loosen the link-to-frame retainers . . .

8. Fingertighten the bolts which retain the U-bolts to the axle.
9. Connect the stabilizer bar link to the frame and finger-tighten the nuts and bolts.
10. Install the inner insulators and washers.
11. Connect the rear stabilizer bar from the stabilizer bar link, then install the outer washer and insulator.
12. Tighten the nut to the lower end of the stabilizer bar link.
13. Tighten the retainers as follows:
- Stabilizer link-to-frame: 41–63 ft. lbs. (55–85 Nm)
- Stabilizer bar retainer-to-axle: 25–34 ft. lbs. (34–46 Nm)
- Stabilizer bar link-to-stabilizer bar: 18–23 ft. lbs. (24–31 Nm)

Rear Wheel Bearings

REMOVAL & INSTALLATION

Refer to the axle removal procedures in Section 7 of this manual for rear wheel bearing removal and installation.

STEERING

Steering Wheel

REMOVAL & INSTALLATION

➡The factory recommends that the front wheels be set in the straight-ahead position and you paint or make chalk marks on the column and steering wheel hub for alignment purposes during installation. Of these two safeguards, it is more important to mark the column so even if the column is moved slightly, the steering wheel can still be repositioned in its original position.

Models Without Air Bag

◆ See Figures 53 thru 59

1. Set the front wheel in the straight ahead position.
2. Disconnect the negative battery cable.
3. Remove the one screw from the underside of each steering wheel spoke, and lift the horn switch assembly (steering wheel pad) from the steering wheel. On vehicles equipped with the sport steering wheel option, pry the button cover off with a screwdriver.
4. Disengage the horn switch wires at the connector and remove the switch assembly. On vans equipped with speed control, squeeze the J-clip ground wire terminal firmly and pull it out of the hole in the steering wheel. Don't pull the wire out without squeezing the clip.
5. Remove the horn switch assembly.
6. Matchmark the relationship of the steering wheel to the steering shaft.
7. Remove the steering wheel retaining nut.
8. Use a steering wheel puller to draw the steering wheel from the shaft.

❊❊ WARNING

Never hammer on the wheel or shaft to remove it! Never use a knock-off type puller.

To install:
9. Position the steering wheel on the shaft so that the marks made during removal are aligned.
10. Install the retaining nut and tighten it to 30–42 ft. lbs. (41–56 Nm).

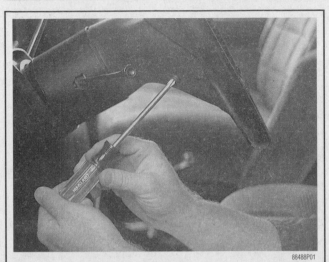

Fig. 53 Loosen the horn pad retaining screws from the underside of the steering wheel

Fig. 56 Matchmark the steering wheel-to-shaft location—this will aid during installation

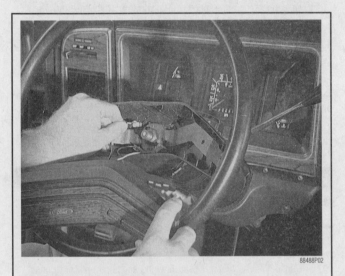

Fig. 54 Disconnect the horn switch wire

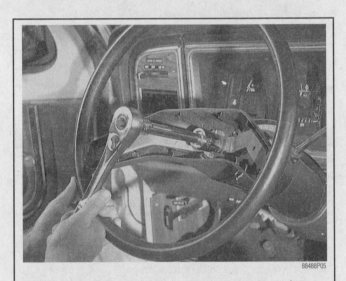

Fig. 57 Loosen the nut from the steering shaft

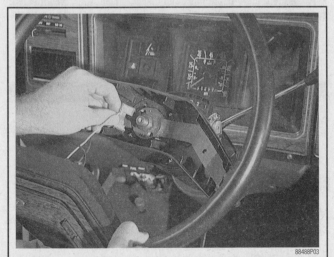

Fig. 55 On models equipped with speed control, squeeze the J-clip terminal to disconnect it

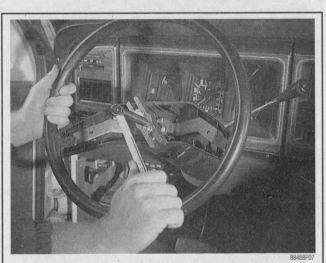

Fig. 58 Install a steering wheel puller—refer to the manufacturer's instructions on use and operation of the tool

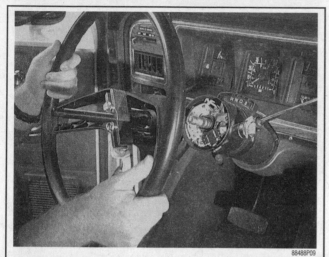

Fig. 59 Tighten the puller until the steering wheel is loose, then remove the wheel from the shaft

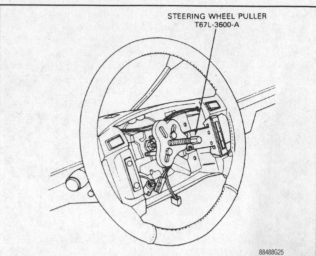

Fig. 61 Use a steering wheel puller to draw the steering wheel from the shaft

11. Engage the horn and speed control wires to the horn pad (if equipped).

12. Install the horn pad and tighten the screws.

13. Connect the negative battery cable.

14. Test drive the van and check for proper operation.

With Air Bag

▶ See Figures 60 and 61

❊❊ CAUTION

Read the air bag service precautions in Section 6 prior to performing any work involving an air bag equipped steering column component. Always wear safety glasses when servicing an air bag vehicle and handling the air bag to avoid possible injury.

1. Turn the front wheels to the straight-ahead position.

2. Disconnect the positive battery cable from the terminal or disengage the positive battery cable-to-starter relay cable for at least one minute to let the air bag back-up power supply discharge.

3. Remove the air bag module from the steering wheel (refer to Section 6).

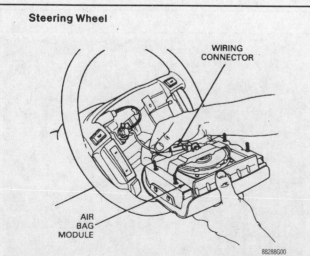

Fig. 60 Remove the air bag module and disconnect the wiring harnesses

4. Disconnect the horn/speed control wiring from the steering wheel.

5. Remove the steering wheel retaining bolt.

6. Use steering wheel puller T67L-3600-A, or equivalent, and remove the steering wheel. Route the contact assembly harnesses through the steering wheel as it is lifted off of the shaft.

To install:

➡**Make sure the front wheels are still in the straight-ahead position prior to installation.**

7. Route the air bag sliding contact wiring through the steering wheel at the 3 o'clock position. Position the steering wheel on the shaft an align the marks. Make sure not to pinch the contact wire.

❊❊ WARNING

Make sure no air gets trapped between the steering wheel and air bag sliding contact.

8. Install a new steering wheel retaining bolt, then tighten to 23–33 ft. lbs. (31–45 Nm).

9. Connect the horn/speed control wiring and clip in place. Connect the air bag wire harness. Tighten the module retaining nuts to 35–53 inch lbs. (4–6 Nm).

➡**When the battery cable has been disconnected, then reconnected, some abnormal driving symptoms may occur for the first 10 miles (16 km) until the PCM relearns it adaptive strategy.**

10. Connect the battery to starter cable. Verify the air bag warning indicator light on the instrument panel.

Turn Signal Switch

REMOVAL & INSTALLATION

1. Disconnect the negative battery cable.

This switch is a separate unit on 1989–91 models. On 1992–96 models the turn signal switch is incorporated into the multi-function switch.

2. Remove the steering wheel.

3. Remove the turn signal lever by unscrewing it from the steering column.

4. Disengage the turn signal indicator switch wiring connector plug by lifting up the tabs on the side of the plug and pulling it apart.

5. On fixed column equipped models with an automatic transmission remove the **PRNDL** lamp assembly and disengage it from the switch

6. Remove the switch assembly attaching screws.

7. On vans with a fixed column, lift the switch out of the column and guide the connector plug through the opening in the shift socket.

8. On vans with a tilt column, remove the connector plug before removing the switch from the column. The shift socket opening is not large enough for the plug connector to pass through. If equipped with an automatic transmission, remove the **PRNDL** lamp wire before removal of the switch.

To install:

9. Guide the disconnected wires of the switch through the opening's provided in the shift socket and left hand side of the brake and clutch pedal support bracket.

10. Engage the **PRNDL** lamp wire.

11. Fasten the switch retaining screws and engage all electrical connections to the switch that were removed.

12. Plug the switch harness into the main harness and make sure the vinyl sleeve cover all the wires were they pass through the brake and clutch pedal support bracket.

13. Install the turn signal lever.

14. Install the steering wheel and connect the negative battery cable.

Multi-Function Switch

REMOVAL & INSTALLATION

▶ See Figure 62

The multi-function switch provides electrical switch for the turn signal switch, headlamp dimmer, headlamp flash-to-pass, hazard warning, windshield washer and wiper switch. The assembly is mounted on the steering column.

✳✳ CAUTION

Read the air bag service precautions in Section 6 prior to doing work involving an air bag equipped steering column component. Always wear safety glasses when servicing an air bag vehicle and handling the air bag to avoid possible injury.

1. Disconnect the negative battery cable.

2. Loosen the retainers and remove the steering column shroud.

3. Loosen the self tapping screws that engage the switch to the column casting.

4. Tag and disengage the electrical connections from the switch being careful not to damage the locking tabs.

5. Remove the switch.

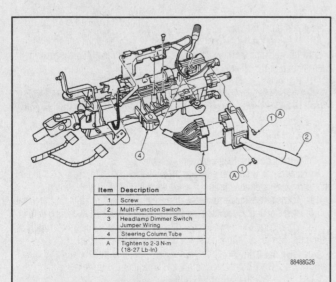

Item	Description
1	Screw
2	Multi-Function Switch
3	Headlamp Dimmer Switch Jumper Wiring
4	Steering Column Tube
A	Tighten to 2–3 N•m (18–27 Lb-In)

88488G26

Fig. 62 Exploded view of the multi-function switch

To install:

6. Engage the electrical connections and install the switch.

7. Install the self tapping screws and tighten them to 18–27 inch lbs. (2–3 Nm).

8. Check the **PRNDL** is correct when the transmission is shifted.

9. Install the shroud and tighten the retainers.

10. Connect the negative battery cable and check for proper switch operation.

Ignition Switch

REMOVAL & INSTALLATION

✳✳ CAUTION

Read the air bag service precautions in Section 6 prior to doing work involving an air bag equipped steering column component. Always wear safety glasses when servicing an air bag vehicle and handling the air bag to avoid possible injury.

1989–91 Models

1. Disconnect the battery ground cable.

2. Remove the steering column shroud and lower the steering column.

3. Disconnect the switch wiring at the multiple plug.

4. Remove the two nuts that retain the switch to the steering column.

5. Lift the switch vertically upward to disengage the actuator rod from the switch and remove the switch.

To install:

6. When installing the ignition switch, both the locking mechanism at the top of the column and the switch itself must be in the LOCK position for correct adjustment. To hold the mechanical parts of the column in the LOCK position, move the shift lever into PARK (with automatic transmissions) or REVERSE (with manual transmissions), turn the key to the LOCK position, and remove the key. New replacement switches, when received, are already pinned in the LOCK position by a metal shipping pin inserted in a locking hole on the side of the switch.

7. Engage the actuator rod in the switch.

8. Position the switch on the column and install the retaining nuts, but do not tighten them.

9. Move the switch up and down along the column to locate the mid-position of rod lash, and then tighten the retaining nuts, top nut first to 40–65 in. lbs. (4.5–7.3 Nm).

10. Remove the locking pin, connect the battery cable, and check for proper start in PARK or NEUTRAL.—Also check to make certain that the start circuit cannot be actuated in the DRIVE and REVERSE position.

11. Raise the steering column into position at instrument panel. Install steering column shroud.

1992–96 Models

▶ See Figure 63

1. Disconnect the positive battery cable from the starter relay.

2. Remove the steering wheel.

3. If necessary, lower the steering column for clearance.

4. Remove the steering column shroud.

5. Disengage the electrical connections from the switch.

6. Loosen the retainers and remove the ignition switch.

To install:

7. Install the switch. Align the pin from the switch with the slot in the column/lock assembly.

8. Position the slot with the index mark on the casting. The ignition switch should be in the run position.

9. Tighten the switch retainers to 44–62 in. lbs. (5–7 Nm).

10. Install the column shroud.

11. If lowered, raise the steering column and install the retainers.

12. Install the steering wheel.

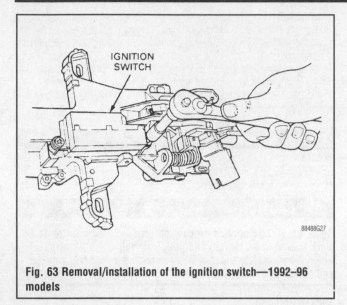

Fig. 63 Removal/installation of the ignition switch—1992–96 models

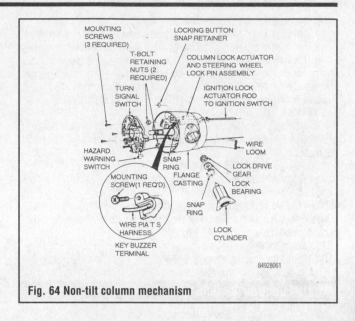

Fig. 64 Non-tilt column mechanism

13. Connect the battery to the starter relay, start the van and check for proper operation.

Ignition Lock Cylinder

REMOVAL & INSTALLATION

✳✳ CAUTION

Read the air bag service precautions in Section 6 prior to doing work involving an air bag equipped steering column component. Always wear safety glasses when servicing an air bag vehicle and handling the air bag to avoid possible injury.

With Key

1. Disconnect the battery ground cable.
2. On tilt columns, remove the upper extension shroud by unsnapping the shroud from the retaining clip at the 9 o'clock position.
3. Remove the trim shroud halves.
4. Unplug the wire connector at the key warning switch.
5. Place the shift lever in **PARK** and turn the key to **ON**.
6. Place a ⅛ in. wire pin in the hole in the casting surrounding the lock cylinder and depress the retaining pin while pulling out on the cylinder.
7. When installing the cylinder, turn the lock cylinder to the **RUN** position and depress the retaining pin, then insert the lock cylinder into its housing in the flange casting. Assure that the cylinder is fully seated and aligned in the interlocking washer before turning the key to the **OFF** position. This will allow the cylinder retaining pin to extend into the cylinder cast housing hole.
8. The remainder of installation is the reverse of removal.

Non-Functioning Cylinder or No Key Available

FIXED COLUMNS

▶ **See Figures 64 and 65**

1. Disconnect the battery ground cable.
2. Remove the steering wheel.
3. Remove the turn signal lever.
4. Remove the column trim shrouds.
5. Unbolt the steering column and lower it carefully.
6. Remove the ignition switch and warning buzzer and pin the switch in the LOCK position.
7. Remove the turn signal switch.

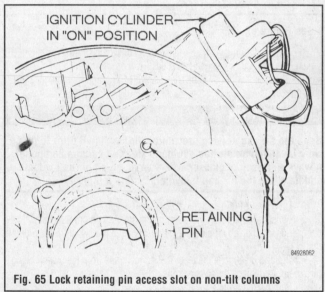

Fig. 65 Lock retaining pin access slot on non-tilt columns

8. Remove the snapring and T-bolt nuts that retain the flange casting to the column outer tube.
9. Remove the flange casting, upper shaft bearing, lock cylinder, ignition switch actuator and the actuator rod by pulling the entire assembly over the end of the steering column shaft.
10. Remove the lock actuator insert, the T-bolts and the automatic transmission indicator insert, or, with manual transmissions, the key release lever.
11. Upon reassembly, the following parts must be replaced with new parts:
- Flange
- Lock cylinder assembly
- Steering column lock gear
- Steering column lock bearing
- Steering column upper bearing retainer
- Lock actuator assembly
12. Assembly is a reversal of the disassembly procedure. It is best to install a new upper bearing. Check that the van starts only in PARK and NEUTRAL.

TILT COLUMNS

▶ **See Figures 66 and 67**

1. Disconnect the battery ground cable.
2. Remove the steering column shrouds.

3. Using masking tape, tape the gap between the steering wheel hub and the cover casting. Cover the entire circumference of the casting. Cover the seat and floor area with a drop-cloth.

4. Pull out the hazard switch and tape it in a downward position.

5. The lock cylinder retaining pin is located on the outside of the steering column cover casting adjacent to the hazard flasher button.

6. Tilt the steering column to the full up position and pre-punch the lock cylinder retaining pin with a sharp punch.

7. Using a ⅛ in. drill bit, mounted in a right angle drive drill adapter, drill out the retaining pin, going no deeper than ½ in. (12.7mm).

8. Tilt the column to the full down position. Place a chisel at the base of the ignition lock cylinder cap and using a hammer break away the cap from the lock cylinder.

9. Using a ⅜ in. drill bit, drill down the center of the ignition lock cylinder key slot about 1¾ in. (44mm), until the lock cylinder breaks loose from the steering column cover casting.

10. Remove the lock cylinder and the drill shavings.

11. Remove the steering wheel.

12. Remove the turn signal lever.

13. Remove the turn signal switch attaching screws.

14. Remove the key buzzer attaching screw.

15. Remove the turn signal switch up and over the end of the column, but don't disconnect the wiring.

16. Remove the 4 attaching screws from the cover casting and lift the casting over the end of the steering shaft, allowing the turn signal switch to pass through the casting. The removal of the casting cover will expose the upper actuator. Remove the upper actuator.

17. Remove the drive gear, snapring and washer from the cover casting along with the upper actuator.

18. Clean all components and replace any that appear damaged or worn.

19. Installation is the reverse of removal.

Steering Linkage

REMOVAL & INSTALLATION

Pitman Arm

▶ **See Figures 68, 69, 70, 71 and 72**

1. Place the wheels in a straight-ahead position.

2. Disconnect the drag link at the Pitman arm. You'll need a puller such as a tie rod end remover.

3. Remove the Pitman arm-to-gear nut and washer.

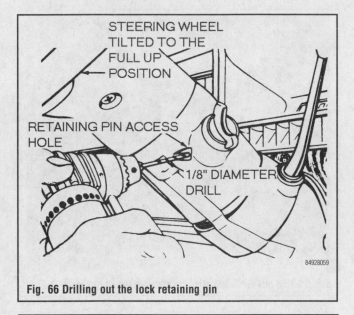

Fig. 66 Drilling out the lock retaining pin

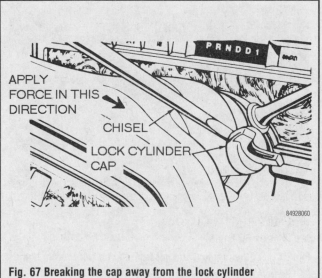

Fig. 67 Breaking the cap away from the lock cylinder

Fig. 68 Remove the cotter pin . . .

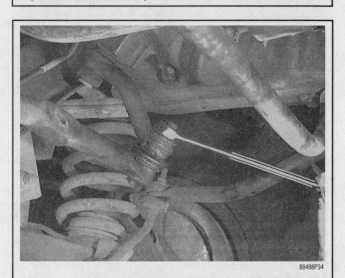

Fig. 69 . . . and loosen the drag link-to-Pitman arm retainer

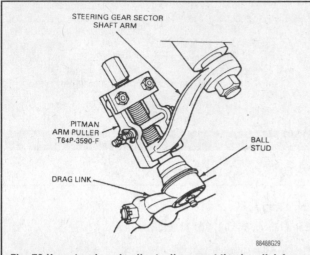

Fig. 70 Use a two-jawed puller to disconnect the drag link from the Pitman arm

4. Matchmark the Pitman arm and gear housing for installation purposes.
5. Using a 2-jawed puller, remove the Pitman arm from the gear.
To install:
6. Install the Pitman arm on the output sector shaft with wheels facing straight ahead.
7. Install the washer and nut or, nut and bolt and tighten to 170–230 ft. lbs. (230–210 Nm).
8. Install the drag link ball stud on the Pitman arm and tighten the ball stud nut to 51–73 ft. lbs. (70–100 Nm). Install the cotter pin.

Tie Rod and Drag Link

EXCEPT RUBBERIZED BALL SOCKET LINKAGE

▶ **See Figures 73, 74, 75 and 76**

1. Place the wheels in a straight-ahead position.
2. Remove the cotter pins and nuts from the drag link and tie rod ball studs.
3. Using a puller such as T64P-3590-F or its equivalent, remove the drag link ball studs from the right-hand spindle and Pitman arm.
4. Remove the tie rod ball studs from the left-hand spindle and drag link.
To install:
5. Position the drag link ball studs into the right hand spindle and Pitman arm. Install the tie rod end ball studs into the left hand spindle and drag link.

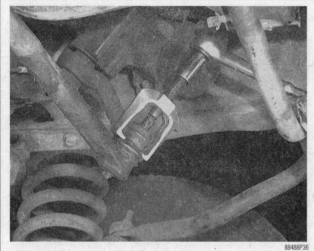

Fig. 71 Tighten the puller's bolt to separate the stud from the Pitman arm

Fig. 73 Use needlenosed pliers to remove the cotter pin . . .

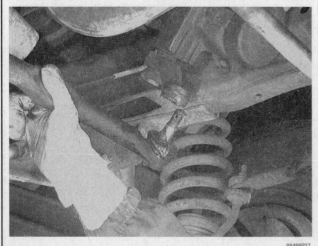

Fig. 72 After the stud is loose, disconnect the drag link from the Pitman arm

Fig. 74 . . . then remove the nut from the tie rod-to-drag link ball stud

Fig. 75 Use a puller to separate the tie rod from the drag link . . .

Fig. 76 . . . then disconnect the tie rod assembly

6. Seat the studs in the tapered hole before tightening the nuts. This will avoid wrap-up of the rubber grommets during tightening of the nuts. Tighten the nuts to 51–73 ft. lbs. (70–100 Nm). Always use new cotter pins.

7. Have the front end alignment checked.

RUBBERIZED BALL SOCKET LINKAGE

1. Raise and support the front end on jackstands.
2. Place the wheels in the straight-ahead position.
3. Remove the nuts connecting the drag link ball studs to the connecting rod and Pitman arm.
4. Disconnect the drag link using a tie rod end remover.
5. Loosen the bolts on the adjuster clamp. Count the number of turns it take to remove the drag link from the adjuster.

To install:

6. Installation is the reverse of the removal procedure. Install the drag link with the same number of turns it took to remove it. Make certain that the wheels remain in the straight-ahead position during installation. Seat the studs in the tapered hole before tightening the nuts. This will avoid wrap-up of the rubber grommets during tightening of the nuts. Tighten the adjuster clamp nuts to 40 ft. lbs. (54 Nm). Tighten the ball stud nuts to 75 ft. lbs. (102 Nm).

7. Have the front end alignment checked.

Connecting Rod

RUBBERIZED BALL SOCKET LINKAGE

1. Raise and support the front end on jackstands.
2. Place the wheels in the straight-ahead position.
3. Disconnect the connecting rod from the drag link by removing the nut and separating the two with a tie rod end remover.
4. Loosen the bolts on the adjusting sleeve clamps. Count the number of turns it takes to remove the connecting rod from the connecting rod from the adjuster sleeve and remove the rod.
5. Installation is the reverse of removal. Install the connecting rod the exact number of turns noted during removal. Tighten the tie rod nuts to 40 ft. lbs. (54 Nm); the ball stud nut to 75 ft. lbs. (102 Nm).
6. Have the front end alignment checked.

Tie Rod Ends

◗ See Figures 77 thru 82

1. Raise and support the front end on jackstands.
2. Place the wheels in a straight-ahead position.
3. Remove the ball stud from the Pitman arm using a tie rod end remover.

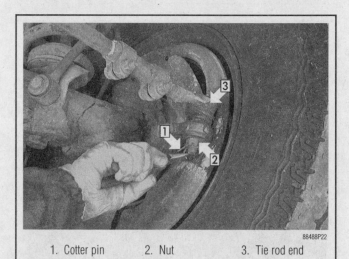

1. Cotter pin   2. Nut   3. Tie rod end

Fig. 77 Use pliers to straighten the ends of the cotter pin, then remove the pin

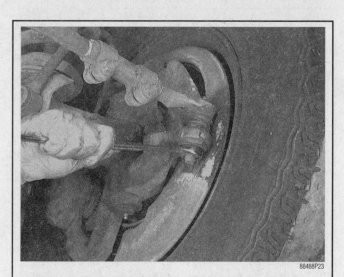

Fig. 78 Loosen the ball stud nut

Fig. 79 Use a pickle fork to separate the ball stud from the spindle

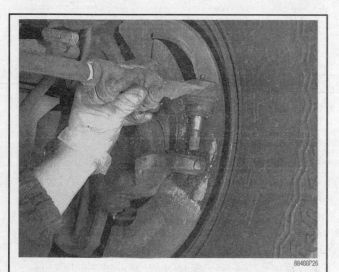

Fig. 80 Lift the tie rod to remove the ball stud from the spindle

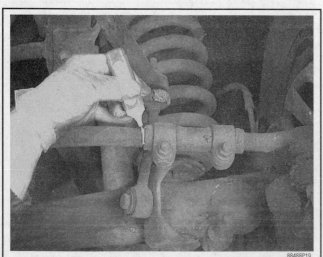

Fig. 81 Mark the threads on the tie rod at the adjusting clamp. This will aid during installation

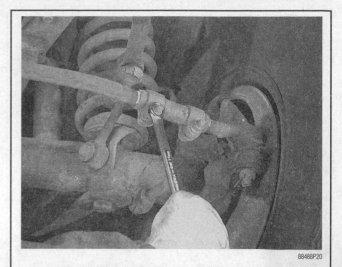

Fig. 82 Loosen the adjuster clamp nuts

➡Optional: paint a mark or measure the length of the tie rod end threads to ease reinstallation in as close to the original position as possible.

4. Loosen the nuts on the adjusting sleeve clamp. Remove the ball stud from the adjuster, or the adjuster from the tie rod. Count the number of turns it takes to remove the sleeve from the tie rod or ball stud from the sleeve.

To install:

5. Install the sleeve on the tie rod, or the ball in the sleeve the same number of turns noted during removal. Make sure that the adjuster clamps are in the correct position, illustrated, and torque the clamp bolts to 30–42 ft. lbs. (40–57 Nm).

6. Keep the wheels facing straight-ahead and install the ball studs. Tighten the nuts to 75 ft. lbs. (102 Nm). Use new cotter pins.

7. Install the drag link and connecting rod.

8. Have the front end alignment checked.

Power Steering Gear

REMOVAL & INSTALLATION

Ford Integral Power Steering Gear

▶ **See Figures 83 and 84**

1. Raise and support the front end on jackstands.
2. Place the wheels in the straight-ahead position.
3. Place a drain pan under the gear and disconnect the pressure (inlet) and return (outlet) lines. Cap the openings.
4. Remove the splash shield from the flex coupling.
5. Disconnect the flex coupling at the gear.
6. Matchmark and remove the Pitman arm from the sector shaft.
7. Support the steering gear and remove the mounting bolts.
8. Remove the steering gear. It may be necessary to work it free of the flex coupling.

To install:

9. Place the splash shield on the steering gear lugs.
10. Slide the flex coupling into place on the steering shaft. Make sure the steering wheel spokes are still horizontal.
11. Center the steering gear input shaft with the indexing flat facing downward.
12. Slide the steering gear input shaft into the flex coupling and into place on the frame side rail. Install the flex coupling bolt and tighten it to 20–35 ft. lbs. (28–47 Nm).

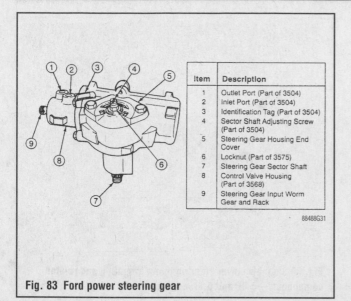

Item	Description
1	Outlet Port (Part of 3504)
2	Inlet Port (Part of 3504)
3	Identification Tag (Part of 3504)
4	Sector Shaft Adjusting Screw (Part of 3504)
5	Steering Gear Housing End Cover
6	Locknut (Part of 3575)
7	Steering Gear Sector Shaft
8	Control Valve Housing (Part of 3568)
9	Steering Gear Input Worm Gear and Rack

Fig. 83 Ford power steering gear

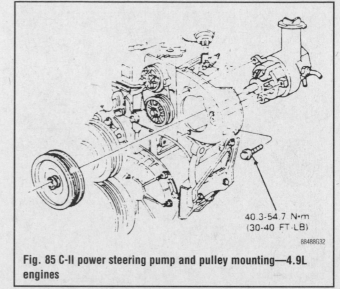

Fig. 85 C-II power steering pump and pulley mounting—4.9L engines

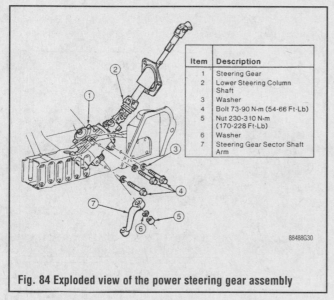

Item	Description
1	Steering Gear
2	Lower Steering Column Shaft
3	Washer
4	Bolt 73-90 N·m (54-66 Ft-Lb)
5	Nut 230-310 N·m (170-228 Ft-Lb)
6	Washer
7	Steering Gear Sector Shaft Arm

Fig. 84 Exploded view of the power steering gear assembly

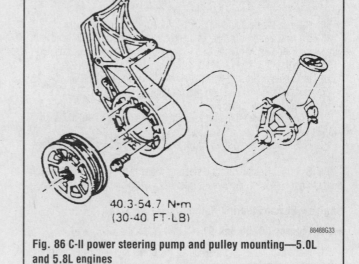

Fig. 86 C-II power steering pump and pulley mounting—5.0L and 5.8L engines

13. Install the gear mounting bolts and tighten them to 54–66 ft. lbs. (74–89 Nm).

14. Make sure that the wheels are still straight-ahead and install the Pitman arm. Tighten the nut to 230 ft. lbs. (312 Nm).

15. Connect the pressure line, and then the return line. Tighten the pressure line to 25 ft. lbs. (34 Nm).

16. Snap the flex coupling shield into place.

17. Fill the steering reservoir.

18. Run the engine and turn the steering wheel lock-to-lock several times to expel air. Check for leaks.

Power Steering Pump

REMOVAL & INSTALLATION

C-II Power Steering Pump

▶ See Figures 85, 86, 87 and 88

1. Disconnect the return line at the pump and drain the fluid into a container.

2. Disconnect the pressure line from the pump.

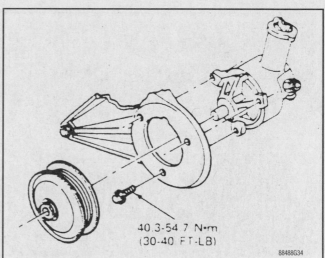

Fig. 87 C-II power steering pump and pulley mounting—7.5L engines

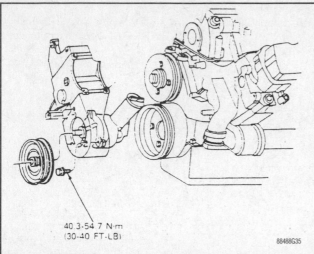

Fig. 88 C-II power steering pump and pulley mounting—7.3L diesel engines

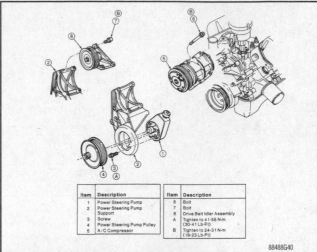

Item	Description	Item	Description
1	Power Steering Pump	6	Bolt
2	Power Steering Pump Support	7	Bolt
3	Screw	8	Drive Belt Idler Assembly
4	Power Steering Pump Pulley	A	Tighten to 41-55 N·m (30-41 Lb-Ft)
5	A/C Compressor	B	Tighten to 24-31 N·m (18-23 Lb-Ft)

Fig. 90 Saginaw power steering pump mounting and related components—5.0L and 5.8L engines

3. Loosen the pump bracket nuts and remove the drive belt. On the 4.9L engine or 5.0L engine with a serpentine drive belt, remove belt tension by lifting the tensioner out of position.

4. Remove the nuts and lift out the pump/bracket assembly.

5. If a new pump or bracket is being installed, you'll have to remove the pulley from the present pump. This is best done with a press and adapters.

To install:

6. Install the pump and tighten the retainer to 30–40 ft. lbs. (40–54 Nm).

7. Install the power steering pump pulley.

8. Install the drive belt.

9. Install and tighten the pressure hose tube nut to 30–40 ft. lbs. (40–54 Nm).

10. Fill the reservoir with the correct grade and amount of power steering fluid.

11. Start the van and turn the steering wheel to the left or the right without hitting the stops to remove air from the system and check for leaks.

Saginaw Power Steering Pump

▶ **See Figures 89, 90 and 91**

1. Place a suitable container under the power steering reservoir pump hose, then disconnect the hose from the pump and drain the fluid.

2. Disconnect the power steering pressure hose from the pump.

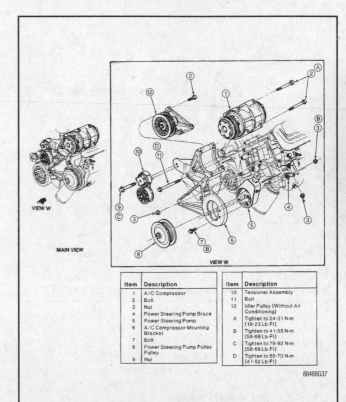

Item	Description	Item	Description
1	A/C Compressor	10	Tensioner Assembly
2	Bolt	11	Bolt
3	Nut	12	Idler Pulley (Without Air Conditioning)
4	Power Steering Pump Brace	A	Tighten to 24-31 N·m (18-23 Lb-Ft)
5	Power Steering Pump	B	Tighten to 41-55 N·m (58-68 Lb-Ft)
6	A/C Compressor Mounting Bracket	C	Tighten to 78-92 N·m (58-68 Lb-Ft)
7	Bolt	D	Tighten to 55-70 N·m (41-52 Lb-Ft)
8	Power Steering Pump Pulley Pulley		
9	Nut		

Fig. 91 Saginaw power steering pump mounting and related components—7.5L engine

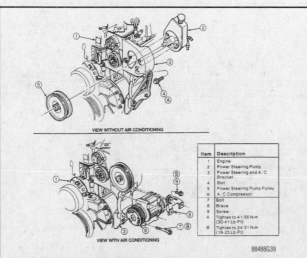

Item	Description
1	Engine
2	Power Steering Pump
3	Power Steering and A/C Bracket
4	Bolt
5	Power Steering Pump Pulley
6	A/C Compressor
7	Bolt
8	Brace
9	Screw
A	Tighten to 41-55 N·m (30-41 Lb-Ft)
B	Tighten to 24-31 N·m (18-23 Lb-Ft)

Fig. 89 Saginaw power steering pump mounting and related components—4.9L engine

3. Remove the drive belt.

4. Remove the pump pulley as follows:

a. If necessary, remove the fan shroud.

b. Install pulley removal tool T69L-10300-B or equivalent onto the hub of the pulley.

c. While holding the nut of the removal tool stationary, rotate the inner spindle of the tool clockwise until the pulley is pulled from the shaft.

5. Loosen the pump retainers and remove the pump from the engine compartment.

To install:

6. Install the pump and tighten the retainers to 30–40 ft. lbs. (41–55 Nm).

7. Install the pulley as follows:

   a. Place the pulley in position and tighten the screw stud of steering pump pulley replacer T65P-3A733-C or equivalent into the end of the pump rotor shaft.

   b. While holding the inner spindle of the tool, rotate the tool nut clockwise until the hub face of pulley is flush with end of the pump rotor shaft.

8. Install the drive belt and fan shroud.
9. Connect the pressure lines and tighten to 22–29 ft. lbs. (30–40 Nm).
10. Fill the reservoir with the correct grade and amount of power steering fluid.
11. Start the van and turn the steering wheel to the left or the right without hitting the stops to remove air from the system and check for leaks.

TORQUE SPECIFICATIONS

System	Component	Ft. Lbs.	Nm
Wheels			
	Lug nuts		
	1989-95 E-150 models	100	135
	1989-95 E-250 and 350 models	140	190
	1996 E-150 models	74-133	100-180
	1996 E-250 and 350 models	126-170	170-230
Front suspension			
	Coil Springs		
	1989-91 Models		
	Upper retaining bolts	20-30	28-40
	Lower attaching nuts	70-100	95-135
	1992-96 Models		
	Upper retaining bolts	19-26	25-35
	Lower attaching nuts	191-245	255-345
	Shock Absorbers		
	1989-91 models		
	Hex	18-28	25-37
	Bolt and nut	40-60	55-81
	1992-96 models	25-35	34-47
	Hex	25-35	34-47
	Bolt and nut	50-68	68-92
	Front Wheel Spindle Pins		
	Lockwasher and nut	40-60	54-81
	Spindle pin plugs	35-50	48-67
	Steering linkage-to-spindle nut	70-100	95-135
	Radius Arm		
	1989-94 Models		
	Radius arm attaching nut	120	162
	Radius arm-to-axle bolt	240-320	326-433
	1995-96 Models		
	Radius arm-to-axle bolt	188-254	255-345
	Stabilizer Bar		
	1989-91 Models		
	Locknut	40-60	55-81
	Stabilizer bar retainers	18-28	25-37
	1992-96 Models		
	Stabilizer bar screws	15-21	21-29
	Front Wheel Spindle		
	Upper and lower ball joint stud nut	109-149	148-202
Rear Suspension			
	Springs		
	1989-91 E-150 Models		
	Leaf spring-to-front bracket nut and bolt	150-204	204-276
	Leaf spring-to-rear bracket nut and bolt	74-107	101-145
	Rear shackle-to-frame nut and bolt	74-107	101-145
	Leaf spring-to-axle U-bolt nut	74-107	101-145
	1989-91 E-250 and 350 Models		
	Leaf spring-to-front bracket nut and bolt	150-204	04-276
	Leaf spring-to-rear bracket nut and bolt	74-107	101-145
	Rear shackle-to-frame nut and bolt	74-107	101-145
	Leaf spring-to-axle U-bolt nut E-250 Light duty models	74-107	101-145

88488C01

TORQUE SPECIFICATIONS

System	Component	Ft. Lbs.	Nm
Rear Suspension	Leaf spring-to-axle U-bolt nut E-250 and 350 models	150-180	204-244
	1992-96 E-150 models		
	Leaf spring-to-front bracket bolt	110-137	150-185
	1992-96 E-250 and 350 models		
	Leaf spring-to-front bracket bolt	240-290	325-393
	Leaf spring-to-rear shackle nut and bolt	153-207	113-253
	Leaf spring-to-axle U-bolt nut E-150 models	72-98	98-133
	Leaf spring-to-axle U-bolt nut E-250 and 350 models	109-149	148-202
Shock Absorbers	1989-91 models		
	Upper mount nut	25-35	33-47
	Lower mount nut and bolt	52-74	70-100
	1992-96 models		
	Upper mount nut	26-33	35-44
	Lower mount nut and bolt	51-67	68-92
Stabilizer Bar	Stabilizer link-to-frame	41-63	55-85
	Stabilizer bar retainer-to-axle	25-34	34-46
	Stabilizer bar link-to-stabilizer bar	18-23	24-31
Steering	Steering Wheel retaining nut		
	Models Without Airbag	30-42	41-56
	With Air Bag	23-33	31-45
	Multi-Function Switch		
	Self tapping screws	18-27 inch lbs.	2-3
	Ignition Switch		
	1989-91 Models		
	Switch retaining nuts	40-65 inch lbs.	4.5-7.3
	1992-96 Models		
	Switch retainers	44-62 inch lbs	5-7
	Pitman Arm		
	Nut or, nut and bolt	170-230	230-210
	Ball stud nut	51-73	70-100
	Tie Rod and Drag Link		
	Except rubberized ball socket linkage		
	Retaining nuts	51-73	70-100
	Rubberized ball socket linkage		
	Adjuster clamp nuts	40	54
	Ball stud nuts	75	102
	Tie Rod Ends		
	Adjuster clamp	30-42	40-57
	Power Steering Gear		
	Ford Integral Power Steering Gear		
	Flex coupling bolt	20-35	28-47
	Gear mounting bolts	54-66	74-89
	Pressure line	25	34
	Power Steering Pump		
	C-II Power Steering Pump		
	Pump bolt and pressure hose tube nut	30-40	40-54
	Saginaw Power Steering Pump		
	Pump retainers	30-40	41-55

88488C02

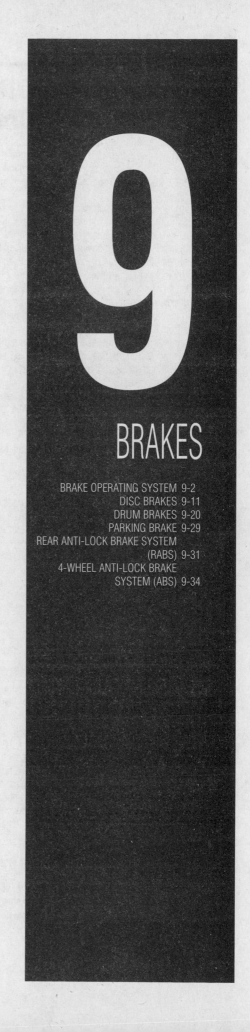

9

BRAKES

BRAKE OPERATING SYSTEM

Basic Operating Principles

Hydraulic systems are used to actuate the brakes of all modern automotive vehicles. The system transports the power required to force the frictional surfaces of the braking system together from the pedal to the individual brake units at each wheel. A hydraulic system is used for two reasons.

First, fluid under pressure can be carried to all parts of a vehicle by small pipes and flexible hoses without taking up a significant amount of room or posing routing problems.

Second, a great mechanical advantage can be given to the brake pedal end of the system, and the foot pressure required to actuate the brakes can be reduced by making the surface area of the master cylinder pistons smaller than that of any of the pistons in the wheel cylinders or calipers.

The master cylinder consists of a fluid reservoir along with a double cylinder and piston assembly. Double type master cylinders are designed to separate the front and rear braking systems hydraulically in case of a leak. The master cylinder coverts mechanical motion from the pedal into hydraulic pressure within the lines. This pressure is translated back into mechanical motion at the wheels by either the wheel cylinder (drum brakes) or the caliper (disc brakes).

Steel lines carry the brake fluid to a point on the vehicle's frame near each of the vehicle's wheels. The fluid is then carried to the calipers and wheel cylinders by flexible tubes in order to allow for suspension and steering movements.

In drum brake systems, each wheel cylinder contains two pistons, one at either end, which push outward in opposite directions and force the brake shoe into contact with the drum.

In disc brake systems, the cylinders are part of the calipers. At least one cylinder in each caliper is used to force the brake pads against the disc.

All pistons employ some type of seal, usually made of rubber, to minimize fluid leakage. A rubber dust boot seals the outer end of the cylinder against dust and dirt. The boot fits around the outer end of the piston on disc brake calipers, and around the brake actuating rod on wheel cylinders.

The hydraulic system operates as follows: When at rest, the entire system, from the piston(s) in the master cylinder to those in the wheel cylinders or calipers, is full of brake fluid. Upon application of the brake pedal, fluid trapped in front of the master cylinder piston(s) is forced through the lines to the wheel cylinders. Here, it forces the pistons outward, in the case of drum brakes, and inward toward the disc, in the case of disc brakes. The motion of the pistons is opposed by return springs mounted outside the cylinders in drum brakes, and by spring seals, in disc brakes.

Upon release of the brake pedal, a spring located inside the master cylinder immediately returns the master cylinder pistons to the normal position. The pistons contain check valves and the master cylinder has compensating ports drilled in it. These are uncovered as the pistons reach their normal position. The piston check valves allow fluid to flow toward the wheel cylinders or calipers as the pistons withdraw. Then, as the return springs force the brake pads or shoes into the released position, the excess fluid reservoir through the compensating ports. It is during the time the pedal is in the released position that any fluid that has leaked out of the system will be replaced through the compensating ports.

Dual circuit master cylinders employ two pistons, located one behind the other, in the same cylinder. The primary piston is actuated directly by mechanical linkage from the brake pedal through the power booster. The secondary piston is actuated by fluid trapped between the two pistons. If a leak develops in front of the secondary piston, it moves forward until it bottoms against the front of the master cylinder, and the fluid trapped between the pistons will operate the rear brakes. If the rear brakes develop a leak, the primary piston will move forward until direct contact with the secondary piston takes place, and it will force the secondary piston to actuate the front brakes. In either case, the brake pedal moves farther when the brakes are applied, and less braking power is available.

All dual circuit systems use a switch to warn the driver when only half of the brake system is operational. This switch is usually located in a valve body which is mounted on the firewall or the frame below the master cylinder. A hydraulic piston receives pressure from both circuits, each circuit's pressure being applied to one end of the piston. When the pressures are in balance, the piston remains stationary. When one circuit has a leak, however, the greater pressure in that circuit during application of the brakes will push the piston to one side, closing the switch and activating the brake warning light.

In disc brake systems, this valve body also contains a metering valve and, in some cases, a proportioning valve. The metering valve keeps pressure from traveling to the disc brakes on the front wheels until the brake shoes on the rear wheels have contacted the drums, ensuring that the front brakes will never be used alone. The proportioning valve controls the pressure to the rear brakes to lessen the chance of rear wheel lock-up during very hard braking.

Warning lights may be tested by depressing the brake pedal and holding it while opening one of the wheel cylinder bleeder screws. If this does not cause the light to go on, substitute a new lamp, make continuity checks, and, finally, replace the switch as necessary.

The hydraulic system may be checked for leaks by applying pressure to the pedal gradually and steadily. If the pedal sinks very slowly to the floor, the system has a leak. This is not to be confused with a springy or spongy feel due to the compression of air within the lines. If the system leaks, there will be a gradual change in the position of the pedal with a constant pressure.

Check for leaks along all lines and at wheel cylinders. If no external leaks are apparent, the problem is inside the master cylinder.

DISC BRAKES

Instead of the traditional expanding brakes that press outward against a circular drum, disc brake systems utilize a disc (rotor) with brake pads positioned on either side of it. An easily-seen analogy is the hand brake arrangement on a bicycle. The pads squeeze onto the rim of the bike wheel, slowing its motion. Automotive disc brakes use the identical principle but apply the braking effort to a separate disc instead of the wheel.

The disc (rotor) is a casting, usually equipped with cooling fins between the two braking surfaces. This enables air to circulate between the braking surfaces making them less sensitive to heat buildup and more resistant to fade. Dirt and water do not drastically affect braking action since contaminants are thrown off by the centrifugal action of the rotor or scraped off the by the pads. Also, the equal clamping action of the two brake pads tends to ensure uniform, straight line stops. Disc brakes are inherently self-adjusting. There are three general types of disc brake:

1. A fixed caliper.
2. A floating caliper.
3. A sliding caliper.

The fixed caliper design uses two pistons mounted on either side of the rotor (in each side of the caliper). The caliper is mounted rigidly and does not move.

The sliding and floating designs are quite similar. In fact, these two types are often lumped together. In both designs, the pad on the inside of the rotor is moved into contact with the rotor by hydraulic force. The caliper, which is not held in a fixed position, moves slightly, bringing the outside pad into contact with the rotor. There are various methods of attaching floating calipers. Some pivot at the bottom or top, and some slide on mounting bolts. In any event, the end result is the same.

DRUM BRAKES

Drum brakes employ two brake shoes mounted on a stationary backing plate. These shoes are positioned inside a circular drum which rotates with the wheel assembly. The shoes are held in place by springs. This allows them to slide toward the drums (when they are applied) while keeping the linings and drums in alignment. The shoes are actuated by a wheel cylinder which is mounted at the top of the backing plate. When the brakes are applied, hydraulic pressure forces the wheel cylinder's actuating links outward. Since these links bear directly against the top of the brake shoes, the tops of the shoes are then forced against the inner side of the drum. This action forces the bottoms of the two shoes to contact the brake drum by rotating the entire assembly slightly (known as servo action). When pressure within the wheel cylinder is relaxed, return springs pull the shoes back away from the drum.

Most modern drum brakes are designed to self-adjust themselves during application when the vehicle is moving in reverse. This motion causes both shoes to rotate very slightly with the drum, rocking an adjusting lever, thereby causing rotation of the adjusting screw. Some drum brake systems are designed to self-adjust during application whenever the brakes are applied. This on-board adjustment system reduces the need for maintenance adjustments and keeps both the brake function and pedal feel satisfactory.

POWER BOOSTERS

Virtually all modern vehicles use a vacuum assisted power brake system to multiply the braking force and reduce pedal effort. Since vacuum is always available when the engine is operating, the system is simple and efficient. A vacuum diaphragm is located on the front of the master cylinder and assists the driver in applying the brakes, reducing both the effort and travel he must put into moving the brake pedal.

The vacuum diaphragm housing is normally connected to the intake manifold by a vacuum hose. A check valve is placed at the point where the hose enters the diaphragm housing, so that during periods of low manifold vacuum brakes assist will not be lost.

Depressing the brake pedal closes off the vacuum source and allows atmospheric pressure to enter on one side of the diaphragm. This causes the master cylinder pistons to move and apply the brakes. When the brake pedal is released, vacuum is applied to both sides of the diaphragm and springs return the diaphragm and master cylinder pistons to the released position.

If the vacuum supply fails, the brake pedal rod will contact the end of the master cylinder actuator rod and the system will apply the brakes without any power assistance. The driver will notice that much higher pedal effort is needed to stop the vehicle and that the pedal feels harder than usual.

Vacuum Leak Test

1. Operate the engine at idle without touching the brake pedal for at least one minute.
2. Turn off the engine and wait one minute.
3. Test for the presence of assist vacuum by depressing the brake pedal and releasing it several times. If vacuum is present in the system, light application will produce less and less pedal travel. If there is no vacuum, air is leaking into the system.

System Operation Test

1. With the engine **OFF**, pump the brake pedal until the supply vacuum is entirely gone.
2. Put light, steady pressure on the brake pedal.
3. Start the engine and let it idle. If the system is operating correctly, the brake pedal should fall toward the floor if the constant pressure is maintained.

Power brake systems may be tested for hydraulic leaks just as ordinary systems are tested.

Brake Light Switch

REMOVAL & INSTALLATION

♦ See Figure 1

1. Lift the locking tab on the switch connector and disconnect the wiring.
2. Remove the hairpin retainer, slide the stop lamp switch, pushrod and nylon washer off of the pedal. Remove the washer, then the switch by sliding it up or down.

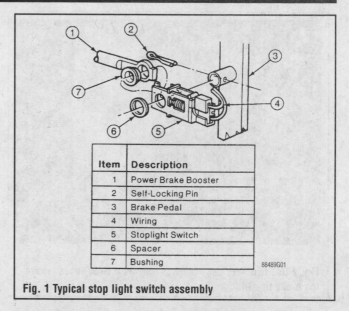

Item	Description
1	Power Brake Booster
2	Self-Locking Pin
3	Brake Pedal
4	Wiring
5	Stoplight Switch
6	Spacer
7	Bushing

88489G01

Fig. 1 Typical stop light switch assembly

➡**On vans equipped with speed control, the spacer washer is replaced by the dump valve adapter washer. To install:**

3. Position it so that the U-shaped side is nearest the pedal and directly over/under the pin.
4. Slide the switch up or down, trapping the master cylinder pushrod and bushing between the switch side plates.
5. Push the switch and pushrod assembly firmly towards the brake pedal arm. Assemble the outside white plastic washer to the pin and install the hairpin retainer.

✳✳ CAUTION

Don't substitute any other type of retainer. Use only the Ford specified hairpin retainer.

6. Assemble the connector on the switch.
7. Check stop lamp operation.

✳✳ CAUTION

Make sure that the stop lamp switch wiring has sufficient travel during a full pedal stroke!

Master Cylinder

REMOVAL & INSTALLATION

♦ See Figures 2, 3, 4, 5 and 6

1. Disconnect the negative battery cable and if necessary, remove the battery.
2. Apply the brake pedal several times to exhaust all the vacuum in the system.
3. If equipped with a Hydro-boost booster, loosen the two power steering fluid line bracket nuts, then remove the bracket.
4. If equipped, detach the brake warning indicator connector.
5. Detach and cap the brake lines from the master cylinder.

➡**A turkey baster (tapered tube with a squeeze ball on top) works well for removing fluid from the reservoir (see photo).**

6. Siphon off the fluid from the master cylinder reservoir to minimize spillage when lines are disconnected.
7. If applicable, disconnect and cap the Hydraulic Control Unit (HCU) supply hose at the master cylinder reservoir and secure in a position to prevent loss of fluid.

Fig. 2 Use two flare nut wrenches (one as a back-up) to loosen the brake line fittings

Fig. 5 Remove the master cylinder-to-booster retaining nuts . . .

Fig. 3 Disconnect the brake line from the master cylinder, being careful not to kink or break it

Fig. 6 . . . and remove the master cylinder from the engine compartment

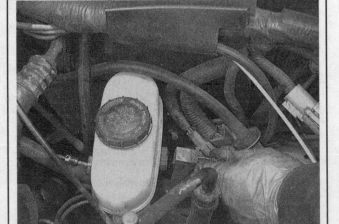

Fig. 4 Unplug the brake warning indicator light, if equipped

8. Unfasten the nuts that attach the master cylinder to the brake booster.

9. Remove the master cylinder from the booster by sliding it forward and upward from the vehicle.

To install:

10. Before installation on models equipped with a brake booster, check the distance from the outer end of the booster assembly pushrod, to the front face of booster assembly and turn the rod adjusting screw until the desired length is achieved. Refer to the accompanying illustration for specifications.

11. Position the master cylinder assembly over the booster pushrod and onto the 2 studs on the booster assembly.

12. Install the retaining nuts, then tighten to 18–25 ft. lbs. (24–34 Nm).

13. Uncap and connect the brake lines to the master cylinder.

14. On 1989–93 models, tighten the fittings to 18–25 ft. lbs. (24–34 Nm). On 1994–96 models, tighten the front fitting to 16–21 ft. lbs. (21–29 Nm), and the rear fitting to 10–15 ft. lbs. (15–20 Nm).

15. If equipped, uncap and connect the HCU hose to the master cylinder reservoir fitting and secure with a hose clamp.

16. If equipped, connect the brake warning indicator.

17. Fill the master cylinder with Heavy Duty Brake Fluid

6AZ-19542-AA or equivalent DOT 3 brake fluid from a clean, sealed container. Bleed the entire brake system, as outlined in this section.

18. Connect the negative battery cable.

19. Operate the brake several times, then check for external hydraulic leaks.

Power Brake Booster

REMOVAL & INSTALLATION

Single and Tandem Diaphragm Models

E-150–350 MODELS

▶ **See Figure 7**

1. Disconnect the brake light switch wires.

2. If equipped, remove the wraparound clip from the booster inboard stud.

3. Support the master cylinder from below, with a prop of some kind.

4. Loosen the clamp and remove the booster check valve hose.

5. Remove the master cylinder from the booster. Keep it supported. It will not be necessary to disconnect the brake lines.

6. Working inside the van below the instrument panel, remove the cotter pin and slide the stop lamp switch, spacers and the bushing off the brake pedal arm.

7. Remove the booster-to-bracket panel attaching nuts.

8. Remove the booster from the engine compartment.

To install:

9. Install the booster in the engine compartment by sliding the bracket mounting bolts and valve operating rod through the holes in the dash panel. Install the attaching nuts and tighten to 10–18 ft. lbs. (13–25 Nm).

10. Install the check valve and connect the manifold vacuum hose to the booster.

11. Install the master cylinder. Tighten the nuts to 18–25 ft. lbs. (24–34 Nm) on 1989–90 models, 13–25 ft. lbs. (17–34 Nm) on 1992–94 models and 15–21 ft. lbs. (20–28 Nm).

12. Install the wraparound clip.

13. Connect the stop light switch wires.

14. Working inside the van below the instrument panel, connect the pushrod and stop light switch.

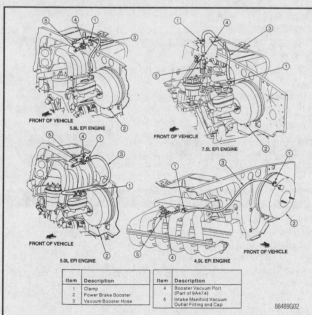

Item	Description
1	Clamp
2	Power Brake Booster
3	Vacuum Booster Hose

Item	Description
4	Booster Vacuum Port (Part of 9A474)
5	Intake Manifold Vacuum Outlet Fitting and Cap

88489G02

Fig. 7 Single and tandem power brake booster hose routing

RV CHASSIS

▶ **See Figure 8**

1. Disconnect the brake light switch wires.

2. Support the master cylinder from below, with a prop of some kind.

3. Loosen the clamp and remove the booster check valve hose and valve.

4. Remove the master cylinder from the booster. Keep it supported. It will not be necessary to disconnect the brake lines.

5. Working inside the van below the instrument panel, remove the 4 nuts attaching the booster to the bell crank.

6. Remove the booster from the bell crank.

To install:

7. Install the booster on the bell crank and make sure the pushrod engages the bell crank arm.

8. Installing the attaching nuts and tighten them to 13–25 ft. lbs. (17–34 Nm) on 1992–94 models and .

9. Install the master cylinder.

10. Connect the manifold vacuum hose to the booster.

11. Connect the stop light switch wires.

12. Working inside the van below the instrument panel, connect the pushrod and stoplight switch.

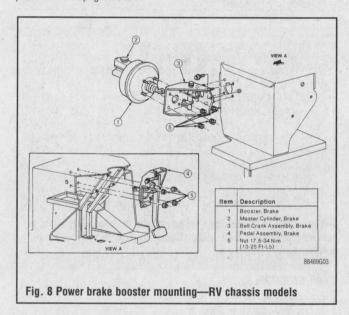

Item	Description
1	Booster, Brake
2	Master Cylinder, Brake
3	Bell Crank Assembly, Brake
4	Pedal Assembly, Brake
5	Nut 17.5-34 N·m (13-25 Ft-Lb)

88489G03

Fig. 8 Power brake booster mounting—RV chassis models

Hydro-Boost

The Hydro-Boost assembly contains a valve which controls pump pressure while braking, a lever to control the position of the valve and a boost piston to provide the force to operate a conventional master cylinder attached to the front of the booster. The Hydro-Boost also has a reserve system, designed to store sufficient pressurized fluid to provide at least 2 brake applications in the event of insufficient fluid flow from the power steering pump. The brakes can also be applied unassisted if the reserve system is depleted.

❋❋ WARNING

Before removing the Hydro-Boost, discharge the accumulator by making several brake applications until a hard pedal is felt.

1989–94 MODELS

1. Disconnect the negative battery cable.

2. Apply the brake pedal several times to exhaust all the vacuum in the system.

3. Remove the master cylinder from the booster. Keep it supported. It will not be necessary to disconnect the brake lines.

Do not depress the brake pedal with the master cylinder removed!

4. Disconnect the hydraulic lines from the booster.
5. Disconnect the input pushrod from the brake pedal bell crank assembly.
6. Loosen the booster retaining nuts and remove the booster.

Do not drop the booster or carried by the accumulator. Check the accumulator snapring for proper seating. The accumulator contains high pressure nitrogen gas and can be dangerous if mishandled or exposed to excessive heat.

To install:

7. Install the booster and tighten the retainers to 16–22 ft. lbs. (22–30 Nm).
8. Connect the input pushrod to the brake pedal bell crank assembly or pedal-to-pushrod linkage.
9. Install the master cylinder.
10. Connect the hoses to the booster and bleed the system as follows:
   a. Fill the pump reservoir with automatic transmission fluid.
   b. Disconnect the coil wire and crank the engine for several seconds. Do not start the engine.
   c. Check the fluid level and connect the coil wire.
   d. Start the engine and turn the wheels lock-to-lock twice, then turn the engine off.
   e. Depress the brake pedal several times to discharge the accumulator.
   f. Repeat Step D.
   g. If foaming occurs, stop the engine and allow the foam to dissipate.
   h. Repeat Step D until all the air is removed from the system.

➡The system is usually self-bleeding, and the procedure outlined will normally bleed the booster. Normal operation of the van will further remove trapped air.

1995–96 MODELS

▶ **See Figure 9**

1. Disconnect the negative battery cable and if necessary, remove the battery.
2. Apply the brake pedal several times to exhaust all the vacuum in the system.
3. Disconnect the two metal lines and one rubber hose from the booster.
4. Remove the two nuts and the metal line retainer.
5. Disconnect the wire harness retainer from the power steering reservoir bracket.
6. Disengage the low brake fluid switch connector.
7. Remove the master cylinder from the booster. Keep it supported.

Do not depress the brake pedal with the master cylinder removed!

8. Disconnect the pushrod from the brake pedal.
9. Loosen the booster retaining nuts and remove the booster.

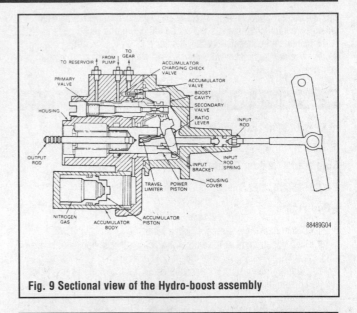

Fig. 9 Sectional view of the Hydro-boost assembly

Do not drop the booster or carried by the accumulator. Check the accumulator snapring for proper seating. The accumulator contains high pressure Nitrogen gas and can be dangerous if mishandled or exposed to excessive heat.

To install:

10. Install the booster and tighten the retainers to 16–21 ft. lbs. (21–28 Nm).
11. Connect the pushrod to the brake pedal.
12. Install the master cylinder.
13. Connect the hoses and tube to the booster.
14. Engage the brake fluid level switch connector.
15. Engage the wire harness retainer to the power steering reservoir bracket.
16. Install the battery and connect the cables.
17. Bleed the system as follows:
   a. Fill the pump reservoir with automatic transmission fluid.
   b. Disconnect the coil wire and crank the engine for several seconds. Do not start the engine.
   c. Check the fluid level and connect the coil wire.
   d. Start the engine and turn the wheels lock-to-lock twice, then turn the engine off.
   e. Depress the brake pedal several times to discharge the accumulator.
   f. Repeat step D.
   g. If foaming occurs, stop the engine and allow the foam to dissipate.
   h. Repeat step D until all the air is removed from the system.

➡The system is usually self-bleeding, and the procedure outlined will normally bleed the booster. Normal operation of the van will further remove trapped air.

Diesel Engine Vacuum Pump

Unlike gasoline engines, diesel engines have little vacuum available to power brake booster systems. The diesel is thus equipped with a vacuum pump, which is driven by a single belt off of the alternator. This pump is located on the top right side of the engine.

Some are also equipped with a low vacuum indicator switch which actuates the BRAKE warning lamp when available vacuum is below a certain level. The switch senses vacuum through a fitting in the vacuum manifold that intercepts the vacuum flow from the pump. The low vacuum switch is mounted on the left side of the engine compartment, adjacent to the vacuum pump.

➡ **The vacuum pump cannot be disassembled. It is only serviced as a unit (the pulley is separate).**

REMOVAL & INSTALLATION

1989–94 Models

◆ **See Figure 10**

1. Remove the hose clamp and disconnect the pump from the hose on the manifold vacuum outlet fitting.
2. Loosen the vacuum pump adjustment bolt and the pivot bolt. Slide the pump downward and remove the drive belt from the pulley.
3. Remove the pivot and adjustment bolts and the bolts retaining the pump to the adjustment plate. Remove the vacuum pump and adjustment plate.

To install:
4. Install the pump-to-adjustment plate bolts and tighten to 14–19 ft. lbs. (19–26 Nm). Position the pump and plate on the vacuum pump bracket and loosely install the pivot and adjustment bolts.
5. Connect the hose from the manifold vacuum outlet fitting to the pump and install the hose clamp.
6. Install the drive belt on the pulley. Place a ⅜ in. drive breaker bar or ratchet into the slot on the vacuum pump adjustment plate. Lift up on the assembly until the proper belt tension is obtained. Tighten the pivot and adjustment bolts to 11–18 ft. lbs. (15–24 Nm).
7. Start the engine and make sure the brake system functions properly.

➡ **The BRAKE light will glow until brake vacuum builds up to the normal level.**

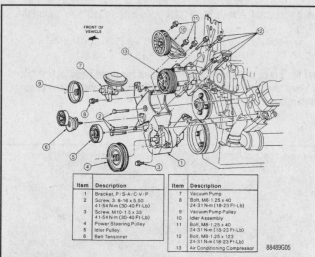

Fig. 10 Exploded view of the vacuum pump and related components' mounting—1989–94 diesel engines

1995–96 Models

◆ **See Figure 11**

1. Remove the air cleaner and drive belt.
2. Partially drain the coolant and remove the upper radiator hose.
3. Disengage the coolant reservoir hose from the radiator and support.
4. Remove the fan blade clutch and shroud.
5. Remove the vacuum pump pulley using pulley removal tool T69L-10300-B or equivalent.

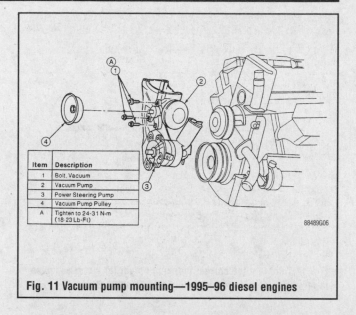

Item	Description
1	Bolt, Vacuum
2	Vacuum Pump
3	Power Steering Pump
4	Vacuum Pump Pulley
A	Tighten to 24-31 N·m (18-23 Lb-Ft)

Fig. 11 Vacuum pump mounting—1995–96 diesel engines

6. Loosen the pump retainers, disengage the hoses and remove the pump.

To install:
7. Connect the hoses to the pump, install the pump and tighten the bolts to 18–23 ft. lbs. (24–31 Nm).
8. Install pump pulley using tool T65P-3A733-C or equivalent.
9. Install the fan shroud, clutch and fan.
10. Connect the cool reservoir hose and radiator hose to the radiator.
11. Refill the cooling system and install the drive belt.
12. Install the air cleaner assembly.

Brake Load Proportioning Valve

REMOVAL & INSTALLATION

E-Super Duty Only

◆ **See Figures 12 and 13**

➡ **If the linkage is disconnected from the valve, the proper setting of the valve will be lost and a new valve will have to be installed. The new valve will have the shaft preset and secured internally. If the shaft of the new valve turns freely, DO NOT USE IT! The valve cannot be repaired or disassembled. It is to be replaced as a unit. If the linkage is damaged or broken and requires replacement, a new sensing valve will also be required.**

1. Raise and support the rear end on jackstands.
2. Raise the frame to obtain a clearance of 6 ⅝ in. (168.3mm) between the bottom edge of the rubber jounce bumper and the top of the axle tube—on BOTH sides of the axle. This is the correct indexing height for the valve.
3. Remove the nut holding the linkage arm to the valve and disconnect the arm.
4. Remove the bolt holding the flexible brake hose to the valve.
5. Disconnect the brake line from the valve.
6. Remove the 2 mounting bolts and remove the valve from its bracket.
To install:
7. Place the new valve on the bracket and tighten the mounting bolts to 22–30 ft. lbs. (30–40 Nm).
8. Install the brake hose, using new copper gaskets and tighten the bolt to 17–25 ft. lbs. (23–34 Nm).
9. Attach the brake line to the lower part of the valve.
10. Connect the linkage arm to the valve and tighten the nut to 11–14 ft. lbs. (15–19 Nm).
11. Bleed the brakes.

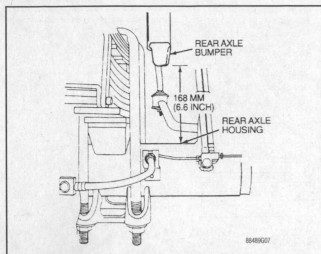

Fig. 12 To obtain the correct indexing height for the valve, raise the frame to obtain a clearance of 6 ⅝ in. (168.3mm)

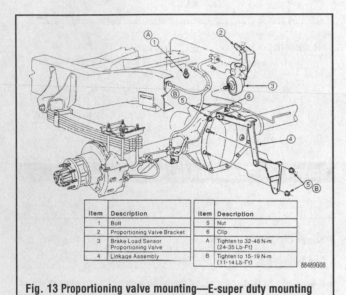

Item	Description	Item	Description
1	Bolt	5	Nut
2	Proportioning Valve Bracket	6	Clip
3	Brake Load Sensor Proportioning Valve	A	Tighten to 32-48 N·m (24-35 Lb-Ft)
4	Linkage Assembly	B	Tighten to 15-19 N·m (11-14 Lb-Ft)

Fig. 13 Proportioning valve mounting—E-super duty mounting

➡When servicing axle or suspension parts which would require disconnection of the valve, instead, remove the 2 nuts that attach the linkage arm to the axle cover plate. This will avoid disconnecting the valve and avoid having to replace the valve.

Brake Hoses and Lines

INSPECTION

▶ See Figure 14

Metal lines and rubber brake hoses should be checked frequently for leaks and external damage. Metal lines are particularly prone to crushing and kinking under the vehicle. Any such deformation can restrict the proper flow of fluid and therefore impair braking at the wheels. Rubber hoses should be checked for cracking or scraping; such damage can create a weak spot in the hose and it could fail under pressure.

Any time the lines are removed or disconnected, extreme cleanliness must be observed. Clean all joints and connections before disassembly (use a stiff bristle brush and clean brake fluid); be sure to plug the lines and ports as soon as they are opened. New lines and hoses should be flushed clean with brake fluid before installation to remove any contamination.

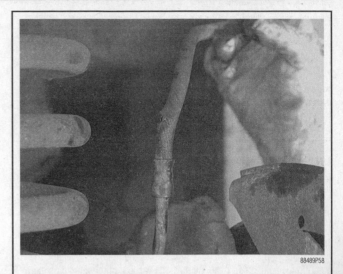

Fig. 14 Check the brake lines for leaks and damage

REMOVAL & INSTALLATION

▶ See Figures 15 thru 22

1. Disconnect the negative battery cable.
2. Raise and safely support the vehicle on jackstands.
3. Remove any wheel and tire assemblies necessary for access to the particular line you are removing.
4. Thoroughly clean the surrounding area at the joints to be disconnected.
5. Place a suitable catch pan under the joint to be disconnected.
6. Using two wrenches (one to hold the joint and one to turn the fitting), disconnect the hose or line to be replaced.
7. Disconnect the other end of the line or hose, moving the drain pan if necessary. Always use a back-up wrench to avoid damaging the fitting.
8. Disconnect any retaining clips or brackets holding the line and remove the line from the vehicle.

➡If the brake system is to remain open for more time than it takes to swap lines, tape or plug each remaining clip and port to keep contaminants out and fluid in.

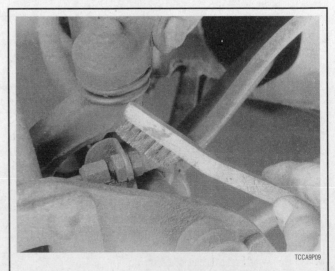

Fig. 15 Use a brush to clean the fittings of any debris

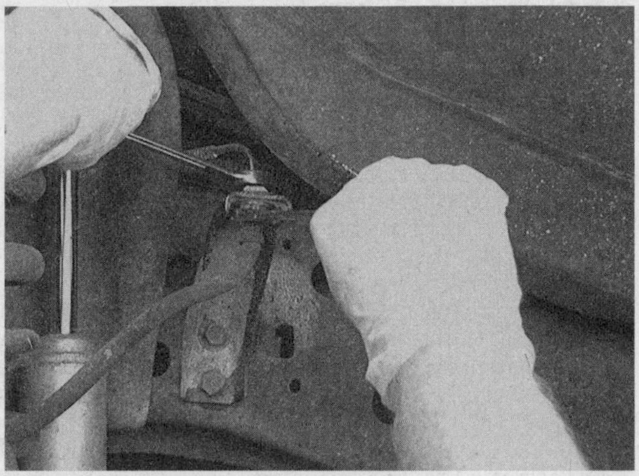

88489P52

Fig. 16 Use two wrenches to loosen the fitting. If available, use flare nut type wrenches

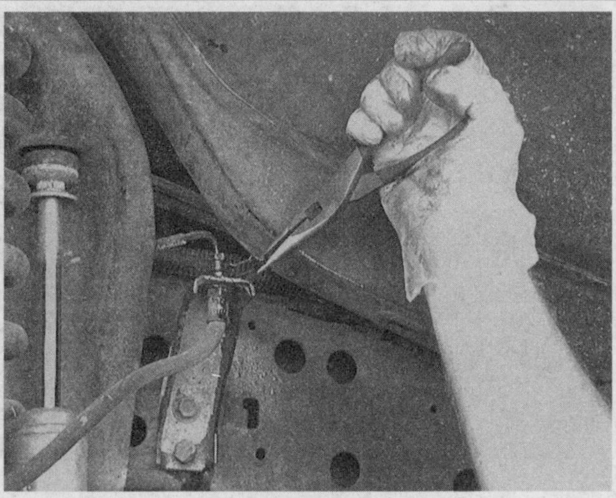

88489P54

Fig. 17 Use pliers to remove the retaining clip

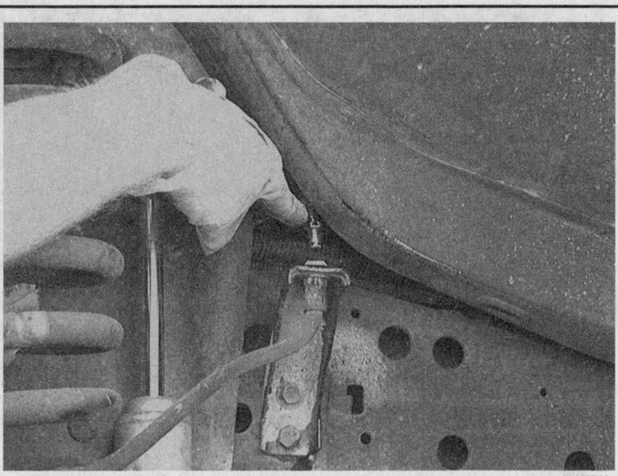

88489P53

Fig. 18 Disconnect the steel brake line from the bracket and hose

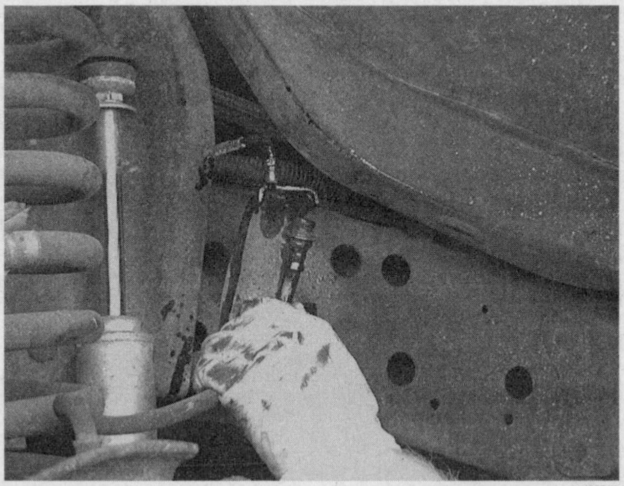

88489P55

Fig. 19 Disconnect the rubber hose from the bracket assembly

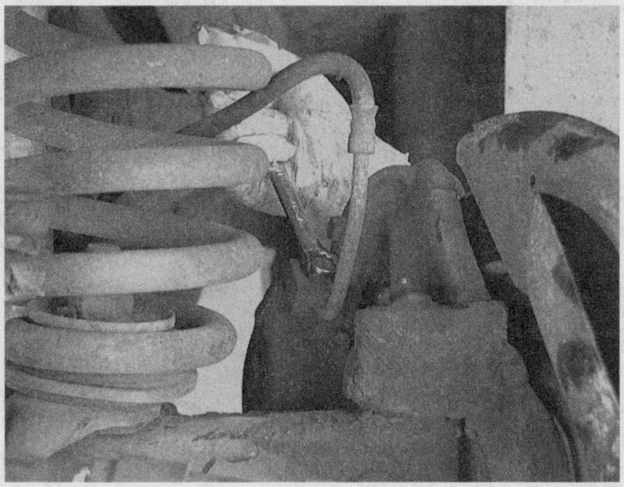

88489P56

Fig. 20 Loosen the brake line-to-caliper banjo bolt

To install:

9. Install the new line or hose, starting with the end farthest from the master cylinder. Connect the other end, then confirm that both fittings are correctly threaded and turn smoothly using finger pressure. Make sure the new line will not rub against any other part. Brake lines must be at least ½ in. (13mm) from the steering column and other moving parts. Any protective shielding or insulators must be reinstalled in the original location.

WARNING

Make sure the hose is NOT kinked or touching any part of the frame or suspension after installation. These conditions may cause the hose to fail prematurely.

10. Using two wrenches as before, tighten each fitting.
11. Install any retaining clips or brackets on the lines.
12. If removed, install the wheel and tire assemblies, then carefully lower the vehicle to the ground.
13. Refill the brake master cylinder reservoir with clean, fresh brake fluid, meeting DOT 3 specifications. Properly bleed the brake system.
14. Connect the negative battery cable.

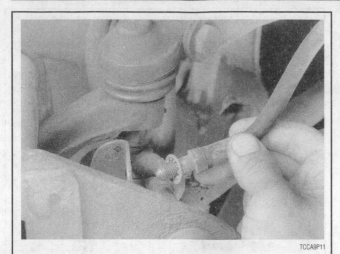

Fig. 21 Any gaskets/crush washers should be replaced with new ones during installation

TCCA9P11

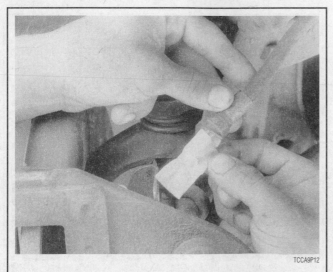

Fig. 22 Tape or plug the line to prevent contamination

TCCA9P12

Bleeding the Brakes

NON-ABS SYSTEMS

When any part of the hydraulic system has been disconnected for repair or replacement, air may get into the lines and cause spongy pedal action (because air can be compressed and brake fluid cannot). To correct this condition, it is necessary to bleed the hydraulic system after it has been properly connected to be sure that all air is expelled from the brake cylinders and lines.

When bleeding the brake system, bleed one brake cylinder at a time, beginning at the cylinder with the longest hydraulic line (farthest from the master cylinder) first. Keep the master cylinder reservoir filled with brake fluid during bleeding operation. Never use brake fluid that has been drained from the hydraulic system, no matter how clean it is.

It will be necessary to centralize the pressure differential valve after a brake system failure has been corrected and the hydraulic system has been bled.

The primary and secondary hydraulic brake systems are individual systems and are bled separately. During the entire bleeding operation, do not allow the reservoir to run dry. Keep the master cylinder reservoirs filled with brake fluid.

Wheel Cylinders and Calipers

▶ **See Figures 23 and 23a**

1. Clean all dirt from around the master cylinder fill cap, remove the cap and fill the master cylinder with brake fluid until the level is within ¼ in. (6mm) of the top of the edge of the reservoir.
2. Clean off the bleeder screws at the wheel cylinders and calipers.
3. Attach the length of rubber hose over the nozzle of the bleeder screw at the wheel to be done first. Place the other end of the hose in a glass jar, submerged in brake fluid.
4. Open the bleed screw valve ½–¾ turn.
5. Have an assistant slowly depress the brake pedal. Close the bleeder screw valve and tell your assistant to allow the brake pedal to return slowly. Continue this pumping action to force any air out of the system. When bubbles cease to appear at the end of the bleeder hose, close the bleed valve and remove the hose.
6. Check the master cylinder fluid level and add fluid accordingly. Do this after bleeding each wheel.
7. Repeat the bleeding operation at the remaining 3 wheels, ending with the one closest to the master cylinder. Fill the master cylinder reservoir.

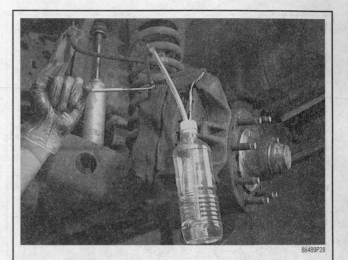

Fig. 23 To bleed the front brakes, place one end of a clear hose on the bleeder screw and the other in a clear container of brake fluid

88489P28

Fig. 23a Place the clear plastic hose over the wheel cylinder bleeder screw and the other in the clear container of brake fluid when bleeding the rear brakes

88489P48

Master Cylinder

1. Fill the master cylinder reservoirs.
2. Place absorbent rags under the fluid lines at the master cylinder.
3. Have an assistant depress and hold the brake pedal.

DISC BRAKES

❋❋ CAUTION

Old brake pads or shoes may contain asbestos, which has been determined to be a cancer causing agent. Never clean the brake surfaces with compressed air! Avoid inhaling any dust from any brake surface! When cleaning brake surfaces, use a commercially available brake cleaning fluid.

There are two types of sliding calipers, the LD sliding caliper unit is operated by one piston per caliper.

The light duty system is used on E-150 models.

The HD slider caliper unit contains 2 pistons on the same side of the rotor. The caliper slides on the support assembly and is retained by a key and spring.

The heavy duty system is used on all E-250–350 models.

Brake Pads

REMOVAL & INSTALLATION

➥**Never replace the pads on one side only! Always replace pads on both wheels as a set!**

Light Duty Vehicles

1989–91 MODELS

▶ See Figures 24, 25 and 26

1. To avoid overflowing of the master cylinder when the caliper pistons are pressed into the caliper cylinder bores, siphon or dip some brake fluid out of the larger reservoir.
2. Jack up the front of the van, support it on jackstands, and remove the wheels.
3. Place an 8 in. (203mm) C-clamp on the caliper and tighten the clamp to bottom the caliper piston in the cylinder bore. Bear the clamp on the outer pad. NEVER PRESS DIRECTLY ON THE PISTON! Remove the C-clamp.

4. With the pedal held down, slowly crack open the hydraulic line fitting, allowing the air to escape. Close the fitting and have the pedal released.
5. Repeat Steps 3 and 4 for each fitting until all the air is released.

4. Clean the excess dirt from around the caliper pin tabs.
5. Drive the upper caliper pin inward until the tabs on the pin touch the spindle.
6. Insert a small prybar into the slot provided behind the pin tabs on the inboard side of the pin.
7. Using needlenose pliers, compress the outboard end of the pin while, at the same time, prying with the prybar until the tabs slip into the groove in the spindle.
8. Place the end of a ½ in. (12mm) punch against the end of the caliper pin and drive the pin out of the caliper slide groove.
9. Repeat this procedure for the lower pin.
10. Lift the caliper off of the rotor.
11. Remove the brake pads and anti-rattle spring.

➥**Do not allow the caliper to hang by the brake hose.**

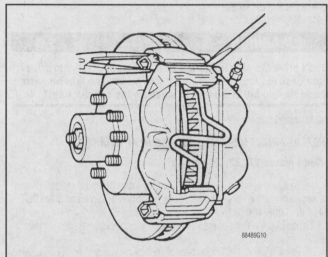

Fig. 25 Insert a prytool into the slot behind the pin and use needlenose pliers to compress the pin

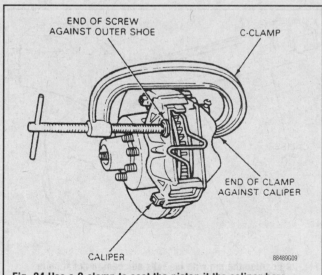

Fig. 24 Use a C-clamp to seat the piston it the caliper bore

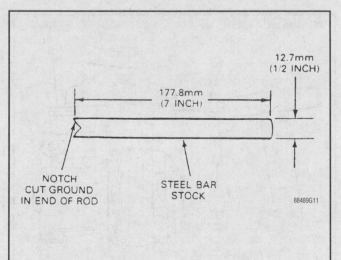

Fig. 26 You can fabricate a pin removal tool using the specifications illustrated

To install:

12. Thoroughly clean the areas of the caliper and spindle assembly which contact each other during the sliding action of the caliper.

13. Place a new anti-rattle clip on the lower end of the inboard shoe. Make sure that the tabs on the clip are positioned correctly and the loop-type spring is away from the rotor.

14. Place the lower end of the inner brake pad in the spindle assembly pad abutment, against the anti-rattle clip, and slide the upper end of the pad into position. Be sure that the clip is still in position.

15. Check and make sure that the caliper piston is fully bottomed in the cylinder bore. Use a large C-clamp, bearing on a piece of wood, to bottom the piston, if necessary.

16. Position the outer brake pad on the caliper, and press the pad tabs into place with your fingers. If the pad cannot be pressed into place by hand, use a C-clamp. Be careful not to damage the lining with the clamp. Bend the tabs to prevent rattling.

17. Position the caliper on the spindle assembly. Lightly lubricate the caliper sliding grooves with caliper pin grease.

18. Position the a new upper pin with the retention tabs next to the spindle groove.

➡**Don't use the bolt and nut with the new pin.**

19. Carefully drive the pin, at the outboard end, inward until the tabs contact the spindle face.

20. Repeat the procedure for the lower pin.

※ WARNING

Don't drive the pins in too far, or it will be necessary to drive them back out until the tabs snap into place. The tabs on each end of the pin MUST be free to catch on the spindle sides!

21. Install the wheels.

1992–93 FRONT BRAKES AND 1996 REAR BRAKES

♦ **See Figures 27, 28, 29 and 30**

1. To avoid overflowing of the master cylinder when the caliper pistons are pressed into the caliper cylinder bores, siphon or dip some brake fluid out of the larger reservoir.

2. Jack up the front of the van, support it on jackstands, and remove the wheels.

3. Place an 8 in. (203mm) C-clamp on the caliper and tighten the clamp to bottom the caliper piston in the cylinder bore. Bear the clamp on the outer pad. NEVER PRESS DIRECTLY ON THE PISTON! Remove the C-clamp.

4. Clean the excess dirt from around the caliper pin tabs.

5. Drive the upper caliper pin inward until the tabs on the pin touch the spindle.

6. Use pin remover D89T-2196-A or equivalent, drive the upper pin from the caliper.

7. Repeat this procedure for the lower pin.

8. Lift the caliper off of the rotor.

9. Remove the brake pads and anti-rattle spring.

➡**Do not allow the caliper to hang by the brake hose.**

To install:

10. Thoroughly clean the areas of the caliper and spindle assembly which contact each other during the sliding action of the caliper.

11. Place a new anti-rattle clip on the lower end of the inboard shoe. Make sure that the tabs on the clip are positioned correctly and the loop-type spring is away from the rotor.

12. Place the lower end of the inner brake pad in the spindle assembly pad abutment, against the anti-rattle clip, and slide the upper end of the pad into position. Be sure that the clip is still in position.

13. Check and make sure that the caliper piston is fully bottomed in the cylinder bore. Use a large C-clamp, bearing on a piece of wood, to bottom the piston, if necessary.

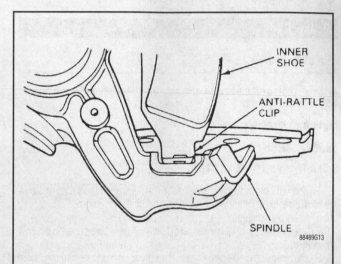

Fig. 28 When installing the brake pad, make sure the anti-rattle clip is fully engaged

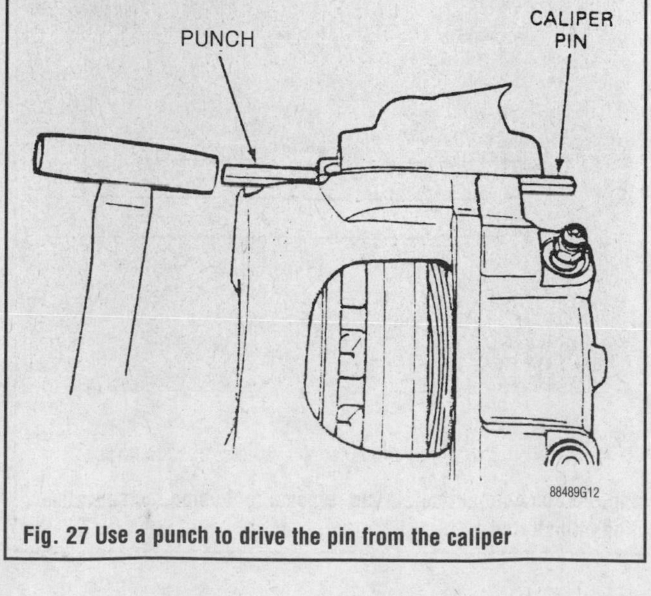

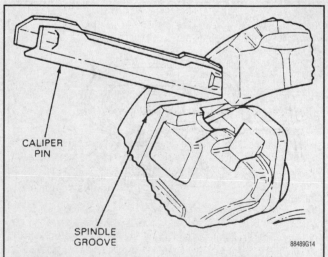

Fig. 29 Position the pin with the tabs adjacent to the spindle groove

Fig. 27 Use a punch to drive the pin from the caliper

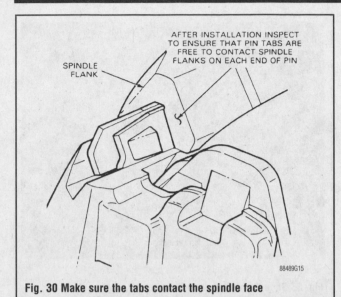

Fig. 30 Make sure the tabs contact the spindle face

14. Position the outer brake pad on the caliper, and press the pad tabs into place with your fingers. If the pad cannot be pressed into place by hand, use a C-clamp. Be careful not to damage the lining with the clamp. Bend the tabs to prevent rattling.

15. Position the caliper on the spindle assembly. Lightly lubricate the caliper sliding grooves with caliper pin grease.

16. Position the a new upper pin with the retention tabs next to the spindle groove.

→**Don't use the bolt and nut with the new pin.**

17. Carefully drive the pin, at the outboard end, inward until the tabs contact the spindle face.

18. Repeat the procedure for the lower pin.

✷✷ WARNING

Don't drive the pins in too far, or it will be necessary to drive them back out until the tabs snap into place. The tabs on each end of the pin MUST be free to catch on the spindle sides!

19. Install the wheels.

1994–96 MODELS—EXCEPT 1996 REAR BRAKES

1. To avoid overflowing of the master cylinder when the caliper pistons are pressed into the caliper cylinder bores, siphon or dip some brake fluid out of the larger reservoir.

2. Jack up the front of the van, support it on jackstands, and remove the wheels.

3. Loosen the caliper retaining bolts.

4. Lift the caliper off of the rotor.

5. Remove the brake pads and anti-rattle spring.

→**Do not allow the caliper to hang by the brake hose.**

To install:

6. Install the brake pad hold-down springs by placing the lower edge of the pad anti-rattle clip beneath the abutment surface of the knuckle and rotating the pad clip up and into position. Press against the slide surfaces of the pad anti-rattle clip to make sure the clip is seated properly.

7. Place the inner shoe in position so that it is caught by the hold-down springs. Slide the pad past the knuckle tabs and wedge one end into position against the pad hold-down spring. Lift the top spring of the outer pad hold-down spring, slide the pad onto the abutment and against the hub and rotor.

8. Install the outer shoe in the same manner as the inner.

9. Pull back the slide pins and install the caliper over the pads while sliding it down into the outer brake shoe clip, making sure the tips of the clip are seated in the retention holes of the caliper.

10. Install and tighten the caliper mounting bolts to 22–26 ft. lbs. (30–36 Nm).

11. Install the wheels and check the brake fluid level, replenish as necessary.

Heavy Duty Vehicles

1989–91 MODELS

♦ **See Figures 31 thru 36**

1. To avoid overflowing of the master cylinder when the caliper pistons are pressed into the caliper cylinder bores, siphon or dip some brake fluid out of the larger reservoir.

2. Jack up the front of the van, support it on jackstands, and remove the wheels.

3. Place an 8 in. (203mm) C-clamp on the caliper and tighten the

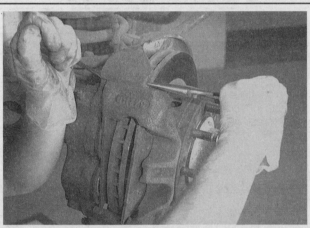

Fig. 31 Compress the outboard end of the pin with needlenose pliers while applying a prybar until the tabs slip into the groove on the spindle

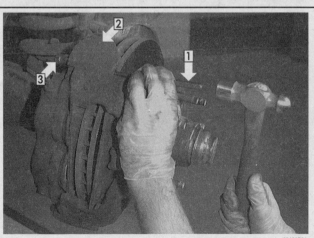

| 1. Punch | 2. Caliper | 3. Pin |

Fig. 32 Drive the upper pin from the caliper groove with a punch . . .

Fig. 33 . . . then withdraw the pin from the caliper

Fig. 35 Slide the caliper from the rotor

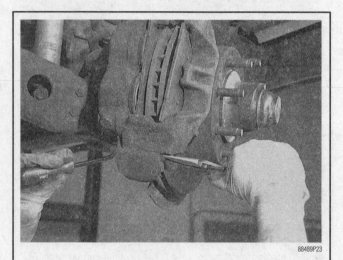

Fig. 34 Remove the lower pin in the same manner as the upper one

Fig. 36 Remove the inboard and outboard brake pads from the caliper

clamp to bottom the caliper piston in the cylinder bore. Bear the clamp on the outer pad. NEVER PRESS DIRECTLY ON THE PISTON! Remove the C-clamp.

4. Clean the excess dirt from around the caliper pin tabs.

5. Drive the upper caliper pin inward until the tabs on the pin touch the spindle.

6. Insert a small prybar into the slot provided behind the pin tabs on the inboard side of the pin.

7. Using needlenose pliers, compress the outboard end of the pin while, at the same time, prying with the prybar until the tabs slip into the groove in the spindle.

8. Place the end of a $7/16$ in. (11mm) punch against the end of the caliper pin and drive the pin out of the caliper slide groove.

9. Repeat this procedure for the lower pin.

10. Lift the caliper off of the rotor.

11. Remove the brake pads and anti-rattle spring.

➡ Do not allow the caliper to hang by the brake hose.

To install:

12. Thoroughly clean the areas of the caliper and spindle assembly which contact each other during the sliding action of the caliper.

13. Place a new anti-rattle clip on the lower end of the inboard shoe. Make sure that the tabs on the clip are positioned correctly and the loop-type spring is away from the rotor.

14. Place the lower end of the inner brake pad in the spindle assembly pad abutment, against the anti-rattle clip, and slide the upper end of the pad into position. Be sure that the clip is still in position.

15. Check and make sure that the caliper piston is fully bottomed in the cylinder bore. Use a large C-clamp, bearing on a piece of wood, to bottom the piston, if necessary.

16. Position the outer brake pad on the caliper, and press the pad tabs into place with your fingers. If the pad cannot be pressed into place by hand, use a C-clamp. Be careful not to damage the lining with the clamp. Bend the tabs to prevent rattling.

17. Position the caliper on the spindle assembly. Lightly lubricate the caliper sliding grooves with caliper pin grease.

18. Position the a new upper pin with the retention tabs next to the spindle groove.

➡**Don't use the bolt and nut with the new pin.**

19. Carefully drive the pin, at the outboard end, inward until the tabs contact the spindle face.

20. Repeat the procedure for the lower pin.

❄❄ WARNING

Don't drive the pins in too far, or it will be necessary to drive them back out until the tabs snap into place. The tabs on each end of the pin MUST be free to catch on the spindle sides!

21. Install the wheels.

1992–94 MODELS

▶ See Figures 27, 28, 29 and 30

1. To avoid overflowing of the master cylinder when the caliper pistons are pressed into the caliper cylinder bores, siphon or dip some brake fluid out of the larger reservoir.

2. Jack up the front of the van, support it on jackstands, and remove the wheels.

3. Place an 8 in. (203mm) C-clamp on the caliper and tighten the clamp to bottom the caliper piston in the cylinder bore. Bear the clamp on the outer pad. NEVER PRESS DIRECTLY ON THE PISTON! Remove the C-clamp.

4. Remove the upper anchor bolt and swing the caliper down.

5. Remove the brake shoes.

➡**Do not allow the caliper to hang by the brake hose.**

To install:

6. Check the slide pin assemblies and rubber boots for damage and replace them if they are defective.

7. Lubricate the slide pins with D7AZ-19590-A or its equivalent and install them.

8. Install the shoes and rotate the caliper into position.

9. Install the anchor bolt and tighten it to 85–100 ft. lbs. (115–135 Nm).

10. Install the wheels and check the brake fluid level, replenish as necessary.

1995–96 MODELS

▶ See Figures 37, 38 and 39

1. To avoid overflowing of the master cylinder when the caliper pistons are pressed into the caliper cylinder bores, siphon or dip some brake fluid out of the larger reservoir.

2. Jack up the front of the van, support it on jackstands, and remove the wheels.

3. Place an 8 in. (203mm) C-clamp on the caliper and tighten the clamp to bottom the caliper piston in the cylinder bore. Bear the clamp on the outer pad. NEVER PRESS DIRECTLY ON THE PISTON! Remove the C-clamp.

4. Remove the caliper slide pins. Examine the slide pins and caliper pin insulators for damage and replace as necessary.

5. Remove the caliper.

6. Remove the brake pads.

➡**Do not allow the caliper to hang by the brake hose.**

To install:

7. Install the pads and anti-rattle clips (if equipped).

8. Install the caliper and slide pins. Tighten the pins to 85–100 ft. lbs. (115–135 Nm) on 1995 models or 141–191 ft. lbs. (191–259 Nm) on 1996 models.

9. Install the wheels and check the brake fluid level; replenish as necessary.

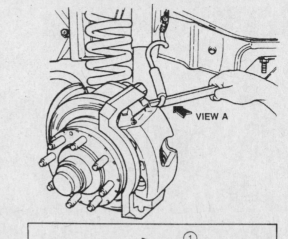

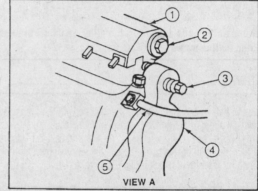

Item	Description
1	Anchor Bracket
2	Anchor Bolt, M16 x 2.0 (2 Req'd)
3	Caliper Pin
4	Front Disc Brake Caliper
5	Front Brake Hose

88489G16

Fig. 37 Loosen the slide pins, at the rear of the caliper, with an appropriate wrench

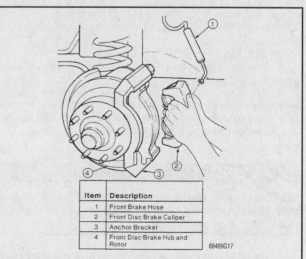

Item	Description
1	Front Brake Hose
2	Front Disc Brake Caliper
3	Anchor Bracket
4	Front Disc Brake Hub and Rotor

88489G17

Fig. 38 Lift the caliper from its mounting and support it with a piece of wire

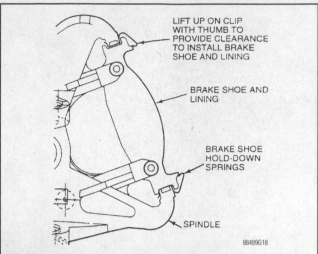

Fig. 39 Install the pads and anti-rattle clips, making sure they are seated as illustrated

INSPECTION

Remove the brake pads and measure the thickness of the lining. If the lining thickness at any point on the pad assembly is less than 1/16 in. (1.5mm) for LD brakes or 1/32 in. (0.8mm) for HD brakes, (as measured above the backing plate or rivets), or there is evidence of the lining being contaminated by brake fluid or oil, replace the brake pad.

Brake Caliper

REMOVAL & INSTALLATION

1. Raise and support the front end on jackstands.
2. Remove the wheels.
3. Remove the caliper and the brake pads as outlined under Disc Brake Pad Removal and Installation.
4. Disconnect the brake hose from the caliper.
To install:
5. Connect the brake hose to the caliper. When connecting the brake fluid hose to the caliper, it is recommended that a new copper washer be used at the connection of the brake hose and caliper.
6. Install the brake caliper and pads onto the vehicle as outlined in this section.
7. Install the wheels and lower the vehicle. Bleed the brake system.

OVERHAUL

▶ **See Figures 40 thru 47**

➡Some vehicles may be equipped dual piston calipers. The procedure to overhaul the caliper is essentially the same with the exception of multiple pistons, O-rings and dust boots.

1. Remove the caliper from the vehicle and place on a clean workbench.

❈❈❈ CAUTION

NEVER place your fingers in front of the pistons in an attempt to catch or protect the pistons when applying compressed air. This could result in personal injury!

➡Depending upon the vehicle, there are two different ways to remove the piston from the caliper. Refer to the brake pad replacement procedure to make sure you have the correct procedure for your vehicle.

2. The first method is as follows:
   a. Stuff a shop towel or a block of wood into the caliper to catch the piston.
   b. Remove the caliper piston using compressed air applied into the caliper inlet hole. Inspect the piston for scoring, nicks, corrosion and/or worn or damaged chrome plating. The piston must be replaced if any of these conditions are found.
3. For the second method, you must rotate the piston to retract it from the caliper.
4. If equipped, remove the anti-rattle clip.
5. Use a prytool to remove the caliper boot, being careful not to scratch the housing bore.
6. Remove the piston seals from the groove in the caliper bore.
7. Carefully loosen the brake bleeder valve cap and valve from the caliper housing.
8. Inspect the caliper bores, pistons and mounting threads for scoring or excessive wear.
9. Use crocus cloth to polish out light corrosion from the piston and bore.
10. Clean all parts with denatured alcohol and dry with compressed air.
To assemble:
11. Lubricate and install the bleeder valve and cap.

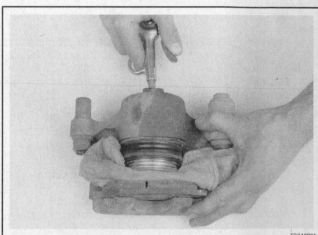

Fig. 40 For some types of calipers, use compressed air to drive the piston out of the caliper, but make sure to keep your fingers clear

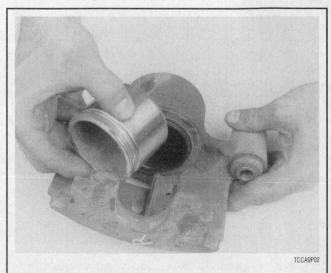

Fig. 41 Withdraw the piston from the caliper bore

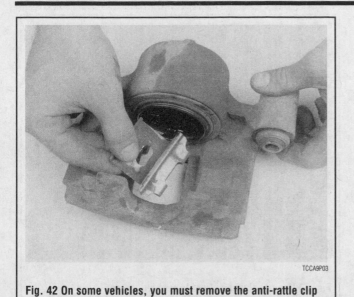

Fig. 42 On some vehicles, you must remove the anti-rattle clip

Fig. 43 Use a prytool to carefully pry around the edge of the boot . . .

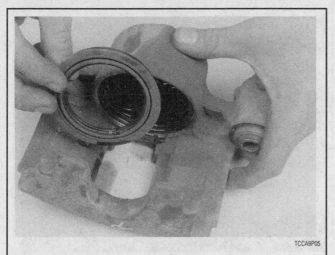

Fig. 44 . . . then remove the boot from the caliper housing, taking care not to score or damage the bore

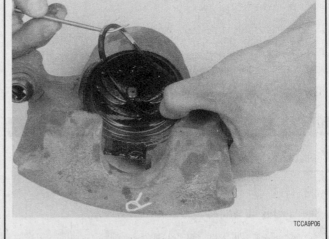

Fig. 45 Use extreme caution when removing the piston seal; DO NOT scratch the caliper bore

Fig. 46 Use the proper size driving tool and a mallet to properly seal the boots in the caliper housing

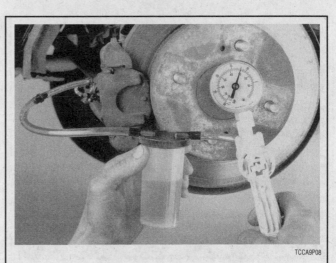

Fig. 47 There are tools, such as this Mighty-Vac, available to assist in proper brake system bleeding

12. Install the new seals into the caliper bore grooves, making sure they are not twisted.

13. Lubricate the piston bore.

14. Install the pistons and boots into the bores of the calipers and push to the bottom of the bores.

15. Use a suitable driving tool to seat the boots in the housing.

16. Install the caliper in the vehicle.

17. Install the wheel and tire assembly, then carefully lower the vehicle.

18. Properly bleed the brake system.

Brake Disc (Rotor)

REMOVAL & INSTALLATION

Front

▶ See Figures 48 thru 54

1. Jack up the front of the van and support it with jackstands. Remove the front wheel.

2. Remove the caliper assembly and support it on the frame with a piece

Fig. 50 Use needlenose pliers to remove the cotter pin

Fig. 48 Use a prytool to loosen the dust cap from its mounting . . .

Fig. 51 Remove the nut washer . . .

Fig. 49 . . . then remove the dust cap from the hub

Fig. 52 . . . then unthread the nut from the spindle

Fig. 53 Remove the outer wheel bearing and set it aside

Fig. 54 Remove the rotor from the van

of wire (or something equally secure) without disconnecting the brake fluid hose.

3. Remove the dust cap, cotter pin, nut washer, nut and outer bearing.
4. Remove the rotor assembly.
5. Install the rotor in the reverse order of removal, and adjust the wheel bearings as outlined in Section 1.

Rear

♦ **See Figure 55**

1. Raise the van and support it with safety stands.
2. Remove the wheel.
3. Remove the caliper.
4. Lift the lockwasher tab from the slot in the outer locknut.
5. Using wheel bearing spanner D78T-1197-A or its equivalent, remove the outer lock nut.
6. Remove the axle shaft. Refer to Section 8.
7. Lift the lockwasher tab from the inner locknut and remove the outer rear wheel pinion nut locking washer.

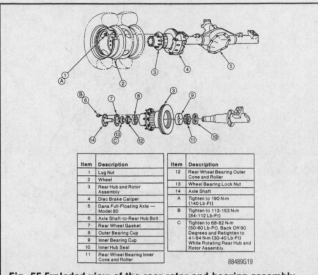

Fig. 55 Exploded view of the rear rotor and bearing assembly

8. Using wheel bearing spanner D78T-1197-A or its equivalent, remove the inner lock nut.
9. Remove the inner rear wheel pinion nut locking washer and the outer bearing cone and roller.
10. Being careful not to damage the axle spindle threads, remove the rear hub and rotor.
11. Loosen the hub-to-rotor bolts and separate the two components.
To install:
12. Install the rotor on the hub and tighten the bolts 84–112 ft. lbs. (113–153 Nm).
13. Install the rear hub and rotor on the axle spindle.
14. Install the outer bearing cone and roller.
15. Install the inner pinion nut locking washer, making sure the washer tab is engaged in the keyway at the rear of the axle spindle.
16. Using wheel bearing spanner D78T-1197-A or its equivalent, install the inner lock nut and tighten to 50–60 ft. lbs. (68–82 Nm). Back off the locknut 90 degrees and retighten to 30–40 ft. lbs. (41–54 Nm) while rotating the hub and rotor.
17. Back off the inner lock nut again 135–150 degrees.
18. Install the lockwasher with the flat side facing in and make sure the flat tabs are positioned in the slots of the inner lock nut.
19. Tighten the inner lock nut until one of the tabs aligns with a slot. Bend the tab a minimum of 30 degrees to fully engage the slot.
20. Install the outer lock nut and tighten it to 65 ft. lbs. (88 Nm) and then keep tightening the nut until one of the eight L-shaped tabs on the lockwasher aligns with one of the six slots on the outer lock nut.
21. Mount a dial indicator with a magnetic base and measure the end-play on the hub. The end-play should be 0.001–0.010 inch (0.025–0.250mm).
22. Bend the L-tab of the lockwasher a minimum of 60 degrees over the outer lock nut to fully engage the slot.
23. Install the axle shaft.
24. Install the brake caliper and the wheel.
25. Test drive the van and check for proper operation.

INSPECTION

♦ **See Figure 56**

If the rotor is deeply scarred or has shallow cracks, it may be refinished on a disc brake rotor lathe. Also, if the lateral run-out exceeds specification within a 6 in. (152mm) radius when measured with a dial indicator, with the

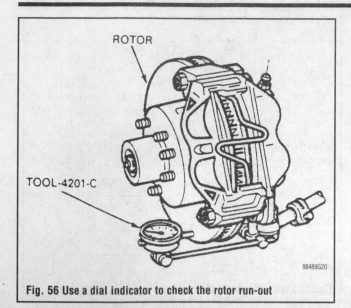

Fig. 56 Use a dial indicator to check the rotor run-out

stylus 1 in. (25mm) in from the edge of the rotor, the rotor should be refinished or replaced. Attach the dial indicator as illustrated.

The lateral run-out should be as follows:
- E-150–350: 0.003 inch (0.08mm)
- E-350 with Dual Rear Wheels (DRW): 0.005 inch (0.13mm)

A maximum of 0.020 in. (0.5mm) of material may be removed equally from each friction surface of the rotor. If the damage cannot be corrected when the rotor has been machined to the minimum thickness shown on the rotor, it should be replaced.

The maximum thickness of the rotor on all models should be 1.18 inch (30.00mm). Use a micrometer in at least six different locations on the rotor.

DRUM BRAKES

✳✳ CAUTION

Older brake pads or shoes may contain asbestos, which has been determined to be a cancer causing agent. Never clean the brake surfaces with compressed air! Avoid inhaling any dust from any brake surface! When cleaning brake surfaces, use a commercially available brake cleaning fluid.

DRUM BRAKE COMPONENTS

1. Adjusting screw
2. Brake shoes
3. Pins
4. Hold-down spring
5. Return springs
6. Parking brake lever
7. Adjusting cable
8. Wheel cylinder

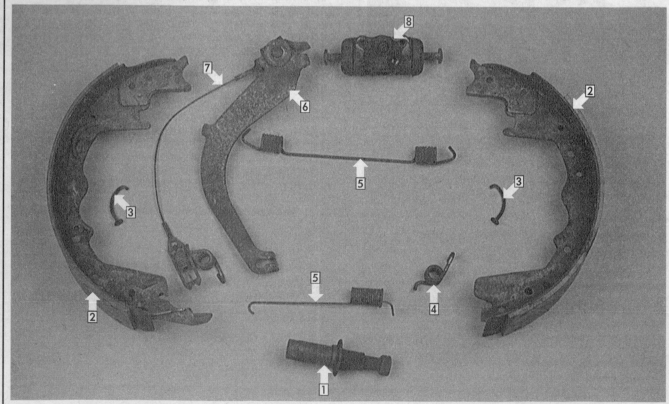

Brake Drums

REMOVAL & INSTALLATION

▶ **See Figures 57 and 58**

1. Raise the vehicle so that the wheel to be worked on is clear of the floor and install jackstands under the vehicle.
2. Remove the wheel.
3. Remove the spring retaining nuts.
4. Remove the brake drum. It may be necessary to back off the brake shoe adjustment in order to remove the brake drum. This is because the drum might be grooved or worn from being in service for an extended period of time.
5. If the inside of the drum has a coating of rust or a ridge, clean it with a piece of coarse sandpaper before installation.
6. Before installing a new brake drum, be sure to remove any protective coating with brake cleaner or a suitable fast-drying degreaser.
7. Install the brake drum in the reverse order of removal and adjust the brakes.

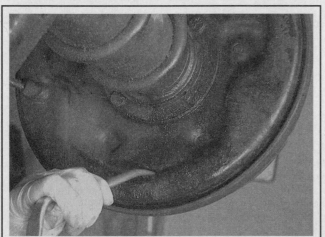

88489P47

Fig. 57 Use a brake adjusting tool to back off the adjuster screw . . .

88489P17

Fig. 58 . . . and remove the drum from the van

INSPECTION

Check that there are no cracks or chips in the braking surface. Excessive bluing indicates overheating and a replacement drum is needed. The drum can be machined to remove minor damage and to establish a rounded braking surface on a warped drum. Never exceed the maximum oversize of the drum when machining the braking surface. The maximum inside diameter is stamped on the rim of the drum.

Brake Shoes

REMOVAL & INSTALLATION

Light Duty Systems

▶ **See Figures 59, 60 and 61**

1. Raise and support the vehicle and remove the wheel and brake drum from the wheel to be worked on.

➡**If you have never replaced the brakes on a van before and you are not too familiar with the procedures involved, only dissemble and**

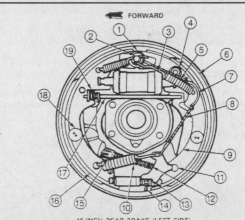

10-INCH REAR BRAKE (LEFT SIDE)

Item	Description
1	Brake Shoe Anchor Pin Guide Plate
2	Anchor Pin
3	Rear Wheel Cylinder
4	Washer
5	Brake Shoe Retracting Spring
6	Rear Brake Shoe and Lining Secondary
7	Cable Guide
8	Brake Shoe Adjusting Lever Cable
9	Parking Brake Lever
10	Brake Shoe Adjusting Screw Spring
11	Pivot Hook
12	Rear Parking Brake Cable
13	Brake Shoe Adjusting Lever Kit
14	Brake Adjuster Screw
15	Parking Brake Cable Housing Retainer
16	Rear Brake Shoe and Lining Primary
17	Primary Brake Shoe Parking Brake Lever Link
18	Brake Shoe Hold Down Spring
19	Parking Brake Link Spring

88489G21

Fig. 59 Light duty brake system components

assemble one side at a time, leaving the other side intact as a reference during reassembly.

2. Install a clamp over the ends of the wheel cylinder to prevent the pistons of the wheel cylinder from coming out, causing loss of fluid and much grief.

3. Contract the brake shoes by pulling the self-adjusting lever away from the starwheel adjustment screw and turn the starwheel up and back until the pivot nut is drawn onto the starwheel as far as it will come.

4. Pull the adjusting lever, cable and automatic adjuster spring down and toward the rear to unhook the pivot hook from the large hole in the secondary shoe web. Do not attempt to pry the pivot hook from the hole.

5. Remove the automatic adjuster spring and the adjusting lever.

6. Remove the secondary shoe-to-anchor spring with a brake tool. (Brake tools are very common implements and are available at auto parts stores). Remove the primary shoe-to-anchor spring and unhook the cable anchor. Remove the anchor pin plate.

7. Remove the cable guide from the secondary shoe.

8. Remove the shoe hold-down springs, shoes, adjusting screw, pivot nut, and socket. Note the color of each hold-down spring for assembly. To remove the hold-down springs, reach behind the brake backing plate and place one finger on the end of one of the brake hold-down spring mounting

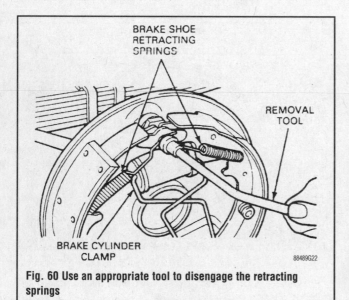

BRAKE SHOE RETRACTING SPRINGS

REMOVAL TOOL

BRAKE CYLINDER CLAMP

88489G22

Fig. 60 Use an appropriate tool to disengage the retracting springs

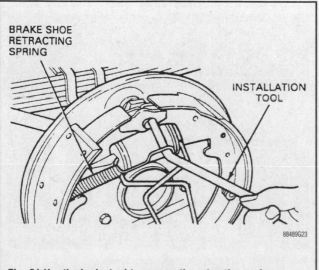

BRAKE SHOE RETRACTING SPRING

INSTALLATION TOOL

88489G23

Fig. 61 Use the brake tool to engage the retracting spring

pins. Using a pair of pliers, grasp the washer type retainer on top of the hold-down spring that corresponds to the pin which you are holding. Push down on the pliers and turn them 90° to align the slot in the washer with the head on the spring mounting pin. Remove the spring and washer retainer and repeat this operation on the hold down spring on the other shoe.

9. Remove the parking brake link and spring. Disconnect the parking brake cable from the parking brake lever.

10. After removing the rear brake secondary shoe, disassemble the parking brake lever from the shoe by removing the retaining clip and spring washer.

To install:

11. Assemble the parking brake lever to the secondary shoe and secure it with the spring washer and retaining clip.

12. Apply a light coating of Lubriplate®, or equivalent, at the points where the brake shoes contact the backing plate.

13. Position the brake shoes on the backing plate, and install the hold-down spring pins, springs, and spring washer type retainers. On the rear brake, install the parking brake link, spring and washer. Connect the parking brake cable to the parking brake lever.

14. Install the anchor pin plate, and place the cable anchor over the anchor pin with the crimped side toward the backing plate.

15. Install the primary shoe-to-anchor spring with the brake tool.

16. Install the cable guide on the secondary shoe web with the flanged holes fitted into the hole in the secondary shoe web. Thread the cable around the cable guide groove.

17. Install the secondary shoe-to-anchor (long) spring. Be sure that the cable end is not cocked or binding on the anchor pin when installed. All of the parts should be flat on the anchor pin. Remove the wheel cylinder piston clamp.

18. Apply Lubriplate®, or equivalent, to the threads and the socket end of the adjusting starwheel screw. Turn the adjusting screw into the adjusting pivot nut to the limit of the threads and then back off ½ turn.

➡**Interchanging the brake shoe adjusting screw assemblies from one side of the vehicle to the other would cause the brake shoes to retract rather than expand each time the automatic adjusting mechanism is operated. To prevent this, the socket end of the adjusting screw is stamped with an "R" or an "L" for "RIGHT" or "LEFT". The adjusting pivot nuts can be distinguished by the number of lines machined around the body of the nut; one line indicates left-hand nut and two lines indicate a right-hand nut.**

19. Place the adjusting socket on the screw and install this assembly between the shoe ends with the adjusting screw nearest to the secondary shoe.

20. Place the cable hook into the hole in the adjusting lever from the backing plate side. The adjusting levers are stamped with an **R** (right) or a **L** (left) to indicate their installation on the right or left-hand brake assembly.

21. Position the hooked end of the adjuster spring in the primary shoe web and connect the loop end of the spring to the adjuster lever hole.

22. Pull the adjuster lever, cable and automatic adjuster spring down toward the rear to engage the pivot hook in the large hole in the secondary shoe web.

23. After installation, check the action of the adjuster by pulling the section of the cable guide and the adjusting lever toward the secondary shoe web far enough to lift the lever past a tooth on the adjusting screw starwheel. The lever should snap into position behind the next tooth, and release of the cable should cause the adjuster spring to return the lever to its original position. This return action of the lever will turn the adjusting screw starwheel one tooth. The lever should contact the adjusting screw starwheel one tooth above the centerline of the adjusting screw.

If the automatic adjusting mechanism does not perform properly, check the following:

24. Check the cable and fittings. The cable ends should fill or extend slightly beyond the crimped section of the fittings. If this is not the case, replace the cable.

25. Check the cable guide for damage. The cable groove should be parallel to the shoe web, and the body of the guide should lie flat against the web. Replace the cable guide if this is not so.

26. Check the pivot hook on the lever. The hook surfaces should be square with the body on the lever for proper pivoting. Repair or replace the hook as necessary.

27. Make sure that the adjusting screw starwheel is properly seated in the notch in the shoe web.

Heavy Duty Systems

♦ **See Figures 62 thru 71**

1. Raise and support the vehicle.
2. Remove the wheel and drum.
3. Remove the parking brake lever assembly retaining nut from behind the backing plate and remove the parking brake lever assembly.
4. Remove the adjusting cable assembly from the anchor pin, cable guide and adjusting lever.
5. Remove the brake shoe retracting springs.
6. Remove the brake shoe hold-down spring from each shoe.
7. Remove the brake shoes and adjusting screw assembly.
8. Disassemble the adjusting screw assembly.
9. Clean the ledge pads on the backing plate. Apply a light coat of Lubriplate®, or equivalent, to the ledge pads (where the brake shoes rub the backing plate).

Fig. 64 Remove the parking brake lever retaining nut, located behind the backing plate

Fig. 62 Common heavy duty drum brake assembly

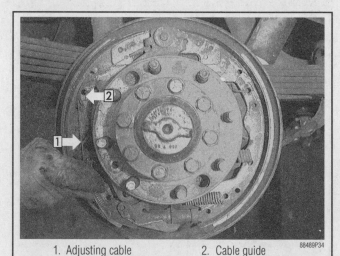

1. Adjusting cable   2. Cable guide

Fig. 65 Disconnect the adjusting cable from the anchor pin, cable guide and lever

Fig. 63 Remove the brake drum from the rear axle

Fig. 66 Slide the parking brake lever out from its mounting

Fig. 67 Disconnect the parking brake cable from the lever

Fig. 68 Use an appropriate tool to disconnect the return springs from their retaining holes

Fig. 69 Disengage the hold-down springs from the retaining clips on the backing plate

Fig. 70 Back off the adjusting screw and remove it from the brake assembly

Fig. 71 Spread the shoes apart and remove them from the backing plate

To install:

10. Apply Lubriplate® to the adjusting screw assembly and the hold-down and retracting spring contacts on the brake shoes.

11. Install the upper retracting spring on the primary and secondary shoes and position the shoe assembly on the backing plate with the wheel cylinder pushrods in the shoe slots.

12. Install the brake shoe hold-down springs.

13. Install the brake shoe adjustment screw assembly with the slot in the head of the adjusting screw toward the primary shoe, lower retracting spring, adjusting lever spring, adjusting lever assembly, and connect the adjusting cable to the adjusting lever. Position the cable in the cable guide and install the cable anchor fitting on the anchor pin.

14. Install the adjusting screw assemblies in the same locations from which they were removed. Interchanging the brake shoe adjusting screws from one side of the vehicle to the other will cause the brake shoes to retract rather than expand each time the automatic adjusting mechanism is operated. To prevent incorrect installation, the socket end of each adjusting screw is stamped with an **R** or an **L** to indicate their installation on the right or left side of the vehicle. The adjusting pivot nuts can be distinguished by the number of lines machined around the body of the nut. Two lines indicate a right-hand nut; one line indicates a left-hand nut.

15. Install the parking brake assembly in the anchor pin and secure with the retaining nut behind the backing plate.

16. Adjust the brakes before installing the brake drums and wheels. Install the brake drums and wheels.

17. Lower the vehicle and road test the brakes. New brakes may pull to one side or the other before they are seated. Continued pulling or erratic braking should not occur.

ADJUSTMENTS

The drum brakes are self-adjusting and require a manual adjustment only after the brake shoes have been replaced, or when the length of the adjusting screw has been changed while performing some other service operation, as, for example, when taking off brake drums.

To adjust the brakes, perform the procedures that follow:

Drum Installed

◗ See Figure 72

1. Raise and support the rear of the vehicle on jackstands.
2. Remove the rubber plug from the adjusting slot on the backing plate.
3. Insert a brake adjusting spoon into the slot and engage the lowest possible tooth on the starwheel. Move the end of the brake spoon downward to move the starwheel upward and expand the adjusting screw. Repeat this operation until the brakes lock the wheels.
4. Insert a small screwdriver or piece of firm wire (coat hanger wire) into the adjusting slot and push the automatic adjusting lever out and free of the starwheel on the adjusting screw and hold it there.
5. Engage the topmost tooth possible on the starwheel with the brake adjusting spoon. Move the end of the adjusting spoon upward to move the adjusting screw starwheel downward and contract the adjusting screw. Back off the adjusting screw starwheel until the wheel spins freely with a minimum of drag. Keep track of the number of turns that the starwheel is backed off, or the number of strokes taken with the brake adjusting spoon.
6. Repeat this operation for the other side. When backing off the brakes on the other side, the starwheel adjuster must be backed off the same number of turns to prevent side-to-side brake pull.
7. When the brakes are adjusted, make several stops while backing the vehicle, to equalize the brakes at both of the wheels.
8. Remove the jackstands and lower the vehicle. Road test the vehicle.

Drum Removed

◗ See Figures 73, 74 and 75

✺✺ CAUTION

Brake shoes may contain asbestos, which has been determined to be a cancer causing agent. Never clean the brake surfaces with compressed air! Avoid inhaling any dust from any brake surface! When cleaning brake surfaces, use a commercially available brake cleaning fluid.

1. Make sure that the shoe-to-contact pad areas are clean and properly lubricated.
2. Using an inside caliper, check the inside diameter of the drum.

➡**Replace any drum which exceeds the maximum allowable diameter, as indicated on the drum.**

3. Measure across the diameter of the assembled brake shoes, at their widest point.

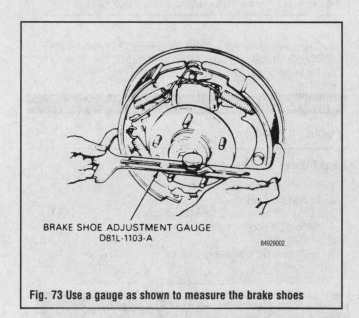

BRAKE SHOE ADJUSTMENT GAUGE
D81L-1103-A

84929002

Fig. 73 Use a gauge as shown to measure the brake shoes

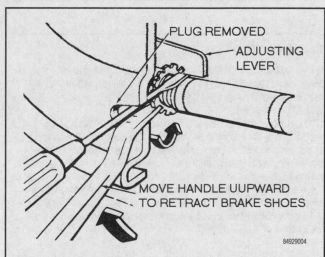

PLUG REMOVED
ADJUSTING LEVER

MOVE HANDLE UUPWARD TO RETRACT BRAKE SHOES

84929004

Fig. 72 Insert an adjusting tool through the slot in the rear of the backing plate

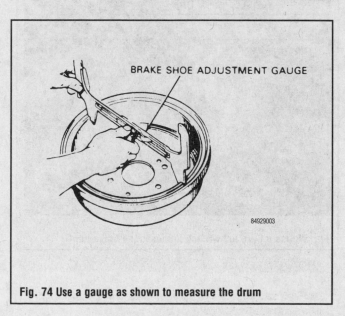

BRAKE SHOE ADJUSTMENT GAUGE

84929003

Fig. 74 Use a gauge as shown to measure the drum

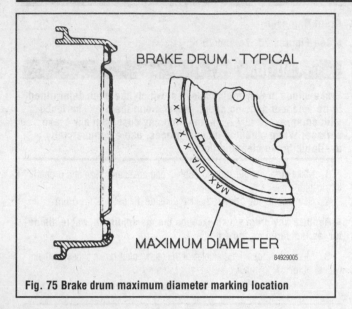

Fig. 75 Brake drum maximum diameter marking location

Fig. 77 Disconnect the brake line from the wheel cylinder, being careful not to kink or break it

4. Turn the adjusting screw so that the diameter of the shoes is 0.030 in. (0.76mm) less than the brake drum inner diameter.
5. Install the brake drum.

Wheel Cylinders

REMOVAL & INSTALLATION

▶ **See Figures 76, 77 and 78**

1. Remove the brake drum.
2. Remove the brake shoes.
3. Loosen the brake line at the wheel cylinder.
4. Remove the wheel cylinder attaching bolt and unscrew the cylinder from the brake line.
5. Installation is the reverse of removal.

Fig. 78 Loosen the retainers at the rear of the backing plate and remove the wheel cylinder

OVERHAUL

▶ **See Figures 79 thru 88**

Wheel cylinder overhaul kits may be available, but often at little or no savings over a reconditioned wheel cylinder. It often makes sense with these components to substitute a new or reconditioned part instead of attempting an overhaul.

If no replacement is available, or you would prefer to overhaul your wheel cylinders, the following procedure may be used. When rebuilding and installing wheel cylinders, avoid getting any contaminants into the system. Always use clean, new, high quality brake fluid. If dirty or improper fluid has been used, it will be necessary to drain the entire system, flush the system with proper brake fluid, replace all rubber components, then refill and bleed the system.

1. Remove the wheel cylinder from the vehicle and place on a clean workbench.

Fig. 76 Use a flare nut wrench to loosen the brake line

Fig. 79 Remove the outer boots from the wheel cylinder

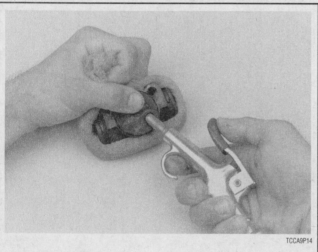

Fig. 80 Compressed air can be used to remove the pistons and seals

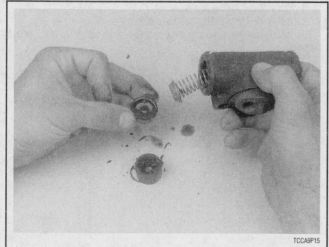

Fig. 81 Remove the pistons, cup seals and spring from the cylinder

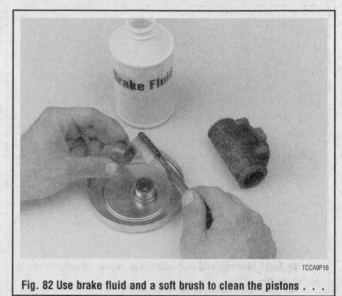

Fig. 82 Use brake fluid and a soft brush to clean the pistons . . .

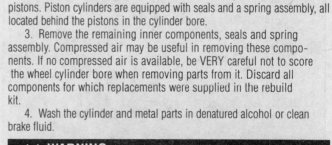

Fig. 83 . . . and the bore of the wheel cylinder

2. First remove and discard the old rubber boots, then withdraw the pistons. Piston cylinders are equipped with seals and a spring assembly, all located behind the pistons in the cylinder bore.

3. Remove the remaining inner components, seals and spring assembly. Compressed air may be useful in removing these components. If no compressed air is available, be VERY careful not to score the wheel cylinder bore when removing parts from it. Discard all components for which replacements were supplied in the rebuild kit.

4. Wash the cylinder and metal parts in denatured alcohol or clean brake fluid.

✳✳ WARNING

Never use a mineral-based solvent such as gasoline, kerosene or paint thinner for cleaning purposes. These solvents will swell rubber components and quickly deteriorate them.

5. Allow the parts to air dry or use compressed air. Do not use rags for cleaning, since lint will remain in the cylinder bore.

6. Inspect the piston and replace it if it shows scratches.

7. Lubricate the cylinder bore and seals using clean brake fluid.

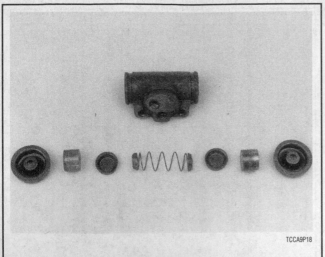

Fig. 84 Once cleaned and inspected, the wheel cylinder is ready for assembly

Fig. 87 Lightly lubricate the pistons, then install them

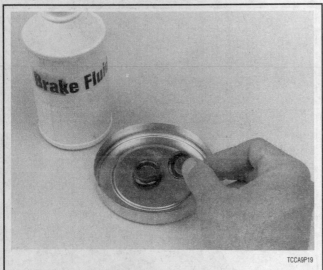

Fig. 85 Lubricate the cup seals with clean brake fluid

Fig. 88 The boots can now be installed over the wheel cylinder ends

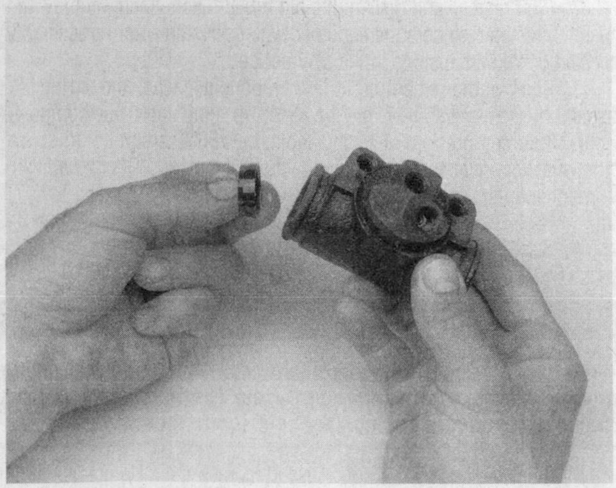

8. Position the spring assembly.
9. Install the inner seals, then the pistons.
10. Insert the new boots into the counterbores by hand. Do not lubricate the boots.
11. Install the wheel cylinder.

Fig. 86 Install the spring, then the cup seals in the bore

PARKING BRAKE

Cables

REMOVAL & INSTALLATION

1989–91 Models

EQUALIZER-TO-CONTROL ASSEMBLY CABLE

▶ **See Figure 89**

1. Raise the van and support it with safety stands.
2. Back off the equalizer nut and remove slug of front cable from the tension limiter.
3. Disengage the cable from the retaining clips.
4. Lower the van and remove the forward ball end of the parking brake cable from the control assembly clevis.
5. Remove the cable from the control assembly by compressing the conduit end fitting prongs with a half inch box wrench.
6. Attach a cord to the control lever end of the cable and remove the cable from the van.

To install:

7. Transfer the cord to the new cable. Place the cable in position, route the cable through the dash panel, remove the cord and connect the cable to the control lever.
8. Connect the ball end of the cable to the clevis of the control assembly.
9. Raise the van and support it with safety stands.
10. Route the cable through the crossmembers and engage it in the retaining clips.
11. Connect the slug of the cable to the tension limiter connector and adjust the cable as outlined in this section.

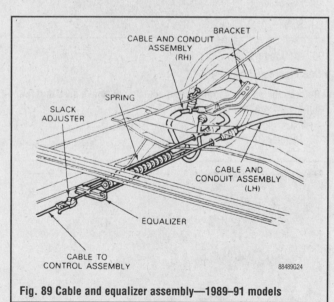

Fig. 89 Cable and equalizer assembly—1989–91 models

EQUALIZER-TO-REAR WHEEL CABLE

▶ **See Figures 90 and 91**

1. Raise and support the rear end on jackstands.
2. Remove the wheels and brake drums.
3. Remove the tension limiter.
4. Remove the locknut from the threaded rod and disconnect the cable from the equalizer.
5. Disconnect the cable housing from the frame bracket and pull the cable and housing out of the bracket.

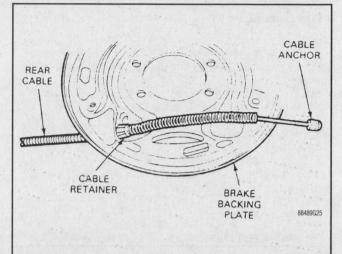

Fig. 90 Compress the prongs on the cable using a ½ inch box end wrench

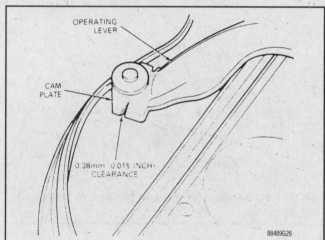

Fig. 91 On models equipped with web ledge brakes, check the clearance between the parking brake operating lever and the cam plate

6. Disconnect the cable from the brake backing plate by compressing the prongs (cable retainer).
7. With the spring tension removed from the lever, lift the cable out of the slot in the lever and remove the cable through the backing plate hole.

To install:

8. Pull the cable through the backing plate until the end of the cable is inserted over the slot in the parking brake lever.
9. Pull the excess slack from the cable and insert the housing into the backing plate access hole until the prongs expand.
10. Insert the front end of the cable housing through the frame cross-member bracket until the prong expands.
11. Insert the ball end of the cable into the equalizer 90 degrees and recouple the tension limiter rod to the equalizer.
12. On models with web ledge brakes, check the clearance between the parking brake operating lever and the cam plate. Clearance should be 0.015 in. (0.38mm) with the brakes fully released.
13. Install the drum and wheel. Adjust the brake shoes.
14. Adjust the parking brake.

1992–96 Models

FRONT CABLE

▶ **See Figures 92 and 93**

1. Remove the control assembly.
2. Relieve tension on the parking brake system by having an assistant pull on the intermediate cable until the cable is unwound from the control assembly.
3. Insert a 5/32 inch (1992–94 models) or a 0.156 inch (4mm) drill (1995–96 models) into the hole in the control assembly.
4. Disconnect the front cable from the connector.
5. Remove the cable from the van.

To install:

6. Route the cable through the left stepwell.
7. Route the cable end fitting over the cable shoe, then snap the fitting into the control assembly. Insert the barrel end into the hole in the track.
8. Install the control assembly.

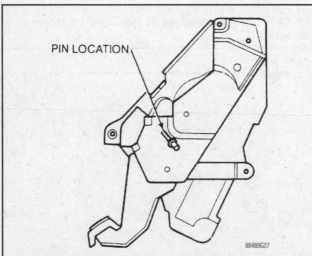

Fig. 92 Place a suitable drill bit or pin into the hole on the control assembly

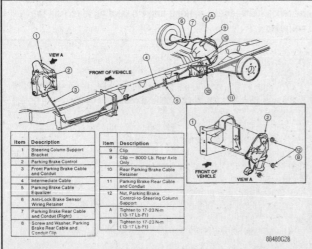

Fig. 93 Exploded view of the parking brake and control assembly—1992–96 models

REAR CABLE

1. Relieve tension on the parking brake system by having an assistant pull on the intermediate cable until the cable is unwound from the control assembly.
2. Insert a 5/32 inch (1992–94 models) or a 0.156 inch (4mm) drill (1995–96 models) into the hole in the control assembly.
3. Raise the van and support it with safety stands. Remove the wheel and brake drum.
4. Disconnect the cable from the equalizer.
5. Use a ½ inch box end wrench to compress the prongs that attach the cable to the frame bracket.
6. Lift the cable out of the slot in the lever and remove the cable through the brake backing plate by compressing the prongs with the ½ inch box end wrench.

To install:

7. Push the cable through the slot in the backing plate until the end of the cable is inserted through the slot in the parking brake lever.
8. Pull the excess slack from the cable and insert the cable housing into the brake backing plate until the prongs expand.
9. Insert the front end of the cable housing through the frame bracket until the prong expands.
10. Install the drum and wheel. Adjust the brake shoes.
11. Remove the drill bit from the control assembly to tension the system.

INTERMEDIATE CABLE

▶ **See Figures 92 and 93**

1. Remove the left-hand cowl panel.
2. Relieve tension on the parking brake system by having an assistant pull on the intermediate cable until the cable is unwound from the control assembly.
3. Insert a 5/32 inch (1992–94 models) or a 0.156 inch (4mm) drill (1995–96 models) into the hole in the control assembly.
4. Disconnect the cable from the connector and equalizer.
5. Remove the cable from the van.
6. Installation is the reverse of removal.

ADJUSTMENT

1989–91 Models

▶ **See Figures 91 and 94**

➡ **Before making any parking brake adjustment, make sure that the drum brakes are properly adjusted.**

1. Raise and support the rear end on jackstands.
2. The brake drums should be cold.

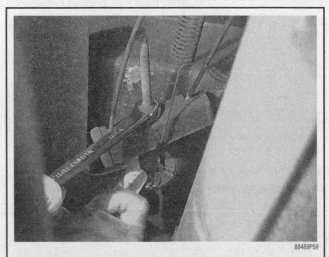

Fig. 94 Hold the equalizer while turning the nut to adjust the parking brake cable

3. Make sure that the parking brake pedal is fully released.
4. While holding the tension equalizer, tighten the equalizer nut 6 full turns past its original position.
5. Fully depress the parking brake pedal. Using a cable tension gauge, check rear cable tension. Cable tension should be 350 lbs. minimum.
6. Fully release the parking brake. No drag should be noted at the wheels.
7. If drag is noted on E-250 and E-350 models, you'll have to remove the drums and adjust the clearance between the parking brake lever and cam plate. Clearance should be 0.015 in. (0.38mm). Clearance is adjusted at the parking brake equalizer adjusting nut.

➡ If the tension limiter on the E-150 models doesn't release the drag, the tension limiter will have to be replaced.

1992–96 Models

The parking brake systems on these models are self-adjusting and require no adjustment.

Brake Shoes

REMOVAL & INSTALLATION

E-Super Duty Model

➡ This procedure only applies to vehicles equipped with a transmission mounted parking brake.

A transmission mounted parking brake is used on some E-super duty models. The unit is mounted to the transmission extension housing; it incorporates a case assembly and a cable actuated drum brake assembly.

The replacement of the parking brake shoes involves the removal and disassembly of the unit and requires the use of several specialized tools. The cost of purchasing the tools needed for this procedure far outweighs the cost of having the unit repaired by a shop; therefore, we recommend that you have this procedure performed by a qualified technician or shop.

REAR ANTI-LOCK BRAKE SYSTEM (RABS)

Operation

The RABS constantly monitors rear wheel speed and, in the event of impending rear wheel lock-up in a sudden stop, regulates the brake fluid hydraulic pressure at the rear brakes to prevent total wheel lock-up, thus reducing the possibility of skidding.

COMPONENT LOCATION

The RABS consists of the following components:
1. RABS module—located in the cab on the driver's side inside the cowl panel, just outboard of the parking brake mechanism.
2. Dual Solenoid Electro-Hydraulic Valve is located on the left inside frame rail, behind the engine mount crossmember.
3. Speed Sensor and Exciter Ring—located in the rear axle carrier.
4. Yellow REAR ANTI-LOCK Warning Light—located in the instrument cluster.
5. RABS Diagnostic Connector is located just off the module connector harness.
6. Diode/Resistor Element is located on the main trunk of the instru-

ADJUSTMENT

➡ See Figure 95

1. Place the transmission in Neutral, then raise the van and support it with safety stands.
2. Loosen the adjusting clevis jam nut several turns.
3. Disconnect the parking brake lever return spring from the clevis pin.
4. Remove the self-locking and clevis pins from the clevis.
5. Hold the lever in the applied position and screw the clevis onto the threaded end of the parking brake cable until the actuating lever hole and clevis lever holes align.
6. Lengthen the parking brake cable 0.5 inch (13mm).
7. Position the clevis over the lever and install the clevis and self-locking pins.
8. Connect the return spring to the head of the clevis pin.
9. Rotate the driveshaft to ensure the brake shoes are not dragging against the drum.
10. Lower the van and check for proper parking brake operation.

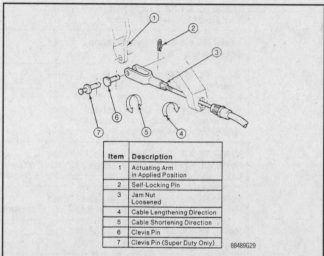

Item	Description
1	Actuating Arm in Applied Position
2	Self-Locking Pin
3	Jam Nut Loosened
4	Cable Lengthening Direction
5	Cable Shortening Direction
6	Clevis Pin
7	Clevis Pin (Super Duty Only)

Fig. 95 The clevis lever must be adjusted so that its holes align with the one in the actuating lever

ment panel wiring harness where the RABS module connector pigtail intersects with the main trunk.
7. Sensor test Connector—located under the hood between the battery and the right side engine compartment wall.
The RABS II consists of the following components:
8. RABS module—located in the cab mounted to the instrument panel lower brace behind the passenger side trim cover.
9. Dual Solenoid Electro-Hydraulic Valve is located left inside frame rail behind the engine mount crossmember.
10. Speed Sensor and Exciter Ring—located in the rear axle carrier.
11. Yellow REAR ANTI-LOCK Warning Light—located in the instrument cluster.
12. RABS Diagnostic Connector is located behind the trim panel at the far right side of the instrument panel, just below the brace.
13. Diode/Resistor Element is located on the main trunk of the instrument panel wiring harness where the (RABS) module connector pigtail intersects with the main trunk.
14. Sensor test Connector—located under the hood between the battery and the right side engine compartment wall.

System Self-Test

▶ See Figure 96

The RABS module performs system tests and self-tests during startup and normal operation. The valve, sensor and fluid level circuits are monitored for proper operation. If a fault is found, the RABS will be deactivated and the REAR ANTI LOCK light will be lit until the ignition is turned OFF. When the light is lit, the diagnostic flashout code may be obtained. Under normal operation, the light will stay on for about 2 seconds while the ignition switch is in the ON position and will go out shortly after. A flash code may be obtained only when the yellow light is ON. Before reading the code, drive the vehicle to a level area and place the shift lever in the PARK or NEUTRAL position. Keep the vehicle ignition ON.

➡ Starting in 1993, all vehicles use the RABS II system. The major difference between the two systems is the addition of a "keep alive memory" (codes are stored, even if ignition is turned off), and a code 16 can be set, which means the system is operating properly.

TO OBTAIN THE FLASH CODE:

1. Locate the RABS diagnostic connector (orange/black wire) and attach a jumper wire to it and momentarily (1 to 2 seconds) ground it to the chassis.

2. Quickly remove the ground. When the ground is made and then removed, the RABS light will begin to flash.

3. The code consists of a number of short flashes and ends with a long flash. Count the short flashes and include the following long flash in the count to obtain the code number. Example 3 short flashes and one long flash indicated Code No. 4. The code will continue until the ignition is turned **OFF**. Refer to the flashcode diagnosis charts for further instructions.

FLASHOUT CODES CHART
CONDITION
No Flashout Code
Yellow REAR ABS Light Flashes 1 Time This Code Should Not Occur
Yellow REAR ABS Light Flashes 2 Times Open Isolate Circuit
Yellow REAR ABS Light Flashes 3 Times Open Dump Circuit
Yellow REAR ABS Light Flashes 4 Times Red Brake Warning Light Illuminated RABS Valve Switch Closed
Yellow REAR ABS Light Flashes 5 Times System Dumps Too Many Times in 2WD (2WD and 4WD vehicles). Condition Occurs While Making Normal or Hard Stops. Rear Brake May Lock
Yellow REAR ABS Light Flashes 6 Times (Sensor Signal Rapidly Cuts In and Out). Condition Only Occurs While Driving
Yellow REAR ABS Light Flashes 7 Times No Isolate Valve Self Test
Yellow REAR ABS Light Flashes 8 Times No Dump Valve Self Test
Yellow REAR ABS Light Flashes 9 Times High Sensor Resistance
Yellow REAR ABS Light Flashes 10 Times Low Sensor Resistance
Yellow REAR ABS Light Flashes 11 Times Stoplamp Switch Circuit Defective. Condition Indicated Only When Driving Above 35 mph
Yellow REAR ABS Light Flashes 12 Times Fluid Level Switch Grounded During a RABS Stop
Yellow REAR ABS Light Flashes 13 Times Speed Processor Check
Yellow REAR ABS Light Flashes 14 Times Program Check
Yellow REAR ABS Light Flashes 15 Times Memory Failure
Yellow REAR ABS Light Flashes 16 Times or More 16 or More Flashes Should Not Occur

NOTE: Refer to Obtaining the Flashout Code in this section for procedure to obtain flashout code.

CAUTION: WHEN CHECKING RESISTANCE IN THE RABS SYSTEM, ALWAYS DISCONNECT THE BATTERY. IMPROPER RESISTANCE READINGS MAY OCCUR WITH THE VEHICLE BATTERY CONNECTED.

85559099

Fig. 96 RABS trouble code index

Trouble Codes

Count the number of times the yellow ABS system light illuminates to determine the Diagnostic Trouble Code. The codes listed are for both systems unless specified in the text.
- Code 2: Light flashes 2 times; open isolation valve circuit
- Code 3: Light flashes 3 times; open dump valve circuit
- Code 4: Light flashes 4 times and red brake warning switch illuminated; RABS valve switch closed or open dump valve
- Code 5: Light flashes 5 times; System dumps too many times
- Code 6: Light flashes 6 times; Sensor signal rapidly cuts in and out
- Code 7: Light flashes 7 times; No isolate valve self-test
- Code 8: Light flashes 8 times; No dump valve self-test
- Code 9: Light flashes 9 times; High sensor resistance
- Code 10: Light flashes 10 times; Low sensor resistance
- Code 11: Light flashes 11 times; Defective stoplamp switch circuit
- Code 12: Light flashes 12 times; Base brake hydraulic loose or worn/damaged master cylinder switch/wiring
- Code 13 RABS system: Light flashes 13 times; Speed processor check
- Code 13 RABS II system: Light flashes 13 times; Module failure
- Code 14 RABS system: Light flashes 14 times; Program check
- Code 15 RABS system: Light flashes 15 times; Memory failure
- Code 16: Light flashes 16 times; System Pass

Computer (RABS) Module

REMOVAL & INSTALLATION

▶ **See Figures 97 and 98**

1. On RABS equipped models, remove the parking brake actuator assembly.
2. Remove any instrument panel covers to gain access to the module.
3. Disconnect the wiring harness to the module.
4. Remove the retaining screws and remove the module.

To install:

5. Place the module in position. Install and tighten the retainers.
6. Connect the wiring harness to the module.
7. Install any instrument panels which were removed.
8. On RABS equipped models, install the parking brake actuator assembly.
9. Check the system for proper operation.

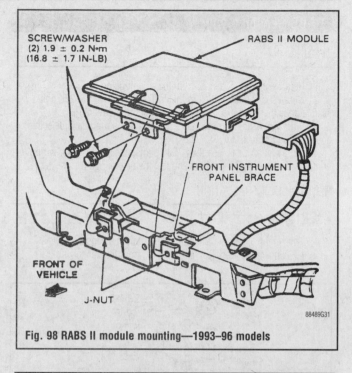

Fig. 98 RABS II module mounting—1993–96 models

RABS Valve

REMOVAL & INSTALLATION

▶ **See Figure 99**

1. Disconnect the brake lines from the valve and plug the lines.
2. Disconnect the wiring harness at the valve.
3. Remove the 3 nuts retaining the valve to the frame rail and lift out the valve.
4. Installation is the reverse of removal. Don't overtighten the brake lines. Bleed the brakes.

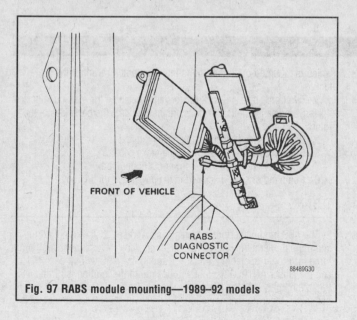

Fig. 97 RABS module mounting—1989–92 models

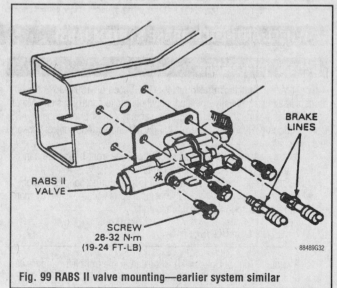

Fig. 99 RABS II valve mounting—earlier system similar

RABS Sensor

TESTING

1. Remove the RABS sensor from the axle housing.
2. Connect a Digital Volt/Ohm Meter (DVOM) set on the 20K ohms scale across the two sensor terminals and record the reading.
3. If the resistance is more than 2500 ohms, the module is defective and must be replaced.
4. If the resistance is less than 2500 ohms, check the sensor wiring for an open circuit. Repair the circuit and test the sensor again.

REMOVAL & INSTALLATION

▶ **See Figure 100**

1. Thoroughly clean the axle housing around the sensor.
2. Disconnect the electrical harness plug from the sensor.

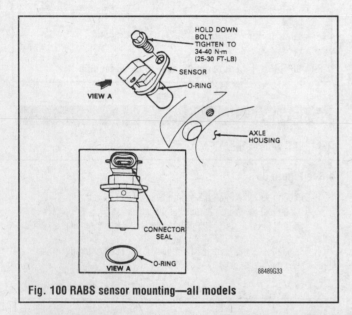

Fig. 100 RABS sensor mounting—all models

3. Remove the sensor hold-down bolt.
4. Remove the sensor by pulling it straight out of the axle housing.
5. Ensure that the axle surface is and that no dirt can enter the housing.
6. If a new sensor is being installed, lubricate the O-ring with clean engine oil. Carefully push the sensor into the housing aligning the mounting flange hole with the threaded hole in the housing. Tighten the hold-down bolt to 30 ft. lbs. (41 Nm). If the old sensor is being installed, clean it thoroughly and install a new O-ring coated with clean engine oil.

Exciter Ring

The ring is located on the differential case inside the axle housing. Once it is pressed off the case, it cannot be reused. This job should be left to a qualified service technician, as it requires the rear differential to be disassembled.

Bleeding The ABS System

On 1989–92 models, the RABS system is bled in the same manner as the hydraulic system.

On 1993–96 models, bleed the system as follows:
1. Disengage the ECU harness connector.
2. Engage Anti-Lock Brake Adapter T90P-50-ALA (bleeder box) to the ECU harness connector.
3. Engage the 55 way connector to Anti-Lock Adapter T93T-50-ALA (jumper cable) and EEC-IV breakout box T83L-50EEC-IV.
4. Slide the bleeder box switch to the bleed position.
5. Turn the key **ON**. The **OFF** indicator light should be illuminated.
6. Depress the MOTOR START button. The **ON** indicator light should illuminate.
7. The pump will run for 60 seconds, then push the abort button and this will turn the pump OFF.
8. After the first 20 seconds have passed, push and hold old the VALVES button for 20 seconds. The pump will continue to run 20 seconds after the VALVES button is released.
9. Turn the key **OFF** and disconnect the bleeder box and adapter.
10. Connect the ECU harness.
11. Bleed the brake system in the conventional manner.

4-WHEEL ANTI-LOCK BRAKE SYSTEM (ABS)

General Information

The 4-Wheel Anti-lock Brake System (ABS) used on 1995–96 Econoline models is an electronically operated, all wheel brake control system. Major components include the master cylinder, vacuum power brake booster, ABS Control Module, Hydraulic Control Unit (HCU) and various control sensors and switches.

The brake system is a three channel design. The front brakes are controlled individually and the rear brakes in tandem.

The system is designed to retard wheel lockup during periods of high wheel slip when braking. Retarding wheel lockup is accomplished by modulating fluid pressure to the wheel brake units.

COMPONENT LOCATIONS

1. Hydraulic Control Unit (HCU) is located in the front left-hand frame inboard liner just under the driver's seat.
2. Anti-lock brake control module is located on the fuel filter bracket which is mounted on the left-hand inboard frame in front of the fuel tank.
3. Two front brake anti-lock sensors are located on the steering knuckles.
4. Speed sensor indicator rings are pressed onto the backsides of the rotors.
5. Rear axle speed sensor is integrated into the rear axle housing.
6. Stoplight switch is attached to the brake pedal.
7. ABS relay is located in the power distribution box.
8. Pump motor relay is located in the power distribution box.

TESTING

The ABS module performs system tests and self-tests during startup and normal operation. The valve, sensor and fluid level circuits are monitored for proper operation. If a fault is found, the ABS will be deactivated and the amber ANTI LOCK light will be lit until the ignition is turned OFF. When the light is lit, the Diagnostic Trouble Code (DTC) may be obtained. Under normal operation, the light will stay on for about 2 seconds while the ignition switch is in the ON position and will go out shortly after.

The Diagnostic Trouble Codes (DTC) are an alphanumeric code and a scan tool, such as Rotunda NGS Tester 007-00500 or its equivalent, is required to retrieve the codes. Refer to the manufacturers instructions for operating the tool and retrieving the codes.

Trouble Codes

A scan tool, such as Rotunda NGS Tester 007-00500 or its equivalent, is required to retrieve the codes. Refer to the manufacturers instructions for operating the tool and retrieving the codes.
- Code C1220: Amber ABS warning lamp failure
- Codes C1225 or C1226: Shorted red brake system warning lamp failure, Foundation brake system
- Codes C1198 or C1200: Front left isolation dump valve
- Codes C1194 or C1196: Front left dump valve
- Codes C1214 or C1216: Front right isolation dump valve
- Codes C1210 or C1212: Front right dump valve
- Codes C1206 or C1208: Rear axle isolation valve
- Codes C1202 or 1204: Rear axle dump valve
- Code C1155: Left front brake anti-lock sensor open circuit
- Code C1258: Left front brake anti-lock sensor output fault
- Code C1145: Right front brake anti-lock sensor diagnosis (electrical/static)

- Codes C1148, C1234 or C1259: Right front brake anti-lock sensor diagnosis (Dynamic)
- Code C1230: Vehicle speed sensor diagnosis (electrical/static)
- Codes C1229, C1237 or C1260: Rear axle speed sensor diagnosis
- Code C1238: Shuttled reset switch concern diagnosis
- Codes C1095 or C1096: Pump motor circuit failure diagnosis
- Codes C1113, C1115 or C1185: Pump motor circuit/relay failure diagnosis
- Codes C1184 or C1222: Generic sensor indicator diagnosis (dynamic)

Hydraulic Control Unit

REMOVAL & INSTALLATION

◆ **See Figure 101**

1. Disconnect the battery ground cable.
2. Unplug the 12-pin connector from the unit, and the 2-pin connector from the pump motor.
3. Disconnect the 5 inlet and outlet tubes from the unit. Immediately plug the ports.

➡**The HCU assembly bracket contains locating hooks on top of the frame. The assembly must be lifted prior to pulling it away from the frame.**

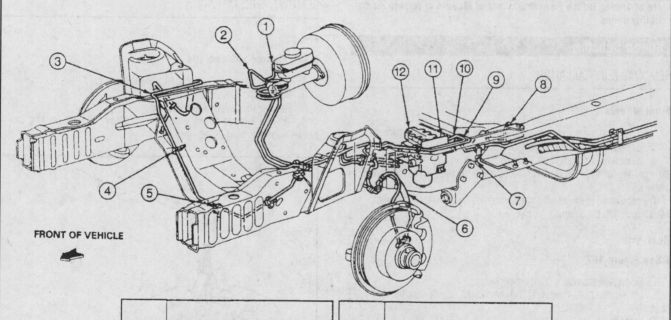

FRONT OF VEHICLE

Item	Description		Item	Description
1	Tube Assembly (Secondary)		7	Union Assembly
2	Tube Assembly (Primary)		8	Anti-Lock Brake Module
3	Front Brake Tube (RH)		9	Front Brake Tube (LH)
4	Clip 2-Way		10	Front Brake Tube (RH)
5	Clip 3-Way		11	Intermediate Brake Tube
6	Front Brake Hose (LH)		12	Hydraulic Control Unit (HCU)

88489G34

Fig. 101 Exploded view of the 4-wheel anti-lock brake system components

4. Remove the 3 unit attaching nuts and lift out the unit.

5. Installation is the reverse of removal. Tighten the mounting nuts to 12–18 ft. lbs. (16–24 Nm) and the tube fittings to 10–18 ft. lbs. (13–24 Nm).

➡**After reconnecting the battery, it may take 10 miles or more of driving for the Powertrain Control Module to relearn its driveability codes.**

6. Bleed the brakes.

Control Module

REMOVAL & INSTALLATION

▶ **See Figure 101**

1. Disconnect the battery ground cable.
2. Locate the module on the ABS bracket. The bracket is located in the front left-hand frame inboard liner just under the driver's seat.
3. Unplug the 40-pin connector from the module.
4. Remove the retainers, slide the module off its bracket.

To install:

5. Install the module and tighten the mounting screws to 62–80 inch lbs. (7–9 Nm).
6. Engage the connector and tighten the bolt to 53–62 inch lbs. (6–7 Nm).

➡**After reconnecting the battery, it may take 10 miles (16 km) or more of driving for the Powertrain Control Module to relearn its driveability codes.**

Speed Sensors

REMOVAL & INSTALLATION

Front Wheels

1. Disengage the sensor two-pin connector from the wiring harness.
2. Disengage the sensor cable from the brake hose clips.
3. Loosen the retaining bolt from the front spindle (E-150 only) and slide the sensor from the mating hole. Remove the rotor on E-250 and 350 models.
4. Installation is the reverse of removal. Tighten the retaining bolt to 44–53 inch lbs. (5–6 Nm).

Rear Axle

▶ **See Figure 102**

1. Disengage the wiring from the sensor.
2. Loosen the hold-down bolt and remove the sensor from the axle housing.

To install:

3. Thoroughly clean the mounting surfaces. Make sure no dirt falls into the axle. Clean the magnetized sensor pole piece. Metal particles can cause sensor problems. Replace the O-ring.
4. Coat the new O-ring with clean engine oil.
5. Position the new sensor on the axle. It should slide into place easily. Correct installation will allow a gap of 0.005–0.045 in. (0.13–1.14mm).
6. Tighten the hold-down bolt to 25–30 ft. lbs. (34–41 Nm).
7. Connect the wiring.

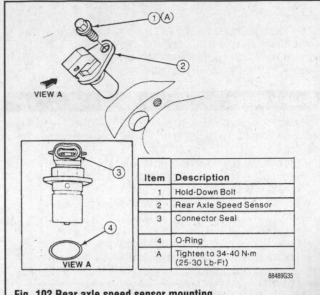

Item	Description
1	Hold-Down Bolt
2	Rear Axle Speed Sensor
3	Connector Seal
4	O-Ring
A	Tighten to 34-40 N·m (25-30 Lb-Ft)

88489G35

Fig. 102 Rear axle speed sensor mounting

Speed Sensor Rings

REMOVAL & INSTALLATION

Front

▶ **See Figures 103 and 104**

1. Raise and support the front end on jackstands.
2. Remove the wheels.
3. Remove the caliper, rotor and hub.
4. Using a 3-jawed puller, remove the ring from the hub. The ring cannot be reused; it must be replaced.

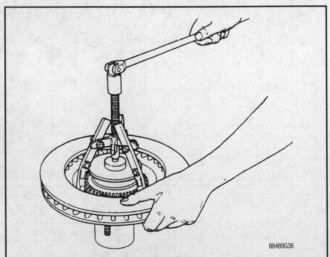

88489G36

Fig. 103 Use a 3-jawed puller to remove the front speed sensor ring from the hub

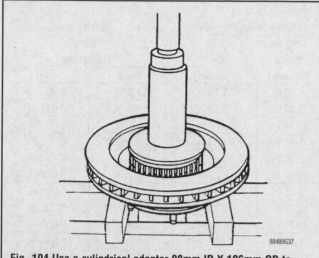

Fig. 104 Use a cylindrical adapter 98mm ID X 106mm OD to press the ring into place

To install:

5. Support the hub in a press so that the lug studs do not rest on the work surface.

6. Position the **new** sensor ring on the hub. Using a cylindrical adapter with a 98mm ID X 106mm OD, press the ring into place. The ring **must** be fully seated!

7. The remainder of installation is the reverse of removal.

Rear

The rear speed sensor ring is located on the differential case inside the axle housing. Once it is pressed off the case, it cannot be reused. This job should be left to a qualified service technician, as it requires the rear differential to be disassembled.

Bleeding The ABS System

The 4-wheel anti-lock brake system can be bled in the conventional manner unless the Hydraulic Control Unit (HCU) has been replaced. Only perform this procedure if the HCU has been replaced.

→Brake fluid absorbs moisture from the air. Don't leave the master cylinder or the fluid container uncovered any longer than necessary. Be careful handling the fluid—it will damage the vehicle's paint.

1. Pressure bleed the brake system as follows:

   a. Remove the master cylinder cap and ensure the reservoir is filled.

   b. Install a pressure bleeder adapter such as Rotunda brake bleeder 104-00064 or equivalent to the master cylinder reservoir and attach a bleeder tank to the adopter. Refer to the manufactories safety and operating instructions when operating the equipment.

   c. Place a ⅜ inch box wrench on the right-hand bleeder screw and attach a bleeder tube around the screw.

   d. Open the valve on the bleeder tank to release the pressurized brake fluid into the master cylinder reservoir.

   e. Submerge the free end of the bleeder tube into a clear container with fresh brake fluid and loosen the bleeder screw.

   f. When all air bubbles have disappeared, close the bleeder screw and remove the tube.

   g. Repeat this procedure, going in order from the left-hand rear wheel cylinder, right-hand front caliper and left-hand front caliper.

   h. When the bleeding is complete, remove the bleeding equipment.

   i. Fill the master cylinder and replace the cap.

2. Disengage the ECU harness connector.

3. Engage Anti-Lock Brake Adapter T90P-50-ALA (bleeder box) to the ECU harness connector.

4. Engage the 55-way connector to Anti-Lock Adapter T93T-50-ALA (jumper cable) and EEC-IV breakout box T83L-50EEC-IV.

5. Slide the bleeder box switch to the bleed position.

6. Turn the key **ON**. The **OFF** indicator light should be illuminated.

7. Depress the MOTOR START button. The **ON** indicator light should illuminate.

8. Let the pump run for 20 seconds, then push and hold the VALVES button for 20 seconds and release the VALVES button. The pump will continue to run 20 seconds after the VALVES button is released and the **OFF** indicator lamp will illuminate when the operation is complete.

9. Turn the key **OFF** and disconnect the bleeder box and adapter.

10. Connect the ECU harness.

11. Pressure bleed the brake system.

BRAKE SPECIFICATIONS

Year	Model	Brake Disc		Maximum Run-out	Brake Drum Diameter		Minimum Lining Thickness	
		Original Thickness	Maximum Refinish		Original Inside Diameter	Max. Wear Limit	Front	Rear
1987	E-150	1.160 in.	1.120 in.	0.003 in.	11.03 in.	11.09 in.	0.030 in.	0.030 in.
	E-250	1.220 in.	1.180 in.	0.003 in.	12.00 in.	12.09 in.	0.030 in.	0.030 in.
	E-350	1.220 in.	1.180 in.	0.003 in.	12.00 in.	12.09 in.	0.030 in.	0.030 in.
1988	E-150	1.160 in.	1.120 in.	0.003 in.	11.03 in.	11.09 in.	0.030 in.	0.030 in.
	E-250	1.220 in.	1.180 in.	0.003 in.	12.00 in.	12.09 in.	0.030 in.	0.030 in.
	E-350	1.220 in.	1.180 in.	0.003 in.	12.00 in.	12.09 in.	0.030 in.	0.030 in.
1989	E-150	1.160 in.	1.120 in.	0.003 in.	11.03 in.	11.09 in.	0.030 in.	0.030 in.
	E-250	1.220 in.	1.180 in.	0.003 in.	12.00 in.	12.09 in.	0.030 in.	0.030 in.
	E-350	1.220 in.	1.180 in.	0.003 in.	12.00 in.	12.09 in.	0.030 in.	0.030 in.
1990	E-150	1.160 in.	1.120 in.	0.003 in.	11.03 in.	11.09 in.	0.030 in.	0.030 in.
	E-250	1.220 in.	1.180 in.	0.003 in.	12.00 in.	12.09 in.	0.030 in.	0.030 in.
	E-350	1.220 in.	1.180 in.	0.003 in.	12.00 in.	12.09 in.	0.030 in.	0.030 in.
1991	E-150	1.160 in.	1.120 in.	0.003 in.	11.03 in.	11.09 in.	0.030 in.	0.030 in.
	E-250	1.220 in.	1.180 in.	0.003 in.	12.00 in.	12.09 in.	0.030 in.	0.030 in.
	E-350	1.220 in.	1.180 in.	0.003 in.	12.00 in.	12.09 in.	0.030 in.	0.030 in.
1992	E-150	1.160 in.	1.120 in.	0.003 in.	11.03 in.	11.09 in.	0.030 in.	0.030 in.
	E-250	1.220 in.	1.180 in.	0.003 in.	12.00 in.	12.09 in.	0.030 in.	0.030 in.
	E-350	1.220 in.	1.180 in.	0.003 in.	12.00 in.	12.09 in.	0.030 in.	0.030 in.
1993	E-150	1.160 in.	1.120 in.	0.003 in.	11.03 in.	11.09 in.	0.030 in.	0.030 in.
	E-250	1.220 in.	1.180 in.	0.003 in.	12.00 in.	12.09 in.	0.030 in.	0.030 in.
	E-350	1.220 in.	1.180 in.	0.003 in.	12.00 in.	12.09 in.	0.030 in.	0.030 in.
1994	E-150	1.160 in.	1.120 in.	0.003 in.	11.03 in.	11.09 in.	0.030 in.	0.030 in.
	E-250	1.220 in.	1.180 in.	0.003 in.	12.00 in.	12.09 in.	0.030 in.	0.030 in.
	E-350	1.220 in.	1.180 in.	0.003 in.	12.00 in.	12.09 in.	0.030 in.	0.030 in.
1995	E-150	1.160 in.	1.120 in.	0.003 in.	11.03 in.	11.09 in.	0.030 in.	0.030 in.
	E-250	1.220 in.	1.180 in.	0.003 in.	12.00 in.	12.09 in.	0.030 in.	0.030 in.
	E-350	1.220 in.	1.180 in.	0.003 in.	12.00 in.	12.09 in.	0.030 in.	0.030 in.
1996	E-150	1.160 in.	1.120 in.	0.003 in.	11.03 in.	11.09 in.	0.030 in.	0.030 in.
	E-250	1.220 in.	1.180 in.	0.003 in.	12.00 in.	12.09 in.	0.030 in.	0.030 in.
	E-350	1.220 in.	1.180 in.	0.003 in.	12.00 in.	12.09 in.	0.030 in.	0.030 in.

88489C01

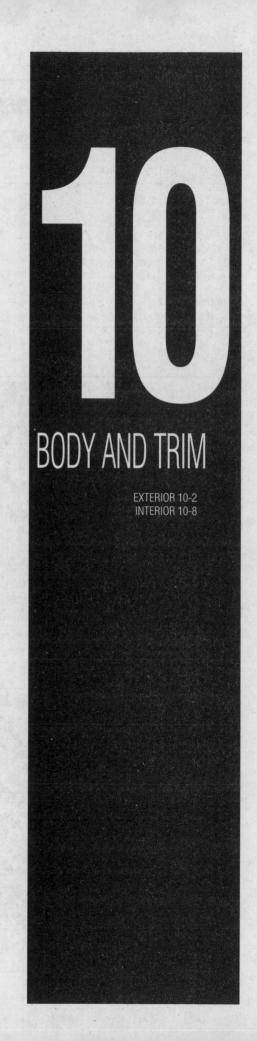

10

BODY AND TRIM

EXTERIOR

Doors

REMOVAL & INSTALLATION

▶ **See Figures 1, 2 and 3**

1. If equipped, disengage any door electrical wiring.
2. Matchmark the hinge-to-body locations. Support the door either on jackstands or have somebody hold it for you.
3. Remove the lower hinge-to-frame bolts.
4. Remove the upper hinge-to-frame bolts and lift the door off of the body.

To install:

5. Install the door and hinges with the bolts finger-tight.
6. Adjust the door and tighten the hinge bolts to 18–25 ft. lbs. (25–35 Nm).

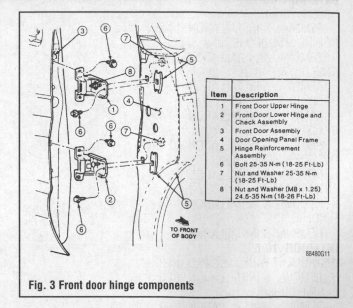

Item	Description
1	Front Door Upper Hinge
2	Front Door Lower Hinge and Check Assembly
3	Front Door Assembly
4	Door Opening Panel Frame
5	Hinge Reinforcement Assembly
6	Bolt 25-35 N·m (18-25 Ft-Lb)
7	Nut and Washer 25-35 N·m (18-25 Ft-Lb)
8	Nut and Washer (M8 x 1.25) 24.5-35 N·m (18-26 Ft-Lb)

TO FRONT OF BODY

88480G11

Fig. 3 Front door hinge components

Sliding Side Doors

REMOVAL & INSTALLATION

▶ **See Figures 4, 5 and 6**

1. Open the door and remove the upper garnish moldings, quarter trim panel, lower stepwell panel and door lower latch cover, if equipped.
2. Remove the lower latch from the guide assembly.
3. Remove the upper and/or lower track stop assembly.
4. Remove the center track shield and slide the door rearward, then tilt the upper corner inward until the upper roller is off the track.
5. Lift the lower roller off the track and the center roller from its track.
6. Remove the door from the body.

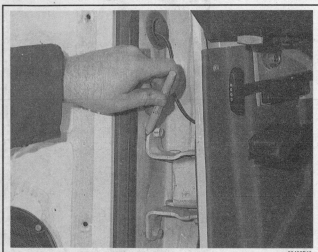

88480P40

Fig. 1 Mark the front door hinge-to-body locations. This will aid during installation

88480P41

Fig. 2 Loosen the bolts, disengage the electrical connections and remove the door

88480P18

Fig. 4 Loosen the upper sliding assembly retaining bolt

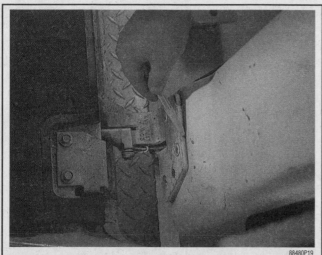

Fig. 5 Mark the location of the lower sliding assembly-to-door attachment . . .

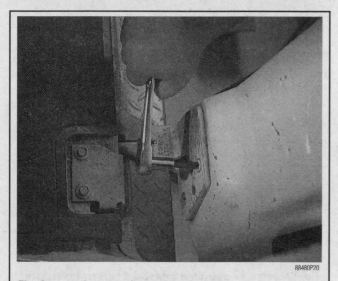

Fig. 6 . . . and remove the retaining screws

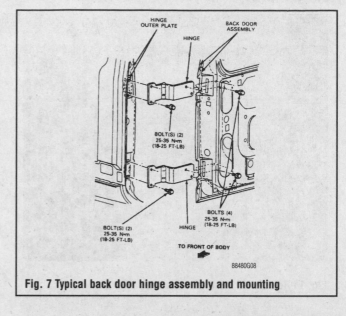

Fig. 7 Typical back door hinge assembly and mounting

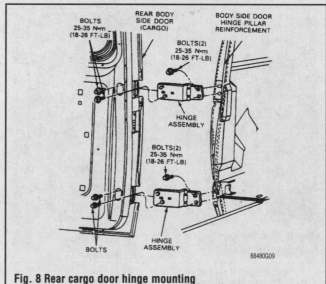

Fig. 8 Rear cargo door hinge mounting

To install:

7. Install the door on the body and engage the lower and center rollers on their tracks.

8. Install the upper roller on its track and slide the door forward.

9. Install the center track.

10. Install the upper and/or lower track stop assembly, as applicable.

11. Install the lower on the guide assembly.

12. Install the upper garnish moldings, quarter trim panel, lower step-well panel and door lower latch cover, if equipped.

Rear Doors

REMOVAL & INSTALLATION

♦ See Figures 7, 8, 9, 10 and 11

➡The hinges are riveted to the doors and bolted to the door frames. If the hinges are to be replaced, remove the door and drill out the rivets.

1. If equipped, disengage the electrical connections.
2. Matchmark the hinge-to-body locations. Support the door either on jackstands or have somebody hold it for you.

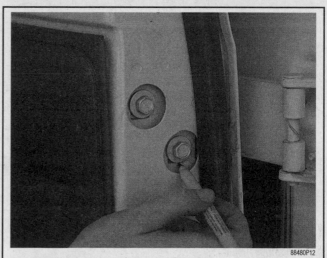

Fig. 9 Mark the hinge-to-body locations; this will aid during installation

Fig. 10 Remove the door retaining strap pin

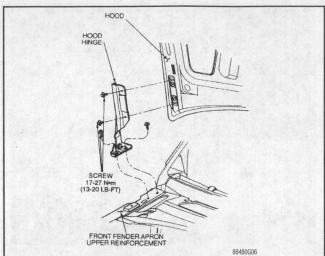

Fig. 12 The hood is attached to the body of the van via a hinge which allows the hood to swing open

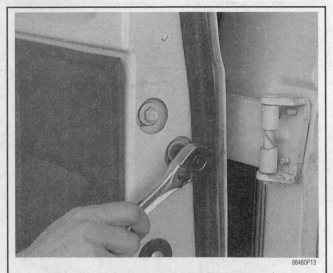

Fig. 11 Loosen the hinge-to-body bolts and remove the door

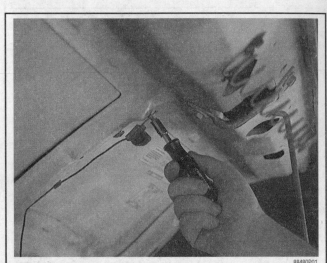

Fig. 13 Loosen the underhood light socket retainer and remove the light assembly

3. Remove the lower hinge-to-frame bolts.
4. If equipped, remove the door strap pin.
5. Remove the upper hinge-to-frame bolts and lift the door off of the body.

To install:

6. If the hinges are being replaced, drill out the rivets using a 1 inch drill bit. New hinges are to be attached to the door with bolts, lockwashers and nuts. Use only hardened bolts of at least Grade 5.
7. Install the door and hinges with the bolts finger-tight.
8. Adjust the door and tighten the hinge bolts to 18–25 ft. lbs. (25–35 Nm).

Hood

REMOVAL & INSTALLATION

▶ See Figures 12, 13 and 14

1. Open and prop up the hood.
2. If equipped, remove the electrical wiring for the underhood light.
3. Matchmark the hinge-to-hood location.

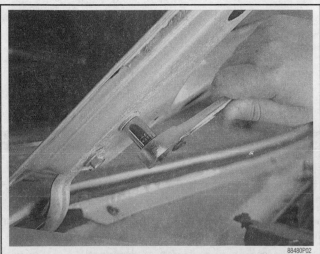

Fig. 14 Loosen the hinge-to-hood bolts and, with the aid of an assistant, remove the hood

4. Remove the bolts from each hinge and with the help of an assistant, lift off the hood.

To install:

5. Install the hood and line up the hinges with the marks made during installation.

6. Install the hood retainers and tighten the m to 13–19 ft. lbs. (17–27 Nm).

7. If equipped, install the underhood light electrical wiring.

8. Align the hood.

Grille

REMOVAL & INSTALLATION

1989–91 Models

▶ **See Figures 15 thru 20**

1. Prop the hood in the open position.

2. Remove the screws which retain the grille center to the radiator grille support.

3. Remove the screws along the bottom of the grille.

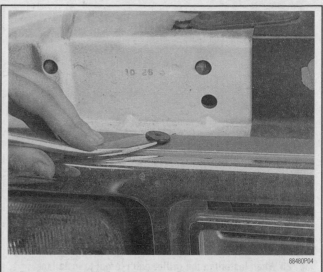

Fig. 17 Use a prytool to remove the grille retaining clips

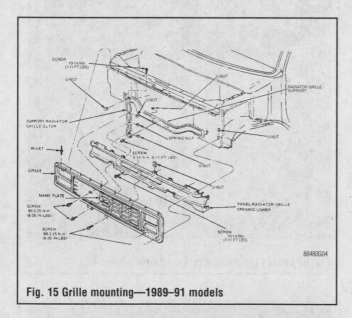

Fig. 15 Grille mounting—1989–91 models

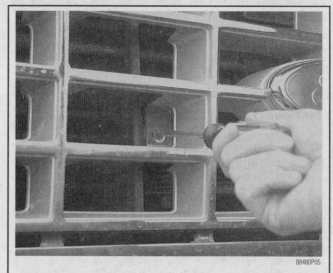

Fig. 18 Loosen the grille retaining screws

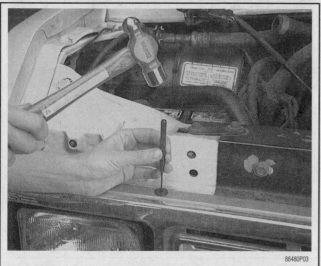

Fig. 16 Use a thin punch to remove the plastic rivets

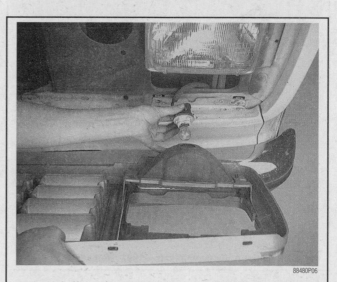

Fig. 19 Disengage the signal/marker light electrical connections

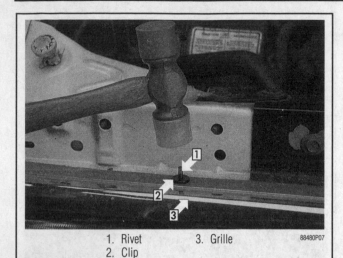

1. Rivet
2. Clip
3. Grille

88480P07

Fig. 20 When installing the grille, don't forget to install the plastic rivets in the clips

4. Remove the 9 plastic rivets which attach the upper grille flange to the radiator support.
5. Disconnect the bulb socket assembly from the signal/marker light lens.
6. Pull the grille from the van.
7. Installation is the reverse of removal. Don't tighten any fasteners until the grille is aligned. Install the plastic rivets last.

1992–96 Models

▶ See Figure 21

1. Raise and support the hood.
2. Remove the two plastic rivets that retain the grille to the opening panel. The rivets are located at each of the lower attaching tabs.
3. Loosen the three screws from the top of the grille.
4. If equipped, depress the snap tabs on the lower outboard corners.
5. Remove the grille.
To install:
6. Place the grille in position.
7. If equipped, engage the tabs on the lower outboard corners.
8. Tighten the screws at the top of the grille.

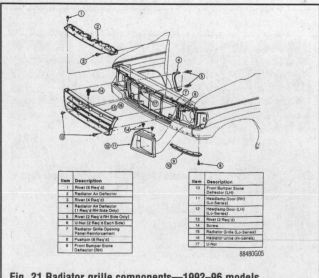

Item	Description
1	Rivet (6 Req'd)
2	Radiator Air Deflector
3	Rivet (4 Req'd)
4	Radiator Air Deflector (1 Req'd RH Side Only)
5	Rivet (2 Req'd RH Side Only)
6	U-Nut (2 Req'd Each Side)
7	Radiator Grille Opening Panel Reinforcement
8	Pushpin (6 Req'd)
9	Front Bumper Stone Deflector (RH)

Item	Description
10	Front Bumper Stone Deflector (LH)
11	Headlamp Door (RH) (Lo-Series)
12	Headlamp Door (LH) (Lo-Series)
13	Rivet (2 Req'd)
14	Screw
15	Radiator Grille (Lo-Series)
16	Radiator Grille (Hi-Series)
17	U-Nut

88480G05

Fig. 21 Radiator grille components—1992–96 models

9. Install the two plastic rivets that retain the grille to the opening panel. The rivets are located at each of the lower attaching tabs.
10. Lower and support the hood.

Outside Mirrors

REMOVAL & INSTALLATION

Conventional

1. Loosen the retainers and remove the mirror.
2. Installation is the reverse of removal.

Swing Away

▶ See Figures 22 and 23

1. Loosen the retainers and remove the bracket and mirror.
2. Installation is the reverse of removal.

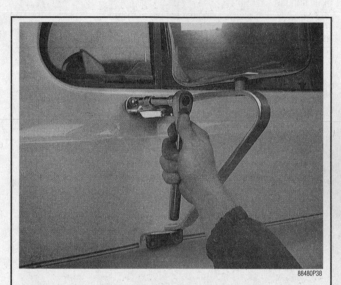

88480P38

Fig. 22 Loosen the mirror bracket-to-door retainers . . .

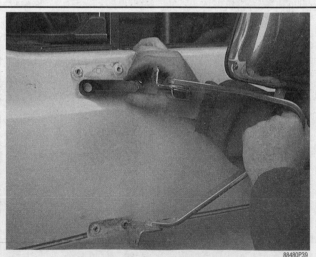

88480P39

Fig. 23 . . . then remove the mirror and bracket assembly from the door

Sail Mount

1989–94 MODELS

◆ **See Figure 24**

1. Remove the outside hole mounting cover.
2. Remove the inner trim panel.
3. If equipped with power mirrors, remove the door mounted speaker, then disengage the wiring.
4. Loosen the mirror retainer and remove the mirror and gasket.
5. Installation is the reverse of removal. Tighten the retainers to 53–79 inch lbs. (6–9 Nm).

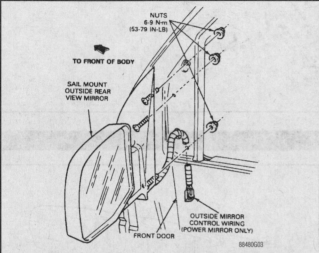

Fig. 24 If equipped with a power mirror, disengage the electrical connection before removal

1995–96 MODELS

◆ **See Figure 24**

1. Remove the outside hole mounting cover.
2. Remove the inner trim panel.
3. If equipped with power mirrors, remove the window regulator switch housing screw.
4. Lift the switch housing and use a prytool to disengage mirror control from the mirror wiring.
5. Disengage the mirror control wiring.
6. Loosen the mirror retainer and remove the mirror and gasket.
7. Installation is the reverse of removal. Tighten the retainers to 53–79 inch lbs. (6–9 Nm).

Antenna

REMOVAL & INSTALLATION

◆ **See Figure 25**

1. Remove the cowl top grille panel above the radio.
2. Disconnect the antenna lead from the back of the radio.
3. Unsnap the 2 retaining clips from the cable.
4. Unsnap the cap from the base of the antenna.
5. Remove the 4 attaching screws and lift off the antenna, carefully pulling the cable through the opening.

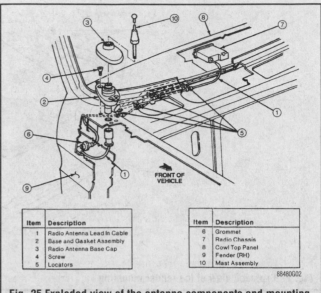

Item	Description
1	Radio Antenna Lead In Cable
2	Base and Gasket Assembly
3	Radio Antenna Base Cap
4	Screw
5	Locators

Item	Description
6	Grommet
7	Radio Chassis
8	Cowl Top Panel
9	Fender (RH)
10	Mast Assembly

Fig. 25 Exploded view of the antenna components and mounting

To install:

6. Insert the tip of the antenna cable through the fender opening and thread the cable to the base. Plug the cable in to the base.
7. Install base attaching screws.
8. Install the cap on the base.
9. Snap the cable into the clips.
10. Insert the cable through the hole and engage it to the radio. Pull the cable until the rubber grommet is seated and seals the entry hole.
11. Install the cowl top grille panel above the radio.

Fenders

REMOVAL & INSTALLATION

◆ **See Figure 26**

1. Remove the grille.
2. Loosen the two side bolts attaching the end of the grille opening lower panel to the fender.
3. Loosen the three screws connecting the lower edge of the fender to the wheel housing.
4. Loosen the lower fender rear attaching screw and remove the shims.
5. Open the door and remove the upper fender rear screw and shim.
6. Loosen the two screws connecting the front edge of the fender to the radiator support.
7. Loosen the three screws and shims retaining the top of the fender, then remove the fender.
   To install:
8. Place the fender in position and install all the retainers finger tight.

➡ **Do not exceed two shims at any location except the lower fender rear attaching screw.**

9. Adjust the fender until proper fit and appearance have been achieved, then tighten the retainers.
10. Install the grille.

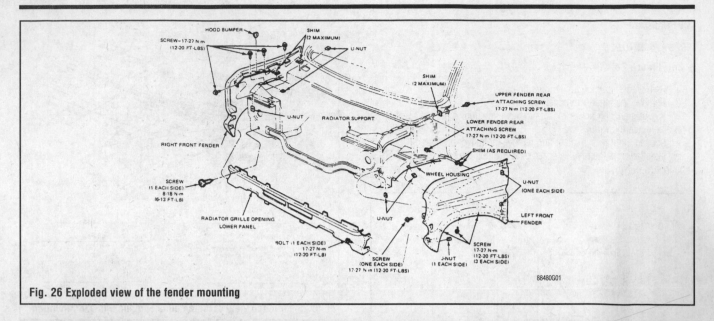

Fig. 26 Exploded view of the fender mounting

INTERIOR

Instrument Panel and Pad

REMOVAL & INSTALLATION

1989–91 Models

▶ **See Figure 27**

1. Disconnect the negative battery cable.
2. Remove the steering wheel.
3. Remove the instruments, clusters and controls.
4. Remove the A/C heater control and the cigar lighter.
5. If equipped, remove the radio and instrument panel mounted speaker.
6. Remome the 11 nuts retaining the pad to the panel.
7. Remove the steering column cover.
8. Remove the instrument upper molding.
9. Remove the two screws and the washers attaching the panel to the brake and clutch (if equipped) support bracket.
10. Remove the screw and washer attaching the panel at the lower support brace.
11. Support the instrument panel and remove the two side attaching screws and washers.
12. Remove the instrument panel.
To install:
13. Install the panel and tighten the two side attaching screws and washers to 11–21 ft. lbs. (15–28 Nm).
14. Install the instrument panel-to-support brace retainers and tighten to 12–20 ft. lbs. (17–27 Nm).
15. Install the upper molding and tighten the retainers to 10–15 inch lbs. (14–20 Nm).
16. Install the steering column cover and tighten the retainers to 10–15 inch lbs. (14–20 Nm).
17. Install the pad and tighten the nuts to 8–20 inch lbs. (11–27 Nm).
18. Install the radio, speaker, A/C heater control and cigar lighter.
19. Install the instruments, clusters and controls.
20. Install the steering wheel.
21. Connect the negative battery cable.

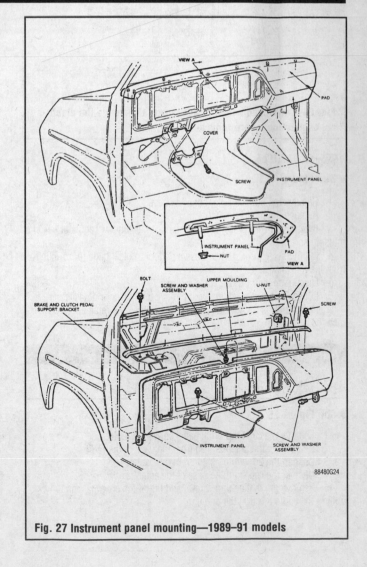

Fig. 27 Instrument panel mounting—1989–91 models

1992–96 Models

◆ **See Figure 28**

1. Disconnect the negative battery cable.
2. Disengage the panel wiring in the engine compartment by loosening the connector center bolt.
3. Remove the left and right windshield moldings.
4. Remove the engine cover.
5. Remove the left and right snap-in molding on each side of the steering column.
6. Loosen the five screws retaining the steering column cover and remove the cover.
7. Loosen the nine bolts from the steering column opening reinforcement and remove the assembly.
8. If equipped, disengage the three wiring connectors located at the bottom of the steering column.
9. Remove the steering column shrouds.
10. If equipped, engage the three wiring connectors located at the bottom of the steering column.
11. If necessary, loosen the retaining bolt and disengage the ignition switch connector from the steering column.
12. If necessary, remove the right-hand side lower trim panel.
13. If necessary, remove the right and left side cowl panels and disengage the park brake wiring.
14. If necessary, loosen the parking brake release lever retainers and lay the lever on the floor.
15. If necessary, disengage the wiring from the right cowl panel and the radio antenna.
16. If necessary, disengage the wiring from the brake light switch.
17. Disconnect the heater control cables and if equipped, disengage the A/C vacuum line connector on the right side of the panel.
18. Loosen the one bolt connecting the right side of instrument panel and the bolt connecting the center of the instrument panel below the register.
19. Remove the pinch bolt from the steering column-to-extension shaft. Compress the extension shaft towards the engine and separate it from the column U-joint.
20. Disconnect the transmission shift cable from the steering column.
21. Loosen the four bolts attaching the left side panel to the cowl side.
22. Loosen the screws attaching the top of the instrument panel.

23. Support the instrument panel and pull it rearward to gain access to the rear and disengage any remaining electrical connections.
24. Remove the instrument panel from the van.

To install:

25. Install the instrument panel in the van and engage the electrical connections to the rear of the panel.
26. Install the screws attaching the top of the instrument panel.
27. Tighten the four bolts attaching the left side panel to the cowl side.
28. Connect the extension shaft to the column U-joint.
29. Install the pinch bolt that attaches the steering column-to-extension shaft
30. Tighten the one bolt connecting the right side of instrument panel and the bolt connecting the center of the instrument panel below the register.
31. Connect the heater control cables and if equipped, engage the A/C vacuum line connector on the right side of the panel.
32. Install the steering column shrouds.
33. If equipped, disengage the three wiring connectors located at the bottom of the steering column.
34. Remove the steering column shrouds.
35. If necessary, engage the ignition switch connector and tighten the retaining bolt.
36. If removed, install the right hand side lower trim panel.
37. If removed, engage the parking brake wiring and install the right and left side cowl panels.
38. If removed, install the parking brake release lever and tighten the retainers.
39. If removed, engage the wiring to the right cowl panel and the radio antenna.
40. If removed, engage the wiring to the brake light switch.
41. Install the reinforcement assembly and tighten the nine bolts.
42. Install the steering column cover and tighten the five screws.
43. Install the left and right snap-in molding on each side of the steering column.
44. Install the engine cover.
45. Install the left and right windshield moldings.
46. Engage the panel wiring in the engine compartment and tighten the connector center bolt.
47. Connect the negative battery cable.

Center Console

REMOVAL & INSTALLATION

1. Open the console door.
2. Reach into the compartment and pull the release handle while lifting the console.

To install:

3. Engage the console tabs into the tracks on the engine cover and push down until the latch engages the engine cover hook.
4. Close the door.

Engine Cover

REMOVAL & INSTALLATION

◆ **See Figures 29, 30 and 31**

1. Slide the front seats to their full rear position.
2. Unfasten the retaining clips and if equipped, bolts.
3. Pull the engine cover from its mounting and remove it from the van via the passenger door.
4. Installation is the reverse of removal.

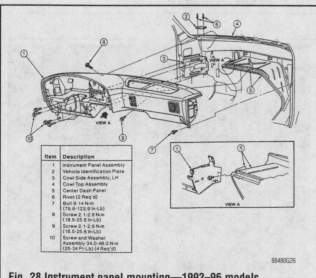

Item	Description
1	Instrument Panel Assembly
2	Vehicle Identification Plate
3	Cowl Side Assembly, LH
4	Cowl Top Assembly
5	Center Dash Panel
6	Rivet (2 Req'd)
7	Bolt 9-14 N-m (79.6-123.9 In-Lb)
8	Screw 2.1-2.9 N-m (18.5-25.6 In-Lb)
9	Screw 2.1-2.9 N-m (18.5-25.6 In-Lb)
10	Screw and Washer Assembly 34.0-46.0 N-m (25-34 Ft-Lb) (4 Req'd)

88480G26

Fig. 28 Instrument panel mounting—1992–96 models

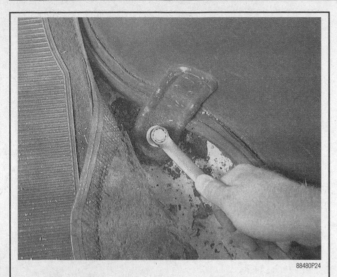

Fig. 29 Loosen the engine cover-to-floor bolts

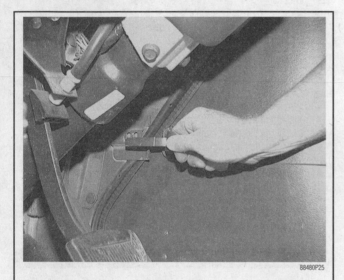

Fig. 30 Unsnap the cover retaining clips

Fig. 31 Pull the cover backwards and remove it

Door Panels

REMOVAL & INSTALLATION

Front Doors

1989–91 MODELS

▸ **See Figures 32 thru 41**

1. Remove the armrest.
2. Remove the door handle and trim cup.
3. If the van is equipped with a stereo radio, remove the speaker grille.
4. Remove the setscrew and remove the window crank handle. On models with power windows, remove the window switch trim cup and switch.
5. Remove the door handle and trim piece.
6. Using a trim panel removal tool, insert it carefully behind the panel and slide it along to find the push-pins. When you encounter a pin, pry the pin outward. Do this until all the pins are out. NEVER PULL ON THE PANEL TO REMOVE THE PINS!
7. Remove the trim panel.

Fig. 32 Unfasten the armrest retainers . . .

Fig. 33 . . . and remove the armrest from the door panel

Fig. 34 Loosen the speaker grille retainers . . .

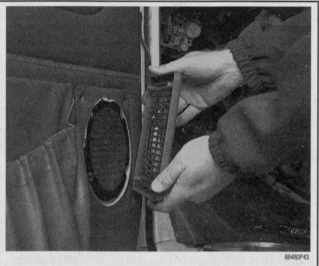

Fig. 35 . . . and remove the speaker grille from the door panel

Fig. 36 Loosen the window crank handle retaining screw . . .

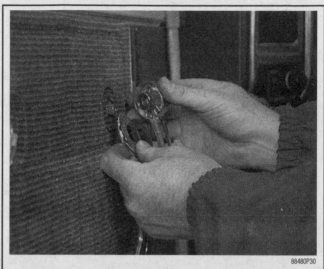

Fig. 37 . . . then remove the handle, trim piece and washer

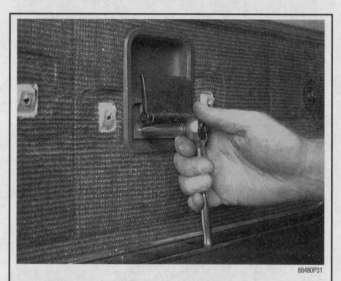

Fig. 38 Loosen the inside door handle retainers

Fig. 39 Disconnect the handle assembly . . .

Fig. 40 . . . then remove the trim piece and set it aside

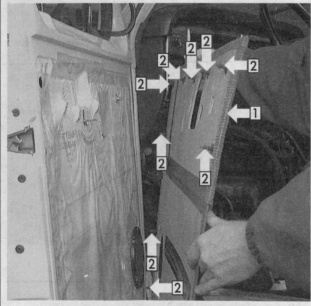

1. Trim panel   2. Retaining clips

Fig. 41 Use a trim panel tool to carefully disengage the clips and remove the panel

To install:

8. Replace any damaged pins.
9. Install the trim panel and located the pins in their holes.
10. Firmly push the panel at the pin locations to seat the pins.
11. Install the door handle and trim cup and tighten the retainers.
12. If removed, install speaker grille.
13. Install the window regulator and tighten the screw.
14. Install the armrest.

1992–96 LO-SERIES MODELS

▶ See Figure 42

1. Loosen the screw in the sill panel and remove the panel.
2. Loosen the screws in the upper panel and remove the panel by lifting it upward.

3. Remove the window crank.
4. Loosen armrest screws and remove the armrest.
5. Remove the "scrivets" (rivet/screw combinations) by turning the heads clockwise using a screwdriver until they are loose.
6. Remove the trim panel.

To install:

7. Install the panel and push the scrivets into the holes and keep pushing on the screw heads until they bottom out.
8. Install the armrest and window crank.
9. Install the upper panel and sill.

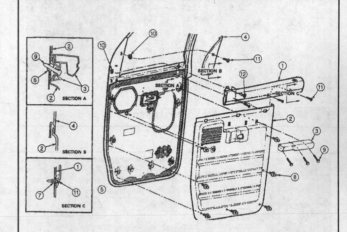

1. Front door upper trim panel
2. Front door lower trim panel
3. Door trim armrest
4. Outside mirror mounting—hole cover
5. Windshield
6. Spring nut
7. Push-in nut
8. Scrivet (7 required each side)
9. Hex head screw (3 required each side)
10. Push-in nut (2 required each side)
11. Screw, oval trim heading—tapping
12. Screw, round washer head—tapping

Fig. 42 Front door trim panel components—1992–96 Lo-series models

1992–96 HI-SERIES MODELS

▶ See Figure 43

1. Loosen the screw in the sail panel and remove the panel.
2. Loosen the inside handle cup screw and remove the cup.
3. Loosen the window regulator switch housing.
4. Lift the swltch and slide if forward to gain access to the retaining screws.
5. Remove the door lock and regulator switches. On the left side, disengage the power mirror connector, if equipped.
6. Loosen the trim retaining screw which is located inside the front of the armrest.
7. Loosen the screw inside the map pocket.
8. Loosen the screw at the top front of the panel.
9. Lift the panel up to disengage the clips.
10. Disengage the wiring connectors from the panel and remove the panel.

To install:

11. Engage the wiring to the door panel.
12. Lift the panel, push forward and insert the lock button. Pull the inside door handle to raise the lock button, this will aid in installation.

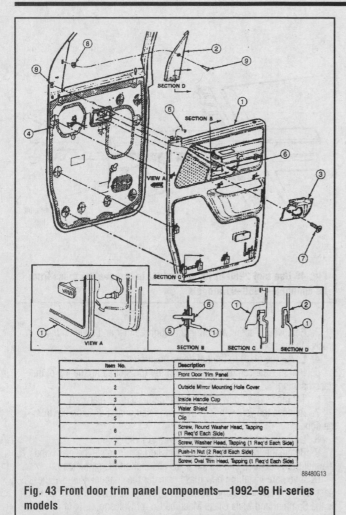

Item No.	Description
1	Front Door Trim Panel
2	Outside Mirror Mounting Hole Cover
3	Inside Handle Cup
4	Water Shield
5	Clip
6	Screw, Round Washer Head, Tapping (1 Req'd Each Side)
7	Screw, Washer Head, Tapping (1 Req'd Each Side)
8	Push-In Nut (2 Req'd Each Side)
9	Screw, Oval Trim Head, Tapping (1 Req'd Each Side)

88480G13

Fig. 43 Front door trim panel components—1992–96 Hi-series models

13. Align the retaining clips with the holes and push firmly on the panel to engage the clips.

14. Install all screws.

15. Install the door handle cup, the switches and the sail panel.

Side and Rear Hinged Door

1. Loosen the retaining screws and remove the panel.
2. Installation is the reverse of removal.

Sliding Doors

1989–91 CARGO VAN

1. Loosen the retaining screws and remove the panel.
2. Installation is the reverse of removal.

1989–91 CLUB WAGON

1. Carefully pry the pull-strap end-caps off.
2. Loosen the retaining screws and remove the strap. The screws will remain attached to the strap.
3. Using a trim panel removal tool, insert it carefully behind the panel and slide it along to find the push-pins. When you encounter a pin, pry the pin outward. Do this until all the pins are out. NEVER PULL ON THE PANEL TO REMOVE THE PINS!
4. Remove the trim panel.

To install:
5. Replace any damaged pins.
6. Install the trim panel and located the pins in their holes.
7. Firmly push the panel at the pin locations to seat the pins.
8. Install the pull strap.

1992–96 LO-SERIES MODELS

▶ See Figure 44

1. Loosen and remove all scrivets.
2. To disengage the hidden hook at the door handle, pull the top of the panel and bow it, while pushing the door handle.
3. Lift the panel to disengage the bottom four hooks. Remove the panel.
4. Install the panel and engage all the hooks.
5. Engage all the scrivets.

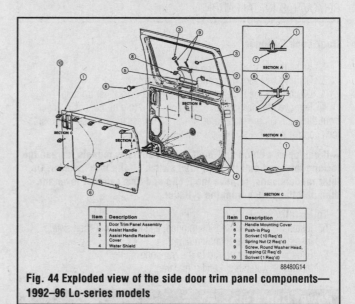

Item	Description	Item	Description
1	Door Trim Panel Assembly	5	Handle Mounting Cover
2	Assist Handle	6	Push-in Plug
3	Assist Handle Retainer Cover	7	Scrivet (10 Req'd)
4	Water Shield	8	Spring Nut (2 Req'd)
		9	Screw, Round Washer Head, Tapping (2 Req'd)
		10	Scrivet (1 Req'd)

88480G14

Fig. 44 Exploded view of the side door trim panel components—1992–96 Lo-series models

1992–96 HI-SERIES MODELS

▶ See Figure 45

1. Partially open the door.
2. Remove the door pull handle retainer cover and screws.
3. Loosen the flipper window latch screws. Push the window out and rest the latches on the outside of the door.
4. Pull the rear door garnish molding away from the window starting at the front lower corner and working rearward.
5. Loosen all screws, then lift panel up and remove it.

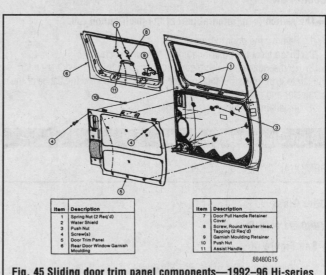

Item	Description	Item	Description
1	Spring Nut (2 Req'd)	7	Door Pull Handle Retainer Cover
2	Water Shield	8	Screw, Round Washer Head, Tapping (2 Req'd)
3	Push Nut	9	Garnish Molding Retainer
4	Screw(s)	10	Push Nut
5	Door Trim Panel	11	Assist Handle
6	Rear Door Window Garnish Moulding		

88480G15

Fig. 45 Sliding door trim panel components—1992–96 Hi-series models

To install:

6. Install the panel on the door and tighten the screws.
7. Install the garnish molding starting at the front edge and working back.
8. Engage the flipper window latches and tighten the screws.
9. Install the door handle cover and tighten the screws.
10. Close the door.

Manual Door Locks

REMOVAL & INSTALLATION

Door Lock Cylinder

1. Raise the window all the way.
2. Remove the door trim panel and watershield.
3. Disconnect the lock actuating rod from the lock control clip.
4. Remove the lock cylinder retaining clip and pull the lock cylinder from the door. On the side doors, it will be necessary to loosen the inside lock control knob set screw and remove the knob.

➡️**If equipped with an anti-theft system on early models, spread the locking tabs and pull the anti-theft switch off the lock cylinder. On later models vans, remove the E-clip and lock cylinder lever and then pull the switch from the cylinder.**

To install:

5. Install the cylinder and if equipped, engage the anti-theft switch.
6. Install the cylinder retaining clip.
7. Engage the actuating rod to the rod control clip.
8. Install the watershield and trim panel.

Power Door Locks

REMOVAL & INSTALLATION

Actuator Motor

1. Remove the door trim panel.
2. Disconnect the motor from the door latch.
3. Remove the motor and swivel bracket from the door by drilling out the pop rivet.
4. Disconnect the wiring harness.
5. Installation is the reverse of removal. Make sure that the pop rivet is tight.

Control Switch

➡️**The switch is an integral part of the push-button rod.**

1. Remove the door trim panel.
2. Disconnect the push-button rod from the latch.
3. To disengage the wiring connector, insert a thin screwdriver under the tab to exert pressure, then pry the locking tab up from the flange of the connector and pull the halves apart.
4. Installation is the reverse of removal.

Door Glass and Regulator

REMOVAL & INSTALLATION

Door Glass

1989–91 MODELS

▶ See Figure 46

1. Remove the trim panel from the door.
2. Remove the 3 screws attaching the vent window to the upper leading edge of the door.

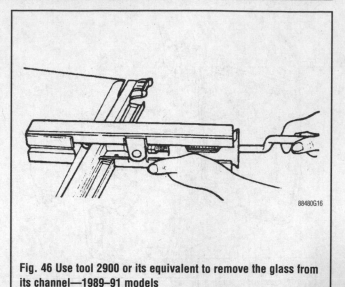

Fig. 46 Use tool 2900 or its equivalent to remove the glass from its channel—1989–91 models

3. Remove the screw attaching the front retainer and division bar bracket to the door.
4. Lower the glass to the full down position.
5. Pull the rear run down and out of the run slot along the top of the glass opening.
6. Tilt the vent window and division bar assembly rearward.
7. Remove the vent window, front run retainer and division bar from the door.
8. Unsnap and remove the belt line weatherstripping.
9. Rotate the front of the glass downward and remove the glass and channel from the door, sliding the glass channel off the regulator arm.
10. If you are installing new glass, transfer the channel. Remove the glass from the channel using Glass and Channel Removal Tool 2900, made by the Sommer and Mala Glass Machine Co. of Chicago, ILL., or its equivalent.

To install:

11. Lubricate the window mechanism.
12. Place the glass assembly in the door inserting the regulator arm roller in the glass channel.
13. Place the vent window and division bar in the door.
14. Install the rear run retainer in the door.
15. Position the glass and channel assembly in the front run retainer and division bar and the rear run. Place the vent window assembly into position in the door and install the 3 attaching screws along the upper edge.
16. Install the front run in the division bar.
17. Install the screw attaching the division bar to the door.
18. Install the belt line weatherstripping.
19. Adjust the glass as necessary.
20. Install the trim panel.

1992–96 MODELS

▶ See Figure 47

1. Remove the trim panel and the door belt line inside weatherstrip.
2. Remove the door belt line outside weatherstrip.
3. Lower the glass to gain access to the two glass bracket retaining rivets.

✳✳ CAUTION

Do not attempt to pry out the rivets as you could break the glass. Before drilling out the rivets, place a suitable block support between the door outer panel and glass bracket to stabilize the glass.

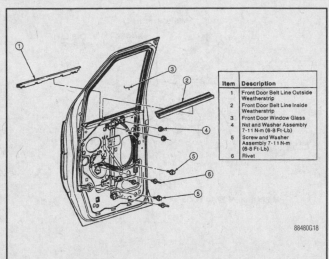

Fig. 47 Front door glass and related components—1992–96 models

Item	Description
1	Front Door Belt Line Outside Weatherstrip
2	Front Door Belt Line Inside Weatherstrip
3	Front Door Window Glass
4	Nut and Washer Assembly 7-11 N·m (6-8 Ft-Lb)
5	Screw and Washer Assembly 7-11 N·m (6-8 Ft-Lb)
6	Rivet

4. Use a drift to remove the center pins from the rivets, then drill out the center of the rivets with a ¼ inch drill bit.
5. Remove the glass.
To install:
6. Install the glass into the bracket.
7. Install two ¼ inch rivets to retain the glass in the bracket.
8. Install the door inside and outside weatherstrip.
9. Install the trim panel.

Regulator

1989–91 MODELS

▶ **See Figure 48**

1. Lower the glass.
2. Remove the window handle setscrew and remove the handle.
3. Remove the door panel access cover.
4. Support the glass in the full up position.
5. Drill out the regulator attaching rivets with a ¼ inch drill bit and punch out the rivets.
6. Disengage the regulator arm from the regulator and lift out the regulator.
7. Installation is the reverse of removal. In place of the rivets you can use ¼ inch-20 x ½ inch bolts and nuts with lockwashers.

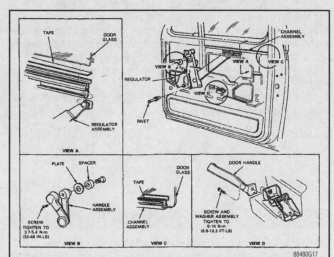

Fig. 48 Exploded views of the regulator and related components—1989–91 models

1992–96 MODELS

1. Remove the trim panel.
2. Remove the glass.
3. Remove the regulator retaining rivets by, using a drift to remove the center pins from the rivets, then drill out the center of the rivets with a ¼ inch drill bit.
4. Loosen the regulator upper bracket and remove the regulator.
To install:
5. Install the regulator.
6. Install the regulator retaining rivets. Equivalent threaded fasteners may be used.
7. Install the two regulator upper bracket nuts.
8. Install the glass.
9. Install the trim panel.

Electric Window Motor

REMOVAL & INSTALLATION

1989–91 Models

1. Disconnect the negative battery cable.
2. Remove the trim panel and watershield.
3. Disengage the connector from the motor.
4. Use a ½ inch (12.7mm) drill bit, drill two holes in the door inner panel at the drill dimples located opposite the two unexposed motor retainer screws.
5. Remove the motor retaining screws using the two drilled holes and the existing hole.
6. Disengage the motor from the drive and regulator gear and prop up the in the full up position.
7. Remove the motor.
To install:
8. Install the motor and engage it to the regulator.
9. Install the retaining screws and tighten them to 50–85 inch lbs. (6–9 Nm).
10. Install some pressure sensitive tape over the drilled holes and engage the motor electrical connection.
11. Connect the negative battery cable and check for proper operation and that the door drain holes are open.
12. Install the trim panel.

1992–96 Models

1. Disconnect the negative battery cable.
2. Remove the trim panel and watershield.
3. Disengage the connector from the motor.
4. Remove the motor retaining rivets, by using a drift to remove the center pins from the rivets, then drill out the center of the rivets with a ¼ inch drill bit.
5. Working through the access hole, remove the motor bracket from the inner panel.
6. Rotate the motor to gain access to the three retaining screws.
7. Loosen the retaining screws and separate the motor from the cable drum housing. Remove the motor.
To install:
8. Install the motor, drive to cable-drum-housing, and motor mounting bracket.
9. Install the retaining screws and tighten them to 53–62 inch lbs. (5–7 Nm).
10. Install the regulator retaining rivets. Equivalent threaded fasteners may be used.
11. Install the motor mounting bracket retaining rivets. Equivalent threaded fasteners may be used.
12. Connect the negative battery cable and check for proper operation and that the door drain holes are open.
13. Install the trim panel.

Inside Rear View Mirror

REMOVAL & INSTALLATION

1989–91 Models

▶ See Figure 49

The mirror is held in place with a single setscrew. Loosen the screw and lift the mirror off. Repair kits for damaged mirrors are available and most auto parts stores.

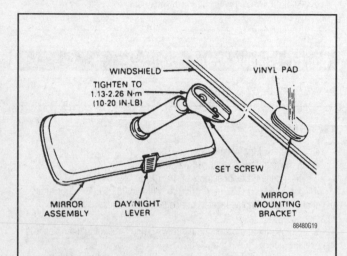

Fig. 49 Loosen the setscrew before withdrawing the mirror from the bracket

1992–96 Models

▶ See Figure 50

1. Grasp the mirror as illustrated and install a small prytool into slot until the spring is contacted.
2. While pushing on the spring, pull up on the mirror to remove it.

To install:

3. Slide the mirror into the bracket until it is fully seated.

Windshield and Fixed Glass

REMOVAL & INSTALLATION

If your windshield, or other fixed window, is cracked or chipped, you may decide to replace it with a new one yourself. However, there are two main reasons why replacement windshields and other window glass should be installed only by a professional automotive glass technician: safety and cost.

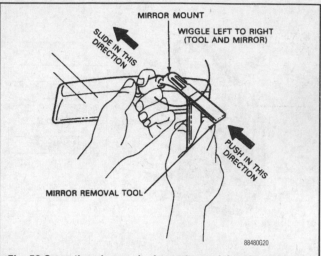

Fig. 50 Grasp the mirror and release the retaining ring with a prytool

The most important reason a professional should install automotive glass is for safety. The glass in the vehicle, especially the windshield, is designed with safety in mind in case of a collision. The windshield is specially manufactured from two panes of specially-tempered glass with a thin layer of transparent plastic between them. This construction allows the glass to "give" in the event that a part of your body hits the windshield during the collision, and prevents the glass from shattering, which could cause lacerations, blinding and other harm to passengers of the vehicle. The other fixed windows are designed to be tempered so that if they break during a collision, they shatter in such a way that there are no sharp or pointed edges on the glass pieces. The professional automotive glass technician knows how to install the glass in a vehicle so that it will function optimally during a collision. Without the proper experience, knowledge and tools, installing a piece of automotive glass yourself could lead to additional harm if an accident should ever occur.

Cost is also a factor when deciding to install automotive glass yourself. Performing this could cost you much more than a professional may charge for the same job. Since the windshield is designed to break under stress, an often life saving characteristic, windshields tend to break VERY easily when an inexperienced person attempts to install one. Do-it-yourselfers buying two, three or even four windshields from a salvage yard because they have broken them during installation are common stories. Also, since the automotive glass is designed to prevent the outside elements from entering your vehicle, improper installation can lead to water and air leaks. Annoying whining noises at highway speeds from air leaks or inside body panel rusting from water leaks can add to your stress level and subtract from your wallet. After buying two or three windshields, installing them and ending up with a leak that produces a noise while driving and water damage during rainstorms, the cost of having a professional do it correctly the first time may be much more alluring.

We at Chilton, therefore, advise that you have a professional automotive glass technician service any broken glass on your vehicle.

TORQUE SPECIFICATIONS

System	Component	Ft. Lbs.	Nm
Exterior			
	Door hinge bolts	18-25	25-35
	Hood Bolts	13-19	17-27
	Sail Mount Mirror retainers	53-79 inch lbs.	6-9
Interior			
1989-91 Models			
	Instrument panel and pad side attaching retainers	11-20	15-28
	Instrument panel-to-support brace retainers	12-20	17-27
	Upper molding retainers	10-15 inch lbs.	14-20
	Steering column cover retainers	10-15 inch lbs.	14-20
	Pad retaining nuts	8-20 inch lbs.	11-27
1992-96 Models			
	Lower center moulding screws	18-27 inch lbs.	2-3
	Ash tray screws	18-27 inch lbs.	2-3
	Steering column cover bolts	97-115 inch lbs.	11-13
	Steering column cover screws	18-27 inch lbs.	2-3
	Instrument panel finish panel screws	18-27 inch lbs.	2-3
	Instrument panel right cowl trim panel bolt	80-124 inch lbs.	9-14
	Instrument panel-to-center dash panel screw	18-27 inch lbs.	2-3
	Instrument panel-to-cowl top assembly screw	18-27 inch lbs.	2-3
	Steering column wiring support screw	9-18 inch lbs.	1-2
	Anti-theft ground screw	31-39 inch lbs.	3.5-4.5

88480C01

GLOSSARY

AIR/FUEL RATIO: The ratio of air-to-gasoline by weight in the fuel mixture drawn into the engine.

AIR INJECTION: One method of reducing harmful exhaust emissions by injecting air into each of the exhaust ports of an engine. The fresh air entering the hot exhaust manifold causes any remaining fuel to be burned before it can exit the tailpipe.

ALTERNATOR: A device used for converting mechanical energy into electrical energy.

AMMETER: An instrument, calibrated in amperes, used to measure the flow of an electrical current in a circuit. Ammeters are always connected in series with the circuit being tested.

AMPERE: The rate of flow of electrical current present when one volt of electrical pressure is applied against one ohm of electrical resistance.

ANALOG COMPUTER: Any microprocessor that uses similar (analogous) electrical signals to make its calculations.

ARMATURE: A laminated, soft iron core wrapped by a wire that converts electrical energy to mechanical energy as in a motor or relay. When rotated in a magnetic field, it changes mechanical energy into electrical energy as in a generator.

ATMOSPHERIC PRESSURE: The pressure on the Earth's surface caused by the weight of the air in the atmosphere. At sea level, this pressure is 14.7 psi at 32°F (101 kPa at 0°C).

ATOMIZATION: The breaking down of a liquid into a fine mist that can be suspended in air.

AXIAL PLAY: Movement parallel to a shaft or bearing bore.

BACKFIRE: The sudden combustion of gases in the intake or exhaust system that results in a loud explosion.

BACKLASH: The clearance or play between two parts, such as meshed gears.

BACKPRESSURE: Restrictions in the exhaust system that slow the exit of exhaust gases from the combustion chamber.

BAKELITE: A heat resistant, plastic insulator material commonly used in printed circuit boards and transistorized components.

BALL BEARING: A bearing made up of hardened inner and outer races between which hardened steel balls roll.

BALLAST RESISTOR: A resistor in the primary ignition circuit that lowers voltage after the engine is started to reduce wear on ignition components.

BEARING: A friction reducing, supportive device usually located between a stationary part and a moving part.

BIMETAL TEMPERATURE SENSOR: Any sensor or switch made of two dissimilar types of metal that bend when heated or cooled due to the different expansion rates of the alloys. These types of sensors usually function as an on/off switch.

BLOWBY: Combustion gases, composed of water vapor and unburned fuel, that leak past the piston rings into the crankcase during normal engine operation. These gases are removed by the PCV system to prevent the buildup of harmful acids in the crankcase.

BRAKE PAD: A brake shoe and lining assembly used with disc brakes.

BRAKE SHOE: The backing for the brake lining. The term is, however, usually applied to the assembly of the brake backing and lining.

BUSHING: A liner, usually removable, for a bearing; an anti-friction liner used in place of a bearing.

CALIPER: A hydraulically activated device in a disc brake system, which is mounted straddling the brake rotor (disc). The caliper contains at least one piston and two brake pads. Hydraulic pressure on the piston(s) forces the pads against the rotor.

CAMSHAFT: A shaft in the engine on which are the lobes (cams) which operate the valves. The camshaft is driven by the crankshaft, via a belt, chain or gears, at one half the crankshaft speed.

CAPACITOR: A device which stores an electrical charge.

CARBON MONOXIDE (CO): A colorless, odorless gas given off as a normal byproduct of combustion. It is poisonous and extremely dangerous in confined areas, building up slowly to toxic levels without warning if adequate ventilation is not available.

CARBURETOR: A device, usually mounted on the intake manifold of an engine, which mixes the air and fuel in the proper proportion to allow even combustion.

CATALYTIC CONVERTER: A device installed in the exhaust system, like a muffler, that converts harmful byproducts of combustion into carbon dioxide and water vapor by means of a heat-producing chemical reaction.

CENTRIFUGAL ADVANCE: A mechanical method of advancing the spark timing by using flyweights in the distributor that react to centrifugal force generated by the distributor shaft rotation.

CHECK VALVE: Any one-way valve installed to permit the flow of air, fuel or vacuum in one direction only.

CHOKE: A device, usually a moveable valve, placed in the intake path of a carburetor to restrict the flow of air.

CIRCUIT: Any unbroken path through which an electrical current can flow. Also used to describe fuel flow in some instances.

CIRCUIT BREAKER: A switch which protects an electrical circuit from overload by opening the circuit when the current flow exceeds a predetermined level. Some circuit breakers must be reset manually, while most reset automatically.

COIL (IGNITION): A transformer in the ignition circuit which steps up the voltage provided to the spark plugs.

COMBINATION MANIFOLD: An assembly which includes both the intake and exhaust manifolds in one casting.

COMBINATION VALVE: A device used in some fuel systems that routes fuel vapors to a charcoal storage canister instead of venting them into the atmosphere. The valve relieves fuel tank pressure and allows fresh air into the tank as the fuel level drops to prevent a vapor lock situation.

COMPRESSION RATIO: The comparison of the total volume of the cylinder and combustion chamber with the piston at BDC and the piston at TDC.

CONDENSER: 1. An electrical device which acts to store an electrical charge, preventing voltage surges. 2. A radiator-like device in the air conditioning system in which refrigerant gas condenses into a liquid, giving off heat.

CONDUCTOR: Any material through which an electrical current can be transmitted easily.

CONTINUITY: Continuous or complete circuit. Can be checked with an ohmmeter.

COUNTERSHAFT: An intermediate shaft which is rotated by a mainshaft and transmits, in turn, that rotation to a working part.

CRANKCASE: The lower part of an engine in which the crankshaft and related parts operate.

CRANKSHAFT: The main driving shaft of an engine which receives reciprocating motion from the pistons and converts it to rotary motion.

CYLINDER: In an engine, the round hole in the engine block in which the piston(s) ride.

CYLINDER BLOCK: The main structural member of an engine in which is found the cylinders, crankshaft and other principal parts.

CYLINDER HEAD: The detachable portion of the engine, usually fastened to the top of the cylinder block and containing all or most of the combustion chambers. On overhead valve engines, it contains the valves and their operating parts. On overhead cam engines, it contains the camshaft as well.

DEAD CENTER: The extreme top or bottom of the piston stroke.

DETONATION: An unwanted explosion of the air/fuel mixture in the combustion chamber caused by excess heat and compression, advanced timing, or an overly lean mixture. Also referred to as "ping".

DIAPHRAGM: A thin, flexible wall separating two cavities, such as in a vacuum advance unit.

DIESELING: A condition in which hot spots in the combustion chamber cause the engine to run on after the key is turned off.

DIFFERENTIAL: A geared assembly which allows the transmission of motion between drive axles, giving one axle the ability to turn faster than the other.

DIODE: An electrical device that will allow current to flow in one direction only.

DISC BRAKE: A hydraulic braking assembly consisting of a brake disc, or rotor, mounted on an axle, and a caliper assembly containing, usually two brake pads which are activated by hydraulic pressure. The pads are forced against the sides of the disc, creating friction which slows the vehicle.

DISTRIBUTOR: A mechanically driven device on an engine which is responsible for electrically firing the spark plug at a predetermined point of the piston stroke.

DOWEL PIN: A pin, inserted in mating holes in two different parts allowing those parts to maintain a fixed relationship.

DRUM BRAKE: A braking system which consists of two brake shoes and one or two wheel cylinders, mounted on a fixed backing plate, and a brake drum, mounted on an axle, which revolves around the assembly.

DWELL: The rate, measured in degrees of shaft rotation, at which an electrical circuit cycles on and off.

ELECTRONIC CONTROL UNIT (ECU): Ignition module, module, amplifier or igniter. See Module for definition.

ELECTRONIC IGNITION: A system in which the timing and firing of the spark plugs is controlled by an electronic control unit, usually called a module. These systems have no points or condenser.

END-PLAY: The measured amount of axial movement in a shaft.

ENGINE: A device that converts heat into mechanical energy.

EXHAUST MANIFOLD: A set of cast passages or pipes which conduct exhaust gases from the engine.

FEELER GAUGE: A blade, usually metal, or precisely predetermined thickness, used to measure the clearance between two parts.

FIRING ORDER: The order in which combustion occurs in the cylinders of an engine. Also the order in which spark is distributed to the plugs by the distributor.

FLOODING: The presence of too much fuel in the intake manifold and combustion chamber which prevents the air/fuel mixture from firing, thereby causing a no-start situation.

FLYWHEEL: A disc shaped part bolted to the rear end of the crankshaft. Around the outer perimeter is affixed the ring gear. The starter drive engages the ring gear, turning the flywheel, which rotates the crankshaft, imparting the initial starting motion to the engine.

FOOT POUND (ft. lbs. or sometimes, ft.lb.): The amount of energy or work needed to raise an item weighing one pound, a distance of one foot.

FUSE: A protective device in a circuit which prevents circuit overload by breaking the circuit when a specific amperage is present. The device is constructed around a strip or wire of a lower amperage rating than the circuit it is designed to protect. When an amperage higher than that stamped on the fuse is present in the circuit, the strip or wire melts, opening the circuit.

GEAR RATIO: The ratio between the number of teeth on meshing gears.

GENERATOR: A device which converts mechanical energy into electrical energy.

HEAT RANGE: The measure of a spark plug's ability to dissipate heat from its firing end. The higher the heat range, the hotter the plug fires.

HUB: The center part of a wheel or gear.

HYDROCARBON (HC): Any chemical compound made up of hydrogen and carbon. A major pollutant formed by the engine as a byproduct of combustion.

HYDROMETER: An instrument used to measure the specific gravity of a solution.

INCH POUND (inch lbs.; sometimes in.lb. or in. lbs.): One twelfth of a foot pound.

INDUCTION: A means of transferring electrical energy in the form of a magnetic field. Principle used in the ignition coil to increase voltage.

INJECTOR: A device which receives metered fuel under relatively low pressure and is activated to inject the fuel into the engine under relatively high pressure at a predetermined time.

INPUT SHAFT: The shaft to which torque is applied, usually carrying the driving gear or gears.

INTAKE MANIFOLD: A casting of passages or pipes used to conduct air or a fuel/air mixture to the cylinders.

JOURNAL: The bearing surface within which a shaft operates.

KEY: A small block usually fitted in a notch between a shaft and a hub to prevent slippage of the two parts.

MANIFOLD: A casting of passages or set of pipes which connect the cylinders to an inlet or outlet source.

MANIFOLD VACUUM: Low pressure in an engine intake manifold formed just below the throttle plates. Manifold vacuum is highest at idle and drops under acceleration.

MASTER CYLINDER: The primary fluid pressurizing device in a hydraulic system. In automotive use, it is found in brake and hydraulic clutch systems and is pedal activated, either directly or, in a power brake system, through the power booster.

MODULE: Electronic control unit, amplifier or igniter of solid state or integrated design which controls the current flow in the ignition primary circuit based on input from the pick-up coil. When the module opens the primary circuit, high secondary voltage is induced in the coil.

NEEDLE BEARING: A bearing which consists of a number (usually a large number) of long, thin rollers.

OHM: (Ω) The unit used to measure the resistance of conductor-to-electrical flow. One ohm is the amount of resistance that limits current flow to one ampere in a circuit with one volt of pressure.

OHMMETER: An instrument used for measuring the resistance, in ohms, in an electrical circuit.

OUTPUT SHAFT: The shaft which transmits torque from a device, such as a transmission.

OVERDRIVE: A gear assembly which produces more shaft revolutions than that transmitted to it.

OVERHEAD CAMSHAFT (OHC): An engine configuration in which the camshaft is mounted on top of the cylinder head and operates the valve either directly or by means of rocker arms.

OVERHEAD VALVE (OHV): An engine configuration in which all of the valves are located in the cylinder head and the camshaft is located in the cylinder block. The camshaft operates the valves via lifters and pushrods.

OXIDES OF NITROGEN (NOx): Chemical compounds of nitrogen produced as a byproduct of combustion. They combine with hydrocarbons to produce smog.

OXYGEN SENSOR: Use with the feedback system to sense the presence of oxygen in the exhaust gas and signal the computer which can reference the voltage signal to an air/fuel ratio.

PINION: The smaller of two meshing gears.

PISTON RING: An open-ended ring with fits into a groove on the outer diameter of the piston. Its chief function is to form a seal between the piston and cylinder wall. Most automotive pistons have three rings: two for compression sealing; one for oil sealing.

PRELOAD: A predetermined load placed on a bearing during assembly or by adjustment.

PRIMARY CIRCUIT: the low voltage side of the ignition system which consists of the ignition switch, ballast resistor or resistance wire, bypass, coil, electronic control unit and pick-up coil as well as the connecting wires and harnesses.

PRESS FIT: The mating of two parts under pressure, due to the inner diameter of one being smaller than the outer diameter of the other, or vice versa; an interference fit.

RACE: The surface on the inner or outer ring of a bearing on which the balls, needles or rollers move.

REGULATOR: A device which maintains the amperage and/or voltage levels of a circuit at predetermined values.

RELAY: A switch which automatically opens and/or closes a circuit.

RESISTANCE: The opposition to the flow of current through a circuit or electrical device, and is measured in ohms. Resistance is equal to the voltage divided by the amperage.

RESISTOR: A device, usually made of wire, which offers a preset amount of resistance in an electrical circuit.

RING GEAR: The name given to a ring-shaped gear attached to a differential case, or affixed to a flywheel or as part of a planetary gear set.

ROLLER BEARING: A bearing made up of hardened inner and outer races between which hardened steel rollers move.

ROTOR: 1. The disc-shaped part of a disc brake assembly, upon which the brake pads bear; also called, brake disc. 2. The device mounted atop the distributor shaft, which passes current to the distributor cap tower contacts.

SECONDARY CIRCUIT: The high voltage side of the ignition system, usually above 20,000 volts. The secondary includes the ignition coil, coil wire, distributor cap and rotor, spark plug wires and spark plugs.

SENDING UNIT: A mechanical, electrical, hydraulic or electro-magnetic device which transmits information to a gauge.

SENSOR: Any device designed to measure engine operating conditions or ambient pressures and temperatures. Usually electronic in nature and designed to send a voltage signal to an on-board computer, some sensors may operate as a simple on/off switch or they may provide a variable voltage signal (like a potentiometer) as conditions or measured parameters change.

SHIM: Spacers of precise, predetermined thickness used between parts to establish a proper working relationship.

SLAVE CYLINDER: In automotive use, a device in the hydraulic clutch system which is activated by hydraulic force, disengaging the clutch.

SOLENOID: A coil used to produce a magnetic field, the effect of which is to produce work.

SPARK PLUG: A device screwed into the combustion chamber of a spark ignition engine. The basic construction is a conductive core inside of a ceramic insulator, mounted in an outer conductive base. An electrical charge from the spark plug wire travels along the conductive core and jumps a preset air gap to a grounding point or points at the end of the conductive base. The resultant spark ignites the fuel/air mixture in the combustion chamber.

SPLINES: Ridges machined or cast onto the outer diameter of a shaft or inner diameter of a bore to enable parts to mate without rotation.

TACHOMETER: A device used to measure the rotary speed of an engine, shaft, gear, etc., usually in rotations per minute.

THERMOSTAT: A valve, located in the cooling system of an engine, which is closed when cold and opens gradually in response to engine heating, controlling the temperature of the coolant and rate of coolant flow.

TOP DEAD CENTER (TDC): The point at which the piston reaches the top of its travel on the compression stroke.

TORQUE: The twisting force applied to an object.

TORQUE CONVERTER: A turbine used to transmit power from a driving member to a driven member via hydraulic action, providing changes in drive ratio and torque. In automotive use, it links the driveplate at the rear of the engine to the automatic transmission.

TRANSDUCER: A device used to change a force into an electrical signal.

TRANSISTOR: A semi-conductor component which can be actuated by a small voltage to perform an electrical switching function.

TUNE-UP: A regular maintenance function, usually associated with the replacement and adjustment of parts and components in the electrical and fuel systems of a vehicle for the purpose of attaining optimum performance.

TURBOCHARGER: An exhaust driven pump which compresses intake air and forces it into the combustion chambers at higher than atmospheric pressures. The increased air pressure allows more fuel to be burned and results in increased horsepower being produced.

VACUUM ADVANCE: A device which advances the ignition timing in response to increased engine vacuum.

VACUUM GAUGE: An instrument used to measure the presence of vacuum in a chamber.

VALVE: A device which control the pressure, direction of flow or rate of flow of a liquid or gas.

VALVE CLEARANCE: The measured gap between the end of the valve stem and the rocker arm, cam lobe or follower that activates the valve.

VISCOSITY: The rating of a liquid's internal resistance to flow.

VOLTMETER: An instrument used for measuring electrical force in units called volts. Voltmeters are always connected parallel with the circuit being tested.

WHEEL CYLINDER: Found in the automotive drum brake assembly, it is a device, actuated by hydraulic pressure, which, through internal pistons, pushes the brake shoes outward against the drums.

MASTER
INDEX